Rome

Sally Webb
Stefano Cavedoni
Helen Gillman

LONELY PLANET PUBLICATIONS
Melbourne • Oakland • London • Paris

Rome
2nd edition – September 2001

Published by
Lonely Planet Publications Pty Ltd ABN 36 005 607 983
90 Maribyrnong St, Footscray, Victoria 3011, Australia

Lonely Planet Offices
Australia Locked Bag 1, Footscray, Victoria 3011
USA 150 Linden St, Oakland, CA 94607
UK 10a Spring Place, London NW5 3BH
France 1 rue du Dahomey, 75011 Paris

Photographs
Many of the images in this guide are available for licensing from
Lonely Planet Images.
Web site: www.lonelyplanetimages.com

Front cover photograph
Statue at Capitoline Museums, Rome
Photographer: Christopher Groenhout

ISBN 1 86450 311 4

Printed through Colorcraft Ltd, Hong Kong
Printed in China

Although the authors and Lonely Planet try to make the information as accurate as possible, we accept no responsibility for any loss, injury or inconvenience sustained by anyone using this book.

Contents – Text

2 Contents – Text

INDEX 305

MAP SECTION 313–36

MAP LEGEND back page

METRIC CONVERSION inside back cover

The Authors

Sally Webb

After living and working in Rome for four years, Sally swapped the cobblestone streets of Trastevere for harbour views in Sydney. The end of an era was nigh and she's now in therapy for the absence of fresh *mozzarella di bufala* and centuries-old mosaics in her life.

Sally has authored/co-authored many Lonely Planet guides, including the first edition of this guide (with Helen Gillman and Stefano Cavedoni), *Rome Condensed*, *Italy* (4th and 5th editions), *Corfu & the Ionians*, *Western Australia* and *New South Wales*. She has also eaten her way around Sydney and Melbourne for Lonely Planet's *Out to Eat* guides.

An art historian by training, journalist by profession and travel writer by choice, Melbourne-born Sally has contributed to publications in Australia, the UK and Italy, including the *Independent on Sunday*, the *Sunday Age*, *Vive*, the *Australian Financial Review Magazine*, *Australian Gourmet Traveller*, *Vacations and Travel*, *Qantas Club*, *Wanted in Rome* and *Vogue Entertaining & Travel*, where she now works as Features Editor.

Helen Gillman & Stefano Cavedonini

Husband-and-wife team Helen and Stefano are based in Italy and have written or contributed to *Italy*, *Walking in Italy*, *Mediterranean Europe*, *Western Europe* and the 1st edition of *Rome* for Lonely Planet.

FROM THE AUTHOR

It wasn't until I lived in Rome that I realised you could fall desperately and hopelessly in love with a place. *Mille grazie* to *bella Roma* and to the many friends, Romans and countrymen and women (by birth or adoption) who have shared their passion for the Eternal City with me: Laura Clarke, Sabina Triulzi and all at *Wanted in Rome*; Nick Rigillo and Lisbeth Davidsen; Michele Pozzi; Rory Carroll and Stéphanie Savariaud (for late-night Piaf singalongs and *vin chaud*); Alessandro and Sari Taddei (my restaurant and shopping gurus); James Walston for his political and historical insight; Lisa Triulzi for hotel tips; Rob Allyn & Rosario Gorgone at Through Eternity; Alice Baker for opera background; Claudio at Babele bookshop; and Vezio and Maria for knowing exactly how I like my cappuccino.

Special thanks to Celia and Markus Bockmuehl, Karen Freeman and Mark Banning-Taylor, and Orla Guerin for delightful company during my research, and to Mary Wilsey who gave me my first journalistic break in Rome and to whom I owe so much.

This Book

This is the 2nd edition of Lonely Planet's *Rome* city guide and was written and updated by Sally Webb. Helen Gillman, Stefano Cavedoni and Sally wrote the 1st edition.

From the Publisher

This edition of *Rome* was produced in Lonely Planet's London office. Heather Dickson was the coordinating editor and Jolyon Philcox handled the mapping, design and layout. Michala Green, Jenny Lansbury, Helen Parry and Sam Trafford helped with editing and proofing. Jimi Ellis drew the climate chart, Andrew Weatherill designed the cover and Lachlan Ross drew the back-cover map. Lonely Planet Images provided the photographs and illustrations were drawn by Asa Andersson and Trudi Canavan. Ed Pickard and Angie Watts also chipped in at the final stages.

Many thanks to Quentin Frayne for the language chapter, Rachel Suddart for Getting There and Away information and Tom Hall for his sporting expertise. Thanks also to Amanda Canning, Tim Fitzgerald and the stalwart Tim Ryder for all their help and advice.

Thanks

Many thanks to the travellers who used the last edition and contacted us with helpful hints, advice and interesting anecdotes:

Alan Bowie, Andrew Charleston, Catherine Cochrane, Maureen Crabb, Kathy Crone, Kristy Dyer, Anne Fleming, Michael Friend, Carmen Hagenaars, Jane Higgins, J Kamea, Karen Keen, Irene Kontje, Miriam Kramer, Sam MacDonald, Orlaith Mannion, Eileen Marner, Kathryn McDonnell, David Meldrum, Dulani Mendis, Sarah Michael, Kristin Radcliffe, Dr Reuven Schossen, Danielle Schubert, John Simpson, Victorien Slomp, Emma Strugnell, Stephen Targett, Jane Walveranta, Rebecca Whitfield, Miriam Wittmann.

Foreword

ABOUT LONELY PLANET GUIDEBOOKS

The story begins with a classic travel adventure: Tony and Maureen Wheeler's 1972 journey across Europe and Asia to Australia. Useful information about the overland trail did not exist at that time, so Tony and Maureen published the first Lonely Planet guidebook to meet a growing need.

From a kitchen table, then from a tiny office in Melbourne (Australia), Lonely Planet has become the largest independent travel publisher in the world, an international company with offices in Melbourne, Oakland (USA), London (UK) and Paris (France).

Today Lonely Planet guidebooks cover the globe. There is an ever-growing list of books and there's information in a variety of forms and media. Some things haven't changed. The main aim is still to help make it possible for adventurous travellers to get out there – to explore and better understand the world.

At Lonely Planet we believe travellers can make a positive contribution to the countries they visit – if they respect their host communities and spend their money wisely. Since 1986 a percentage of the income from each book has been donated to aid projects and human rights campaigns.

Updates Lonely Planet thoroughly updates each guidebook as often as possible. This usually means there are around two years between editions, although for more unusual or more stable destinations the gap can be longer. Check the imprint page (following the colour map at the beginning of the book) for publication dates.

Between editions up-to-date information is available in two free newsletters – the paper *Planet Talk* and email *Comet* (to subscribe, contact any Lonely Planet office) – and on our Web site at www.lonelyplanet.com. The *Upgrades* section of the Web site covers a number of important and volatile destinations and is regularly updated by Lonely Planet authors. *Scoop* covers news and current affairs relevant to travellers. And, lastly, the *Thorn Tree* bulletin board and *Postcards* section of the site carry unverified, but fascinating, reports from travellers.

Correspondence The process of creating new editions begins with the letters, postcards and emails received from travellers. This correspondence often includes suggestions, criticisms and comments about the current editions. Interesting excerpts are immediately passed on via newsletters and the Web site, and everything goes to our authors to be verified when they're researching on the road. We're keen to get more feedback from organisations or individuals who represent communities visited by travellers.

> Lonely Planet gathers information for everyone who's curious about the planet – and especially for those who explore it first-hand. Through guidebooks, phrasebooks, activity guides, maps, literature, newsletters, image library, TV series and Web site we act as an information exchange for a worldwide community of travellers.

Research Authors aim to gather sufficient practical information to enable travellers to make informed choices and to make the mechanics of a journey run smoothly. They also research historical and cultural background to help enrich the travel experience and allow travellers to understand and respond appropriately to cultural and environmental issues.

Authors don't stay in every hotel because that would mean spending a couple of months in each medium-sized city and, no, they don't eat at every restaurant because that would mean stretching belts beyond capacity. They do visit hotels and restaurants to check standards and prices, but feedback based on readers' direct experiences can be very helpful.

Many of our authors work undercover, others aren't so secretive. None of them accept freebies in exchange for positive write-ups. And none of our guidebooks contain any advertising.

Production Authors submit their raw manuscripts and maps to offices in Australia, USA, UK or France. Editors and cartographers – all experienced travellers themselves – then begin the process of assembling the pieces. When the book finally hits the shops, some things are already out of date, we start getting feedback from readers and the process begins again...

WARNING & REQUEST

Things change – prices go up, schedules change, good places go bad and bad places go bankrupt – nothing stays the same. So, if you find things better or worse, recently opened or long since closed, please tell us and help make the next edition even more accurate and useful. We genuinely value all the feedback we receive. A well-travelled team reads and acknowledges every letter, postcard and email and ensures that every morsel of information finds its way to the appropriate authors, editors and cartographers for verification.

Everyone who writes to us will find their name in the next edition of the appropriate guidebook. They will also receive the latest issue of *Planet Talk*, our quarterly printed newsletter, or *Comet*, our monthly email newsletter. Subscriptions to both newsletters are free. The very best contributions will be rewarded with a free guidebook.

Excerpts from your correspondence may appear in new editions of Lonely Planet guidebooks, the Lonely Planet Web site, *Planet Talk* or *Comet*, so please let us know if you *don't* want your letter published or your name acknowledged.

Send all correspondence to the Lonely Planet office closest to you:

Australia: Locked Bag 1, Footscray, Victoria 3011
USA: 150 Linden St, Oakland, CA 94607
UK: 10a Spring Place, London NW5 3BH
France: 1 rue du Dahomey, 75011 Paris

Or email us at: talk2us@lonelyplanet.com.au

For news, views and updates see our Web site: www.lonelyplanet.com

HOW TO USE A LONELY PLANET GUIDEBOOK

The best way to use a Lonely Planet guidebook is any way you choose. At Lonely Planet we believe the most memorable travel experiences are often those that are unexpected, and the finest discoveries are those you make yourself. Guidebooks are not intended to be used as if they provide a detailed set of infallible instructions!

Contents All Lonely Planet guidebooks follow roughly the same format. The Facts about the Destination chapters or sections give background information ranging from history to weather. Facts for the Visitor gives practical information on issues like visas and health. Getting There & Away gives a brief starting point for re-searching travel to and from the destination. Getting Around gives an overview of the transport options when you arrive.

The peculiar demands of each destination determine how sub-sequent chapters are broken up, but some things remain constant. We always start with background, then proceed to sights, places to stay, places to eat, entertainment, getting there and away, and getting around information – in that order.

Heading Hierarchy Lonely Planet headings are used in a strict hierarchical structure that can be visualised as a set of Russian dolls. Each heading (and its following text) is encompassed by any preceding heading that is higher on the hierarchical ladder.

Entry Points We do not assume guidebooks will be read from beginning to end, but that people will dip into them. The tradi-tional entry points are the list of contents and the index. In addition, however, some books have a complete list of maps and an index map illustrating map coverage.

There may also be a colour map that shows highlights. These highlights are dealt with in greater detail in the Facts for the Visitor chapter, along with planning questions and suggested itin-eraries. Each chapter covering a geographical region usually begins with a locator map and another list of highlights. Once you find something of interest in a list of highlights, turn to the index.

Maps Maps play a crucial role in Lonely Planet guidebooks and include a huge amount of information. A legend is printed on the back page. We seek to have complete consistency between maps and text, and to have every important place in the text captured on a map. Map key numbers usually start in the top left corner.

Although inclusion in a guidebook usually implies a recommen-dation we cannot list every good place. Exclusion does not necessarily imply criticism. In fact there are a number of reasons why we might exclude a place – sometimes it is simply inappropriate to encourage an influx of travellers.

Introduction

Rome is a beautiful, beguiling, chaotic, fascinating, frustrating and romantic city that has always inspired wonder and awe in its visitors.

Its innumerable monuments are evidence of the city's transformation through the imperial, medieval, Renaissance and Baroque periods, and from a pagan to a Christian world. In fact, from the time of the Roman Empire, through the development of Christianity to the present day – a period of more than 2500 years – Rome has produced an archaeological archive of Western culture.

Tourists wandering round the city with their eyes raised to admire the architecture should know that about 4m under their feet exists another city, with traces of other settlements deeper still. St Peter's Basilica stands on the site of an earlier basilica, which was built by Emperor Constantine in the 4th century over the necropolis where St Peter was buried. Castel Sant'Angelo was the tomb of Emperor Hadrian before it was converted into a fortress. The form of Piazza Navona is suggestive of a hippodrome and, in fact, it was built on the ruins of the Emperor Domitian's stadium. Understanding this can help you interpret this complex and sometimes confusing city.

Ancient history is only part of Rome's charm. Much of the city you see today is a legacy of the Renaissance and Baroque popes who spared no expense to rebuild an all-but-ruined medieval town. The greatest artists and architects of their day, including Michelangelo and Bernini, built basilicas and churches, and designed piazzas, palaces and fountains, as well as producing astounding sculptures and paintings to decorate them.

Although new-millennium Rome has no great architectural geniuses who can leave a mark on the city the way Michelangelo and Bernini did, there is a greater understanding of (and respect for) the city's existing cultural patrimony and laudable efforts are being made to preserve it for future generations.

In the wake of the Jubilee Year of 2000, when around 16 million Catholic pilgrims joined the regular tourist hordes, the Eternal City has never looked better. Its beautiful monuments, churches, *palazzi*, bridges and fountains have undergone major cosmetic surgery, and everything is sparkling. The city's infrastructure has been improved – roads widened, car parks built, underpasses dug and transport boosted – and new museums have been opened and old ones renovated. The improvements are ongoing, with several public works projects, including a new music auditorium, expected to be completed within the next few years.

Rome has been the capital of a united Italy only since 1870 but to Roman emperors Rome was always *caput mundi* (capital of the world). To pilgrims, historians, artists, writers and plain old tourists who have spent time here, it has always been the Eternal City. However, among the phenomenal concentration of history, legend and monuments there is an equally phenomenal concentration of people busily going about everyday life. It is easy to spot today's tourists because they are the only ones to turn their heads as the bus passes the Colosseum.

The minutiae of daily existence in Rome possess a charm unimaginable in other capitals. It doesn't matter how much time you spend in Rome, it won't be enough. The popular saying *'Roma, non basta una vita'* ('Rome, a lifetime isn't enough') couldn't be more accurate. There is more to see here than in any other city in the world. And it is constantly changing, as new excavations unearth yet more ancient treasures. So get your cultural fill but make sure you leave time for more hedonistic concerns, from food and wine to sunshine and shopping. After all, when in Rome... Just make sure you throw a coin in the Trevi Fountain so you'll be guaranteed to return.

Facts about Rome

HISTORY
The Foundation of Rome

It is generally agreed that Rome's origins lie in a group of Etruscan, Latin and Sabine settlements on the Palatine, Esquiline and Quirinal hills. Ancient Romans put the date of their city's foundation at 21 April 753 BC, and indeed archaeological discoveries have confirmed the existence of a settlement on the Palatine dating from the 8th century BC. In 1999, archaeologists excavating in the Foro di Cesare found traces from the 9th century BC, indicating that Roman history could be a century older than previously thought.

However, it is the legend of Romulus and Remus that prevails. According to this legend, the twin sons of Rhea Silvia (a Latin princess) and the war god Mars were raised by a she-wolf after being abandoned on the banks of the River Tiber. The myth says Romulus killed his brother during a battle over who should govern, and then established the city of Rome on the Palatine, making himself the first king. Later he disappeared, poetically taken up by the gods or, more prosaically, secretly murdered by senators.

The next seven kings of Rome were elected from the ranks of the nobles. Most notably, Numa Pompilius is credited with installing the state religion and the Etruscan Servius Tullius built the first walls around the city state, establishing the basic organisation of the political and military system. The last king, Tarquinius Superbus (Tarquin the Proud), was expelled from Rome after his son raped a nobleman's wife. The Etruscan royal house was overthrown and the Roman Republic was born.

The Republic

In government, the Romans combined the best of all the known systems and held them in a state of equilibrium. Monarchy was represented by two consuls who were also the alternating commanders-in-chief; oligarchy came from the Senate, to which all higher magistrates, including the consuls, belonged; and democracy came from the direct election to almost all political offices. To keep the magistrates in check, all offices were changed annually; re-election was originally forbidden, then later allowed only after a 10-year gap. No man was permitted to stand for high office until he had progressed through the sequence of junior posts, and all magistracies were held jointly. The exception was the dictator, appointed along with a subordinate Master of the Horse for six months during periods of crisis.

The Romans also developed a unique system for dealing with the other peoples (eg, the Sabines and Etruscans to the north, the Oscans, Samnites, Hernici, and Greek colonies to the south) in the region. Defeated city states were not taken over but became allies. Allowed to retain their own government and lands, they were required to provide troops to serve alongside Roman soldiers in future wars. This naturally increased Rome's military strength, and the protection offered by the Roman hegemony induced many cities to become allies voluntarily.

The civic structure also expanded. In 450 BC, the existing laws were codified as the Law of the Twelve Tables, which remained in force for the next 1000 years. Construction of the Via Appia began in 312 BC and in 244 BC the road was extended to the eastern port of Brindisi.

Not everything, however, went the Romans' way. In 390 BC, Gauls swept down from the north and besieged Rome. The populace retreated to the Capitoline, which was saved on one occasion when Juno's sacred geese alerted the defenders to a nocturnal attack. The invaders were finally bought off with a massive bribe.

Punic Wars

The other Mediterranean power during this period was Carthage, a kingdom of traders based in North Africa (modern Tunis).

The First Punic War (264–241 BC) was the result of the internal politics of Messina, a Greek colony in Sicily. One faction, thrown out of the city, sought Carthaginian support, while the other party appealed to Rome. During the resulting 23-year war the Romans learned the lesson of naval power. Eventually victorious, they forced the Carthaginians to abandon their colonies in western Sicily and, for good measure, they also seized Sardinia.

One of the defeated and aggrieved Punic generals was Hamilcar Barca, who turned to building a personal fiefdom in southern Spain, where he taught his sons, Hannibal and Hamilcar, to view Rome with a profound hatred. Hannibal inherited the command and provoked war in 219 BC by attacking Saguntum. This city lay within the agreed Carthaginian area but it appealed to Rome for help. In 218 BC, the Roman Senate declared war on Carthage again.

With the Romans controlling the seas, Hannibal daringly crossed into Italy by leading his army over the Alps. Despite losing up to half his troops and almost all of his war elephants in the crossing, Hannibal was able to inflict several crushing defeats on the Romans at Ticinus, Trebia and Lake Trasimeno in 217 BC, and at Cannae in the following year. The Romans were also hampered by the system that saw command alternating between the two consuls and had Hannibal attacked Rome in 216 BC, the city would have fallen. Instead, he chose to consolidate his position in southern Italy.

During this stalemate, the Romans discovered their own military genius to match Hannibal – Publius Cornelius Scipio. Granted military command before he had held any public office, Scipio struck first at Hannibal's power base in Spain and then, in 204 BC, attacked Africa itself, forcing the Carthaginians to recall Hannibal to defend their own capital. Scipio won the battle of Zama in 202 BC; Hannibal committed suicide in exile some 20 years later.

Philip V of Macedon had been Hannibal's ally and, through the ensuing Macedonian Wars, the Romans came into contact with the splendour and wealth of the Hel-

lenistic Empire left by Alexander the Great. Since a Roman politician alternated between military and civilian offices, the astute and the ambitious quickly made the connection between the prestige – and riches – won in overseas conquest and electoral success at home. Using the same system of alliance, rather than direct conquest, Rome established a series of 'client kingdoms' ruled by local princes who fully understood that their bread was buttered on the Roman side.

From Republic to Empire

With Rome's expansion eastwards came the rise of the generalissimo. In 107 BC, Gaius Marius replaced the increasingly unpopular system of conscription by accepting volunteers from the ranks of the landless urban poor. The result was that Roman armies now looked to their individual generals for recompense after a campaign and the commanders soon realised the unlimited political potential of conquest.

Meanwhile Roman politics was increasingly polarised into two factions, linked as much by marriage as by policies: the Optimates (conservatives), who upheld the primacy of the Senate; and the Populares (populists), who preferred to take their bills before the people's assemblies. This split in political methods was the cause of civil conflict between the supporters of Marius, a Populare, and his erstwhile lieutenant Cornelius Sulla, an Optimate.

Sulla twice threatened to invade Rome and in 82 BC, after he committed a string of political murders, the Senate gave in to his demands and he was voted dictator for the extraordinary period of 10 years.

One of Sulla's proteges, Gnaeus Pompeius Magnus (Pompey the Great), was allowed by Sulla to leapfrog his way up the political ladder. In 71 BC, the fabulously wealthy Marcus Licinius Crassus finally mopped up the dramatic slave rebellion led by the gladiator Spartacus, which had been raging through Italy for two years. At its conclusion, 6000 slaves who did not die in battle were crucified along the Via Appia. Crassus and Pompey together campaigned

Rome Timeline

Foundation of Rome

753 BC Foundation of Rome by Romulus

700–396 Etruscan civilisation

715–673 Numa Pompilius becomes first Etruscan king of Rome; State religion established

578–535 Servius Tullius reforms social and military structure

509 Expulsion of monarchy; dedication of the first temple on the Capitoline

501 Senatorial appointment of first dictator

450 Law of the Twelve Tables

396 Etruscan stronghold of Veio captured

390 Sack of Rome by Gauls

386–5 Defeat of Latins, Volsci and Hernici

338 Rome subsumes Latin League

312 Construction of Via Appia starts

Republic

264–241 First Punic War

218–202 Second Punic War

217 Hannibal defeats Roman army; consul killed at Lake Trasimeno

216 Roman defeat at Cannae

214–205 First Macedonian War

192–189 Syria defeated; Roman client kingdoms established in the East

146 Carthage destroyed

144 Construction of Aqua Marcia

142 First stone bridge over River Tiber

Late Republic

107 Gaius Marius becomes consul

82 Cornelius Sulla becomes dictator

73–71 Revolt of Spartacus

70 Marcus Crassus and Pompey the Great made consuls

59–54 First Triumvirate

Transition to Empire

50–45 Civil war between Julius Caesar and Pompey

44 Caesar assassinated

42 'Liberators' defeated at Philippi

40–31 Second Triumvirate

27 Pantheon built

23 Augustus' constitutional position regularised

19 Death of Virgil

Early Empire

13 Teatro di Marcello dedicated

9 Ara Pacis dedicated

AD 17 Death of Livy

27 Tiberius continues to rule from Capri

45 Port facilities at Ostia extended

58 Emperor Claudius assassinated

59 Murder of Agrippina, Nero's mother

64 Great Fire, Nero's persecution of Christians and martyrdom of Sts Peter and Paul

68 Year of the Four Emperors

Zenith

79 Eruption of Mt Vesuvius

80 Dedication of the Colosseum

92 Palatine palace complex completed

116 Parthia conquered

118–25 Pantheon rebuilt

174 *Meditations* of Marcus Aurelius

193 Civil war

Decline & Fall

211–16 Construction of Baths of Caracalla

271 Aurelian Wall begun

285 East and West division of Empire, formalised in 395

313 Christianity legalised

(and bribed) their way to the consulships of 70 BC. Pompey later took an army as far east as Syria.

In 59 BC, Gaius Julius Caesar was running for consulship, and made a deal with Crassus and Pompey. In return for their electoral and financial support, Caesar as consul would ensure that his allies' interests would be looked after despite Optimate opposition. The three men became known as the First Triumvirate and their pact was reinforced by

Pompey's marriage to Caesar's daughter, Julia. After his consulship, Caesar left to win military glory in Gaul. The First Triumvirate was renewed in 56 BC, and with Caesar's electoral support, Crassus and Pompey shared another consulship in 55 BC. The alliance was shaken, however, when Julia died in 54 BC and Crassus was heavily defeated and killed in Parthia the following year.

Pompey became increasingly influenced by the Optimates, who wanted to impeach

Rome Timeline

330 Constantinople founded as new capital

382–420 Vulgate Bible produced

455 Vandals sack Rome

Middle Ages

c.520 St Benedict codifies rules of monastic life

536 Rome briefly 'liberated' from Goths

597 St Augustine sent by Gregory I to Christianise England

653 Martin I captured and humiliated in Constantinople

754 Papal States created

774 Charlemagne crowned Holy Roman Emperor

846 Saracens sack Rome; Vatican fortified

1300 First Jubilee Year proclaimed

Renaissance

1309–79 Papacy based in Avignon

1425 San Giovanni in Laterano rebuilt by Martin V

1471 Capitoline Museum and Sistine Chapel founded

1500 *Pietà* sculpted by Michelangelo

1505 Pope Julius II hires 200 Swiss mercenaries

1506 Rebuilding of St Peter's starts

1508 Sistine Chapel frescoes begun

1517 Martin Luther begins Reformation

1527 Sack of Rome by Charles V of Spain

1532 Henry VIII rejects papal authority

1540 Foundation of the Society of Jesus (Jesuits)

1547 Michelangelo appointed architect of St Peter's

1555 Paul IV establishes the Ghetto

1585 Accademica di Santa Cecilia founded

1600 Giordano Bruno burned for heresy

1610 Death of Caravaggio

1624 Bernini commissioned to create the baldachino in St Peter's

1680 Death of Gian Lorenzo Bernini

1723 Construction of the Spanish Steps

1763 Creation of the Trevi Fountain

1796 Napoleon annexes papal lands, forces armistice

1848 Garibaldi and Mazzini begin the Risorgimento

1870 Victor Emmanuel II enters Rome; unification of Italy

1922 Mussolini marches on Rome

20th Century

1929 Mussolini and Pius XI sign Lateran Treaty

1936 Rome-Berlin Axis

1944 Fosse Ardeatine massacre

1946 Italian monarchy abolished

1953 Treaty of Rome

1960 Olympic Games; Fellini makes *La Dolce Vita*

1962–5 Second Vatican Council

1975 Death of Pasolini

1978 Murder of Aldo Moro

1981 Attempted assassination of John Paul II

1990 World Cup held in Rome

1992 Tangentopoli bribery scandal unfolds

1994 Restoration of Sistine Chapel frescoes

1998 John Paul II celebrates 20 years as pope

2000 Jubilee Year

2001 Berlusconi becomes prime minister

Caesar for irregularities in Gaul, causing civil war when Caesar crossed into Italy with his army of devoted veterans in 49 BC. Pompey and his supporters evacuated Italy for Spain, Africa and Greece, where their main force was defeated by Caesar at Pharsalus a year later. Pompey fled to Egypt, where he was assassinated.

In 47 BC, Caesar returned to Rome, where he began to institute a series of reforms, overhauling both the calendar and the Senate. Of his extensive building programme, the Curia (Senate House) and the Basilica Guilia remain. Initially declared dictator for one year, Caesar had this extended to 10 years and then, in 44 BC, was proclaimed dictator for life. This accumulation of power fatally alienated even those who had initially supported him, and Caesar was famously assassinated in the portico of the Teatro di Pompeo on the Ides of March (15 March) 44 BC.

However, the Liberators, as Caesar's assassins called themselves, found that they had severely underestimated Caesar's popularity with the military and the general populace: the people regarded the dead dictator as a new god. Caesar's lieutenant, Marcus Antonius (Mark Antony), took command of the city, aided by the troops under the command of Lepidus. Caesar's will had declared the adoption of his 18-year-old great-nephew, Octavian, as his son and heir. Octavian, then studying in Greece, returned to Rome to claim his inheritance. Now calling himself Gaius Julius Caesar Octavianus, the young man first sided with the Liberators against Antony, then switched sides and fought with Antony against Brutus and Cassius who were defeated at Philippi. The orator Cicero, who had attacked Antony in a series of speeches and then underestimated Octavian, became a victim of the political murders that followed.

Lepidus was quickly frozen out of the Second Triumvirate and the Roman world was divided in two, with the new Caesar raising troops in the western half while Antony administered the wealthy provinces and client kingdoms in the east. Although Antony married Octavian's sister, the situation inevitably deteriorated again into civil war, with Octavian making brilliant propagandist use of Antony's affair with Cleopatra VII, queen of Egypt.

Octavian's general, Marcus Agrippa, defeated Antony and Cleopatra in a naval battle off the coast of Actium in 31 BC. They committed suicide in Alexandria the following year.

The Empire

Octavian was left the sole ruler of the Roman world, but, remembering Caesar's fate, trod very carefully. In 27 BC, he officially surrendered his extraordinary powers to the Senate, which promptly gave most of them back, making him the first emperor of Rome and voting him the unique title Augustus (Your Eminence).

The new era of political stability allowed the arts to flourish. Augustus was exceptionally fortunate in having the poets Virgil,

Horace and Ovid, as well as the historian Livy, as his contemporaries. He encouraged the visual arts, restored existing buildings and commissioned many new ones, including the Ara Pacis (Altar of Peace) explicitly to commemorate his achievement. He boasted in his memoirs that 'he found Rome in brick, and left it in marble'.

Augustus succeeded because instead of trying to reinvent the political system, he simply made room for himself at the top. He never called himself a king or an emperor, but only *princeps* (the leading man). The Republic, as it was still known, continued as usual from the consuls down. He died aged 75 after a 40-year reign (27 BC–AD 14).

His successor, Tiberius, enjoyed a stable reign (AD 14–37), ruling from his villa in Capri for the last decade. Gaius Caligula (AD 37–45) had little time for the political niceties that the Senate expected; his increasingly extravagant and bizarre behaviour led to his assassination by an officer of the Praetorian Guard, the imperial bodyguard.

A return to a truly republican form of government was contemplated but the Praetorians, with an eye on job security, declared Claudius, Caligula's uncle, emperor. Despite his unexpected elevation, Claudius proved to be a conscientious ruler. He extended the port facilities at Ostia and constructed a new aqueduct, the Acqua Claudia, to service Rome's growing population. He also strengthened Rome's hold on Britain, first invaded by Caesar.

Probably poisoned in AD 58 by his wife, Agrippina, Claudius was succeeded by Nero, her 17-year-old son by a previous marriage. Nero gradually showed his preference for Gaius Caligula's style of government. In the ultimate act of youthful rebellion, he had his mother assassinated, then began to impose his passion for all things Greek on an increasingly resentful Roman aristocracy. With revolt spreading among the provincial governors, who commanded armies, the Senate declared Nero a public enemy in AD 68 and he committed suicide while on the run. In the 'Year of the Four Emperors' that followed, Galba, Otho and Vitellius came and went in quick succession. For more on Nero see the boxed text 'Nero Rules, OK?' on this page.

Stability was restored when Vespasian, sent to Judaea to crush the Great Rebellion of AD 66, was proclaimed emperor by his troops and the exhausted Senate agreed. A practical man, Vespasian (AD 69–79) made a point of rebuilding the temple on the Capitoline, which had been burned down during the civil wars, and constructing a huge amphitheatre (the Colosseum) in the grounds of Nero's Domus Aurea.

Vespasian celebrated the return of normality by building the Foro di Pace (Forum of Peace). The brief reign of his successor Titus (AD 79–81) is chiefly remembered for the catastrophic eruption of Mt Vesuvius, which buried Pompeii and Herculaneum. He did find time to construct public baths, the Terme di Tito, as well as the Arco di Tito, which commemorates him as the captor of Jerusalem.

Domitian, Titus' younger brother, built the Forum Transitorio (for which his successor, Nerva, took the credit and the name, calling it the Foro di Nerva) and greatly extended the palace complex on the Palatine. Domitian had the corridors lined with highly polished stone to allow him to detect lurking assassins. In AD 96, his paranoia was justified when he was murdered in a palace plot.

After the brief reign of Nerva (AD 96–98), the elderly stop-gap emperor, came Trajan, an experienced general of Spanish birth. His victories over the Dacians are depicted on the column erected in the forecourt of his forum, which also contained separate Greek and Latin libraries. Other public works constructed at this time included his market and the Via Traiana, linking Benevento with Brindisi. Trajan was the first Roman general to conquer Parthia, the traditional eastern enemy. He died while on campaign in AD 117 and his ashes were buried in the base of his column.

Hadrian (117–138) is known as a prodigious traveller and a keen architect. He remodelled the Pantheon and built an extensive and elaborate holiday villa at Tivoli, outside Rome. This era was the peak of the Roman Empire, when stability on the borders was matched in internal politics. By 100, the city of Rome had more than 1.5 million inhabitants and all the trappings of the capital of an empire, its wealth and prosperity obvious in the rich mosaics, marble temples, public baths, theatres, circuses and libraries. An extensive network of aqueducts fed the baths and provided private houses with running water and flushing toilets.

The reigns of Antonius Pius (138–161) and the philosopher-emperor Marcus Aurelius (161–180) were stable, but the latter ominously spent 14 years fighting northern invaders. A slow decline began with the disturbed Commodus (180–192) and, with his assassination, the events of AD 68 and 69 were repeated. Pertinax, Didius Julianus and Pescennius Niger came and went before North-African-born Septimius Severus (193–211) defeated the other challengers to become emperor. Serious cracks were beginning to appear in the Empire.

Nero Rules, OK?

Although Nero was in Anzio when the great fire of Rome broke out in AD 64, rumour quickly spread that he was responsible. One tale was that he callously used the burning city as a backdrop for a recital on the fall of Troy; even worse was the rumour that he had actually started the fire. The pleasure with which he used a large amount of the ruined city for his new palace, the Domus Aurea, hardly helped calm popular feeling.

Unnerved, Nero looked for scapegoats, and chose the early-Christian community, for whom the rest of the population had little understanding and no sympathy. Some were thrown to wild animals in the circus, and others, in perverse retribution for arson, were burned alive as human torches.

St Peter and St Paul are said to have been martyred during this period. Peter was crucified (upside down at his own request so as not to imitate the death of Jesus too closely) near Nero's racetrack in the Vatican, and Paul, a Roman citizen, was given the privilege of decapitation.

Severus was jointly succeeded by the brothers Caracalla and Geta, with Caracalla predictably having his sibling assassinated. Despite some financial problems, Caracalla's building programme included refurbishing roads as well as building his monumental public baths. When he was throttled in 213, chaos ensued. Some 24 assorted emperors and pretenders violently rose and fell until Diocletian (284–305) realised that increasing instability on the borders made central government impossible. He therefore split the administration of the Empire, looking after the east himself and allocating the west to Maximian, who based himself in Milan. This arrangement worked so well that in 293 Diocletian created two junior rulers.

In 305, Maximian and Diocletian abdicated simultaneously, leaving the Empire to Constantius in the west and Galerius in the east. A four-way tug-of-war ensued until, in 312, Constantine (Constantius' son) faced Maxentius, his last rival, just outside Rome at Saxa Rubra. After claiming to have seen a vision of the Christian monogram and the message 'with this sign you will conquer', Constantine prevailed at the Battle of Ponte Milvio. The new emperor converted to Christianity and in 313 granted the Edict of Milan, which enshrined religious freedom in law.

Constantine's highly ambitious building programme included churches such as St Peter's, San Lorenzo Fuori-le-Mura and Santa Croce, the Basilica di Costantino in the Roman Forum and his own triumphal arch, the Arco di Costantino. However, he accepted Diocletian's view that Rome could no longer serve as the Empire's capital, being too far removed from the northern and eastern frontiers, and in 324 he founded the new Christian capital – Constantinople – in Byzantium.

Division of the Empire

The demise of the Roman Empire continued when the ruling brothers Valentian and Valens divided the Empire into western and eastern halves in 364, a division that was formalised after the death of Emperor Theodosius I in 395. One of his sons, Honorius, ruled the Western Roman Empire, while his other son, Arcadius, ruled the Eastern Roman Empire.

Separated from its Roman roots the Eastern Roman Empire embraced Hellenistic culture and went on to develop into the mighty Byzantine Empire, the most powerful Mediterranean state throughout the Middle Ages. It existed until the capture of Constantinople by the Turks in 1453.

The Decline of the Empire

Rome became increasingly insignificant to the Byzantine Empire. In 408, a Gothic army commanded by Alaric surrounded Rome and forced its way into the city in 410. Some districts were sacked and many temples destroyed, but the intercession of Pope Innocent I averted a massacre. This act of papal heroism was repeated even more dramatically in 440 when Pope Leo I persuaded Attila the Hun not to attack Rome. Less fortunately, the city was thoroughly plundered 15 years later by the Vandals, whose name became a byword for wanton destruction. Normality returned quickly, however, and church construction flourished.

In 476, the year traditionally recognised as the end of the great period of the Roman Empire, the last Western Roman emperor, Romulus Augustulus, was deposed. Gothic rule in Italy reached its zenith with the Ostrogothic Emperor Theodoric (493–526) who shifted the power base to Ravenna. By 500, the aqueducts feeding into Rome had been deliberately cut by invaders or had been looted for the lead piping: the swamps created by the leaking water were to last until the 20th century.

Medieval Rome

In 590, Pope Gregory I, son of a rich Roman family, returned from self-imposed exile in a monastery, having given all his wealth to the poor. He set the pattern of Church administration, which was to guide Catholic services and rituals throughout history. Gregory oversaw the Christianisation of Britain, improved conditions for slaves, provided free bread in Rome and repaired Italy's extensive network of aqueducts, as well as leaving an enormous volume of writing on which much Catholic dogma was subsequently based.

After Gregory's death, Rome was threatened first by waves of barbarians and then, from the mid-7th century, by Islamic armies that swept through the Mediterranean world. To make matters worse, relations between Rome and Constantinople deteriorated to the extent that Martin I was held under house arrest in San Giovanni in Laterano for over a month before being taken to Constantinople to be humiliated and flogged.

Pepin, the Merovingian king, offered to conquer Lombard territory for Pope Stephen II in return for papal recognition of the legitimacy of his line of succession. The relationship between the Church and the Frankish kings was further cemented in 774 when Leo III, continuing in the footsteps of Hadrian I, crowned Pepin's son Charlemagne as Holy Roman Emperor during Christmas Mass at St Peter's in 800. The bond between the papacy and the Byzantine Empire was thus forever broken and political power shifted north of the Alps.

In the 9th century, southern Italy prospered under Arab rule but the rest of the peninsula was not so calm. A Saracen fleet sailed up the Tiber and attacked Rome in 846, prompting Pope Leo IV to build a protective wall around the Vatican. Following the end of the Carolingian Empire in 887, warfare broke out in earnest between local Italian rulers, who were divided in their support of Frankish and Germanic claimants to the imperial crown.

In 962, the Saxon Otto I was crowned emperor in Rome and formally founded the Holy Roman Empire. His son, Otto II, and later his grandson, Otto III, also took the title Holy Roman Emperor, cementing a tradition that was to remain the privilege of Germanic emperors until 1806.

The campaign of Hildebrand (who was to become Pope Gregory VII in 1073) to bring the world under the rule of Christianity was, in reality, a struggle for power between Church and State. The papacy, based in Rome, and the Holy Roman Empire, with its power base north of the Alps, were compelled to agree in order to reconstruct political and cultural unity, which had been lost with the fall of the Western Roman Empire. The two powers were in perennial conflict and the consequences of this dual leadership dominated Rome throughout the Middle Ages.

Meanwhile, the fiercely Christian Normans moved into southern Italy and Sicily, succeeded by the Swabian ruler Frederick II, who was both a warrior and an enlightened scholar. As a half-Norman southerner, Frederick rejected the tradition that Holy Roman Emperors lived north of the Alps, and established his power base in southern Italy.

The 11th and 12th centuries saw arguments over temporal and spiritual power rage unabated. Rome was the battleground over which popes fought anti-popes and supporters of the papacy attacked supporters of the emperor. Norman troops under Robert Guiscard sacked the city in 1084.

Rome's aristocratic families continued to engage in battles for the papacy but a new force of Roman society (composed of artisans, financiers, lawyers and traders) was developing. Organised into guilds, they demanded the establishment of a Republic and in 1188 Pope Clement III recognised the city as a commune with rights to appoint senators and a prefect. A proportion of papal income was set aside for maintenance in the city and payment of its officials. In exchange the senators recognised the pope's temporal powers, allowing the Church to regain its influence and re-establish itself as the ultimate spiritual authority in Europe. With stability restored, the popes turned their attention to the city's material improvement, building ecclesiastical and secular buildings including a fortified mansion on the site of the present Vatican, the Tor de' Conti (near the Foro di Nerva).

In 1300, Pope Boniface VIII proclaimed the first Holy (Jubilee) Year, with the promise of a full pardon for those who made the pilgrimage to St Peter's and San Giovanni in Laterano. It is said that there were 200,000 pilgrims in Rome at any one time during that year. Dante was among them, and made Holy Week 1300 the central point in his *Divina Commedia*.

Boniface also used his power to continue his family feud with the Colonna clan. When he was preparing to excommunicate King Philip of France, the Colonna family helped French forces to break into the papal palace at Anagni and threaten the life of the pope. Boniface died a month later and the next eight popes based themselves in Avignon.

During this period, goats and cows grazed on the Capitoline and in the Roman Forum, and residential support for the city's many churches and cathedrals disappeared. Ancient marble was burned to make lime for cement. The city became a battleground for the struggles between the powerful Orsini and Colonna families. The ruling families challenged the papacy's ongoing claim to be temporal rulers of Rome and the papal state began to fall apart.

After the failed attempt of Cola di Rienzo, a popular leader, to wrest the control of Rome from the nobility in 1347, Cardinal Egidio d'Albornoz managed to restore the Papal State with his Egidian Constitutions, thereby enabling Pope Gregory XI to return to Rome in 1379. When he found a ruined and almost deserted city, Gregory transferred the papal residence from the Lateran Palace to the Vatican because it was fortified and close to the formidable Castel Sant'Angelo. When Gregory died a year after returning to Rome, Roman cardinals tried to ensure their continuing power by electing the unpopular Urban VI as pope. This sparked off a renegade movement of (mainly French) cardinals who soon elected a second pope, Clement VII. Clement set up his claim in Avignon and so began the Great Schism, which continued until 1417.

Renaissance Rome

The election of Nicholas V as pope in 1447 marked the beginning of a new era for Rome, at the time when the Renaissance was flowering in Florence. The prestige of the papacy was restored under such popes as Sixtus IV, who built the Sistine Chapel and initiated an urban plan that was to link the areas that had been cut off from one another during the Middle Ages. The artists Donatello, Sandro Botticelli and Fra Angelico lived and worked in Rome at this time.

In 1471, Sixtus IV effectively created one of the oldest museums in the world, the Capitoline Museum, when he handed over to the people of Rome a selection of bronzes. At the beginning of the 16th century, Pope Julius II opened Via del Corso and Via Giulia and in 1506 ordered that the old St Peter's Basilica be demolished, commissioning Bramante to build a new church. In 1508, Raphael started painting the rooms in the Vatican known today as the Stanze di Raffaello (Raphael Rooms), and Michelangelo began work Sistine Chapel vaults.

All the great artists of the epoch were influenced by the ever more frequent discoveries of marvellous pieces of classical art, such as the Laocoön (now in the Vatican Museums), found in 1506 in the area of Nero's Domus Aurea. Rome had 100,000 inhabitants at the height of the Renaissance and was the major centre for Italian political and cultural life. Pope Julius II was succeeded by Pope Leo X, a Medici, and the Roman Curia (or Papal Court) became the meeting place for learned men such as Baldassar Castiglione and Ludovico Ariosto.

But the papacy was also deeply involved in the power struggles that kept Europe in turmoil. In 1527, Pope Clement VII was forced to take refuge in Castel Sant'Angelo when the troops of Charles V of Spain sacked Rome – an event that is said to have deeply influenced Michelangelo's vision of *The Last Judgment*, which he began for Clement VII only two years later.

Rome owes much of its present splendour to 16th-century popes Paul III and Sixtus V, who altered the urban plan, opening up straight avenues, raising obelisks and laying out grand piazzas. In 1538, Paul III asked Michelangelo to lay out the Piazza del Campidoglio, which included the placement of the bronze statue of the Emperor Marcus Aurelius in its centre. Under Sixtus V, the dome of St Peter's was completed.

The Counter-Reformation

By the third decade of the 16th century, the broad-minded curiosity of the Renaissance had begun to give way to the intolerance of the Counter-Reformation. This was the response of the Catholic Church to the Reformation, a collective term for the movement led by Martin Luther that aimed to reform the Church and led to the rise of Protestantism in its many forms.

The transition was epitomised by the reign of Pope Paul III (1534–49), who promoted the building of the classically elegant Palazzo Farnese but who also, in 1540, allowed the establishment of Ignatius Loyola's order of the Jesuits and the organisation in 1542 of the Holy Office. This was the final (and ruthless) court of appeal in the trials that began to gather momentum with the increased activities of the Inquisition (1232–1820), the judicial arm of the Church whose aim was to discover and suppress heresy.

Pope Paul III's opposition to Protestantism and his purging of clerical abuse, as he saw it, resulted in a widespread campaign of torture and fear. In 1559, the Church published the *Index Librorum Prohibitorum,* the Index of Prohibited Books, and the Roman Church's determination to regain papal supremacy over the Protestant churches set the stage for the persecution of intellectuals and freethinkers.

Two great Italian intellectuals who felt the force of the Counter-Reformation were Giordano Bruno (1548–1600) and Galileo Galilei (1564–1642). Bruno, a Dominican monk, philosopher, astronomer and mathematician, was forced to flee Italy for Calvinist Geneva, from where he travelled extensively throughout Europe before being arrested by the Inquisition in Venice in 1592. A statue of Bruno now stands on the site in the Campo de' Fiori where he was burned at the stake in 1600.

A native of Pisa and an advocate of Aristotelian science, Galileo was forced by the Church to renounce his approval of the Copernican astronomical system, which held that the earth moved round the sun rather than the reverse. He was summoned by the Inquisition to Rome in 1632, deemed by the Jesuits to be as dangerous to the Church as 'Luther and Calvin put together'

and exiled to Florence for the rest of his life. But whereas Bruno had spurned the Catholic Church, Galileo never deviated from the faith that rejected him.

However, the latter years of the 16th century were not all counterproductive. Pope Gregory XIII (1572–85) replaced the Julian calendar with the Gregorian one in 1582, fixing the start of the year on 1 January and adjusting the system of leap years to align the 365-day year with the seasons.

The Chiesa del Gesù was the prototype of Rome's great Counter-Reformation churches, built to attract huge congregations. In the 17th century, under the popes and grand families of Rome, the theatrical exuberance of the Baroque found masterful interpreters in Bernini and Borromini. The designs of Piazzas Navona and San Pietro, and the sculptures in Rome's churches and museums, confirm Bernini's genius as both architect and artist.

Napoleonic Occupation

Over the centuries the popes had acquired a group of provinces in central Italy that were known as the Papal States, with Rome as their capital. They constituted a strategic prize that Napoleon set out to win as he made his bid for power in Europe. In 1796, he forced a humiliating armistice on Pope Pius VI, including the choice of any 100 works of art and 500 manuscripts to be taken to France. In 1805, Napoleon crowned himself king of Italy (later naming his infant son king of Rome) and three years later demanded the abdication of the pope, annexing Rome.

Goethe's 1816 account of his travels in Italy, *Italian Journey*, opened the way for a flow of literary and artistic visitors to Rome, which became the principal destination for cultivated travellers on the Grand Tour.

Risorgimento

After Napoleon's defeat, action to unify Italy under a modern Roman Republic took the form of revolt in 1849. Patriot Giuseppe Mazzini and soldier Giuseppe Garibaldi led an assault on Rome that failed miserably after a few initial successes. But the Risorgimento (Resurgence) movement proved irresistible.

At the head of a band of militia, Garibaldi took Sicily and Naples. In 1861, the kingdom of Italy was declared and Victor Emmanuel II was proclaimed king. But the pope, supported by the French, was still sovereign of Rome.

In 1870, the French were busy defending themselves from the Prussians, thus enabling Italian troops to breach Rome's city walls at Porta Pia. King Victor Emmanuel entered the city and Pope Pius IX, who had rejected war with Austria, a Catholic country, retired behind the walls of the Vatican, refusing to recognise Italy.

At last Rome was capital of the newly united kingdom of Italy. The city was soon transformed by a scandal-ridden building boom, land speculation and an influx of bureaucrats, politicians and labourers.

Fascism & WWII

Discontent and social unrest after WWI favoured the rise of Benito Mussolini, who founded the Fascist Party (with its hallmarks of the black shirt and Roman salute) in 1919. These were to become the symbols of violent oppression and aggressive nationalism for the next 23 years. In 1921, the party won 35 of the 135 seats in parliament. In October 1922, Mussolini staged the March on Rome by 40,000 members of his Fascist militia. King Victor Emmanuel III invited him to form a government. In April 1924, following a campaign marked by violence, the Fascist Party won the national elections and Mussolini created the world's first Fascist regime. By 1925, the term 'totalitarianism' had entered the language. By the end of 1925, Mussolini had expelled opposition parties from parliament, gained control of the press and trade unions and reduced the voting public by two-thirds.

In 1929, Mussolini and Pope Pius XI signed the Lateran Pact, whereby Catholicism was declared the sole religion of Italy and the Città del Vaticano was recognised as an independent state with extraterritorial rights to the patriarchal basilicas of Santa Maria Maggiore, San Giovanni in Laterano and San Paolo Fuori-le-Mura, among other sites.

With the intent of glorifying Rome's imperial past, Mussolini's regime initiated radical, often destructive, public works. Via dei Fori Imperiali and Via della Conciliazione were laid out, parks were opened at the Colle Oppio and Villa Celimontana, the Imperial Fora and the temples at Largo Argentina were excavated, and the monumental Foro Italico sports complex and the Esposizione Universale di Roma (EUR) district were built.

Dreams of imperial glory also led Mussolini to invade Abyssinia (present-day Ethiopia) in 1935 and to form the Rome-Berlin Axis with Hitler in 1936. In 1940, from the balcony of Palazzo Venezia, Mussolini announced Italy's entry into WWII to a vast, cheering crowd. Declared an open city, Rome was largely spared from destruction during the war, although many members of the city's Jewish community were deported and killed in the Nazi death camps. Although there were many acts of individual heroism, the official silence from the Vatican during the Holocaust continues to be controversial, especially with the rumoured plans to canonise Pius XII.

One of the worst atrocities of WWII in Italy occurred in Rome. In March 1944, urban partisans blew up 32 German military police in Via Rasella. In reprisal, the Germans rounded up 335 people who had no connection with the incident, and shot them at the Fosse Ardeatine, just outside the city. A monument was constructed at the site.

In a 1946 referendum the Italian people voted to abolish the monarchy and adopt a republican form of government. The first president of Italy was installed in Palazzo del Quirinale, former residence of popes and kings.

Immediately after the war there was a series of three coalition governments, particularly dominated by the newly formed Democrazia Cristiana Party (DC; Christian Democrats), which remained the most powerful party in subsequent coalition governments until the '80s.

Rome was the scene in 1953 of the signing of the Treaty of Rome, which established the European Economic Community and laid the groundwork for the present European Union.

From 1948 to the early '60s, Rome was the centre of Italy's film industry, with the Cinecittà studios acting as Rome's answer to Hollywood. Federico Fellini's film *La Dolce Vita* made a modern legend of the lifestyle of the rich and famous in Rome during that period.

In 1960, the city hosted the Olympic Games.

Protest & Terrorism

Influenced by similar events in France, the late 1960s were marked by student revolt. University students in Rome and throughout the country rose up in protest, ostensibly against poor conditions in universities but, in reality, against authority and what they saw as the impotence of the left. The movement resulted in the formation of many small revolutionary groups that attempted to fill an ideological gap in Italy's political left wing.

But as the new decade began, a new phenomenon – terrorism – began to overshadow this turbulent era of protest and change. By 1970, a group of young left-wing militants had formed the Brigate Rosse (Le BR). While it was the most prominent of Italy's terrorist groups, the Brigate Rosse was by no means the only such group operating in the country during the Anni di Piombo (Years of the Bullet) from 1973 to 1980.

The most notorious of a chain of political killings in those years was the 1978 kidnapping and murder of former prime minister Aldo Moro, who had been moving towards a compromise that would have allowed the Partito Comunista Italiano (PCI; Communist Party) to become part of a coalition government. During the 54 days that Moro was held captive by the BR, his colleagues laboured over whether to bargain with the terrorists to save his life or to adopt a position of no compromise. In the end, they took the latter path and the BR killed Moro on 9 May 1978, leaving his body in the boot of a car parked in Via Caetani in the centre of Rome, precisely halfway between the headquarters of the Communist Party and that of the Christian Democrats.

In the same year, Karol Wojtyla was elected pope and took the name John Paul II. He is the first non-Italian pope since 1522, and the first Polish pope in the history of the Church. In 1981, a Turkish gunman severely wounded him in front of a crowd in Piazza San Pietro.

1980s & 1990s

Italy enjoyed significant economic growth throughout the 1980s, during which it became one of the world's leading economic powers.

The proposed compromise with the communists was never to eventuate but, in 1983, the DC government was forced to hand over the prime ministership to socialist Bettino Craxi, who held the post from 1983 to 1989. These were Rome's golden years of fat expense accounts and unlimited excesses. The Hotel Raphael, Craxi's powerbase in the capital, became the fulcrum of Rome, and the upmarket shops and restaurants in the historic centre had never seen better times. A skilled politician, Craxi continued to wield considerable power until he fled the country in 1993 after being implicated in the Tangentopoli national bribery scandal (see the boxed text 'Tangentopoli' overleaf). Convicted in absentia on corruption charges, he remains in self-imposed exile in Tunisia.

Rome at this time was governed by a series of undemocratically elected Socialist and Christian Democrat mayors. Corruption flourished, the worst episodes occurring during the lead up to the 1990 World Cup (for which Rome was the epicentre).

During this period, the PCI reached a watershed and internal ideological clashes led to an early-1990 party split. The old guard is now the Partito Rifondazione Comunista (PRC) and the breakaway, more moderate wing of the party reformed itself as the Partito Democratico della Sinistra (PDS; Democratic Party of the Left). This party went on to become the largest in the centre-left Ulivo (Olive Tree) coalition.

Tangentopoli

The Tangentopoli (literally 'kickback cities') scandal broke in Milan in early 1992 when a functionary of the PSI was arrested on charges of accepting bribes in exchange for public works contracts. Led by Milanese magistrate Antonio di Pietro, dubbed the 'reluctant hero', investigations known as Mani Pulite (clean hands) eventually implicated thousands of politicians, public officials and businesspeople.

Charges ranged from bribery, making illicit political payments and receiving kickbacks, to blatant thievery. It is ironic that few ordinary Italians were surprised that many politicians, at all levels of government, were entrenched in this corrupt system that affected the whole country.

The 1990s heralded a new period of economic and political crisis. High unemployment and inflation rates, combined with a huge national debt and an extremely unstable lira, led the government to introduce Draconian measures to revive the economy.

In post-Tangentopoli elections, voters expressed their discontent and the DC's share of the vote dropped by 5%. Umberto Bossi's Lega Nord (Northern League) made its first appearance as a force to be reckoned with at national level, winning 7% of the vote on a federalist, anticorruption platform. After the elections, parliament chose Christian Democrat, Oscar Luigi Scalfaro, a man noted for his personal integrity, as President of the Republic.

As Tangentopoli continued to unfold, the main parties – the DC and the PSI – were in tatters and the centre of the Italian political spectrum was effectively demolished.

In 1993, Francesco Rutelli – at that stage nominally part of the Verdi (Green Party) – became the first mayor of Rome to be directly elected by the inhabitants of the city. With movie-star good looks and charisma to match, the suave, media-savvy Rutelli set to cleaning up the city. Inspired by both the impending Jubilee Year of 2000 and

Rome's (unsuccessful) bid for the 2004 Olympics, the Rutelli *giunta* (group of councillors) targeted transport, infrastructure, pollution, conservation and protection of cultural patrimony.

At the 1994 national elections, voters continued to express their disgust with the old order. The elections were won by a new right-wing coalition known as the Polo per le Libertà (Freedom Alliance), whose members included the newly formed Forza Italia (Go Italy), the Neo-Fascist Alleanza Nazionale (National Alliance) and the federalist Northern League. Its leader, billionaire media magnate Silvio Berlusconi, who had entered politics only three months before the elections, was appointed prime minister. After a turbulent nine months in power, Berlusconi's volatile coalition government collapsed when Bossi, in an extremely controversial move, withdrew the support of his Northern League.

Berlusconi himself was under investigation by the Milano Mani Pulite judges and court proceedings against him continued into 1997.

In the chaos following the fall of Berlusconi's government, President Scalfaro appointed an interim government of 'technocrats' who set about running the show and confronting the country's economic problems until the April 1996 elections. By that time, there was a fairly clear division of the parties into two main groups: *centro-destra* (centre-right) and *centro-sinistra* (centre-left). Berlusconi's party, Forza Italia, remained aligned with the National Alliance, a repackaged and sanitised MSI, led by Gianfranco Fini. Their alliance, the Polo per le Libertà, has gathered other small parties of the centre-right under its umbrella.

However, it was the centre-left Ulivo coalition, led by Bolognese university professor Romano Prodi, which claimed victory at the 1996 elections, winning 50% of seats in the Senate and 45% in the House of Deputies. As prime minister, Prodi worked hard to ensure that Italy joined Europe's Economic and Monetary Union (EMU) in the first intake in 1988. His government drastically reduced public spending and introduced new taxes, enabling Italy to join the single currency as planned.

Despite its minor economic miracle, the road was far from smooth for Prodi's government, and proved to be a succession of trials of strength between the Ulivo and its coalition partner, the far-left Partito Rifondazione Comunista, which gave conditional support on increased spending and job creation. The impasse reached its height in September 1998.

Faced with the prospect of bringing down the second-longest lasting government of the Republic, the PRC split into those who supported the PRC leader Fausto Bertinotti, and a new grouping, Comunisti Italiani, who wanted to maintain the Prodi government. At the same time, the Unione Democratica per la Repubblica (UDR), a centrist group seeking a share of political power, offered its (conditional) support. Prodi refused to compromise and opted to face parliament in a vote. He lost by one vote.

During the Prodi government the Partito Democratico della Sinistra (PDS), under party secretary Massimo D'Alema, had remodelled itself as the Democratici di Sinistra (DS; Democrats of the Left), moving yet further from its communist roots. D'Alema had been manoeuvring for months (if not years) into a position where he could take over from Prodi. Prepared to compromise where Prodi wouldn't, he brokered an agreement with the centrist UDR, and was asked by President Scalfaro to form a government. Thus Italy gained its first former-communist prime minister (ironically leading a governing coalition closer to the centre than that of his predecessor), who clearly believed that it was better to be in power with an uncomfortable ally than not be in power at all.

In 1998, Francesco Rutelli was re-elected mayor of Rome. The 1999 election of Carlo Azeglio Ciampi as the 10th president of the Republic marked a new age of Italian politics. The highly respected former Bank of Italy governor was elected by a strong left and right parliamentary consensus.

What goes around comes around and in the wake of regional elections in 2000, which saw a huge swing to the right, Massimo D'Alema resigned as prime minister. Centre-left stalwart Giulio Amato formed a new government – Italy's 56th since the 1946 referendum.

2001 & Beyond

The May 2001 elections saw Silvio Berlusconi clinch victory over Francesco Rutelli, giving Italy another centre-right coalition. The charismatic Berlusconi has bounced back after disasterous times in the ministerial arena in the mid-1990s but with Italy's ever-changing political record, be sure to watch this space.

GEOGRAPHY

The Comune di Roma covers an expanse of roughly 150,000 hectares, of which 37% is built-up urban area, 15% is parkland and 48% is under agricultural use.

Rome's best known geographical features are its seven hills: the Palatine (Palatino), Capitoline (Campidoglio), Aventine (Aventino), Caelian (Celio), Esquiline (Esquilino), Viminal (Viminale) and Quirinal (Quirinale). Two other hills, the Gianicolo, which rises above Trastevere, and the Pincio, above Piazza del Popolo, were never actually part of the ancient city.

The Gianicolo is, in fact, a good vantage point from which to survey Rome's geography. From there it is possible to identify each of the seven hills, although two of them – the Viminal and Quirinal – are swallowed up by the city sprawl and seem not much more than gentle slopes. From here you can see how the River Tiber winds like a green ribbon through town, a handy thing to understand since the river is a good point of reference for navigating your way around the city centre.

The Tiber, which has its source in the Apennines north of Arezzo (in Tuscany) and runs into the sea at Ostia, is subject to sudden flooding. Until the late 19th century this caused significant problems for the areas bordering the river, including Trastevere. There were 46 devastating floods on record up to 1870. The problem was solved in 1900 by raising the level of the river's embankments. It is still possible to see markers around Trastevere denoting the water level reached by various floods. The ancient Romans built a major sea port, Ostia Antica, at the mouth of the Tiber but the harbour silted up long ago. Today the area is Rome's closest beach resort, known as Lido di Ostia.

In ancient times the city covered what is now called the *centro storico* (historical centre) and was enclosed by defensive walls (see the boxed text 'Within these Walls').

Modern Rome is divided into 22 *rioni*, 35 *quartieri* and six *suburbi*. The rioni, which are all in or near the city centre, trace their origins back to the regions of the city of the Roman Republic. The regions evolved into rioni during the Middle Ages and by the late 16th century there were 14. Another eight rioni were declared in 1921. Based on what might be called neighbourhoods, some of the rioni still retain a strong sense of history and tradition, notably Monti, the area incorporating the Esquiline, Viminal and Caelian; Borgo, next to St Peter's and the Vatican; and Trastevere, bordered by the Gianicolo hill and the Tiber.

CLIMATE

Spring and autumn are the best times to visit Rome, when the weather is warm and generally sunny. In September it is often still warm enough to head for the beach and well into October you'll be able to sit comfortably at an outside table while drinking your cappuccino. In a good year, mild weather can continue right up to December, punctuated by occasional days of icy winds that blow in from northern Europe. However, in a bad year, you might strike heavy rain in October.

July and August are generally extremely hot, with temperatures often reaching as high as 37°C for days on end, making sightseeing unpleasant, particularly if you are travelling with children. Romans desert their city in droves, heading for the beaches or mountains, which means that tourists (and the few remaining residents) can enjoy light traffic and semi-deserted footpaths.

From November to February the weather can be unpredictable, with heavy rain, particularly in November, and icy winds. However, even when it's chilly in January and February you'll often find blue skies and sunshine.

Within these Walls

The earliest defensive wall was, according to tradition, built by Romulus around the first settlement on the Palatine. As the city grew during the Republican era, it was divided into four *regiones* (known as the Palatino, Suburra, Esquilino and Collina), which were surrounded by the Servian Wall (Mura Serviane) started in 378 BC, following a surprise attack by the Gauls. Today only traces of the wall and its 12 entrances *(porte)* remain.

Emperor Aurelian started building a second wall in AD 271 to defend the city, which by then had about one million inhabitants, from barbarian attack. The huge, 19km-long wall had not been completed in 275 when Aurelian died, and was finished by his successor, Probus. Much of the Aurelian Wall (Mura Aureliane) still stands, along with many of its entrances, including Portas Maggiore, San Giovanni, Latina, San Sebastiano, San Paolo, San Pancrazio, del Popolo and Pia.

Over the centuries the wall was frequently consolidated and adapted for military use. In 536, Byzantine emperor Justinian sent his general Belisarius to Rome from Constantinople to snatch Italy from the reign of the Goths. His officials counted 383 towers, 7020 battlements, 14 main entrances, 116 latrines and 2066 external windows in the Aurelian Wall. In 1870, troops supporting Victor Emmanuel II breached the wall near the Porta Pia entrance and took Rome from Pope Pius IX.

The independent enclave known as the Vatican City, established in 1929 with signing of the Lateran Treaty between Mussolini and Pius XI, is also securely surrounded by walls.

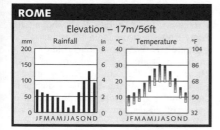

ROME
Elevation – 17m/56ft

Rome's sunniest months are May, June and July; its hottest months are June, July and August; its coldest are December, January and February; and the wettest are October, November and December.

ECOLOGY & ENVIRONMENT
Cleaning Up
Any large city can seem chaotic and claustrophobic and Rome is certainly no exception. Its traffic problems are appalling and the air pollution caused by vehicles idling in traffic jams can be choking at times, just ask anyone riding around on a moped! Efforts have increased in recent years to steer the traffic away from the city's historic centre and its main monuments, and only holders of special permits are allowed to drive in certain restricted areas of the centre. However, many of the city's most important monuments, the Colosseum included, remain at risk from pollution.

At the same time, there has been a massive clean-up and restoration effort, partly in preparation for the Jubilee Year of 2000 but also as part of a major effort by the Comune di Roma (City of Rome) to modernise the city for the new millennium. The effort has seen many of Rome's historic churches and palaces emerging from behind scaffolding with their facades finally cleaned of the dirt and grime built up over centuries.

Much as when Michelangelo's ceiling in the Sistine Chapel was revealed in all its glorious colour, many Romans have expressed some shock at seeing so many dazzling white marble buildings, after becoming so accustomed to their former dirty grey colour. Among the highlights of these restorations has been the opening of the restored Museo e Galleria Borghese in the Villa Borghese, and the opening of the Palazzo Altemps and Palazzo Massimo as two new seats of the Museo Nazionale Romano.

Rome's former mayor, Francesco Rutelli, oversaw a huge public works programme, mainly concentrated on improving roads, public transport and other infrastructure. Works are still underway to create an integrated railway network, to further develop the subway and tramlines and to create plans for traffic and pedestrian areas.

In this important process, the challenge is to modernise the city while preserving its extraordinary historical, architectural and artistic heritage. In Rome, where there is such an incredible concentration of monuments – many yet to be excavated – the Comune has regularly fallen foul of the Sovrintendenza dei Beni Culturali, the body responsible for protecting and maintaining the city's art and architectural patrimony. Over the years, many public works projects have been halted or delayed by the Sovrintendenza when it was discovered that they could have interfered with monuments.

Parks
Rome has an extensive network of parks, many of which were the former private gardens and parklands of the city's nobility. According to figures provided by the Comune di Roma, 64% of the territory of the Comune is 'green', although this includes agricultural land as well as parkland. The Villa Borghese, just north of the city centre, was once the estate of Cardinal Scipione Borghese, whose villa now houses the Museo e Galleria Borghese. The Villa Doria Pamphilj in Trastevere is Rome's largest park. It was the private estate of Prince Camillo Pamphilj, whose uncle was Pope Innocent X, and it features a number of different environments, including a small forest of *pini domesticii* (stone pines) and a large lake. Other large parks include the Villa Ada and Villa Glori, north of the city, and the Villa Celimontana, on the Caelian.

FLORA & FAUNA
Flora
Most of Rome's parks were formerly the private gardens of the city's aristocrats and they were designed and planted according to the fashion of the relevant periods. Accordingly, they generally contain a wide variety of exotic species – plants indigenous to the city were rarely considered fashionable.

But long before the nobles started to plant their spectacular gardens, the Etruscans and ancient Romans had been chopping down trees, trampling the native vegetation and importing exotic species. The stone pine *(pino domestico)*, considered a symbol of the city, was in fact imported, probably by the Etruscans, from the Middle East and botanists debate whether or not it should be considered indigenous to Rome.

Despite thousands of years of interference, Rome still manages to maintain almost 1300 native plants. Typical trees include about 10 species of oak *(quercia)*, including the holm oak *(leccio)* and the cork oak *(sughera)*, both of which grow spontaneously in small forests in the Roman countryside.

Rome's archaeological sites provide an ideal environment for the caper *(cappero)*. This plant, which usually grows only in the hot, dry climate of the country's south, has found ideal conditions in the rocks of Rome's ruined monuments. In spring, the caper forms cascading, puffy bushes, which in June become masses of pink flowers. You will see them growing in areas including the Palatine, the Terme di Caracalla (Baths of Caracalla), the Aurelian Wall and on the Ponte Rotto near the Isola Tiberina.

Rome's native plants also find an ideal environment along the banks of the Tiber. These include the willow *(salice)* and the poplar *(pioppo)*. In the uncultivated areas of the countryside, there are hundreds of species of daisies, grasses, grains and clover.

Rome's botanical gardens *(orto botanico)* are at the base of the Gianicolo in Trastevere, at Largo Cristina Svezia. Originally part of the grounds of the Palazzo Corsini, the gardens were handed over to the University of Rome in 1883. There are more than 7000 plant species from around the world in the gardens and the collection of orchids is particularly notable.

Fauna
The animals you are most likely to observe in Rome are cats, dogs and perhaps the odd rat, although you might be lucky to spot a squirrel or fox in one of Rome's numerous parks. However, in the green areas and even while walking around the city streets, you can observe a surprising variety of birdlife. More than 100 different types of birds are said to nest in Rome's parks and rooftops, including kingfishers, kites, woodpeckers, kestrels, barn owls and horned owls. You'll have no trouble spotting red robins, sparrows, finches, tits, swallows and seagulls, as well as ducks, moorhens and swans on lakes. Some of the lakes in Rome's parks

Fellini's Felines

While animal rights is not a major consideration for the average Roman, the welfare of the city's huge stray cat population is a fascinating exception. Most of the city's feline residents are semi-wild, although it can be hard to pick the strays from the pets just out for a stroll.

The strays are often as well fed and contented, thanks to the army of women who feed them leftover pasta. There are an estimated 10,000 cat colonies in Rome, many located in archaeological areas, such as the Colosseum, Foro di Traiano and in Largo di Torre Argentina. Some 500 of these colonies are under veterinary supervision, either by private animal welfare groups or by the city's own services.

Since the introduction of an extraordinarily humane law in 1988, Rome's stray cats are guaranteed the right to live where they're born – meaning that locals can't chase them away, whatever problems they cause. This right is also included in the model for national legislation.

are also occasional refuges for cormorants and grey herons.

If you have a particular passion for bird-watching, you might like to pick up the *Atlante degli Uccelli Nidificanti a Roma* (Atlas of Nesting Birds in Rome), by Bruno Cignini and Mario Zapparoli (€25.82).

GOVERNMENT & POLITICS

Rome's municipal government is located on the Capitoline, which has been the seat of the city's civic government since the late 11th century. The city has a *sindaco* (mayor) elected by the public, who appoints a *giunta*, a group of councillors called *assessori* who hold ministerial positions as heads of municipal departments. The assessori are appointed from the *consiglio comunale*, a body of elected officials, much like a parliament.

Rome is also the seat of national government. A parliamentary republic, Italy is headed by a president, who appoints the prime minister. The parliament consists of two houses – a Senate and a Chamber of Deputies – both with equal legislative power.

The president resides in the Palazzo del Quirinale, on Rome's Quirinal hill, the Chamber of Deputies sits in the Palazzo di Montecitorio, just off Via del Corso, and the Senate sits in the Palazzo Madama, near Piazza Navona.

Italy's electoral system generally forces the formation of unstable coalition governments. Since the declaration of the republic in 1946 there have been 58 governments with an average lifespan of 11 months. For further information see 2001 & Beyond under History earlier in this chapter.

ECONOMY

Rome generates 12% of its economy from tourism. Other stalwarts of the Roman economy are banking, insurance, printing, publishing and fashion. Unemployment in Rome is around 12.5%, although the figure is much higher for people aged between 14 and 29 – around 22%. The Comune itself is one of the city's biggest employers and a good proportion of Romans employed in the private sector are self-employed.

The mainstays of the city's budget are the annual 'garbage tax' paid by residents (a form of municipal tax or rates) and its share of national taxes. In comparison with other cities, Rome receives a fairly low share of the tax pool – €149.77 annually per capita – while Milan receives €231.89 and Naples €524.20 for every resident. Over the past decade, Rome's municipal government has been very proactive in attracting international investment in Rome by selling city bonds and seeking sponsorship for high-profile restoration projects.

Recent spending on infrastructure has soared, including more than €1 billion on a much improved rail network. After a slow start Rome has taken a great leap forward in digital communications and almost €1 billion has been invested in laying fibre optic cables to modernise the city's telecommunication network.

POPULATION & PEOPLE

The Comune di Roma has a population of some 2.6 million people. The Provincia di Roma (Rome Province) – encompassing areas such as: Ostia to the south-west of the city; Castelli Romani and Colli Albani to the south-east; Tivoli to the east; Cerveteri and Lago di Bracciano to the north-east; and the Monti Sabini to the north – has a population of 3.8 million. The Regione Lazio (Lazio Region), which comprises the provinces of Roma, Rieti, Viterbo, Latina and Frosinone, has a total population of 5.2 million.

Of the Roman population, 17.1% are aged under 20, 65.5% are aged between 20 and 64, and 17.4% are over 65. The ageing population echoes the demographic trend throughout Italy, which is one of the only countries in the world where the old outnumber the young. Demographic estimates suggest that by 2040, those over 65 will represent 41% of Italy's population.

In the Lazio region in 1997 there were 47,172 births and 48,807 deaths, following national trends. Italy has had a negative birth rate for the past five years and things do not seem to be changing. In fact Italy's current birth rate is the lowest in the world and the lowest in its history. International demographers have warned that if the current levels of generation replacement remain, the Italian population will become extinct in 200 years. The trend is unlikely to reverse itself in the short term. A recent survey conducted by a leading women's magazine found that more than half of the young women in Italy do not want to have children. For those between the ages of 16 and 24 a staggering 52% claimed already to have decided against having children. Only 19% of those surveyed were in favour of having children and of those most wanted only one child.

However, the population of the Lazio region actually increased in 1997 thanks to the arrival of around 30,000 immigrants from around the globe.

Estimates of the number of foreigners in Rome vary, although it is thought that one fifth of the total number of immigrants in Italy live in Rome. The official number is around 211,000 (or around 8% of the city's population). However, there are also around 33,000 illegal immigrants living in the city. Of the foreigners in Rome, around 21% are in the city for religious reasons.

Around 11% of the foreigners in Rome come from the Philippines, 6% from Poland, 4.2% from the USA, 3.8% from India, 3.7% from Bangladesh and 3.7% from Spain. The majority of immigrants (35.5%) come from other countries in Europe (EU, central and eastern Europe) followed by Asia (29.4%), the Americas (17.2%) and Africa (16.9%). The immigrant population is essential to the Italian economy, as the immigrants tend to do jobs such as domestic work, manual labour and seasonal agricultural jobs, which Italians themselves seem to be increasingly less willing to take on.

EDUCATION

The Italian state-school system is free of charge and consists of several levels. Attendance is compulsory from the ages of six to 14 years, although children can attend a *scuola materna* (nursery school) from the ages of three to five years before starting the *scuola elementare* (primary school) at

six. After five years they move on to the *scuola media* (secondary school) until they reach the age of 14.

The next level, the *scuola secondaria superiore* (higher secondary school), is voluntary and lasts a further five years until the student is 19 years old. It is, however, essential if young people want to study at university. At this level there are several options: four types of *liceo* (humanities-based school), four types of technical school, and teacher-training school.

The government is in the process of reforming the education system. The standards of education in the state-run system compare well with those in other countries, although the system does have its problems, compounded by relatively low standards in teacher-training and poor government management. Officially at least, only 3% of Italians over the age of 15 are illiterate.

Private schools in Rome are run mainly by religious institutions, notably the Jesuits. There are also 21 private international schools, which provide education for English-, French-, German-, Spanish- and Japanese-speaking children.

In Rome there are three state universities, one private university, several Catholic universities and several international universities (see Universities in the Facts for the Visitor chapter). The largest Italian university, La Sapienza, has around 150,000 students. Courses are usually from four to six years, although students are under no obligation to complete them in that time. Students in fact often take many more years to fulfil their quota of exams and submit their final thesis. Attendance at overcrowded lectures is optional and for scientific courses, practical experimentation is done. Students therefore tend to study at home. All state-school and university examinations are oral, rather than written.

Italy produces far fewer graduates per capita than most other countries in the West. Of the 65% of Italian secondary school students who enrol at university, only a third ever actually graduate. Despite that, unemployment among graduates is estimated at higher than 40%.

ARTS
Architecture
Pre-Roman There are archaeological and architectural remains dating back to the 4th millennium BC in Italy, but the earliest well preserved Italian art and architecture dates from the 1st millennium BC. It comes from three cultures: Latin and Roman culture in Lazio; Etruscan culture, from what is now northern Lazio and southern Tuscany (see Etruscan Sites in the Excursions chapter for more details); and the culture of Magna Grecia, in southern Italy and Sicilia, where city states were founded in the 8th and 7th centuries BC by Greek colonists who settled alongside the Italic peoples.

Like the Greeks, the early Romans built temples of stone. Whereas the Greek temples (of southern Italy and Sicilia) had steps and colonnades on all sides, the Roman variety had a high podium with steps and columns only at the front, forming a deep porch. The Romans also favoured fluted Ionic columns with volute capitals and Corinthian columns with acanthus leaf capitals (rather than the Greek Doric columns with cushion-like capitals). Examples still standing today in Rome include the Republican Tempio di Ercole Vincitore and the Tempio di Portunus by the Tiber near Piazza della Bocca della Verità and, though not so well preserved, the temples in the Area Sacra di Largo Argentina.

Roman The Romans' great achievement was in perfecting existing construction techniques and putting these skills to use in the service of the Republic and later the Empire. For example, they learnt how to build roads and bridges from the Etruscans, and used these skills to create aqueducts and arches on a grandiose scale, the likes of which had never been seen before.

From the 1st century BC the Romans, using volcanic sand, made a quick-curing, strong concrete for vaults, arches and domes. It was used especially in Rome to roof vast areas such as the Pantheon, which was until the 20th century the largest poured concrete dome in existence. Pumice was used in the concrete at the top to reduce the weight. Huge vaults covered the hot baths and other rooms in complexes such as the Terme di Caracalla built in AD 217.

Brick-faced concrete was also used for *insulae* (multistorey apartment blocks) and basilicas such as the massive Basilica di Costantino (completed in 315). Dry-stone masonry was used for some temples, aqueducts and for the vaulted substructures to support the seating of theatres and amphitheatres such as the Teatro di Marcello and the Colosseum.

Marble was a popular building material in both Republican and Imperial Rome and was used from the 2nd century BC. As Rome's power grew, new buildings were needed to reflect the city's status in the Mediterranean world. The Romans developed complexes used for commercial and political activities such as Trajan's Forum and Markets. Building projects became increasingly ambitious. Artistic concerns took second place to size and impressive engineering, evident in structures such as the huge Terme di Diocleziano (built in AD 298).

In the 4th century, an ambitious building programme financed by Constantine saw the erection of several places of worship, most of which followed the basilican style of late antiquity, although little of the original buildings remains. A notable exception is the domed baptistry of San Giovanni in Laterano, built by Constantine between 315 and 324 and remodelled into its present octagonal shape in the 5th century; it became the model for many baptistries throughout the Christian world.

Middle Ages Early-medieval architecture in Italy (around 600 to 1050) involved mainly the construction and decoration of Christian churches and monasteries, much of which took place outside Rome, notably in Ravenna. Among the most important churches in Rome of this period were Santa Maria in Cosmedin, built in the 8th century, and the 9th-century Santa Prassede.

The basilican style survived into the so-called Romanesque period (11th to 13th centuries), which saw a revival of buildings whose size and structure resembled those of the Roman Empire. Many Romanesque basilican churches were built throughout Italy with rounded arch forms echoing those of classical and late antiquity.

Late-medieval Gothic architecture, influenced by northern European styles of pointed arches and vaults, never took off in Rome the way it did in northern Italy. The city's only Gothic church is the Chiesa di Santa Maria sopra Minerva.

Renaissance Almost all the artistic and architectural activity of the early Renaissance was in Tuscany and Venice. However, with the revival of the papacy, Rome was on course to take over the limelight. The 15th-century popes saw that the best way to ensure political power was to rebuild the city and the leading artistic and architectural masters were summoned to Rome. The Venetian Paul II (1464–71) commissioned many works including Palazzo Venezia, Rome's first great Renaissance *palazzo* (palace), built in 1455 when he was still a cardinal and enlarged when he became pope in 1464. The pontificate of Julius II (1503–13) marks the true beginning of the high Renaissance in Rome.

Domes, vaults and arches and the model of classical Rome provide the key to Renaissance architecture. The first such buildings were by Donato Bramante (1441–1514), who had already made a name for himself in Milan when he arrived in Rome. Impressed by the ruins of ancient Rome, he created a refined classicism that embodied the concerns of the Renaissance more fully than any previous architecture. Bramante's respect for the ancients and understanding of Renaissance ideals can be seen in his Tempietto (1502), next to the Chiesa di San Pietro in Montorio on the Gianicolo, and in the perfectly proportioned cloister (1504) of the Chiesa di Santa Maria della Pace near Piazza Navona. The circular Tempietto, surrounded by 16 Doric columns, was the first building to depend entirely on the proportions of the classical orders and the most sophisticated attempt that had yet been made to combine the highest ideals of faith and art in order to create a perfect temple.

In 1506, Bramante was commissioned by Julius II to start work on St Peter's Basilica, the reconstruction of which under Nicholas V had virtually ground to a halt 50 years earlier. Bramante's original design was based on a Greek cross plan topped by a huge central dome and flanked by four smaller cupolas. Bramante died in 1514, at which time the four central piers and the arches of the dome had been completed.

St Peter's Basilica occupied most of the other notable architects of the high Renaissance including Raphael (1483–1520), Giuliano da Sangallo (1443–1517), Baldassarre Peruzzi (1481–1537) and Antonio da Sangallo the Younger (1483–1546). Commissioned by Paul III, Michelangelo Buonarroti (1475–1564) took over the task and created the magnificent light-filled dome, 42m wide, based on Brunelleschi's design for the Duomo cupola in Florence, the first major architectural achievement of the early Renaissance.

Paul III also commissioned Michelangelo to create a new civic square on the Capitoline, for which he adapted the vocabulary of classicism to suit his own ends, creating columns and pilasters that rose through two or more storeys of the *palazzi* facades.

Counter-Reformation During the period of Counter-Reformation both art and architecture were entirely at the service of the Church. A costly building programme was begun, largely under the direction of the Jesuits, to create massive and impressive churches to attract and overawe worshippers.

Giacomo della Porta (1539–1602) was the leading architect of the age and the last of the Renaissance tradition. He designed the mannerist facade of the main Jesuit church in Rome, the Gesù (1568–75). In a move away from the style of earlier Renaissance churches, the facade has pronounced architectural elements that create a contrast between surfaces and a play of light and shade. The building's exterior, as well as the interior – a wide nave and side chapels instead of aisles – was widely copied throughout Italy. Della Porta also designed the Sant'Andrea della Valle church in 1591 and the Palazzo della Sapienza, which was the seat of Rome's university until 1935.

The end of the 16th century and the papacy of Sixtus V (1585–90) marked the beginning of major urban planning schemes as the city became a symbol of the resurgent Church. Domenico Fontana (1543–1607) and other architects created a network of major thoroughfares to connect previously disparate parts of the sprawling medieval city and erected obelisks at various vantage points. Fontana also designed the large-scale but uninspiring Palazzo Laterano (1607) next to the Basilica di San Giovanni in Laterano.

In his design for the facade of Chiesa di Santa Susanna (1603), Fontana's nephew, Carlo Maderno (1556–1629) created his masterpiece, which was regarded as a forerunner of Baroque.

Baroque The two great artistic figures of 17th-century Rome are the architect Francesco Borromini (1599–1667) from Lombardy and the Neapolitan-born architect and sculptor Gian Lorenzo Bernini (1598–1680).

No other architect before or since has had such an impact on a city as Bernini did on Rome. His patron was the Barberini pope, Urban VIII, who appointed him as the official architect of St Peter's from 1629. Bernini designed towers for Carlo Maderno's facade (which were structurally problematic and later demolished) and the baldacchino or altar canopy above St Peter's grave, for which ancient bronze was stripped from such places as the Pantheon.

Under Urban VIII's patronage, Bernini had an opportunity, afforded to no other man before or since, to transform the face of the city, and his churches, palaces, piazzas and fountains are Roman landmarks to this day. However, things soured for a short time on the death of Urban VIII in 1644 and the accession of Innocent X, who wanted as little contact as possible with the favoured artists and architects of his detested predecessor. Instead he turned to Borromini, Alessandro Algardi (1598–1654) and Girolamo and Carlo Rainaldi.

The son of an architect and well versed in stone masonry and construction techniques, Borromini created buildings involving complex shapes and exotic geometry. Distinctive features of his designs were windows, often oval-shaped and positioned for maximum illumination. His most memorable works are Chiesa di San Carlo alle Quattro Fontane (1634), which has an oval-shaped interior, and Chiesa di Sant'Ivo alla Sapienza, which combines a unique arrangement of convex and concave surfaces and is topped by an innovative spiral campanile.

Stories abound about the rivalry between Bernini and Borromini. Certainly, the latter was envious of Bernini's early success. Bernini came back into favour with his magnificent design for the Fontana dei Quattro Fiumi (1651) in the centre of Piazza Navona, opposite Borromini's Chiesa di Sant'Agnese in Agone. It is said that Bernini's figure of the Nile is holding up his arm to shield his eyes from the sight of Borromini's church. In fact the fountain was built several years before the church so the story, while engaging, doesn't stand up. What is true is that together they were the dominating architectural forces of the Baroque period.

Like Michelangelo, Bernini thought of himself first and foremost as a sculptor, and his best known works fall somewhere between sculpture and architecture. He was responsible for the setting for the throne and tombs for Urban VIII and Alexander VII in St Peter's and the magnificent sweeping colonnade in Piazza di San Pietro (1656–67) as well as the church of Sant'-Andrea al Quirinale (1658). His most endearing works include the small obelisk set on the back of an elephant in Piazza della Minerva, near the Pantheon, and the angels set on the parapets of the Ponte Sant' Angelo bridge over the Tiber.

Late 17th to 20th Centuries The early 18th century saw a brief flurry of surprisingly creative architecture such as the Scalinata di Spagna (Spanish Steps) built between 1723 and 1726 by Francesco de Sanctis, which provided a focal point for the many Grand Tourists who came to re-discover Rome's classical past. The rococo Piazza di Sant'Ignazio designed by Filippo Raguzzini (1680–1771) in 1728, with its curved facades, gives Sant'Ignazio, Rome's second Jesuit church, a theatrical setting.

Carlo Fontana (1634–1714), the most popular architect at the tail end of the Baroque era, designed various palaces and churches.

The Baroque love of grand gesture continued with the Trevi Fountain, one of the city's most exuberant and enduringly popular monuments. It was designed in 1732 by Nicola Salvi (1697–1751) and completed three decades later.

The beginning of modern architecture in Italy is epitomised by the late-19th-century iron and glass-roofed shopping galleries in Milan, Naples, Genoa and Turin. However, this fashion never quite made it to Rome, which instead received the massive white-marble monument – the so-called 'wedding cake' or 'typewriter' – to Victor Emmanuel II built between 1885 and 1911. Its enormous colonnade alludes to ancient precedents.

There was still time for flights of fancy such as the wonderfully frivolous Art Nouveau palazzi of Coppedè, north-east of the city centre near Via Salaria, before Mussolini and the Fascist era made its architectural mark with grandiose building schemes, such as the Foro Italico sports centre at the foot of Monte Mario (1928–31) and EUR (Esposizione Universale di Roma), a complete district on the outskirts of Rome that has a classicising, axial monumentality, massive statues and under-utilised museums.

Other than rather hideous and anonymous apartment buildings in the outer suburbs of the city, Rome has seen little new architecture in the second half of the 20th century. Exceptions are the Stadio Flaminio built for the 1960 Olympics, the Stadio Olimpico also built for the Olympics and revamped for the 1990 World Cup, the mosque in the Parioli area, designed by Paolo Portoghesi, and the new auditorium north of the city centre designed by Renzo Piano (see the boxed text 'A New Auditorium for a New Millennium' in the Entertainment chapter for further details).

However, new-millennium architecture may soon be another drawcard for Rome, with two projects by the American architect Richard Meier currently under way. One of these is a church officially known as Dio Padre Misericordioso, in Tor Tre Teste, a suburb east of the city centre. The church was destined to be the symbol of the Holy Year 2000 and *should* have been consecrated in 2000 by Pope John Paul II as an important part of Rome's Jubilee celebrations. Administrative and technical problems have delayed the construction of the church and it is now due for completion in 2002.

Five years of mainly bureaucratic and political obstacles have delayed another project by Richard Meier, who was commissioned by Rome's mayor Francesco Rutelli in 1995 to build a new museum complex for the Ara Pacis (see the Things to See & Do chapter) in Piazza Augusto Imperatore. Rutelli had a vision for Rome, along the lines of Barcelona or London, which included an important contemporary building in the heart of the ancient city. When it is completed in 2002, the Ara Pacis museum will be the first new building in Rome's historic centre in 60 years.

Painting & Mosaics

Roman The Romans used painting and mosaic work, both legacies from Etruscans and Greeks, to decorate houses and palaces from at least the 1st century BC. Although very little decoration of this type survives, there are some magnificent examples in the Museo Nazionale Romano collection at Palazzo Massimo alle Terme.

Roman wall-paintings, including those of the catacombs, were in true fresco technique with water-based pigments applied to wet plaster. The frescoes represent four styles: the first imitates stonework; the second creates illusions of architectural settings and dates to the last century BC; the third has a pattern of delicate architectural tracery combined with imitations of panel paintings; and the fourth, from the mid-1st century, combines features of the second and third styles and is the most common.

Later frescoes, found at Ostia Antica and in the catacombs, tend towards simpler decoration and are often on a white background.

Christian At first, black-and-white mosaic cubes were used for floors; later coloured stones were employed. By the 4th century, glass tesserae were used to splendid effect in the apses of the early Christian churches of Rome including Santa Costanza, Santa Pudenziana, Santi Cosma e Damiano and the Basilica di Santa Maria Maggiore.

During the 5th and 6th centuries the only art permitted was Christian art, which changed little in style but broadened its subject matter, including scenes from the Old Testament and the Passion of Christ. The tradition of mosaic decoration of churches continued from the 7th to the 9th century in Chiesa di Santa Prassede and the Basilica di Santa Cecilia in Trastevere, and the influence of Byzantine mosaic artists who created images against a gold background, became more widespread.

Middle Ages Local artists were employed to decorate churches and palaces when Rome started building again in the 12th century. The most famous decorative artists of the day were the Cosmati, originally a single family of artisans, whose title eventually became a name for a whole school.

The Cosmati revolutionised the already well established art of mosaic by reusing fragments of coloured glass from the ruins of ancient Rome. They also sliced up ancient columns of coloured marble and other precious stones into circular slabs, which were used to create intricate patterned pavements, altars, paschal candlesticks, pulpits and other decoration. Their work is referred to as 'Cosmati' or 'Cosmatiesque' and can be found in churches all over Rome.

Some of the Cosmati school eventually became accomplished sculptors, architects and mosaicists, such as Pietro Vassalletto (died 1186) who built the cloisters at San Giovanni in Laterano and San Paolo Fuorile-Mura, two of the best surviving examples of Cosmatiesque decoration in Rome.

One of the greatest Roman artists of the Middle Ages, and a precursor of the Renaissance, was Pietro Cavallini (c.1250–1330) who switched effortlessly between fresco painting (found in Santa Cecilia in Trastevere) and mosaic work (in Santa Maria in Trastevere).

Renaissance The main artistic activity of the early Renaissance took place in Florence, Siena and Venice. However, painting flourished once again as Rome was rebuilt after the 15th-century restoration of the papacy.

Between 1481 and 1483 some of the country's greatest painters were employed by Sixtus IV to decorate the walls in his newly rebuilt Sistine Chapel in the Vatican. The frescoes of the lives of Moses and Christ and portraits of popes were done by Perugino (1446–1523), Sandro Botticelli (1444–1510), Domenico Ghirlandaio (1449–94), Cosimo Rosselli (1439–1507) and Luca Signorelli (c.1441–1523). These artists were assisted by members of their workshops, including Pinturicchio (1454–1513), who subsequently frescoed the Borgia apartments between 1492 and 1494, Piero di Cosimo (1462–1521) and Bartolomeo della Gatta (1448–1502).

The decoration of the official apartments of Pope Julius II (the Stanze di Raffaello or Raphael Rooms), marked the beginning of the brilliant Roman career of Urbino-born Raphael (Raffaello Sanzio, 1483–1520) who arrived from Florence in 1508. In true Renaissance spirit, he absorbed the manner of classical Rome and became the most influential painter of his time.

Raphael was also adept at portraiture and mythological paintings. Wonderful frescoes in this vein, painted between 1508 and 1511, can be found in the Villa Farnesina in Trastevere. Other leading artists who worked on the villa, designed by Baldassarre Peruzzi, were Sebastiano del Piombo (c.1485–1547), Sodoma (1477–1549) and Giulio Romano (c.1492–1546), one of the few native Roman artists of the Renaissance.

The greatest achievement of the period was by Raphael's contemporary, Michelangelo Buonarroti (1475–1564) on the Sistine

Hidden Treasures

Few tourists know that within Rome's medieval churches lie some of the most beautiful Byzantine mosaics in Italy. Many decorate the apses of the city's important churches, including Santa Maria Maggiore, Santa Maria in Trastevere and San Clemente. The oldest mosaics date from the 4th century, when the Roman art of mosaic-making was evolving into early-Christian and Byzantine styles. Those depicting Santa Costanza retain some Roman characteristics: a white background, geometric composition and ornamental motifs.

During the reign of Constantine, who decriminalised the Christian religion, many churches were built and ornamental mosaic became the main form of decoration. Often used to cover vast wall areas inside new churches, they were a form of architectural tapestry that, with their uneven tesserae of coloured glass and gold, brilliantly reflected light to create strong effects and sharp colour contrasts.

Rome's early-Christian mosaics also illustrate the progression from the naturalism of Roman art to the symbolism of Christian art, often reflected in the various representations of Jesus Christ. A mosaic in a mausoleum under St Peter's Basilica shows Christ in the form of Apollo. In Chiesa di Santa Pudenziana (390) he is enthroned between the apostles (who are dressed as Roman senators) and his magisterial air is reminiscent of Jupiter. By the 9th century, in Santa Prassede, he has become the Lamb with his faithful flock.

The mosaics of Rome's medieval churches are a fascinating and often overlooked treasure for those who cannot spare time to visit Ravenna or Monreale. The following suggested itinerary covers some of the lesser-known churches. The mosaics in major churches are described in the Things to See & Do chapter.

The mid-4th-century **Mausoleo di Santa Costanza** was built by Constantia, daughter of Constantine, as a mausoleum for herself and her sister Helen. This round church is in the same grounds as the **Basilica di Sant'Agnese Fuori-le-Mura**, Via Nomentana, a few kilometres north of the centre (catch bus No 62 from Piazza Venezia). As well as the fascinating paleo-Christian mosaics on the barrel-vaulting of the ambulatory, the 7th-century mosaic of St Agnes and Popes Symmachus and Honorius I in the apse of the basilica are also worth a look.

Chapel ceiling (1508–12). The dramatically foreshortened figures are the most striking examples of the mannerist style of the 16th century. The ceiling is the most moving and original combination of art and faith in Renaissance Rome, and one of the greatest artistic achievements of all time – by an artist who didn't think of himself as a painter. Three decades later, after the Sack of Rome, Michelangelo returned to the Vatican to adorn the altar wall of the Sistine Chapel with *The Last Judgment* (1535–1541). For more details see the boxed text 'Michelangelo in Rome' in the Things to See & Do chapter.

Counter-Reformation Both painting and sculpture hit a low point in the late 16th century, although there were some high-

lights at the very end of the century. Annibale Carracci (1560–1609) left his mark on Rome with magnificent frescoes (1597–1603) of mythological subjects in the Palazzo Farnese and the technically proficient, if uninspiring, Cavalier d'Arpino (1568–1640) designed the mosaics covering the inside of St Peter's dome.

The arrival of Michelangelo Merisi da Caravaggio (1573–1610) heralded a move away from the confines of the high Renaissance towards a new naturalism. In Caravaggio's case, his naturalism was often regarded as being just a little too 'real' and his paintings, using street urchins and prostitutes as models for biblical subjects, were often rejected. However, his innovative sense of light and shade and supreme draughting ability meant that he was

According to tradition, **Santa Pudenziana**, one of the oldest churches in Rome, was founded on the site of a house where St Peter was given hospitality. The structure actually incorporated the internal thermal hall of the house. The mosaic in the apse dates from 390 and is the earliest of its kind in Rome but, unfortunately, was partially destroyed by a 16th century restoration. The church is in Via Urbana.

Santi Cosma e Damioano, Via dei Fori Imperiali, harbours magnificent 6th-century mosaics on the triumphal arch (Christ as the Lamb enthroned, surrounded by candlesticks and angels, as well as the symbols of the evangelists) and mosaics in the apse feature Cosma and Damian being presented to Christ by Peter and Paul and, underneath, Christ as the Lamb, with the 12 apostles also represented as lambs. Bethlehem and Jerusalem are portrayed on either side.

The 9th-century **Chiesa di Santa Prassede**, Via Santa Prassede, was founded in honour of St Praxedes, by Pope Paschal I, who transferred the bones of 2000 martyrs there from the catacombs. The rich mosaics of the apse date from the 9th century and feature Christ in the centre of the semi-dome, surrounded by St Peter, St Pudentiana and St Zeno (to the right) and St Paul, St Praxedes and St Paschal (to the left). Below is Christ as the Lamb and his flock.

The **Cappella di San Zenone**, inside the church, is the most important Byzantine monument in Rome, built by Paschal I as a mausoleum for his mother. Known as the Garden of Paradise, the chapel has a vaulted interior covered in mosaics, including Madonna with Saints, Christ with Saints and, in the vault, Christ with Angels. The chapel pavement is an early example of *opus sectile* (polychrome marble), and in a small niche on the right are fragments of a column brought from Jerusalem in 1223. It's said to be the one at which Christ was scourged.

Across the Tiber is the **Basilica di Santa Cecilia in Trastevere,** Piazza dei Mercanti, built in the 9th century by Paschal I over the house of St Cecilia, where she was martyred in 230. The impressive mosaic in the apse was executed in 870 and features Christ giving a blessing. To his right are St Peter, St Valerian (St Cecilia's husband) and St Cecilia herself. To his left are St Paul, St Agatha and St Paschal. The holy cities are depicted underneath.

---

courted by contemporary collectors. who wanted to cash in on his talent, and was an influential figure for centuries. See the boxed text 'On the Caravaggio Trail' in the Things to See & Do chapter.

More successful in their day, though less-highly revered afterwards, were the dryly academic painters Guido Reni (1575–1642) and Domenichino (1581–1641). Their immediate contemporaries and successors considered them to be on a par with Raphael and Michelangelo.

Domenichino was a native of Bologna and a pupil of Annibale Carracci. He was one of the most prodigious and admired masters in early-17th-century Rome and, for a time at least, so in favour with the aristocratic clergy of the day that he received innumerable commissions. His best works were his fresco cycles, which adorn nine churches in Rome.

Baroque Michelangelo had started a fashion for ceiling frescoes that continued well into the 17th century. Pietro da Cortona (1596–1669) was one of the most sought-after decorators of Baroque Rome. His fresco on the ceiling of the Salone Grande in Palazzo Barberini, begun in 1632, paved the way for numerous other commissions including the ceiling frescoes in Chiesa Nuova. Many painters tried, but failed, to match his talent.

The Jesuit artist Andrea Pozzo (1642–1709) made a name for himself creating trompe l'oeil perspectives on ceilings and walls of Jesuit churches and buildings, while serene landscapes were being produced by

Salvator Rosa (1615–73) and the Italianised French painters Nicolas Poussin (1594–1665) and Claude Lorrain (1600–82).

The 18th to 20th Centuries By the 18th century, Rome's artistic heyday was over; the attention of the many foreign artists who settled in Rome turned to the antique. The widely disseminated etchings of the city and its ancient ruins by Giovanni Battista Piranesi attracted Grand Tourists and artists alike. The Swiss-born Angelica Kauffmann was just one example of a foreign artist who settled in the Eternal City and produced proficient, if ordinary, academic art.

Painting and sculpture since Italian unification in 1870 are most readily found in the Galleria Nazionale d'Arte Moderna. The late 19th century saw the emergence of Italian post-impressionism with the *Macchiaioli* school ('*macchia*' means 'stain' or 'spot') who produced a version of pointillism using thousands of dots of pure colour to build up the picture, and Italian symbolists.

The Italian futurists were inspired by urbanism, industry and the idea of progress. Umberto Boccioni (1882–1916) and Giacomo Balla (1871–1958) aligned themselves with the futurist manifesto (1909) of writer Emilio Marinetti, whereas Carlo Carrà (1881–1996) had much in common with cubists such as Pablo Picasso. Giorgio Morandi (1890–1964) consistently depicted bottles and jars as forms rather than objects, while the surrealist Giorgio De Chirico (1888–1978) painted visionary empty streetscapes with disconcertingly juxtaposed elements, which often incorporated allusions to classical antiquity.

Amedeo Modigliani (1884–1920) spent most of his adult life in Paris. However, his art – mainly arresting portraits and sensuous reclining female nudes – was firmly rooted in the Italian Renaissance.

Important post-WWII and contemporary artists include Burri, Colla, Manzoni, Pascali and the Transavanguardia, whose exponents such as Enzo Cucchi, Francesco Clemente (born 1952), Mimmo Paladino and Sandro Chia (born 1946) have gained success both in Italy and abroad.

Sculpture

Etruscan Most evidence of Etruscan art has come from their tombs, richly furnished with carved stone sarcophagi, fabulous gold jewellery, ceramic and bronze statues and utilitarian objects, as well as frescoes, fine examples of which are displayed in the Villa Giulia. The Etruscan artists learned Greek artistic techniques and transformed them into a unique style of their own.

The Etruscans were famous for metalwork such as the bronze *Lupa Capitolina* (Capitoline Wolf) in the Capitoline Museums, though such a large piece is a rarity. The made-to-measure figures of Romulus and Remus were added during the Renaissance. Most of the surviving Etruscan pieces are small figurines and household items, such as engraved mirrors. The techniques used to make the amazingly intricate filigree work, which decorates Etruscan gold jewellery, were only rediscovered in the 20th century.

Roman During both the Republic and the Empire, sculpture was very much at the service of the Roman state (and the emperor), and more than any other art form provides a compelling record of the city's history.

The first 'Roman' sculptures were actually made by Greek artists or were copies of imported classical Greek works. An exception was Roman portrait sculpture, derived from the Etruscans who aimed for naturalism and the honest representation of the subject. A popular form of sculpture for the Romans was to have statues made of themselves in the guise of Greek gods or heroes. However, the most interesting Roman sculpture is that of the 1st and 2nd centuries AD, commemorating the city's history and its citizens, or the type carved for specific architectural settings such as the Villa Adriana at Tivoli.

The Emperor Augustus was an expert at exploiting the possibilities of sculpture as a propaganda tool. One of the most important works of Roman sculpture is the Ara Pacis (Altar of Peace; 9 BC), made to celebrate the peace that he had brought to the Empire – and established at home. The reliefs, exemplified by clarity and classical restraint, mark the point at which Roman art gained its own identity. The Prima Porta statue of Augustus himself, now in the Vatican Museums, is another masterpiece of intricate symbolism combined with idealised portraiture.

Later commemorative works include the early-2nd-century AD Colonna di Traiano, celebrating Trajan's military achievements in the Dacian campaigns, and the Colonna Antonina (180–196) built to commemorate Marcus Aurelius' victories over the Germans and Sarmatians between 169 and 176.

In the 3rd and 4th centuries there was little public sculpture, although a notable exception is the 4th-century statue of Constantine, a 10m colossus, which stood at his basilica in the Roman Forum. Pieces of it (namely the head, a hand and a foot) are now in the Capitoline Museums.

Christian The early-Christian period saw an almost total rejection of sculpture, except for carved decoration on sarcophagi. The 5th-century carved-wood panels depicting scenes of the Passion of Christ on the doors of the Basilica di Santa Sabina are a significant but rare exception.

Sculpture took centuries to recover and longer to do so in Rome than in other parts of the country where stonemasons and sculptors carved notable church porticoes, pulpits and facade decorations.

Arnolfo di Cambio (c.1245–1302) is best known for his work in Florence but, together with his pupils, he created a number of interesting works in Rome in the late 13th century, including a bronze statue of St Peter in St Peter's Basilica, tombs in Santa Prassede and the Basilica di San Giovanni in Laterano, and wall tabernacles at San Clemente and San Paolo Fuori-le-Mura.

Renaissance Michelangelo Buonarroti (1475–1564) already had an established reputation as a sculptor when he arrived in Rome from Florence at the end of the 15th century. His staggeringly beautiful *Pietà* in St Peter's, sculpted when he was only 25 years old, amazed the Roman public.

Julius II immediately put him to work on the massive project to create a tomb for the pope, involving 40 sculptured pieces. The tomb occupied the artist for his entire career but was never completed. For more details see the boxed text 'Michelangelo in Rome' in the Things to See & Do chapter.

Baroque In Rome, Baroque meant one thing: Gian Lorenzo Bernini (1598–1680). A visit to the Museo Borghese, which houses many of Bernini's early and best works, gives a clear idea of the sculptor's astounding talent.

Bernini could do things with marble that no-one before or since has managed. He could make the cold hard stone appear to be soft flesh and a solid static figure seem to be dynamic. Not only was he a virtuoso carver but he also took risks using the marble blocks, breaking all sorts of unwritten sculptors' rules about wasting expensive stone by creating an outflung limb or a figure that genuinely appears to be in motion.

Baroque sensibilities gave a new importance to exaggerated poses, cascading drapery and primacy of emotions and Bernini was an unequalled master. His were not sculptures but rather theatrical and emotional spectacles set in stone that unfolded before the viewers' eyes. His *David*, *Rape of Persephone* and *Apollo and Dafne*, all in the Museo Borghese, and *The Ecstasy of St Teresa* in Santa Maria della Vittoria, are cases in point.

Bologna-born Alessandro Algardi (1595–1654) was one of the few sculptors in Rome not totally overshadowed by Bernini, his great rival. He received commissions from Pope Innocent X and noble Roman families, and his bronze and marble grace several Roman churches and palazzi. His white-marble monument to Pope Leo XI (1650) is in St Peter's.

The 18th to 20th Centuries The neo-classicism of the late 18th and early 19th centuries was a reaction to the excesses of Baroque and a response to the renewed interest in the classical world, sparked by the excavations of Pompeii and Herculaneum.

The neoclassical sculptural style was best represented by Antonio Canova (1757–1822), an accomplished modeller, whose work is often devoid of obvious emotion. His most famous piece is a daring sculpture of Paolina Bonaparte Borghese as a reclining *Venere Vincitrice* in the Museo Borghese. Her diaphanous drapery leaves little to the imagination and is typical of the mildly erotic sculptures for which Canova became known. One of his best works is the majestic *Ercole* in the Galleria Nazionale d'Arte Moderna, where every muscular ripple of the dynamic, straining figure of Hercules is clearly evident.

The Sicilian-born sculptor Mario Rutelli (1859–1941), great-grandfather of Rome's former mayor, left his mark on the city with a series of fountains, monuments and mainly academic equestrian statues, including that of Anita Garibaldi on the Gianicolo. One of his most visible and delightful works is the theatrical Fontana delle Naiadi (1901) in Piazza della Repubblica.

Giacomo Manzù (1908–91) revived the Italian religious tradition. His best-known work is a bronze door (to the left of the central Holy Door) in St Peter's, which he was awarded after a competition in 1949.

Alberto Giacometti, Lucio Fontana, Alberto Burri and Mimmo Paladino are a few among many Italian sculptors to have achieved widespread international success.

Music

Choral Music The Italians have played a pivotal role in the history of music: they invented the system of musical notation in use today; a 16th-century Venetian printed the first musical scores with movable type; Cremona produced immortal violins; and Italy is the birthplace of the piano.

Not surprisingly, the medieval and Renaissance popes had a strong influence on music in Rome. The Church was by far the most stable employer for talented musicians, and individual popes established the great musical institutions, many of which have survived. It is unlikely that Gregory I actually had any hand in creating the liturgical music known as Gregorian Chant, but this certainly provided the basis for the uniform liturgical music still in use. Sixtus IV greatly increased the status of the papal choir, not the least by having a new chapel commissioned – the Sistine Chapel.

The greatest musicians of the day served as papal choirmasters, including Giovanni Pierluigi da Palestrina (c.1525–1594) and Domenico Scarlatti (1685–1757). Girolamo Frescobaldi (1583–1643), admired by the young JS Bach, was twice an organist at St Peter's Basilica.

The papal choirs, originally composed of priests, were closed to women, and the high parts were originally taken by men singing in falsetto. The *falsetti* were gradually supplanted by *castrati*, boys surgically castrated before puberty to preserve their high voices for life. Although castration was punishable by excommunication, the Sistine Chapel and other papal choirs contained castrati as early as 1588; the last known castrato, Alessandro Moreschi (1858–1922), had been a member of the Sistine Chapel choir. Moreschi even made a primitive recording in 1903, the very year that Pius X banned castrati from the papal choirs. Boy sopranos were introduced in the 1950s.

As well as liturgical singing, castrati, whose unique voices combined a female register with the lung power of a man, were also in demand for the operatic stage and are known to have taken female roles even before Sixtus V, worried about society's morals, banned women from performing in public. The castrati were the pop stars of their day, with voices described as 'the singing of angels'.

The Sistine Chapel choir now consists of 20 men and 30 to 40 boys. It is regarded as the pope's personal choir and accompanies him whenever he celebrates a papal mass (three or four times a month). The choir also sings at any festivities on the church calendar, such as beatifications, canonisations, funerals, and papal anniversaries.

In 1585, Sixtus V formally established the Accademia di Santa Cecilia, originally called the Congregazione dei Musici di Roma and formed as a support organisation (perhaps even an early trade union) for papal musicians. From its 17th-century role

God's Choirmaster

ASA ANDERSSON

Giovanni Pierluigi da Palestrina (c.1525– 1594) was born in the town from which he took his name and began his musical career as a choirboy at Santa Maria Maggiore, later serving as organist and singing teacher in Palestrina's cathedral. When the bishop of Palestrina, Cardinal Giovanni Maria del Monte, was elected Pope Julius III, he took Palestrina to Rome with him as director of the papal choir.

Two popes later, Paul IV was scandalised to find that a married man was directing his choir and Palestrina was sacked. In 1555, he moved on to San Giovanni in Laterano where he was choirmaster and, six years later, came full circle to become maestro at Sant Maria Maggiore. He spent the last 20 years of his long life again as choirmaster to the pope and was buried in St Peter's.

Palestrina's greatest contribution was his ability to combine complex polyphonic music with the requirements laid down by the Council of Trent (who met at South Tyrol and set the ideals of the Counter-Reformation) that the words of liturgical music must be clearly heard – the Council had even considered banning polyphony from sacred music until they heard Palestrina's *Messa Papae Marcelli* (Mass for Pope Marcellus).

in musical education and the publication of sacred music, it developed a teaching function (Arcangelo Corelli was an early maestro of the instrumental section in 1700), and in 1839 it reinvented itself as an academy with wider cultural and academic goals – including even the admission of women! It is today one of the most highly respected conservatories in the world, with its own orchestra and chorus.

Ottorino Respighi (1879–1936) came to Rome from Bologna as Professor of Composition at the Accademia di Santa Cecilia and later served as its director. His works include three sets of tone poems evoking various features of his adopted city: *Pini di Roma* (Pines of Rome); *Fontane di Roma* (Fountains of Rome); and *Feste Romane* (Roman Festivals).

Outside the Vatican precinct, music publishing came to Rome soon after its birth in Venice. Music was printed in Rome from 1510 and Roman music publication was the first to replace movable type with copperplate engraving.

Opera Ballet and opera developed in Rome as they did in Florence and Venice – out of the lavish musical entertainment that diverted the nobility. The Barberini were particularly noted for the extravagance of their 17th-century spectacles, held either in their new palace at Piazza Barberini or in the Cardinal's residence in the Palazzo della Cancelleria.

The melodramatic story of Giacomo Puccini's opera *Tosca* (1900) is set entirely in Rome during Napoleonic occupation. The first act takes place in the Chiesa di Sant'- Andrea della Valle, the second in Palazzo Farnese and the final act is set at Castel Sant'Angelo, from which Tosca jumps to her death. Neither the diva Floria Tosca nor her revolutionary lover Mario Cavaradossi existed but the villainous police chief, Baron Scarpia, may well have been based on Baron Sciarpa, a Bourbon officer. In 1992, an Emmy Award-winning television broadcast was made of the opera (starring Catherine Malfitano and Placido Domingo), shot on location and at the precise times specified by the libretto.

Tenor Luciano Pavarotti (born 1935) is still the best known of Italian opera singers, though he is well past his prime. The remarkable blind tenor Andrea Bocelli (born 1958) has taken his fine voice to the pop charts and some see him as Pavarotti's natural successor. Bocelli's *Con Te, Partirò* was a huge hit in 1998 and he has since given concerts around the world, even if his voice is not in the calibre of Pavarotti.

Other current operatic talents include home-grown mezzo-soprano superstar Cecilia Bartoli, Barbara Frittoli, Cecilia Gasdia, Anna Caterina Antonacci, Luciana Serra, Sonia Ganassi, Ruggero Raimondi, Renato Bruson, Ferruccio Furlanetto and Giuseppe Sabbatini, many of whom regularly sing in Rome.

Rome's opera season runs from December to June, with festivals and special outdoor performances during summer. See under Opera in the Entertainment chapter.

Contemporary Music Few modern Italian singers or groups have made any impact outside Italy, and contemporary Italian music tends to be nonregional. The best vocalist to emerge since the war is probably Mina, who cut dozens of records during the 1960s. Many of her songs were written by Giulio Rapetti, better known as Mogol, the undisputed king of Italian songwriters.

The 1960s and '70s produced various *cantautori* (singer-songwriters), vaguely reminiscent of some of the greats of the UK and USA. Lucio Dalla, Vasco Rossi and Pino Daniele have been successfully hawking their versions of protest music since the early 1970s. The strength of their music lies in lyrics occasionally laced with venom portraying the shortcomings of modern

society. Daniele brings an unmistakably bluesy flavour to his music. The Singer-songwriter Lucio Battisti (who died in 1998) was less inclined towards social critique and, from the 1960s until his death, his music never lost its popularity.

Zucchero (Adelmo Fornaciari) is a phenomenon on the Italian music scene. Starting out as a session musician with the likes of Joe Cocker, he has aimed at both the Italian and international markets as few other Italians have, earning many sour grapes along the way. Lots of his songs are sung in Italian *and* English.

Since the early 1990s, Eros Ramazzotti has been one of the country's top male artists. Most other pop singers and groups fall squarely into the 'middle-of-the-road' (or unexceptional) category, and include Alexia, Ambra, Claudio Baglioni, Luca Barbarossa, Alex Britti and Patty Pravo. Others to look out for include Luca Carboni, Francesco de Gregori, Antonello Venditti, Fiorella Mannioa, and the group RAF.

Home-grown bands include Prozac+, Afterhours and high-profile indie band Litfiba. Jovanotti's thoughtful and entertaining lyrics make him Italy's top rap exponent. He recently declared that Italian music is largely uninspired because the younger generation is too rich and privileged to produce the necessary sentiment to make good music. Watch the national pop song contest held in San Remo each February (and televised ad nauseum for a week) and you'll get a clearer idea of what he means.

Literature

Latin of the Republic Marcus Tullius Cicero (106–143 BC) stands out as the pre-eminent prose author of the Roman Republic. A 'new man' without consuls in his family tree, Cicero won his way to the consulship of 63 BC through his brilliance as a barrister. As well as his philosophical works, he tidied up many of his notable speeches for publication, and his secretary later published many of his letters to family and friends. Fancying himself as the senior statesman, Cicero took the young Octavian under his wing and attacked Mark Antony in a series of 14 speeches, the *Philippics*. These soon proved fatal when Octavian changed sides and joined Mark Antony, who then demanded – and got – Cicero's head.

Golden-Age Latin This era centred around the reign of Augustus. With the *Aeneid*, Virgil (70–19 BC) transformed the various Aeneas legends into the great foundation myth of Rome. This blend of legend, history and moral instruction immediately became a school text, and remained one for the next 1700-odd years. The *Aeneid* acquired such an aura that a popular method of fortune telling involved interpreting the significance of a randomly selected passage – the same process used by some with the Bible.

Silver-Age Latin As Roman society began to change over the century, so too did the Latin language and the people who used it. While Livy, Virgil's contemporary, had written the history of Rome's glorious past, Tacitus (c. AD 56–116) viewed more recent history with a decidedly colder eye.

Emperors also left their versions of history, often following the example set by Julius Caesar's war *Commentaries*. As well as his autobiography, the scholarly Claudius produced volumes of Etruscan, Carthaginian and Augustan history. Agrippina, Nero's mother, wrote her own autobiography. All of these are, unfortunately lost but the philosophical *Meditations* of Marcus Aurelius (161–180) have survived.

Vulgate Bible Pope Damasus (333–384) made the first concerted effort to Christianise Roman culture. As part of his programme, he commissioned his secretary, Eusebius Hieronymous (St Jerome), to render the Bible in elegant but accessible Latin. The Vulgate Bible has been used ever since.

Italian Literature Middle Ages From before the final collapse of Rome till the Middle Ages, creative literary production declined, kept barely alive in western Europe by clerics and erudites who debated theology, wrote histories and handbooks of rhetoric, translated or interpreted classical literature and used Latin as their lingua franca. The 12th-century *Mirabilia Romae* were effectively the first guidebooks to the monuments of the ancient city.

Although 13th-century popes wrote great books, instructive sermons and issued laws and official acts, the removal of the papacy to Avignon in 1309 meant that 14th-century literary activity in Rome was less noteworthy. Throughout the Italian peninsular, Latin had already ceased to be a living language. Florence was the most productive centre and the period was marked by the production of literature in Italian, in the highly influential work of Dante, Boccaccio and Petrarch (Francesco Petrarca).

Dante (1265–1321) was probably the greatest figure in Italian literature. His *Divina Commedia* (Divine Comedy) is an allegorical masterpiece that takes his protagonist on a search for God through hell, purgatory and paradise. It confirmed the Italian vernacular (in its Tuscan form) as a serious medium for poetic expression and was highly influential on subsequent writers. Dante's Latin work *De Monarchia* reflects his preference for a return of imperial power and his vision of a world where the roles of pope and emperor complemented each other.

Even more influential than Dante was the Tuscan humanist Petrarch (1304–74). Petrarch was the most important Latinist of his day and was crowned poet laureate in Rome in 1341 after earning a reputation throughout Europe as a classical scholar. He had sought to win recognition through his Latin writings but in fact the reverse happened. His lyrical works in the Tuscan vernacular, such as his epic poem *Africa*, and the sonnets of *Il Canzoniere*, have had a permanent influence on Italian poetry.

The humanist movement that swept Italy and Europe in the 14th and 15th centuries put Rome in the spotlight. After centuries of religion-dominated writing, scholars and intellectuals became more interested in the secular aspects of antiquity, and the idea of classical Rome began to play a crucial role in the evolution of western culture.

Flavio Biondo (1392–1463) was a disciple of Petrarch and the founder of modern archaeology. His *Decades*, a history of Christendom from the fall of Rome to the 1440s, was effectively the first history of the Middle Ages.

Lorenzo Valla (1407–57) was the greatest Roman humanist. He bravely challenged Church administration and was sceptical about various aspects of papal primacy. He also produced a humanist commentary on the New Testament, pioneering a new critical attitude to the text – at times he was branded a heretic because of his philosophy. He was renowned for his vigorous mind, sharp tongue and expert command of Latin (exhibited in his *Opus elegantiarum linguae Latinae*) to which few of his contemporaries could aspire.

Renaissance By the end of the 15th century, Rome was a cultural capital of Europe due to the papal and ecclesiastical patronage of artists, architects and a multitude of Latinists. However, the most significant 14th- and 15th-century literary activity actually took place outside Rome in the courts of Milan, Ferrara, Mantua and in the kingdom of Naples. It appears that Roman humanists were, on the whole, less noteworthy and less original thinkers than those in northern Italy.

In the 16th century, the qualities inherent in the Petrarchan and Neo-Platonic tradition became more pronounced. Although better known as a painter, sculptor and architect, Michelangelo Buonarroti (1475–1564) was also one of the great poets of the time. At an early age, in the Florentine court of Lorenzo de' Medici, he was exposed to Neo-Platonist writers and began writing poetry in his youth. His most outstanding works – mainly sonnets and madrigals – were composed in Rome during the last 20 years of his life and are regarded as the finest Italian poems since Petrarch and Dante (in whose praise Michelangelo wrote two sonnets).

It is through one of Michelangelo's sonnets that we learn more about the strains and difficulties that he encountered while he was painting the ceiling of the Sistine Chapel:

> My beard turns up to heaven; my nape falls in
> Fixed on my spine: my breast-bone visibly
> Grows like a harp: a rich embroidery
> Bedews my face from brush-drops thick and thin

His writing was not actually published until 1623, when his great-nephew released a slightly edited version of the poems, suppressing the fact that many of them were written for Tommaso Cavalieri (a young man Michelangelo fell in love with in 1532) and explored the dilemma of a homosexual whose moral beliefs conflict with his sexuality. It was mistakenly thought for several centuries that they were love poems for the Roman noblewoman, Vittoria Colonna.

Vittoria Colonna (1490–1549) was a member of the noble Roman Colonna family. She spent much of her early life on Ischia, an island in the Bay of Naples, but visited Rome regularly. Her unusual intellectual abilities won her a considerable reputation and she formed friendships with many outstanding writers, reformers and religious figures. After the loss of her philandering husband, she wrote a series of around 100 poems lamenting his death and idealising his character. Later in her life she wrote poems on sacred and spiritual themes. Her poetry – skilful but not strikingly original – was written in the Petrarchan and Neo-Platonic style. Her friendship with Michelangelo was truly 'Platonic', marked by frequent exchanges of philosophical sonnets and letters. Michelangelo was at her bedside when she died in 1549.

Giorgio Vasari's *Vite dei Più Eccellenti Pittori* (Lives of the Painters; 1550, republished 1568) a treatise on the lives of his artist predecessors and contemporaries, remains one of the most informative works of Renaissance art history. Vasari was a close contemporary of Michelangelo and spent several years in Rome as chief architect of St Peter's (to which he was appointed in succession to Michelangelo).

The sculptor and goldsmith Benvenuto Cellini (1500–71) began his autobiography,

Vita, in 1558. A native of Florence, Cellini spent many years in Rome working for eminent ecclesiastical figures including popes Clement VII and Paul III. In his writing, Cellini used an uninhibited spoken manner, which was unparalleled for several centuries. It has been described as a narrative made up of fact, fiction, self-justification and technical information. The story reaches its dramatic climax with the 1527 Sack of Rome and the author's escape in 1538 from Castel Sant'Angelo, where he had been imprisoned.

Censorship became institutionalised under Paul IV with the 1554 publication of the Index of Prohibited Books. The publication of the list, which concerned itself not only with faith but also morals, was accompanied by public book-burnings and many printers were forced to flee the city.

Giordano Bruno (1548–1600) was one of the earliest champions of freedom of speech and thought. His fiery temperament brought him into conflict with one form of Counter-Reformation establishment after another. Originally a Dominican priest, his interests included natural magic, cosmology and astrology – one of his assertions was that the earth was not the centre of the universe, a belief that Galileo was also forced to renounce. Among the orthodox Church doctrines that he questioned was the notion of the Immaculate Conception. He spent many years in exile outside Italy, returning only in 1591. In 1600, after an eight year trial, he was branded a heretic and burned at the stake in Campo de' Fiori. In 1603, all Bruno's books were placed on the Index of Prohibited Books.

The absence of free speech in Counter-Reformation Rome is one explanation for the lack of significant literature from that period; anything the Church and State disapproved of was suppressed. But in 17th-century Rome an 'underground' literary form emerged, in the posting of anonymous satirical writings or *pasquinades* (named after the first person identified as having written one), which criticised the Church and authoritative figures. One of the most popular places for such notices to be left was on the torso of a Roman statue, near Piazza Navona (in a small square today known as Piazza Pasquino). The epigrams were usually posted in the dark of night and then gleefully circulated around town the following day.

The 18th Century Rome soon became a hotbed for many 18th-century historians and Grand Tourists from northern Europe. Edward Gibbon penned his influential *The History of the Decline and Fall of the Roman Empire* between 1776 and 1778. Johann Wolfgang von Goethe, already a celebrated poet when he arrived in Rome in 1786, found the city an inspiration for his literary and artistic travails. His *Italian Journey* captures better than any other text the elation of the northern travellers as they discovered the ruins of ancient Rome and the colours of the modern city. 'In Rome I found myself for the first time,' he wrote.

Rome was also a magnet for the English Romantics. Keats, Byron, Shelley, Mary Shelley and other writers all spent time in the city. Byron claimed Rome as the city of his soul even though he only visited it fleetingly. John Keats came to Rome in 1821 in the hope that it would cure his ill health but he died of tuberculosis in his lodgings at the foot of the Spanish Steps after only a few months in the city.

Percy Bysshe Shelley (1792–1822) wrote his most important works in Italy between 1818 and 1822, including the powerful verse drama *The Cenci,* based on the true story of Beatrice Cenci, a tragic young Roman woman who was dominated and abused by her father, killed him and then was put to death herself for the murder.

The 19th Century Italy's home-grown Romantic, Giacomo Leopardi (1798–1837) was less inspired by the wonders of Rome than his northern counterparts and spent only a few months in Rome from 1822 to 1823.

The American author Nathaniel Hawthorne lived in Italy between 1857 and 1859. *The Marble Faun* (1860) recreates his impressions of Rome in a narrative context.

FACTS ABOUT ROME

In 1869, Henry James made the first of 14 trips to Italy, which inspired his enduringly popular classic, *The Portrait of a Lady* (1881), and his book of essays, *Italian Hours* (1909).

Romans are particularly proud of their most famous local poets, Gioacchino Belli (1791–1863), Carlo Alberto Salustri (1871–1950), better known as Trilussa, and Cesare Pescarella (1858–1940), who all wrote in Roman dialect.

Belli started his career with conventional and undistinguished verse but found the medium for his expression in the crude and colourful dialect of the Roman people, making use of its puns and obscenities. He was a savage satirist and outspoken in his attacks on all classes and institutions. Belli also often painted vulgar caricatures of important Risorgimento figures.

The 20th Century Gabriele D'Annunzio (1863–1938) is the most flamboyant Italian literary figure of the turn of the 20th century and into the modern era. Born in Pescara, D'Annunzio settled in Rome in 1881. An ardent nationalist, his virulent poetry was perhaps not of the highest quality, but his voice was a prestigious tool for Mussolini's Fascists.

Italy's richest contribution to modern literature has been in the novel and short story, and two of the most popular figures were closely tied to the capital.

Alberto Moravia (1907–90) grew up in the residential area east of the Villa Borghese. He describes Rome and its people in his prolific novels, such as *La Romana* (A Woman of Rome), which conveys the detail and sharp sense of social decay that make his storytelling so compelling. The alienated individual and the emptiness of Fascist and bourgeois society are common themes in his writing. *Racconti Romani* (Roman Tales; 1954) and *Nuovi Raconti Romani* (New Roman Tales; 1960) offer amusing sketches of the lives of Roman characters including plumbers, servants and hoodlums.

The novels of Elsa Morante (1912–85) are characterised by a subtle psychological appraisal of her characters and can be seen as a personal cry of pity for the sufferings of individuals and society. Her 1974 novel *La Storia* follows the fortunes of a half-Jewish woman in occupied Rome.

Pier Paolo Pasolini (1922–75) moved to Rome in 1950 in the wake of a sex scandal in his native Friuli. Rome gave him an opportunity to explore both his homosexuality and different ways of writing. His first novel, *Ragazzi di Vita* (1955) explores the violent, linguistically explosive and sordid world of the dilapidated suburbs of Rome, in which theft, card-sharping, prostitution and murder are commonplace. These were subjects Pasolini returned to in later works such as *Una Vita Violenta* (1956) and in many of his (often controversial) films. For books set in Rome, see Fiction under Books in the Facts for the Visitor chapter.

Rome is a continual source of inspiration for foreign writers. It is becoming increasingly fashionable for many contemporary novelists to use ancient and modern Rome as a backdrop for their stories.

Cinema

Rome has always played a major role in Italian cinema, both as a subject and as a production centre. Born in Torino in 1904, the Italian film industry originally made an impression with silent spectaculars. By 1930 it was virtually bankrupt and Mussolini began moves to nationalise the industry. These culminated in 1940, when Rome's version of Hollywood, Cinecittà, was ceded to the State. Set up in 1937, this huge complex was fitted out with the latest in film equipment. Half the nation's production took place here – 85 pictures in 1940 alone – and in its glory days it was labelled 'Hollywood on the Tiber'.

Abandoned later in the war, Cinecittà only went timidly back into action in 1948, although its absence had not bothered the early neo-realist directors. In 1950, an American team arrived to make *Quo Vadis?*, and for the rest of '50s, film-makers from Italy and abroad moved in to use the site's huge lots.

Major American productions at Cinecittà included William Wyler's *Ben Hur* (1959) with Charlton Heston, Stanley Kubrick's *Spartacus* (1960) starring Kirk Douglas, and Joseph Mankiewicz's *Cleopatra* (1963) with Elizabeth Taylor and Richard Burton. By the early 1960s, however, this symbol of Italian cinema had again begun to wane as location shooting became more common. The main moneymakers for the Italian film industry in the 1960s and '70s were Sergio Leone's 'spaghetti westerns' shot near Viterbo.

In the three years following the close of hostilities in Europe, Roberto Rossellini (1906–77) produced a trio of neo-realist masterpieces. The first and most famous of these was *Roma Città Aperta* (Rome Open City; 1945), set in German-occupied Rome and starring Anna Magnani. It was filmed in the working-class district of Via Prenestina east of the city centre. For many cinophiles the film marks the true beginning of neo-realism, uniting a simplicity and sincerity peculiar to Italian film-making; often heart-rending without ever descending into the bathos to which so many Hollywood products fall victim.

Vittorio de Sica (1901–74) kept the neo-realist ball rolling in 1948 with another classic set in Rome, *Ladri di Biciclette* (Bicycle Thieves), the story of a man's frustrated fight to earn a crust and keep his family afloat. It was filmed in the outskirts of the city where the ugly purpose-built suburbs meet the countryside.

Federico Fellini (1920–94) took the creative baton from the masters of neo-realism and carried it into the following decades. Some of his best known films were set in Rome, his adopted home (he lived for many years in Via Margutta). His disquieting style demands more of audiences, abandoning realistic shots for pointed images at once laden with humour, pathos and double-meaning – all cleverly capturing not only the Rome of the day, but the human foibles of his protagonists. Fellini's greatest international hit was *La Dolce Vita* (1968), starring Marcello Mastroianni and Anita Ekberg, with memorable scenes set in the Trevi Fountain (for which a Cinecittà set was actually used) and Via Veneto. *Roma* (1972) could almost be described as a sur-

real and poetic documentary about Rome. It satirised the Church and used relatively unpicturesque parts of Rome as a backdrop, including the Grand Raccordo Anulare, the city's motorway ring road.

Pier Paolo Pasolini (1922–75) used his local neighbourhood, Pietralata, in his films and books. Homosexual, Catholic and Marxist, Pasolini's films reflect his ideological and sexual tendencies and are a unique portrayal of Rome's urban wasteland. In his earlier work he was preoccupied with the condition of the subproletariat in films like *Accattone* (1961), set in the forgotten suburbs of Rome, and *Teorema* (1968). Later he became obsessed with human decay and death as reflected in *Il Decamerone, I Racconti di Canterbury* and *Il Fiore delle Mille e Una Notte*. Pasolini was murdered in mysterious circumstances in 1975.

Nanni Moretti (born 1953), who first came to the silver screen in the late 1970s, has proved to be a highly individualistic actor-director. *Caro Diario* (Dear Diary), his whimsical, self-indulgent, autobiographical three-part film won the prize for best director at Cannes in 1994. A major part of the film involved a camera recording Moretti driving through the streets of Rome on a Vespa.

A wonderful homage to film-making is *Nuovo Cinema Paradiso* (1988), by Giuseppe Tornatore (born 1956). Tornatore was back in 1995 with *L'Uomo delle Stelle* (The Starmaker), the story of a fraud touring around Sicily and peddling hopes of a screen career in Cinecittà, and again in 2000 with *La Leggenda del 1900*.

According to recent reports, the glory days of Italian cinema are back and the future for Cinecittà looks rosy with increased private investment in state-of-the-art digital technology and special effects equipment. There has also been a revival of interest in ancient Rome by leading Hollywood directors. See also Films in the Facts for the Visitor chapter.

SOCIETY & CONDUCT

The family remains of central importance in the fabric of Italian society. Most young

Italians tend to stay at home until they marry, a situation admittedly partly exacerbated by the lack of affordable housing. Still, modern attitudes have begun to erode the traditions, especially in Rome and Milan where many young people (particularly students from regional Italy) are forced to live away from home.

Statistics show that one in three married couples have no children and one in nine children is born out of wedlock.

Dos and Don'ts

Italians tend to be tolerant but despite an apparent obsession with (mostly female) nakedness, especially in advertising, they are not excessively free and easy.

In churches you are expected to dress

Roman Rules

'I love Italians. They're so spontaneous, chaotic and easygoing.'

You often hear statements like this from foreigners. Because that's what Italians are like, right? Well, yes... and no.

The common perception that all Italians are as hilarious as comedian Roberto Benigni is a misconception. They *can* be hilarious and they *can* be spontaneous. But Romans in particular can also be completely conformist and inflexible.

Conformity comes out in the way they dress. In winter in particular, the men seem to be in a uniform – albeit an elegant one with more than a passing resemblance to an English country squire – of well cut sports jacket, casual trousers, shirt and large-knotted tie, topped by a Barbour-style waxed jacket.

It also comes out in the way they behave. For Italians in general and Romans in particular, one of the most important things of life is the *bella figura*, which roughly translates as making a good impression. Few Italians drink much alcohol, and being drunk – especially if you are a woman – is *really* frowned upon.

There are also accepted methods of culinary conduct. Take drinking coffee, for example. A cappuccino is taken at breakfast only and never after a meal. And parmesan cheese never tops pasta with a seafood or fish sauce.

Commercial conduct can also be totally inflexible. Shopkeepers are completely bound by the traditional way of doing things. Despite deregulation of commercial shopping hours, many shops still close for the traditional afternoon rest, the daily siesta being regarded as more important than any commercial concerns.

Then there are the laborious procedures you have to go through to do the simplest things – such as buy a tub of gelato from a gelateria. A rigorous system must be followed: one person will scoop out the ice cream, you'll probably have to wait around for another person to weigh and price it and a third person will take your money. Then you'll wait again while your polystyrene carton is wrapped in shiny paper and tied up with a ribbon.

Italians *can* be the friendliest race on earth. But centuries of unwelcome visitors, dating back to Hannibal coming over the Alps with his elephants and Saracen invaders reaching the Mediterranean shores, have left the Romans with a deep-seated mistrust of foreigners, bordering on xenophobia. Non-European foreign immigrants are referred to as *extracomunitari* and often face a covert form of racism. What tourists are most likely to experience are impolite waiters and indifferent shop assistants – but fortunately it's just as likely that you'll come across Romans who go out of their way to be friendly and polite.

What all Italians share is a healthy distrust of authority. When confronted with a silly rule or an unjust law (and they are regularly confronted with many), they don't complain, they simply try to find the quickest way around it. In this way they *do* fit the stereotype of cheeky irreverence, humour and spontaneity.

Latin Lovers & Mummies' Boys

The rough charm of the unshaven Italian Lothario mounted jauntily on his Vespa is an inescapable image; one redolent of the Latin lover. The truth is perhaps a little less alluring.

According to figures published in 1997 by Istat (Istituto Centrale di Statistica), the country's main statistics body, Italian men actually constitute an *esercito di mammoni* (army of mummies' boys). Forget Oedipus, these boys know which side their bread is buttered. Perhaps they are not so different from men the world over but the numbers are certainly telling.

If you can believe Istat, 66.5% of single Italian men remain at home with mum (and dad) up to the age of 34 at least. Granted, this is partly caused by problems of unemployment, the cost of housing and so on. Of the remainder who do move out of home, some 42% do not shift more than 1km away and only 20% dare to move more than 50km beyond the maternal home. Of all these 'independent' single men, 70% manage to stop off at mum's place every day of the week. The unkind might be led to believe (as was the author of at least one newspaper story on the subject) that apart from filial devotion, the lads may well bring with them a bag of dirty washing and time the visit to coincide with lunch.

But even if the washing and lunch are taken care of by their wives (not an uncommon situation among Italian couples), married men still find time to pop in to see mamma at least a few times a week. When marriage fails, a quarter of ex-husbands go home to mother, as opposed to 17% of wives.

The chances of the marriage taking place at all is also looking grim. Research carried out by the Italian Institute of Andrology reveals that many young Italian men are struggling to live up to the stereotype of the Latin lover. Around 18% of 18 to 30-year-olds admitted to having no sex life at all, with a further 20% stating that they suffered serious problems in sexual performance, blaming it on work stress and fatigue. But things picked up in the older age group, with 75% of men between the ages of 60 and 70 claiming that they had a happy sex life.

So if it's a Latin lover you're after, find one of pensionable age... or go to Spain.

---

modestly. This means no shorts (for men or women) or short skirts, and shoulders should be covered. Strict dress codes are enforced at St Peter's Basilica – turn up in the wrong gear and the Vatican dress police simply won't let you in.

RELIGION

Some 85% of Italians profess to be Catholic. Of the remaining 15%, there are about 500,000 evangelical Protestants and 140,000 Jehovah's Witnesses. Other small groups include a Jewish community in Rome, which has re-established itself after virtually being annihilated by the Nazis. There are also communities of orange-clad followers of the Bhagwan Rajneesh, known in Italy as the *arancioni*.

The big surprise on this front is the growth of the Muslim population, currently estimated at over 700,000, and thus the second largest religious community in Italy after the Catholics. A fitting symbol of demographic shift in the heart of Christendom was the inauguration in 1995 of the first mosque in Rome.

Although the fabric of life is profoundly influenced by the presence of the Church, surprisingly few Italian Catholics practise their religion these days. Church attendance is low – an average of only 25% attend Mass regularly – and many children are never baptised. However, a child's first communion remains a popular event, many Italian couples marry in a church and religious festivals never fail to attract a large turnout. Most Italians are also generally familiar with saints' feast days and legends, and they keenly follow the various activities of the pope.

A Pilgrim's Progress

Rome has always been a destination for Christian pilgrims. For the celebrations of the Jubilee Year of 2000, around 16 million of them converged on the city to bear witness to their faith.

Holy Years (also called Jubilee Years) are celebrated every 25 years (or by extraordinary papal decree) and are extremely important events for devout Catholics. The practice of making pilgrimages began with the early Church, when believers started to visit the holy lands of Judaea and Rome.

Pope Boniface VIII instituted the first Christian Jubilee in 1300, when pilgrims visited the major religious sites in Rome. For their efforts the pilgrims were granted indulgences, which would effectively annul their time in purgatory due for sins committed during their lifetimes. In the Middle Ages indulgences were sold, which was one of Martin Luther's objections; today the Church is a little stricter about what constitutes a plenary (full) indulgence for all sins.

Pilgrims traditionally visit seven Roman churches: the four patriarchal basilicas (St Peter's, Santa Maria Maggiore, San Giovanni in Laterano and San Paolo Fuori-le-Mura), and three minor ones (San Lorenzo Fuori-le-Mura, Santa Croce in Gerusalemme and San Sebastiano). They also visit the catacombs, the shrines of Christian martyrs and the places where important Christian relics were kept. Pilgrims also have to attend confession and participate in a communion Mass.

While the Jubilee of 2000 has been hailed as a great success for the Church and for Rome, it hasn't always been the case in the past. In the Jubilee of 1300, for instance, Ponte Sant'Angelo collapsed because of overcrowding and many pilgrims perished. In the 1450 Jubilee, there were food shortages and 172 pilgrims were killed by stampeding crowds. In 1750, Leonardo da Porto Maurizio, a famed preacher (later beatified) was almost trampled to death in the Colosseum, where he had set up the Stations of the Cross.

LANGUAGE

In addition to Italian many Romans also converse among themselves in *romanaccia*, or the rough Roman dialect.

English is the most commonly spoken foreign language, although many Italians (especially those working in the tourism industry) speak French, German and Spanish. See the Language chapter for an introduction to Italian and some vocabulary.

ANCIENT RUINS
Colosseum
More than any other monument, the Colosseum is *the* symbol of the Eternal City. The massive amphitheatre seated over 50,000 spectators, who witnessed bloody gladiatorial contests, wild-beast shows and mock sea battles. See Map 7.

Domus Aurea
In its day, Emperor Nero's extravagant imperial residence covered a third of the city. The facade was covered in gold leaf and the pavilions and loggias were decorated with frescoes, which inspired many Renaissance artists. Excavations over the past three decades have opened up part of the massive complex. See Map 5.

Palatine
Rome's mythical founding place was chosen by wealthy Romans and emperors for their homes and palaces. Emperor Domitian built a private residence and an official palace, the ruins of which can best be seen from the Circo Massimo. Frescoes from patrician villas are a highlight and the shady gardens are great for picnics. See Map 7 & Palatine map.

Terme di Caracalla
Most of the internal walls of the Baths of Caracalla are still intact and it's easy to make out the various bathing rooms. Many mosaic floors have also been preserved, hinting at the opulence of this impressive imperial bath complex. See Map 7.

JONATHAN SMITH

Title Page: Minds have met on the Spanish Steps for centuries. (photograph: Jon Davison)

Left: Go back to the days of swords and sandals at the Colosseum, begun by Emperor Vespasian in AD 72.

MARTIN MOOS

NEIL SETCHFIELD

MARTIN MOOS

JON DAVISON

Top: Arches on the Palatine line Domitian's private garden.

Middle Left: Bath time at the Terme di Caracalla

Middle Right: Ancient Romans shopped till they dropped at Mercati di Traiano.

Bottom: The mighty Roman Forum

Mercati di Traiano

Built in the early 2nd century AD, Trajan's Markets comprised six floors of shops and offices and can be seen as precursor to today's shopping centre. Goods sold included wine, oil and imported silks. See Map 5.

Roman Forum

The Forum was the centre of ancient Rome from the Republic until the 4th century AD. In the Middle Ages the area was heavily plundered for its precious marbles. During the Renaissance, with renewed regard for all things classical, it provided inspiration for artists and architects. See Map 7 & Roman Forum map.

PIAZZAS & FOUNTAINS

Rome's piazzas (squares) are more than public meeting spaces. Like the city's churches they can be fabulous open-air repositories for sculpture by the greatest artists of the Renaissance and Baroque periods.

Campo de' Fiori

By day the occupants of this lively square are Roman mammas with their market baskets and by night they're beer-clutching bright young things. Towering over them all is Giordano Bruno, who was burned at the stake for heresy here in 1600. See Map 8.

Piazza Mattei & Fontana delle Tartarughe

Rome's most delightful fountain, designed by Giacomo della Porta, features young boys lifting their arms to help tortoises into the basin above. It sits in a quiet residential square in the Ghetto area. See Map 4.

Piazza Barberini & Fontana del Tritone

Bernini's Triton Fountain was created in 1643 for Pope Urban VIII, patriarch of the Barberini family. What wouldn't anyone give for a six-pack like that of the muscular Triton kneeling in a scallop shell? See Map 5.

Piazza della Repubblica & Fontana delle Naiadi

This square – formerly known as Piazza dell'Esedra – follows the line of the exedra of the adjacent Terme di Diocleziano, where ancient Romans indulged in exercise and sport. The Fontana delle Naiadi in its centre features a bronze Glaucus wrestling with a fish, surrounded by four water nymphs. See Map 5.

Piazza del Popolo

The 'people's piazza', at the northern gateway to the city, has been freed from the traffic that was choking it for years. This magnificently restored square features an Egyptian obelisk from Heliopolis surrounded by 19th-century lions, 'twin' (but not identical) Baroque churches and the art treasure-trove of Santa Maria del Popolo. See Map 2.

JONATHAN SMITH

Left: The lion's share of peace and quiet in Piazza del Popolo

MARTIN MOOS

LAUREN SUNSTEIN

MARTIN MOOS

Top: Plucky pigeons in Piazza San Pietro

Bottom Left: Glaucus tackles a fish at Fontana delle Naiadi.

Bottom Right: A helping hand at Fontana delle Tartarughe

Piazza di Spagna & Barcaccia

This Baroque square and its magnificent Spanish Steps were a magnet for travellers doing the Grand Tour, and attracted the likes of Byron, Keats and Shelley. It's still a popular meeting place. The fountain of a sinking boat, the Barcaccia, is by Pietro Bernini, father of the famous Gian Lorenzo. See Map 4.

Trevi Fountain & Piazza di Trevi

This stunning Baroque fountain has been recently cleaned and is one of Rome's most famous landmarks. Go along in the evening to avoid the worst of the crowds. See Map 4.

Piazza Navona & Fontana dei Quattro Fiumi

This vast and beautiful square, following the shape of the ancient stadium beneath it, is lined with Baroque palaces. Bernini's Fontana dei Quattro Fiumi is a magnificent and dramatic centrepiece, depicting four rivers – the Nile, Ganges, Danube and Rio Plata. See Map 8.

Piazza San Pietro

Bernini's monumental square in front of St Peter's Basilica is bordered by two semicircular colonnades. On either side of the central Egyptian obelisk are twin fountains, one designed by Carlo Maderno and the other built later to match it. See Map 4.

Piazza Santa Maria in Trastevere

This traffic-free square is unadorned with Baroque architecture or classical monuments, and is the peaceful heart of the Trastevere district as well as a popular meeting spot for the locals. Children play ball games during the day, while in the evening artisans sell their work alongside young Romans looking for a good time. See Map 6.

Piazza Venezia

To Romans it's a giant traffic roundabout good for target practice in running down pedestrians, but a glance at any map will tell you that this grand square really is the fulcrum of the city. It is bordered by Palazzo Venezia, the first great Renaissance building in Rome, and the Vittoriano monument, which was built to commemorate Italian unification. See Map 4.

ERIC L WHEATER

Left: Your chariot awaits in Piazza San Pietro.

GEOFF STRINGER

GUY MOBERLY

Top: The theatrical Trevi Fountain was designed by Nicola Salvi in 1732.

Right: Let the conversation flow at Fontana dei Quattro Fiumi on Piazza Navona.

GREEN SPOTS

If you can't take Rome's summer heat or the noisy traffic in this chaotic city is getting you down, then head to one of Rome's tranquil green spots to chill out and cool off. The Orto Botanico and Vatican Gardens have admission charges; the rest are free.

Orto Botanico

Formerly the private gardens of Palazzo Corsini, the botanical garden in Trastevere has some exceptionally rare plants. See Map 4.

Pincio

The shady gardens above Piazza del Popolo and next to Villa Borghese park are peopled by Roman families, cyclists and rollerbladers. One of the main draws is the exceptional view of St Peter's. See Map 2.

Vatican Gardens

Originally just lawns, these formal gardens were laid out in the 17th and 18th centuries. Guided tours take you through the flower-filled French parterre, the formal Italian garden and the naturalistic English wood. See Map 4.

SALLY WEBB

Left: Two's company: larking about in Villa Borghese

Villa Ada

This is a popular park year round and it hosts music and cinema festivals in summer. You can relax in the shade under its massive trees or stroll across its magnificent lawns. See Map 1.

Villa Borghese

Rome's most popular park offers stunning views across the city and many wonderful statue-lined footpaths. It also encompasses art galleries, a lake, riding schools and a zoo. See Maps 2 & 3.

Villa Celimontana

When it's not overrun by newly wed couples seeking photo opportunities, Villa Celimontana park is a peaceful haven just a stone's throw from the Colosseum. Kids will enjoy the playground and jazz aficionados will love the outdoor jazz festival in summer.

Right: Whatever your pace there's always something on offer in Rome's exquisite parks and gardens.

Villa Doria Pamphilj

Rome's largest park is a pretty place to relax and is blessed with abundant parasol pines and fine views over the city. See Map 1.

CHRISTOPHER GROENHOUT

MARKETS

Whether it's fresh fruit and vegetables, antique furniture or second-hand clothes, Rome will have a market for your needs.

Campo de' Fiori

This lively daily market offers an excellent array of food, fish, flowers and bric-a-brac and is undoubtedly the most colourful in the city, even though locals complain that it isn't what it used to be. See Map 8.

Mercato delle Stampe

For antique prints and second-hand books, this is your one-stop shop. Early music scores, architectural engravings, chromolithographs of fruit and flowers and views of Rome are among the stunning objects for sale. See Map 4.

Piazza San Cosimato

This traditional neighbourhood market is an excellent place to stock up on fruit, vegetables, meat and fish, as the Trastevere locals will tell you. Nearby is one of the best food-shopping streets in Rome, Via Natale del Grande. See Map 6.

Piazza Vittorio Emanuele

Rome's biggest produce market in the multicultural Esquiline area has Asian and Middle-Eastern goodies alongside the usual fare. See Map 5.

Ponte Milvio

Antique and bric-a-brac stalls today cover the area where Constantine

Left: Pick of the crop: Campo de' Fiori market offers an array of fresh produce.

defeated Maxentius in AD 312. Bargains can be found – on the first Sunday of each month. See Map 1.

Porta Portese
Rome's largest and best-known flea market has an enormous mishmash of new and old on sale, from bags to bikes and frocks to furniture. See Map 6.

Testaccio
The covered stalls of the Testaccio market sell fruit, vegetables, meats, cheeses, herbs and flowers. The market is noted for its good prices and the excellent quality of its produce. Cheap shoes are its other drawcard. See Map 6.

Via Sannio
If your life won't be complete without a full-length leather coat, then this covered market's for you. It boasts leather in all shapes and shades, bargain shoes, retro jeans, fluffy fleeces and sports gear. The pre-loved cashmere in the second-hand section is a bargain. See Map 7.

MARTIN MOOS

Top: Keep 'em rolling: fruit and veg arrives in the traditional way.

Bottom Left: Socks and the city – mementoes for everyone!

Bottom Right: Just odds and ends? You might strike it lucky among the bric-a-brac.

NEIL SETCHFIELD

MARTIN MOOS

BASILICAS & CHURCHES

Not surprisingly for the centre of the Christian world, Rome has its fair share of churches – over 400 in the *centro storico* alone – many of which are repositories for some of the city's great artworks.

The history of Rome's churches mirrors the history of the city. There are former pagan temples from Imperial Rome, early Christian basilicas, some of which retain their original structure and many their superb mosaic decoration, Renaissance masterpieces such as St Peter's and Baroque extravaganzas by Bernini, Borromini and other architects designed to lure potential congregations.

Rome's newest church is still being built. Located in the far eastern suburbs of the city, Dio Padre Misericordioso, designed by American architect Richard Meier, was destined to be the symbol of the Holy Year 2000. Construction and administrative problems held it up and it's now due for completion in 2002.

NEIL SETCHFIELD

Left: The elaborate interior of Chiesa del Gesù has enticed worshippers and visitors since the 16th century.

Chiesa del Gesù

The first Jesuit church in Rome represents the epitome of Counter-Reformation architecture. The intention was to attract and overawe worshippers with splendour and breathtaking artworks. No expense was spared, as St Ignatius' opulent marble and bronze tomb with lapis lazuli-encrusted columns illustrates. See Map 4.

Pantheon

The Pantheon, the 'temple to all the gods', is the best-preserved building of ancient Rome. It was converted into a Christian church in 608. The interior's height and diameter both measure 43.3m and the extraordinary dome – the largest masonry vault ever built – is considered a mighty achievement of ancient-Roman architecture. See Map 8.

Chiesa di Santa Prassede

The stunning mosaics of this 9th-century church are possibly the best in Rome and are the work of mosaic artists brought over especially from Byzantium (now Constantinople). Don't miss those on the triumphal arch, apse and especially in the small Cappella di San Zenone, the church's jewel. See Map 5.

Santa Cecilia in Trastevere

This 9th-century basilica was built on the spot where St Cecilia was martyred in 230. The impressive apse mosaic (870) and Pietro Cavallini's magnificent 13th-century fresco of the *Last Judgment* are stunning, while the marble statue of the saint at her death is eerily alluring. See Map 6.

Santa Maria in Trastevere

This is the only church in Rome to have retained its complete medieval appearance. According to tradition it was established by Pope Calixtus in the early 3rd century and rebuilt by Julius I in 337. The outstanding 12th-century mosaics in the apse and on the triumphal arch are among the best in the city. See Map 6.

Left: The Pantheon, a remarkable architectural treasure, stands boldly on Piazza della Rotonda.

Right: Time ticks by for age-old Santa Maria in Trastevere.

Santa Maria Maggiore

There's an harmonious blend of architectural styles in this great basilica: a triple nave from the original 5th-century building, a Romanesque bell-tower, Cosmatesque marble floor, and an altar canopy decorated with bronze cherubs. The 5th-century mosaics of biblical scenes are the most important of this period in Rome. See Map 5.

Santa Sabina

Many people consider this early-Christian basilica to be the loveliest church in Rome. The carved wooden door features one of the oldest crucifixion scenes in existence. See Map 6.

San Clemente

This basilica defines better than any other the multilevel history of Rome. The 12th-century church was built over a 4th-century church which was, in turn, built over a 1st-century Roman house. The stunning mosaics are its highlight. See Map 7.

San Giovanni in Laterano

The first Christian basilica in Rome, San Giovanni was built between 314 and 318, and served as a model for all subsequent Christian churches. It has been destroyed by fire twice and rebuilt several times, most notably between 1646 and 1649 when Borromini transformed the interior. See Map 7.

St Peter's Basilica

A church has stood on the Vatican hill since 315, when Constantine ordered construction of a basilica on the site of the apostle's tomb. It was reconstructed in the 15th century when, over 150 years, Bramante, Raphael, Sangallo, Michelangelo, Giacomo della Porta, Maderno and Bernini all contributed to its realisation. Michelangelo's 136m-high dome is the world's tallest. See Map 4 & floor plan.

MARTIN MOOS

Left: The impressively lit dome of St Peter's Basilica towers over the Eternal City.

MARTIN MOOS

MARTIN MOOS

CAFES & BARS

You'll never be stuck for a decent coffee in Rome. The problem is just choosing one to suit your mood – whether it's a bar for a quick espresso or a nostalgic trip down Rome's memory lane.

Babington's Tea Rooms

English-style tea and cakes are on offer in these old-fashioned tea rooms at the bottom of the Spanish Steps. See Map 4.

Camilloni a Sant'Eustachio

It won't be just the excellent coffee you'll consume at this place on Piazza Sant'Eustachio. There's a counter full of cakes to make your mouth water. See Map 8.

Bar Vezio

If you fancy a bit of communism with your coffee, Vezio's bar in the Ghetto should fit the bill; the place abounds with Italian communist memorabilia, and the faces of Stalin and Che Guevera stare down from the walls. See Map 3.

Top: If you're dashing about, grab a *caffè latte* to go from one of Rome's many bars.

Bottom: Fancy the slow lane instead? Try Babington's for a less-hectic option.

BEST OF ROME

Caffè Farnese

This place on one corner of the lovely Piazza Farnese is ideal for people-watching, especially on Saturday morning when the nearby Campo de' Fiori market is at its busiest. See Map 8.

Caffè Greco

In its heyday this elegant antique-mirrored and wood-panelled cafe near the Spanish Steps was a favourite haunt of Keats, Byron, Goethe, Liszt, Wagner, Bizet and Casanova. See Map 4.

Caffè Sant'Eustachio

This is one of the best coffee bars in Rome, famous for *gran caffè*, a wonderful coffee made by beating the first drops of espresso and several teaspoons of sugar into a frothy paste, then adding the coffee on top. See Map 8.

SALLY WEBB

MARTIN MOOS

MARTIN MOOS

Top Left: Coffee with Che at Bar Vezio

Top Right: Caffè Greco – the literati's top haunt

Bottom: Typically bubbly at Caffè Sant' Eustachio

Facts for the Visitor

WHEN TO GO

Rome's mild climate makes it visitable year-round, but you will be likely to strike unpleasantly hot weather in July and August, and briskly cold weather from December to February when icy winds blow in from northern Europe. Spring and autumn are without doubt the best times to visit, with generally sunny skies and mild temperatures, although late autumn (November) can be rainy.

The main tourist season starts at Easter and runs until October, building to peak periods in spring and autumn, when the tour buses pour in and tourists are herded around like cattle. In July and August it is almost heartbreaking to observe the suffering of heat-exhausted travellers as they drag screaming, dehydrated kids around the historic centre. Temperatures can soar to around 37°C and humidity is often close to 100% in Rome during those months, but there are some advantages: Romans desert the city for the beaches and mountains, which means very light traffic and a consequent reduction in air pollution, as well as a less-crowded city centre. In summer there are also numerous outdoor festivals and concerts. If you must visit in summer, try to hit the sights early, take a long lunch and a nap, and then head out again around 6 pm to take advantage of the cooler evening.

While November is noted for heavy rain and December to February can bring icy weather, in recent years there has been unseasonably warm weather right up to Christmas. In any case, Rome is hardly Moscow! In fact, the city is less overrun with tourists and there are some fun events around Christmas time, including free concerts of sacred music in churches and the traditional Christmas market held in Piazza Navona.

ORIENTATION

Rome is a vast city but the historic centre is relatively small, defined by the twisting River Tiber to the west, the sprawling Villa Borghese park to the north, the Roman Forum and Palatine to the south and the central train station, Stazione Termini, to the east. Most of the major sights are within a reasonable distance of the train station. It is, for instance, possible to walk from the Colosseum, through the Roman Forum and the Palatine, up to Piazza di Spagna and across to the Vatican in one day, although such a crowded itinerary is hardly recommended even for the most dedicated tourist.

One of the great pleasures of being in Rome is wandering through the many beautiful squares. Make sure you use a map. While it can be enjoyable to get off the beaten track in Rome, it can also be very frustrating and time-consuming.

Most new arrivals in Rome will end up at Stazione Termini, the terminus for all international and national trains. The station is commonly referred to as Termini. The main city bus station is in Piazza dei Cinquecento, directly in front of the station. Many intercity buses depart from and arrive at Piazzale Tiburtina, in front of Stazione Tiburtina, accessible from Termini on the Metro Linea B. Buses serving towns in the Lazio region depart from various points throughout the city, usually corresponding to stops on the Metro lines. See the Getting There & Away and Excursions chapters for details.

The main airport is Leonardo da Vinci at Fiumicino – about 30 minutes by the special airport–Termini train or 45 minutes to one hour by car from the city centre. A second airport, Ciampino, south of the city on the Via Appia Nuova, serves most charter flights to Rome.

If you're arriving in Rome by car, invest in a good road map of the city beforehand so as to have an idea of the various routes into the city centre. Rome is encircled by a ring road, called the Grande Raccordo Anulare (GRA), which is connected to the A1 autostrada (the main north–south route in Italy, extending from Milan to Reggio di Calabria). The main access routes from the GRA into the city centre include Via Salaria from the north, Via Aurelia from the north-west and Via Cristoforo Colombo from the south.

MAPS

Lonely Planet's fold-out *Rome City Map* is perfect for sightseeing. It is plastic-coated, virtually indestructible and indicates all the major landmarks, museums and shops. There's also a street index.

Editrice Lozzi publishes a street map and bus guide simply entitled *Roma* (€3.10); it is available at any newsstand in Termini. It lists all streets, with map references, as well as bus and tram routes. Lozzi also publishes the very good *Archaeo Map*, a plan of the Roman Forum, Palatine, Fori Imperiali and Colosseum.

The free city map, *Charta Roma*, has a reasonable map of the city centre with major monuments and sights indicated. It also details the city's public transport routes, including buses, trams and the Metro. Information is in English and Italian. Pick it up at tourist offices or at the ATAC booth in Piazza dei Cinquecento, in front of Stazione Termini (Map 5).

City maps are available at good bookshops (such as Feltrinelli) or newsstands. Excellent city plans and maps are published by the Istituto Geografico de Agostini, the Touring Club Italiano and Michelin.

TOURIST OFFICES
Local Tourist Offices

There is an information office run by the Comune di Roma at Stazione Termini (Map 5), at the end of Platform 4 (open 8 am to 9 pm). Free city maps, transport guides, accommodation booklets (one on hotels and the other on B&Bs) and brochures on museums, festivals and events are available here. The Comune di Roma operates a tourism infoline ☎ 06 360 04 399 (9 am to 7 pm).

There are also 10 Comune di Roma tourist information kiosks dotted around the city: Piazza dei Cinquecento outside Stazione Termini (Map 5); Via dei Fori Imperiali near Largo Ricci (Map 5); Via Nazionale, next to the Palazzo del Esposizione (Map 5); Via del Corso, at Via

Minghetti (Map 4); Via del Corso, at Largo Goldoni (Map 4); Castel Sant'Angelo, at Piazza Pia (Map 4); Trastevere, at Piazza Sonnino (Map 6); Santa Maria Maggiore at Via dell'Olmata (Map 5); Piazza Navona at Piazza delle Cinque Lune (Map 8); Piazza San Giovanni in Laterano opposite the basilica (Map 7). All open 9 am to 6 pm daily.

The Azienda di Promozione Turistica (APT; Map 5; ☎ 06 488 99 253), Via Parigi 5, opens 8.15 am to 7.15 pm Monday to Friday and 7.15 am to 1.45 pm on Saturday. APT is operated by the regional authorities and has information (including brochures, maps and accommodation listings) on destinations outside the city centre. There is another office in the arrivals hall at Fiumicino airport.

Enjoy Rome (Map 5; ☎ 06 445 18 43), Via Marghera 8, is a privately run tourist office a few minutes' walk north-east of the train station. The office (which provides a complete range of travel-agency services including free hotel reservations in Rome and other parts of Italy) is brimming with information about the city including the free *Rome City Guide* pamphlet, packed with practical information. Check out its Web site at www.enjoyrome.com. Walking, bike and sightseeing tours are offered daily (see Organised Tours in the Getting Around chapter). The office opens 8.30 am to 2 pm and 3.30 to 6.30 pm Monday to Friday and 8.30 am to 2 pm on Saturday.

Tourist Offices Abroad

Italy's national tourist board, ENIT, has offices throughout the world. Check out its Web site at www.enit.it for contact details as well as information on museum opening hours and places to visit in Italy. Rome's ENIT office (Map 5; ☎ 06 497 11, fax 06 446 33 79, ✉ sedecentrale.enit@interbusiness.it) is at Via Marghera 2.

Australia
(☎ 02-9262 1666, ✉ enitour@ihug.com.au) Level 26, 44 Market Street, Sydney, NSW 2000
Austria
(☎ 0900-970 228, ✉ enit-wien@aon.at) Kaerntnerring 4, 1010 Vienna

Canada
(☎ 416-925 4882, e enit.canada@on.aibn.com) Suite 907, South Tower, 17 Bloor Street East, Toronto, Ont M4W 3R8
France
(☎ 01 42 66 03 96, e enit.parigi@wanadoo.fr) 23 rue de la Paix, 75002 Paris
Germany
(☎ 030-247 83 97, e enit-berlin@t-online.de) Karl Liebknecht Strasse 34, 10178 Berlin
(☎ 089-531 317, e enit-muenchen@t-online.de) Goethestrasse 20, 80336 Munich
(☎ 069-259 126, e enit.ffm@t-online.de) Kaiserstrasse 65, 60329 Frankfurt-am-Main
Netherlands
(☎ 020-616 82 44, e enitams@wirehub.nl) Stadhouderskade 2, Amsterdam 1054 ES
Spain
(☎ 091 559 97 50, e italiaturismo@retemail.es) Gran Via 84, Madrid 28013
Switzerland
(☎ 01-211 7917, e enit@bluewin.ch) Uraniastrasse 32, 8001 Zurich
UK
(☎ 020-7355 1557, e enitlond@globalnet.co.uk) 1 Princess St, London W1R 9AY
USA
(☎ 312-644 0996, e enitch@italiantourism.com) 500 North Michigan Avenue, Suite 2240, Chicago, IL 60611
(☎ 310-820 1898, e enitla@earthlink.net) 12400 Wilshire Blvd, Suite 550, Los Angeles, CA 90025
(☎ 212-245 4822, e enitny@italiantourism.com) 630 Fifth Avenue, Suite 1565, New York, NY 10111

Compagnia Italiana di Turismo (CIT) is an international network of travel agencies which promotes tourism in Italy. It has offices in various countries, can provide extensive information on travelling in Italy and will organise tours, as well as book hotels. CIT can also make train bookings and sells Eurail passes and discount passes for train travel in Italy. Offices include:

Australia
(☎ 02-9267 1255) 263 Clarence St, Sydney, NSW 2000
(☎ 03-9650 5510) Level 4, 227 Collins St, Melbourne, Vic 3000
Web site: www.cittravel.com.au
Canada
(☎ 800-361 7799, e tours@cittours.com) 666 Sherbrooke St, Suite 901, Montreal, Que H3A 1E7
(☎ 800-387 0711) 80 Tiverton Court, Suite 401, Markham, Ont L3R 0G4
France
(☎ 01 44 51 39 51, fax 01 44 51 39 67) 3 blvd des Capucines, 75002 Paris
Germany
(☎ 0211-690 030, fax 690 03 19) Geibelstrasse 39, 40235 Düsseldorf
UK
(☎ 020-8686 0677, 8686 0328) Marco Polo House, 3–5 Lansdowne Rd, Croydon, Surrey CR9 1LL
Web site: www.citalia.co.uk
USA
(☎ 800-248-8687, e tour@cittours.com) 15 West 44th St, 10th floor, New York, NY 10036
(☎ 800 248 8687) 9501 West Devon Ave, Suite 1, Rosemont, IL 60018

The Italian cultural institutes based in major cities throughout the world have information on opportunities to study in Rome and other cities throughout Italy.

TRAVEL AGENCIES

Really cheap airfares are hard to come by in Rome where bucket shops don't exist. However, there are a few agencies specialising in youth and budget travel. Bear in mind that even in these days of electronic transactions, there are still some agencies that don't accept credit cards – check first.

The Centro Turistico Studentesco (CTS; Map 4; ☎ 06 687 26 72), Corso Vittorio Emanuele II 297, is Italy's official student travel service and offers discounted air, rail and bus tickets to students and travellers aged under 30. CTS also issues ISIC cards. It opens 9.30 am to 1 pm and 3.30 to 7 pm Monday to Friday and 9.30 am to 1 pm on Saturday. There are other branches at Via Genova 16 (Map 5; ☎ 06 467 92 71) and near La Sapienza university, at Via degli Ausoni 5 (Map 5; ☎ 06 445 01 41). Note that to take advantage of CTS fares if you are not a student, you have to have a CTS card, which costs around €25 and is valid for a year. Get information online at www.cts.it.

The well run private tourist office Enjoy Rome (Map 5; ☎ 06 445 18 43, fax 06 445 07 34), Via Marghera 8, also operates as a travel agency, selling discount tickets for

FACTS FOR THE VISITOR

air, bus and rail travel, and dealing with everything from car hire to Vatican tours. There's always someone who speaks English in the office and staff are friendly and helpful. The office opens 8.30 am to 2 pm and 3.30 to 6.30 pm Monday to Friday and 8.30 am to 2 pm Saturday. For online bookings visit www.enjoyrome.com.

Nouvelles Frontières (Map 2; ☎ 06 322 24 63 or toll-free 147 88 99 00) at Via A Brunetti 25, off Via del Corso near Piazza del Popolo, is another popular travel agency catering for the youth and budget travel markets. Elsy Viaggi (Map 8; ☎ 06 688 01 372), Via di Torre Argentina 80, offers cheap fares for flights to other European cities as well as good deals on long-haul flights. It opens 9 am to 1 pm and 3.30 to 6.30 pm Monday to Friday and 9 am to 1 pm on Saturday. Credit cards are not accepted.

CIT (Compagnia Italiana Turismo) offers a full range of travel services, although not necessarily cheap fares. There are several CIT offices in Rome. The most central are at Piazza della Repubblica 65 (Map 5; ☎ 06 462 03 11) and Via Nazionale 196 (Map 5; ☎ 06 47 86 41).

DOCUMENTS
Passport
Citizens of European Union (EU) member states can travel to Italy with their national identity cards alone. People from countries that do not issue ID cards, such as the UK, must carry a valid passport. All non-EU nationals must have a full valid passport.

If you've had your passport for a while, check that the expiry date is at least some months off, otherwise you may not be granted a visa (if you need one). If you travel a lot, keep an eye on the number of pages you have left in the passport. US consulates will generally insert extra pages if you need them but others may ask for a new passport.

If your passport is stolen or lost while in Italy you should notify the police and obtain a statement, and then contact your embassy or consulate as soon as possible.

The only time you are likely to have your passport stamped is when you arrive by air – although even at Rome's airport there's a good chance they won't stamp it. If you are entering Italy for any reason other than tourism (eg, to study) or if you plan to remain in the country for an extended period, you should insist on having the entry stamp. Without it you could encounter problems when trying to obtain a *permesso di soggiorno* – in effect, permission to remain in the country for a nominated period – which is essential for everything from enrolling at a language school to applying for residency in Italy (see Permesso di Soggiorno later in this section).

Visas
Italy is one of 15 countries that have signed the Schengen Convention, an agreement whereby all EU member countries (except the UK and Ireland) plus Iceland and Norway agreed to abolish checks at common borders. Legal residents of one Schengen country do not require a visa for another Schengen country. Citizens of the UK and Ireland are also exempt from visa requirements for Schengen countries and nationals of a number of other countries (including Australia, Canada, Israel, Japan, New Zealand, Switzerland and USA), do not require visas for tourist visits of up to 90 days. If you are a citizen of a country not mentioned in this section, you should check with an Italian consulate whether you need a visa.

The standard tourist visa issued by Italian consulates is the Schengen visa, valid for up to 90 days. A Schengen visa issued by one Schengen country is generally valid for travel in other Schengen countries. However, individual Schengen countries may impose additional restrictions on certain nationalities. It is therefore worth checking visa regulations with the consulate of each Schengen country you plan to visit.

Rules for obtaining Schengen visas have been tightened and it's now mandatory that you apply in your country of residence. You can apply for no more than two Schengen visas in any 12-month period and they are not renewable inside Italy. If you are going to visit more than one Schengen country, you are supposed to apply for the visa at a consulate of your main destination country or of the first country you intend to visit.

EU citizens do not require any permits to live or work in Italy. They are, however, required to register with a *questura* (police station) if they take up residence and obtain a permesso di soggiorno.

Study Visas Non-EU citizens who want to study at a university or language school in Italy must have a study visa. These visas can be obtained from your nearest Italian embassy or consulate. It should be noted that you will normally require confirmation of your enrolment, proof of payment of fees and adequate funds to support yourself before a visa is issued. The visa will then cover only the period of the enrolment. This type of visa is renewable within Italy but, again, only with confirmation of ongoing enrolment and proof that you are able to support yourself – bank statements are preferred.

Travel Insurance
Don't leave home without it! It will cover you for medical expenses, luggage theft or loss and unexpected changes in your travel arrangements (eg, ticket cancellation etc). Cover depends on your insurance and type of ticket, so ask both your insurer and ticket-issuing agency to explain where you stand. Ticket loss is also covered by travel insurance but keep a separate record of your ticket details (see under Copies later in this chapter). Buy travel insurance as early as possible. If you buy it the week before you fly or hop on the bus, you may find that you are not covered for delays to your trip.

Paying for your ticket with a credit card often provides limited travel accident insurance, and you may be able to reclaim the payment if the operator doesn't deliver. Ask your credit-card company what it will cover.

Driving Licence & Permits
If you plan to drive while in Rome, you will need to carry your driving licence. Either an international driving licence or a translation of your licence (available from ENIT – see Tourist Offices earlier in this chapter) might also be useful. EU citizens and foreigners who have held residency in Italy for one year or more are required to have an Italian

licence. If you are driving your own car, you must carry an International Insurance Certificate, known as a Green Card, and the car's registration papers.

Hostel Card
A valid HI (Hostelling International) card is required in all associated youth hostels (Associazione Italiana Alberghi per la Gioventù; AIG) in Italy. You can get this in your home country or at the youth hostel in Rome. In the latter case you apply for the card and must collect six stamps costing €2.58 each. You pay for a stamp on each of the first six nights you spend in the hostel. With six stamps you are considered a full member. HI is on the Web at www.iyhf.org.

Student & Youth Cards
An ISIC (International Student Identity Card) or similar card will get you discounted admission prices into some museums and other sights and is an asset for other purposes. It can help for cheap flights out of Italy and can also come in handy for such things as cinema and theatre and other travel discounts. Similar cards are available to teachers (ITIC). They are good for various discounts and carry a travel insurance component. If you're aged under 26 but not a student you can apply for a Euro<26 card, which gives much the same discounts as ISIC.

These student cards are issued by student unions, hostelling organisations and some youth travel agencies (such as usit Campus in the UK). They don't always automatically entitle you to discounts but you won't find out until you flash the card.

In Rome, the Centro Turistico Studentesco e Giovanile (CTS) office issues ISIC, ITIC and Euro<26 cards.

Seniors' Cards
EU citizens aged over 65 are often entitled to discount or free admission to museums and monuments. Your travel documents are adequate identification. See Senior Travellers later in this chapter for further details.

The Italian rail network offers discounts on train fares for those aged over 60 but you need to purchase a Carta d'Argento (see under Italian Rail Passes in the Getting There & Away chapter).

Other Documents

Permesso di Soggiorno Visitors are technically obliged to report to the questura if they plan to stay at the same address for more than one week, to receive a *permesso di soggiorno* (permit to remain in the country). Tourists who are staying in hotels are not required to do this because hotel owners are required to register all guests with the police.

A permesso di soggiorno only becomes a necessity if you plan to study, work (legally) or live in Italy. Obtaining one is never a pleasant experience. It involves enduring long queues and the frustration of arriving at the counter (after a two-hour wait) to find that you don't have all the necessary documents.

The exact requirements, such as documents and official stamps *(marche da bollo)*, can change from year to year. In general, you will need: a valid passport, containing a visa stamp indicating your date of entry into Italy; a special visa issued in your own country if you are planning to study; four passport-style photographs; and proof of your ability to support yourself financially.

It is best to go to the questura to obtain precise information on what is required. Sometimes there is a list posted, otherwise you will need to join a queue at the information counter.

The main Rome questura, in Via Genova (Map 5), is notorious for delays and best avoided if possible. This problem has been solved by decentralisation: in Rome it is now possible to apply at the *ufficio stranieri* (foreigners' bureau) of the police station closest to where you are staying.

Work Permits Non-EU citizens wishing to work in Italy will need to obtain a *permesso di lavoro* (work permit). If you intend to work for an Italian company, the company must organise the permesso and forward it to the Italian consulate in your

country – only then will you be issued an appropriate visa.

If non-EU citizens intend to work for a non-Italian company or will be paid in foreign currency, or wish to go freelance, they must organise the visa and permesso in their country of residence through an Italian consulate. This process can take many months, so look into it early.

In any case it's advisable to seek detailed information from an Italian embassy or consulate on the exact requirements before attempting to organise a legitimate job in Italy. Many foreigners, however, don't bother with such formalities, preferring to work 'black' in areas such as teaching English, bar work and seasonal jobs (see under Work later in this chapter).

Copies

All important documents (passport data page and visa page, credit cards, travel insurance policy, air/bus/train tickets, driving licence and so on) should be photocopied before you leave. Give a copy to someone at home and keep another with you, separate from the originals.

It's also a good idea to store details of your vital travel documents in Lonely Planet's free online Travel Vault in case you lose the copies or can't be bothered with them. Your password-protected Travel Vault is accessible online anywhere in the world – create it at www.ekno.lonelyplanet.com.

EMBASSIES & CONSULATES
Italian Embassies & Consulates

Italian diplomatic missions abroad include:

Australia
Embassy: (☎ 02-6273 3333, fax 6273 4223, ⓔ embassy@ambitalia.org.au) 12 Grey St, Deakin, ACT 2600
Consulate: (☎ 02-9392 7900, fax 9252 4830, ⓔ itconsydn@itconsyd.org) Level 43, The Gateway, 1 Macquarie Place, Sydney, NSW 2000
Consulate: (☎ 03-9867 5744, fax 9866 3932, ⓔ itconmel@netlink.com.au) 509 St Kilda Rd, Melbourne, Vic 3004
Web site: www. ambitalia.org.au

Austria
Embassy: (☎ 01-712 51 21, fax 713 97 19, 📧 ambitalviepress@via.at) Metternichgasse 13, Vienna 1030

Canada
Embassy: (☎ 613-232 2401, fax 233 1484) 21st floor, 275 Slater St, Ottawa, Ont K1P 5H9
Consulate: (☎ 604-684 7288, fax 685 4263, 📧 consolato@italianconsulate.bc.ca) Standard Building #1100, 510 West Hastings St, Vancouver, BC V6B 1L8
Web site: www.italyincanada.com

France
Embassy: ☎ 01 49 54 03 00, fax 01 45 49 35 81, 📧 ambasciata@amb-italie.fr) 47 rue de Varenne, 75007 Paris

Ireland
Embassy: (☎ 01-660 1744, fax 668 2759, 📧 italianembassy@eircom.net) 63–65 Northumberland Rd, Dublin
Web site: http://homepage.tinet.ie/~italianembassy

Netherlands
Embassy: (☎ 070-302 10 30, fax 361 4932, 📧 italemb@worldonline.nl) Alexanderstraat 12, The Hague 2514 JL
Web site: www.italy.nl

New Zealand
Embassy: (☎ 04-473 53 39, fax 472 72 55, 📧 ambwell@xtra.co.nz) 34 Grant Rd, Thorndon, Wellington

Switzerland
Embassy: (☎ 031-352 4151, fax 351 1026, 📧 ambital.berna@spectraweb.ch) Elfenstrasse 14, 3006 Bern
Web site: www3.itu.int/embassy/italy

UK
Embassy: (☎ 020-7312 2200, fax 7312 2230, 📧 emblondon@embitaly.org.uk) 14 Three Kings Yard, London W1K 4EH
Web site: www.embitaly.org.uk
Consulate in Edinburgh: (☎ 0131-226 3631, fax 226 6260, 📧 consedimb@consedimb.demon.co.uk) 32 Melville St, Edinburgh EH3 7HA

USA
Embassy: (☎ 202-612 4400, fax 518 2154, 📧 stampa@itwash.org) 1601 Fuller St, NW Washington, DC 20009
Web site: www.italyemb.org
Consulate: (☎ 212-7737 9100, fax 249 4945, 📧 italconsulnyc@italconsulnyc.org) 690 Park Ave, New York, NY 10021
Web site: www.italconsulnyc.org
Consulate: (☎ 213-826 6207, fax 820 0727, 📧 cglos@conlang.com) Suite 300, 12400 Wilshire Blvd, West Los Angeles, CA 90025
Web site: www.conlang.com

Embassies & Consulates in Rome

Foreign embassies and consulates in Rome include:

Australia
(Map 3; ☎ 06 85 27 21) Via Alessandria 215

Austria
Embassy: (Map 3; ☎ 06 844 01 41) Via Pergolesi 3
Consulate: (☎ 06 855 29 66) Viale Liegi 32

Canada
Embassy: (Map 1; ☎ 06 44 59 81) Via G B de Rossi 27
Consulate: (Map 3; ☎ 06 44 59 81) Via Zara 30

France
Embassy: (Map 8; ☎ 06 68 60 11) Piazza Farnese
Visas: (Map 8; ☎ 06 688 02 152) Via Giulia 251

Germany
(Map 5; ☎ 06 492 131) Via San Martino della Battaglia 4

Ireland
(Map 4; ☎ 06 697 91 21) Piazza Campitelli 3

Netherlands
(Map 3; ☎ 06 322 11 41) Via M Mercati 8

New Zealand
(Map 3; ☎ 06 441 71 71) Via Zara 28

Switzerland
(Map 1; ☎ 06 80 95 71) Via Barnarba Oriani 61

UK
(Map 3; ☎ 06 482 54 41) Via XX Settembre 80a

USA
(Map 5; ☎ 06 467 41) Via Vittorio Veneto 119a–121
Web site: www.usis.it

For other diplomatic missions in Rome, look under 'Ambasciate' or 'Consolati' in the telephone book. The tourist offices will also generally have a list.

CUSTOMS

There is no limit on the amount of euros brought into the country. Goods brought in and exported with the EU incur no additional taxes, provided duty has been paid somewhere within the EU and the goods are for personal consumption.

Duty-free sales within the EU no longer exist. Travellers coming into Italy from non-EU countries can import, duty free, 200 cigarettes, 1L of spirits, 2L wine, 60mL perfume, 250mL eau de toilette and other goods up to a total of €175.60; anything over this limit must be declared on arrival and the appropriate duty paid.

MONEY
Currency

From January 1 2002, Italy will have a new currency, the euro. It is one of 11 EU countries in the first intake for European Monetary Union (EMU). The euro has been traded on international exchanges since January 1999. The actual notes and coins will be phased in over the first two months of 2002. The Italian lira (plural: lire) will remain legal currency until 28 February 2002. For further details see the boxed text 'Euros Will Do Nicely, Thank You'.

Exchange Rates

country	unit		lire/euros
Australia	A$1	=	L1151.40/€0.59
Canada	C$1	=	L1428.53/€0.71
France	10FF	=	L2951.82/€1.52
Germany	DM1	=	L989.99/€0.51
Japan	¥100	=	L1797.84/€0.89
New Zealand	NZ$1	=	L930.31/€0.47
UK	UK£1	=	L3147.44/€1.57
USA	US$1	=	L2214.65/€1.06

Exchanging Money

You can change money in banks, at the post office or in a *cambio* (exchange office). Banks are generally the most reliable and tend to offer the best rates. However, you should look around and ask about commissions. These can fluctuate considerably and a lot depends on whether you are changing cash or cheques.

While the post office charges a flat rate of €0.62 per cash transaction, banks charge €1.55 or more. Travellers cheques attract higher fees. Some banks charge €0.55 *per cheque* with a €1.55 minimum, while the post office charges a maximum €2.60 per transaction. Other banks will have different arrangements again, and in all cases you should compare the exchange rates too. Exchange booths often advertise 'no commission' but the rate of exchange can often be inferior to that in the banks.

Balanced against the desire to save on such fees by making occasional large trans-

actions should be a healthy fear of pickpockets – you don't want to be robbed the day you have exchanged a huge hunk of money to last you weeks!

Cash There is little advantage in bringing more than a small amount of foreign cash with you. True, exchange commissions are often lower than for travellers cheques, but the danger of losing the lot far outweighs such petty gains.

It is worth having some cash on you when you arrive especially with early morning arrivals at Fiumicino where nothing much operates until about 8 am.

Travellers Cheques These are a safe way to carry money and are easily cashed at banks and exchange offices in Rome and throughout Italy. Always keep the bank receipt listing the cheque numbers separate from the cheques and keep a list of the numbers of those you have already cashed – this will reduce problems in the event of loss or theft. Check the conditions applying to such circumstances before buying the cheques.

If you buy your travellers cheques in euros (or lire), there should be no commission charge when cashing them. Most hard currencies are widely accepted, although you may have occasional trouble with the New Zealand dollar. Buying cheques in a third currency (such as US dollars if you are not coming from the USA) means you pay commission when you buy the cheques and again when cashing them in Italy. Get most of the cheques in fairly large denominations to save on per-cheque exchange charges.

Travellers using the better-known cheques, such as Visa, American Express (Amex) and Thomas Cook, will have little trouble in Rome. Amex, in particular, has offices in all the major Italian cities and agents in many smaller cities. If you lose your Amex cheques while in Rome, you can call a 24-hour toll-free number (☎ 800 87 20 00). For Thomas Cook or MasterCard cheques call ☎ 800 87 20 50 and for Visa cheques call 800 87 41 55.

Take along your passport when you go to cash travellers cheques.

Euros Will Do Nicely, Thank You

On January 1 2002, the euro will become the currency of cash transactions in all of Italy (including the Vatican City and the Republic of San Marino) and throughout the EU (except for the three foot-draggers: Denmark, Sweden and the UK).

From January 2002 there will be a two-month transition period, during which lire and euros will circulate side by side and lire can be exchanged for euros free of charge at banks. From 28 February 2002, the euro is Italy's sole currency, though unused banknotes and coins can be exchanged at central banks for at least two years beyond that date but will only issue euros.

The euro is divided into 100 cents. Coin denominations are one, two, five, 10, 20 and 50 cents, €1 and €2. The notes are €5, €10, €20, €50, €100, €200 and €500. All euro coins across the EU will be identical on the side showing their value, but there will be 12 different obverses, each representing one of the 12 euro zone countries. All euro notes of each denomination will be identical on both sides. All euro coins and notes will be legal tender throughout the euro zone.

Travellers will probably find varying degrees of 'euro-readiness' in Rome in the lead up to the introduction of the euro as legal tender. Legally, shops, hotels and restaurants should list prices in both lire and euros, but at the time of writing this wasn't always the case.

Once euro notes and coins are issued in 2002, you won't need to change money at all when travelling to other single-currency members and prices in the member states will be immediately comparable. Banks may still charge a handling fee (yet to be decided) for travellers cheques but they won't be able to profit by buying the currency from you at one rate and selling it back to you at another. And even EU countries not participating in the single currency may price goods in euros and accept euros over shop counters.

This book was researched during the transition period, when not all prices were available in euros. Prices quoted, eg by hotels, restaurants and entertainment venues, in the national currency have been converted to euros at the fixed conversion rate (€1 is equal to L1936.27) – these may undergo further change as the euro comes into use.

For more information check out the Web site www.europa.eu.int/euro.

Credit/Debit Cards & ATMs Carrying plastic (whether a credit or ATM card) is the simplest way to organise your holiday funds. You don't have large amounts of cash or cheques to lose, you can get money after hours and on weekends and the exchange rate is better than that offered for travellers cheques or cash exchanges. By arranging for payments to be made into your credit card account while you are travelling, you can avoid paying interest.

Major credit cards, such as Visa, MasterCard, Eurocard, Diners Club and JCB, are accepted in Rome and throughout Italy, as are Cirrus and Eurocheque cards. They can be used for many purchases (including in many supermarkets) and in hotels and restaurants (although *pensioni* and smaller trattorie and pizzerie still tend to accept cash only).

Credit cards can also be used in ATMs *(bancomat)* displaying the appropriate sign or (if you have no PIN number) to obtain cash advances over the counter in many banks – Visa and MasterCard are among the most widely recognised for such transactions. Check charges with your bank but, as a rule, there is no charge for purchases on major cards and a 1.5% charge on cash advances and ATM transactions in foreign currencies.

It is possible to use your own ATM card in machines in Rome and throughout Italy to obtain money from your own bank account. This is without doubt the simplest way to handle your money while travelling.

If an ATM rejects your card, don't despair or start wasting money on international calls to your bank. Try a few more

ATMs displaying your credit card's logo at major banks before assuming the problem lies with your card rather than with the local system. Italian ATMs are notoriously fickle.

If your credit card is lost, stolen or swallowed by an ATM, you can telephone toll-free to have an immediate stop put on its use. For MasterCard the number in Italy is ☎ 800 87 08 66, or make a reverse-charges call to St Louis in the USA on ☎ 314-275 66 90; for Visa, phone ☎ 800 87 72 32 in Italy. If, by chance, you have a credit card issued in Italy call ☎ 800 82 20 56 to have it blocked.

Amex is also widely accepted (although not as common as Visa or MasterCard). Amex's full-service offices (such as those in Rome and Milan) will issue new cards, usually within 24 hours and sometimes immediately, if yours has been lost or stolen. Some Amex offices have ATMs that you can use to obtain cash advances if you have made the necessary arrangements in your own country.

The toll-free emergency number to report a lost or stolen Amex card varies according to where the card was issued. Check with Amex in your country or contact the office in Rome on ☎ 06 722 82, which itself has a 24-hour cardholders' service.

International Transfers One reliable way to send money to Rome is by TT or Swift transfer through the foreign office of a large Italian bank, or through major banks in your own country, to a nominated bank in Rome. It is important to have an exact record of all details associated with the money transfer, particularly the exact address of the Italian bank to where the money has been sent. The money will always be held at the head office of the bank in the town to which it has been sent. Swift transfers should take only a few days, while other means, such as telegraphic transfer or draft, can take weeks.

It is also possible to transfer money through Amex and Thomas Cook. You will be required to produce ID, usually a passport, in order to collect the money. It is also a good idea to take along the details of the transaction.

One of the speedier options is to send money through Western Union (☎ 800 01 38 39). This service functions in Rome through a number of different outlets and it is best to call the toll-free number in order to get the address of the closest outlet. The sender and receiver have to turn up at a Western Union outlet with passport or other form of ID and the fees charged for the virtually immediate transfer depend on the amount sent.

Costs

A *very* prudent traveller could get by on €40 per day but only by staying in a youth hostel, eating one hot meal a day (at the hostel), buying a sandwich or pizza (by the slice) for lunch and minimising the number of galleries and museums visited, since the admission cost to most museums is cripplingly expensive at around €6.20. You can save on transport costs by buying tourist or day tickets for the city bus and Metro services. Museums and galleries usually give discounts to students but you will need a valid student card, which you can obtain from CTS offices if you have documents proving you are a student (see Travel Agents earlier in this chapter).

One step up, you can get by on about €56 per day if you stay in one of the cheaper hotels, and keep sit-down meals and museums to one a day. Lone travellers may find even this budget hard to maintain, since single rooms tend to be pricey.

With a generous budget, you'll find your niche in Rome. There's no shortage of luxury hotels, expensive restaurants and shops. Realistically, a traveller wanting to stay in comfortable lower- to mid-range hotels, eat two square meals a day, not feel restricted to one museum a day and be able to enjoy the odd drink and other minor indulgences should reckon on a minimum daily average of €100 to €130 per day.

A basic breakdown of costs during an average day could be: €13 (hostel) to €105 (top-end hotel) for accommodation; €1.55 (coffee and croissant) to €10 (sit-down meal at an outdoor cafe) for breakfast; €2.50 (sandwich and mineral water) to €25 (sit-down meal in a mid-range restaurant) for lunch; €3.10 (day pass for bus and

Metro) for public transport; €6.20 admission fee for one museum; €13 to €50 for a sit-down dinner.

Tipping & Bargaining

You are not expected to tip on top of restaurant service charges but it is common to leave a small amount. If there is no service charge, the customer might consider leaving a 10% tip but this is by no means obligatory. In bars, Italians often leave any small change as a tip, often only €0.05 or €0.10. Tipping taxi drivers is not common practice but you should tip the porter at higher-class hotels.

Bargaining is common in flea markets but not in shops. At the Porta Portese market in Rome, for instance, don't hesitate to offer half the asking price for any given item. Don't be deterred by stallholders who dismiss you with a wave of the arm: the person at the next stall will be just as likely to accept your offer after a brief (and obligatory) haggle. While bargaining in shops is not acceptable, you might find that the proprietor is disposed to give a discount if you are spending a reasonable amount of money. It is quite acceptable to ask if there is a special price for a room in a *pensione* if you plan to stay for more than a few days.

Taxes & Refunds

A value-added tax (VAT) of around 19%, known as IVA (Imposta di Valore Aggiunto), is slapped onto just about everything in Italy. If you are resident outside the EU and you spend more than €154.91 in the same shop on the same day, you can claim a refund on this tax when you leave the EU. The refund only applies to purchases from affiliated retail outlets which display a 'Tax free for tourists' sign. You have to complete a form at the point of sale, then get it stamped by Italian customs as you leave. At major airports you can then get an immediate cash refund; otherwise it will be refunded to your credit card.

Receipts

Laws aimed at tightening controls on the payment of taxes in Italy mean that the onus is on the buyer to ask for and retain receipts for all goods and services. This applies to everything from a litre of milk to a haircut. Although it rarely happens, you could be asked by an officer of the *guardia di finanza* (fiscal police) to produce the receipt immediately after you leave a shop. If you don't have it, you may be obliged to pay a fine of up to €1033.

POST & COMMUNICATIONS
Post

Italy's postal system is notoriously unreliable, although things look better than they did a decade ago now that there is a more efficient but also more expensive *posta prioritaria* service for some domestic and all international mail. Ironically, the introduction of this additional service has reduced the demand on the regular mail system, which in turn is functioning better.

Stamps *(francobolli)* are available at post offices and authorised tobacconists; look for the official *tabacchi* sign: a big 'T', usually white on black. Since letters often need to be weighed, what you get at the tobacconist's for international air mail will occasionally be an approximation of the proper rate.

Information about postal services can be obtained on ☎ 800 22 26 66 or online at www.poste.it. Rome's main post office is at Piazza San Silvestro 18–20 (Map 4). It opens 8.30 am to 6 pm Monday to Friday, 8.30 am to 2 pm Saturday and 9 am until 2 pm on Sunday.

There are local post offices in every district of the city. They usually open 8.30 am to 1.50 pm Monday to Friday and 8.30 to 11.50 on Saturday. All post offices close two hours earlier than normal on the last business day of each month.

Postal Rates The cost of sending a letter air mail *(via aerea)* depends on its weight, destination and method of postage. For regular post, letters up to 20g cost €0.41 within Europe, €0.67 to the USA and €0.77 to Australia and New Zealand. Postcards cost the same. (As only a small percentage of postcards sent to, from or within Italy are delivered, it's worth putting your postcards in envelopes and sending them as letters.)

However, few people use the regular post any more, preferring the slightly more expensive priority mail service *(posta prioritaria)*, guaranteed to deliver letters sent to Europe within three days and to the rest of the world within four to eight days. Letters up to 20g sent *posta prioritaria* cost €0.62 within Europe, €0.77 to the Americas, Africa, Asia, Australia and New Zealand. Letters weighing 21g to 100g cost €1.24 within Europe, €1.55 to Africa, Asia and the Americas and €1.81 to Australia and New Zealand.

For more important items, use registered mail *(raccomandato)* – €2.58 on top of the normal cost of the letter – or insured mail *(assicurato)*, the cost of which depends on the value of the object being sent (€5.16 for objects valued up to €51.64). Insured mail is not available to the USA.

Parcels Parcels *(pacchetti)* can be sent from any post office. You can buy posting boxes or padded envelopes from most post offices. Stationery shops *(cartolerie)* and some tobacconists also sell padded envelopes. There are some strange regulations about how parcels should be sealed, and these appear to vary from one post office to another.

Don't tape up or staple envelopes – they should be sealed with glue. Your best bet is not to close the envelope or box completely and ask at the counter how it should be done. Parcels usually take longer to be delivered than letters. A different set of postal rates apply.

Express Mail Urgent mail can be sent by *postacelere* (also known as CAI Post), the Italian post office's courier service. Letters up to 500g cost €15.50 in Europe, €23.76 to the USA and €35.12 to Australia. A parcel weighing 1kg will cost €17.56 to a destination in Europe, €27.89 to the USA and Canada, and €41.32 to Australia and New Zealand. CAI post is not necessarily as fast as private courier services. It will take three to five days for a parcel to reach the USA, Canada or Australia and one to three days to European destinations. Ask at post offices for addresses of CAI post outlets or check out www.postacelere.com.

Vatican Post Many people, both Romans and tourists, choose to use the Vatican postal system instead of the Italian one. There is a post office in Piazza di San Pietro (Map 4) next to the information office and another one inside the Vatican Museums. Rates are similar to those of the Italian postal system. The Vatican post is run in association with the Swiss postal service and has always been considered to be more reliable than the Italian system, especially for overseas mail.

However, this is not always the case. A letter sent by this author via Vatican post from Rome to Australia took five months to reach its destination. Also, the Vatican post offices don't accept poste restante mail.

Couriers Several international couriers operate in Italy: DHL has three offices in Rome and two others at Fiumicino and Ciampino airports and a 24-hour toll-free phone line ☎ 800 34 53 45; Federal Express is located centrally in Via Barberini 115 and has a toll-free number ☎ 800 83 30 40; for UPS call toll-free ☎ 800 82 20 54. Note that if you are having articles sent to you by courier in Italy, you might be obliged to pay IVA of up to 20% to retrieve the goods.

Receiving Mail Poste restante is known as *fermo posta* in Italy. Letters marked thus will be held at the counter of the same name in the main post office. Poste restante mail sent to Rome should be addressed as follows:

> John SMITH,
> Fermo Posta,
> Posta Centrale,
> Piazza San Silvestro,
> 00186 Roma

You will need to pick up your letters in person and present your passport as ID.

Amex-card or travellers-cheque holders can use the free client mail-holding service at the Amex office, Piazza di Spagna 38 (Map 4). You can obtain a list of other branches throughout Italy from Amex offices inside or outside Italy. Take your passport when you go to pick up mail.

Telephone

The state-run Telecom Italia is the largest telecommunications organisation in Italy and its orange public pay phones are liberally scattered throughout Rome. The most common accept only phonecards *(carte/ schede telefoniche)*, although you will still find plenty that accept cards and coins (L100, L200 and L500). Machines will be altered to accept euros when lire are taken out of circulation in 2002. Some card phones now also accept special Telecom credit cards and even ordinary credit cards. Among the latest generation of pay phones are those that also send faxes.

Telecom pay phones can be found in the streets, train stations and some large stores as well as in Telecom offices. Some of the latter are staffed and a few have telephone directories for other parts of the country. Where these offices are staffed it is possible to make international calls and pay at the desk afterwards. There is a Telecom office at Stazione Termini (Map 5).

You can buy phonecards at post offices, tobacconists, newsstands and from vending machines in Telecom offices. To avoid the frustration of trying to find one of the fast-disappearing coin telephones, always keep a phonecard to hand. They come with a value of L5000/€2.58, L10,000/ €5.16 or L50,000/€25.82 but be prepared for changes when the euro is Italy's sole currency.

Public phones operated by the private telecommunications companies, Infostrada and Albacom, can be found in airports and stations. These phones accept Infostrada or Albacom phonecards (available from post offices, tobacconists and newsstands), which come with a value of L5000/€2.58 and L10,000/€5.16. The rates are slightly cheaper than Telecom's for long-distance and international calls.

Rates The cost of calls, particularly long-distance ones, are among the highest in Europe, although deregulation of the telecommunications industry has helped to reduce rates. The cheapest time for domestic calls is between 10 pm and 8 am. For international calls, off-peak hours are 10 pm to 8 am and all of Sunday.

A local call *(comunicazione urbana)* from a public phone will cost €0.10 for three to six minutes, depending on the time of day. Peak call times are 8 am to 6.30 pm Monday to Friday and 8 am to 1 pm Saturday.

Rates for long-distance calls *(comunicazione interurbana)* within Italy depend on the time of day and the distance involved. At the worst, one minute will cost about €0.20 in peak periods.

If you need to call overseas, beware of the cost – even a call of less than five minutes to Australia after 10 pm will cost around €3.82 from a private phone (more from a public phone). Calls to most European countries cost about €0.26 per minute and closer to €0.62 from a public phone.

Travellers from countries that offer direct dialling services paid for at home country rates (such as AT&T in the USA and Telstra in Australia) should think seriously about taking advantage of them.

Domestic Calls Telephone area codes all begin with 0 and consist of up to four digits. The area code is followed by a number of anything from four to eight digits.

Area codes are an integral part of all telephone numbers in Italy, even if you are calling within a single zone. If you are in Rome and are calling another fixed line in Rome (except toll-free numbers beginning with 800 or 147) the first two digits of the phone number will be 06. So any number you're calling in Florence will start with 055, in Venice 041, in Naples 081 and in Milan 02, regardless of whether you're in that place or in another part of Italy.

Mobile-phone numbers begin with a four-digit prefix such as 0330, 0335, 0347, 0368 and so on. Free-phone or toll-free numbers are called *numeri verdi* and start with 800 or 147. Dial ☎ 12 for directory enquiries.

International Calls Direct international calls can easily be made from public telephones by using a phonecard. Dial ☎ 00 to get out of Italy, then the relevant country and area codes, followed by the telephone number. Useful country codes are: Australia ☎ 61; Canada and USA ☎ 1; New Zealand ☎ 64; and the UK ☎ 44. Codes for other countries in Europe include: France ☎ 33; Germany ☎ 49; Greece ☎ 30; Ireland ☎ 353; and Spain ☎ 34. Other codes are listed in Italian telephone books.

To make international reverse-charge (collect) calls from a public telephone, dial ☎ 170. For European countries dial ☎ 15. All operators speak English.

Using the Country Direct service for your country is easier and often cheaper. You dial the number and request a reverse-charge call through the operator in your country. Numbers for this service include:

Australia (Telstra)	☎ 172-10 61
Australia (Optus)	☎ 172-11 61
Canada	☎ 172-10 01
France	☎ 172-00 33
New Zealand	☎ 172-10 64
UK (BT)	☎ 172-00 44
UK (BT Chargecard Operator)	☎ 172-01 44
USA (AT&T)	☎ 172-10 11
USA (IDB)	☎ 172-17 77
USA (MCI)	☎ 172-10 22
USA (Sprint)	☎ 172-18 77

For international directory enquiries call ☎ 176.

Call Centres Cut-price call centres are all over Rome, especially near Stazione Termini (Map 5), the Vatican (Map 4) and in the city centre. These are run by various companies and rates are significantly lower for international calls than Telecom pay phones. The other advantages are that it's usually a little less noisy than making a call from a pay phone in a busy street and you don't need a phonecard. You simply place your call from a private booth inside the centre and pay for it when you've finished. Not all phone centres accept credit cards.

Calling Italy from Abroad The country code for Italy is ☎ 39. You must always include the initial 0 in area codes. For example to call the number ☎ 06 777 77 77 in Rome you need to dial the international access code followed by ☎ 39 06 777 77 77. However, for mobile phones in Italy you should still drop the initial 0 of the prefix. For example, to call the mobile number ☎ 0335 77 77 77, you need to dial the international access code followed by ☎ 39 335 77 77 77.

Mobile Phones Italy uses the GSM cellular-phone system, compatible with phones sold in the UK, Australia and most of Asia, but not those from North America or Japan. Check with your service provider before you leave home that they have a roaming agreement with a local counterpart.

eKno Communication Service
Lonely Planet's eKno global communication service provides low-cost international calls – for local calls you're better off with a local phonecard. eKno also offers free messaging services, email, travel information and an online travel vault, where you can securely store all your important documents. You can join online at www.ekno .lonelyplanet.com, where you will find the local-access numbers for the 24-hour customer-service centre. Once you have joined, always check the eKno Web site for the latest access numbers for each country and updates on new features.

Fax
You can send faxes from post offices and some tobacconists, copy centres and stationers. Faxes can also be sent from some Telecom public phones. To send a fax within Italy, expect to pay €1.55 for the first page and €1.03 for each page thereafter, plus €0.03 per second for the actual call. International faxes can cost €3.10 for the first page and €2.07 per page thereafter, and €0.05 per second for the call.

Email & Internet Access
If you are bringing your laptop to Rome and want access to the Internet you will need to have a server that operates in Italy too. AOL (www.aol.com), CompuServe

(www.compuserve.com) and IBM Net (www.ibm.net) have dial-in nodes in Rome and Milan as well as slower-access numbers in other towns. It's best to download a list of the dial-in numbers before you leave home. If you access your Internet email account at home through a smaller ISP or your office or school network, your best option is either to open an account with a global ISP, such as those mentioned above, or rely on Internet cafes and other public access points to collect your mail.

If you do intend to rely on Internet cafes, you'll need to carry three pieces of information with you to enable you to access your Internet mail account: your incoming (POP or IMAP) mail server name, your account name and your password. Your ISP or network supervisor will be able to give you these. Armed with this information, you should be able to access your Internet mail account from any net-connected machine in the world, provided it runs some kind of email software (remember that Netscape and Internet Explorer both have mail modules). It pays to become familiar with the process for doing this before you leave home.

Keep in mind that the telephone socket in each country you visit will probably be different from the one at home, so ensure that you have at least a US RJ-11 telephone adapter that works with your modem. Most electronics shops in Rome sell adapters that convert from RJ-11 to the local three-pinned plug variety; more modern phone lines take the RJ-11 jack directly. Consider bringing an extension cord and a female-to-female RJ-11 adapter to make life easier. Also make sure you've got the right AC adapter for your computer, which enables you to plug it in anywhere without frying the innards. For further information on travelling with a portable computer, see www.teleadapt.com or www.warrior.com.

Some Italian servers can provide short-term accounts for local Internet access. Agora Telematica (☎ 06 699 25 693 42), online at www.agoratelematica.it, is one of them. Several Italian ISPs offer free Internet connections: check out Tiscalinet (www.tiscalinet.it), kataweb (www.kataweb.it and

www.kataweb.com); and Libero (www.libero.iol.it).

Internet Cafes Rome has dozens Internet cafes and new ones are opening up continually. These allow you to surf the Net and send email. Some places also provide email accounts. Costs vary but are usually in the region of €5.16 per hour, with hefty discounts or bonus hours if you take out a subscription, and discounts for students.

The Netgate (Map 8; ☎ 06 689 34 45), Piazza Firenze 25, in the heart of the historic centre near the Pantheon, offers Internet access at €5.16 per hour including an email account. There are discounts for students, and there's a welcome bonus for first-time clients: if you pay for 10 hours you get another six hours free. It opens 10.30 am to 9 pm daily (to 10 pm in summer). There are two other locations: near St Peter's Basilica at Borgo Santo Spirito 17–18 (Map 4; ☎ 06 681 34 082) and in the underground Forum shopping area at Stazione Termini (Map 5; ☎ 06 874 06 008).

Rimaweb Internet Point (Map 4; ☎ 06 688 91 356, ⓔ info@rimaweb.com) is in the heart of the Ghetto at Via del Portico d'Ottavia 2a. Internet access costs €1.55 for 15 minutes, or €25.82 for five hours. It opens 9.30 am to 7.30 pm Monday to Friday and 11 am to 7 pm on Saturday and Sunday. Visit online at www.rimaweb.com.

Bibli Bookshop (Map 6; ☎ 06 588 40 97), Via dei Fienaroli 28 in Trastevere, is a popular Internet spot for foreign students. It opens 11 am to midnight Tuesday to Saturday and 5.30 pm to midnight on Monday. Access costs €25.82 for 10 hours or €51.64 for 25 hours and when you buy access time you get your own email account.

Also in Trastevere is Globalservice (Map 6; ☎ 06 583 33 316, ⓔ globalservice@mclink.it), Piazza Sonnino 27, which opens 8 am to midnight daily. Internet access costs €5.16 per hour.

Kill two birds with one stone at Splashnet (Map 5; ☎ 06 493 82 073, ⓔ splashnet@yahoo.com), an Internet cafe near Termini station where you can also do your washing. It costs €3.10 per hour but if you're doing your laundry you get 10 minutes free. Their Web site is at www.splashnet.it.

Located in the university district, the imaginatively named Internet Café (Map 5; ☎ 06 445 49 53), Via Marrucini 12, is popular with students and offers one-/10-hour access for €4.13/30.99. It opens 9 am to 2 am Monday to Friday and 5 pm to 2 am on Saturday and Sunday. Another place also called Internet Café and charging the same prices is at Via Cavour 213 (Map 5; ☎ 06 47 82 30 51).

DIGITAL RESOURCES
Web Sites
The World Wide Web is a rich resource for travellers. You can research your trip, hunt down bargain air fares, book hotels, check on weather conditions or chat with locals and other travellers about the best places to visit (or avoid!).

There's no better place to start your Web explorations than the Lonely Planet Web site (www.lonelyplanet.com). Here you'll find succinct summaries on travelling to most places on earth, postcards from other travellers and the Thorn Tree bulletin board, where you can ask questions before you go or dispense advice when you get back. You can also find travel news and updates to many of our most popular guidebooks, and the sub-WWWay section links you to the most useful travel resources elsewhere on the Web.

Italy's leading student travel organisation, CTS, is online at www.cts.it and offers information on Rome. Other sites packed with tourist advice are Enjoy Rome at www.enjoyrome.com and Travel Italy at www.travel.it.

Roma's municipal government, the *comune*, has its own Web page (www.comune .roma.it), which provides information about everything from rubbish collection, health, social services and education to cultural listings. The site is geared towards residents of Rome, though the section on tourism and culture provides a good overview of current and forthcoming major events. The comune's database (www.informaroma.it) has details on the city's monuments and museums, virtual tours and links to other sites.

If you're planning a few museum visits and want to book tickets, then the culture ministry's Web site, www.beniculturali.it, has information on museums and galleries and an online reservation service.

The Vatican's official Web site is at www.vatican.va, where you can take a virtual tour of the Vatican Museums.

The Web site of the fortnightly magazine *Wanted in Rome*, www.wantedinrome.com, has listings and reviews of current exhibitions and cultural events as well as informative articles on aspects of Rome and the surrounding region. It also has classified ads online, which are helpful if you're planning a longer stay in the city and want to find a room in a shared flat (see Newspapers and Magazines later in this section).

The *English Yellow Pages* is a useful directory of English-speaking professionals, commercial activities, organisations and services in Rome. Its Web site, www .mondoweb.it/eyp, could be a good first stop and has lots of useful links.

CitySync
CitySync Rome is Lonely Planet's digital city guide for Palm OS handheld devices. With CitySync you can quickly search, sort and bookmark hundreds of Rome's restaurants, hotels, attractions, clubs and more – all pinpointed on scrollable street maps. Sections on activities, transport and local events means you get the big picture plus all the little details. Purchase or demo CitySync Rome at www.citysync.com.

BOOKS
Most books are published in different editions by different publishers in different countries. As a result, a book might be a hardcover rarity in one country while it is readily available in paperback in another. Fortunately, bookshops and libraries search by title or author, so your local bookshop or library is best placed to advise you on the availability of these recommendations.

Lonely Planet
If this book's too heavy for you then grab a copy of LP's *Rome Condensed*. If Rome is

not your only destination in Italy, consider buying LP's *Italy*. Hikers who are planning to visit other parts of the country should definitely consult LP's *Walking in Italy* guide. *Mediterranean Europe* and *Western Europe* include chapters on Italy and are recommended for those planning further travel in Europe. Also published by Lonely Planet, the *Italian phrasebook* lists all the words and phrases you're likely to need when travelling in Italy. LP's *World Food Italy* by Australia's leading food writer Matthew Evans is a great read, has fabulous photos and will make sure you don't miss any taste sensation during your Italian travels.

Guidebooks

The decades-old *Companion Guide to Rome* by Georgina Masson is packed with historical detail and fascinating anecdotes. The paperback edition, revised by Tim Jepson, was published in 1998.

Amanda Claridge's *Oxford Archaeological Guide to Rome* (1998) is an extremely detailed guide to ancient Rome, with descriptions, maps, plans and photos of more than 150 archaeological sites.

City Secrets Rome (2000), edited by Robert Kahn, is a guidebook with a difference. Contemporary artists, art historians, archaeologists, writers and historians, many of them Americans who have lived, worked and studied in Rome, give personal insights into Rome's monuments.

Travel

The list of books written by travellers to Italy, many of which describe sojourns in Rome, is endless but there are a few which stand out. For a potted idea of how the great writers saw the country, it's worth reading the *Traveller's Literary Companion to Italy* (1998) by Martin Garrett.

Three Grand Tour classics are Johann Wolfgang von Goethe's *Italian Journey*, Charles Dickens' *Pictures from Italy*, and Henry James' *Italian Hours*. James also used Rome as a backdrop for part of *Portrait of a Lady*. DH Lawrence wrote three short travel books while living in Italy, now combined in one volume entitled *DH Lawrence and Italy*.

HV Morton's *A Traveller in Rome*, written in the 1950s, is still a useful guide to the city and its people. The same author also wrote *A Traveller in Italy* and *A Traveller in Southern Italy*.

History & Politics

If you want a first-hand account of life in ancient Rome, and can handle the ancient philosophers and writers, try Plutarch, Tacitus and Livy, all of whom are available in the Penguin Classics series. Edward Gibbon's 18th-century *History of the Decline and Fall of the Roman Empire* (1994; available in six hardback volumes, or an abridged, single-volume paperback) is as much a masterpiece of literature as history; for an overview of Rome from Romulus to Constantine, try M Carey & HH Scullard's *History of Rome* (1980). *Rome: Biography of a City* (1987) by Christopher Hibbert is one of the most readable studies of Rome's multilayered history, and an excellent reference book.

Other history books include: *The Oxford History of the Roman World* (1991) edited by J Boardman et al; *The Oxford Illustrated History of Italy* (2001) edited by G Holmes; *Daily Life in Ancient Rome* (1991) by J Carcopino; *Italy: A Short History* (1991) by Harry Hearder; *Concise History of Italy* (1994) by C Duggan; *History of the Italian People* (1991) by G Procacci; *The Oxford Dictionary of Popes* (1992) compiled by JND Kelly; *The Penguin Historical Atlas of Ancient Rome* (1995) by C Scarre; *Rome in the Dark Ages* by P Llewellyn (1996); and *The Transformation of the Roman World AD 400–900* (1997) edited by L Webster and M Brown.

A History of Contemporary Italy (1990) by Paul Ginsburg, is an absorbing and well written book that will help Italophiles place the country's modern society in perspective. *Modern Italy: A Political History* (1997) by Denis Mack Smith is a complete and absorbing account of the fate of Italy from Risorgimento to the present. Mack Smith is widely regarded as the most authoritative historian on the subject writing in English.

Art

Useful references for fans of Italian art include: *A Handbook of Roman Art* (1983) edited by Martin Henig; *Roman Architecture* (1998) by Frank Sear; and *Art and Architecture in Italy 1600–1750* (1999) by Rudolf Wittkower. On the Renaissance, *The Penguin Book of the Renaissance* (1991) by JH Plumb, *Painters of the Renaissance* (1997) by Bernard Berenson and Giorgio Vasari's *Lives of the Artists* (1998) should keep you going for quite a while.

There is also a series of guides to Italian art and architecture, published under the general title World of Art. These include: *Roman Art and Architecture* (1964) by Mortimer Wheeler; *Michelangelo* (1980) by Linda Murray and *Italian Renaissance Sculpture* (1992) by Roberta JM Olson.

General

People For background on the Italian people and their culture, as seen by an Italian, there is the classic, *The Italians* (1996), by Luigi Barzini. Charles Richards' *The New Italians* (1995) is an absorbing account of modern Italy, its people and its political upheavals. *Italy – The Unfinished Revolution* (2001) by Matt Frei, a former Rome correspondent for the BBC, challenges the notion of Italy as a disordered society and catalogues the changes it has undergone in the past decade.

Italian Neighbours (2001) by Tim Parks is an often hilarious account of the life of an expatriate in Verona. Parks' *An Italian Education* (2001) is in the same vein and looks at child rearing, bilingual style.

The Church For a trip behind the scenes of the Vatican look no further than *His Holiness* (1997) by journalists Carl Bernstein (of Watergate fame) and Marco Politi (the Vatican correspondent for *La Repubblica*). It examines the influence of Pope John Paul II on Church doctrine and Italian society. *Man of the Century* (1998) by Jonathan Kwitny looks at the life and times of John Paul II. *Saints and Sinners* (1997) by Eamon Duffy is an illustrated history of the papacy from St Peter to John Paul II.

Food The eponymously titled *Diane Seed's Rome for All Seasons* (1997) concentrates on the seasonal flavours of Rome. *The Food of Italy* (1992) by Waverley Root is an acknowledged classic and will prepare the tastebuds for what awaits the traveller in Italy. Marcella Hazan is arguably Italy's most famous cook and any of her cookbooks will provide useful information about the history of the various regional cuisines.

Fiction Many contemporary authors regularly use ancient Rome as a backdrop for their stories. Robert Graves' classics *I, Claudius* and *Claudius the God* (1934) were brilliantly dramatised by the BBC with Derek Jacobi in the title role; try also novels by Allan Massie. Steven Saylor and Lindsey Davis both set detective novels in ancient Rome; Saylor's books are set in the dying Republic, and Davis' series revolves around Marcus Didius Falco, best described as a Philip Marlowe of Imperial Rome.

Michael Didbin's thrillers follow the travails of the slightly corrupt police inspector Aurelio Zen – including *Ratking*, *Vendetta* and *Cabal* – and are richly evocative of contemporary Rome as well as other Italian cities.

Morris West has written a trilogy of Vatican novels: *Shoes of the Fisherman*, *Lazarus* and *Eminence* (1999); and Peter Robb's *M* (2000), a 'faction' biography of Caravaggio, brings 16th- and 17th-century Rome to life.

Living in Rome An invaluable resource for those planning to linger in Rome is Travis Neighbor's *Living, Studying and Working in Italy* (1998). Although the book was written for a US audience, most of the information is applicable to visitors from other non-EU countries and can help to guide you through Italian bureaucracy. *Getting it Right in Italy: A Manual for the 1990s* by William Ward aims to provide accessible, useful information about Italy, while also providing a reasonable social profile of the people. However, it is increasingly out of date and should be used with caution.

FILMS

Rome has starred in many movies. Who can forget Audrey Hepburn and Gregory Peck causing havoc around the streets of Rome in the 1953 romantic comedy *Roman Holiday*? Or Marcello Mastroianni and Anita Ekberg frolicking in the Trevi Fountain in Fellini's 1960 film *La Dolce Vita*? Other memorable movies with Rome as subject or backdrop include: Roberto Rossellini's *Roma Città Aperta* (Rome Open City; 1945), which is set in German-occupied Italy; *Ladri di Biciclette* (Bicycle Thieves; 1948), by neo-realist director Vittorio de Sica, set in poverty-stricken postwar Rome; Fellini's surreal *Rome* and the famous *Three Coins in the Fountain* (1955).

Rome the movie star had a busy time in recent years. Actor-director Nanni Moretti set a number of his films in Rome, including the award-winning *Caro Diario* (1994; Dear Diary). Anthony Minghella depicted Rome at its most beautiful in *The Talented Mr Ripley* (1999), starring Matt Damon, Gwyneth Paltrow, Cate Blanchett and Jude Law. And the buildings of ancient Rome (albeit generated by computer) were on show in Ridley Scott's box-office smash *Gladiator* (2000).

NEWSPAPERS & MAGAZINES
English Language

Wanted in Rome (€0.77) is a fortnightly English-language news and listings magazine directed towards Rome's foreign residents. It contains informative articles about Italian politics and bureaucracy, city news, history and culture, plus arts and entertainment listings and reviews. It also has hundreds of classified ads that are useful for those seeking accommodation or jobs.

The *International Herald Tribune* (€1.65) is available Monday to Saturday. It has a daily four-page supplement, *Italy Daily*, on specifically Italian news.

British daily papers, including the *Guardian* (€1.86), the *Times* (€2.58), the *Daily Telegraph* (€3.00), the *Independent* (€2.32) and the *Financial Times* (€1.81) as well as various tabloids, are sent from London. They are available from newsstands towards lunchtime on the day of publication. British Sunday papers are usually available on the following Monday.

US newspapers such as *USA Today* (€1.55), the *Wall Street Journal Europe* (€1.81) and the *New York Times* (€6.20) are also available. The major German, French, Spanish dailies and some Scandinavian papers can also be found fairly easily. If you can't find any foreign papers try one of the larger central newsstands on Via del Corso, Piazza Navona, Via Veneto, Largo di Torre Argentina or at Stazione Termini.

News magazines such as *Time* (€3.00), *Newsweek* (€3.10) and the *Economist* (€4.13) are available weekly.

Italian Language

Italian newspapers can be frustrating, even for fluent Italian readers. Don't expect the Italian press to give you a balanced view of current events as most newspapers reflect the political or business interests of those who control them. The articles tend to be long-winded and the point, if indeed there is one, is usually buried in the final paragraphs. The domestic politics section, which normally occupies the first four or five pages of the newspaper, is difficult to follow even for the most dedicated reader and if you miss an instalment it's almost impossible to catch up on events.

Il Messaggero is the most popular broadsheet in Rome. It is especially good for news about Rome itself and the Vatican, and has a weekly listings supplement, *Metro*. Milan-based *Corriere della Sera* is the country's leading daily and has the best foreign news pages and the most comprehensive and comprehensible political coverage.

The Rome-based tabloid, *La Repubblica*, usually has great photos but it also has a reputation for sloppy reporting. Its Thursday supplement, *Trovaroma*, provides entertainment listings. The conservative paper *L'Osservatore Romano* is published daily in Italian (with weekly editions in English and other foreign languages) and is the official voice of the Vatican. There are several other daily papers. Most Italian daily newspapers cost €0.77 (or €1.03 if a supplement is

FACTS FOR THE VISITOR

included) and are available from all news-stands. *Porta Portese* costs €1.03.

Roma C'é (€1.03) is a weekly listings booklet that is published every Thursday. There is a small section in English towards the end.

RADIO & TV
Radio
You can pick up the BBC World Service on medium wave at 648kHz, short wave at 6.195MHz, 9.410MHz, 12.095MHz and 15.575MHz, and on long wave at 198kHz, depending on where you are and the time of day. Voice of America (VOA) can usually be found on short wave at 15.205MHz.

Vatican Radio (1530kHz AM, 93.3MHz FM and 105MHz FM) broadcasts the news in English at 7 am, 8.30 am, 6.15 pm and 9.50 pm. The reports usually include a run-down on what the pope is up to on any particular day. Pick up a pamphlet at the Vatican information office.

There are three state-owned stations: RAI-1 (1332kHz AM or 89.7MHz FM), RAI-2 (846kHz AM or 91.7MHz FM) and RAI-3 (93.7MHz FM). They combine classical and light music with news broadcasts and discussion programmes. RAI-2 broadcasts news in English every day from 1 to 5 am at three minutes past the hour.

Commercial radio stations are a better bet if you're after contemporary music. Popular stations include: Radio Centro Suono (101.3MHz FM); the Naples-based Radio Kiss Kiss (97.25MHz FM); and Radio Città Futura (97.7MHz FM), which broadcasts a listing of the day's events in Rome at 10 am daily.

TV
Italian television is so bad that it is compelling. There is an inordinate number of quiz shows and variety programmes with troupes of scantily clad women prancing and thrusting across the set. The home-bred soap operas are so dreadful that it's sometimes embarrassing to watch, but they attract a huge following. So, too, do the many imported soaps, mainly from the USA, all of which are dubbed into Italian. Current-release films transfer to the small screen relatively quickly in Italy but they are always dubbed.

The state-run channels are RAI-1, RAI-2 and RAI-3. The main commercial stations are Canale 5, Italia 1, Rete 4 and Telemontecarlo (TMC). CNN is broadcast nightly on TMC from around 1 am. The French-language TV channel, Antenne 2, can sometimes be received on Channel 10.

Most of Rome's mid- to top-range hotels, as well as many bars and restaurants, have satellite TV and can receive BBC World, Sky Channel, CNN and NBC Superchannel.

VIDEO SYSTEMS
Italy uses the PAL video system (the same as in Australia and throughout Europe, except in France). This system is not compatible with NTSC (used in North America, Japan and Latin America) or Secam (used in France and other Francophone countries). However, modern video players are often multisystem and can read all three.

PHOTOGRAPHY & VIDEO
Film & Equipment
A roll of 36 exposure 100 ASA Kodak film costs around €5. It costs between €6.20 and €9.30 to have 36 exposures developed and between €4 and €6 for 24 exposures. A roll of 36 slides costs from €3.10 to €7.75 and between €4 and €6 to develop.

Numerous outlets sell and process films but beware of poor quality processing. A roll of film is called a *pellicola* but you will be understood if you ask for film. Plenty of places offer one-hour photo developing; others can do it in a few hours or in a day. Slides *(diapositive)* will take several days to be processed. Photo processing outlets are open normal shop hours, although some close on Saturday afternoon.

Photokina (Map 4) at Via dei Pettinari 4, near Ponte Sisto, has its own processing equipment and can usually develop photos within an hour or slides within a few days. Leon Foto (Map 4) at Via del Banco di Santo Spirito 28, just off Corso Vittorio Emanuele, also offers one-hour service. There are several photo processing outlets in the city centre near the Pantheon. Professional photographers use Fotoservice (Map 2; ☎ 06 321 66 46) on Via Marcantonio Colonna, just by the Lepanto Metro station on the corner of Viale Giulio Cesare in Prati. They can develop slides in three hours and open Monday to Friday.

Tapes for video cameras are often available at the same outlets or can be found at stores selling electrical goods.

TIME
Italy operates on a 24-hour clock, which will take some getting used to for travellers accustomed to the 12-hour system. Daylight-saving time starts on the last Sunday in March, when clocks are put forward one hour. Clocks are put back an hour on the last Sunday in October. Ensure that when telephoning home you also make allowances for daylight saving in your own country.

Italy is in a single time zone. Countries such as France, Germany and Spain are in the same zone. Greece and Israel are one hour ahead, the UK one hour behind. When it's noon in Rome, it's 3 am in San Francisco, 6 am in New York, 11 am in London, 7 pm in Perth, 9 pm in Sydney and 11 pm in Auckland.

ELECTRICITY
The electric current in Italy is 220V, 50Hz, but make a point of checking with the hotel management because some places, especially those in older buildings, may still use 125V.

Power points have two or three holes and do not have their own switches, while plugs have two or three round pins. Some power points have larger holes than others. Italian homes are usually full of plug adapters to cope with this anomaly.

Make sure you bring international plug adapters for your appliances. It is a good idea to buy these *before* leaving home as they are virtually impossible to get in Italy. If you do forget, there is always the option of taking your appliance to an electrical store and having them replace the foreign plug with an Italian one. Travellers from North America need a voltage converter (although many of the more expensive hotels have provision for 110V appliances such as electric razors).

WEIGHTS & MEASURES
Italy uses the metric system. Basic terms for weight include *un etto* (100g) and *un chilo* (1kg). Travellers from the USA will have to cope with the change from pounds to kilograms, miles to kilometres and gallons to litres. A standard conversion table can be found at the back of this book.

Note that Italians generally indicate decimals with commas and thousands with points.

LAUNDRY
Coin laundrettes, where you can do your own washing, were once a rarity in Rome but fortunately for the traveller are now much more common. In most cases, a 6–8kg load costs L6000/€3.10 to wash and L6000/€3.10 to dry. There are several self-service laundrettes in the streets north-east of Stazione Termini. Bolle Blu has two outlets, at Via Palestro 59–61 (Map 5) and Via Milazzo 20b (Map 5), which open 8 am to 10 pm daily. In the same area, Oblo Service (Map 5), Via Vicenza 50, opens 9 am to 9 pm daily.

Near the Vatican, Onda Blu (Map 2) at Via Vespasiano 50, off Piazza del Risorgimento, opens 8 am to 10 pm daily. Wash & Dry Lavarapido has two outlets, open 8 am to 10 pm daily, at Via della Chiesa Nuova 15–16 (Map 8) off Corso Vittorio Emanuele II and in Trastevere at Via della Pelliccia (Map 6).

Dry-cleaning *(lavasecco)* charges range from around €3.10 for a shirt to €6.20 for a jacket. Be careful, though – the quality can be unreliable.

TOILETS
Public toilets are not exactly widespread in Rome (it is estimated that there are less than 40 of them in the whole city). Residents and tourists alike are waiting with crossed legs to see whether all the 'portaloos' brought in for the Jubilee year will remain. Most people use the toilets in bars and cafes – although you might need to buy a coffee first.

FACTS FOR THE VISITOR

At Stazione Termini there are two sets of public toilets on the lower-ground level that charge €0.52. The toilets on the Via Giolitti side also have showers (€7.75).

LEFT LUGGAGE

There are left-luggage services at Stazione Termini on the lower-ground level under platform 24. They open 7 am to midnight daily. The rate is an exorbitant €3.10 for the first five hours then €0.52 per hour for each additional hour (so you'll pay €12.91 for 24 hours). There are also self-service luggage lockers at the start of platform 24. They cost L3000/€1.55, L4000/€2.07 and L5000/€2.58 (according to size) for each six-hour period. Lockers will be altered to accept euros when the currency changes in 2002 and prices may change.

At Fiumicino airport there is a 24-hour left-luggage facility in the international arrivals area on the ground floor. It costs €2.12 per item per day. For luggage over 160cm long, you pay an extra €2.12 per day. Make sure you have your passport handy, as a photocopy will be made when you leave your luggage.

HEALTH

You are unlikely to have any serious health problems in Rome – except maybe a little indigestion from overeating the delicious food, or blisters on your feet from too much walking. The water in Rome is perfectly safe to drink, although it has a relatively high calcium content, and many Romans prefer to drink bottled water.

Air pollution can be a problem, particularly in summer. If you suffer from asthma or other respiratory problems, consider bringing a face mask. There are periodic pollution alerts when it is best to stay indoors; keep yourself informed through your hotel proprietor or a tourist office.

Another problem in summer is the severe heat and humidity, which can be debilitating. Pace yourself, wear a hat, apply sunscreen and make sure you drink plenty of water. Do as the Romans do and rest indoors during the hottest part of the day.

Tiger mosquitoes can be a problem in Rome, especially during the spring and summer. Use insect repellent to keep them and other biting insects at bay.

No vaccinations are required for Italy unless you are coming from an infected area but it is recommended that everyone keeps up to date with vaccinations such as tetanus, polio and diphtheria.

The public health system is administered by local centres generally known as Unità Sanitaria Locale (USL), usually listed in the telephone directory under 'A' for Azienda USL. Under these headings you'll find long lists of offices – look for *poliambulatorio* (polyclinic) and the telephone number for Accetazione Sanitaria. You need to call this number to make an appointment – there is no point in just rolling up.

Opening hours vary widely but most, at least, open 8 am to 12.30 pm Monday to Friday. Some open for a couple of hours in the afternoon and on Saturday morning too.

Medical Cover

All foreigners have the same right as Italians to free emergency medical treatment in a public hospital.

EU citizens are entitled to the full range of health care services free of charge, but you will need to present your E111 form (enquire at your national health service before leaving home). Australia has a reciprocal arrangement with Italy which entitles Australian citizens to free health care. Medicare in Australia publishes a brochure with the details, and it is advisable to carry your Medicare card.

Citizens of New Zealand, the USA, Canada and other countries have to pay for any treatment other than emergency treatment. Most travel insurance policies will include medical cover (see Travel Insurance earlier in this chapter).

Private hospitals and clinics throughout the country generally provide excellent services but are expensive for those without medical or travel insurance. That said, certain treatments, tests or referrals to specialists in public hospitals may also have to be paid for and in such cases can be equally costly.

Your embassy in Rome can recommend where to go for medical treatment and should be able to refer you to doctors who speak your language. However, if you have a specific health complaint, it would be wise to obtain the necessary information and referrals for treatment before leaving home. In the USA, the International Association for Medical Assistance to Travellers, 417 Center Street, Lewiston, NY 14092 (IAMAT; ☎ 716-754 4883, fax 519-836 3412), a nonprofit organisation based in New York, can provide you with a list of English-speaking doctors in Rome who have been trained in the USA, the UK or Canada.

Hospitals & Clinics

The quality of medical treatment in public hospitals in Rome is well below the standards of many other major Western European cities, but not so much due to a lack in professional expertise – Italy's doctors are highly regarded on an international level, particularly in the area of research – but more because hospital administration is appalling, the facilities and equipment are outdated, the services are oversubscribed and the standard of nursing care is low. In recent years there have been serious hygiene scares, and some of Rome's main hospitals were threatened with closure.

If you need an ambulance call ☎ 118. For emergency treatment, go straight to the casualty *(pronto soccorso)* section of a public hospital *(ospedale)*, where you'll also receive emergency dental treatment. You are likely to find doctors who speak English, or a volunteer translator service.

Ospedale Bambino Gesù
(Map 4; ☎ 06 685 92 351) Piazza Sant' Onofrio; paediatric hospital on Giancolo
Ospedale Fatebenefratelli
(Map 6; ☎ 06 683 71) Piazza Fatebene-fratelli, Isola Tiberina
Ospedale Nuova Regina Margherita
(Map 6; ☎ 06 581 06 58) Via Morosini 30, Trastevere
Ospedale San Camillo
(Map 1; ☎ 06 587 01) Circonvallazione Gianicolense 87; free clinic

Ospedale San Gallicano
(Map 6; ☎ 06 588 23 90) Via San Gallicano; skin problems and venereal diseases
Ospedale San Giacomo
(Map 2; ☎ 06 362 61) Via Canova 29, off Via del Corso near Piazza del Popolo
Ospedale San Giovanni
(Map 7; ☎ 06 770 51) Via Amba Aradam 8, near Piazza San Giovanni in Laterano
Ospedale Santo Spirito
(Map 4; ☎ 06 683 51) Lungotevere in Sassia 1
Policlinico Umberto I
(Map 5; ☎ 06 499 71) Via del Policlinico 155, near Stazione Termini

Private Hospitals Rome has several international private hospitals. Use their services only if you have health insurance and have consulted your insurance company. The American Hospital (☎ 06 225 51), Via E Longoni 69, is a long way east of the city centre off Via Collatina. The European Hospital (☎ 06 65 97 59), Via Portuense 696, is a fair distance south-west of the centre.

Guardia Medica This private association of doctors, the Guardia Medica, can make house calls (or visits to hotels) at any hour of the day or night. They are listed in the telephone directory under *Guardia Medica*. This is not a free service and calling out a doctor for a general medical problem will cost from €61.97. If you need a specialist or have a more complicated problem it costs from €77.47. Most travel insurance policies will cover you for these consultations.

Bear in mind that if the problem is very serious you will be sent to casualty anyway, so you might do better to avoid the wait and head for the nearest hospital yourself. Guardia Medica SPRIM (☎ 06 582 04 006) has English speaking doctors. Other associations include Guardia Medica Circelli (☎ 06 785 84 70) and Associazione Professionale Medica (☎ 06 884 11 81).

Pharmacies

Pharmacies or chemists *(farmacie)* usually open 9 am to 1 pm and 4 to 7.30 pm Monday to Saturday. They open on Sunday, at night and for emergencies on a rotation basis. Night pharmacies are listed in the daily newspapers (usually at the back near the cinema listings). When a pharmacy is closed, it is required by law to post on the door a list of others open nearby. There is a 24-hour pharmacy at Piazza dei Cinquecento 51, just outside Stazione Termini (Map 5; ☎ 06 488 00 19). Within the station, a pharmacy on the lower-ground floor opens 7.30 am to 10 pm daily.

The Farmacia del Vaticano (Map 4; ☎ 06 698 83 422), just inside the Porta Sant' Anna, sells certain drugs that are not available in Italian pharmacies, and will also fill prescriptions from some other countries, which Italian pharmacies cannot do (though apparently it doesn't stock Viagra).

If you take a regular medication, make sure you bring an adequate supply. Also make sure you note the drug's generic name (rather than the brand name) in case you need a prescription written in Italy.

Opticians

If you lose or break your glasses, you will be able to have them replaced within a few days (sometimes a few hours) by an optician (ottico) as long as you have your prescription. The Italians are specialists in making glasses frames and you'll probably find a good range of frames at reasonable prices.

HIV/AIDS

The national AIDS hotline is ☎ 800 86 10 61. For HIV/AIDS treatment, contact the Clinica Dermosifilpatica at Ospedale Spallanzani (Map 1; ☎ 06 582 37 639), Via Portuense 332. The Circolo Mario Mieli di Cultura Omosessuale (☎ 06 541 39 85; see also Gay & Lesbian Travellers later in this chapter) runs a free AIDS testing centre at Ospedale San Giovanni (entrance at Via di San Giovanni in Laterano 155). For information and operating hours, call Mario Mieli or visit online at www.mariomieli.org.

STDs

Gonorrhoea, herpes and syphilis are among these diseases; sores, blisters or rashes around the genitals, discharges or pain when urinating are common symptoms. In some STDs, such as wart virus or chlamydia, symptoms may be less marked or not observed at all, especially in women. Syphilis symptoms eventually disappear completely but the disease continues and can cause severe problems in later years. While abstinence from sexual contact is the only 100% effective way of prevention, using condoms can help reduce risks. The different STDs are treated with specific antibiotics. There is no cure for herpes or AIDS.

Women's Health

Each USL (Unità Sanitaria Locale) area has its own Family Planning Centre (Consultorio Familiare), where you can go for advice on gynaecological problems, contraceptives, pregnancy tests and information about abortion. These centres are listed under each USL office in the telephone book, otherwise ask at the USL office.

There is a gynaecological/family-planning clinic, known by its acronym AIED (Map 3; ☎ 06 428 25 314), Via Toscana 30, where foreign women can seek medical advice and assistance. It opens 9 am to 7 pm Monday to Friday and 9 am to 1 pm on Saturday. Consultations cost €41.32. There are usually English-speaking doctors working there.

Pharmacies can provide creams and pessaries for common fungal infections (candida). Cystitis is known as cistiti; you can buy capsules (called Pipram) to treat it over the counter.

WOMEN TRAVELLERS

Rome is not a dangerous city for women but women travelling alone will often find themselves plagued by unwanted attention from men. This attention usually involves catcalls, whistles and the occasional 'ciao bella' and is more annoying than threatening. Lone women will also find it difficult to remain alone – you will have Italian men harassing you as you walk along the street, drink a coffee in a bar or try to read a book in a park. Usually the best response is to ignore them, but if that doesn't work, politely tell them that you are waiting for your husband (marito) or boyfriend (fidanzato) and, if necessary, walk away.

Avoid becoming aggressive as this almost always results in an unpleasant confrontation. If all else fails, approach the nearest member of the police or *carabinieri* (see under Police later in this chapter).

Basically, most of the attention falls into the nuisance/harassment category. However, women should use their common sense. Avoid walking alone in deserted and dark streets and look for centrally located hotels within easy walking distance of places where you can eat at night.

Rome is fundamentally a very safe city, especially compared with other European capitals (see the 'Safe City' boxed text later in this chapter). The city centre is well lit, and there is always lots of activity late into the night. However, foreigners in general and women on their own in particular are regarded as prime targets for bag-snatchers, who rush past on a motorbike and grab your handbag in a split second. Be alert, use a backpack if you can (it's harder to pull off) or keep one hand on your bag, and be very careful about walking in deserted streets at night.

Watch out for men with wandering hands on crowded buses. The No 64 bus, which travels from Stazione Termini to the Vatican, is notorious for over-attentive males who take advantage of the fact that many passengers on the route are tourists and that the bus is generally packed. If someone starts fondling your backside or rubbing up against you, make a huge fuss. A loud '*che schifo!*' ('how disgusting!') will usually do the trick. The locals will sympathise with you and the culprit will almost certainly make a hasty exit at the next stop.

Hitching is not recommended for lone women in the city or elsewhere. The *Handbook for Women Travellers* by M and G Goss is a good read for women who travel solo.

GAY & LESBIAN TRAVELLERS

Homosexuality is legal in Italy and well tolerated in Rome, that is if you ignore the Vatican's periodic antigay diatribe such as Pope John Paul II referring to homosexual men and women as 'morally corrupt'. The legal age of consent is 16. A few years ago the gay capitals of Italy were Milan and Bologna but Rome is now giving both cities

some strong competition. Previously a subculture that operated behind closed doors, Rome's gay scene is now a lot more open and there are numerous bars and clubs, with new venues opening all the time.

On a political level, Italy is still a long way behind most Western countries in making gay rights a major issue. During his first term, Rome's former mayor, Francesco Rutelli, had a brief courtship with the gay community, appointing an adviser on gay rights and issues, and even leading part of the Gay Pride march in 1994. However, as he climbed the political ladder Rutelli let go of his more 'radical' agenda and aligned himself more closely with the Vatican establishment and 'traditional' family values.

The year 2000 was a watershed for gay Rome, when the city hosted World Pride, a week-long festival of parties and cultural events, bang in the middle of the Roman Catholic Jubilee year. Just prior to the July event, however, the Vatican announced its disapproval. The then prime minister did the same. Mayor Rutelli, whose council had demonstrated no problems with the event's organisation during the preceding two years of organisation, suddenly became indecisive about where the city stood on the issue. What World Pride brought to the fore – other than gay rights – was that many of Italy's politicians still look to the Vatican for signals before they act.

In recent years in Rome there has been a spate of murders of middle-aged and older men who happened to be gay. The jury is out as to whether they were murdered because of their sexuality, but it is fair to say that the link is strong. As in all places, you should exercise caution and judgment as to whom you leave a bar or club with and where you go.

The lesbian scene is less active than the gay scene and there is not yet any permanent lesbian nightclub, although there are various associations that organise events.

Rome has several gay bars and discos and there is even a gay beach (see Gay & Lesbian Venues in the Entertainment chapter). These can be tracked down through local gay organisations and publications such as *Pride* (€3.10), a national monthly magazine, and *AUT* (free) published by Circolo Mario Mieli (see Organisations below) both available at the various gay and lesbian organisations and bookshops.

The Italian magazine *Time Out Roma* (€1.03), published weekly and available from newsstands, has good coverage of gay and lesbian venues and events. The international gay guide *Spartacus* also has listings of gay venues in Rome.

Organisations

In Rome, the main cultural and political organisation is the Circolo Mario Mieli di Cultura Omosessuale (☎ 06 541 39 85, e info@mariomieli.it) at Via Efeso 2a, off Via Ostiense near the Basilica di San Paolo, which organises debates, cultural events and social functions. It also runs a free AIDS/HIV testing and care centre (see Health earlier in this chapter). Mario Mieli organises Rome Pride, which takes place in June every year. Its Web site, www.mariomieli.org, has information and listings of forthcoming social and political events. Mario Mieli also publishes a free monthly magazine *AUT* (predominantly in Italian) available from gay bookshops and organisations.

Another good Web site, www.gay.it/guida/Lazio/Roma, features club and event listings for Rome and the Lazio region.

The national organisation for lesbians is Co-ordinamento Lesbiche Italiano (CLI), also known as the Buon Pastore Centre (Map 4; ☎ 06 686 42 01, e cli_network@iol.it), on the corner of Via San Francesco di Sales and Via della Lungara in Trastevere. The weekly political meetings of the Centro Femminista Separatista are held here, as well as conferences and literary evenings. A women-only restaurant, Le Sorellastre, and a hostel/hotel are due to open, ask for details.

Zipper Travel Association (Map 5; ☎ 06 488 27 30, Via Castelfidardo 18), north-east of Stazione Termini, specialises in customised travel for gays and lesbians.

Gay and lesbian bookshops are also good sources of information; for further details of these see under Books in the Shopping chapter.

DISABLED TRAVELLERS

Rome is not an easy city for disabled travellers, who will almost certainly need to depend on other people more than they would in their home countries. Getting around can be a problem for the wheelchair bound. Even a short journey can become a major expedition if cobblestone streets have to be negotiated and in some areas of the historic centre and Trastevere, for example, there are simply no footpaths. Although many buildings have lifts, they are not always wide enough to accommodate a wheelchair.

Public transport is improving. There are wheelchair-accessible buses on several busy routes, although if the bus is very crowded it will still be difficult to get on. Rome's newer trams are generally accessible. On the Metro system, only the more recent stations at the end of the lines have lifts. Bus No 590 follows the route of Metro Linea A and is specially equipped for disabled passengers and wheelchairs. For information on transport for disabled passengers, check out the Web site at www.atac.roma.it or call ☎ 800 43 17 84 (from 8 am to 6 pm).

Some taxis are equipped to carry passengers in wheelchairs. It is advisable to book a taxi by phone, rather than heading for a taxi rank or trying to hail one on the street. Inform the operator that you need a taxi for a wheelchair *(sedia a rotelle)*. See the Getting Around chapter for further details on public transport information and taxi company numbers.

Airline companies should be able to arrange assistance at airports if you notify them of your needs in advance. If you are travelling by train from Stazione Termini to Fiumicino airport or elsewhere, call ☎ 06 488 17 26 in advance in order to arrange for assistance.

Many of the city's main museums have been overhauled in recent years so things are looking better for disabled travellers than ever before. Tourists in wheelchairs will find access ramps, special toilets and spacious lifts in the Vatican and Capitoline Museums, the Galleria Borghese, the Galleria Nazionale d'Arte Moderna, the Palazzo delle Esposizioni and Palazzo Massimo.

Organisations

The best point of reference for disabled travellers is Consorzio Cooperative Integrate (COIN), which can provide information about services for the disabled in Rome (including transport and museum access). It operates a telephone help line ☎ 06 712 90 11 (9 am to 5 pm Monday to Friday) and information is also available online at www.coinsociale.it or via email at ✉ turismo@coinsociale.it.

COIN publishes a multilingual guide, *Roma Accessibile*, which lists the facilities available at museums, department stores, theatres and Metro stations. The guide is available from public offices and by mail order; some tourist offices might have copies. Call COIN for information about availability; the staff are very helpful and can arrange for guides to be waiting for you at your hotel in Rome.

Tourist offices can provide some information about museum access and transport for disabled travellers. The Italian State Tourist Office in your country may be able to provide advice on tour operators which organise holidays for the disabled. It may also carry a small brochure, *Services for Disabled People*, published by the Italian railways, which details facilities at stations and on trains.

The Italian travel agency, CIT, can advise on hotels with special facilities, such as ramps and so on. It can also request that wheelchair ramps be provided on arrival of your train if you book travel through CIT. See under Travel Agencies earlier in this chapter.

SENIOR TRAVELLERS

Senior citizens are entitled to discounts on public transport in Rome, but only for monthly passes (not daily or weekly tickets). The minimum qualifying age is 65.

For rail travel on the Ferrovie dello Stato, seniors (over 60) can get 30% to 40% reductions on full fares if by purchasing an annual seniors pass for €23.24 (see Getting There & Away).

Admission to most museums in Rome is free for those aged over 60. You should also seek information in your own country on travel packages and discounts for senior travellers, through travel agents and senior citizens' organisations.

ROME FOR CHILDREN

Sightseeing in Rome will wear out adults – so imagine how the kids feel! If the weather isn't too hot, children of all ages should appreciate a wander through the Roman Forum and up to the Palatine. Another interesting, if not tiring, experience is the climb to the top of the dome of St Peter's Basilica for a spectacular view of the city. A museum, which might amuse the kids, is the Museo Nazionale delle Paste Alimentari (Pasta Museum), Piazza Scanderberg 117, between the Trevi Fountain and Palazzo del Quirinale. The well organised museum traces the history of the nation's favourite dish and has old-fashioned pasta-making machinery on display. A portable CD player provides the commentary. The museum opens 9.30 am to 5.30 pm daily. Admission costs €6.20.

During the Christmas period Piazza Navona is transformed into a festive market place, with stalls selling puppets, figures for nativity scenes *(presepio)* and Christmas stockings. Most churches set up nativity scenes, many of them elaborate arrangements, which will fascinate kids and adults alike. The most elaborate is an 18th-century Neapolitan presepio at the Basilica di Santi Cosma e Damiano.

If you can spare the money, take the family on a tour of Rome by horse and cart. You'll pay through the nose at around €92.96 for what the driver determines is the 'full tour' of the city. Make sure you agree on a price and itinerary before you get in the cart – even though prices are supposedly regulated, horror stories abound about trusting tourists who forgot to ask the price!

Fortunately the city has plenty of parks. Take a break for a picnic lunch and an afternoon in the Villa Borghese. Near the Porta Pinciana there are bicycles for rent, as well as pony rides, mini-train rides and a merry-go-round. Rollerblading exhibitions often take place on weekends and are fun to watch. In the Villa Celimontana, on the western slopes of the Caelian (entrance from Piazza della Navicella), is a lovely public park and a children's playground.

The Gianicolo hill, between the St Peter's Basilica and Trastevere, with its panoramic view of Rome, is a good place to take the kids if they need a break. At the top of the hill, just off Piazza Garibaldi, there is a permanent merry-go-round and pony rides, and on Sunday a puppet show is often held. In the square there is a small bar. Bus No 870 (from the end of Corso Vittorio Emanuele where it meets the Lungotevere) will take you to the Gianicolo and also within easy walking distance of the nearby Villa Doria Pamphilj, the largest park in Rome and a lovely quiet spot for a walk and a picnic. Ask for directions to the lake inside the park, which is home to a large population of ducks, a few herons and some strange little rodents known as *nutrie*. A short distance from the southern end of the lake is a children's playground.

Villa Sciarra in Monteverde Vecchio is an uphill hike from Trastevere (from Piazza San Cosimato take Via Roma Libera and Via Dandolo) but the kids will really love it. There's a permanent fun fair, lots of shady trees, water fountains and sprinklers (to cool off in during summer).

Italians love children and they will be made a fuss of wherever they go. It is not unusual to see Italian children out with their families even very late at night. Most restaurants can provide high chairs *(seggioloni)*. You can usually ask for a child's portion *(mezzo porzione)* and most fussy eaters can be tempted by a delicious pizza.

All city transport is free for children under 1m tall. Most museums, galleries and archaeological sites are free for those aged under 18. At some, children are entitled to discounts.

Chemists sell baby formula in powder or liquid form as well as sterilising solutions such as Milton. Disposable nappies (diapers) are widely available at supermarkets, chemists (where they are more expensive) and sometimes in larger *cartolerie* (stationery suppliers). A pack of around 30 disposable nappies costs around €9. Fresh cow's milk is sold in cartons in bars (look

for a 'Latteria' sign) and in supermarkets. If it is essential that you have milk you should carry an emergency carton of UHT milk, since bars usually close at 8 or 9 pm.

Many car-rental firms rent out children's safety seats, however, it is strongly advised that you book them in advance.

Information about current events for children can be found in *Roma C'è* (see its Children's Corner in the English section) and in *Trovaroma*, the Thursday supplement to *La Repubblica*, under Città dei Ragazzi. For more general information on how to keep the kids amused while travelling, see Lonely Planet's *Travel with Children*.

LIBRARIES

There are over 700 libraries *(biblioteche)* in Rome. Some have important historical collections with books dating from the 15th century. Admission is sometimes restricted to members of the library (where an annual fee is paid) or to readers with an appropriate letter of presentation stating their area of research. Each of the city's districts or *circoscrizioni* has at least one local library; these are listed under Comune di Roma in the telephone directory.

The main public library is the Biblioteca Nazionale Centrale Vittorio Emanuele II (Map 5; ☎ 06 49 89), Viale Castro Pretorio 105. It is the national repository of books published in Italy and also has periodicals, newspapers, official acts, drawings, engravings and photographs. It opens 8.30 am to 7 pm Monday to Friday and 8.30 am to 1.30 pm on Saturday. Readers will need an identity document in order to get a day pass.

The Vatican library or the Biblioteca Apostolica Vaticana (Map 4; ☎ 06 69 82; fax 06 698 84 795) at Cortile Belvedere, Porta Sant'Anna, in the Vatican City has one of the world's richest collections of illuminated manuscripts and early printed books. However, only serious scholars will be given permission to consult its treasures. Potential readers should apply in writing stating their area of research.

The library at Palazzo Venezia, the Biblioteca di Archeologia e Storia dell'Arte (Map 4; ☎ 06 678 30 34), Piazza Venezia 3, is useful for texts on archaeology and art history. The Biblioteca Casanatense (Map 4; ☎ 06 679 89 88), Via di Sant'Ignazio 52, in the heart of the city centre, has a specialist collection of manuscripts and rare books on Rome, religion, philosophy, theatre and music. It opens 8.30 am to 1.30 pm Monday, Wednesday and Saturday 8.30 am to 7 pm Tuesday, Thursday and Friday.

If it's fiction in English that you are after, try the Santa Susanna Lending Library (Map 5; ☎ 06 482 75 10), Via XX Settembre 15 (1st floor), which usually opens 10 am to 1 pm Tuesday and Thursday, 3 to 6 pm Wednesday, 1 to 4 pm Friday and 10 am to 12.30 pm Saturday and Sunday. You'll have to pay a modest annual fee but you can then borrow all the books you want.

The Biblioteca Centrale per Ragazzi (Map 4; ☎ 06 686 51 16), Via San Paolo alla Regola 16, is a children's library not far from Campo de' Fiori which lends books and videos to members.

UNIVERSITIES

Rome has three state universities, La Sapienza, Tor Vergata and Roma Tre. The latter two are in outlying areas of the city and student life tends to centre around the San Lorenzo area close to La Sapienza. (Unfortunately none of them has facilities useful to the traveller – stick to Internet cafes and English bookshops.) There is also a private Italian university LUISS (Libera Università Internazionale degli Studi Sociali). There are also about 20 pontifical universities run by different religious orders.

There are a number of private international universities in Rome. Tuition fees and course requirements vary from one institution to another. The American University of Rome (Map 6; ☎ 06 583 30 919), Via Pietro Roselli 4, offers degree programmes in international business, international relations and liberal arts. Visit online at www.aur.edu. The European School of Economics (Map 4; ☎ 06 678 05 03), Largo del Nazareno 15, has degree programmes in international business (including MBAs) and a Web site at www.uniese.it. John Cabot University (Map 4; ☎ 06 681 91 21) at

Via della Lungara 233 in Trastevere offers courses in business administration, international affairs, political science and art history. Check out its Web site at www.johncabot.edu. St John's University (Map 1; ☎ 06 63 69 37), Via Santa Maria Mediatrice 24 (near the Vatican), offers MBA degrees and MA programmes in government and politics. It's online at www.stjohns.edu.

There are also a number of schools and study abroad programmes affiliated with US universities. For more information visit www.studyabroad.com.

CULTURAL CENTRES

In addition to the many museums, galleries and theatres, there are a large number of foreign cultural academies and institutes in Rome, where artists, writers, performing artists and academics come from their home countries to spend several months in Rome, creating, researching and absorbing Italian history and culture. The academies organise exhibitions, poetry readings, drama and dance performances, lectures and conferences. Both *Time Out Roma* and *Wanted in Rome* carry regular listings of the events and they are sometimes listed in *Roma C'è*.

DANGERS & ANNOYANCES
Theft & Loss

Pickpockets and bag-snatchers are particularly active in Rome. The best way to avoid being robbed is to wear a money belt under your clothing. You should keep all important items, such as money, passport, other papers and tickets, in your money belt at all times. If you are carrying a bag or camera, ensure that you wear the strap across your body and have the bag on the side away from the road to deter snatch thieves who often operate from motorcycles and scooters. Since the aim of young motorcycle bandits is often fun rather than gain you are just as likely to find yourself relieved of your sunglasses – or worse, of an earring.

You should also watch out for groups of dishevelled-looking women and children. They generally work in groups of four or five and carry paper or cardboard, which

A Safe City

Italian cities, Rome among them, have a bad reputation for crime that is not always deserved. According to a 1997 report by the Lazio regional authorities, Rome is one of the safest cities in Europe as far as personal security is concerned.

The report compared crime statistics in Rome, Milan, Berlin, Hamburg, London and Paris. Rome was the safest city as far as rape and assault were concerned, and compared favourably with regard to burglary and bag snatching.

Berlin had the highest rate of violent assault (325 attacks for every 100,000 inhabitants) followed by Paris (254 per 100,000) and Hamburg (172 per 100,000). In Rome there were only 22 assaults for every 100,000 inhabitants. London had the highest incidence of rape (25 for every 100,000 inhabitants) followed by Paris and Berlin. Rome, at the bottom of the list, recorded the figure of 3.1 rapes for every 100,000 inhabitants. London also had the highest level of household burglaries, while Milan was top of the list for bag snatching.

However, Rome had the highest incidence of car theft. In the period 1996–97, 38,956 cars were reported stolen, or 1471 for every 100,000 inhabitants, three times the frequency of Paris or Berlin.

they use to distract your attention while they swarm around and rifle through your pockets and bag. Never underestimate their skill – they are lightning fast and very adept. Their favourite haunts are in and near major train stations, at tourist sights (such as the Colosseum) and in shopping areas. If you notice that you have been targeted by a group, either take evasive action, such as crossing the street, or shout *'va via!'* ('go away!') in a loud, angry voice.

Pickpockets often hang out on crowded buses (the No 64 bus, which runs from Stazione Termini to the Vatican, is notorious) and in crowded areas such as markets. There is only one way to deter pickpockets: simply *do not* carry any money or valuables in your pockets and be very careful about your bags. Be cautious, even in hotels, and don't leave valuables lying around.

Parked cars, particularly those with foreign number plates or rental company stickers, are also prime targets for thieves. Try removing or covering the stickers and leave a local newspaper on the seat to make it look like a local car.

Never leave valuables in your car – in fact, try not to leave anything on display if you can help it and certainly not overnight. It is a good idea to pay extra to leave your car in supervised car parks, although there is no guarantee it will be completely safe. Throughout Italy, particularly in the south, service stations along the autostradas are favourite haunts of thieves who can clean out your car in the time it takes to have a cup of coffee. If possible, park the car where you can keep an eye on it.

When driving in cities you also need to beware of snatch thieves when you pull up at traffic lights. Keep the doors locked and, if you have the windows open, ensure that there is nothing valuable on the dashboard or on the back seats.

Horror tales abound about women being dragged to the ground by thieves trying to snatch their bags, of people losing wallets, watches and cameras on crowded buses or in a flurry of newspaper-waving children. These things really do happen! Certainly even the most cautious travellers are still prey to expert thieves but there is no need to be paranoid. By taking a few basic precautions, you can greatly lessen the risk of being robbed.

Unfortunately, some Italians practise a more insidious form of theft: short-changing. Numerous travellers have reported losing money this way. Take the time to acquaint yourself with euro (and lira) denominations. When paying for goods, or tickets, or a meal, or whatever, keep an eye on the notes you hand over and then count your change carefully. One popular dodge occurs when you hand over a banknote, receive some change and, while the person who sold you the goods hesitates, you hurry off without checking it. If you'd stayed for another five seconds, the rest of the change probably would have been handed over without any fuss.

In case of theft or loss, always report the incident to the police within 24 hours and ask for a statement, otherwise your travel insurance company won't pay out.

In case of emergency, you can contact the police throughout Italy on ☎ 112 or 113.

Traffic & Pedestrians

Roman traffic can at best be described as chaotic, at worst downright dangerous, for the unprepared tourist. Many drivers, particularly motorcyclists and scooter riders, do not stop at red lights. Drivers are not keen to stop for pedestrians, even at pedestrian crossings, and are more likely to swerve. Romans simply step off the footpath and walk through the (swerving) traffic with determination – it is a practice which seems to work, so if you feel uncertain about crossing a busy road, wait for the next Italian. Better still, cross with God! If you see a priest or nun in the vicinity, stick to them like glue, as even the craziest driver tends to slow down for them. If you wait for the traffic to stop, you'll be there all day. Roads that appear to be for one-way traffic sometimes have special lanes for buses travelling in the opposite direction – always look both ways before stepping onto the road.

Pollution

Italy has a poor record when it comes to environmental concerns. Few Italians would think twice about dropping litter in the streets, illegally dumping household refuse in the country or driving a car or motorcycle with a faulty or nonexistent muffler.

Tourists will be affected in a variety of ways by the surprising disregard Italians have for their country, which is of considerable natural and artistic beauty. Noise and air pollution are problems in major cities, caused mainly by heavy traffic. A headache after a day of sightseeing in Rome is likely to be caused by breathing carbon monoxide and lead, rather than simple tiredness. While most traffic is banned from the historic centre, there are still plenty of cars,

buses and motorcycles in and around the inner city to pollute the air.

Particularly in summer, there are periodic pollution alerts. The elderly, children and people with respiratory problems are warned to stay indoors. If you fit into one of these categories, keep yourself informed through the tourist office or your hotel proprietor.

When booking a hotel room it is a good idea to ask if it is quiet – although this might mean you will have to decide between a view and sleep.

One of the most annoying things about Rome is that the footpaths are littered with dog droppings – so be careful where you put your feet (see the boxed text 'Oh Poo!').

The beaches near Rome – Ostia, Fregene and Anzio – are generally heavily polluted by industrial waste, sewage and oil spills from the Mediterranean's considerable sea traffic. The farther south you go, towards Terracina, Gaeta and Sperlonga, the cleaner the beaches are. Even better beaches can be found in Sardinia, Sicily and the less-populated areas of the south.

Roman-Style Service

It requires a lot of patience to deal with the Roman concept of service. What for Italians is simply a way of life can be horrifying for the foreigner – like the bank clerk who wanders off to have a cigarette just as it is your turn (after a one-hour wait) to be served, or the postal worker who has far more important work to do at a desk than sell stamps to

---

Oh Poo!

Just a short note on another 'pollution' problem which tourists will doubtless encounter in Rome: dog poo! Literally, no footpath is without it, so watch your step.

A brief effort by the Comune di Roma to raise public awareness of this issue came and went with little effect and, while the law fines owners of offending pooches €103.29, no-one seems to worry much, not least the *vigili urbani* (urban police) who do little to enforce the law.

---

customers. Anyone in a uniform or behind a counter (including police officers, waiters and shop assistants) is likely to regard you with imperious contempt. Long queues are the norm in banks, post offices and any government offices.

It pays to remain calm and patient. Customers who become aggressive, demanding and angry stand virtually no chance of getting what they want.

EMERGENCIES
In case of emergency, call the following numbers:

Police	☎ 113
Carabinieri	☎ 112
Ambulance	☎ 118
Fire	☎ 115

For a list of hospitals see under Hospitals & Clinics earlier in this chapter.

LEGAL MATTERS
For many Italians, finding ways to get around the law (any law) is a way of life. They are likely to react with surprise, if not annoyance, if you point out that they might be breaking a law. Few people pay attention to speed limits, most motorcyclists and many drivers don't stop at red lights – and certainly not at pedestrian crossings. No-one bats an eyelid about littering or dogs pooping in the middle of the footpath – even though many municipal governments have introduced laws against these things. But these are minor transgressions when measured up against the country's organised crime, the extraordinary levels of tax evasion and corruption in government and business.

The average tourist will probably have a brush with the law only after being robbed by a bag-snatcher or pickpocket.

Drugs
Italy has introduced new drug laws that are lenient on drug users and heavy on pushers. If you're caught with drugs which the police determine are for your own personal use, you'll be let off with a warning – and, of course, the drugs will be confiscated. If, instead, it is determined that you intend to sell

the drugs in your possession, you could find yourself in prison. It's up to the discretion of the police to determine whether or not you're a pusher, since the law is not specific about quantities. The sensible option is to avoid illicit drugs altogether.

Drink Driving
The legal blood alcohol level is 0.08% and breath tests are common. Drink driving is not a major problem in Italy where heavy alcohol consumption is frowned upon. See Road Rules in the Getting There & Away chapter for more information.

Police
If you run into trouble in Italy, you're likely to end up dealing with either the *polizia* (police) or the *carabinieri* (military police). The police are a civil force and take their orders from the Ministry of the Interior, while the carabinieri fall under the Ministry of Defence. There is a considerable duplication of their roles, despite a 1981 reform of the police forces that was intended to merge the two. Both forces are responsible for public order and security which means that you can call either in the event of a robbery or violent attack.

The carabinieri wear a dark-blue uniform with a red stripe and drive dark-blue cars with a red stripe. They are well trained and tend to be helpful. You are most likely to be pulled over by the carabinieri rather than the police when you are speeding and so on. Their police station is called a *caserma*.

The police wear powder-blue trousers with a fuchsia stripe and a navy-blue jacket and drive light-blue cars with a white stripe, with 'polizia' written on the side. Tourists who want to report thefts, and people wanting to get a residence permit, will have to deal with them. The police headquarters is called the *questura*. It is located at Via San Vitale 15 (Map 5; ☎ 46 86). The Ufficio Stranieri (Foreigners' Bureau; Map 5; ☎ 46 86 29 87) is around the corner at Via Genova 2. It opens 24 hours a day and thefts can be reported here. You need to go here if you want to apply for a permesso di soggiorno. For immediate police attendance, call ☎ 113.

JON DAVISON

Circo Massimo, the ancient-Roman chariot racetrack, is a popular spot for walking the dog.

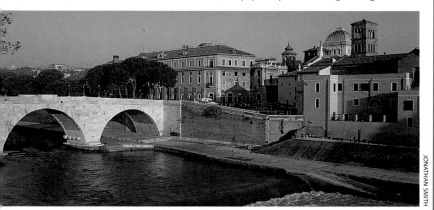
JONATHAN SMITH

Spanning the River Tiber, Ponte Cestio links the tiny Isola Tiberina and Trastevere.

CHRIS IVIN

The Vittoriano monument in Piazza Venezia is mockingly known as the 'typewriter'.

Get closer to God – lick a lollipope.

A Swiss Guard for a Polish pope

Down to business in Chiesa del Gesù

A cross to bear at Ponte Sant'Angelo

The local police station is called the *commissariato*. Most areas of Rome have either a commissariato or a carabinieri caserma, sometimes both. Shopkeepers or newsstand proprietors should be able to point you in the direction of the nearest one.

Other varieties of police in Italy include the *vigili urbani*, basically traffic police, with whom you will have to deal if you get a parking ticket, or if your car is towed away; and the *guardia di finanza*, who are responsible for fighting tax evasion and drug smuggling. You could be stopped by them if you leave a shop without a receipt for your purchase – although it's a long shot.

Your Rights

Italy still has some antiterrorism laws on its books, which could make life very difficult if you happen to be detained by the police. You can be held for 48 hours without a magistrate being informed and you can be interrogated without the presence of a lawyer. It is difficult to obtain bail and you can be held legally for up to three years without being brought to trial. These same laws require that all foreigners must report to the police within eight days of arriving in the country, even if you are here only for a holiday (see under Permesso di Soggiorno earlier in this chapter).

BUSINESS HOURS

Shops generally open 9 am to 1 pm and 3.30 to 7.30 pm (or 4 to 8 pm) Monday to Friday. In some cities, grocery shops might not re-open until 5 pm and, during the warmer months, they could stay open until 9 pm. Most food shops close on Thursday afternoon and some close on Saturday afternoon too. Shops, department stores and supermarkets tend to be closed on Monday morning. Department stores, such as Coin and Rinascente, and most larger supermarkets open continuously from 9 am to 7.30 pm Monday to Saturday. Some even open from 9 am to 1 pm (or longer) on Sunday. Great revolutions were expected of Italy's shopping hours after a government bill to liberalise opening hours was passed in 1998. However, shops which took advantage of the new bill are generally only those located in central or touristy areas.

Banks tend to open 8.30 am to 1.30 pm and 2.45 to 4.30 pm Monday to Friday, though hours can vary. Some banks in the city centre also open Saturday morning. It is always possible to find an exchange office open in major tourist areas.

For post office and pharmacy hours see under Post and Pharmacies, respectively, earlier in this chapter.

Bars (in the Italian sense, ie coffee and sandwich places) and cafes generally open 7.30 am to 8 pm, though some stay open after 8 pm and turn into pub-style drinking and meeting places. Discos and clubs open around 10 pm but often there'll be no-one there until around midnight. Restaurants open midday to 3 pm and 7.30 to 11 pm (later in summer). Restaurants and bars are required to close for one day each week, which varies between establishments.

Museum and gallery opening hours vary, although there is a trend towards continuous opening hours from 9 am to 7 pm. Most of Rome's museums are closed on Monday.

PUBLIC HOLIDAYS & SPECIAL EVENTS

Most Romans take their annual holidays in August, deserting the city for the cooler seaside or mountains. This means that many businesses and shops close for at least a part of the month, particularly during the week around Ferragosto (Feast of the Assumption) on 15 August. The city is left to the tourists, who may be frustrated that many restaurants and clothing and grocery shops are closed until early September. National public holidays include the following:

Epiphany 6 January
Easter Monday March/April
Liberation Day 25 April
Labour Day 1 May
Feast of the Assumption 15 August
All Saints' Day 1 November
**Feast of the Immaculate
   Conception** 8 December
Christmas Day 25 December
Feast of Santo Stefano 26 December

Rome also has its own public holiday to celebrate the Feast of Sts Peter and Paul, its patron saints, on 29 June.

Year-round, Italy's calendar bursts with cultural events ranging from colourful traditional celebrations with a religious and/or historical flavour, through to festivals of the performing arts, including opera, music and theatre.

Summer is definitely the best time to visit if you want to catch the best of the festivals, where opera, dance and music (classical, jazz, contemporary or ethnic) share the spotlight. However, the Romaeuropa festival (dance, theatre and opera) is now a feature of the autumn calendar, the Rome opera season runs from December until June and the classical and contemporary music scene is lively all year round.

See the boxed text 'Rome, Festival Town' in the Entertainment chapter for music- and film-festival listings.

February
Carnevale Children in fancy dress parade the streets and adults eat *bigné* and *fritelle* pastries.

March/April
Festa della Primavera The Spanish Steps are filled with azaleas – a perfect photo occasion.
Settimana dei Beni Culturali Culture for the populace – museums open free of charge and free guided tours aim to get Italians (and foreigners) back into their heritage.

April
Natale di Roma The Eternal City celebrates her birthday. She was 2754 in 2001. Bands and standard bearers perform in Piazza del Campidoglio; 21 April.

May
Primo Maggio May Day rock concert in Piazza di Porta di San Giovanni; 1 May.

July
Festa di Noantri Trastevere's residents celebrate their individuality and have a good excuse to drink local wine and eat *porchetta* (roasted suckling pig, stuffed with herbs and cooked on the spit); last two weeks of the month.
Rome Pride Festival celebrating gay rights and culture.

August
Ferragosto *Everything* shuts down, and the only

thing you can eat in the few places still open is *pollo con peperoni*; 15 August.

September
Via dell'Orso Craft Fair Artisans in and around this characteristic street near Piazza Navona open their studios and workshops to browsers and buyers.

October/November
Via dei Coronari Mostra-Mercato Antiques fair.

December/January
Piazza Navona Christmas Fair The gaudy stalls and kitsch souvenirs get tackier each year but, like a bad case of herpes, they keep coming back; early December to 6 January.
Presepi Churches around Rome set up their nativity scenes.

DOING BUSINESS
Milan, not Rome, is Italy's business centre. The stock exchange is based there, as are the Italian headquarters of many multinational companies including Fiat, Blockbuster Video and IBM. However, in the provinces around Rome there are significant manufacturing facilities in a range of sectors, including domestic appliances, pharmaceuticals, steel, electronic components, clothing and footwear.

If you are dealing with multinationals you will probably find that most people you come into contact with speak a certain amount of English. However, this is by no means assured in smaller businesses where fluency, or at least competence in Italian, is an enormous advantage.

Useful Contacts Abroad
The trade office of the Italian Embassy in your home country can probably provide initial information and help you establish contacts.

In the USA, the Italy-America Chamber of Commerce (IACC) has branches in a number of cities including Chicago, Los Angeles and New York. It publishes an annual directory of Italian companies that do business in the USA and vice versa. Check out the Web site www.italian-chamber.com. The Italian Trade Commission (☎ 212-980

1500, fax 758 1050), 499 Park Avenue, New York, NY 10022, also has offices in Atlanta, Los Angeles and Chicago.

Useful Contacts in Italy

The trade office of your embassy can provide tips and contacts. The *English Yellow Pages*, a telephone directory of English-speaking professionals, commercial activities and organisations in Rome (as well as Florence, Bologna and Milan) might be of use. It is available in English-language bookshops.

Rome's Istituto Nazionale per il Commercio Estero (☎ 06 599 21; ℮ ice@ice.it), Via Liszt 21, is the main foreign trade commission in Italy. Its Web site is at www.ice.it. The British Chamber of Commerce in Italy (℮ bcci@britchamitaly.com) is based in Milan but has a Rome representative (☎ 06 862 06 459). Online information can be found at www.britchamitaly.com.

The American Chamber of Commerce in Italy is based in Milan (☎ 02 869 06 61, ℮ amcham@amcham.it), Via Cantù 1, 20123, and online at www.amcham.it.

Office Services

A GSM mobile phone and a good laptop computer will probably be all you need to do business in Rome. However, some of the better hotels in the city have business centres or secretarial assistance for guests.

Executive Services Business Centres (☎ 06 852 37 250), Via Savoia 78, can provide secretarial services, meeting rooms with video conferencing facilities, company addresses, voice mailboxes, translators and interpreters and other services. Check out its Web site at www.executivenetwork.it.

World Translation Centre (☎ 06 488 10 39, ℮ wtc@iol.it), Via Merulana 259, can provide sworn translations for legal and corporate needs.

Couriers

There are several motorcycle courier companies, which are known as 'ponies'. Two of the largest are Speedy Boys (☎ 06 398 88) and Presto (☎ 06 398 90).

WORK

It is illegal for non-EU citizens to work in Italy without a work permit but trying to obtain one can be time consuming. EU citizens are allowed to work in Italy but they still need to obtain a permesso di soggiorno

FACTS FOR THE VISITOR

Business Etiquette

Italians are extremely polite, especially in the business world. If you speak Italian, always use the formal mode of address, *lei* rather than the familiar *tu*. If your contact reverts to the familiar form, only then should you do it too. See the Language chapter at the back of this book for further details.

Use correct titles if you know them. Anyone with a university degree is referred to as *Dottore* (doctor), a lawyer is *Avvocato* and an engineer, *Ingeniere*. If in doubt, ask.

Be flexible and don't expect your appointments to run like clockwork. Romans are very relaxed about timekeeping. It is not unusual for a meeting scheduled for 11 am to start at 11.30 or even midday. But it works both ways – if you're running a little late, don't work yourself into a lather.

Make sure you reconfirm any appointment you make, especially if there's more than a few days between the last contact and the meeting. Italians are notorious for not turning up to appointments (both business and social) if there is no prior reconfirmation.

Never mix business with food. If a meeting is scheduled over lunch, make sure you don't bring up the deal or negotiations until the meal is finished. In Italy it's important to pay full attention to the food, *then* get down to business.

Don't plan any business in Rome for late July or for the month of August when the whole country goes on holiday and it's difficult, if not impossible, to get anything done. It's too hot anyway and you'll have more fun (and possibly make better business contacts) at the beach.

(see that section earlier in this chapter) from the main questura. New immigration laws require foreign workers to be 'legalised' through their employers, which can apply even to cleaners and babysitters. The employers then pay pension and health insurance contributions. This doesn't mean that 'black' work can't still be found.

Jobs are advertised in *Porta Portese* and in *Wanted in Rome*. You could also look in *Il Messaggero* and *The Herald Tribune* for job ads, and on the bulletin boards of English-language bookshops (see the Shopping chapter).

Working Holiday

The best options, once you're in the country, are restaurant, bar and nightclub work during the tourist season. Babysitting is a good possibility. You may be able to pick up a summer job accompanying a family on their annual beach holiday – you could look in *Wanted in Rome* or even place an advertisement. Another option is au pair work, organised before you come to Italy. Two useful guides are *The Au Pair and Nanny's Guide to Working Abroad* (1997), by S Griffith and S Legg, and *Work Your Way Around the World* (2001) by S Griffith.

Teaching English

The easiest source of work for foreigners is teaching English, but even with full qualifications an American, Australian, Canadian or New Zealander might find it difficult to secure a permanent position. Most of the larger, more reputable schools will hire only people with work permits, but their attitude can become more flexible if demand for teachers is high and they come across someone with good qualifications. The more professional schools will require a TEFL (Teaching English as a Foreign Language) certificate. It is advisable to apply for work early in the year, in order to be considered

for positions available in October (language school years correspond roughly to the Italian school year which is late September to the end of June).

Numerous schools hire people without work permits or qualifications but the pay is usually low (around €7.75 per hour). It is more lucrative to advertise your services and pick up private students (although rates vary wildly, ranging from as low as €7.75 up to €26 per hour). The average rate is around €15.50. Although you can get away with absolutely no qualifications or experience, it might be a good idea to bring along a few English grammar books (including exercises) to help you at least appear professional.

Most people get started by placing advertisements in shop windows and on university notice boards, or in a local publication, such as *Wanted in Rome* or *Porta Portese*.

International Organisations and Embassies

Several international organisations are based in Rome, including the Food and Agriculture Organization of the United Nations and the UN World Food Program. However, unless you've got very specific skills, they are hard to get into. Foreign embassies sometimes require administrative or domestic staff and prefer to employ their own nationals.

Tour Guiding

If you've got strong vocal chords, plenty of stamina and an encyclopedic knowledge of Rome's ancient ruins (or willingness to learn about it) then tour guiding could be a good option. There are plenty of companies that run 'promotional' tours of the Roman Forum and Colosseum – designed as a sweetener to get tourists to sign up for another paid tour – and they sometimes need more tour leaders. Try out a tour and go from there.

Getting There & Away

If you live outside Europe, flying is by far the easiest way to get to Rome. Competition between the airlines means you should be able to pick up a reasonably priced fare, even if you are coming from as far away as Australia. If you live in Europe, you can often find enticing deals from all the major European hubs.

AIR

Rome's main airport is Leonardo da Vinci, commonly referred to as Fiumicino after the town nearby. Rome's smaller second airport, Ciampino, is used by low-cost airlines and charter flights.

Italy's national carrier is Alitalia (www .alitalia.it), which operates direct flights between Rome and most European cities. Many of Alitalia's intercontinental flights (and intercontinental flights by other carriers) fly into Malpensa 2000 airport in Milan, connecting with domestic services to Rome, though there are still a limited number of direct flights to Rome. In 2000, Alitalia cut a number of its long-haul routes altogether and it no longer flies from Italy to Bangkok, Singapore, Sydney, Nairobi or Addis Ababa.

Airlines with direct connections to Rome include British Airways, American Airlines, Emirates Airlines, Qantas Airways, Lufthansa Airlines, Singapore Airlines and Malaysia Airlines.

Buying Tickets

World aviation has never been so competitive, making air travel better value than ever. However, research the options carefully to secure the best deal. The Internet is a useful resource for checking fares.

Full-time students and those aged under 26 (under 30 in some countries) have access to better deals than other travellers. You have to show a document proving your date of birth or a valid International Student Identity Card (ISIC) when buying your ticket and boarding the plane.

Generally, there is nothing to be gained by buying tickets direct from the airline. Discounted tickets are released to selected travel agents and specialist discount agencies, and these are usually the cheapest deals going.

One exception is the expanding number of no-frills carriers, which mostly sell only direct to travellers. Unlike full-service airlines, no-frills carriers often make one-way tickets available at around half the return fare, meaning that it is easy to put together an open-jaw ticket.

Many airlines, full-service and no-frills, offer some excellent fares to Web surfers. They may sell seats by auction or simply cut prices to reflect the reduced cost of electronic selling.

Online ticket sales work well if you are doing a simple one-way or return trip on

Air Travel Glossary

Alliances Many of the world's leading airlines are now intimately involved with each other, sharing everything from reservations systems and check-in to aircraft and frequent-flyer schemes. Opponents say that alliances restrict competition. Whatever the arguments, there is no doubt that big alliances are the way of the future.

Cancelling or Changing Tickets If you have to cancel or change a ticket, you need to contact the original travel agent who sold you the ticket. Airlines only issue refunds to the purchaser of a ticket – usually the travel agent who bought the ticket on your behalf. There are often heavy penalties involved; insurance can sometimes be taken out against these penalties.

Courier Fares Businesses often need to send urgent documents or freight securely and quickly. Courier companies hire people to accompany the package through customs and, in return, offer a discount ticket which is sometimes a bargain. However, you may have to surrender all your baggage allowance and take only carry-on luggage.

Fares Airlines traditionally offer 1st class (coded F), business class (coded J) and economy class (coded Y) tickets. These days there are so many promotional and discounted fares available that few passengers pay full fare.

Lost Tickets If you lose your airline ticket, an airline will usually treat it like a travellers cheque and, after inquiries, issue you with another one. Legally, however, an airline is entitled to treat it like cash and if you lose it then it's gone forever. Take very good care of your tickets.

Onward Tickets An entry requirement for many countries is that you have a ticket out of the country. If you're unsure of your next move, the easiest solution is to buy the cheapest onward ticket to a neighbouring country or a ticket from a reliable airline which can later be refunded if you do not use it.

Open-Jaw Tickets These are return tickets where you fly out to one place but return from another. If available, this can save you backtracking to your arrival point.

Overbooking Since every flight has some passengers who fail to show up, airlines often book more passengers than they have seats. Usually excess passengers make up for the no-shows, but occasionally somebody gets 'bumped' onto the next available flight. Guess who it is most likely to be? The passengers who check in late. If you do get 'bumped', you are normally offered some form of compensation.

Reconfirmation Some airlines require you to reconfirm your flight at least 72 hours prior to departure. Check your documents to see if this is the case.

Restrictions Discounted tickets often have various restrictions on them – such as needing to be paid for in advance and incurring a penalty to be altered or cancelled. Others are restrictions on the minimum and maximum period you must be away.

Round-the-World Tickets RTW tickets give you a limited period (usually a year) in which to circumnavigate the globe. You can go anywhere the carrying airlines go, as long as you don't backtrack. The number of stopovers or total number of separate flights is decided before you set off and they usually cost a bit more than a basic return flight.

Ticketless Travel Airlines are gradually waking up to the realisation that paper tickets are unnecessary encumbrances. On simple one-way or return trips, reservations details can be held on computer and the passenger merely shows ID to claim their seat.

Transferred Tickets Airline tickets cannot be transferred from one person to another. Travellers sometimes try to sell the return half of their ticket, but officials can ask you to prove that you are the person named on the ticket. On an international flight, tickets are compared with passports.

specified dates. However, online superfast fare generators are no substitute for a travel agent who knows about special deals, has

strategies for avoiding stopovers and can offer advice.

You may find the cheapest flights are

advertised by obscure agencies. Most such firms are honest and solvent but there are some rogue fly-by-night outfits around. Paying by credit card generally offers protection, as most card issuers provide refunds if you can prove you didn't get what you paid for. Similar protection can be obtained by buying a ticket from a bonded agent, such as one covered by the Air Travel Organiser's Licence (ATOL) scheme in the UK. Agents who accept only cash should hand over the tickets straight away and not tell you to 'come back tomorrow'.

After you've made a booking with an agency or paid your deposit, call the airline and confirm your flight. It's generally not advisable to send money (even cheques) through the post unless the agent is very well established – some travellers have reported being ripped off by unreliable mail-order ticket agents.

If you purchase a ticket and later want to make changes to your route or get a refund, you need to contact the original travel agent. Airlines issue refunds only to the purchaser of a ticket – usually the travel agent who bought the ticket on your behalf. Many travellers change their routes halfway through their trips, so think carefully before you buy a ticket that is not easily refunded.

Travellers with Specific Needs

If they're warned early enough, airlines can often make special arrangements for travellers, such as wheelchair assistance at airports or vegetarian meals on the flight. Children under two years of age travel for 10% of the standard fare (or free on some airlines) as long as they don't occupy a seat. They don't get a baggage allowance. 'Skycots', baby food and nappies should be provided by the airline if requested in advance. Children aged between two and 12 can usually occupy a seat for half to two-thirds of the full fare, and do get a baggage allowance.

The disability-friendly Web site www .everybody.co.uk has an airline directory that provides information on the facilities offered by various airlines.

Departure Tax

The departure tax payable when you leave Italy by air is always factored into your airline ticket.

Other Parts of Italy

Regular domestic flights connect Rome to all major Italian airports. The majority of these are operated by Alitalia and its subsidiary airlines. Other domestic airlines include Air One (Map 3; ☎ 06 47 87 61), Via Sardegna 14, with a Web site at www.air -one.it, for flights between Rome, Milan, Turin, Bologna, Naples, Bari, Reggio Calabria and Crotone; and Meridiana (Map 5; ☎ 06 47 80 41), Via Barberini 67, online at www.meridiana.it, for flights to Milan, Catania, Verona and Sardinia. New player National Jet Italia (☎ 848 812 266 within Italy), a British Airways franchise, offers flights from Rome to Palermo and Catania.

The UK & Ireland

Discount air travel is big business in London. Advertisements for a variety of travel agencies appear in the travel pages of the weekend broadsheet newspapers, in *Time Out*, in the *Evening Standard* and in the free magazine *TNT*.

Popular travel agencies in the UK catering mainly for students or travellers aged under 26 include STA Travel (☎ 020-7361 6262), with a main office at 86 Old Brompton Rd, London SW7; and usit Campus (☎ 0870 240 1010), with an office at 52 Grosvenor Gardens, London SW1. Both agencies have offices throughout the UK and you can visit them online at www.statravel.co.uk and www.usitcampus.co.uk respectively.

Another good agency is Trailfinders (☎ 020-7937 5400), with a main booking centre at 215 Kensington High St, W8 and a Web site at www.trailfinders.com.

Two reliable airlines linking the UK and Rome are British Airways (BA; www .british-airways.com) and Alitalia (www .alitalia.co.uk). They operate regular direct flights (usually several a day) to Rome, Milan, Venice, Florence, Turin, Naples and Pisa. The regular published fares for both airlines tend to be the same. Flexible economy fares on a scheduled BA flight from London to Rome cost UK£557 return. At the time of writing BA had a low-season 'world offer' fare from London to Rome for UK£99 return. The standard return Apex fare costs around UK£199 in high season. An Apex ticket must be booked seven or 10 days in advance and allows no changes or refund; regulations vary so check when you buy your ticket.

Several no-frills airlines offer great deals for scheduled flights to Rome. On these airlines passengers are not always issued with a ticket but given a booking reference/itinerary instead, which is transferred directly into a boarding pass at the check-in. In general there is no complimentary food or drink served on the flight, although you can buy refreshments.

Go (☎ 0870 607 6543), a BA subsidiary operating out of Stansted airport, offers return flights to Ciampino airport ranging from UK£88 to UK£273. Go also flies to Milan, Venice, Bologna and Naples. Prices for flights from Rome are similar to fares from Britain (from €160 to €460 return). The cheaper flights have a number of conditions and are nonrefundable and nontransferable. Go is contactable in Rome toll-free on ☎ 14 788 77 66. You can book online at www.go-fly.com in both the UK and Italy.

Virgin Express (☎ 0800 891 199) flies from Heathrow, Gatwick and Stansted airports to Brussels with a connection to Rome. The fares are competitive if you've got the extra time to spare and don't mind changing planes. In Rome call ☎ 16 709 70 97 or visit online at www.virgin-express.com.

Charter flights are a cheap way to get to Italy from the UK and are often advertised in British weekend newspapers. If you're booking a charter flight, remember to check what time you'll be flying; many charter flights arrive very late at night. Transport into the city centre from either Fiumicino or Ciampino can be difficult after about 11 pm (see the Getting Around chapter).

If you're coming from Ireland, it might be worth comparing what is available direct with what is available from London – getting across to London first may save you some money. The Irish no-frills airline Ryanair, with a Web site at www.ryanair.com, offers charter flights to Ciampino from Dublin; ask a travel agent for details. You cannot purchase Ryanair flights to Ireland from Italy.

Continental Europe

Air travel between Rome and other cities in continental Europe is worth considering if you are pushed for time. Short hops can be expensive but good deals are available from some major hubs.

Several airlines offer cut-rate fares on legs of international flights between European cities. These are usually cheap but often involve flying at night or early in the morning. In addition, days on which you can fly are often restricted. Ask a travel agent for advice.

France Travel agencies catering especially to students and young people, with branches throughout France, include usit Connect Voyages (☎ 01 42 44 14 00), 14 rue de Vaugirard, 75006 Paris; and OTU Voyages (☎ 01 40 29 12 12), 39 ave Georges-Bernanos, 75005 Paris, with a Web site at www.otu.fr. Other recommendations include Voyageurs du Monde (☎ 01 42 86 16 00), 55 rue Ste-Anne, 75002 Paris; and Nouvelles Frontières (☎ 08 25 00 08 25, ☎ 01 45 68 70 00), 87 blvd de Grenelle, 75015 Paris, with branches country-wide. Visit online at www.nouvelles-fron tieres.fr.

High-season return fares from Paris to Rome cost from €265.

Germany STA Travel (☎ 030-311 0950), Goethestrasse 73, 10625 Berlin, and usit Campus (☎ 01805 788336 or ☎ 0221-923990 in Cologne), Zülpicher Strasse 2a, 50674 Cologne, are two recommended agencies. Both have several offices in Germany and details can be found online at www.statravel.de and www.usitcampus.de.

High-season return fares from Munich or Frankfurt-am-Main to Rome cost from €250.

The Netherlands Recommended agencies include NBBS Reizen (☎ 020-620 5071), 66 Rokin, Amsterdam; Budget Air (☎ 020-

627 1251), 34 Rokin, Amsterdam; and Holland International (☎ 070-307 6307). These agencies have offices in most cities and NBBS has a Web site at www.nbbs.nl.

High-season return fares from Amsterdam to Rome cost from €300.

Spain Travel agencies with branches in major cities include usit Unlimited (☎ 91 225 25 75), Plaza de Callao 3, 28013 Madrid, which is online at www.unlimited .es; Barcelo Viajes (☎ 91 559 1819), Princesa 3, 28008 Madrid; and Nouvelles Frontières (☎ 91 547 42 00), Plaza de España 18, 28008 Madrid, which has a Web site at www.nouvelles-frontieres.es.

High-season return fares from Madrid to Rome cost from €260.

The USA

The North Atlantic is the world's busiest long-haul air corridor and the flight options are bewildering. Several airlines fly direct to Rome, including American Airlines, Alitalia, TWA and Delta Air Lines. United Airlines flies to Milan's Malpensa airport. However, if your trip will not be confined to Italy, consult your travel agent on whether cheaper flights are available to other European cities.

Discount travel agents in the USA are known as consolidators. San Francisco is the ticket consolidator capital of America, though good deals can be found in Los Angeles, New York and other major cities.

Council Travel, the largest US student travel organisation, has around 60 offices in the USA; details can be obtained from its Customer Contact Center (☎ 800-226 8624), Boston, MA 02108, or online at www .counciltravel.com. STA Travel (☎ 800-777 0112) has offices in Boston, Chicago, Miami, New York, Philadelphia, San Francisco and other major cities. Call the toll-free 800 number for office locations or visit www.statravel.com on the Web.

Ticket Planet is a recommended, leading ticket consolidator in the USA. See online at www.ticketplanet.com.

Low-season return tickets from New York to Rome or Milan cost from US$500.

Return air fares from Rome to New York can be found for as little as €410 to €465 in low season, and €620 to Los Angeles.

Canada

Canadian discount air ticket sellers are also known as consolidators and their fares tend to be about 10% higher than those sold in the USA.

Travel CUTS (☎ 800-667 2887) is Canada's national student travel agency and has offices in all major cities. Its Web address is www.travelcuts.com.

Both Alitalia and Air Canada have direct flights to Rome and Milan from Toronto and Montreal. Low-season return fares from Rome to Toronto start from around €515.

Australia

Cheap flights from Australia to Italy generally go via South-East Asian capitals or the Middle East.

Quite a few travel offices specialise in discount air tickets and some travel agents, particularly smaller ones, advertise cheap fares in the travel sections of weekend newspapers.

Two well known agents for cheap fares are STA Travel and Flight Centre. STA Travel (☎ 03-9349 2411) has its main office at 224 Faraday St, Carlton, Melbourne, with offices in all major cities and on many university campuses. Call ☎ 131 776 Australia-wide for the location of your nearest branch or visit its Web site at www.statravel.com .au. Flight Centre (☎ 131 600 Australia-wide) has a central office at 82 Elizabeth St, Sydney. You can visit its Web site at www.flightcentre.com.au.

Qantas Airways flies from Melbourne and Sydney to Rome three times a week. Singapore Airlines, Emirates Airlines and Malaysia Airlines all fly directly to Rome. Some airlines fly to their European hub and throw in a return flight to another European city; for example, British Airways will fly you return to London with a London–Rome–London flight included in the price.

Discounted return fares on mainstream airlines through reputable agents can be surprisingly cheap. Low-season fares from

GETTING THERE & AWAY

Melbourne or Sydney to Rome cost around A$1800 return but can go as low as A$1500. High-season fares range from about A$1800 to A$2600, depending on the airline and ticket conditions. Flights from Perth are generally a few hundred dollars cheaper.

New Zealand

Flight Centre (☎ 09-309 6171) has a large central office in Auckland at National Bank Towers (corner of Queen and Darby Sts) and many branches throughout the country. STA Travel (☎ 0880 874 773 or 09-309 0458) has its main office at 10 High St, Auckland, as well as other offices in Hamilton, Palmerston North, Wellington, Christchurch and Dunedin. Its Web address is www.statravel.com.au.

The cheapest fares to Italy are routed through the USA or South-East Asia, and a round-the-world ticket may be cheaper than a return. Thai Airways International, Singapore Airlines and Cathay Pacific Airways all have some good fare deals to Rome. Low-season return fares from Auckland start from around NZ$2149 or NZ$2549 in high season.

Airline Offices

All the airlines have counters in the departure hall at Fiumicino. Many of the head offices are now based at or near the airport, although most have ticket offices in the area around Via Veneto and Via Barberini, northwest of Stazione Termini, including:

Alitalia (☎ 06 6 56 42) Via Bissolati 20
  Web site: www.alitalia.it
Air France (☎ 06 48 79 11) Via Sardegna 40
  Web site: www.airfrance.it
British Airways (☎ 147 812 266) Via Bissolati 54
  Web site: www.british-airways.com
Air Canada (☎ 06 655 15 06) Via C Veneziani 58
  Web site: www.aircanada.ca
Cathay Pacific Airways (☎ 06 482 09 30) Via Barberini 3
  Web site: www.cathaypacific.com
Delta Air Lines (☎ 800 864 114) Via Sardegna 40
  Web site: www.delta.com
Lufthansa Airlines (☎ 06 65 68 40 04) Via di San Basilio 41
  Web site: www.lufthansa.com

Qantas Airways (☎ 06 52 48 27 25) Via Bissolati 54
  Web site: www.qantas.com
Singapore Airlines (☎ 06 47 85 51) Via Barberini 11
  Web site: www.singaporeair.com
TWA (☎ 800 841 843) Via Barberini 67
  Web site: www.twa.com

BUS
Other Parts of Italy

Lazio Blue COTRAL buses (now officially known as Linee Laziali or LiLa), which service the Lazio region, depart from numerous points throughout the city, depending on their destinations (see the Getting Around chapter). The company is linked with Rome's public transport system, meaning that day tickets are valid for city and regional buses, trams, the Metropolitana (Metro) and other train lines. The official information line is ☎ 800 431 784, but expect a long delay before someone (and not necessarily an English speaker) answers.

Buses for Palestrina and Tivoli depart from Ponte Mammolo Metro station on Linea B (also stopping at Rebbibia); buses for Bolsena, Saturnia, Toscana and Viterbo depart from Saxa Rubra, on the Ferrovia Roma Nord train line; buses for the Castelli Romani depart from Anagnina, the last stop on Metro Linea A; buses for beaches south of Rome depart from the EUR-Fermi station (Metro Linea B); and for Bracciano, Cerveteri and Tarquinia take a bus from the Lepanto stop (Metro Linea A). See also the destinations in the Excursions chapter.

Other Regions The main station for intercity buses is in Piazzale Tiburtina, in front of Stazione Tiburtina. Catch Metro Linea B from Stazione Termini to Tiburtina. The more centrally located Eurojet agency (Map 5; ☎ 06 474 28 01) in Piazza della Repubblica 54 sells tickets for some bus lines.

Useful bus lines include:

ARPA, SIRA, Di Fonzo, Di Febo & Capuani Services to Abruzzo, including L'Aquila, Pescasseroli and Pescara; tickets and information from ARPA (☎ 8488 654 14 toll-free), Via Teodorico 24

Bonelli Services to Emilia-Romagna, including Ravenna and Rimini; information and tickets from Picarozzi (☎ 06 440 44 95), Via Guido Mazzoni 12–14
Web site: www.autolinee.it

Interbus Services to Sicily; information at Piazza dell Repubblica or Piazzale Tiburtina

Lirosi Services to Calabria; information at Eurojet (☎ 06 474 28 01)

Marozzi Services to Bari and Brindisi, Sorrento, the Amalfi coast and Pompeii; information and tickets from Eurolines (☎ 06 440 40 09), Circonvallazione Nomentana 574, and Eurojet (☎ 06 474 28 01), Piazza della Repubblica 54
Web site: www.eurolines.it

SAIS Services to Sicily; tickets from Picarozzi (☎ 06 440 44 95), Via Guido Mazzoni 12–14
Web site: www.autolinee.it

Segesta Services to Sicily (Messina, Palermo, Trapani); information and tickets from Tiburviaggi (☎ 06 442 90 091), Via Guido Mazzoni 12–14

Sena Services to Siena; information at Picarozzi (☎ 06 440 44 95), Via Guido Mazzoni, and Eurojet (☎ 06 474 28 01)

SULGA Services to Perugia, Assisi and Fiumicino airport; information at Eurojet (☎ 06 474 28 01) or SULGA Perugia (075 500 96 41)

Europe

Eurolines (☎ 06 440 40 09) is the main carrier for European destinations and is connected with coach operators throughout Europe. The office in Rome is at Circonvallazione Nomentana 574, opposite Stazione Tiburtina. Its Web site, www.eurolines.com, is linked with the Web sites of national bus lines in other countries.

The prices quoted in this section are for the high season. There is a 10% reduction for people aged under 26 or over 60. Children aged four to 11 years pay 50% of the full fare; those aged under three years travel free if they are not occupying a seat.

Bear in mind that a discounted air fare might work out cheaper than a long bus trip, allowing for food and drink bought en route.

UK Eurolines (☎ 0990 143219) runs buses twice a week from London's Victoria Coach Station to Rome (33 hours) and other Italian destinations including Turin, Genoa, Milan, Florence, Rimini and Ancona. Up to four services a week run during the summer. The lowest one-way fare from London

for those aged under 26 costs UK£72; the full adult fare costs UK£81. Fares rise in the peak summer season.

A one-way adult fare from Rome to London costs €113.62.

France Eurolines has offices in several French cities. The Paris office (☎ 01 49 72 51 51) is at 28 ave du Général de Gaulle. A one-way/return ticket from Paris to Rome costs €71.65/118.91 (under-26) and €79.27/131.10 (those aged 26 and over). A one-way adult fare from Rome to Paris costs €96.57 in the high season.

Germany Eurolines and associated companies have stations at major cities across Germany, including Hamburg, Frankfurt-am-Main and Munich. For the latter, head for Deutsche Touring GmbH (☎ 089-545 87 00) at Amulfstrasse 3, Stamberger Bahnhof. Otherwise, SITA has buses from Hamburg, Frankfurt and Munich to Padua, where you can pick up a connection for Rome. In Frankfurt, SITA (☎ 069-790 3240) is at Am Römerhof 17. A full-price ticket from Frankfurt to Rome costs €86.92/156.45 one-way/return.

A one-way adult fare from Rome to Frankfurt (via Siena) with Eurolines costs €88.83.

The Netherlands Eurolines (☎ 020-627 51 51) is at Rokin 10 in Amsterdam. The cheapest fare between Amsterdam and Rome is €36.30/72.60 one-way/return. The adult one-way fare from Rome to Amsterdam costs €100.71.

Spain Eurolines and associated companies have representatives across the country, including the Estación Sur de Autobuses (☎ 91 528 11 05), Calle de las Canarias 17, Madrid, and the Estación Autobuses de Sants (☎ 93 490 40 00), Calle del Viriato s/n, Barcelona.

The Madrid to Rome fare costs €120.80/161.67 one-way/return. Between Barcelona and Rome fares cost €96.76/124.41. There are at least two weekly services between Rome and Barcelona (€100.71 one-way) and between Rome and Madrid.

GETTING THERE & AWAY

TRAIN

Almost all trains arrive at and depart from Stazione Termini. There are regular connections to other European countries, all the major cities in Italy and many smaller towns. There are eight other train stations scattered throughout Rome. Some northbound trains depart from or stop at Stazione Ostiense and Stazione Trastevere.

For train information (in Italian only), ring ☎ 14 788 80 88 from 7 am to 9 pm or go to the information office at the train station, where English is spoken. The office opens 7 am to 9.45 pm but be aware that there are always lengthy queues. If you are doing a reasonable amount of travelling, it is worth buying a train timetable. There are several available, including the official Ferrovie dello Stato (FS) timetables, which can be purchased at newsstands in or near train stations for around €2.60.

Remember to validate your train ticket in one of the yellow machines on the station platforms. If you don't, you may be forced to pay a fine on the train.

Other Parts of Italy

Travelling by train in Italy is simple, cheap and generally efficient. The Ferrovie dello Stato (FS), which has a Web site at www.fs -on-line.com, is the partially privatised state train system and there are several private train services throughout the country.

There are different types of train, including Regionale (R), which stop at all stations and can be very slow; interRegionale (iR), which run between the regions and can also be slow; and Intercity (IC), Eurostar (ES) and Euro-City (EC), which service the major cities and towns and are usually express services.

There are 1st and 2nd classes on all Italian trains, with a 1st-class ticket costing a bit less than double the price of 2nd class. On the Eurostar trains, 2nd class is much like 1st class on other trains.

It is recommended that you book train tickets for long trips, particularly if you're travelling at the weekend or during holiday periods, otherwise you could find yourself standing in the corridor for the entire journey. Reservations are obligatory for most Eurostar services. You can get timetable information and make bookings at most travel agencies in Rome, including CTS (see Travel Agencies in the Facts for the Visitor chapter), or you can simply buy your ticket at the station. There are special Eurostar booking offices at the relevant train stations.

There are 24-hour left-luggage facilities at all train stations. They open seven days a week (some may close for a couple of hours after midnight) and charge from €0.77 per day for each piece of luggage.

Costs To travel on the Intercity, Eurostar and EuroCity (see under Europe later in this section), you are required to pay a *supplemento*, an additional charge determined by the distance you are travelling. For instance, on the Intercity train between Rome and Florence you will pay an extra €7.54. The cost of a Eurostar ticket includes the supplement and booking fee. The one-way fare from Rome to Florence on the Eurostar costs €26.60 in 2nd class and €42.09 in 1st class. The difference in price between the Eurostar (1½ hours) and the cheaper Intercity (around two hours) is only €5.47. For the extra money you get a faster, much more comfortable service, with some nuts or biscuits thrown in. The Eurostar always takes priority over other trains, so there's less risk of delays in the middle of nowhere.

Always check whether the train you are about to catch is an Intercity or Eurostar and pay the appropriate supplement before you get on, otherwise you will pay extra on the train. On overnight trips within Italy it can be worth paying extra for a *cuccetta* – a sleeping berth (commonly known as a couchette) in a four-bed compartment, costing between €16.53 and €23.24 extra (depending on the train).

Some examples of 2nd-class, one-way train fares on Intercity/Eurostar trains (including supplements) are Rome–Milan €36.77/42.35; Rome–Venice €36.77/42.35; and Rome–Naples €15.49/20.40. Return fares are double the one-way fare.

Italian Rail Passes It is not worth buying a Eurail or Inter-Rail pass if you are going to travel only in Italy, since train fares are reasonably cheap.

The FS offers its own discount passes for travel within the country. These include the Carta Verde for those aged from 12 to 26 years. It costs €20.66, is valid for one year and entitles you to a 20% discount on all train travel, but you'll need to do a fair bit of travelling to get your money's worth. The Carta d'Argento entitles those aged 60 years and over to a 20% discount on 1st- and 2nd-class travel for one year. It also costs €20.66. Children aged between four and 12 years are automatically entitled to a 50% discount; those aged under four travel free.

A *biglietto chilometrico* (kilometric ticket) is valid for two months and allows you to cover 3000km, with a maximum of 20 trips. It costs €110.52 (2nd class) and you must pay the supplement if you catch an Intercity or Eurostar train. Its main attraction is that it can be used by up to five people, either singly or together.

Two other useful passes (only for foreign visitors) are the Italy Railcard and Italy Flexi Rail. With both passes, prices include supplements for travel on Intercity trains but not for Eurostar trains. You should have your passport for identification when purchasing either pass. The Italy Railcard is valid for eight, 15, 21 or 30 consecutive days of travel and is available for 1st- or 2nd-class travel. An eight-day pass costs €275.01/182.98 for 1st/2nd class. A 21-day pass costs €397.98/264.99 for 1st/2nd class. Italy Flexi Rail is valid for four, eight or 12 cumulative days of travel within one month. A four-day pass costs €215.98/143.99 for 1st/2nd class. A 12-day pass costs €388.99/259.01 for 1st/2nd class.

Europe

Train travel is a convenient and simple means of travelling from most parts of Europe to Italy. It is certainly a popular way of getting around for backpackers and other young travellers, and even the more well heeled travellers will find European trains a comfortable and reliable way to reach their destination.

If you plan to travel extensively by train in Europe it might be worth getting hold of the *Thomas Cook European Timetable*, which gives a complete listing of train schedules and indicates where supplements apply and where reservations are necessary. It is updated monthly and is available from Thomas Cook offices and agents worldwide. In Rome it is also available at the Anglo-American Bookshop (Map 4), Via delle Vite 102, near Piazza di Spagna. The European Railway Server Web site, http://mercurio.iet.unipi.it, is also helpful.

EuroCity (EC) is a fast train service with both 1st and 2nd classes. Its trains run from major destinations throughout Europe – including Paris, Geneva, Zürich, Frankfurt-am-Main, Vienna and Barcelona – direct to major Italian cities. On most overnight hauls you can book a *cuccetta* (couchette) for around €23. Sleepers are more expensive but also much more comfortable.

It is always advisable to book a seat on EuroCity trains, or on any long-distance train to Italy, since frequent overcrowding (particularly in summer) means you could find yourself standing in the corridor for the whole trip.

When crossing international borders on overnight trips, train conductors will usually collect your passport before you go to sleep and hand it back the following morning.

Some of the main international services include transport for private cars – an option worth examining to save wear and tear on your vehicle before it arrives in Italy.

The UK The Channel Tunnel allows for land transport links between Britain and continental Europe. The Eurostar passenger train service (☎ 0870 518 6186), with a Web site at www.eurostar.com, travels between London and Paris and London and Brussels. The Eurotunnel vehicle service (☎ 0870 535 3535) travels between terminals in Folkestone and Calais. Visit its Web site at www.eurotunnel.com.

Alternatively, you can get a train ticket that includes the Channel crossing by ferry or SeaCat (catamaran). After that you can travel to Rome via Paris and southern

France or by swinging from Belgium down through Germany and Switzerland.

The cheapest standard fares from London to Rome cost around UK£85/170 one-way/return for students and those aged under 26, while the full adult fares cost around UK£110/190. You need to add the price of a couchette to this fare.

For the latest fare information on journeys including the Eurostar, call the Rail Europe Travel Centre (☎ 0870 584 8848). For information on trips using normal trains and ferries only, contact Wasteels (☎ 020-7834 7066), whose office is opposite platform 2 at Victoria train station in London.

France & Spain Standard one-way, 2nd-class fares from Rome to Paris cost from €100.71, including a reserved couchette.

There are no direct trains from Rome to Barcelona (you have to change in Milan and France); the one-way fare costs €92.96 but does not include a reservation or couchette.

Switzerland & Austria One-way fares (excluding a seat/couchette reservation) from Rome to Geneva cost from €111.55. There are several daily trains to Vienna (some involve a change at Venezia-Mestre, near Venice); the one-way fare costs from €95.54 (again excluding a seat/couchette reservation).

CAR & MOTORCYCLE

The main road connecting Rome to the north and south of Italy is the Autostrada del Sole, extending from Milan to Reggio di Calabria. On the outskirts of the city it connects with the Grande Raccordo Anulare, the ring road encircling Rome. From here, there are several exits into the city.

If you are approaching from the north, take the Via Salaria, Via Nomentana or Via Flaminia exits. From the south, Via Appia Nuova, Via Cristoforo Colombo and Via del Mare (which connects Rome to the Lido di Ostia) all provide reasonably direct routes into the city. The A12 connects the city to Civitavecchia and then runs along the coast to Genoa (it also connects the city to Fiumicino airport).

The Grande Raccordo Anulare and all arterial roads in Rome are clogged with traffic on weekday evenings from about 5 to 7.30 pm, and on Sunday evening, particularly in summer, all approaches to the city are subject to traffic jams as Romans return home after weekends away.

Signs from the centre of Rome to the *autostrada* (motorway) can be vague and confusing, so invest in a good road map. It is best to stick to the arterial roads to reach the Grande Raccordo Anulare and then exit at the appropriate point.

The main roads out of Rome basically follow the same routes as the ancient consular roads. The seven most important are:

Via Aurelia (S1) Starts at the Vatican and leaves the city to the north-east, following the Tyrrhenian coast to Pisa, Genoa and France.

Via Cassia (S2) Starts at Ponte Milvio and heads north-westwards to Viterbo, Siena and Florence.

Via Flaminia (S3) Starts at Ponte Milvio and goes north-westwards to Terni, Foligno and over the Apennines into Le Marche, ending on the Adriatic coast at Fano.

Via Salaria (S4) Heads northwards from near Porta Pia in central Rome to Rieti and into Le Marche, ending at Porto d'Ascoli on the Adriatic coast.

Via Tiburtina (S5) Links Rome with Tivoli and Pescara, on the coast of Abruzzo.

Via Casilina (S6) Heads south-eastwards to Anagni and into Campania, terminating at Capua near Naples.

Via Appia Nuova (S7) Heads southwards along the coast of Lazio into Campania and inland across the Apennines into Basilicata, through Potenza and Matera to Taranto in Apulia, and on to Brindisi.

Documents

Proof of ownership or registration of a private vehicle should always be carried when driving in Italy. Third party insurance is a minimum requirement throughout Europe and it is compulsory to have a Green Card, an internationally recognised proof of insurance, which can be obtained from your insurer.

Every vehicle travelling across an international border should display a nationality plate of its country of registration.

Roadside Assistance

The Automobile Club Italiano (ACI) will provide free emergency roadside assistance once only to members of foreign automobile associations, taking you and the car to the nearest ACI-registered mechanic (which is not always convenient). If you are not a member of a foreign automobile association, you'll pay a minimum fee of €82.63, but again this only gets you and the vehicle to the nearest garage. If you want to get your car to a specialist mechanic or to a more distant destination, you will have to shell out the towing costs. To get roadside assistance call ☎ 116.

ACI has offices at Via Marsala 8, Rome (☎ 06 499 81); and Corso Venezia 43, Milan (☎ 02 774 51).

A European breakdown assistance policy such as the AA's Five Star Service or the RAC's Eurocover Motoring Assistance is a good investment.

Road Rules

In Italy, as throughout continental Europe, people drive on the right side of the road and overtake on the left.

Carrying a warning triangle (to be used in the event of a breakdown) is compulsory throughout Europe. Recommended accessories are a first-aid kit, a spare bulb kit and a fire extinguisher. It is compulsory to wear seat belts if fitted to the car (ie, front seat belts in all cars, rear seat belts in cars produced after 26 April 1990). If caught without seat belts, you will be required to pay a €29.95 on-the-spot fine, although this doesn't seem to deter Italians, many of whom wear them only on the autostradas.

Tolls apply on most of the main autostradas. You pick up a ticket as you enter and pay as you exit (the amount depends on the distance travelled).

Random breath tests now take place in Italy. If you're involved in an accident while under the influence of alcohol, the penalties can be severe. The limit on blood-alcohol content is 0.08%.

Speed limits, unless otherwise indicated by local signs, are: on autostradas 130km/h for cars of 1100cc or more and 110km/h for smaller cars and motorcycles under 350cc; on all main, non-urban highways 110km/h; on secondary, non-urban highways 90km/h; and in built-up areas 50km/h. Speeding fines follow EU standards and are €30.47 for up to 10km/h over the limit, €121.36 for up to 40km/h over the limit and €303.16 for more than 40km/h over the limit. The penalty for driving through a red light is €60.42.

See Documents in the Facts for the Visitor chapter for driving licence requirements.

You don't need a licence to ride a moped under 50cc but you should be aged 14 years or over. You may not carry passengers or use the autostradas and the speed limit for a moped is 40km/h. To ride a motorcycle or scooter up to 125cc, you must be at least 16 years old and have a licence (a car licence will do). Helmets are compulsory for everyone riding a motorbike of more than 50cc. The days of the Italian scooter rider with free-flowing locks came to an abrupt end in 2000 when police started applying the rules and issuing hefty fines.

For motorcycles over 125cc you need a motorcycle licence. You will be able to enter restricted traffic areas in Italian cities without any problems and Italian traffic police generally turn a blind eye to motorcycles parked on footpaths. There is no lights-on requirement for motorcycles during the day.

For information about renting cars, motorbikes and mopeds see the Getting Around chapter.

Fuel

The cost of leaded petrol in Italy is very high, at around €1.08 per litre; unleaded costs slightly less at €1.03. Leaded petrol is *benzina*, unleaded petrol is *benzina senza piombo* and diesel is *gasolio*. If you are driving a car which uses LPG (liquid petroleum gas), you will need to buy a special guide to service stations that have *gasauto* or GPL. By law these must be located in nonresidential areas and they are usually in the country or on the outskirts of cities, although you'll find plenty on the autostradas. GPL costs around €0.46 per litre.

GETTING THERE & AWAY

BICYCLE

Cycling is a favourite national sport in Italy but there are surprisingly few dedicated cycle paths, so most of the time you'll be sharing the tarmac with traffic. Local tourist offices have information about trails in their area.

Bikes can be taken very cheaply on trains (€5.16), though only some trains will actually carry them. Fast trains (IC, EC etc) will generally not accommodate bikes and they must be sent as registered luggage. This can take a few days and will probably mean that your bike won't be on the same train that you travel on. It might be an idea to send your bike in advance, if possible. Check with the FS or a travel agent for more information.

Bikes can usually be transported by air for a low fee, or even for free. Ask your airline or travel agent for details.

For information on hiring bikes and bike tours see the Getting Around chapter.

HITCHING

Hitching is never entirely safe in any country, and we don't recommend it. Travellers who decide to hitch should understand they are taking a small, but potentially serious, risk. People who choose to hitch will be safer if they travel in pairs and let someone know where they are planning to go. Women travelling alone should be extremely cautious about hitching anywhere in Italy.

It is illegal to hitch on Italy's autostradas, but quite acceptable to stand near the entrance to the toll booths. You could also approach drivers at petrol stations and truck stops. To head northwards on the A1, take bus No 319 from Stazione Termini, get off at Piazza Vescovio and then take bus No 135 to Via Salaria. To go south to Naples on the A2, take Metro Linea A to Anagnina and hitch from Via Tuscolana.

It is sometimes possible to arrange lifts in advance – ask around at youth hostels. Enjoy Rome (see Tourist Offices in the Facts for the Visitor chapter) may be able to help.

BOAT

The nearest port to Rome is at Civitavecchia, from where ferries depart for Sardinia. Regular trains run from Stazione Termini to Civitavecchia (1½ hours). Services are run by Tirrenia (online at www.tirrenia.de) and the FS. Ticket prices vary according to the time of year and are at their most expensive during summer. Travel agencies in Rome will be able to provide information on fares and bookings.

ORGANISED TOURS

There are many options for organised travel to Rome. Tours can save you hassle but they do rob your independence. The Italian Tourist Office can sometimes provide a list of tour operators noting what each specialises in. Offices of CIT (see under Tourist Offices in the Facts for the Visitor chapter) abroad can also help. It is always worth shopping around for good-value deals but such tours rarely come cheap. The weekend newspapers and glossy travel magazines in the UK, the USA and Australia carry ads for various tours ranging in theme from cooking to architecture.

The major airlines often offer short city-break packages, which include air fares, accommodation and transfers but leave you free to do your sightseeing independently. Again, these deals are usually advertised in newspaper travel sections. Prices vary depending on the time of year you travel (always cheaper in the low season) and the type of accommodation you choose.

Hop on a tram and see where you end up.

Horsing around in Campo de' Fiori

Traffic chaos, one of Rome's more frenzied aspects, is averted by a carabiniere in Piazza Navona.

CHRISTOPHER WOOD

Bell tower of Chiesa di Sant'Ivo alla Sapienza

MICHELLE LEWIS

All roads lead to Rome – ask a gladiator.

MARTIN MOOS

The twin churches of Santa Maria dei Miracoli and Santa Maria in Montesanto with St Peter's behind

Getting Around

TO/FROM THE AIRPORTS
Fiumicino

Rome's main airport, Leonardo da Vinci (commonly known as Fiumicino), is 30km south-west of the city centre. The Leonardo Express, the direct Fiumicino–Stazione Termini train (follow the signs to the train station from the airport arrivals hall), costs €8.78. The train arrives at and leaves from platforms 25 to 29 at Stazione Termini (Map 5) and takes about 30 minutes. The first direct train leaves the airport for Termini at 7.37 am, then runs half-hourly until the last train at 10.37 pm. From Termini to the airport, trains start at 6.51 am and run half-hourly until the last train at 9.21 pm.

Another train from Fiumicino stops at Trastevere, Ostiense and Tiburtina stations (€4.65). From the airport, trains run about every 20 minutes from 5.57 am to 11.27 pm and from Tiburtina from 5.06 am until 10.36 pm. You should allow more time on Sundays and public holidays when there is a reduced service. This train does not stop at Termini.

Tickets for both trains can be bought from vending machines in the main airport arrivals hall. Make sure you have some small notes as these machines rarely have much change. Tickets can also be bought from the ticket office, tobacconist or vending machines in the train stations.

From midnight to 5 am an hourly bus runs from Stazione Tiburtina via Stazione Termini to the airport. The same bus departs for the city from outside the arrivals hall. Tickets cost €3.62. Don't hang around Tiburtina at night – it's not safe.

Fiumicino airport is connected to the city by an autostrada. Follow the signs for Rome out of the complex and exit from the autostrada at EUR. From there, you'll need to ask directions to reach Via Cristoforo Colombo, which will take you directly into the centre.

Taxis leave from outside the arrivals hall. They are expensive: a taxi to the centre of Rome will cost from €36, including a special airport surcharge of €7.75.

Several private companies run limousine services which work out the same price as a taxi but are usually a lot more comfortable. Airport Connection Services (☎ 06 338 32 21) has two deals: a minivan shuttle service for €17 per person (minimum two people); or a chauffeur-driven Mercedes for €39. Coop Airport (☎ 06 65 08 81 41 Monday to Saturday or 06 65 95 49 10 Sunday) has an office in the domestic arrivals area at Fiumicino and offers a limousine service for €41 to/from central Rome (with a 20% supplement 11 pm to 7 am). Both services can be booked for airport pick-ups and drop-offs.

Ciampino

Ciampino airport, about 15km south-east of the city, caters to charter companies and discount airlines. Ciampino is connected to Rome by the Via Appia Nuova. Public transport to the city centre is ridiculously inefficient; if you arrive late or very early, you have little option other than to catch a taxi, which will cost upwards of €31 (depending on the traffic), including an airport surcharge of €7.75. Knowing they have a captive market, the taxi drivers often (illegally) add huge surcharges to the fare, or quote an exorbitant flat fee to take you into town. It's worth asking fellow passengers if they want to share a cab.

Blue COTRAL buses (officially known as Linee Laziali or LiLa) running between 5.45 am and 10.30 pm, about every 60 to 90 minutes, will take you to the Anagnina Metro station (€0.62), from where you can catch the Linea A to Stazione Termini (€0.77). Buses for Ciampino leave from Anagnina every hour or so from 6.10 am to 11 pm.

At the time of writing, the low-cost airline Go was providing a bus service for their passengers from Ciampino to Piazza Santa Maria Maggiore (a few blocks south of Stazione Termini) and back out to the airport for around €11. You can buy tickets on inbound flights; ask about this bus when you make your booking. Some charter companies do the same – be sure to ask.

BUS & TRAM
ATAC Services
ATAC (☎ 06 46 95 22 52 or 06 46 95 22 56) is the city's public transport company. Many of the main bus routes terminate in Piazza dei Cinquecento in front of Stazione Termini where there's an information booth, on stand C in the centre of the square.

Another central point for the main bus routes is Largo di Torre Argentina, near Piazza Navona (Map 8). Buses generally run from about 6 am to midnight, with limited services throughout the night on some routes. If you're planning on using the buses and trams a lot, pick up a free transport map from the information kiosk at Termini or from any tourist information booth.

Travel on Rome's buses, trams, Metro and suburban railways is part of the same system and the same Metrebus ticket, also known as *biglietto integrato a tempo* (BIT), is valid for all modes of transport. Single tickets cost €0.77 for 75 minutes' travel. Children up to 1m tall travel free. Daily tickets cost €3.09, weekly tickets €12.39 and monthly tickets €25.82. Travel to destinations in Lazio can usually be done with a *biglietto integrato regionale giornaliero* (BIRG), a ticket valid for one day's travel on COTRAL buses and Ferrovia dello Stato (FS; State Railway) trains (within specified zones on the Lazio region) and all all public transport in Rome. These tickets range in price depending on the number of zones travelled. You can purchase them from all Metro, bus and train stations.

Tickets must be purchased *before* you get on the bus or train and then validated in the machine as you enter. On the Metro tickets must be validated as you go through the electronic barriers before you descend to the platform. If changing from bus to Metro, the ticket should be validated a second time. The minimum fine for travelling without a validated ticket is €51.64 (but it can be as much as €258) and inspectors are growing tired of the same old explanations from tourists that they 'didn't know'. Tickets can be bought in Piazza dei Cinquecento, at tobacconists and newsstands and from vending machines at main bus stops.

Information about all public transport services can be obtained by calling ☎ 800-431 784 (from 8 am to 6 pm) or from www.atac.roma.it.

Useful routes include:

No 46 Piazza Venezia to St Peter's and Via Aurelia
No 64 Stazione Termini to St Peter's
No 40 Stazione Termini to St Peter's (Express route with fewer stops than No 64)
No 27 Stazione Termini to the Colosseum, Circo Massimo and the Aventine hill
No 36 Stazione Termini along Via Nomentana (for foreign embassies)
No 116 (small electric bus) Via Giulia through the city centre to Villa Borghese park
No 175 Piazzale Partigiani car park at Stazione Ostiense to Stazione Termini
No 218 Piazza San Giovanni in Laterano to the Via Appia Antica and the catacombs
No 910 Stazione Termini to the Villa Borghese
No 590 Follows the route of Metro Linea A (includes facilities for disabled passengers)

Trams
There is a growing network of trams in Rome. Especially useful to tourists are routes Nos 2 (Piazzale Flaminio to Viale delle Belle Arti, for the Galleria Nazionale di Arte Moderna and Villa Borghese) and 8, from Largo di Torre Argentina to Trastevere (and on to Stazione Trastevere for trains to the airport).

J Buses
In addition to the ATAC system, Rome also has a private network of J buses (☎ 800-076 287) – express services covering a limited number of routes. They were introduced during the Jubilee Year of 2000 and it is expected (although not confirmed) that they will remain in operation throughout 2001 and beyond.

Tickets cost €0.98 and last 75 minutes. Day tickets cost €2.43, two-day tickets €4.13, three-day tickets €5.89 and weekly tickets €9.30.

Of the various routes, J4 and J5 are the most useful for tourists. Linea J4 runs from San Paolo Fuori-le-Mura via Stazione Ostiense, Circo Massimo, the Colosseum, Roman Forum, Teatro Marcello to Castel Sant'Angelo and the Stadio Olimpico. J5 runs from Stazione Tiburtina to San Giovanni, the Colosseum, Roman Forum, Largo di Torre Argentina and Corso Vittorio Emanuele to St Peter's.

Linea J3 goes to the catacombs from Termini via Piazza Santa Maria Maggiore and the Terme di Caracalla.

For further information visit online at www.linee-j.com (Italian only).

TRAIN
Apart from connections to the airports, Rome's overground rail network is useful only if you are heading out of town to the Castelli Romani, the beaches at Lido di Ostia or the ruins at Ostia Antica (see the Excursions chapter).

METRO
The Metropolitana (Metro) has two lines, Linea A and Linea B. Both pass through Stazione Termini. The Metro operates from 5.30 am to 11.30 pm (one hour later on Saturday) and trains run approximately every 5 to 10 minutes. See Map 1 for routes around the city. Useful Metro stations include:

station	line	attractions
Spagna	Linea A	Piazza di Spagna
Flaminio	Linea A	Villa Borghese
Ottaviano	Linea A	Vatican
Colosseo	Linea B	Colosseum
Circo Massimo	Linea B	Circo Massimo, Aventine, Caelian, Terme di Caracalla
Piramide	Linea B	Stazione Ostiense (for trains to Fiumicino and Lido di Ostia)

On Sundays you can take your bike on the Metro Linea B and the connecting Lido di Ostia train. You'll have to stamp two tickets – one for you and one for the bike – before you get on the train (front carriage only).

CAR & MOTORCYCLE
Negotiating Roman traffic by car is difficult enough but you may be taking your life into your hands if you ride a motorcycle or moped in the city. The rule in Rome is to look straight ahead to watch the vehicles in front, and hope that the vehicles behind are watching you!

Most of the historic centre of Rome is closed to normal traffic. Police control some of the entrances to the centre, while other entrances have electronic gates. Check with your hotel about gaining access (they may provide you with a special pass) – traffic officers might let you through if they see your car full of luggage but an electronic gate can't make a judgment so you'd probably receive a fine.

Traffic police are getting very tough on illegally parked cars. At best you'll get a heavy fine (around €100), at worst a wheel clamp or your car towed away. In the event that your car goes missing after it was parked illegally, always check first with the traffic

Stuck for a Parking Spot

Drive in Rome at your peril. According to the Italian newsagency Ansa, Italians spend an average of seven years of their lives sitting in their cars, and two years in the desperate search for a place to park them. The average time spent in getting from home to work by car rose from 45 minutes in 1994 to over an hour and a quarter in 2001.

ASA ANDERSSON

GETTING AROUND

police (☎ 06 676 91). You will have to pay about €95 to get it back, plus a hefty fine.

A pay parking system has been introduced around the periphery of Rome's city centre. Spaces are denoted by a blue line in most areas including the Lungotevere (the roads beside the River Tiber) and near Stazione Termini (Map 5). You'll need small change to get tickets from vending machines, otherwise scratch tickets are available from tobacconists. Parking costs €1.03/L2000 per hour.

The major parking area closest to the centre is at the Villa Borghese (Map 3); entry is from Piazzale Brasile at the top of Via Veneto. There is also a supervised car park at Stazione Termini. Other car parks are at Piazzale dei Partigiani, just outside Stazione Ostiense (Map 1; you can then take the Metro into central Rome from nearby Piramide Metro station) and at Stazione Tiburtina (Map 1), from where you can also catch the Metro into the centre.

Car Rental

There's no point renting a car to tour the city but it could be useful if you are travelling to destinations outside Rome. It is cheaper to arrange car rental before leaving your own country, for instance through some sort of fly/drive deal. Most major firms, including Hertz, Avis and Budget, will arrange this, and you simply pick up the vehicle at a nominated point upon arrival or on a specified day.

You will need to be aged 21 years or over (23 years or above for some companies) and possess a valid driving licence to rent a car in Italy. You will find the deal far easier to organise if you have a credit card. No matter where you rent, make sure you understand what is included in the price (unlimited kilometres, tax, insurance, collision damage waiver etc) and what your liabilities are. In some cases you are liable for penalties of between €260 to €520 if the car is stolen.

At the time of writing, Avis offered a special weekend rate for unlimited kilometres which compared well with rates offered by other firms: €150.81 for a Fiat Punto or

€255.13 for a Fiat Brava, from Friday 9 am to Monday 9 am. Maggiore National offered a weekend deal of €119.30 for a Fiat Punto, with a limit of 100km/day. If you pick up or drop off the car at an airport there is a surcharge of around €26. Renting the same car for five to seven days, with a limit of 1400km, costs €307.29.

Major rental companies include:

Avis
  24-hr booking (☎ 199 100 133)
  Ciampino airport (☎ 06 79 34 01 95)
  Fiumicino airport (☎ 06 65 01 15 31)
  Stazione Termini (☎ 06 481 43 73)
Europcar
  Central booking (☎ 06 52 08 11)
  Fiumicino airport (☎ 06 65 01 08 79)
  Stazione Termini (☎ 06 488 28 54)
Maggiore National
  Central booking (☎ 147 867 067)
  Fiumicino airport (☎ 06 65 01 06 78)
  Stazione Termini (☎ 06 488 00 49)

Motorcycle & Moped Rental

Motorcycles, scooters and mopeds can be rented from Happy Rent (Map 5; ☎ 06 481 81 85), Via Farini 3, off Via Cavour between Stazione Termini and Piazza Esquilino. Motorcycle (600cc) rental costs €103.29 per day and scooters and mopeds (50cc to 125cc) cost from €30.99 to €67.14 per day. Happy Rent also rents cars and minivans (baby seats are available) but prices are higher than the major car rental companies. All major credit cards are accepted.

Another option is Bici e Baci (Map 5; ☎ 06 482 84 43), Via del Viminale 5, near Piazza della Repubblica. Scooter rental starts at €25.82 per day. All major credit cards are accepted.

Treno e Scooter (Map 5; ☎ 06 48 90 58 23) at Stazione Termini, on the north-eastern side of the bus terminus at Piazza dei Cinquecento, also rents mopeds and scooters. A 50cc moped costs €23.24 for four hours, €41.32 for a day and €165.27 for a week. A 125cc scooter costs €41.32 for four hours, €59.39 per day or €237.57 per week. The organisation operates in conjunction with the railways and various environmental groups and if you show a train ticket, you are entitled to a 10% discount on the first day's rental. Chains, locks, helmet and goggles are included, and the organisation will also provide assistance if you break down during office hours. A cash or credit-card deposit is required. It opens 8.30 am to 7.30 pm daily.

See also the Bicycle section later in this chapter.

TAXI

Taxis are on radio call 24 hours a day in Rome. Cooperativa Radio Taxi Romana (☎ 06 3570), La Capitale (☎ 06 4994) and Samarcanda (☎ 06 5551) are three of the many operators.

Strictly speaking, taxis are not allowed to be hailed in the street. Major taxi ranks are at the airports, Stazione Termini, Largo di Torre Argentina, Piazza San Silvestro and Piazza Venezia.

There are surcharges for luggage, night service, public holidays and travel to and from the airports. The minimum charge is €2.32 (for the first 3km), then €0.62 per kilometre. There is a €2.58 supplement from 10 pm to 7 am and €1.03 from 7 am to 10 pm on Sunday and public holidays. Each large bag or suitcase costs €1.03 extra. If you phone for a taxi, the driver will turn on the meter immediately and you will pay the cost of travel from wherever the driver was when the call was received.

BICYCLE

If you ignore the fact that Rome was built on seven hills and that most Roman drivers are crazy, cycling is a good way to cover a lot of ground quickly. There are some cycle paths along the River Tiber to the north and south of the city centre, but it's you against the traffic in most areas. The Comune di Roma is planning to create more cycle paths but, as with many city council projects, their realisation is a slow process. Via dei Fori Imperiali is closed to traffic on Sunday, and you can cycle virtually all the way to the Appia Antica from Piazza Venezia on traffic-free roads.

Uneven cobblestones are the most common hazard for cyclists, followed by potholes and very slippery roads when it rains.

Bicycle Rental

Bici e Baci (see Motorcycle & Moped Rental earlier in this chapter) rents bicycles from €7.75 per day.

Treno e Scooter (see Motorcycle & Moped Rental earlier in this chapter) rents bikes for €2.06 per hour, €5.16 per day or €18.07 per week. Mountain bikes can be hired for €3.61 per hour, €9.29 per day and €27.89 per week. Chains and locks are included in the price. As the organisation is linked with the railways, if you show a train ticket you get a 20% discount on the first day's rental. A cash or credit-card deposit is required.

Cicli Collati (Map 8; ☎ 06 68 80 10 84), at Via del Pellegrino 80–82 near Campo de' Fiori, rents bikes by the hour (€2.58), half-day (€5.16) and day (€7.75). Discounts are given for longer-term rentals. Baby seats and kids' bikes are also available.

Bicycles are usually available for rent in Piazza del Popolo and at the Villa Borghese.

WALKING

The historic centre of Rome is relatively small and quite manageable on foot. Walking is a great way to see the city, as around every corner there's another pretty square, magnificent building or picturesque fountain to appreciate. Make sure you wear comfortable shoes. See the Rome Walks chapter for detailed routes.

ORGANISED TOURS
Bus Tours

ATAC operates a special air-conditioned tourist bus, No 110, which leaves from the bus terminus in front of Stazione Termini every half-hour from 9 am to 8 pm daily. Commentary is provided in English, Italian and several other languages. The tour takes three hours and the bus stops at Piazza del Popolo, Piazza San Pietro, Piazza del Campidoglio, Circo Massimo and the Colosseum. Tickets cost €7.75 and are available from the ATAC information booth on stand C at the terminus. For more information see under Bus & Tram earlier in this chapter.

Green Line Tours (Map 5; ☎ 06 482 74 80), Via Farini 5a, near Piazza Esquilino, operates various tours including Classical,

GETTING AROUND

Imperial and Christian Rome designed for lazy tourists. The night-time tour of illuminated Rome gives you a different perspective on the city. Each tour costs €25.82.

Ciao Roma (Map 5; ☎ 06 87 40 64 81), Via Giolitti 34, organises similar classic and religious tours with recorded commentary in ten languages. A small bus (painted to look like an old trolley car) zips you around Rome. Each tour costs €15.49.

Walking & Cycling Tours

Enjoy Rome (Map 5; ☎ 06 445 18 43), Via Varese 39, organises walking tours of the major sights for groups of 15 to 20 people most days of the week. The tour lasts three hours and tickets cost €15.49. Enjoy Rome also organises bicycle tours, which last 3½ hours. Tickets (€18.07) include bike and helmet rental.

Scala Reale (Map 5; ☎ 06 474 56 73), Via Varese 52, is run by an American-Italian couple who organise (by prior arrangement) themed walks in small groups with knowledgeable guides. Bike and scooter tours can also be arranged. Visit online at www.scalareale.org.

Through Eternity (☎ 06 700 9335) gives tours led by enthusiastic 'storytellers' who are passionate about their subject and make Rome come alive. Twilight tours (€15.49) of Renaissance and Baroque Rome show the city in arguably its best light, and 'Feast of Bacchus' wine sampling tours combine aesthetic and gastronomic pleasures. Check out its Web site at www.througheternity.com.

Things to See & Do

The historic centre of Rome is small, and most of the major attractions are packed within the city walls. However, there are a number of sights farther afield that are well worth the extra effort to visit, including the catacombs dotted along the Appia Antica. Most of these locations are easily reached by Metro, bus or tram (for information on Rome's public transport system see the Getting Around chapter).

Be flexible with your sightseeing, as unpredictability is a fact of life in Rome. It's not unusual to find that churches, museums or archaeological sites on your well planned itinerary are closed when you get there. This could be due to any number of factors, from ongoing excavations to lack of personnel. Relax, have a *cappuccino* or a *gelato*, and head for the next ancient wonder or Baroque architectural extravagance on your list.

Most churches open around 7 am to midday, and reopen around 3.30 or 4 pm to 6 or 6.30 pm daily. Opening hours that vary drastically have been listed. In some of the larger churches you may be able to wander around during Mass without disturbing worshippers, particularly if the service is being held in one of the side chapels.

Museum admission is generally free for those aged under 18 or over 65 and there are usually discounts for students and those aged under 26. The prices here indicate full admission.

Culture vultures in Rome for several days who really want to *do* the sights should consider buying a five-day ticket (€15.49), which gives admission to the Colosseum, Palatine, and the four Museo Nazionale Romano sights – Palazzo Massimo alle Terme, Terme di Diocleziano, Palazzo Altemps and Crypta Balbi.

PIAZZA DEL CAMPIDOGLIO (Map 4)

Designed by Michelangelo in 1538 and located on the Capitoline, this square is bordered by three palaces: the Palazzo Nuovo on the northern side, the Palazzo Senatorio at the rear, and the Palazzo dei Conservatori on the southern side. The palace facades were also designed by Michelangelo.

This hill, now the seat of the city's municipal government, was the political centre of ancient Rome and where Nelson hoisted the British flag in 1799 before he prevented Napoleon from entering the city. The Palazzo Senatorio opens to the public 9 am to 4 pm on Sunday. Admission is free but you need to bring some identification.

For the greatest visual impact, approach the square from Piazza d'Aracoeli and ascend the *cordonata*, a stepped ramp also designed by Michelangelo. It is guarded at the bottom by two ancient-Egyptian granite lions and at the top by two mammoth statues of Castor and Pollux, which were found in the nearby Ghetto in the 16th century.

The bronze, equestrian statue of Marcus Aurelius in the centre of the square is a copy. The original, which dates from the 2nd century AD, was badly damaged by pollution, weather and pigeon poo, and was removed in

Roma Gratis

The following sights won't burn a hole in your pocket – they're free:

- Roman Forum
- Pantheon
- Views from the Pincio, the Gianicolo and the Capitoline
- Trevi Fountain
- Bocca della Verità
- St Peter's Basilica
- Every church in Rome
- Sistine Chapel and Vatican Museums on the last Sunday of the month
- Walking through Villa Borghese or Villa Pamphilj parks

1981. See the boxed text 'A Case of Mistaken Identity'.

In front of the Palazzo Senatorio's double staircase is a fountain displaying a marble and porphyry statue of a sitting **Minerva**, which dates from the time of Domitian. The statue sits uncomfortably on an elevated plinth and is about the only thing in the square that seems out of proportion. On either side of it are colossal statues representing the Tiber (on the right) and the Nile (on the left). Martino Longhi il Vecchio's bell tower replaced an old medieval tower in 1578.

At the bottom of the Capitoline, next to the staircase leading up to Santa Maria in Aracoeli, are the ruins of a Roman apartment block or *insula*. Only the upper storeys are visible; three lower levels are buried below current street level. Buildings of this type were used to house the urban poor, who lived in cramped and squalid conditions.

Capitoline Museums

The Capitoline Museums (Musei Capitolini) is the world's oldest public sculpture gallery and was started in 1471, when Pope Sixtus IV donated the first group of bronze sculptures to the city. Subsequent popes followed suit as the city expanded and further ancient statues were unearthed. The museums are comprised of the Palazzo Nuovo on the left side of the square (looking at Palazzo Senatorio) and the Palazzo dei Conservatori opposite. Together they form one of the world's most impressive collections of ancient sculpture.

The Capitoline Museums open 10 am to 9 pm (last tickets 8 pm) Tuesday to Sunday. Admission costs €6.19.

The **Palazzo Nuovo** is the permanent home of many important works, including statues of Roman emperors and other famous personages. The beautiful and sensual

A Case of Mistaken Identity

The original equestrian statue of Marcus Aurelius is one of only a handful of ancient bronzes not to have been melted down. This statue survived because it had been incorrectly identified as Constantine, the first Christian emperor, an opinion which was maintained for centuries.

Marcus Aurelius was emperor from AD 161 to 180 and is remembered as both a warrior and a philosopher. He spent almost 10 years of his reign on the Danube fighting the local tribes which threatened the border; his victories are commemorated on his Column.

This statue represents him mounted on his horse, addressing his people. The horse's right hoof, now hanging loose, originally rested on the head of a defeated barbarian. Traces of the gold plating that once covered the statue are still visible on the emperor's face and coat and on the horse's head and back. Legend has it that when the gold plating is restored, an owl's hoot will sound from the tuft of hair between the horse's ears, announcing the Last Judgment.

Since the Renaissance, the statue has been used as a model for equestrian monuments. Paul III ordered it to be brought to the Campidoglio from Piazza di San Giovanni in Laterano in 1538. He replaced it in San Giovanni with the 31m obelisk of Tutmosis III which had been found at the Circo Massimo.

The statue on display in the square is a very good modern copy, executed using a computer. Having recently undergone 10 years of restoration, the original was put on display behind glass in the safety of the Palazzo Nuovo.

ASA ANDERSSON

Venere Capitolina (Capitoline Venus), a Roman copy of a 3rd-century-BC Greek original, is on display in a small chamber of her own. Busts of philosophers, poets and politicians, among them Sophocles, Homer, Epicuros and Cicero line the Sala dei Filosofi, while the walls of this and other galleries are punctuated by marble epigraphs originally in the Tabularium. Other impressive pieces include the *Galata Morente* (Dying Gaul), a Roman copy of an original 3rd-century-BC Greek work, a *Satiro in Riposo* (Resting Satyr) and the red-marble *Satiro Ridente* (Laughing Satyr) holding a bunch of grapes – the Marble Faun of Nathaniel Hawthorne's novel.

Stairs to the lower-ground floor lead to a tunnel between Palazzo Nuovo and Palazzo dei Conservatori. A connecting passage leads to the **Tabularium** of Palazzo Senatorio, the state archive of ancient Rome, which was built in 78 BC and turned into a salt deposit and prison in the early Middle Ages. The superb views over the Roman Forum from here are unparalleled.

The most famous piece in the **Palazzo dei Conservatori** is the *Lupa Capitolina* (Capitoline Wolf), an Etruscan bronze statue from the 6th century BC. The figures of Romulus and Remus were added by Antonio Pollaiuolo around 1509. It stands in a room of its own, the Sala della Lupa, on the 1st floor. Also of interest in this wing is the *Spinario*, a delicate bronze statue of a boy taking a thorn from his foot, dating from the 1st century BC.

The inner court of the ground floor of the Palazzo dei Conservatori contains the fascinating remains of a colossal statue of Constantine – the head, a hand and a foot – which were once part of a 12m high acrolith (a composition made of marble and cloth held together by a frame) originally in the apse of the Basilica di Constantino in the Roman Forum. It depicted the seated emperor with his index finger raised to symbolise the direct contact with God that enabled him to govern with divine inspiration. In the portico on the far side of the courtyard there is a huge Trajanic statue representing Rome. It stands between two grey-marble statues of captive barbarian kings (2nd century AD) and another marble head from a colossal statue of Constantine's son and successor, Constans II.

The wall on the left displays high reliefs representing the provinces under Roman dominion, taken from the inner sanctuary in Hadrian's Temple. Above them is an inscription from a triumphal arch, which once stood in Via Lata, commemorating Claudius' conquest of Britain in AD 43.

The **Pinacoteca** on the 2nd floor contains fine paintings and is well worth a visit if the sculpture hasn't worn you out. Artists from the Venetian school, including Giovanni Bellini, Paolo Veronese, Titian and Tintoretto are represented and there are works by Guido Reni, Federico Zucchari, Salvator Rosa, Van Dyck and Rubens. There are also paintings by Domenichino, Guido Reni, Poussin, the Carracci family, Pietro da Cortona and others. Highlights include Caravaggio's sensual *San Giovanni Battista* in his fully fledged realist style and Guercino's immense *Santa Petronilla*, a mosaic of which is in St Peter's Basilica. Both are in the Sala di Santa Petronilla.

The cafe on the 2nd floor of the Palazzo dei Conservatori has decent snacks and fabulous views.

Many of the sculptures from the Palazzo dei Conservatori, including pieces which have rarely or never been on display before, have been transferred to a former thermoelectric plant in Via Ostiense, south of the city centre. See Capitoline Museums at Centrale Montemartini later in this chapter.

Chiesa di Santa Maria in Aracoeli

The church of Santa Maria in Aracoeli is between Piazza del Campidoglio and the Vittoriano monument at the highest point of the Capitoline hill. It is accessible either by a long flight of steps from Piazza d'Aracoeli or from behind the Palazzo Nuovo.

The austere brick church is built on the site where legend says the Tiburtine Sybil told Augustus of the coming birth of Christ and dates from before the 7th century. In the 10th century it belonged to Benedictine monks and in the 13th century it was rebuilt in the Romanesque style by the Franciscans but the facade was never completed. The church features frescoes by Pinturicchio, painted in the 1480s, in the first chapel of the southern aisle. It is noted for a statue of the baby Jesus said to have been carved from the wood of an olive tree from the garden of Gethsemane. In 1994 the statue was stolen and a replica is on display. The ceiling is decorated with naval motifs, commemorating the Battle of Lepanto.

PIAZZA VENEZIA (Map 4)

The square is overshadowed by **Il Vittoriano**, definitely one of Italy's more unusual monuments, which was begun in 1885 to commemorate Italian unification and to honour Victor Emmanuel II, the first king of united Italy. Since its inauguration in 1911, it has often been mockingly referred to by Italians as the *macchina da scrivere* (typewriter). The monument incorporates the Altare della Patria (Altar of the Fatherland) and the tomb of the unknown soldier.

Witty commentators have suggested that the Vittoriano is the best address in the city as it's the only place you can't see the structure itself. But this much maligned monument is in fact Italy's biggest open-air museum of Art Nouveau, with some fabulous sculptures, and the view from its highest level (a portico with 15m-high columns) gives a new perspective on Rome – north to Piazza del Popolo and St Peter's and south over the Roman Forum. It opens 10 am to one hour before sunset Tuesday to Sunday. Admission is free.

The **Museo del Risorgimento** (☎ 06 678 06 64) is located beneath the Vittoriano; it hosts temporary exhibitions. The entrance is on Via di San Pietro in Carcere.

On the western side of the square is the **Palazzo Venezia**, the first great Renaissance palace in Rome, which was partially built with materials quarried from the Colosseum. It was built for the Venetian cardinal Pietro Barbo, who later became Pope Paul II. Work began on the square in 1455 but bits were added until the 16th century. Mussolini used it as his official residence and

made some of his famous speeches from the balcony. Major art exhibitions are held here and part of the building houses the Museo del Palazzo di Venezia. For information on exhibitions contact the museum (see that section later in this chapter).

Actually part of the Palazzo Venezia, but facing onto Piazza San Marco, the **Basilica di San Marco** was founded in the 4th century in honour of St Mark the Evangelist. After undergoing several major transformations over the centuries, the church has a Renaissance facade, a Romanesque bell tower and a largely Baroque interior. The main attraction is the 9th-century mosaic in the apse, which depicts Christ with saints and Pope Gregory IV.

Museo del Palazzo di Venezia

The rooms of the former Appartamento Cybo in Palazzo Venezia house the Museo del Palazzo di Venezia, which exhibits a fine collection of paintings and decorative arts.

The painted, coffered ceilings are particularly notable. The first room as you enter contains medieval altarpieces and panel paintings. Paolo Veneziano's 14th-century *Coro di Angeli*, depicting a group of angels with musical instruments, Jacopo da Montagnana's triptych and Pisanello's *Testa di Donna*, a fresco fragment of a woman's head with delicately worked hair, all stand out.

Among the paintings by artists of the 14th- and 15th-century Tuscan school are two beautiful reliquaries (decorated with delicate images of the Madonna and saints) by the so-called Master of Santa Chiara da Montefalco and a splendid, well preserved triptych *Madonna col Bambino, Santa Lucia e Santa Caterina d'Alessandria* by Giovanni Antonio da Pesaro, with the Crucifixion and the Annunciation depicted in the upper panels. Also of note is the two-sided altarpiece of *La Madonna della Misericordia*, with St John the Baptist and St Sebastian on the reverse.

Notable late-15th-century Tuscan works include a remnant of Benozzo Gozzoli's fresco of *Il Redentore* (The Redeemer), a beautiful *Natività* (Nativity) from the workshop of Filippo Lippi and a small oblong panel in vibrantly rich colours of the *Matirio di Santa Caterina d'Alessandria* showing the moment when the saint is beheaded.

Other highlights of the painting collection are: Guercino's canvas of *San Pietro*; Carlo Maratta's *Cleopatra*, which clothes the Egyptian queen in 17th-century fashion; and Orazio Borgianni's late-16th-century *Cristo Deposto* (The Deposition), a prostrate Christ viewed from his feet, which recalls Mantegna's famous foreshortened image of *Cristo Morto* in the Pinacoteca di Brera in Milan. One room is devoted exclusively to 18th- and 19th-century pastels.

The decorative arts collection contains jewellery, tapestries, silver, ivories, ceramics, hundreds of 15th- to 17th-century bronze figurines spread over several rooms and carved wooden wedding chests as well as a collection of arms and armour.

The entrance to the museum (☎ 06 679 88 65) is at Via del Plebiscito 118. It opens 8.30 am to 7.30 pm Tuesday to Sunday (closed Monday). Admission costs €4.13.

FORI IMPERIALI (Maps 4 & 5)

The Fori Imperiali (Imperial Forums) – Foro di Traiano, Foro di Augusto, Foro di Cesare, Foro di Nerva and Foro di Vespasiano – were built by various emperors between 42 BC and AD 112. In 1933, Mussolini built a grand thoroughfare, the Via dei Fori, as a symbolic link of the Fascist regime with the marvels of ancient Rome and a practical link between Piazza Venezia and the Colosseum. In the process, many 16th-century buildings were destroyed and the Fori Imperiali were almost completely covered. Archaeological excavations are continuing on both sides of Via dei Fori Imperiali to recover some of the buried treasures. Admission to the public is prohibited. For details on accessing other closed archaeological sites see the boxed text 'Open Only on Request' later in this chapter.

The most extensively excavated of the Fori Imperiali is the **Foro di Traiano** (Trajan's Forum; Map 4), the last of the forums. Designed by Apollodorus of Damascus for Trajan and constructed at the beginning of the 2nd century AD, it was a vast complex, measuring 300m by 185m, and comprised a basilica for the judiciary, two libraries – one Greek and one Latin – a temple, a triumphal arch, and the **Colonna di Traiano** (Trajan's Column; Map 4). Restored in the late 1980s, the column was erected to mark the victories of Trajan over the Dacians, who lived in what is now Romania. After it was built, Trajan's ashes were interred in a golden urn at the base of the column. The urn, along with the ashes, disappeared during one of the barbarian sacks of Rome.

The column is decorated with a spiral series of reliefs depicting the battles between the Roman and Dacian armies, which are regarded as among the finest examples of ancient-Roman sculpture. A golden statue of Trajan once topped the column but it was lost during the Middle Ages and replaced with a statue of St Peter. Apart from the column, all that remains of the forum are some pillars which once formed part of the Basilica Ulpia, ancient Rome's largest basilica.

In comparison, the **Mercati di Traiano** (Trajan's Markets; Map 5) are well preserved. Also designed by Apollodorus, the markets were constructed on three levels, comprising six floors of shops and offices in a semicircle. This was the ancient equivalent of a modern multilevel shopping centre, selling everything from wine and oil to fresh fruit, vegetables and flowers to imported silks and spices. You can get an idea of their grandeur from the high vaulted roofs. It's worth paying the admission fee if only to reach the high levels of the market, from where there are spectacular views across to the Roman Forum.

The entrance to Trajan's Markets (☎ 06 679 00 48) is at Via IV Novembre 94. They open 9 am to 7 pm, Tuesday to Sunday. Admission costs €6.19. Theoretically the ticket also gives admission to the Foro di Traiano, although parts of it are often off limits due to excavations.

The tall red-brick tower above the market buildings, the **Torre delle Milizie**, was built in the 13th century for defensive purposes. There is a delightful walkway beneath the loggia of the 12th-century **Casa dei Cavalieri di Rodi** (Ancient Seat of the Knights of St John of Jerusalem), which is between the Foro di Traiano and the Foro di Augusto, and accessible from either Via dei Fori Imperiali or Piazza del Grillo. The building itself, which contains a beautiful chapel, is open only by appointment.

Augustus ordered the **Foro di Augusto** (Forum of Augustus; Map 5) to be built in 42 BC but it was not completed and dedicated until 40 years later. Three columns of a temple dedicated to Mars the Avenger are still standing and others have been reconstructed from fragments, but over half the original area is now covered by Via dei Fori Imperiali. The 30m-high wall behind the Foro di Augusto was built to protect the area from the fires that frequently swept through the area known as the Suburra.

Next to the Foro di Augusto is the **Foro di Nerva** (Map 5), much of which is also covered by Via dei Fori Imperiali. Part of a temple dedicated to Minerva still remains on the site. The temple was still standing in the 17th century when Pope Paul V had it pulled down to provide marble for the Fontana dell'Acqua Paola on the Gianicolo. The Foro di Nerva connected the Foro di Augusto to the **Foro di Vespasiano**, also known as the Forum of Peace, which was built in AD 70 by Vespasian. A large hall was converted in the 6th century into a church, Santi Cosma e Damiano (see that section later).

Across the Via dei Fori Imperiali is the **Foro di Cesare** (Caesar's Forum; Roman Forum map), built by Julius Caesar at the foot of the Capitoline. It is not open to the public but can be viewed from Via dei Fori Imperiali. Caesar claimed the goddess Venus in his family tree and his forum included a temple to her as Venus Genetrix – Venus the Ancestor. All that remains today are three columns on a platform. Trajan made various additions to the forum, including the Basilica Argentaria, a financial exchange, some shops and a heated public lavatory.

Following Via di San Pietro in Carcere you come to the ancient **Carcere Mamertino** (Mamertine Prison), where condemned prisoners were garrotted. St Peter is believed to have been held here prior to his trial and to have created a miraculous stream of water to baptise his jailers and his fellow prisoners. The site was later consecrated and is now the church of San Pietro in Carcere.

ANCIENT ROME
Roman Forum (Maps 5 & 7)
The commercial, political and religious centre of ancient Rome, the Roman Forum (Foro Romano) stands in a valley between the Capitoline and Palatine hills. Originally marshland, the area was drained during the early Republican era and became a centre for political rallies, public ceremonies and Senate meetings. The forum was constructed over 900 years, with later emperors erecting buildings next to those from the Republican era. Its importance declined along with the Roman Empire after the 4th century AD, and the temples, monuments and buildings constructed by successive emperors and senators fell into ruin, eventually leading to the site being used as pasture land. In the Middle Ages the area was known as the Campo Vaccino (literally 'cow field'), an interesting example of history repeating itself, since the valley in which the forum stood was used as pasture land in the earliest days of Rome's development.

During medieval times the area was extensively plundered for its stone and precious marble. Many temples and buildings had been converted to other uses and other monuments lay half-revealed. Ironically, the physical destruction of ancient Rome can be blamed not on the invading barbarians or natural disasters but on Romans themselves. Over the centuries, in the name of progress, Romans dismantled the ancient city brick by brick and marble block by marble block in order to build their own palaces, churches and monuments.

With renewed appreciation of all things classical during the Renaissance, the forum provided inspiration for artists and architects. The area was systematically excavated in the 18th and 19th centuries and excavations are still continuing today. You can watch archaeological teams at work in several locations.

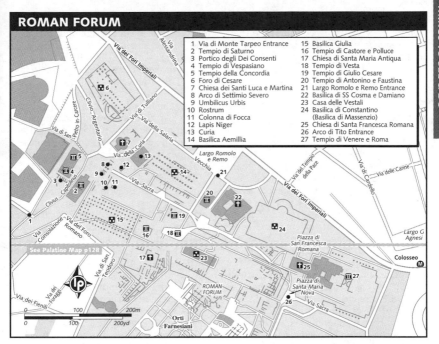

ROMAN FORUM

1 Via di Monte Tarpeo Entrance
2 Tempio di Saturno
3 Portico degli Dei Consenti
4 Tempio di Vespasiano
5 Tempio della Concordia
6 Foro di Cesare
7 Chiesa dei Santi Luca e Martina
8 Arco di Settimio Severo
9 Umbilicus Urbis
10 Rostrum
11 Colonna di Focca
12 Lapis Niger
13 Curia
14 Basilica Aemillia
15 Basilica Giulia
16 Tempio di Castore e Polluce
17 Chiesa di Santa Maria Antiqua
18 Tempio di Vesta
19 Tempio di Giulio Cesare
20 Tempio di Antonino e Faustina
21 Largo Romolo e Remo Entrance
22 Basilica di SS Cosma e Damiano
23 Casa delle Vestali
24 Basilica di Constantino
  (Basilica di Massenzio)
25 Chiesa di Santa Francesca Romana
26 Arco di Tito Entrance
27 Tempio di Venere e Roma

There are three entrances to the forum: Largo Romolo e Remo off Via dei Fori Imperiali; at the eastern end near the Arco di Tito at Piazza di Santa Maria Nova; and from the Capitoline at Via di Monte Tarpeo. It opens 9 am to 6 pm (to 4 pm in winter) Monday to Saturday and 9 am to 2 pm on Sunday. Admission is free. There are guided tours in English every day at noon €3.10.

If you enter from Via dei Fori Imperiali, to your left is the **Tempio di Antonino e Faustina**, erected by the Senate in AD 141 and dedicated to the Empress Faustina and later, after his death, to Antoninus Pius. It was transformed into the Chiesa di San Lorenzo in Miranda in the 8th century. To your right is the **Basilica Aemilia**, built in 179 BC. The building was 100m long and its facade was a two-storey portico lined with shops. Destroyed and rebuilt several times, the basilica was almost completely demolished during the Renaissance, when it was plundered for its precious marble.

The **Via Sacra**, which traverses the forum from north-west to south-east, runs in front of the basilica. Continuing along Via Sacra in the direction of the Capitoline, you will reach the **Curia**, just after the Basilica Aemilia on the right. Once the meeting place of the Roman Senate, it was rebuilt successively by Julius Caesar, Augustus, Domitian and, after a fire in the 3rd century AD, by Diocletian. It was converted into a church in the Middle Ages. The church was dismantled and the Curia restored in the 1930s to the form it had under Diocletian. The bronze doors are copies – the Roman originals were moved by Borromini to San Giovanni in Laterano.

In front of the Curia is the **Lapis Niger**, a piece of black marble, which covered a sacred area. According to legend, the tomb of Romulus was beneath it. Down a flight of stairs (rarely open to the public), under the Lapis Niger, is the oldest known Latin inscription, dating from the 6th century BC.

The **Arco di Settimio Severo** (Arch of Septimius Severus) is considered one of Italy's major triumphal arches. According to the inscription on both sides of the arch, it was erected in AD 203 in honour of Emperor Septimius Severus and his sons, Caracalla and Geta. After Caracalla murdered his brother, the inscription was altered so that the words *optimis fortissimisque principibus* were inscribed over Geta's name. If you look closely at the fourth line of the inscription, you can see the original lettering.

To the south is the **Rostrum**, used in ancient times by public speakers and once decorated with the rams of captured ships. A circular-based stone, the Umbilicus Urbis (Navel of the World), beside the arch marks the symbolic centre of ancient Rome.

Southwards along the Via Sacra lies the **Tempio di Saturno** (Temple of Saturn), inaugurated in 497 BC and one of the most important temples in ancient Rome. It was used as the city's treasury and during Caesar's rule contained 13 tonnes of gold, 114 tonnes of silver and 30 million *sestertii* in coined silver. Eight granite columns are all that remain. Behind the temple and backing onto the Capitoline are (roughly from north to south) the ruins of the **Tempio della Concordia** (Temple of Concord), the three remaining columns of the **Tempio di Vespasiano** (Temple of Vespasian) and the **Portico degli Dei Consenti**, of which 12 columns remain (five are restorations). The remains of the **Basilica Giulia**, which was the seat of civil justice, are just across from Basilica Aemilia, at what is known as Piazza del Foro. The square was the site of the original forum, which served as the main meeting place during the Republican era.

The **Colonna di Foca** (Column of Phocus), which stands in the square and dates from AD 608, was the last monument erected in the forum. It honoured the Byzantine emperor Phocus who donated the Pantheon to the church. At the south-eastern end of the square is the **Tempio di Giulio Cesare** (Temple of Julius Caesar), which was erected by Augustus in 29 BC on the site where Caesar's body was burned and Mark Antony delivered his famous speech.

Back towards the Palatine is the **Tempio dei Castore e Polluce** (Temple of Castor and Pollux; also known as the Tempio dei Dioscuri), built in 489 BC to mark the defeat of the Etruscan Tarquins and in honour of the Heavenly Twins, or Dioscuri, who miraculously appeared to deliver the news of an important victory. Three elegant Corinthian columns from the temple, which served at times as a banking hall and also housed the city's weights and measures office, survive today. The temple was restored during the 1980s.

In the area south-east of the temple is the **Chiesa di Santa Maria Antiqua**, the oldest Christian church in the forum. Inside the church are some early Christian frescoes. This area, including the church, has been closed to the public since 1992.

Back on the Via Sacra is the **Casa delle Vestali** (House of the Vestal Virgins), home of the virgins who tended the sacred flame in the adjoining **Tempio di Vesta**. The six virgin priestesses, aged between six and 10 years, were selected from patrician families. They had to serve in the temple for 30 years and during this time they were bound by a vow of chastity. The Tempio di Vesta was a circular building surrounded by columns. The sacred flame burnt in the inner chamber, known as the *cella*, and was regarded as the hearth fire of Rome itself. Any priestess who allowed it to go out was beaten. A Vestal accused of breaking her vows of chastity was entombed alive on the reasoning that if she were innocent, then Vesta herself would rescue her. The man involved was taken outside the city walls and clubbed to death.

The next major monument is the vast **Basilica di Costantino**, also known as the Basilica di Massenzio. Maxentius initiated work on the basilica and it was finished in AD 315 by Constantine. Its impressive design provided inspiration for Renaissance architects, possibly including Michelangelo, who is said to have studied its construction when he was designing the dome for San Pietro. The basilica was the largest building in the forum, covering an area of approximately 100m by 65m, and was used for business and the administration of justice. The three massive barrel-vaulted aisles that remain today were used as law courts. One of the basilica's original columns now stands in Piazza Santa Maria Maggiore. A colossal statue of Constantine was unearthed at the site in 1487. Pieces of this statue are on display in the courtyard of the Palazzo dei Conservatori in the Capitoline Museums (see that section earlier in this chapter).

The **Arco di Tito** (Arch of Titus), at the Colosseum-end of the forum, was built in AD 81 in honour of the victories of the future emperor Titus against the Jewish rebels in Jerusalem. Titus is represented with Victory personified on one of the reliefs on the inside of the arch; the spoils of Jerusalem are paraded in a triumphal procession on the other. Along with the Arco di Costantino (see that section later in the chapter), this arch was incorporated into a fortress by the Frangipani family in the Middle Ages.

Santi Cosma e Damiano & Santa Francesca Romana (Roman Forum Map)

East towards the Colosseum along Via dei Fori Imperiali, past the entrance to the Roman Forum, is the 6th-century Basilica di Santi Cosma e Damiano dedicated to the brothers St Cosmas and St Damian who were doctors with miraculous healing powers.

The church once incorporated a large hall, which formed part of the Foro di Vespasiano. The 6th-century mosaics, located in the apse, were restored in 1989 and are among the most beautiful in Rome. The central figure of Christ against a deep-blue background is flanked by St Peter and St Paul (in white robes), who are presenting St Cosmas and St Damian to him. On the far left is St Felix, holding up a model of the church, and on the right is St Theodore. Below this scene is a frieze of the Lamb of God (representing Christ) and his flock of 12 lambs (representing the Apostles). These mosaics were copied in several Roman churches, especially during the 9th century. Make sure you have plenty of spare change as this is the meanest mosaic lighting system in Rome – €0.26 gives you the briefest of glimpses of these stunning mosaics.

In a room off the 17th-century cloisters is a vast Neapolitan *presepio* (nativity scene), dating from the 18th century. Children in particular will love this wonderful model, which places the birth of Jesus among Neapolitan folk going about their daily business. Dotted around the finely crafted wooden and terracotta figures are animals, a chestnut vendor, a fruit seller, grape harvester, a soldier and an innkeeper. It can be viewed (a donation of €0.52 is requested) 9.30 am to 12.30 pm and 3 to 6.30 pm.

Past the Basilica di Costantino there is a small stairway leading to Chiesa di Santa Francesca Romana. Built in the 9th century over an earlier oratory, the church (also known as Santa Maria Nova) incorporates part of the Tempio di Venere e Roma (Temple of Venus and Rome). It has a lovely Romanesque bell tower.

There is a 12th-century mosaic in the apse of the Madonna and child and saints, as well as a 7th-century painting of the Madonna and child above the high altar. During restoration works in 1949, another painting of the Madonna and child was discovered beneath the 7th-century work. Dating from the early 5th century and probably taken from the Chiesa di Santa Maria Antiqua in the Roman Forum, this precious painting is now in the sacristy which you can enter if the sacristan is around.

Francesca Romana is the patron saint of motorists; on 9 March (her feast day) drivers park their vehicles close to the church to be blessed. Her skeleton, wrapped in a white diaphanous cloth, holding a book and wearing rather modern-looking, black-leather slippers, is in a chapel under the altar (steps lead down from both sides).

Palatine (Map 7)

The Palatine hill (Palatino) was the mythical founding place of Rome and where the remains of Iron Age huts have been unearthed. You reach the Palatine from the forum by following the Clivio Palatino to the right from the Arco di Tito. There is another entrance at Via di San Gregorio 30. It opens 9 am to 6 pm March and April, 9 am to 7 pm May to August, 9 am to 6.30 pm

PALATINE

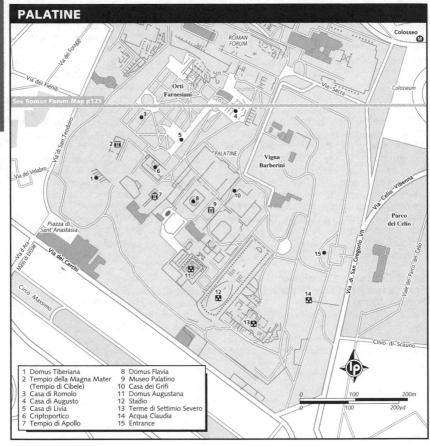

Key to map:

1 Domus Tiberiana	8 Domus Flavia
2 Tempio della Magna Mater	9 Museo Palatino
(Tempio di Cibele)	10 Casa dei Grifi
3 Casa di Romolo	11 Domus Augustana
4 Casa di Augusto	12 Stadio
5 Casa di Livia	13 Terme di Settimio Severo
6 Criptoportico	14 Acqua Claudia
7 Tempio di Apollo	15 Entrance

September and October and 9 am to 4.30 pm November to February. Admission costs €6.19 and includes entry to the Museo Palatino (see later in this section).

Favoured by its situation above the Tiber and its exposure to sea breezes, the Palatine was the most desirable spot for wealthy Romans to build their homes during the Republican era. It later became the realm of the emperors. Augustus was born on the Palatine and lived there throughout his life, although his residences were modest compared to those of subsequent rulers. This was extended first into the Domus Tiberiana

and further grand complexes were added by subsequent emperors, including Caligula and Domitian – inspiring, in fact, the very word 'palace'.

The Palatine became an important centre in Roman life and remained so into the early Middle Ages. Representatives of the Byzantine emperors lived on the Palatine in the 7th century, as did some popes.

Like those of the forum, the temples and palaces of the Palatine fell into ruin and in the Middle Ages a few churches, monasteries and castles were built over the remains. During the Renaissance, wealthy families established their gardens on the hill, notably Cardinal Alessandro Farnese, who had elaborate gardens laid out over the ruins.

The largest part of the Palatine as it appears today is covered by ruins of a vast complex built for Emperor Domitian, which served as the main imperial palace for 300 years. This was an ambitious project to create an official imperial palace, the Domus Flavia (the emperor's private residence), the Domus Augustana and a stadium. The complex was designed by the architect, Rabirius, who levelled a crest of land, the Palatium, on the steep eastern side of the Palatine, and filled in the depression between it and the next crest, the Germalus, demolishing or burying many Republican era houses in the process. Some of these buried buildings have since been unearthed, and excavations are continuing.

On entering from the Roman Forum, take the path straight ahead past a grassy area on the right, to the ruins of the **Domus Augustana**. The path from the entrance at Via di San Gregorio leads to the same place.

The Domus Augustana was built on two levels, with rooms leading off a *peristilio* (peristyle or garden courtyard) on each floor. You can't get down to the lower level but from above you can see the basin of a fountain and beyond it rooms which were paved with coloured marble. The palace had an elaborate two-storey colonnaded facade to the south overlooking Circo Massimo (from where you get the clearest indication of the grand scale of the complex).

East of the Domus Augustana is the **Stadio** (stadium) probably used by the emperors for private games and events. An oval recess in the eastern wall is thought to have served as the emperor's private viewing area. Next to the stadio are the scant remains of baths built by Septimius Severus, the **Terme di Settimio Severo**. Considerable engineering skill was required to build this complex on an extension of the southernmost point of the Palatine. It was supported by enormous arched substructures, best seen from Circo Massimo.

The **Museo Palatino** is the big white building (a former convent) located between

the Domus Augustana and the Domus Flavia. It was established in the 1860s and houses artworks and artefacts found on the Palatine. For the past century, the most important of the excavated pieces from the Palatine were kept in the Museo Nazionale Romano. Some objects remain in the Museo Nazionale Romano collection (including stuccoes from the Palatine criptoportico) but many were transferred to the restored Museo Palatino in 1998. Admission is with the same ticket as for the Palatine (see earlier in this section). Note that the museum closes one hour earlier than the Palatine itself.

The ground floor illustrates the history of the hill from its origins to the Republican age. In Sale I, II and III there are pots, eating and cooking utensils from the Palaeolithic Age to the Bronze Age as well as models of how the Iron Age huts and tombs might have appeared. Sala IV contains artefacts from the Archaic and Republican Ages (6th to 1st centuries BC) including an altar to a pagan god and ceramic masks.

On the 1st floor, the entrance hall contains statuary that decorated the various imperial palaces on the Palatine. On display in Sala V are artefacts from the Augustan period (27 BC–AD 14) including reliefs and black marble statues from the Tempio di Apollo, which was located next to the Casa d'Augusto. Sala VI contains objects pertaining to Nero's reign (54–68 AD), including remnants of decorative frescoes. Sculpted heads and busts dating from the 1st to the 4th century AD can be seen in Sale VII and VIII.

North of the Museo Palatino is the **Domus Flavia**, which was connected to the Domus Augustana. The palace comprised three large halls to the north, the central one of which was the emperor's throne room, and a large banqueting hall or triclinium *(triclinio imperiale)* to the south, which was paved in coloured marble that can still be seen. The triclinium looked out onto an oval fountain whose remains are clearly visible. Domitian was terrified of being assassinated and had the peristyle of the Domus Flavia lined with shiny marble slabs so that, from whichever room he was in, he could see who was approaching. Nonetheless he ended up being murdered in his bedroom, possibly with the connivance of his wife. The Domus Flavia was constructed over earlier edifices. One of these, which can sometimes be visited (ask at the Palatine entrance), is the **Casa dei Grifi** (House of the Griffins), so called because of a stucco relief of two griffins in one of the rooms. It is the oldest building on the Palatine and dates from the late 2nd or 1st century BC. It was excavated in the 18th century.

Among the best-preserved buildings on the Palatine is the **Casa di Livia**, west of the Domus Flavia. It is well below current ground level and is reached by steps down to a mosaic-covered courtyard. Livia, the wife of Augustus, owned this house and a larger villa at Prima Porta to the north of Rome (see the Palazzo Massimo alle Terme section later in this chapter). The Casa di Livia contains a forecourt, or *atrium*, leading onto what were once reception rooms. The walls of the house were decorated with frescoes – of mythological scenes, landscapes, fruits and flowers – some of which can still be seen, although they have been detached from the walls for preservation purposes. In front of the Casa di Livia is the **Casa d'Augusto**, Augustus' own residence – the two constructions were most likely part of the same complex. Both casas are being restored and have been closed to the public for several years, though they can sometimes be visited by appointment; ask at the entrance to the Palatine.

Next to the Casa d'Augusto is the **Casa di Romolo** (House of Romulus) where, it is thought, Romulus and Remus were brought up after their discovery by the shepherd Faustulus. Excavations in the 1940s revealed evidence of supports for wattle and daub huts dating from the 9th century BC. The **Tempio della Magna Mater** is just north of the huts. Also known as the Tempio di Cibele, it was built in 204 BC to house a black stone connected with the Asiatic goddess of fertility, Cybele.

North of the Casa di Livia is the **criptoportico**, a 128m tunnel, built by Nero to connect his Domus Aurea with the imperial palaces on the Palatine. Unfortunately you can't walk into it. The tunnel had windows on one side which provided light and ventilation. Elaborate stucco decorations once lined part of the criptoportico but these have been replaced by copies. The originals are in the Museo Nazionale Romano. A second tunnel was later added to link it with the Domus Flavia.

The area west of the criptoportico was once the **Domus Tiberiana**, Tiberius' palace, which Gaius Caligula extended farther north towards the forum. Today it is the site of the **Orti Farnesiani**. Cardinal Alessandro Farnese, a grandson of Pope Paul III, bought the ruins of Tiberius' palace in the mid-16th century. He had the ruins filled in and asked the acclaimed and fashionable architect Vignola to design a garden for him. One of Europe's earliest botanical gardens, it contained a number of plant species that had never before been planted in Italy. The garden originally extended from the forum up terraced levels connected with steps. There are various paths, rose gardens and shady parasol pines and it's a great place for a picnic. Twin pavilions stand at the northern end of the garden, from where the view over the forum and the rest of Rome is breathtaking.

Arco di Costantino (Map 7)

North-east of the Palatine, beside the Colosseum is the triumphal arch built to honour Constantine following his victory over Maxentius at the battle of the Milvian Bridge (near the present-day Zona Olimpica, northwest of the Villa Borghese) in AD 312.

However, the arch was not built completely from scratch. Its decorative reliefs are an assemblage of pieces taken from earlier structures, probably to speed up construction in order to celebrate Constantine's triumph. The lower stonework dates from Domitian's reign (AD 81–96), and the eight large medallions depicting hunting scenes are Hadrianic (AD 117–138). Four enormous reliefs, on the inside of the central archway and on the sides of the arch, depict Trajan's battle against the Dacians. Removed from the Foro di Traiano, these reliefs are believed to be by the same sculptor who carved Trajan's column.

Incorporated into the Frangipani fortress, the arch was 'liberated' in 1804. Major restoration work was completed in 1987.

Walk back towards Via dei Fori Imperiali and turn left into Via Sacra, towards the Arco di Tito and one of the Roman Forum exits. Just before the gate, head uphill to the left for another panoramic view of the forum.

Colosseum (Map 7)

Construction of the Colosseum was started by Vespasian in AD 72 in the grounds of Nero's private Domus Aurea. Originally known as the Flavian Amphitheatre, after the family name of Vespasian, it was inau-gurated by his son Titus in 80. The massive structure could seat more than 50,000 spectators who came to watch gladiatorial combat and gory wild-beast shows (see the boxed text 'Go, Go Gladiators'). The splendid games held at the inauguration of the Colosseum lasted for 100 days and nights, during which some 5000 animals were slaughtered. Trajan once held games that lasted for 117 days, during which 9000 gladiators fought to their death.

The outer walls of the Colosseum have three levels of arches, articulated by columns topped by capitals of the Ionic (at the bottom), Doric and Corinthian (at the top)

Go, Go Gladiators

Gladiatorial combat originated as part of Etruscan funerary rites as a form of human sacrifice. By the 1st century BC, gladiatorial games had far outstripped this ritual context; Caesar exhibited 320 pairs of gladiators in 65 BC, Augustus and Trajan each showed 5000 pairs of gladiators on different occasions during their reigns.

Gladiators were prisoners of war, slaves sold to gladiatorial schools or volunteers. Some were equipped with heavy swords and shields and others were almost naked, armed with a net and a trident. Pairings were made to match a heavily armed gladiator against a lightly armed one.

Bouts were not necessarily to the death. A defeated gladiator could appeal to the crowd and the presiding magistrate who could signal that he had fought well and deserved to be spared. Thumbs down, however, meant death, which the defeated man was expected to face with quiet courage.

Although gambling was technically illegal in Rome, vast sums were wagered on gladiatorial combats. Successful gladiators were popular heroes and lived to enjoy a comfortable retirement, with some running their own training schools.

As with the other blood sports held in Rome, gladiatorial games were more than just particularly gruesome entertainment. This state-run public spectacle was a demonstration of Empire through the display of exotic beasts and prisoners of war, and the people's judgment of the defeated allowed them to share in the Roman State's authority over life and death.

Inspired as much by Russell Crowe in the recent box-office hit *Gladiator* as by the history of ancient Rome, the Gruppo Storico Romano, an association of history enthusiasts, has established Rome's first gladiator school on the Via Appia. Romans are enrolling in courses over several months to transform themselves into gladiators under the direction of a *magister*. Short intensive courses (☎ 0338 243 6678, fax 06 301 70 14, ℮ gruppo_storicoromano@libero.it) have also been introduced to cater for tourists keen to get a grip on gladiatorial combat in three days. Further details can be found online at www.gsr.3000.it.

---

orders. The external walls were covered in travertine and marble statues once filled the niches on the second and third storeys. The upper level, punctuated by windows and slender Corinthian pilasters, had supports for 240 masts, which held up a canvas awning over the arena, shielding the spectators from sun and rain. The 80 entrance arches allowed the spectators to enter and be seated in a matter of minutes.

The interior of the Colosseum was divided into three parts: the arena, the cavea and the podium. The arena originally had a wooden floor covered in sand to prevent the combatants from slipping and to soak up the blood spilt there. It could also be flooded for mock sea battles. Trapdoors led down to the underground chambers and passageways beneath the arena floor, which can be clearly seen today. Animals in cages and sets for the various battles were hoisted onto the arena by a complicated system of pulleys. The cavea, for spectator seating, was divided into three tiers. Knights sat in the lowest tier, wealthy citizens in the middle and the populace in the highest tier. The podium, a broad terrace in front of the tiers of seats, was reserved for emperors, senators and other VIPs.

With the fall of the Empire, the Colosseum was abandoned and gradually became overgrown. Exotic plants grew there for centuries; seeds had inadvertently been transported from Africa and Asia with the wild beasts that appeared in the arena (including crocodiles, bears, lions, tigers, elephants, rhinos, hippos, camels and giraffes). In the Middle Ages the Colosseum became a fortress, occupied by two of the city's warrior families: the Frangipani and the Annibaldi. Its reputation as a symbol of Rome, the Eternal City, also dates to the Middle Ages, with Bede writing that: 'While the Colosseum stands, Rome shall stand, but when the Colosseum falls, Rome shall fall – and when Rome falls, the world will end.'

Damaged several times by earthquakes, it was later used as a quarry for travertine and marble for the Palazzo Venezia, Palazzo Barberini and Palazzo Cancelleria among other buildings. Pollution and the vibrations caused by traffic and the Metro have also taken their toll. Restoration works have periodically been carried out, the latest starting in 1992 but suspended in 2000. Despite this it remains an evocative spot to explore while imagining yourself in the latest Hollywood sword-and-sandals epic, giving Russell Crowe a run for his money.

The Colosseum (☎ 06 39 96 77 00) opens 9 am to 6 pm March and April, 9 am to 7 pm May to August, 9 am to 6.30 pm September and October and 9 am to 4.30 pm November to February. Admission costs €5.16.

Domus Aurea (Map 5)

The megalomaniac emperor Nero didn't do things by halves. His massive Domus Aurea (Golden House), built after the fire of AD 64, extended over the Palatine, Oppian and Caelian hills. The gold leaf that covered the facade gave the Domus Aurea its name and the banqueting halls, nymphaeums, baths and terraces were decorated with frescoes and mosaics, a few of which remain. The extensive grounds had vineyards, game and an artificial lake.

Nero didn't have long to enjoy his palace. After his death in 68, his successors were quick to remove all trace of his excesses, razing much of the Domus Aurea to the ground and filling it up with earth. Vespasian drained the lake and built the Colosseum in its place, Domitian built his palace on the Palatine, and Trajan constructed a baths complex on top of the Oppian ruins using the Domus Aurea as a foundation. Archaeologists have spent 25 years excavating this area.

Many of the original loggias and halls were walled in when Trajan's baths were built and the light, which filtered through the Domus Aurea's loggias and pavilions, was completely lost. It is quite confusing trying to identify parts of the original complex and the later baths. Among the scant fresco remnants are mythical creatures, flowers, fruit, vines and human figures staring out of illusionary windows. The best preserved of them illustrate scenes from Homer's *Iliad* where Achilles is disguised as a woman on the island of Skyros. The octagonal room at the end of the tour has been identified as the circular dining room described by the ancient writer Suetonius, where Nero sang and played the lyre on a revolving stage.

Nero was a great pillager and had hundreds of Greek bronzes and marble copies of Greek statues placed in his palace. Among them were the *Galata Morente* and *Galata Suicida* (now in the Capitoline Museums and Palazzo Altemps respectively; see those sections for details), which were displayed in the octagonal room of the Domus Aurea. The *Laocoön*, now in the Vatican Museums, is also thought to have once been in the Domus Aurea.

The baths and underlying ruins were abandoned by the 6th century. During the Renaissance, artists (including Ghirlandaio, Perugino and Raphael) lowered themselves into the ruins in order to study the frescoes. Some left their own graffiti – not quite 'Pinturicchio woz 'ere', but not far off – and all copied motifs from the Domus Aurea frescoes in their work in the Vatican and other parts of Rome.

The excavations of the Domus Aurea and the Colle Oppio are in their early days and archaeologists expect to find many more major discoveries in the area. In 1998, archaeologists found a large wall painting of an unidentified city in a criptoportico of the Domus Aurea. It is the most important archaeological discovery in Rome in recent years and will be a treat for future visitors once excavations are completed.

The Domus Aurea (☎ 06 39 96 77 00), Viale della Domus Aurea, opens 9 am to 8 pm Wednesday to Monday. Admission costs €6.19. Visits are only possible in accompanied groups; you can book to go in or just turn up, buy a ticket for the next available admission time (usually every 15 minutes) and wait for a group to form. You have to follow a set itinerary.

ESQUILINE (Maps 5 & 7)

The Esquiline hill (Esquilino) is the largest and highest of Rome's seven hills. It stretches from the Colosseum to Stazione Termini, encompassing Via Cavour (a major traffic artery between Stazione Termini and Via dei Fori Imperiali), the Basilica di Santa Maria Maggiore, the market square of Piazza Vittorio Emanuele II and the Oppian hill. The Esquiline originally had four summits. In ancient times the lower slope of the western summit, the Suburra, was occupied by crowded slums while the area between Via Cavour and the Colle Oppio was a fashionable residential district for wealthier citizens. Pompey lived here, as did the famous patron of the arts, Maecenas, and Virgil is said to have had a house in the area. Much of the hill was covered with vineyards and gardens, many of which remained until the late 19th century, when they were dug up to make way for grandiose apartment blocks.

Today, the Esquiline is the most multicultural area of Rome and home to thousands of immigrants. It is also popular with trendy, young artists enticed by low rents and spacious lofts.

Santa Maria Maggiore (Map 5)

One of Rome's four patriarchal basilicas (the others being St Peter's, San Giovanni in Laterano and San Paolo Fuori-le-Mura), Santa Maria Maggiore was built on the highest point of the Esquiline in the 5th century, during Pope Sixtus III's era. According to legend, in 352 Pope Liberius had a dream in which he was instructed by the Virgin Mary to build a church in the exact place where he found snow. When, on the following morning (5 August – the middle of a hot Roman summer), snow fell on the Esquiline, he obeyed. The original church was called Santa Maria della Neve. Each year on 5 August there is a service in the basilica, during which white petals are released from the ceiling to commemorate the miracle.

Its main facade was added in the 18th century, preserving the 13th-century **mosaics** of the earlier facade. These are beautifully illuminated at night. The interior is Baroque and the bell tower Romanesque.

The basilican form of the vast interior, a nave and two aisles, remains intact and the most notable feature is the cycle of mosaics, dating from the 5th century, which decorate the triumphal arch and nave, some of which are so high up that they are difficult to see (a pair of binoculars or a telephoto lens would be useful). They are the most important mosaics of this period in Rome and depict biblical scenes, in particular events in the lives of Abraham, Jacob and Isaac (to the left), and Moses and Joshua (to the right). Scenes from the life of Christ decorate the triumphal arch. The central image in the apse, signed by Jacopo Torriti, dates from the 13th century and represents the coronation of the Virgin. The Virgin is seated on the same throne as Christ and it is thought that the artist was influenced by the mosaics of the same scene in Santa Maria in Trastevere. Further scenes of the life of the Virgin are below.

The **baldachino** (canopy) over the high altar is elaborately decorated with gilt cherubs. The altar itself is a porphyry sarcophagus, which is said to contain the relics of St Matthew and other martyrs. Steps lead down to the Confessio where a reliquary preserves a fragment of baby Jesus' crib. Note the Cosmati pavement of the nave and aisles, dating from the 12th century. The sumptuously decorated **Cappella Sistina** (not to be confused with the Sistine Chapel in St Peter's), last on the right, was built by Domenico Fontana in the 16th century and contains the tombs of popes Sixtus V and Pius V. Opposite is the **Cappella Borghese** (or Cappella Paolina), also full of elaborate decoration, erected in the 17th century by Pope Paul V. The *Madonna and Child* panel above the altar, surrounded by lapis lazuli and agate, is believed to date from the 12th to the 13th century.

Monti (Map 5)

The western side of the Esquiline is known as Rione Monti (or simply Monti) and includes some of Rome's most famous smaller churches. The late-4th-century **Chiesa di Santa Pudenziana**, on Via Urbana just off Piazza dell'Esquilino, is dedicated to Pudentiana, the daughter of a Roman senator, who is said to have given hospitality to St Peter on the site, which is now occupied by the church. Most of the facade was added in the 19th century although elements from the earlier buildings, such as the delicately

carved frieze and medallions dating from the 11th century, were retained. The Romanesque arched windows and the bell tower date from the 12th century.

The interior is noted for its magnificent apse mosaic. An enthroned Christ is flanked by two female figures who are crowning St Peter and St Paul; on either side of them are the Apostles as Roman senators dressed in togas. Dating from AD 390, this is the oldest mosaic of its kind in Rome. You can only see 10 out of the original 12 Apostles; the two outer figures were cut off in a 16th-century restoration which also sliced off the bottom of the mosaic, amputating the legs of the outer Apostles. See the boxed text 'Hidden Treasures' in the Facts about Rome chapter for further information on the city's mosaics.

The **Chiesa di Santa Prassede**, Via Santa Prassede 9a, was built in the 9th century by Pope Paschal I on the site of a 2nd-century oratory. It is almost hidden, being hemmed in by a cluster of medieval buildings; you enter through a side door. The church is dedicated to Praxedes, the sister of Pudentiana. Interestingly, the sainthoods of both Pudenziana and Prassede were declared invalid in 1969, although the churches have kept their names. Paschal I had mosaic artists brought from Byzantium (later Constantinople) to decorate his church – the results are breathtaking.

The naturalism evident in earlier mosaics from the late-classical period has been replaced with a marked Christian symbolism. On the first triumphal arch, angels guard the door to the New Jerusalem. On the underside of both arches are beautifully worked garlands of lilies and foliage. The apse mosaics are slightly blocked from view by the Baroque baldachino. Climb up the red marble steps for a better view if you need to. Christ is flanked by St Peter, St Pudentiana and St Zeno (on the right) and St Paul, St Praxedes and Paschal on the left. All the figures have golden halos except for the figure of Paschal, whose head is shadowed by a green square or nimbus, indicating that he was still alive at the time the mosaic was done (but expected to be on a fast track to sainthood). Below are the Lamb of God and the faithful flock.

The small **Cappella di San Zenone** in the southern aisle was built by Paschal as a mausoleum for his mother. The mosaics on the outside show distinctive Roman faces representing the Virgin and Child, Prassede, Pudenziana and other saints (inner group) and Christ and the Apostles. Enter the chapel and you feel like part of the mosaic. It is unlikely that you will get much closer to mosaic decoration anywhere in Rome, and you can really appreciate the skill of the artists. A small mosaic in the altar niche depicts the Virgin and Child with St Praxedes and St Pudentiana; in the vault is Christ with four angels; on the inside of the doorway are St Peter and St Paul supporting the throne; and on the left, facing the altar are St Praxedes, St Pudentiana and St Agnes. The fragment of marble in the glass case on the right is thought to be a piece of the column to which Christ was tied when he was scourged.

If you can tear your eyes away from the mosaics, have a look at the other features of the church, such as the trompe l'oeil frescoes in the nave, which are the work of various artists and were completed in the 16th century. The architrave of the nave is made up of ancient Roman fragments, some with inscriptions. The floor is paved in coloured marble. A large round porphyry disc surrounded by an inscription, located in the nave near the main door, marks the spot where Prassede is thought to have hidden the bones of Christian martyrs. See the boxed text 'Hidden Treasures' in the Facts about Rome chapter for more details.

Following Via San Martino ai Monti, you come to the **Chiesa di San Martino ai Monti**, a Carmelite church originally constructed in the 4th century, subsequently rebuilt in the 6th and 9th centuries and then completely transformed by Filippo Gagliardi in the 1650s. The 24 Corinthian columns in the nave are all that remain of the 6th-century building. Of note are Gagliardi's frescoes of the Basilica di San Giovanni in Laterano before it was rebuilt in the mid-17th century by Borromini, and St Peter's Basilica before it assumed its present appearance in the 16th century by the hands of Bramante, Raphael, Michelangelo, Maderno and others. There are also frescoes by Gaspard Dughet.

The characteristic Via Panisperna, which connects Santa Maria Maggiore to the Fori Imperiali, still gives a clear indication of the topography of the Esquiline. At the western end is **Villa Aldobrandini**, built for the duke of Urbino in the 16th century. It was subsequently acquired by Clement VIII, the Aldobrandini pope, who gave it to his nephews. Now owned by the state, the villa houses an international law library. The extensive formal gardens, which have splendid views over the city, can be reached through a gate at Via Mazzarino 11.

Piazza Vittorio Emanuele II (Map 5)

This square is south-east of Santa Maria Maggiore. From Monday to Saturday it is the scene of Rome's largest and most boisterous food market. Offering a multi-ethnic treat, this market is the place to come for exotic spices, African and Asian produce and Indian and Chinese food shops, which can be found in the vicinity. However, keep an eye on your wallet or handbag as it is also a popular spot for pickpockets.

Within the square are the ruins of the **Trofei di Mario**, once a fountain at the end of an aqueduct. The square itself hosts ethnic food and cultural festivals throughout the year and an outdoor film festival in the summer (see the boxed text 'Rome, Festival Town' in the Entertainment chapter).

In the northern corner of the square is the **Chiesa di Sant'Eusebio**, which was founded in the 4th century and rebuilt twice in the 18th. Each year, worshippers of the four-legged variety – dogs, cats and even horses – attend the annual blessing of the animals, held on the saint's day (17 January) of their protector, St Anthony Abbot.

San Pietro in Vincoli (Map 5)

The Basilica di San Pietro in Vincoli was built in the 5th century by the Empress Eudoxia, wife of Valentinian III, to house the chains of St Peter. Legend has it that when a second part of the chains was returned to Rome from Constantinople, the two pieces miraculously joined together.

While the presence of the chains makes the church an important place of pilgrimage, the church offers another great treasure – Michelangelo's unfinished tomb of Pope Julius II, with his powerful *Moses* and unfinished statues of *Leah* and *Rachel* on either side. Michelangelo was frustrated for many years by his inability to find time to complete work on the tomb. In the end, Pope Julius was buried in St Peter's without the great tomb he had envisioned and the unfinished sculptures, which were to have adorned it, are in the Louvre (Paris) and the Galleria dell'Accademia (Florence). A flight of steps through a low arch leads down from the church to Via Cavour.

San Clemente (Map 7)
At the base of the Colle Oppio near the Colosseum, is the Basilica di San Clemente in Via San Giovanni in Laterano (across Via Labicana). Dedicated to one of the earliest popes, the basilica is one of the best examples in Rome of how the city exists on many levels. The 12th-century church at current street level was built over a 4th-century church which was, in turn, built over a 1st-century Roman house containing a Mithraic temple where practitioners of the eastern fertility cult worshipped in the 2nd century AD. Further, it is believed that Republican foundations lie beneath the house.

It is possible to visit the first three levels. You enter the church through a side door. If the main door at the eastern end of the church is open go through it into the courtyard outside and then come back into the church the way it was designed to be entered. The mosaic decoration is even more stunning and effective.

In the medieval church, note the Schola Cantorum, a marble choir screen dating from the 6th century which was originally in the older church below. It is decorated with panels of white and coloured marble and the early-Christian symbols of the fish, the dove and the vine. The high marble pulpit on the left, together with the beautiful

Paschal candlestick decorated with Cosmati mosaics, was added when the new church was built. High pulpits, common in medieval churches, were probably designed so that the priest could read from illuminated manuscripts in the form of scrolls and, as he read, the congregation could see the pictures. The floor is paved with intricate patterns of coloured marble.

The stunning mosaics in the apse, dating from the 12th century, are the highlight of the church. On the triumphal arch are Christ and the symbols of the four Evangelists. The apse itself depicts the Triumph of the Cross, with 12 doves symbolising the Apostles. Figures around the cross include the Madonna and St John, as well as St John the Baptist and other saints encircled by a vine growing from the foot of the cross. There are also beautifully detailed animals and acanthus leaves. The gold background of the mosaics are typical of the later Byzantine style. However, it is thought that the designs were partially based on mosaics in the earlier church and that some of the mosaic tiles were actually salvaged from it. The early Renaissance frescoes by Masolino da Panicale in the Cappella di Santa Caterina depict scenes from the life of St Catherine of Alexandria.

You have to buy a ticket (€2.06) to descend to the lower levels of the church. Take some time to study the plans of the various levels to orient yourself and follow the suggested route. Not much remains of the 4th-century church that was virtually destroyed by Norman invaders in 1084, though some 11th-century Romanesque frescoes illustrating the life of St Clement can be seen at the eastern end. In a left aisle is a *piscina* or deep pit, discovered by archaeologists in 1967, which was probably used as a font or fountain. Other fresco cycles are faded or damaged beyond repair.

Descending another level, you arrive at the 1st-century Roman house and temple of Mithras. At the eastern end is a catacomb with 16 wall tombs dating from the 5th or 6th century. The temple, probably once the house's *triclinium* or banquet room, is situated directly under the apse of the 4th-century church and dates from the late 2nd century or early 3rd century. It contains an altar with a sculpted relief of Mithras slaying the bull. Don't be afraid if you hear the sound of running water in the deepest level of the church. Behind an iron door at the western end of the excavations is a drain that joins the Cloaca Maxima, the main water drain of ancient Rome, near the Colosseum.

From San Clemente turning right into Via dei Quercei you reach **Chiesa di Santi Quattro Coronati**, a fortified medieval convent. The four crowned saints to whom it is dedicated were four Christian sculptors killed for refusing to make a statue of a pagan god. The squat bell tower dates from the 9th century. Note the extremely well preserved 13th-century frescoes of St Sylvester and Constantine in the **Cappella di San Silvestro**. There is also a pretty early-13th-century cloister and garden off the northern aisle (ring the bell for admission).

SAN GIOVANNI (Map 7)
San Giovanni in Laterano

Founded by Constantine in the 4th century, Basilica di San Giovanni in Laterano was the first Christian basilica constructed in Rome and remains one of the most important in the Christian world. It is Rome's cathedral and the pope's seat as bishop of Rome. It has been destroyed by fire twice and rebuilt several times. In 1425 Martin V had the floor inlaid with stone and mosaic looted from other derelict Roman churches.

Borromini was commissioned to transform its interior into the Baroque style between 1646 and 1649. The eastern facade, which is the basilica's main entrance, faces onto Piazza di Porta San Giovanni. The bronze main doors were moved here by Borromini from the Curia in the Roman Forum. The portico, built by Alessandro Galilei in 1736, is surmounted by colossal statues representing Christ with St John the Baptist, St John the Evangelist and the 12 Apostles. The Gothic baldachino over the papal altar dates from the 14th century and contains many relics, including the heads of St Peter and St Paul and part of St Peter's

wooden altar table. The frescoes in the transepts depict the conversion of Constantine. The apse was rebuilt in the 19th century and the mosaics that we see today are copies of originals, which were destroyed during the rebuilding. One of the nicest architectural features of the basilica is Borromini's treatment of the various funerary monuments in the aisles; he surrounded them with sculptural frames and placed his trademark oval window above each one.

Fortunately the beautiful 13th-century **cloister** escaped the fires which ravaged the rest of the basilica. Built by the Vassalletto family in Cosmati style, the cloister has columns which were once completely covered with inlaid marble mosaics. The damage done by time and pollution is sadly evident and few of the wonderful twisted columns have any mosaic decoration left, although a major restoration is imminent. The central court is off limits so you can't get a really good look at the highly decorated architrave above the columns. The outer walls of the cloister are lined with inscriptions, sarcophagi and various sculptures. Of note on the southern side is the inscription of a Papal Bull of Sixtus IV and, on the western side, four small columns supporting a marble slab, which Christians in the Middle Ages regarded as representing the height of Christ. The cloister opens 9 am to 5 pm (to 6 pm April to October) and admission costs €2.06.

A second entrance into the basilica is through the northern facade, which faces onto Piazza San Giovanni in Laterano. The two-tiered portico, built by Domenico Fontana in 1586, was damaged by a bomb attack in 1993 and has recently been restored. Leaving the church by this door and crossing the square you come to the domed **baptistry**, which was also built by Constantine, but has been remodelled several times. Sixtus III gave it its present octagonal shape, which became the model for many baptistries throughout the Christian world. A green basalt font is in the centre of the baptistry, beneath the dome decorated with modern copies of frescoes by Andrea Sacchi. The outer walls are decorated by 17th-century frescoes. It is surrounded by several chapels with magnificent mosaic decorations.

The **Cappella di Santa Rufina** is decorated with a stunning 5th-century mosaic of vines and foliage against a deep-blue background, while the **Capella di San Giovanni Evangelista** has a mosaic in the vault of the Lamb of God surrounded by birds and flowers. The **Capella di San Venanzio** was added by Pope John IV in the 7th century. It has extremely well preserved mosaics; in the apse are Christ with angels and the Madonna and saints, and on the triumphal arch are Christian martyrs. Right at the top are views of Jerusalem and Bethlehem. The baptistry opens 9 am to 1 pm and 4 to 6 pm Monday to Thursday, and 9 am to 1 pm on Friday and Saturday.

The **Palazzo Laterano**, which adjoins the basilica, was the papal residence until the pope moved to Avignon in the 14th century. It was largely destroyed by fire in 1308 and most of what remained was demolished in the 16th century. The present building houses the Rome Vicariate and offices of the diocese of Rome.

Scala Santa & Sancta Sanctorum

The building on the eastern side of Piazza di Porta San Giovanni is all that remains of the original Palazzo Laterano and contains the Scala Santa and the Sancta Sanctorum. The Scala Santa (Holy Staircase) is said to be from the palace of Pontius Pilate in Jerusalem where Christ himself had trod; people are allowed to climb it only on their knees. To protect them the 28 marble steps are covered with wooden boards. Colourful frescoes by a group of unknown Roman artists from the late 13th century cover the ceiling and walls above the stairs.

The Scala Santa and two other staircases lead to the Sancta Sanctorum, originally the popes' private chapel. The name, meaning 'the holy of holies', refers to the numerous relics that were once housed in the chapel but which have now been moved to the Vatican. The silver panelled altarpiece, originally a painting of Christ said to have been done by St Luke and an angel, has been restored and repainted so many times that it

bears no resemblance to how it once appeared. The vaulted ceiling above it is covered with 13th-century mosaics. The Cosmati marble work on the floor is particularly fine and the lower walls are also adorned with marble. Above are 13th-century frescoes (by the artists who frescoed the stairwells) of the Apostles and saints, separated by swirling Gothic columns and, higher still, frescoes clearly illustrating the various ways that martyrs met their deaths.

The Sancta Sanctorum opens 10.30 to 11.30 am and 3 to 4 pm on Tuesday, Thursday and Saturday. Admission costs €2.58. The Scala Santa (☎ 06 70 49 46 19) opens 6.15 am to noon and 3.30 to 6.45 pm daily April to September, and 6.15 am to noon and 3 to 6.15 pm daily October to March. The rest of the building has been occupied by a Passionist convent since 1953.

Santa Croce in Gerusalemme

Following Viale Carlo Felice east from Piazza di Porta di San Giovanni, you reach the Chiesa di Santa Croce in Gerusalemme in the square of the same name. The church is thought to have been founded in AD 320 by St Helena, Constantine's mother, who brought Christian relics, including a piece of the cross on which Christ was crucified, to Rome from Jerusalem. The church was rebuilt in 1144 by Lucius II who added a bell tower. Benedict XIV made major alterations to the church in 1744, adding the facade and oval vestibule. The frescoes in the apse date from the 15th century and represent the legends of the Cross. The relics are housed in a chapel at the end of the northern aisle.

Next to the church are the columns and bricked-up arches of the 3rd-century-BC **Anfiteatro Castrense**, once part of an imperial palace on the site. The small amphitheatre was used for games and baiting animals. North of the church are former military barracks which house two military museums and the **Museo Nazionale degli Strumenti Musicali** (Map 1), which has a unique collection of musical instruments dating from Roman times to the 19th century, including those from Asia, Africa and the Americas. The museum (☎ 06 701 47

96) opens 9 am to 1.30 pm Tuesday to Saturday. Admission costs €2.58.

Via Eleniana leads northwards from Santa Croce to the **Porta Maggiore**, also known as the Porta Prenestina, a gateway to ancient Rome built by Claudius in AD 52. The main south-bound roads, Via Prenestina and Via Labicana, passed beneath the gateway and ruts made by carriage wheels can still be seen in the basalt flagstones under the arches. The arch supported two aqueducts – the Acqua Claudia and the Acqua Aniene Nuova – one on top of the other. It was later incorporated into the Aurelian Walls of the city.

Just outside the gate is a rather pretentious travertine monument, the **Sepolcro di M Virgilio Eurisace**, commonly known as the Baker's Tomb, built around 30 BC by the widow of the baker Vergilius Eurysaces in memory of her husband. The tomb is decorated with reliefs depicting the industrious baker at work, and the monument itself is in the shape of an enormous bread oven.

CAELIAN TO PORTA SAN SEBASTIANO
Caelian (Map 7)

The Caelian hill (Celio) is accessible either from Via di San Gregorio or, from the other side, from Via della Navicella. The **Villa Celimontana** is a large public park on top of the hill, perfect for a quiet picnic (as long as it isn't overrun by wedding parties having photographs taken – common on Saturday). There is also a children's playground. The Renaissance villa, which originally belonged to the noble family, now houses the Italian Geographical Society.

The 4th-century **Chiesa di SS Giovanni e Paolo**, in the square of the same name on Via di San Paolo della Croce (which runs off Via della Navicella), is dedicated to two Romans, St John and St Paul. They had served Constantine II and were beheaded by his anti-Christian successor, Julian, for refusing to serve in his court. The church was built over their houses. A beautiful 13th-century fresco of Christ with the Apostles is in a small room by the altar. It is usually locked but you can ask the sacristan to let you in. The arches in the square are the remains of 3rd-century Roman shops.

Walk downhill along the Clivio di Scauro, an atmospheric road dating from the 1st century BC. A road to the left leads up to the 8th-century **Chiesa di San Gregorio Magno**, built in honour of Pope Gregory I (the Great) on the site where he dispatched St Augustine to convert the people of Britain to Christianity. The church was remodelled in the Baroque style in the 17th century. The atrium, designed by Giovanni Battista Soria, contains tombs of prominent Englishmen including Sir Edward Carne, an envoy of Henry VIII and Mary I, who was sent to Rome several times. One of his missions was to obtain a papal annulment of the king's marriage to Catherine of Aragon. He died in 1561.

The interior of the church was given a Baroque makeover in the 18th century by Francesco Ferrari. The Cappella di San Gregorio, at the end of the right aisle, contains a 1st-century-BC marble throne. A gate to the left of the church leads to three small chapels among cypress trees. On the right, the Cappella di Santa Silvia (dedicated to Gregory the Great's mother) contains a fresco of angels by Guido Reni. The central chapel, the Cappella di Sant'Andrea, contains a painting by Domenichino of the flagellation of St Andrew and Guido Reni's depiction of St Andrew on his way to martyrdom. Giovanni Lanfranco's fresco on the inside of the entrance depicts St Silvia and St Gregory. The altarpiece, by Pomarancio, features the Madonna with St Andrew and St Gregory. The third chapel is dedicated to Santa Barbara, and along with a statue of St Gregory, contains frescoes illustrating St Augustine's mission. The chapels open 9.30 am to 12.30 pm Tuesday to Sunday.

Santo Stefano Rotondo (Map 7)

The fascinating, round Chiesa di Santo Stefano Rotondo is on Via di S Stefano Rotondo, just across Via della Navicella from Villa Celimontana. Inside the church are two rings of antique granite and marble columns. The circular wall is lined with frescoes depicting the various ways in which saints were martyred. The vivid scenes are quite grotesque and you might not make it through all 34 of them. Watch out for a little priest pointing to your shoes – he is worried you will dirty the polished wooden floor. At the time of writing, the church resembled a building site, due to excavations beneath it, and parts of the wooden floor had been pulled up.

The church opens 9 am to 1 pm and 1.50 to 4.20 pm Tuesday to Saturday, and 1.50 to 4.20 pm on Monday. It also opens 9 am to noon, on the second Sunday of each month, April to October.

Terme di Caracalla (Map 7)

South of the Caelian hill is the Via delle Terme di Caracalla (accessible by bus Nos 160 and 628 from Piazza Venezia). The big white building on the corner of Piazza di Porta Capena houses the **Food and Agriculture Organization of the United Nations**, in front of which is the Axum obelisk taken from Ethiopia by Mussolini as war booty.

In Piazza Santa Balbina (off Viale Guido Baccelli, which runs through the park) is the **Chiesa di Santa Balbina**, one of the oldest churches in Rome, dating from the 4th century. A notable feature is the fine Cosmati tomb of Stefanus de Surdis, which dates from the early 14th century. The church was extensively restored in the 1930s when 1st-century AD Roman mosaics found in other parts of the city were installed there.

Santa Balbina overlooks the magnificent ruins of the Terme di Caracalla (Baths of Caracalla). Begun by Antonius Caracalla and inaugurated in AD 217, the baths were used until the 6th century. They are the best preserved of the Imperial Roman baths in the city. Covering 10 hectares, these baths could hold 1600 people and had shops, gardens, libraries and gym facilities. Men and women bathed at different times of the day and the process was convoluted. Excavations of the baths in the 16th and 17th centuries unearthed important sculptures and statues from the site which found their way into the Farnese family collection. Two enormous basins now serve as twin fountains in Piazza Farnese.

The baths open 9 am to 6 pm Tuesday to Saturday (to 1 pm on Sunday and Monday) April to October, and 9 am to 4 pm November to March. Admission costs €4.13.

Porta San Sebastiano (Maps 1 & 7)

Via di Porta San Sebastiano runs from Piazzale Numa Pompilio in front of the Terme di Caracalla to the beginning of Via Appia Antica (see that section later in this chapter and Walk 3 in the Rome Walks chapter). Behind the high stone walls are luxurious private villas and gardens, and on the eastern side, a small public park.

At the southern end of the road is the Porta San Sebastiano, the largest and best-preserved gateway in the Aurelian Wall. It is now a museum, the **Museo delle Mura**, which documents the history of the wall surrounding the city built by Aurelian (270–275) for defensive purposes and continued by his successor Probus (276–282). The perimeter of the wall measured around 19km with 18 gates and 381 towers; all seven of Rome's hills were incorporated within it. Maxentius (306–312) subsequently doubled its height. Most of the Aurelian Wall survives today (see the boxed text 'Within these Walls', in the Facts about Rome chapter, and the Rome Walks chapter for more details). The museum contains prints, drawings and models, and visitors can walk along the ramparts for about 400m. The museum (☎ 06 70 47 52 84), Via di Porta San Sebastiano 18, opens 9 am to 7 pm Tuesday to Sunday. Admission costs €2.58.

BOCCA DELLA VERITÀ TO TESTACCIO
Piazza Bocca della Verità & the Forum Boarium (Map 6)

Between the Aventine and the Tiber is the recently refurbished **Chiesa di Santa Maria in Cosmedin** in Piazza Bocca della Verità, regarded as one of the finest medieval churches in Rome. Two earlier structures that stood on the site – an arcaded colonnade that was part of an Imperial-era market inspector's office and walls from a 7th-century Christian welfare centre – were incorporated into the church built by Pope Hadrian I in the 8th century. The church was further altered in the 12th century when the seven-storey bell tower and medieval portico were added. The church's interior, including the beautiful floor, high altar and *schola cantorum* (choir), was decorated with Cosmati inlaid coloured marble. There are 12th-century frescoes in the aisles, inside the nave arches and scant remains high up on the nave walls. An 8th-century mosaic fragment is preserved in the souvenir shop.

Under the portico is the famous **Bocca della Verità** (Mouth of Truth), a large disk in the shape of a mask which probably once served as the cover of an ancient drain. Legend says that if you put your right hand into the mouth while telling a lie, it will snap shut. The church opens 10 am to 1 pm and 3 to 5 pm, although the portico opens 9 am to 6 pm.

Opposite Santa Maria in Cosmedin are two tiny Roman temples dating from the Republican era both of which have been recently restored: the round **Tempio di Ercole Vincitore** and the **Tempio di Portunus**. The temples were consecrated as churches in the Middle Ages and stand in an area once known as the Forum Boarium (cattle market), which existed even before the Roman Forum. The Forum Boarium later became an important commercial centre and had its own port on the Tiber. To its north are the ruins of the **Casa dei Crescenzi**, a former tower fortress transformed into a mansion in the 11th century by the powerful Crescenzi family. It is one of the few medieval Roman houses to have survived.

Off Piazza Bocca della Verità, towards the Palatine in Via del Velabro, is the **Arco di Giano** (Arch of Janus), a four-sided Roman arch, which once covered a crossroads. In ancient times, cattle dealers used it to shelter from sun and rain. Beyond the arch, on the northern side of the street is the medieval **Chiesa di San Giorgio in Velabro**. The church's portico, which dates from the 7th century, has been rebuilt after it was completely destroyed by a Mafia bomb attack in 1993. The convent beside the church was also damaged and has been restored.

Turning left into Via di San Teodoro, you reach the circular **Chiesa di San Teodoro** which nestles at the foot of the Palatine. A church was built on this site in the 6th century on the ruins of warehouses that stood between the Roman Forum and the Tiber. The present church dates from the mid-15th century and was built by Pope Nicholas V, but the breathtaking mosaic in the apse has survived from an earlier building. The church was restored in 1704 by Carlo Fontana working under the commission of Pope Clement XI. Fontana designed the double stairway that leads down from street level to a courtyard, in the centre of which is an altar from a pagan temple. The church has inconsistent opening hours. You might be lucky to find it open between 9 am and 1 pm and 3.30 to 6 pm. Otherwise it opens at 10.30 am for Mass on Sunday.

Fascist-era buildings line Via Petroselli, the road from Piazza Bocca della Verità to Teatro di Marcello. These house municipal offices including the Anagrafe, or public records office. To the right, Vico Jugario leads up to Piazza della Consolazione at the top of which is the **Chiesa di Santa Maria della Consolazione**, which has 16th century frescoes by Taddeo Zuccari. On the corner of Via Petroselli and Via del Foro Olitorio is the **Chiesa di San Nicola in Carcere**. It was built in the 11th century and remodelled in 1599 by Giacomo della Porta. The church was built on the site of the Republican era vegetable and oil market, and marble columns from temples that once stood there were used in the church's facade and interior.

Continuing northwards along Via del Teatro di Marcello, you come to the **Teatro di Marcello**, (Map 4) planned by Julius Caesar and built around 13 BC by Augustus. See the boxed text 'Teatro di Marcello' in the Rome Walks chapter.

Circo Massimo (Maps 4 & 6)

The Circo Massimo (Circus Maximus in ancient-Roman times) lies between the Palatine and Aventine in a valley once known as the Vallis Murcia. There is not much to see here: only a few ruins remain of what was once a chariot racetrack, about 600m long and 90m wide, decorated with statues and columns and surrounded by wooden stands, which held more than 200,000 spectators. Races were run anticlockwise around the track, the greatest excitement coming when the chariots had to negotiate the tight turns at each end.

The history of the circo goes back a long way. A brick structure was built to substitute earlier wooden structures in the 2nd century BC. In 46 BC, Julius Caesar had battles re-created here, using prisoners of war and method acting. Augustus erected the obelisk of Ramses II in 10 BC; the obelisk now stands in Piazza del Popolo. The fire of AD 64 that destroyed much of the city is thought to have started in the Circo Massimo's wooden stands. The circo was rebuilt by Trajan in about 100; by this time it could hold 250,000 spectators. It was later expanded by Caracalla and restored by Constantine, who decorated it with a second obelisk, that of Tutmosis III, which was later moved to Piazza San Giovanni in Laterano.

The Circo Massimo remained in use until 549. Today, excavations of the ruins continue at the eastern end and it's a popular place for jogging and walking dogs.

Aventine (Map 6)

South of the Circo Massimo is the Aventine hill (Aventino), best reached from Via di Circo Massimo by either Via di Valle Murcia or Clivo dei Pubblici to Via di Santa Sabina. It is also easily accessible by bus No 81 from Piazza Venezia, or on the Metro Linea B, disembarking at the Circo Massimo station). Along the way, you will pass the **Roseto Comunale**, a beautiful public rose garden, best seen obviously when the roses are in bloom in May and June, and the pretty, walled **Parco Savello**, planted with orange trees. There is a stunning view of Rome from the park.

Next to the Parco Savello is the **Basilica di Santa Sabina**, founded by Peter of Illyria in AD 422, one of the most important and beautiful early-Christian basilicas in Rome. The church was added to in the 9th century

Open Only on Request

Several archaeological sites in Rome are open to the public only on request. To gain entry to a closed site, you should send a letter or fax well in advance of your trip to: Ufficio Monumenti Antichi e Scavi del Comune di Roma, Ripartizione X, Via del Portico d'Ottavia 29, 00186 Roma (fax 06 689 21 15 or 06 67 10 31 18).

You should state the dates of your stay in Rome, the monuments you want to see and how many people are in the party. Letters and faxes can be written in English. The office will then write back to you (probably in Italian) with possible dates and times, and the cost of the visit. A further confirmation from you might also be required.

One confusing thing to note is that there are three different archaeological authorities: at Comune or city level (Ripartizione X), regional level and national level, and that there are further divisions in each of these authorities. Even the people who work in these offices don't always know who is responsible for what.

Ripartizione X governs 21 archaeological areas in Rome, of which eight are described in this chapter: Monte Testaccio, Area Sacra di Largo Argentina, Circo Massimo, Colombario di Pomponio Hylas in Via Latina, Insula Ara Coeli (Roman apartment block at the foot of the Capitoline), Mausoleo di Augusto, Stadio di Domiziano (Piazza Navona) and the Teatro di Marcello. These sites can be visited on request as outlined above.

If you don't manage to organise a special visit in advance of your trip, all is not lost. Archaeological sights are opened periodically by the authorities, so you might strike it lucky. Tourist information booths can provide details.

and again in 1216, just before it was given by Honorius III to the newly founded Dominican order. Of particular note is the 5th-century door carved from cypress wood, to the far left as you stand under the 15th-century portico facing the church. The door features 18 carved wooden panels depicting biblical scenes. The crucifixion scene is one of the oldest in existence but it is interesting to note that Christ's cross is not shown.

The three naves in the solemn interior are separated by 24 Corinthian columns made (strangely enough for the period) specifically for the occasion. They are Rome's first example of columns, based on the Ravenna model, which supported arches rather than architraves. Above and to the sides of the arches there is a red and green frieze in *opus sectile* (5th and 6th century). Light streams into the interior of the church from high nave windows added in the 9th century. Also dating from the 9th century are the carved choir, pulpit and bishop's throne.

In the centre of the nave is a mosaic tombstone of Muñoz de Zamora, one of the first leaders of the Dominicans. Only a small amount of the mosaic decoration that once covered the walls still remains. The fresco in the apse was painted in the 19th century. The 13th-century cloister was recently restored and can be visited with permission of the sacristan. The basilica opens 6.30 am to 12.45 pm and 3.30 to 7 pm daily.

Farther south along Via Santa Sabina is the Piazza Cavalieri di Malta and the **Priorato di Malta**, the headquarters of the Order of the Knights of Malta. The order was founded in the 12th-century in Rhodes and later in Malta to assist pilgrims en route to the Holy Land. The villa is the residence of the grand master of the Knights of Malta and served as the order's embassies to Italy and the Vatican. It is surrounded by a radiant garden with laurel hedges and palm trees.

Piranesi redesigned the **Chiesa di Santa Maria del Priorato** within the compound in 1765. Entering it is like walking into a Piranesi drawing; it is loaded with architectural details and elaborate stucco work. The complex is rarely open to the public. Should you be passing on a day when it is, a visit is a must. If it's closed, peep through the keyhole in the central door of the entrance for a view through a tunnel of trees to St Peter's dome in the distance. Piranesi also designed Piazza Cavalieri di Malta, which is decorated with mini obelisks and coats of arms.

On the other side of the hill is **Chiesa di Santa Prisca** in Piazza Santa Prisca dating from the 4th century AD. The church was built on top of a Mithraic shrine which the Christians all but destroyed. This was extensively excavated in the 1950s and damaged wall paintings, showing the seven stages of initiation into the Mithraic cult, have been restored but are not on show to the public. The church opens 8 am to noon and 4.30 to 7.30 pm daily.

Across Viale Aventina in Via di San Saba is the picturesque **Chiesa di San Saba**, which dates from the 10th century although it has been substantially rebuilt. Cosmati marble work from the 13th century decorates the main door and floor. The portico contains a number of sculptural and intricately carved Roman sarcophagi. Above the portico is a loggia which was added in the 16th century. The church opens 7 am to noon and 4 to 6.30 pm daily.

Porta San Paolo & Testaccio (Map 6)

Porta San Paolo, one of the ancient city gates, is situated south of the Aventine. Via Ostiense runs south from here towards Ostia, once Rome's main commercial sea port (see the Excursions chapter). The area is known as Piramide, after the pyramid monument, 27m high, inside which Gaius Cestius, a plebeian tribune, was buried in 12 BC. The pyramid was incorporated into the Aurelian Wall in the 3rd century AD.

Behind it is the **Cimitero Acattolico per gli Stranieri** (Protestant Cemetery), the final resting place of numerous distinguished foreigners, including John Keats, who died in Rome in 1821. It is a shady and pleasant place for a peaceful wander. Percy Bysshe Shelley certainly thought so: 'It might make one in love with death to think that one should be buried in so sweet a place,' he wrote. His heart was brought to Rome and buried there after his death in 1822. The cemetery (entrance at Via Caio Cestio 5, off Via Nicola Zabaglia) opens 9 am to 6 pm Tuesday to Sunday (to 5 pm from October to March).

Situated south-west of the Aventine, between Via Marmorata and the Tiber, **Testaccio** was the river port of ancient Rome from the 2nd century BC to the 3rd century AD. Supplies of wine, oil and grain were transported from Roman colonies to the city via Ostia and the Tiber. The containers for these goods – huge terracotta amphorae and other pots – were then dumped. At first the pots were tossed into the river; when the Tiber became almost unnavigable as a consequence, the pots were smashed to pieces and stacked methodically in a pile which over time grew into a large hill, the Monte Testaccio.

The word Testaccio comes from the Latin *testae*, meaning potsherds. In the Middle Ages the area was the scene of jousts and particularly vicious carnival games, when pigs, bulls and other animals were packed into carts and sent flying down the 45m hill. Those that survived were slaughtered anyway and eaten.

Most of the area is now occupied by low-cost housing that went up at the end of the 19th century to house workers for the new capital city. Although it is off the regular sightseeing trail, Testaccio is a good place to visit if you want to try the most Roman of Roman culinary specialities – offal (see the Places to Eat chapter). There is an excellent morning market from Monday to Saturday selling fruit, vegetables, herbs, flowers and (rather incongruously) cheap shoes.

The area around Monte Testaccio and the former slaughterhouse (which is now an active social centre) is also becoming increasingly popular for nightlife (see the Entertainment chapter) with some bars and clubs occupying caves carved out of the artificial hill – the neatly stacked amphora pieces are clearly visible. Monte Testaccio itself can only be visited on request (see the boxed text 'Open Only on Request' earlier in this chapter for details).

GHETTO
Via del Portico d'Ottavia (Map 4)

This road is the centre of what remains of the Jewish Ghetto. In the 16th century Pope Paul IV ordered the confinement of Jewish people in this area, marking the beginning of a period of intolerance which continued into the 20th century. There is a certain irony in the fact that Europe's longest surviving Jewish community – there have been Jews in Rome for over 2000 years – can be found in the heart of the city that is the centre of the Christian world.

The tightly packed buildings on the northern side of the street incorporate the remains of old Roman and medieval buildings. The house at No 1 (on the corner of Piazza Costaguti) dates from 1468 and the facade is decorated with pieces of ancient-Roman sculpture including a fragment from a sarcophagus. At street level, in a tiny unmarked shop, an all-female bakery produces traditional Jewish breads, pastries and cakes.

Heading through Piazza delle Cinque Scole, you see the rear of the imposing **Palazzo Cenci**, the biggest palace in the area. In Via dell'Arco dei Cenci you can see the main facade, which is decorated by elaborate stucco work around small balconies. The palace belonged to the family of the ill-fated Beatrice Cenci, who was abused by her tyrannical father; she eventually killed him and was subsequently beheaded. Shelley based his tragedy *The Cenci* on the family and a portrait of her by Guido Reni is one of the most famous works in the Galleria Nazionale d'Arte Antica in Palazzo Barberini.

In the nearby Piazza Mattei is the **Fontana delle Tartarughe** (Tortoise Fountain), one of the most delightful of all Rome's fountains, created in 1585 by Taddeo Landini based on a design by Giacomo della Porta. Landini added the bronze figures between 1581 and 1584. Legend has it that the fountain was built in a single night for the duke of Mattei, who owned the surrounding palaces. The duke had apparently just lost all his money and consequently his fiancée, and wanted to prove to her father that he was still capable of great things.

A nun contemplates temptation on Via dei Fori Imperiali.

See the whole city in one go: take a trip to Piazza Navona and browse around the art stalls.

Hot nuts in Piazza Navona

A mixed bunch at Campo de' Fiori market

Foccacia bread with any filling at Pizza a Taglio

Say goodbye to lire – the euro has arrived.

Sniff out Gorgonzola cheese at Volpetti.

At the end of Via del Portico d'Ottavia is the majestic **Portico d'Ottavia**. The portico was erected in 146 BC and then rebuilt by Augustus in 23. The original builder was called Octavius, and Augustus kept the name since it coincided nicely with that of his sister, Octavia. The few remaining columns and fragmented pediment are a small part of the original vast rectangular portico with about 300 columns. Measuring 132m by 119m, the complex included temples dedicated to Juno and Jupiter (the latter was the first temple in Rome to be built entirely of marble), a Latin and a Greek library, and numerous magnificent statues and works of art. By the Middle Ages the Roman structure had already been sacked for its marble and been pulled down.

The city fish market was established here in the Middle Ages and was operational until the end of the 19th century. Recent excavations have uncovered the remains of a small fishmonger's stand, complete with a bench for displaying the wares, clam shells and a stone basin in which the fish were washed. On one of the brick pillars outside the church a stone plaque states that the fish sellers had to give city officials the head *usque ad primas pinnas inclusive* (up to and including the first fin) of any fish longer than the plaque itself. Fish heads, and particularly those of the sturgeon still living in the Tiber at the time, were prized for soup.

In AD 755, part of the original colonnade was incorporated into the facade of **Chiesa di Sant'Angelo in Pescheria**. To the right of the portico you will notice the stucco facade of the 17th-century oratory of **Sant'Andrea dei Pescivendoli** (1689).

Continuing along Via del Portico d'Ottavia to the river, you come to the 19th-century **synagogue** which also houses the **Museo della Comunità Ebraica**, a museum of Roman Jewish history. The building is under constant armed guard after a bomb exploded there in 1983, killing a small child. The museum opens 9.30 am to 4.30 pm, Monday to Thursday, 9.30 am to 1.30 pm Friday and 9.30 am to noon on Sunday. Tickets cost €4.13 and include a visit to the synagogue. Opposite the synagogue, on the other corner of Via del Portico d'Ottavia, is the little **Chiesa di San Gregorio**, one of the places where Ghetto Jews were forced to attend Mass. An inscription above the door in Hebrew and Latin reproaches the Jews for not converting to Christianity.

Isola Tiberina (Map 6)

The Isola Tiberina (Tiber Island) is the only island in the Tiber and lies between the Ghetto and Trastevere. From the Ghetto, you cross the **Ponte Fabricio** which was built in 62 BC and is Rome's oldest standing bridge.

Reputedly the world's smallest inhabited island, it is only 300m long and 80m wide. According to some ancient writers the island was formed by the grain stores thrown into the river after the expulsion of the Tarquins from the city. Another version states that a Greek ship ran aground at this spot and was later surrounded by a travertine wall. In its shape, the island still resembles a ship but it is in fact made of volcanic rock. The island has been associated with healing since the 3rd century BC when the Romans adopted Aesculapius, the Greek god of healing, as their own and erected a temple to him on the island. Today it is the site of the Ospedale Fatebenefratelli (hospital).

The recently restored **Chiesa di San Bartolomeo** was built in the 10th century on the ruins of the Roman temple. It has a Romanesque bell tower and a marble wellhead, believed to have been built over the same spring which provided healing waters for the temple. The church has suffered damage from floods several times. Floating mills were a feature of the Tiber near the Isola Tiberina (and upstream to the Ponte Sisto) from the 6th to the 19th centuries.

The **Ponte Cestio**, built in 46 BC, connects the island to Trastevere. It was rebuilt in the late 19th century. The remains of a bridge to the south of the island are part of ancient Rome's first stone bridge, the **Ponte Rotto** (Broken Bridge). Most of the bridge was swept away in a terrible flood in 1598.

TRASTEVERE (Maps 4 & 6)

The settlement at Trastevere – the name comes from *trans Tiberim* meaning 'across the Tiber' – was, in early times, separate from Rome. Although it was soon swallowed by the growing city, this sense of separation continued during medieval times when the area developed its own identity. Trastevere residents have always regarded themselves as *noantri* or 'we others'. It is said that even today many of the old people of Trastevere rarely cross the river to the city. In recent years it has become a fashionable place to live and is always busy at the weekend and during summer, when tourists and Romans flock here to eat in the trattorie or to drink at the numerous bars.

Santa Cecilia in Trastevere (Map 6)

The Basilica di Santa Cecilia in Trastevere in Piazza di Santa Cecilia was built in the 9th century by Paschal I over the house of St Cecilia, where she was martyred in 230. Cecilia was the Christian wife of Valerian, a Roman patrician. Despite her marriage, she kept her vow of chastity, and her husband was so impressed by her faith that he too converted. Valerian was martyred for this act; Cecilia was arrested while burying his body and was subsequently martyred too. Her murderers first tried to scald her to death by locking her in the caldarium of the baths in her own house. She emerged unscathed and was then beheaded, but the executioner did such a bad job that she took three days to die. Legend has it she sang as she was dying and, for this reason, she became the patron saint of music and musicians.

An 18th-century facade leads into a pretty courtyard and then to the portico, decorated with colourful 12th-century mosaic medallions, and Baroque facade of the church itself. The impressive mosaic in the apse was executed in 870 and features Christ giving a blessing. To his right are St Peter, St Valerian (husband of St Cecilia) and St Cecilia. To his left are St Paul, St Agatha and St Paschal. The holy cities are depicted underneath. The baldachino over the main altar was carved by Arnolfo di Cambio, and the statue of St Cecilia in front of the altar is by Stefano Maderno. This finely carved statue depicts, with considerable compassion, the body of the saint as she was found when her tomb was opened in 1599.

In the right-hand nave the **Cappella del Caldarium** marks the spot where the saint was allegedly tortured with steam for three days before being martyred. There are two works by Guido Reni here.

Of great interest are the excavations of Roman houses, one of which was perhaps the house of St Cecilia, underneath the church. These ruins are accessible from the room at the end of the left aisle as you enter the church. Admission costs €1.03. Note the large room with deep basins in the floor, thought to have been a tannery, the remains of black-and-white mosaic paving and the elaborate crypt which was decorated in the 19th century in Byzantine style.

There is a superb 13th-century fresco of the Last Judgment by Pietro Cavallini in the nun's choir, entered through the convent. The fresco used to be the inside facade of the old church. It was boarded up for many years and only rediscovered around 1900, hence its excellent state of preservation and amazingly rich colours and clear details. The fresco can be visited 10 to 11.30 am Tuesday and Thursday, and 11.15 (after Mass) to 11.45 am on Sunday. Admission costs €1.03. The church itself opens 10 to 11.45 am and 4 to 5.30 pm daily.

Nearby, in the pretty Piazza in Piscinula is the medieval **Chiesa di San Benedetto**. The church has a roofed bell tower, Cosmati paving and a fine 13th-century fresco depicting St Benedict. On Viale Trastevere, the busy traffic thoroughfare that dissects Trastevere, at Piazza Sonnino is the **Chiesa di San Crisogono**, with a 12th-century Romanesque bell tower and a portico that was added in the 17th century. The columns and some of the marble fragments in the mosaic floor are ancient. A fine mosaic in the apse representing the Madonna and Child flanked by St James and St Chrysogonus is by Pietro Cavallini and his pupils. Beneath the present building (you enter through the sacristy) are the remains of an early-Christian church dating from the 5th century, which was itself built on a *titulus*, a private house used for secret Christian worship.

Piazza Santa Maria in Trastevere (Map 6)

Via della Lungaretta connects Piazza Sonnino to the lovely Piazza Santa Maria in Trastevere, the heart of Trastevere and a popular neighbourhood meeting place. It's a true Roman square – by day peopled by mothers with pushchairs, chatting locals and guidebook-toting tourists, by night with artisans selling their craftwork, young Romans looking for a good time and the odd homeless person looking for a bed. It's worth paying extra for a cappuccino or an aperitvo to sit down at one of the bars in the square. You'll enjoy not only a great view but also the passing people parade.

The fountain in the centre of the square is of Roman origin and was restored by Carlo Fontana in 1692. An ancient legend says that on the day that Christ was born a miraculous fountain of pure oil sprang from the ground in this area and flowed for a whole day down to the Tiber. Via della Fonte d'Olio, a small street leading off the northern side of the square, commemorates this event.

Santa Maria in Trastevere (Map 6)

The Basilica di Santa Maria in Trastevere is believed to be the oldest place of worship dedicated to the Virgin in Rome. Tradition has it that the church was established by Pope Calixtus in the early 3rd century AD and subsequently rebuilt by Julius I in 337. The present structure was built in 1138 by Innocent II and features a Romanesque facade, with a stunning 12th-century mosaic of the Virgin feeding the baby Jesus flanked by 10 women holding lamps. Two tiny figures kneeling at the Virgin's feet were probably donors to the church. At the top of the Romanesque bell tower (whose bells ring every 15 minutes) is a small mosaic of the Virgin. The portico, embedded with fragments of ancient and medieval sculpture, inscriptions and sarcophagi, was added by Carlo Fontana in 1702.

The impressive interior features 21 irregular ancient Roman columns with Ionian and Corinthian capitals, some of which come from the Terme di Caracalla. The wooden ceiling was designed in 1617 by Domenichino, who painted the central panel depicting the Assumption of the Virgin. The mosaics in the apse and on the triumphal arch date from 1140 and are absolutely stunning. At the top of the triumphal arch are the symbols and names of the four Evangelists. On either side are Isaiah and Jeremiah, each with an image of a caged bird representing Christ imprisoned by the sins of humankind. At the top of the apse are the signs of the zodiac, beneath which is a splendid mosaic against a gold background of the Christ and the Virgin enthroned. They are flanked by various saints and, on the far left, Pope Innocent II holding a model of the church. Note the richly patterned and detailed robes of the Virgin. Below this is a series of six mosaics by Pietro Cavallini (c.1291) illustrating the life of the Virgin.

On the right of the altar is a beautiful Cosmati Paschal candlestick placed, it is said, on the exact spot of the miraculous fountain of oil. The small chapel on the left of the altar, the Cappella Altemps, is decorated with frescoes and stuccoes (1588). A Byzantine painting of the Madonna and angels, dating from the 8th century or earlier, was once the altarpiece and is now substituted by a photograph. The badly deteriorated original is displayed in a room to the left. The church opens 7 am to noon and 3 to 7 pm daily.

North of Piazza Santa Maria in Trastevere (Maps 4 & 6)

Heading westwards from Piazza Santa Maria you come to Piazza Sant'Egidio which leads onto the pretty Via della Scala. Residents of the streets east of here have the most photographed washing in the world.

The recently restored **Chiesa di Santa Maria della Scala** (Map 6), in Piazza Santa Maria della Scala, dates from the 16th century. Next to it is the historic Farmacia di Santa Maria della Scala, which is still run by monks from the adjacent monastery. If it's open, go in and have a look.

Passing through the city walls at **Porta Settimiano** (Map 4), you reach the long, straight Via della Lungara, built by Pope Julius II to connect the area of the Borgo (near the Vatican) to Trastevere, and Palazzo Corsini, the Orto Botanico and Villa Farnesina (see those sections later in this chapter).

From Porta Settimiano, Via di Santa Dorotea leads to Piazza Trilussa and **Ponte Sisto**, a footbridge over the river that connects Trastevere to Via Giulia and the Campo de' Fiori area. The bridge was built during the pontificate of Sixtus IV (1471–84) to replace the ancient Pons Janiculensis.

Palazzo Corsini (Map 4)

The large, white Palazzo Corsini dates from the 15th century but was rebuilt in the 18th century for Cardinal Neri Maria Corsini, a nephew of Pope Clement XII. The building had a series of illustrious occupants. Queen Christina of Sweden, who had fled her native country after becoming a Catholic, died there in 1689, and Napoleon's mother Letizia took up residency there in 1800. Cardinal Corsini's valuable art collection was acquired by the state in 1883 and now forms part of the **Galleria Nazionale d'Arte Antica**. The rest of the collection is in Palazzo Barberini.

The galleries are decorated with trompe l'oeil frescoes. Highlights of the collection (of mainly 16th- and 17th-century works) are Van Dyck's superb *Madonna della Paglia* (Madonna of the Straw) in Room 1 and Murillo's *Madonna and Child* in Room 2. The same subject painted by Girolamo Siciolante de Sermoneta demonstrates the difference between a good and a bad artist. Sermoneta's baby is overly flushed and muscular and appears to be choking on its mother's milk.

The paintings of the Bologna school in Room 7 stand out, including Guido Reni's richly coloured and expressive *St Jerome* and melancholy *Salome*, Giovanni Lanfranco's very beautiful *St Peter Healing St Agatha* and a haunting *Ecce Homo* by Guercino.

The museum's (☎ 06 68 80 23 23) entrance is at Via della Lungara 10. It opens 9 am to 7 pm Tuesday to Sunday and admission costs €4.13.

Orto Botanico (Map 4)

The gardens of the Palazzo Corsini subsequently became the Orto Botanico, Rome's botanical garden, which has some of the rarest plants in Europe. Highlights include the Mediterranean succulents, an avenue of palms, a collection of cacti and a rock garden of mountain flowers from the Apennines and other ranges in Europe and Africa. It opens 9 am to 6.30 pm Monday to Saturday, April to September, and 9 am to 5.30 pm Monday to Saturday, October to March. Tickets cost €2.06.

Villa Farnesina (Map 4)

Opposite Palazzo Corsini is the Renaissance Villa Farnesina, built by Baldassarre Peruzzi between 1508 and 1511 for the Sienese banker Agostino Chigi as his suburban residence. Chigi was a patron of Raphael, who devised the decorative scheme of the frescoes and painted the superb *Galatea* in the Loggia della Galatea. The rest of the work was carried out by Raphael's pupils, including Giulio Romano, Giovanni da Udine and Francesco Penni, and also by Peruzzi and Sebastiano del Piombo. Gaspard Dughet added various frescoes in the 17th century. The villa (☎ 06 683 88 31 or 06 68 80 17 67) opens 9 am to 1 pm Monday to Saturday. Admission costs €3.09.

The building also houses the **Gabinetto Nazionale delle Stampe** (National Print Collection), part of the Istituto Nazionale per la Grafica (☎ 06 69 98 01), which can be consulted by scholars.

CAMPO DE' FIORI & AROUND
Campo de' Fiori (Map 8)

This is a lively square where a flower and vegetable market is held Monday to Saturday. Now lined with bars and trattorie, the square was once a flowery meadow before it became a place of execution during the Inquisition. Giordano Bruno was burned at the stake here for heresy in 1600 and his statue now stands at its centre.

Many of the streets near Campo de' Fiori are named after the artisans who traditionally occupied them, for example Via dei Cappellari (hatters), Via dei Baullari (trunk makers) and Via dei Chiavari (key makers). Via dei Giubonnari (jacket makers), still a popular street for clothing shops, runs off the southern corner of the square and leads to the 17th-century **Chiesa di San Carlo ai Catinari**. The church and exquisite dome were designed by Rosato Rasati. Inside, there are altarpieces by Pietro da Cortona and Giovanni Lanfranco among others. It opens 7.30 am to noon and 4.30 to 7 pm.

The northern corner of Campo de' Fiori leads to Piazza della Cancelleria, which is dominated by a late-15th-century Renaissance palace. **Palazzo della Cancelleria**, built for Cardinal Raffaello Riario, once housed the Papal Chancellery and it is still used by the Vatican. It is thought that Bramante designed the double loggia in the magnificent interior courtyard. Recent excavations beneath the palace have revealed ruins of one of the most important early-Christian churches in Rome, the Basilica di San Lorenzo in Damaso, which was finally demolished in the 15th century to make way for a new church (of the same name) and the palace into which it is incorporated.

Heading towards Piazza Navona, on the corner of Via dei Baullari and Corso Vittorio Emanuele II, is a small palace known as the Piccolo Farnesina, built for a French clergyman, Thomas Le Roy, in 1523. It is now home to the **Museo Barracco**, one of the city's most charming museums. Senator Giovanni Barracco presented his exquisite collection of Greek, Roman, Assyrian and Egyptian sculpture and artefacts to the city in 1902. Underneath the museum are remains of what is said to be a Roman fish shop, complete with counter and a water trough (ask for access). Fresco fragments found there are displayed on the ground floor. The museum opens 9 am to 7 pm, Tuesday to Sunday. Admission costs €2.58.

Opposite the Museo Barracco is the Palazzo Braschi, which houses the **Museo di Roma** (☎ 06 687 58 80), founded in 1930 to illustrate the history and life of Rome from the Middle Ages to the present day. Many of the exhibits, which include paintings, statues and architectural decorations, came from buildings that have since been demolished. The museum has been closed for major renovations for several years, and was still closed at the time of writing.

Heading in an easterly direction along Corso Vittorio Emanuele II you come to the late-16th-century **Chiesa di Sant'Andrea della Valle**, the setting for the first act of Puccini's opera *Tosca*. The elaborate facade was completed in the 17th century and is in high-Baroque style. The church's dome is the highest in Rome, after that of St Peter's, and was designed by Carlo Maderno. Frescoes by Giovanni Lanfranco and Domenichino decorate the inside of the dome. The frescoes around the apse and altar were also painted by Domenichino. Competition between the artists was fierce, especially when they were working at the same time, and legend has it that Domenichino once took a saw to Lanfranco's scaffold. The church opens 7.30 am to noon and 4.30 to 7.30 pm.

Piazza Farnese (Map 8)

Piazza Farnese is one of Rome's most elegant squares. It is dominated by the enormous **Palazzo Farnese**, a fine Renaissance building, which was started in 1514 by Antonio da Sangallo, continued by Michelangelo and completed by Giacomo della Porta. Built for Cardinal Alessandro Farnese (later Pope Paul III), it is now the French Embassy. Cleaning of the facade in 1999 revealed interesting polychrome brickwork that no-one ever knew was there. The palace (which is rarely open to the public) is famous for its magnificent frescoes by Annibale and Agostino Caracci.

The twin fountains in the square were enormous granite baths taken from the Terme di Caracalla.

Palazzo Spada (Map 8)

South of Campo de' Fiori in Piazza Capodiferro, this 16th-century palace is probably Rome's prettiest and has an elaborately decorated facade. It was restored by Francesco Borromini a century later, after Cardinal Bernardino Spada had acquired the palace. The building now houses the Italian Council of State (or Supreme Court) and the **Galleria Spada**.

It used to be possible to sneak past the guards to peek at the delightful courtyard and its elaborate stucco decoration, and you could ask the porter to show you Borromini's trompe l'oeil perspective in a lower courtyard. This appears to be a long colonnade stretching out to a large statue at the end; on closer inspection the colonnade is only a quarter of the length it seems, and the statue much smaller than it first appears. But the gallery has wised up to this, and the perspective can only be viewed with a ticket to Galleria Spada.

The private collection of the Spada family was acquired by the state in 1926 and has works by Titian, Andrea del Sarto, Guido Reni, Guercino, Rubens and Caravaggio. Entrance to the museum (☎ 06 686 11 58) is from Vicolo del Polverone 15b. It opens 9 am to 7.30 pm Tuesday to Saturday (to 6.30 pm Sunday). Admission costs €5.16.

Via Giulia (Maps 4 & 8)

Running parallel to the Tiber, Via Giulia was designed by Donato Bramante for Pope Julius II, who wanted a new approach road to St Peter's. It is lined with Renaissance palaces, antique shops and art galleries. The places listed are on Map 8 unless indicated otherwise.

At its southern end, near Ponte Sisto, is the **Fontana del Mascherone** (Map 8), a Baroque fountain made by combining two ancient pieces of sculpture – a grotesque mask and a stone basin. Just beyond it and spanning the road is the **Arco Farnese**, from which ivy tendrils hang like stalactites. Built to a design by Michelangelo, the arch was intended to be part of a bridge across the Tiber connecting the Palazzo Farnese and its gardens with the Villa Farnesina on the opposite side of the river. Note the two giant falcon heads which glare at each other across the doorway of the **Palazzo Falconieri** (Via Giulia 1), which houses the Hungarian Academy. Borromini had a hand in the enlargement and decoration of the building.

To the left, in Via di Sant'Eligio, is **Chiesa di Sant'Eligio degli Orefici** (Map 4), the 16th-century goldsmiths' church, which was designed by Raphael. Farther along on

the right is **Palazzo Ricci**, famous for the 16th-century frescoes on its facade. Beyond the ruined church of San Filippo Neri are the **Carceri Nuove**, built in 1655 and used as a prison until the 19th century when they were replaced by Regina Coeli prison on the other side of the Tiber.

The **Museo Criminologico** in the adjacent building is devoted to crime and punishment throughout the ages. The displays cover instruments of torture and execution, including guillotines that were used by the Papal States until 1860. The museum (☎ 06 68 30 02 34), Via del Gonfalone 29, opens 9 am to 1 pm and 2.30 to 6.30 pm Tuesday, 9 am to 1 pm Wednesday, Friday and Saturday, and 2.30 to 6.30 pm on Thursday. Admission costs €2.06.

There are several massive Renaissance palaces with elaborate facade decoration at the northern end of Via Giulia. This area is sometimes known as the Quartiere Fiorentino because of the Florentine colony that at one time inhabited the area. Many Florentine artists and architects contributed to the construction and decoration of the **Chiesa di San Giovanni Battista dei Fiorentini** (Map 4). Jacopo Sansovino won a competition for its design. The construction of the church took over a century, Sansovino's design being continued by Antonio Sangallo the younger and Giacomo della Porta. Carlo Maderno completed the elongated cupola (a Roman landmark) in 1614. Of note inside are the sculptures on the high altar by Antonio Raggi representing the baptism of Christ. The altar is by Borromini, who is buried in the church.

PIAZZA NAVONA (Map 8)

Lined with Baroque palaces, this vast and beautiful square was laid out on the ruins of a stadium built by Domitian in AD 86, ruins of which can still be seen at its northern end. The stadium had seating for around 30,000 spectators. Originally called Circus Agonalis, it became known in the Middle Ages as the Campus Agonis, which in time became 'n'agona' and eventually 'navona'. The arena was used for festivals and sporting events, including jousts, until the late

15th century, when it was paved over and transformed into a market place and public square. The ruins of the stadium can be visited by appointment only (see the boxed text 'Open Only on Request' earlier in this chapter).

Piazza Navona is a popular gathering place for Romans and tourists alike. Take time to relax on one of the stone benches and watch the artists who gather in the square to do their work, have your *tarocchi* (tarot cards) read, or pay top prices to enjoy a drink at one of the outdoor cafes, such as Tre Scalini. The square is best avoided from early December until 6 January when a gaudy market and mini funfair take over.

There are three fountains, the central one being Bernini's masterpiece, the **Fontana dei Quattro Fiumi** (Fountain of the Four Rivers) depicting the Nile, Ganges, Danube and the Rio Plata. The fountain took four years to build and was completed in 1651; funds to build the fountain were raised by an unpopular tax on bread. Bernini designed the figures but the actual carving was done by assistants. The obelisk once stood in the Circo di Massenzio on Via Appia Antica.

The **Fontana del Moro** at the southern end of square was designed by Giacomo della Porta in 1576. Bernini altered the fountain in the mid-17th century when he designed the central figure of the Moor holding a dolphin. The surrounding tritons are 19th-century copies. The Fontana del Nettuno at the square's northern end dates from the 19th century and has a central figure of Neptune fighting with a sea monster, surrounded by sea nymphs.

In the centre of the square facing the Fontana dei Quattro Fiumi is the **Chiesa di Sant'Agnese in Agone**, its facade designed by Bernini's bitter rival, Borromini. The tradition is that the statues of Bernini's Fontana dei Fiumi are shielding their eyes in disgust from the sight of Borromini's church, but the truth is that Bernini completed the fountain two years before his contemporary started work on the facade. In fact, the figure is shielding its face to indicate that the source of the river at that time was undiscovered.

The largest building in the square is the elegant **Palazzo Pamphilj** built between 1644 and 1650 by Girolamo Rainaldi and Borromini for Giovanni Battista Pamphilj when he became Pope Innocent X. It was later occupied by his domineering sister-in-law, Olimpia Maidalchini, who like other members of the pope's family received enormous riches and favours during his pontificate. It is now the Brazilian Embassy.

AROUND PIAZZA NAVONA (Map 8)
Piazza di Pasquino
At the southern end of Piazza Navona is the small Piazza di Pasquino. A statue, an ancient Roman torso that was much admired by Bernini, was placed in the square in 1501. This became known as a 'talking statue' to which people attached witty or caustic criticisms of the people who ruled the city. A prosperous tailor in the area, Pasquino, was credited with having inaugurated this form of public satire, and the messages left on the statue (and other similar statues around the city) became known as *pasquinade*.

Via del Governo Vecchio
The narrow Via del Governo Vecchio was once part of the papal thoroughfare from the Palazzo Laterano in San Giovanni to St Peter's. It takes its name from the 15th-century Palazzo del Governo Vecchio (also known as the Palazzo Nardini) at No 39, which was the seat of the papal government in the 17th and 18th centuries. Bramante is thought to have lived in the palace opposite (No 123). Former workshops that lined the street have been converted into shops selling second-hand goods such as leather jackets, old linens, lace, watches, clocks and antique furniture. See the Shopping chapter for more details.

Via della Chiesa Nuova, to the left off Via del Governo Vecchio, leads to **Chiesa Nuova**. Formerly known as Santa Maria in Vallicella, it was given to San Filippo Neri by Pope Gregory XIII in 1575 in recognition of the work he and his order did in reviving the spiritual life of the city and caring for the sick, homeless and mentally ill. San Filippo had the church rebuilt and it was decorated after his death.

The interior is elaborately gilded throughout. Pietro da Cortona was responsible for the decoration of the vault, apse and dome, there are paintings by Rubens over the high altar, and there is a beautiful painting in the northern transept by Federico Barocci of the Presentation of the Virgin in the Temple. San Filippo is buried beneath the altar in a chapel to the left of the apse. Next to the church is an **oratory**, mainly by Borromini, which was completed in 1652. Interestingly, San Filippo invented the oratory as a form of spiritual celebration through music.

Behind the Chiesa Nuova is the **Torre dell'Orologio** – a clock tower built by Borromini to decorate one corner of the convent attached to the church. Piazza dell'Orologio takes its name from the clock tower. Via dei Banchi Nuovi continues towards the Tiber. The early-16th-century **Palazzo del Banco di Santo Spirito** (Map 4) at the end of the street was designed by Antonio Sangallo the Younger and was the mint of papal Rome. The facade of the building resembles a Roman triumphal arch and the two statues crowning it represent Charity and Thrift.

Via dei Coronari

This street runs westwards from Piazza Navona towards Via del Banco di Santo Spirito. It follows the course of an ancient-Roman road that ran in a straight line from the area of Piazza Colonna to the Tiber and was a popular thoroughfare for pilgrims. The rosary-bead sellers (coronari) who once lined the street have been replaced by antique shops, though many of the original buildings remain.

The **Chiesa di San Salvatore in Lauro** in the pretty square of the same name, dates from the 16th century and has an altarpiece by Pietro da Cortona. At the eastern end, Vicolo del Montevecchio (off to the right) leads to Piazza Montevecchio and Piazza della Pace.

Santa Maria della Pace

Chiesa di Santa Maria della Pace was built for Pope Sixtus IV in the early 1480s. The church's facade and semicircular portico were added in the 17th century by Pietro da Cortona for Pope Alexander VII. Inside, the church has an octagonal dome. The first chapel on the southern side contains frescoes by Raphael representing the Sibyls having the future revealed to them by angels. These were painted for the banker Agostino Chigi in 1514. The first chapel on the northern side is decorated with frescoes by Baldassare Peruzzi who also did the *Presentation in the Temple* to the right of the high altar. Next to the church is a beautiful **chiostro** (cloister) added by Bramante in 1504 and regarded as one of the architect's finest works in Rome. Bramante employed classical rules of proportion in this two-storey arcade, creating a monumental feeling in a relatively small space.

Palazzo Altemps & Museo Nazionale Romano

Palazzo Altemps, in Piazza Sant'Apollinare, at the northern end of Piazza Navona, was begun around 1477 for Girolamo Riario and altered by its subsequent owner, Cardinal Francesco Soderini, between 1511 and 1523. It was completed in the late 16th century by the Milanese cardinal Marco Sittico Altemps and his heirs. Antonio da Sangallo the Elder, Baldassarre Peruzzi and Martino Longhi all had a hand in its design. For centuries the palace housed the notable Altemps family collection of antiquities as well as an extensive library. It was acquired by the Italian state in 1982 and underwent a careful and lengthy restoration before opening in 1997 as the new home of part of the Museo Nazionale Romano collection.

The Egyptian collection from the Museo Nazionale Romano is housed here together with the Mattei collection, formerly at Villa Celimontana (once the Mattei family estate), and 16 remaining works from the Altemps collection. However, the prestigious Ludovisi Boncompagni collection forms the main body of the exhibits. Cardinal Ludovico Ludovisi was a nephew of Pope Gregory XV and a ravenous collector of the ancient sculpture that was being unearthed and sold off on an almost daily basis in the building boom of Counter-Reformation Rome. He took advantage of his wealth and position to build up one of the most extensive and celebrated private collections of all time. It was displayed in the gardens of his palace in the present-day Via Veneto area, among follies, mazes, orchards and formal gardens, and for two centuries attracted travellers from all over Europe.

Most of the statuary that was dug up was damaged in some way. Ludovico Ludovisi employed the leading sculptors of his day – including Gian Lorenzo Bernini, Alessandro Algardi and Filippo Buzzi – to repair and enhance the works he had acquired. They didn't think twice before replacing a missing limb with one that had been found elsewhere or sculpting a new, 17th-century head to stick on top of a headless torso. Throughout the museum instructive labels illustrate which parts of the statue are original and which are Baroque additions. One of the most interesting things about Palazzo Altemps is that the sculptures are displayed in a way that is very similar to common 16th-century exhibition criteria, so you get a good idea of how a Renaissance palace and collection would have looked.

Most of the rooms are named after the pieces in them. A large hall off the courtyard, the Salone delle Erme, contains six double-faced herms and twin 1st-century AD statues of Apollo playing the lyre. Next to it, the Sala dell'Atena contains an ancient statue of Athena with a serpent, which was restored by Antonio Algardi in the 17th century. In the southern loggia, by the entrance, are several delicately carved sarcophagi reliefs. The most beautiful of these depicts a ritual foot bathing and is probably the work of a 2nd-century Greek sculptor.

Baroque frescoes throughout the building not only provide a decorative backdrop for the ancient sculpture but are fascinating exhibits themselves. The walls of the Sala delle Prospettive Dipinte (on the 1st floor) are decorated with landscapes and hunting scenes seen through trompe l'oeil windows. These frescoes were painted in the 16th century for Cardinal Altemps. The Sala della Piattaia, once the palace's main reception room, has a superb 15th-century fresco by Melozzo da Forlì of a cupboard displaying gifts received by Girolamo Riario and Caterina Sforza on the occasion of their wedding.

One of Bernini's 'touch-ups', the *Ares Ludovisi*, a Roman copy of an original Greek work, can be seen in this room. Bernini added a pointing foot, carved a demon on the hilt of Ares' sword and changed the face of the small cupid at his feet. Another Bernini enhancement is in the Sala con Obelischi (so called because of the obelisks painted on the window frames) where, in a sculptural group of a satyr and nymph, both figures have heads that belong to other statues.

The Sala della Storie di Mosè, decorated with a wall frieze depicting the 10 plagues of Egypt and the Exodus (about half of which remains) contains the *Trono Ludovisi*, one of the prize pieces in the Ludovisi collection. The carved-marble throne was discovered at the end of the 19th century in the grounds of the Villa Ludovisi. Most scholars believe that the Trono Ludovisi came from one of the Greek colonies in Italy and was produced in the 5th or 6th century BC, although its precise date and authenticity is still a subject of debate. The throne shares the room with two colossal heads, one of which is the goddess Juno and dates from around 600 BC.

A series of portrait busts is displayed in the painted loggia on the 1st floor. The loggia is adorned with trompe l'oeil windows, floral arbours, vines, exotic animals, decorative vases, foreign fruits and cherubs. It was commissioned by Cardinal Altemps around 1595 and has been superbly restored. The small fountain at the end, decorated with mosaics, marble sculptures and stuccoes, was completed in 1594.

Two of the highlights of the museum are in the Sala del Camino, named after the monumental fireplace built for Cardinal Altemps. The giant sarcophagus with intricately carved marble depicting a Roman battle scene is breathtaking. The image reads in three levels: at the top are the victors, in the middle the fighters and at the bottom the vanquished. The expression and movement extracted from a huge lump of stone are astonishing. Equally impressive is the sculptural group *Galata Suicida*, depicting a Gaul killing himself and a dead woman at his feet. This marble copy of a Pergamon bronze was commissioned by Julius Caesar. You are spared little of the detail: blood spurts out of his flesh as the Gaul knifes himself to death. The small chapel, entered from the Sala del Camino, was added to in the 17th century and is covered with elaborate gilt stuccoes and richly coloured marble decoration.

Palazzo Altemps (☎ 06 683 35 66), Piazza Sant'Apollinare 46, opens 9 am to 7 pm Tuesday to Sunday. Admission costs €5.16.

Corso del Rinascimento

Piazza delle Cinque Lune, at the northern end of Piazza Navona, leads to **Chiesa di Sant'Agostino**. The plain white facade is one of the earliest of the Renaissance. The church, built in the 15th century and renovated in the 18th, is dedicated to St Augustine and contains two great artworks. A fresco of Isaiah on the third column in the nave was painted by Raphael in 1512. The powerful figure shows the influence of Michelangelo, with whom Raphael was in close contact when both artists were working in the Vatican. A marvellous painting by Caravaggio, the *Madonna dei Pellegrini* (also known as the *Madonna di Loreto*), hangs in the first chapel on the left aisle and is considered one of his best works. See the boxed text 'On the Caravaggio Trail' later in this chapter.

Until 1935 the **Palazzo della Sapienza** housed Rome's university, La Sapienza, which was founded by Pope Boniface VIII in 1303. Giacomo della Porta designed the Renaissance facade. The building now houses the state archives. Borromini designed a library in the palace as well as its courtyard which has porticoes on three sides. The fourth side is occupied by the tiny **Chiesa di Sant'Ivo alla Sapienza**, a masterpiece of Baroque architecture and considered to be one of Borromini's most original creations. The walls alternate between being convex and concave, and the bell tower is crowned by a distinctive twisted spiral.

The 16th-century **Palazzo Madama** was originally the Rome residence of the Medici family. It was enlarged in the 17th century when the Baroque facade was added together with the decorative frieze of cherubs and bunches of fruit. The building is named after 'Madama' Margaret of Parma, the illegitimate daughter of Charles V, who lived here from 1559 to 1567. It has been the seat of the Senate, the upper house of the Italian parliament, since 1871. Unless you're a politician, the only way to get into Palazzo Madama is on a free guided tour (☎ 06 670 61 or 06 67 06 22 25). These take place at regular intervals from 10 am to 6 pm on the first Saturday of the month.

San Luigi dei Francesi

Chiesa di San Luigi dei Francesi in the square of the same name dates from the 16th century and is the French national church in Rome. Giacomo della Porta designed the facade and the interior has elaborate marble decoration. There are tombs of eminent French citizens – artists, cardinals and soldiers – who spent time in Rome, including a monument to Claude Lorrain. Frescoes by Domenichino illustrating the life of St Cecilia decorate the second chapel, although these are in a poor state of repair. St Cecilia is also depicted in the altarpiece by Guido Reni, which is in fact a copy of a work by Raphael. Most people visit the church to see the paintings by Caravaggio illustrating the life of St Matthew in the fifth chapel on the left. These have been recently restored and show Caravaggio's distinctive realism and highly dramatic use of light. See the boxed text 'On the Caravaggio Trail' later in this chapter.

PANTHEON TO GESÙ
Pantheon (Map 8)

The magnificent Pantheon or 'temple to all the gods' is the best-preserved building of ancient Rome. The original temple was built by Marcus Agrippa, top general and son-in-law of Augustus, in 27 BC. It was rebuilt by Domitian after it burned down in AD 80 and rebuilt again after being struck by lightning. Although the temple was rebuilt by Hadrian around 120, Agrippa's name remained inscribed over the entrance, leading historians to believe it was the original building until excavations in the 19th century revealed traces of the earlier temple.

The dramatic, imposing interior is the kind of place that inspires people to become architects. The height and diameter of the interior both measure 43.3m and the extraordinary dome – the largest masonry vault ever built – is considered the most important achievement of ancient Roman architecture. Light is provided by the oculus, a 9m opening in the dome; small holes in the marble floor beneath it allow any rain that enters to drain away.

The weight of the dome is supported by brick arches embedded in the structure of the walls – evident from the exterior. Rivets and holes in the brickwork indicate where the original marble veneer panels have been removed. The 16 massive Corinthian columns of the portico are each a single block of stone.

After being abandoned under the first Christian emperors, the temple was given to the church by the Byzantine emperor Phocus in 608 and dedicated to the Madonna and all martyrs. (A column was erected in honour of Phocus in the Roman Forum to mark the occasion.) Over the centuries the temple has been consistently plundered and damaged. The gilded-bronze roof tiles were removed by an emperor of the Eastern empire and, in the 17th century, the Barberini pope, Urban VIII, had the bronze ceiling of the portico melted down to make the baldachino over the main altar of St Peter's and 80 cannons for Castel Sant'Angelo.

The Italian kings Victor Emmanuel II and Umberto I, and the artist Raphael are buried here. The Pantheon is in the Piazza della Rotonda and opens 8.30 am to 7.30 pm Monday to Saturday and 9 am to 6 pm Sunday and holidays. Admission is free.

Piazza della Minerva (Map 4)

The 13-centruy **Chiesa di Santa Maria Sopra Minerva**, on Piazza della Minerva just east of the Pantheon, was built on the site of an ancient temple of Minerva (Athena).

This Dominican church is one of the few ancient churches in Rome to have been built in the Gothic style. It contains a number of important art treasures dating from the 13th to the 17th century.

There are magnificent frescoes dating from around 1489 by Filippino Lippi (the son of Filippo Lippo) in the Cappella Carafa, the last chapel in the southern transept, depicting events in the life of St Thomas Aquinas. The central *Annunciation* also shows St Thomas Aquinas presenting Cardinal Olivieri Carafa to the Virgin. To the left of the high altar is Michelangelo's statue of Christ bearing the Cross. Michelangelo completed the figure of Christ around 1520; the bronze drapery was added later. An altarpiece of the *Madonna and Child* in the second chapel in the northern transept is attributed to Fra Angelico, the Dominican friar and painter, who is also buried in the church. The body of St Catherine of Siena, minus her head (which is in the Chiesa di San Domenico in Siena) lies under the high altar. The tombs of two Medici popes, Leo X and Clement VII, are in the apse. The church was heavily restored in the Gothic style in the 19th century, when the rose windows were added and the vault painted with overly vibrant colours. It opens 7 am to 7 pm daily.

The delightful statue of an elephant supporting an Egyptian obelisk, known as the **Elefantino**, stands in the centre of the square and is one of Rome's most popular monuments. The obelisk, dating from the 6th century BC, was found among the ruins of a temple to Isis in the garden of the monastery of Santa Maria Sopra Minerva. The white-marble elephant, sculpted in 1667 by Ercole Ferrata to Bernini's design, is a symbol of strength and wisdom. The monument was unveiled in 1667, the result of many consultations between Bernini and Pope Alexander VII, whose reign it was intended to glorify. The pope composed the inscription on its base, which states: 'You who see here the figures of wise Egypt carved on a column carried by an elephant, the strongest of animals, understand it is the proof of a robust mind to sustain solid wisdom.'

On the Caravaggio Trail

Michelangelo Merisi da Caravaggio (1573–1610) arrived in Rome around 1590. Much of the information that scholars have gathered about Caravaggio's time in Rome has been gleaned from police records. Trouble with the law was a fact of daily life for the artist.

He had a reputation for wandering around the streets of the historic centre, from Campo de' Fiori to the Pantheon, brandishing (and sometimes using) a long sword. One of his girlfriends was a prostitute who worked in Piazza Navona and he was arrested on several occasions, once for launching a tray laden with artichokes at a waiter in a restaurant and another time for throwing rocks at the windows of his former landlady's house.

He was, however, fortunate to meet a number of influential churchmen who recognised his artistic genius, provided him with lodgings and introduced him to important dealers and collectors.

He fled Rome in 1606 after a ball game in Campo de' Fiori during which he killed his opponent, and spent four years on the run in Naples, Malta and Sicily. He died in Porto Ercole in Tuscany at the age of 36.

Caravaggio's paintings were controversial. His innovative and dramatic use of lighting influenced generations of subsequent artists. He used peasants, beggars and prostitutes as his models, which gave the Madonnas and saints of his paintings a realism that was not always well received. On several occasions he had to repaint commissions for churches because the subjects were deemed to be too lifelike: saints would *not* have had such dirty feet.

Several of these rejected works were bought by intuitive private collectors, including Cardinal Scipione Borghese. Borghese is said to have used his influence in the Church (he was a nephew of Pope Paul V) to dissuade several religious confraternities, who had commissioned Caravaggio works, to reject the completed paintings for being too 'realistic'. Caravaggio would then be constrained to produce a more acceptable version of the same subject, enabling Scipione to buy the offending work, soon to be considered a masterpiece, at a bargain price.

Caravaggio's work dots Rome, which has more masterpieces by the artist than any other city in the world, and can be seen in a number of churches, museums and private collections. The *Madonna dei Pellegrini* in Chiesa di Sant'Agostino is regarded as one of his most alluring works and features a superbly serene Madonna surrounded by scruffy pilgrims. Two saintly masterpieces in Santa Maria

Largo di Torre Argentina (Map 8)

The four Republican temples of the **Area Sacra di Largo Argentina** get lost amongst the heavy traffic circulating around the square. The ruins were discovered during construction work in the 1920s. The Area Sacra can be visited by appointment only (see the boxed text 'Open Only on Request' earlier in this chapter). However, you can get a good look at it from outside. The ruins are now home to hundreds of stray cats, cared for by the volunteers at the cat sanctuary at the southern end.

Crypta Balbi (Map 4)

The newest seat of the **Museo Nazionale Romano** collection illustrates – almost better than any other museum in Rome – the

city's multilayered history. The museum (part of the Museo Nazionale Romano) is based around the ruins of medieval and Renaissance structures built on top of a grand Roman portico and theatre, the Theatre of Balbus, which was constructed between 19 and 13 BC.

Many of the artefacts on display – including vividly coloured and decorated ceramics whose designs are still used today – were excavated in the immediate area; the rest (including most of the exhibits on the second floor) come from the Museo Nazionale Romano's vast and valuable collection.

The Crypta Balbi (☎ 06 481 55 76), Via delle Botteghe Oscure 31, opens 9 am to 7.30 pm Tuesday to Sunday. Admission costs €5.16.

On the Caravaggio Trail

del Popolo show the *Conversione di San Paolo* (Conversion of St Paul), a bravura composition dominated by the rear end of a horse, below which the saint is sprawled; and the *Crocifissione di San Pietro* (Crucifixion of St Peter), which uses dramatic foreshortened figures and depicts the moment when St Peter is tied upside down on the cross.

Two early works in the Galleria Doria Pamphilj include *Riposo nella Fuga in Egitto* (Rest During the Flight into Egypt) and *Mary Magdalene*, which are interesting but less theatrically illuminated than his later pieces. The Galleria Borghese contains six paintings including the *Ragazzo con Canestro di Frutta* (Boy with a Basket of Fruit), the *Bacchino Malato* (Sick Bacchus) and the famous *Madonna dei Palafrenieri*, commissioned for a chapel in St Peter's but snapped up by Scipione.

The dramatic *Davide con la Testa di Golia* (David with Goliath's Head) and *San Giovanni Battista*, showing a young St John the Baptist, were apparently given to Scipione by the artist in exchange for clemency from Pope Paul V for the murder he committed in 1606. Another *San Giovanni Battista* is in the Pinacoteca of the Capitoline Museums. The Galleria Nazionale d'Arte Antica at Palazzo Barberini has a striking *Narcissus* and a gruesome *Giuditta e Oloferne* (Judith and Holofernes). Caravaggio's *Deposizione* (Descent from the Cross) is in the Pinacoteca of the Vatican Museums.

Caravaggio's first great religious works were the three canvases of the life of St Matthew in the Chiesa di San Luigi dei Francesi. The artist had obtained the commission through the influence of the powerful Cardinal Francesco del Monte. The first version of *San Matteo e l'Angelo* (St Matthew with the Angel), the central canvas in the chapel, was rejected because the saint was depicted as a tired old man with filthy feet.

ASA ANDERSSON

Chiesa del Gesù (Map 4)

The Chiesa del Gesù in the square of the same name was the first Jesuit church in Rome. The Jesuits were founded in 1540 by the Spanish soldier Ignatius Loyola who had joined the Church after being wounded. He came to Rome in 1537 and three years later founded the Society of Jesus (the Jesuits). The order trained missionaries and teachers and sent them all over the world to convert both civilised and uncivilised peoples.

Construction of the church began in 1568 and it was consecrated in 1584. The interior was designed by Vignola and the facade by Giacomo della Porta. The high point of Counter-Reformation Baroque architecture, the Gesù was extremely important to the subsequent design of churches in Rome and throughout the Catholic world. The church's interior is elaborate, following the Jesuits' intention to attract worshippers with splendour and spectacle. It was financed by Alessandro Farnese, who was subsequently regarded as being the owner of the three most beautiful things in Rome – his family palace, his daughter and the church of the Gesù. The church opens 6 am to 12.30 pm and 4 to 7.15 pm daily.

The extraordinary fresco on the vault, depicting the *Triumph of the Name of Jesus*, is by Giovanni Battista Gaulli (known as Il Baciccia). The wonderfully foreshortened figures appear to tumble from the vault onto the coffered ceiling. Baciccia also painted the frescoes inside the cupola and designed the church's stucco decoration. St Ignatius is buried in the Cappella di Sant'Ignazio in the northern transept in an opulent marble and bronze tomb with columns encrusted with lapis lazuli. The tomb, which doubles as an altar, was made by Andrea Pozzo and other artists and is topped by a group of the *Trinity* with a terrestrial globe which is in fact the largest single piece of lapis lazuli in the world. The marble sculpture to the right of the tomb represents *Religion Triumphing over Heresy*, which just about sums up what the Jesuits were all about.

To the right of the church are rooms where St Ignatius lived from 1544 until his death in 1556. They have been restored and display paintings and memorabilia, including a masterful trompe l'oeil perspective by Andrea Pozzo. They can be visited 4 to 6 pm Monday to Saturday, and 10 am to noon on Sunday.

VIA DEL CORSO (Maps 2 & 4)

Via del Corso, known also as *Il Corso*, is a straight street over 1km in length which connects Piazza Venezia to Piazza del Popolo. The name comes from the Carnival races that were transferred there from Piazza Navona and Testaccio by Pope Paul II in 1466. These continued until the late 19th century.

Collegio Romano & Sant'Ignazio (Map 4)

A Jesuit College, the Collegio Romano, was built in 1585 under orders from Pope Gregory XIII. Many future popes studied there, including Urban VIII, Innocent X, Clement IX, Clement X, Innocent XII, Clement XI, Innocent XIII and Clement XII. Dominating the northern side of Piazza del Collegio Romano (take Via del Gesù north from the Chiesa del Gesù and turn right into Via del Piè di Marmo), the building is now used partly by the national heritage ministry.

The Jesuit **Chiesa di Sant'Ignazio di Loyola** occupies the north-eastern corner of the Collegio Romano building (take Via di Sant'Ignazio from Piazza del Collegio Romano) and rivals the Gesù for opulence and splendour. The church was commissioned by Cardinal Ludovico Ludovisi and built by the Jesuit mathematician and architect

Orazio Grassi. The sumptuous interior is covered with paintings, stucco, coloured marble and gilt. Paintings in the nave show the Jesuit fathers doing missionary work and a masterpiece by Andrea Pozzo (1642–1709) shows the *Triumph of St Ignatius*.

A highlight of the Baroque interior is the trompe l'oeil ceiling perspective, also by Pozzo. His ingenious decorative scheme makes the walls appear to extend beyond their limits, and an illusionary dome painted on canvas covers the area where the real thing should have been. A small yellow spot on the floor of the nave indicates the best vantage point.

Piazza Sant'Ignazio, in front of the church, has been described as delightfully frivolous. The theatrical square was designed by Filippo Raguzzini in the early 18th century. The picturesque and elegant buildings opposite the church are wasted as a police station.

Palazzo Doria Pamphilj (Map 4)

The Palazzo Doria Pamphilj takes up an entire block at the southern end of Via del Corso, bordered by Via del Plebiscito, Via della Gatta and Piazza del Collegio Romano. It has been the residence of the Doria Pamphilj family, Roman nobles, since the 17th century.

The **Galleria Doria Pamphilj** contains the family's private art collection, which was started by the Pamphilj pope, Innocent X. It is dazzling even by Roman standards. The elaborate picture galleries, decorated with frescoed ceilings, gilding and mirrors, had a major facelift in 1996. The walls are crammed with paintings from floor to ceiling, hung exactly as they were in the 18th century.

The most famous work in the collection is the Velasquez portrait of Innocent X, in its own room at one corner of the picture galleries. There is also a wonderfully expressive bust of Innocent X by Bernini. Four newer rooms house paintings by Hans Memling, Raphael, Titian, Tintoretto and two early works by Caravaggio (see boxed text 'On the Caravaggio Trail'). There is also a collection of sculpture.

The gallery (☎ 06 679 73 23), Piazza del Collegio Romano 2, opens 10 am to 5 pm daily (except Thursday). Admission costs €7.23. Guided tours of the private apartments (packed with more paintings and furniture) take place every half-hour from 10.30 am to 12.30 pm and cost €3.09.

Piazza Colonna (Map 4)

This square gets its name from the **Colonna Antonina** or Column of Marcus Aurelius in its centre. The column was inspired by Colonna di Traiano which is almost a century older. It was erected after the death of Marcus Aurelius in AD 180 to commemorate his victories over the barbarian tribes of the Danube. It is 30m high and made of 28 marble drums. The carved reliefs on the lower part represent the war between 169 and 173 against the Germanic tribes; those on the upper part commemorate the war against the Sarmatians between 174 and 176. In 1589 the statue of Marcus Aurelius that originally crowned the column was replaced by a bronze figure of St Paul. The column is a pain in the neck (literally) for tourists who want to appreciate the intricate reliefs. An easier option is to study the casts of the reliefs in the Museo della Civiltà Romana in EUR (see that section later).

Palazzo Chigi on the northern side of the square is the prime minister's official residence. The building was started in the 16th century by Matteo di Castello and finished in the 17th century by Felice della Greca.

South of Piazza Colonna in Piazza della Pietra is the **Tempio di Adriano**, which dates from 145 and is one of the most complete relics of antiquity in Rome. However, it is often overlooked since the colonnade of 11 columns, each 15m high, was converted in the 17th century into the former stock exchange building.

Piazza di Montecitorio (Map 4)

To the west of Piazza Colonna is Piazza di Montecitorio and the Palazzo di Montecitorio, which has been the seat of the Chamber of Deputics, the lower house of the Italian parliament, since 1871. Its rear facade is on Piazza del Parlamento.

The original palace was built for the Ludovisi family in 1650 by Gian Lorenzo Bernini. It was enlarged by Carlo Fontana at the end of the 17th century and given a larger facade with steps leading up to the entrance by Art Nouveau architect Ernesto Basile in 1918. A new-look square was unveiled in 1998 which returned to Bernini's original plan of a gently sloping ramp up to the entrance of the building articulated by three radiating semicircles.

The obelisk in the centre of the square was brought to Rome from Heliopolis in Egypt by Augustus to celebrate his victory over Cleopatra VII and her ally Mark Antony in 30 BC. It was originally set up in the area known as Campus Martius and served as part of a huge sundial. It was excavated from an area north of the square and erected on its present site in 1792. Free guided tours (☎ 06 676 01 or 06 67 60 45 65) of Palazzo di Montecitorio take place at regular intervals between 10 am and 5 pm on the first Sunday of each month.

Piazza di San Lorenzo in Lucina (Map 4)

Farther north along Via del Corso is the elegant pedestrian area of Piazza San Lorenzo in Lucina. **Chiesa di San Lorenzo in Lucina** dates from at least the 5th century but was rebuilt in the 12th century. Six ancient Ionic columns support a long portico, and the church has a pretty Romanesque bell tower. The simple facade hides an elaborate interior totally overhauled in the 17th century, when numerous side chapels were added. Guido Reni's *Crucifixion* is positioned above the main altar, and there is a fine portrait bust by Bernini in the stucco Cappella Fonseca, the fourth chapel on the southern side. The French painter Nicholas Poussin is buried in the church.

Piazza Augusto Imperatore (Map 4)

The **Mausoleo di Augusto** in Piazza Augusto Imperatore was once one of the most imposing monuments in ancient Rome. Today it looks like an unkempt mound of earth, overgrown with weeds and covered with litter, although the city council has long-term plans to turn the mausoleum and square into an important urban space. Built in 28 BC, the mausoleum was the tomb of Augustus and his descendants. Nerva was the last to be interred there, in AD 98. It served as a fortress in the Middle Ages and was later used as a vineyard, a private garden and a travertine supply for new buildings. The mausoleum was excavated and restored in the 1920s, not long before the fascist-era buildings went up on three sides of the surrounding square.

Ara Pacis (Map 4)

The fourth side of Piazza Augusto Imperatore is occupied by the Ara Pacis Augustae (Altar of Augustan Peace), which was inaugurated in 13 BC to commemorate the peace that Augustus had established both at home and abroad. The actual altar is enclosed by a marble wall decorated with reliefs – historical scenes on the northern and southern friezes and mythological scenes on the eastern and western. It is one of the most important works in the history of ancient Roman sculpture and represents the point at which Roman art emerged as a distinct entity.

The Ara Pacis was originally located in the Campus Martius, under a palace at the corner of Via del Corso and Via di Lucina (near Piazza del Parlamento). Parts of the altar were unearthed during excavations in the 16th, 17th and 18th centuries and the sculpted reliefs were acquired by the Medici, the Vatican and even the Louvre. Large-scale excavations were carried out in 1903 and again in 1937, when the remaining part of the altar was extracted. The altar was placed in its present site in 1938 under Mussolini's orders and a Fascist-style pavilion hastily erected around it. Some of the missing carvings were returned to Rome and others replaced by facsimiles made from casts of the originals. The inscription on the outer wall of the current Ara Pacis display is the text of the *Res Gestae* (Things Achieved), Augustus' official account of his reign. This was originally inscribed on two bronze pillars set outside his mausoleum.

At the time of writing, a new museum pavilion for the altar was being built. Designed by the American architect Richard Meier, it will be the first modern building to be constructed in Rome's city centre for decades. The Ara Pacis should reopen in mid-2002. Call ☎ 06 68 80 68 48 for details.

Casa di Goethe (Map 2)

Johann Wolfgang von Goethe lived in an apartment at Via del Corso 18 between 1786 and 1788. In 1997 it was transformed into Casa di Goethe (☎ 06 32 65 04 12), a museum containing some interesting drawings and etchings by Goethe as well as documents relating to his Italian sojourn. It opens 10 am to 6 pm Wednesday to Monday. Admission costs €2.58.

Piazza del Popolo (Map 2)

This vast square was laid out in the early 16th century at the point of convergence of the three roads – Via di Ripetta, Via del Corso and Via del Babuino – which form a trident at what was the main entrance to the city from the north. The 'people's piazza' has been recently and magnificently restored, and is now one of the finest of Rome's traffic-free pedestrian areas.

The two Baroque churches that divide the three roads are **Santa Maria dei Miracoli**, bordering Via di Ripetta, and **Santa Maria in Montesanto**. They are often referred to as the twin churches, as their porticoes and domes are almost identical, but on closer inspection the bell towers, lanterns and apse windows are quite different.

The square was redesigned in the neoclassical style by Giuseppe Valadier in the early 19th century. In the square's centre is an obelisk brought by Augustus from Heliopolis, in ancient Egypt, and moved to the square from the Circo Massimo in the mid-16th century. To the east is a ramp leading up to the **Pincio**, a hill which affords a stunning view of the city.

Chiesa di Santa Maria del Popolo, next to the Porta del Popolo at the northern end of the square, was originally a chapel built in 1099 on the site where Nero was buried. It was enlarged in the 13th century and re-

The elegant 13-century cloister of Basilica di San Giovanni in Laterano

Designed to impress – the alluring Cappella Sistina dome in Basilica di Santa Maria Maggiore

Pozzo's ceiling perspectives showing the *Triumph of St Ignatius*, Chiesa di Sant'Ignazio di Loyola

It's well worth the climb to the top of St Peter's for a bird's-eye view of the Vatican City.

built during the early Renaissance. In the 17th century the interior was renovated by Bernini. The apse was designed by Bramante and contains the tombs of Cardinal Ascanio Sforza and Cardinal Girolamo Basso della Rovere, both signed by the Florentine sculptor Andrea Sansovino.

The **Cappella Chigi** (the second chapel in the northern aisle after you enter the church) was designed by Raphael for the famous banker Agostino Chigi. Raphael died, thus leaving the chapel unfinished. It was completed more than 100 years later by Bernini, and contains a mosaic of a kneeling skeleton, representing death.

The frescoes in the vault are by Bernardino Pinturicchio and were painted between 1508 and 1509. They represent classical and biblical scenes. Pinturicchio also painted the lunette frescoes and the *Adoration* above the altar in the Della Rovere chapel (the first chapel in the southern aisle after you enter the church). In the first chapel to the left of the high altar are two paintings by Caravaggio, the *Conversion of St Paul* and the *Crucifixion of St Peter*, and an altarpiece, *The Assumption* by Annibale Carracci. See the boxed text 'On the Caravaggio Trail' earlier in this chapter.

PIAZZA DI SPAGNA TO PINCIO (Maps 2 & 4)

The square, church and famous **Spanish Steps** (Map 4) have long provided a gathering place for foreigners. Built with a legacy from the French in 1725, but named after the Spanish Embassy to the Holy See (which is still located in the square), the steps lead to the French church, **Trinità dei Monti** (Map 4). In the 18th century Italy's most beautiful women and men gathered here, waiting to be chosen as artists' models.

In the square is a boat-shaped fountain, called the **Barcaccia**, believed to be by Pietro Bernini, father of the famous Gian Lorenzo.

In April each year the steps are decorated with pink azaleas. It might look like the perfect spot for a picnic but don't get too enthusiastic. Theoretically you are not allowed to eat while sitting on the steps. The municipal police who patrol the area can be quite

strict and transgressors can be fined. It's all aimed at keeping the steps clean after a major restoration in 1996 but the police would do better catching the vandals who deface Rome's monuments with graffiti.

To the right as you face the steps is the house where John Keats died in 1821, now the **Keats-Shelley House** (Map 4), a small museum that's crammed with memorabilia of Keats, Percy Bysshe Shelley, Mary Shelley, Lord Byron and other Romantics. It opens 9 am to 1 pm and 2.30 to 5.30 pm Monday to Friday. Admission costs €2.58.

Farther to the right, in Piazza Mignanelli, is the **Colonna dell'Immacolata**, crowned with a statue of the Virgin Mary. Rome's firefighters traditionally place a wreath on her arm on 8 December; in his more nimble years, Pope John Paul II climbed up the firemen's ladder to do the same.

Pincio (Map 2)

The Viale della Trinità dei Monti at the top of the Spanish Steps leads to the Pincio, which gets its name from the Pinci family who owned it in the 4th century. (If you can't manage the steps there's a lift to the top outside the Piazza di Spagna Metro station). Halfway along the road on the right is the **Villa Medici**, perhaps Rome's best piece of real estate with undoubtedly one of the city's best views. The palace was built for Cardinal Ricci da Montepulciano in 1540. Ferdinando dei Medici bought it in 1576 and it remained his family's property until Napoleon acquired it in 1801, when the French Academy was transferred here. The academy was founded in 1666 to provide talented French artists, writers and musicians – *Prix de Rome* winners – with an opportunity to study and absorb Rome's enormous classical heritage.

A good way to get inside the building is by seeing one of the regular art exhibitions that are held there. Guided tours of the villa's spectacular gardens are conducted intermittently; call the French Academy (☎ 06 676 11) for details.

The view of St Peter's from the Pincio just *has* to be seen. Giuseppe Valadier designed the shady gardens (which adjoin Villa

Borghese) between 1809 and 1814. Roman families, cyclists and rollerbladers continue the tradition of past strollers, who have included Keats, Severn, Richard Strauss, Mussolini, Ghandi and King Farouk.

Pincio is also accessible from Piazza del Popolo.

Via Condotti (Map 4)

One of Rome's most elegant shopping streets, Via Condotti, runs off Piazza di Spagna towards Via del Corso. The famous Caffè Greco, at No 86, is where artists, musicians and the literati used to meet, including Goethe, Keats, Byron and Wagner. Other top shopping streets in the area include Via Frattina, Via della Croce and Via della Carozza (see the Shopping chapter for more details). Another exclusive shopping street is **Via del Babuino**, which runs off Piazza di Spagna towards Piazza del Popolo. The pretty **Via Margutta** (parallel to Via del Babuino) is lined with art galleries and antique shops. The Italian film director Federico Fellini lived in Via Margutta for many years.

Heading back towards Via del Corso you come to Piazza San Silvestro, where there is a busy bus terminus and the main post office. **Chiesa di San Silvestro in Capite** was given to the English Roman Catholics by Leo XIII in 1890. The original church was built in the 7th century on the site of a Roman building. The current church has a Romanesque bell tower and some interesting 17th-century frescoes. The **Chiesa di Santa Maria in Via** across Via del Tritone, has a display of presepi at Christmas.

VIA VENETO & PIAZZA BARBERINI (Map 5)
Via Veneto

The area around Via Vittorio Veneto was once an estate belonging to Julius Caesar was Rome's hot spot in the 1960s, where film stars could be seen at the expensive sidewalk cafes. The atmosphere of Fellini's Rome is long dead, and the street is little more than a thoroughfare for traffic to and from the centre. The US embassy in the late 19th-century Palazzo Margherita takes up

a sizeable chunk of the street. You can still pay through the nose for a meal or a coffee in one of the glass-enclosed restaurants but you'll get a better *Dolce Vita* feel in the Piazza del Popolo or Piazza Navona.

The **Chiesa di Santa Maria della Concezione** is an austere 17th-century church but the Capuchin cemetery beneath (access is on the right of the church steps) features a bizarre display of the bones of some 4000 monks, used between 1528 and 1870 to decorate the walls of a series of underground chapels. The monks who guard the cemetery request a 'compulsory' donation – so make sure you've got a few small notes handy.

Piazza Barberini

Piazza Barberini is at the southern end of Via Veneto. In its centre is the spectacular **Fontana del Tritone** (Triton Fountain), created by Bernini in 1643 for Pope Urban VIII, patriarch of the Barberini family. It features a Triton (with an enviable washboard stomach) blowing a stream of water from a conch shell. He is seated in a large scallop shell that is supported by four dolphins. The fountain suffers from its traffic-ridden position – it was once the focal point of the Baroque square in front of the Barberini family palace – and has been restored many times, most recently in 1998.

In the north-western corner of the square is another Bernini fountain, the **Fontana delle Api** (Fountain of the Bees), also created for the Barberini family. Their crest, which features three bees, can be seen on many buildings throughout Rome.

Palazzo Barberini

Palazzo Barberini was built for Pope Urban VIII between 1625 and 1633. Carlo Maderno's original design was embellished by both Bernini and Borromini. Bernini was responsible for the monumental staircase on the left (looking at the main facade). Borromini added the elegant oval staircase on the right and the windows of the upper storey. A master of artificial perspective, he created windows that from a distance seem to be the same size as those on the floor below, but are in fact significantly smaller, in keeping with the interior plan. The palace houses part of the **Galleria Nazionale d'Arte Antica**, the other part being in Palazzo Corsini in Trastevere. Large parts of the building have been used as an officers' mess for decades; the new millennium should see the first steps taken in the re-acquisition of the whole building for the museum.

A highlight of the museum is the ceiling fresco of the *Gran Salone* on the 1st floor of the palace, entitled the *Trionfo della Divina Provvidenza* (Triumph of Divine Providence), painted by Pietro da Cortona to glorify Urban VIII's pontificate and the Barberini family.

The collection is arranged chronologically and is particularly strong in 16th- and 17th-century paintings. There are works by Guido Reni, Bronzino and Guercino. Raphael's *La Fornarina* is widely believed to be a portrait of his mistress, a baker's daughter, although some scholars suggest that it was in fact a portrait of a courtesan and not by Raphael at all. An ethereal *Annunziazione* by Filippo Lippi stands out, as does Andrea del Sarto's *Sacra Famiglia*.

Two paintings by Bernini, a portrait of Urban VIII and *Davide con la Testa di Golia*, depicting David with the head of Goliath, show that his skill lay in sculpture and architecture rather than painting. There are two paintings by Caravaggio, *Judith e Holfernes*, a gruesome masterpiece of theatrical lighting, and *Narcissus*. A recent addition to the collection is Jacopo Zucchi's *Il Bagno di Betsabea* (Bethsheba's Bath). Dating from the late 1580s, this piece was lost after WWII, found in Paris, bought by an American museum and returned to Italy in 1998.

The gallery (☎ 06 481 45 91) opens 9 am to 7 pm Tuesday to Saturday, and 9 am to 8 pm on Sunday. The entrance is at Via Barberini 18 and admission costs €6.19.

QUIRINAL TO TREVI FOUNTAIN
Piazza del Quirinale (Map 5)
The Quirinal hill (Quirinale) is the highest of Rome's seven hills. At its summit is the **Palazzo del Quirinale**, in the square of the same name, the official residence of the president of the republic. Built and added

to from 1574 to the early 18th century, the palace was the summer residence of the popes from 1592 until 1870, when it became the royal palace of the kings of Italy.

Several leading architects worked on the building, including Domenico Fontana, who designed the main facade; Carlo Maderno who designed the chapel; and Bernini, who was responsible for the long wing that runs the length of Via del Quirinale. The obelisk in the centre of the square was moved here from the Mausoleo di Augusto in 1786. It is flanked by large statues of the Dioscuri, Castor and Pollux, which are Imperial Roman copies of 5th-century-BC Greek originals.

The palace (☎ 06 46 99 25 68) opens to the public 8.30 am to 12.30 pm each Sunday (unless there are official receptions). Arrive early, since it is not usually possible to join the queue after about 11 am. Admission costs €5.16.

Via del Quirinale to Via XX Settembre (Map 5)
Along Via del Quirinale are two excellent examples of Baroque architecture: the churches of **Sant'Andrea al Quirinale**, designed by Bernini, and **San Carlo alle Quattro Fontane**, designed by Borromini.

Chiesa di Sant'Andrea is considered one of Bernini's masterpieces. He designed it with an elliptical floor plan, and with a series of chapels opening onto the central area. The interior is decorated with polychrome marble, stucco and gilding. Note the cherubs that decorate the lantern of the dome.

Chiesa di San Carlo was the first church designed by Borromini in Rome and was completed in 1641. It is one of his best known buildings and the first project he completed on his own. The small cloister, also designed by Borromini, was restored in 1996. The church stands at the intersection known as **Quattro Fontane**, after the late-16th-century fountains at its four corners which represent Fidelity, Strength and the Rivers Aniene and Tiber. From the intersection you can see Porta Pia and the obelisks of the Quirinal, Trinità dei Monti and the Esquiline.

Via XX Settembre continues in a north-easterly direction to Largo di Santa Susanna and the smaller Piazza San Bernardo, on the southern side of which is **Chiesa di San Bernardo alla Terme**. The late-16th-century church was built into the ruins of a circular tower that had been part of the Terme di Diocleziano. Not dissimilar to the Pantheon, the church has a dome with a small oculus at the top to illuminate the interior. On the western side of the intersection is the **Chiesa di Santa Susanna**, the Catholic church of the American community in Rome. Dating from the 4th century, the church was rebuilt several times. The impressive facade was added by Carlo Maderno in 1603 and is considered his masterpiece.

Maderno also designed **Chiesa di Santa Maria della Vittoria** on the northern side of the intersection, although the facade was by Giovanni Battista Soria. The interior boasts colourful marble decoration in the Baroque style. The second chapel on the left as you enter the church contains an altarpiece by Domenichino, *La Madonna che Porge il Bambino a San Francesco*, depicting the Madonna showing the baby Jesus to St Francis. In the Cappella Cornaro (the fourth chapel on the right) there are two works by Bernini. The spectacular sculptural group above the altar, known as *Santa Teresa trafitta dall'amor di Dio* (The Ecstasy of St Theresa), presents a smiling angel pointing an arrow at the heart of St Teresa's, who is obviously stirred by the experience. Below is a gilded-bronze relief of the Last Supper. The late-19th-century apse fresco commemorates the victory of a Catholic army over Protestant forces in Prague in 1620.

On the corner of Via XX Settembre and Via Vittorio Emanuele Orlando, the **Fontana dell'Acqua Felice** is also known as the Moses Fountain because of the huge figure of Moses in its central niche. It was designed by Domenico Fontana and finished in 1586 to mark the terminus of the Acqua Felice aqueduct, which carried clean water to this part of the city for the first time. The water may still be relatively clean but the statues, which are suffering from pollution caused by passing traffic, are filthy.

Piazza della Repubblica (Map 5)

Formerly known as Piazza Esedra, Piazza della Repubblica follows the line of the exedra of the adjacent Terme di Diocleziano. The fountain in its centre, the **Fontana delle Naiadi**, was designed by Mario Rutelli and features a central figure of Glaucus wrestling a fish, surrounded by four naiads or water nymphs. When the fountain is shooting the right way the nymphs really do look like they are frolicking in the water. The scantily clad figures caused a furore when they were first put in place in 1901. The models for the curvaceous nymphs were two sisters, well known musical stars of their day. It is said that in their old age the sisters visited the fountain daily and that once a year the sculptor would travel from his native Sicily to take them out to dinner.

Museo Nazionale Romano Terme di Diocleziano (Map 5)

The Museo Nazionale Romano Terme di Diocleziano opened in 1889 to showcase some of the many archaeological finds unearthed in Rome and farther afield. The complex incorporates several halls of the ancient Terme di Diocleziano and a huge cloister. The museum (☎ 06 481 55 76) opens 9 am to 7 pm Tuesday to Sunday and admission costs €4.13. The entrance is at Viale Enrico de Nicola 78, opposite Piazza dei Cinquecento.

The **cloister** was for many years attributed to Michelangelo but this is unlikely as it was built in 1565, a year after his death. In the centre is a 17th-century fountain surrounded by cypress trees, one of which dates from the same period. There are also huge statues of animals' heads, thought to have come from the Foro di Traiano. Lining the cloister are ruins of columns and capitals, friezes, sarcophagi and (mostly headless) statues.

The modern and airy ground-floor and first-floor galleries contain a display of epigraphs with informative panels in English and Italian on their production and place in history. A large collection of vases, amphorae and household objects in terracotta and bronze are also on display. Among the highlights are three stunning terracotta statues of seated female figures that were found in the Ariccia area south-east of Rome. The extensive second-floor galleries contain artefacts (mainly burial objects such as jewellery and domestic items) from Italian protohistory – 11th to 6th centuries BC – when communities in the Lazio region evolved from tribal structures towards the beginning of city states. There are also galleries devoted to much more recent ethnographic objects from the Pacific islands.

After a thorough and costly revamp completed in 2000, the extensive collection of priceless antiquities that make up the Museo Nazionale Romano are now split between several locations: Palazzo Massimo alle Terme (diagonally across Piazza dei Cinquecento), Palazzo Altemps (near Piazza Navona), the Museo Palatino (on the Palatine), the Crypta Balbi (near Largo di Torre Argentina) as well as the Terme di Diocleziano. A five-day ticket (€15.50) gives admission to all six museums as well as to the Colosseum. A visit to all six sites gives you an idea of just how vast and rich the Museo Nazionale Romano collection is.

The **Terme di Diocleziano** (Diocletian's Baths) were completed in the early 4th century. The complex of baths, libraries, concert halls and gardens was the largest in ancient Rome, covering about 13 hectares and with a capacity of 3000 people. The *caldarium* (hot room) extended into what is now Piazza della Repubblica. After the aqueduct which fed the baths was destroyed by invaders in about AD 536, the complex fell into disrepair.

Large sections of the baths were incorporated into the Chiesa di Santa Maria degli Angeli, which faces Piazza della Repubblica, and the Museo Nazionale Romano. The rest of what remains of the baths complex is used as a space for temporary exhibitions (with varying admission prices). Some of the original sculptures from the Terme di Diocleziano (as well as pieces found at other Imperial Roman baths) are on display in the **Aula Ottagonale**, a domed octagonal hall which was a main hall in the baths. Roman foundations can be seen through a glass panel in the floor. It opens 9 am to 2 pm,

Tuesday to Sunday. The entrance is on Via Romita and admission is free.

The **Chiesa di Santa Maria degli Angeli** was designed by Michelangelo and incorporates what was the great central hall and *tepidarium* (lukewarm room) of the original baths. During the following centuries his work was drastically changed and little evidence of his design, apart from the great vaulted ceiling, remains. An interesting feature of the church is a double meridian in the transept, one tracing the polar star and the other telling the precise time of the sun's zenith, visible at midday (solar time). The church opens 7.30 am to 6.30 pm. Through the sacristy is an entrance to a stairway leading to the upper terraces of the ruins. A plaque near the stairway records the traditional belief that the baths were built by thousands of Christian slaves.

Palazzo Massimo alle Terme (Map 5)

The Palazzo Massimo alle Terme, part of the **Museo Nazionale Romano** collection, boasts some of the best examples of Roman art in the city. It took 16 years and L68 billion for the 19th-century building, a former Jesuit college, to be transformed into a museum. It is one of Rome's best – light-filled, spacious and blissfully air-conditioned in summer.

The ground and 1st floors are devoted to sculpture and statuary dating from the end of the Republican age (2nd to 1st centuries BC) to the late-Imperial era (4th century AD). Some original 5th-century-BC Greek sculptures are dotted among the numerous Roman copies of Greek originals and the portraits of emperors and their families and of eminent citizens.

One of the first pieces you see as you enter is *Minerva*, a huge polychrome statue of the goddess made of alabaster, white marble and black basalt. The face is a modern plaster cast taken from another statue of Minerva. The statue, possibly inspired by early Greek artists working on the Italian peninsula, was found at the bottom of the Aventine, and probably formed part of a temple to Minerva on the hill.

An airy courtyard is surrounded by three long galleries containing portrait busts, off which are rooms arranged thematically. The first two contain funerary reliefs, portrait busts and statues of emperors, statesmen and their families. These were commissioned works and represented the ruling classes as they wanted to be depicted. Realism had little to do with these idealised statues, which were carved at a time when self-glorification was the order of the day.

An anonymous Republican general (in Sala I) depicted in heroic nudity, semi-draped with his armour next to him, shows evidence of Greek sculpting techniques and dates from the 1st century BC. A full-length portrait of Augustus (in Sala V) depicts him as Pontifex Maximus (Chief Priest), his head covered with a fold of his toga. A portrait head of Augustus' wife Livia, with her distinctive braided hairdo, is one of many images of the emperor's wife which had a strong influence on private portraiture of the period.

Terracottas, reconstructed from various fragments, found in the area of the Domus Tiberiana on the Palatine in the 1980s are on display in Sala VI. Sala VII contains a superb original Greek sculpture, dating from the 5th century BC, of a young woman trying to extract an arrow from her back. The statue, along with other Greek originals, was found in the Horti Sallustiani (now the Via Veneto area), which belonged to Julius Caesar and was later the estate of the Roman historian Sallust. In the 17th century, it was also where Ludovico Ludovisi housed his magnificent collection of ancient statuary, which is now part of the Museo Nazionale Romano (see Palazzo Altemps earlier in this chapter).

Sculptures from the time of the Flavian emperors (late 1st to 4th century AD) demonstrate various iconographic trends in official Roman art. Among the highlights (Sala V) are pieces that come from Nero's residence at Anzio (two full length statues) and a wonderfully naturalistic image of a voluptuous *Afrodite* crouching down, a Roman copy of a Greek original from the Villa Adriana at Tivoli.

The badly damaged *Apollo del Tevere* in Sala VI shows what too long in polluted water can do to marble; this piece was discovered in the banks of the Tiber during the embankment process in the late 19th century. In the same room are the *Discobolus Lancellotti* and the *Discobolus di Castelporziano*, two marble statues of a discus thrower copied from one of the most famous of all Greek bronzes.

The highlight of Palazzo Massimo is the collection of Roman paintings and mosaics displayed on the 2nd floor. Many of these rare pieces have been out of public view for decades and have undergone extensive restoration. Thoughtfully installed in their new home, these examples of Roman interior decoration positively sparkle.

Among the most beautiful are the frescoes (in Sala II) from the Villa Livia, a house that belonged to the wife of Augustus. The villa, located on the Via Flaminia north of Rome, was excavated in the 19th century. The frescoes were removed from the villa in 1951 and transferred to the Museo Nazionale Romano. The room in which they were originally painted was half underground and covered by a barrel vault decorated with stuccoes and reliefs (unfortunately only a small part of this vault decoration has survived and is too delicate to exhibit). It was probably a summer *triclinium*, a large living and dining area protected from the heat, and has been recreated in Palazzo Massimo in a specially constructed gallery space. The frescoes, which totally surround you, depict an illusionary garden with all the plants in full bloom, regardless of the season. There are tall cypresses, pines and oak trees, shrubs and bushes of oleander, myrtle and laurel, and fruit trees abundant with ripe pomegranates and quinces. The style dates from between 20 and 10 BC.

Frescoes from an ancient-Roman villa, found in the grounds of Villa Farnesina, are on display in Galleria II and Sale III, IV and V. The villa was discovered and excavated in the 19th century during the embankment of the Tiber. Dating from around 20 BC, these frescoes are among the most important surviving examples of Roman painting.

It is thought that the villa belonged to an important figure close to Augustus' circle. The substantial fragments illustrate clearly the style and taste of the period. There is a great variety of decoration: landscapes, narrative friezes that have an almost Egyptian appearance, and illusionary architectural elements such as columns, cornices and vases.

The museum also boasts a stunning collection of inlaid marble and mosaics, including (in Sala VII) the surviving wall mosaics from a nymphaeum at Nero's villa in Anzio. In the basement is an extensive display of ancient and medieval coins, including a collection donated to the state by King Victor Emmanuel II.

Palazzo Massimo (☎ 06 48 90 35 00) opens 9 am to 7.30 pm, Tuesday to Sunday. Opening hours are often extended in summer. The entrance is at Largo di Villa Peretti 1 and admission costs €6.19.

Via Nazionale (Map 5)

This busy shopping street and traffic thoroughfare connects Piazza della Repubblica to the Quirinal and Piazza Venezia. To the left (heading towards Piazza Venezia) off Via Torino in Piazza Beniamino Gigli, is Rome's opera house, the **Teatro dell'Opera di Roma** (also known as Teatro Costanzi, after the man who built a private theatre here in 1880). The Fascist-era exterior hides a richly decorated 19th-century interior of plush red-velvet seats, gilded stucco and a glittering chandelier in the centre of the auditorium (see the Entertainment chapter for further details).

On the corner of Via Napoli is **St Paul's Within-the-Walls**, the American Episcopal church famous for its magnificent Pre-Raphaelite mosaics designed by Edward Burne-Jones which were completed in 1907.

It is difficult to miss the **Palazzo delle Esposizioni**, a massive white edifice with triumphal arch and grand Corinthian columns. Rome's purpose-built exhibition centre was designed by Pio Piacentini and opened its doors in 1882. The building has had a chequered history. Apart from serving its original brief, it once housed the Communist Party and was used as a mess for allied servicemen. It also served as a polling station and as a public loo.

After years of restoration it was relaunched in 1990, and is today a vibrant multimedia centre. There is a changing programme of art exhibitions, live performances and cinema, with many films screened in their original language. There's also an excellent book and gift shop and a cafe. It opens 10 am to 9 pm daily (except Tuesday).

Piazza dei Santi Apostoli (Map 4)

The long, thin Piazza dei Santi Apostoli runs off Via Cesare Battisti, east of Piazza Venezia. It is a popular place for political demonstrations. The **Museo delle Cere**, a rather tacky museum of waxworks, is at No 67 (on the corner of Via Cesare Battisti). It opens 9 am to 8 pm daily and admission costs €3.09.

The **Palazzo Colonna** spans one side of the square. It was begun in the 15th century for Pope Martin V (who lived here from 1424 until his death in 1431) although most of the building dates from the 18th century. It is still occupied by members of the Colonna family. The private gardens behind the palace, on the site of a 3rd-century Temple of Serapis, rise in terraces up to the grounds of the Palazzo del Quirinale.

Chiesa di Santi Apostoli is wedged into the front of the palace. Originally built in the 6th century and dedicated to the Apostles James and Philip (whose relics are in the crypt), the church was enlarged in the 15th and 16th centuries and then rebuilt in the early 18th century by Carlo and Francesco Fontana who were responsible for the Baroque interior. The unusual facade with Renaissance arches dates from the early 16th century. The church contains the tomb of Pope Clement XIV by Antonio Canova.

The facade of the building opposite the church, **Palazzo Odelscalchi**, was designed by Bernini in 1664. At the end of the square is the Baroque **Palazzo Muti** which was given to James Stuart, the Old Pretender, in 1719 by Pope Clement XI.

THINGS TO SEE & DO

Galleria Colonna (Map 4)

The entrance to Galleria Colonna is at Via della Pilotta 17, a pretty street spanned by four arches which connect the Palazzo Colonna to its gardens. The gallery contains one of Rome's most important private collections, arranged in magnificent Baroque halls. The vestibule, at the top of the stairs, leads into the Sala della Colonna Bellica lined with fine portraits of Colonna family members and others. In the centre of the room is a carved *colonna* (column) of red marble dating from the 16th century. Steps lead down to the lavishly gilded Salone – don't trip over the cannon ball which became lodged there during the 1849 siege of Rome.

The vibrant ceiling paintings are by Giovanni Coli and Filippo Gherardi and represent the life of Marcantonio Colonna, who commanded the papal forces at the Battle of Lepanto. The paintings on the walls are somewhat overpowered but include a notable *San Giovanni Battista* by Salvator Rosa, Guido Reni's *San Francesco d'Assisi con gli Angeli* (St Francis of Assisi with Angels) and *San Paolo Eremita* (St Paul the Hermit) by Guercino. The Sala degli Scrigni (Room of the Desks) contains classical landscapes by Gaspard Dughet and other artists, ceiling frescoes (depicting the Battle of Lepanto) by Sebastiano Ricci, and two ornate cabinets. One is made of ebony with inlaid carved ivory bas-reliefs reproducing works by Raphael and Michelangelo (the central panel is his *Giudizio Universale* from the Sistine Chapel).

The adjacent room is named after the *Apoteosi di Martino V* fresco by Benedetto Luti, which decorates its ceiling and contains the delightful *Mangi Fagiuoli* (Bean Eater), attributed to Annibale Carracci. It is an amusing departure from more serious religious and historical subjects. In the Sala del Trono beyond it a chair is kept ready (turned to the wall) in case of a papal visit. The gallery (☎ 06 679 43 62) opens 9 am to 1 pm Saturday (closed all of August), with a guided tour in English at 11.45 am. Admission costs €5.16 and the tour is included in the price.

Trevi Fountain (Map 4)

This high-Baroque fountain is one of the city's most famous monuments, and where Marcello Mastroianni and Anita Ekberg (spilling out of a black strapless gown) frolicked in Fellini's *La Dolce Vita*.

The theatrical fountain was designed by Nicola Salvi in 1732. It completely dominates the tiny square and incorporates the facade of the adjacent Palazzo Poli. Neptune's chariot is led by Tritons with seahorses – one wild, one docile – representing the moods of the sea.

Water for the fountain is supplied by one of Rome's earliest aqueducts. Work to clean the fountain and its water supply was completed in 1991, but the effects of pollution have already dulled the brilliant white of the clean marble.

The famous custom is to throw a coin into the fountain (over your shoulder while facing away) to ensure you return to Rome. For a second coin you can make a sure you'll fall in love with an Italian. The third coin will have you marrying him or her. The terraces around the fountain are always packed with tourists throwing coins and, on average, €118,785 (L230 million) is recovered from the basin each year. Euros (and lire) go into the city council's coffers and foreign coins are given to the Red Cross. The name Trevi is thought to come from *tre vie*, referring to the three roads which converged at the fountain.

VILLA BORGHESE (Maps 2 & 3)

This beautiful park, just north-east of the Piazza del Popolo, was once the estate of Cardinal Scipione Borghese. Taking papal nepotism to its extremes, when Camillo Borghese became Pope Paul V in 1605, he granted his nephew Scipione the title of cardinal and gave him a sizeable chunk of Rome, just outside the Aurelian Walls. There, between 1605 and 1614, Scipione built his *casino* (mansion) to house his enormous collection of paintings and sculpture (now the Museo e Galleria Borghese) and had the grounds laid out by leading landscape designers such as Jacob More from Edinburgh.

The main entrance is from Piazzale Flaminio, although it is also accessible through the park at the top of the Pincio hill, from Porta Pinciana at the top of Via Veneto, from Via Mercadante on the north-eastern side and from Viale delle Belle Arti on the northern side. Take a picnic to the park if the tourist trip starts to wear you down and certainly take the kids there for a well deserved break.

The park is divided into different areas by avenues of trees, hedged walks, planted flowerbeds, gravel paths and named roads. The pretty, English-style **Giardino del Lago** (Map 2) in the centre of the park was laid out in the late 18th century. Equestrian events are held in May in **Piazza di Siena**, an amphitheatre built around 1792. The park is dotted with sculptures of various periods, although many of these are not the real thing. The city authorities have been systematically removing the originals for several years and replacing them with resin copies. The originals will eventually be put on display in a museum in the park.

The small **Museo Canonica** (Map 3; ☎ 06 884 22 79) at Viale Pietro Canonica 2 houses the collection, private apartment and studio of the sculptor and musician Pietro Canonica who died in 1959. The building, which formerly belonged to the Borghese family, was acquired by the city and given to Canonica in 1927. It opens 9 am to 7 pm Tuesday to Saturday, and 9 am to 1.30 pm on Sunday. Admission costs €2.58.

Museo e Galleria Borghese (Map 3)

Hailed as the 'queen of all private collections', the Galleria e Museo Borghese is one of the most spectacular displays of art in Rome. Cardinal Scipione Borghese was the most passionate and knowledgeable art collector of his day. He had a keen appreciation for the antique but also patronised his contemporaries including the Caracci, Caravaggio and Gian Lorenzo Bernini. He stopped at nothing to add to his treasures; he had the fashionable painter Cavaliere d'Arpino flung into jail in order to confiscate his canvases, and had Domenichino arrested, to force him to surrender his painting of *The Hunt of Diana*.

Scipione's house, the Casino Borghese, surrounded by formal gardens and parkland, was a private treasure chest where he entertained lavishly. The collection and the building in which it was housed attracted illustrious visitors through the centuries, and both were augmented by the cardinal's heirs. In the late 18th century, Scipione's descendant, Prince Marcantonio Borghese, had the casino redecorated in a neoclassical style with elaborate gilding, faux-marble finishes and trompe l'oeil frescoes, which is how it appears today. The mannerist nude figures and cheeky cherubs surrounded by ornate garlands of golden acanthus leaves are at times over the top. However, not all of the original art collection remains. Much of the antique statuary was carted off to the Louvre under the orders of Napoleon, whose sister Paolina was married to Marcantonio's son Camillo. Other pieces were sold off over time.

The entire collection and the mansion were acquired by the Italian state in 1902, but it was badly neglected. Structural problems in the building became evident in the 1940s. In 1983 part of a ceiling fresco by Giovanni Lanfranco in one of the 1st-floor rooms crashed to the ground. In 1984 the gallery had to be shut down. After 13 years of restoration, it reopened in 1997.

The Museo Borghese (the ground-floor rooms) contains some important classical statuary. In the Salone are intricate floor mosaics of fighting gladiators dating from the 4th century AD and a *Satiro Combattente* (Fighting Satyr) from the 2nd century AD (restored by Bernini). High on the wall opposite the entrance is a gravity-defying bas-relief, *Marco Curzio a Cavallo*, of a horse and rider falling into the void of the room, which was created by Pietro Bernini (Gian Lorenzo Bernini's father) by combining ancient fragments and modern pieces. Throughout the ground-floor rooms there are full-length representations and busts of Roman gods, emperors and public figures. In Sala V, a 1st century AD *Ermafrodito* (Sleeping Hermaphrodite), a Roman copy of a Greek original, faces a wall so you can't see the evidence. She/he lies on a rather comfortable looking bed carved by Bernini.

A daring sculpture by Antonio Canova of Paolina Bonaparte Borghese as a reclining *Venere Vincitrice* (Venus Victorius) in Sala I is one of the most famous works in the collection. Her diaphanous drapery leaves little to the imagination and in its day the statue was considered outrageous and provocative. Paolina Borghese had quite a reputation, and tales abounded of her grand habits, her many lovers and her sometimes shocking behaviour. When asked how she could have posed almost naked she apparently replied: 'Oh, there was a stove in the studio.'

Bernini's spectacular carvings – flamboyant depictions of pagan myths – are the stars of the ground-floor museum. Cardinal Scipione Borghese was one of Bernini's earliest patrons. The sculptor's precocious talent is evident in works such as *Il Ratto di Proserpina* (The Rape of Proserpine) in Sala IV, where Pluto's hand presses into Proserpine's solid marble thigh and in his *Davide* (Sala II), grim-faced and muscular, thought to be a self-portrait produced around 1624. In Sala III, Bernini's stunning, swirling *Apollo e Dafne* depicts the exact moment when the nymph is transformed into a laurel tree, her fingers becoming leaves, her toes turning into tree roots, while Apollo watches helplessly.

Other pieces by Bernini include: an early work, *Enea e Anchise* (Aeneas and Anchises), which shows the sculptor's slight lack of confidence in depicting movement; and *La Verità* (Truth), a rather strange later work done between 1645 and 1652, monumental in character but showing little of the mastery evident in his other significant pieces.

In Sala VIII, a 2nd-century-AD *Satiro Danzante* (Dancing Satyr), a Roman copy of an earlier Greek work, is surrounded by six paintings by Caravaggio. The luscious *Ragazzo con Canestro di Frutta* (Boy with a Basket of Fruit) and the *Bacco Malato* (Sick Bacchus), a self-portrait by Caravaggio painted when he was suffering from malaria, are early works completed between 1593 and 1595, not long after his arrival in Rome. Both include magnificent representations of still life. The *Madonna dei Palafrenieri*, also known as the Madonna of the Serpent, was commissioned in 1605 by the Confraternity of the Palafrenieri (footmen) for their chapel in St Peter's Basilica. This is one of Caravaggio's masterpieces and to our eyes it is a wonderfully naturalistic work. However, its uninhibited realism was incompatible with early-17th-century ecclesiastical sensibilities and, after being rejected by the Palafrenieri, it was snapped up by Scipione. The other works depict *San Girolamo*, *San Giovanni Battista* (a young St John the Baptist), and *Davide con la Testa di Golia*, a dramatic image where Goliath's severed head is said to be a self-portrait. See the boxed text 'On the Caravaggio Trail' earlier in this chapter.

The paintings in the Galleria Borghese on the 1st floor, representing the flowering of the Tuscan, Venetian, Umbrian and northern European schools, are testimony to Scipione's connoisseur's eye. In Sala IX are Raphael's *La Deposizione di Cristo* (Descent from the Cross) dated 1507 and his earlier portraits *Ritratto d'uomo* (1502) and *Dama con Liocorno*, a beautiful woman holding a mythological animal, painted in 1506. In the same room are the superb *Adorazione del Bambino* by Fra Bartolomeo and Perugino's *Madonna col Bambino*. Correggio's rather erotic *Danae* – perhaps an early version of soft porn – is in Sala X. In Sala XX it is interesting to compare Titian's early masterpiece *Amor Sacro e Amor Profano* (Sacred and Profane Love) with his later and less powerful work *Venere che Benda Amore* (Venus Blinding Cupid). There are also pieces by Giovanni Bellini, Giorgione, Veronese, Botticelli, Guercino, Domenichino, Antonello da Messina, Rubens and Cranach, to name a few.

The museum is at Piazzale Museo Borghese in the Villa Borghese park (☎ 06 328 10, fax 06 32 65 13 29). It opens 9 am to 7 pm Tuesday to Sunday, with hourly entry. However, the opening hours vary according to season (call to check) and advance booking is advisable. Don't just turn up as you might not get in. Admission costs €7.23, which includes the compulsory booking fee. The museum is equipped for disabled visitors and there's a bar/cafe serving snacks and light meals.

Bioparco (Map 3)

Rome's zoo, known as Bioparco, is at the north end of the park in Viale del Giardino Zoologico (☎ 06 321 65 64). For many years the zoo suffered from an appalling reputation but a new programme is currently underway to improve the cages and facilities. There are currently 1200 animals on the 17-hectare site; this number is likely to be reduced and the conditions for the remaining animals will be improved. Exotic animals are gradually being phased out and sent to other zoos and ultimately the park will have only animals compatible with the ecosystem and climate of central Italy and animals from the Mediterranean area which are in danger of extinction.

There are better ways to spend €5.16 (€3.62 for children aged five to 12, free for children under five) but kids might enjoy it. It opens 9.30 am to 5 pm daily.

Galleria Nazionale d'Arte Moderna (Map 2)

The Galleria Nazionale d'Arte Moderna, the national collection of modern art, is on the edge of Villa Borghese park, Cesare Bazzini's *belle epoque* palace is one of the few remaining buildings erected for the Rome international exhibition in 1911. Extensive renovations have restored the building to its former glory. Original features such as decorative friezes and columns can be seen again and long-closed wings have been opened up.

The collection covers mostly Italian artists from the 19th and 20th centuries. There is a representative holding of academic history painting (some of it very good, some of it overly sentimental) and works by the *macchiaioli*, who produced an Italian version of pointillism using thousands of dots of pure colour to build up a picture, and by the Italian symbolists. The 20th-century collection includes work by De Chirico, Carrà, Casorati, Marini and Fontana as well as exponents of futurism (Boccioni, Severini, Balla), *Arte Povera* (Burri, Colla, Manzoni, Pascali) and the *Transavanguardia* (Enzo Cucchi, Francesco Clemente and Mimmo Paladino among others). The modern foreign art includes work by Degas, Cézanne, Kandinsky, Duchamp, Mondrian, Henry Moore and Cy Twombly.

The wing to the left of the entrance has been transformed into a sculpture gallery. Dynamic white marble, such as Canova's majestic *Ercole* (Hercules), contrast dramatically against walls painted in rich, solid colours. The museum (☎ 06 32 29 81), Viale delle Belle Arti 131, opens 8.30 am to 7.30 pm Tuesday to Sunday. Admission costs €6.19. There is an excellent bar/restaurant with a lovely outdoor terrace. The museum can be reached by tram No 2, from Piazzale Flaminio, which travels along Viale delle Belle Arti.

Museo Nazionale Etrusco di Villa Giulia (Map 2)

The delightful Villa Giulia (at the top end of the Villa Borghese in the Piazzale di Villa Giulia) was built in the mid-16th century for Pope Julius III. Vignola, Vasari, Bartolomeo Ammannati and Michelangelo all had a hand in its design. As the pope's summer residence, it was made up of numerous courtyards, shady loggias covered in decorative frescoes and an elaborate sunken nymphaeum, which was much copied in later 16th-century villas. During the summer, Villa Giulia hosts classical-music concerts by the Accademia di Santa Cecilia orchestra (see the Entertainment chapter for further details).

Since 1889, Villa Giulia has been home to the national collection of Etruscan treasures, many found in tombs at sites throughout Lazio. If you plan to visit Etruscan sites near Rome (see the Excursions chapter) a visit to the museum before setting out will give you a good understanding of Etruscan culture.

The museum contains thousands of exhibits, ranging from domestic objects such as cooking utensils, terracotta vases and amphoras to the remains of a horse-drawn chariot. There is an instructive reconstruction of an Etruscan tomb (in the basement of the left wing as you enter), divided into male and female areas, and complete with burial objects and armchairs sculpted into the rock. Among the most fascinating exhibits are the personal items, such as safety pins and hairclips, and the small bronze figurines. Have a look at the jewellery and you'll see that designs haven't changed much.

Of particular note is the polychrome terracotta statue of *Apollo* and other pieces found at Veio, dating from the late 6th or early 5th century BC. Another highlight is the *Sarcofago degli Sposi* (Sarcophagus of the Married Couple) in Room 9, presumably made for a husband and wife, from a tomb at Cerveteri. This piece is finely sculpted and demonstrates the heights of creativity and skill that the Etruscan artists could reach. It has been restored several times, most recently in 1998 when a cleaner in the museum knocked one of the wife's arms off. It's now protected in a glass case.

The museum has been extensively refurbished and the galleries show the objects off in a better light than was previously the case. However, the labelling is still rather haphazard and the promised room brochures in English and Italian are not yet available throughout. If museum fatigue hits, go outside and enjoy the gardens and courtyards, and then return for another assault on the exhibits.

Villa Giulia (☎ 06 320 19 51), Piazzale di Villa Giulia 9, opens 9 am to 7 pm, Tuesday to Saturday, and 9 am to 2 pm on Sunday. Admission costs €4.13. It can be reached by tram No 2, from Piazzale Flaminio, which travels along Viale delle Belle Arti to Piazzale di Villa Giulia.

GIANICOLO & VILLA DORIA PAMPHILJ (Maps 1, 4 & 6)

The Gianicolo rises behind Trastevere and stretches to St Peter's Basilica. In 1849 it was the scene of one of the fiercest battles in the struggle for Italian unity, when a makeshift but brave army commanded by Giuseppe Garibaldi defended Rome against French troops sent to restore papal rule. Garibaldi is commemorated by a monument erected at the peak of the hill.

His Brazilian-born wife, Anita, is also commemorated on the Gianicolo with an **equestrian monument** (Map 4) by Mario Rutelli (about 200m away, towards St Peter's) completed in 1932. The statue was presented to the city of Rome by the Brazilian government and shows Anita Garibaldi mounted on a rearing horse, cradling a baby in her left arm and brandishing a pistol in her right. High relief sculptures depicting Anita Garibaldi's heroic activities during her husband's campaign are at the base of the monument.

On a clear day the panoramic view from **Piazza Giuseppe Garibaldi** (Map 4) is breathtaking. This is also a top spot to take the kids if they need a change of scene. Just off Piazza Garibaldi, there is a merry-go-round and pony rides, and a puppet show on most Sundays. In the square there is a small bar. Take bus No 870 from Via Paola at the end of Corso Vittorio Emanuele where it meets the Lungotevere, or walk up the steps from Via Mameli in Trastevere.

About five minutes' walk from Piazza Garibaldi, following the uphill fork of the Passeggiate del Gianicolo past the Porta di San Pancrazio, you reach Rome's largest park, **Villa Doria Pamphilj** (Map 1). Once an enormous private estate – its perimeter measures 9km – the park was laid out around 1650 by Alessandro Algardi for Prince Camillo Pamphilj, a nephew of Innocent X. At its centre is the superb Casino del Belrespiro, also designed by Algardi, surrounded by manicured formal gardens and citrus trees. The casino was acquired by the state in the late 1950s, and is now used for official government functions.

The surrounding grounds were acquired by the city authorities between 1965 and 1971 and turned into a public park. It opens sunrise to sunset daily and is a lovely quiet spot for a walk or a picnic. Even at its most crowded, on weekend afternoons in spring and autumn, you can still find a secluded spot beside a Baroque fountain or beneath parasol pines. The park can also be reached by bus No 870 (from Via Paola at the end of Corso Vittorio Emanuele where it meets the Lungotevere).

Heading downhill from Piazza Garibaldi, you pass the **Fontana dell'Acqua Paola** (Map 6) opposite a terrace with a magnificent panorama of the city. The fountain was built in 1612 for Pope Paul V using marble pillaged from the Roman Forum. Four of the fountain's six pink stone columns came from the facade of the old St Peter's Basilica. The large granite basin was designed by Carlo Fontana in 1690.

Farther downhill along Via Garibaldi is **Chiesa di San Pietro in Montorio** (Map 6) and in a courtyard next to it, Bramante's circular **Tempietto**, built on a site that was once assumed to be the place of St Peter's crucifixion (he was actually crucified in the circus that once occupied the site of St Peter's Basilica). The tempietto, which has just been restored, was built in 1502 and is a Renaissance masterpiece of classical proportion and elegance. See the Rome Walks chapter for more details.

VIAS SALARIA & NOMENTANA
Via Salaria (Map 1)
This road heads northwards from the city centre. One of the oldest Roman roads, used to transport salt *(sale)*, it is now a busy residential and shopping district. Not far out of the city centre, after the intersection with Viale Regina Margherita, is an architecturally interesting area known as **Coppedè**. The streets in this small pocket of an otherwise unexceptional residential zone are lined with villas and palazzi built just after WWI in an extravagant Art Nouveau style. The best examples are in Via Dora and Piazza Mincio, one block east of Viale Regina Margherita. Bus No 56 from Trastevere, Piazza Venezia and Piazza Barberini and bus No 319 from Stazione Termini run along Via Tagliamento, parallel to Via Salaria.

The walls of **Villa Ada** park border much of the Via Salaria. The villa was once the private residence of Victor Emmanuel III but it is now the Egyptian embassy. The villa's grounds are now a huge public park with sloping lawns, shady areas, lakes and ponds. It's great for a picnic year-round and in summer hosts a festival of world music.

The **Catacombe di Priscilla**, north of Villa Ada along Via Nomentana, were originally part of the estate of the patrician Acilii family in the 1st century AD. They were greatly expanded in the 3rd and 4th centuries and became a popular 'society' burial ground – with appropriate upmarket decoration, quite a lot of which has survived. Several popes were buried in the catacombs between 309 and 555. A funerary chapel known as the Cappella Greca is thought to have been part of the criptoportico from the Acilii Villa. It retains good stucco decoration and well preserved, late-3rd-century frescoes of biblical scenes. The catacombs (☎ 06 86 20 62 72), Via Salaria 430, open 8.30 am to noon and 2.30 to 5 pm Tuesday to Sunday. Admission costs €4.13.

Porta Pia & Via Nomentana (Maps 1 & 3)
Bus Nos 36 and 90 from Stazione Termini and bus No 62 from Piazza Venezia and Piazza Barberini take you to Porta Pia and the tree-lined Via Nomentana, which heads north-eastwards out of the city. Porta Pia, built beside the ruins of the ancient Porta Nomentana, was Michelangelo's last architectural work. It was commissioned by Pius IV in 1561 and it was near Porta Pia that the Italian troops entered Rome on 20 September 1870 and brought to an end the temporal power of the popes. The ugly modern building just inside the city walls is the British Embassy. Opposite it is the Villa Paolina, the residence of Napoleon's sister Paolina Bonaparte from 1816 to 1824, and now the French embassy to the Holy See.

About 1km from Porta Pia on the right (heading away from the city) is **Villa Torlonia** park (Map 3), once a splendid estate belonging to the Torlonia family. There are several buildings in the park, including a large, neoclassical villa built by Giuseppe Valadier in 1806, which Mussolini used as his private residence in the 1930s. The villa was occupied by Allied troops after WWII, then abandoned. In 1978, the estate was expropriated by the city council as a public park. A programme is underway to bring the park back to its former glory.

One of the most interesting buildings in the park is the **Casina delle Civette** (Map 3). The house was built between 1840 and 1930 and is an eclectic combination of a Swiss cottage, a turreted Gothic castle and an arts-and-crafts farmhouse with Art Nouveau decoration. It was already in an advanced state of abandon when it was gutted by a fire in 1991. It was reopened as a museum in 1997 after a lengthy and detailed restoration. The museum is dedicated to stained glass and contains the house's original windows, including work done between 1908 and 1930 by leading Italian decorative artists including Duilio Cambelotti, as well as new leadlights based on early-20th-century designs. There are also over 100 designs and sketches for stained glass, decorative tiles, elaborate parquetry floors and boiseries. The museum (☎ 06 44 25 00 72) opens 9 am to 7 pm Tuesday to Sunday, April to September, and 9 am to 5 pm Tuesday to Sunday, October to March. Admission costs €2.58.

Sant'Agnese Fuori-le-Mura & Santa Costanza (Map 1)

Along Via Nomentana, at No 349, is the Basilica di Sant'Agnese Fuori-le-Mura one of a group of early-Christian buildings rebuilt and restored in the 15th, 16th and 19th centuries. The church is named after St Agnes, who was buried here in 304. According to tradition, having rejected the advances of one of Diocletian's courtiers, the 13-year-old Agnes was exposed naked in the Stadium of Domitian. Miraculously, her hair grew to preserve her modesty. She was then burnt at the stake but was untouched by the flames. Eventually, she was beheaded. Her relics are preserved beneath the high altar.

A beautiful apse mosaic dating from the 7th century shows St Agnes, dressed in a purple robe with a golden stole, flanked by two popes. The church opens 9 am to noon and 4 to 6 pm Tuesday to Saturday. On Sunday it opens only in the afternoon and on Monday only in the morning. The Catacombe di Sant'Agnese date from the 3rd century and contain many Christian inscriptions. The entrance is from the left aisle of the basilica; the catacombs keep the same opening hours as the church. Admission costs €4.13.

In the same complex, across the convent courtyard, is the Mausoleo di Santa Costanza, also known as the Chiesa di Santa Costanza. It was built in the 4th century as a mausoleum for Constantine's daughters Constantia and Helena, and later converted into a baptistry. The pretty circular building has a dome supported by 12 pairs of granite columns. The ambulatory that runs outside of the arches has a barrel vaulted ceiling covered with beautiful 4th-century mosaics of fruit, flowers, vines and animals as well as geometric designs. There were once mosaics in the dome – said to be even more astounding than those in the ambulatory – but were destroyed by Paul V in 1622. The original porphyry sarcophagi of Constantia and Helena were moved to the Vatican in 1790 and are on display in the Vatican Museums. Santa Costanza opens the same hours as Sant'Agnese.

SAN LORENZO (Map 1)

Just outside the city walls, San Lorenzo is home of Rome's La Sapienza university and a popular area for student life. It is easily reached by public transport (bus No 71 from Piazza San Silvestro or No 492 from Piazza Venezia and Stazione Termini or tram No 3).

The **Basilica di San Lorenzo Fuori-le-Mura** in the heart of the area, is one of Rome's seven pilgrimage churches and is dedicated to the martyred St Lawrence. One of the most revered of early Christian martyrs, he had been burnt at the stake under the orders of Valerian in AD 258. The original structure was erected by Constantine in the 4th century over St Lawrence's burial place but it was rebuilt in the 579 by Pope Pelagius II. The church was subsequently altered several times between the 8th and 13th centuries; these works included the incorporation of a nearby 5th century church and knocking the two buildings into one. The nave, portico and much of the decoration date from the 13th century. San

Lorenzo was the only church in Rome that suffered serious damage during WWII.

Of note are a restored 6th-century mosaic inside the triumphal arch of Christ with saints and Pelagius offering a model of his church to Christ, the 12th-century Cosmati mosaic on the floor, the medieval frescoes of the life and martyrdom of St Lawrence in the portico, the 13th-century pulpits and the bishop's throne. The remains of St Lawrence and St Stephen are in the church crypt beneath the high altar. A pretty barrel-vaulted cloister contains inscriptions and sarcophagi and leads to the Catacombe di Santa Ciriaca where St Lawrence was initially buried (ask the sacristan for admission). The church, on Piazzale del Verano 3, opens 7.30 am to noon and 4 to 6.30 pm daily.

The **Cimitero di Campo Verano**, to the right of the basilica is the city's largest cemetery. It was designed by Giuseppe Valadier between 1807 and 1812. From the 1830s to the 1980s virtually all Catholics who died in Rome (with the exception of popes, cardinals and royalty) were buried here, although the main cemetery and crematorium is now located north of Rome at Prima Porta. Campo Verano gets particularly crowded with people and flowers on *I Morti* (All Souls' Day), 2 November, when thousands of Romans flock to visit their dear departed.

VIA APPIA ANTICA & THE CATACOMBS (Map 1)

Known to ancient Romans as the *regina viarum* (queen of roads), the Via Appia Antica (Appian Way) extends from the Porta San Sebastiano, near the Terme di Caracalla, to Brindisi on the coast of Puglia. It was started around 312 BC by the censor Appius Claudius Caecus, but did not connect with Brindisi until around 190 BC. The first section of the road, which extended 90km to Terracina, was considered revolutionary in its day because it was almost perfectly straight – perhaps the world's first motorway.

Every Sunday, a long section of the Via Appia Antica becomes a no-car zone. You can walk or ride a bike from the Porta di San Sebastiano for several kilometres.

Monuments along the road near Rome include the catacombs, listed later in this section, and Roman tombs. The **Chiesa di Domine Quo Vadis** is built at the point where St Peter had a vision of Christ as he was escaping the Neronian persecution. Noticing that he was going towards the city, Peter asked: 'Domine, quo vadis?' – 'Lord, where are you going?' When Jesus replied that he was going to Rome to be crucified again, Peter took the hint and returned to the city, where he was arrested and martyred.

To get to Via Appia Antica, catch bus No 218 from Piazza San Giovanni in Laterano or bus No 660 from the Colle Albani station on Metro Linea A. For more detailed information about these and other monuments on the Via Appia Antica, see the Rome Walks chapter.

Circo di Massenzio

This circus, built around AD 309 by Maxentius, is in almost perfect condition. Maxentius was emperor from 306 to 312, when he was challenged and killed by Constantine at the battle of Ponte Milvio.

Entrance to the circus is through two towers on the curved side (west). Here you will also find traces of the 12 stalls *(carceres)* for the horse chariots. It is interesting to note that this side is positioned at a slight oblique angle to allow all the quadrigae to cover an identical distance before reaching the beginning of the low wall in the centre. The wall, 1000 Roman feet or 296m in length, consisted of a channel formed by a series of basins. These contained sculptures and tabernacles on columns displaying the seven eggs and the seven dolphins that represented the seven laps that had to be completed to cover a distance of three Roman miles (approximately 4.44km). The centre was dominated by the obelisk of Domitian, brought here from Campo Marzio and later removed to Bernini's fountain in Piazza Navona on the order of Pope Innocent X in 1650.

The spectators would have been able to watch the race from steps that rested on sloping vaults, now largely collapsed. The disintegration of the structure has, however, revealed a curious but effective method of engineering typical of the time: the insertion of amphorae into the brickwork to lighten the structure. However, it seems that the circus did not reach completion before the owner Maxentius died, and scholars think it unlikely that it ever actually saw a chariot race.

Above the circus are the unexcavated ruins of Maxentius' imperial residence, most of which are still covered in vegetation. In front of the circus is the **Tomba di Romolo** (Tomb of Romulus), built by Maxentius for his young son, Romulus. It stands on a circular base measuring 33m in diameter. It was crowned with a large dome and had a rectangular portico similar to the Pantheon. The monument was surrounded on all sides by an imposing colonnade measuring 107m by 121m, in part still visible. In the 19th century the tomb was incorporated into a country villa.

The circus (☎ 06 780 13 24) opens 9 am to 2.30 pm Tuesday to Sunday. Admission costs €2.58.

Tomba di Cecilia Metella

Money talked in Roman times, and Cecilia Metella's fabulously wealthy father-in-law Marcus Crassus made sure she was buried in style. Cylindrical in shape and 11m high and roughly 30m in diameter, the mausoleum encloses an interesting burial chamber, now roofless. The walls are made of travertine and decorated with a lovely sculpted frieze featuring Gaelic shields, ox skulls and festoons. The Ghibelline battlements were added in the Middle Ages. Because of its location, the mausoleum was turned into a keep for the 14th-century castle built by the Caetani astride the road to extract money, rather like a modern motorway toll booth. It opens 9 am to 6 pm, Tuesday to Saturday and 9 am to 1 pm Sunday and Monday, from April to October; and 9 am to 4 pm Tuesday to Saturday and 9 am to 1 pm Sunday and Monday from November to March. Admission costs €2.06.

Not far past the tomb is a section of the actual ancient road, excavated in the mid-19th century. It is very picturesque, lined with fragments of ancient tombs. Although it is in an area where the rich have built their villas, the road is in a bad state, littered with rubbish and the ruins vandalised. It's not a good idea to wander there alone after dark.

The Catacombs

There are several catacombs along and near Via Appia Antica – kilometres of tunnels carved out of the soft tufa rock, which were the meeting and burial places of early Christians in Rome from the 1st to the early 5th centuries. People were buried wrapped in simple white sheets, and usually placed in rectangular niches carved into the tunnel walls, which were closed with marble or terracotta slabs.

The catacombs can be visited only with a guide. The visit is limited to specially adapted areas, with exhaustive multilingual commentaries. In winter the catacombs operate a system of rotating closure, so that one catacomb always remains open (San Sebastiano closes from mid-November to mid-December roughly and San Callisto closes in or around February). The same applies to weekly closure. For more details see 'The Catacombs' boxed text in the Rome Walks chapter.

Catacombe di San Callisto These catacombs are the largest and most famous, and contain the tomb of the martyred St Cecilia (although her body was moved to the Basilica di Santa Cecilia in Trastevere). Founded at the end of the 2nd century on private land, these catacombs became the official cemetery of the newly established Roman Church. Fifty martyrs from the time of persecution and 16 of the first popes, themselves mostly martyrs, are buried here. The catacombs are named after Pope Calixtus I, who was killed in Trastevere in 222 while saying Mass. He had been responsible for the catacombs for 20 years. They cover an area of 15 hectares and 20km of tunnels have been explored to date. Archaeologists have found the sepulchres of some 500,000 people, as well as Greek and Latin inscriptions and frescoes.

The catacombs (☎ 06 51 30 15 80), Via

An elderly resident in the Palestrina district

Lighting-up time in Pincio park

Dioscuri and a group of local youngsters are captivated by the vista.

Balcony plants wilt in the Roman heat.

Shutting out the city: it's time for *il resto*.

All aglow in the backstreets of Rome: a lamp flickers in a shadowy alley, close to the Trevi Fountain.

Appia Antica 110, open 8.30 am to noon and 2.30 to 5.30 pm (5 pm in winter) daily (except Wednesday). Admission is with a guide only and costs €4.13. The catacombs close late January to late February each year.

Basilica & Catacombe di San Sebastiano The basilica was built in the 4th century over the catacombs, which were used as a safe haven for the remains of St Peter and St Paul during the reign of the Vespasian, who repressed and persecuted the Christians. Originally know as the *Memoria Apostolorum* (Memory of the Apostles), the basilica was dedicated to St Sebastian, after he was martyred and buried here in the late 3rd century.

Preserved in the Capella delle Reliquie, in the right-hand nave of the basilica, is one of the arrows used to kill the saint and the column to which he was tied.

The Catacombe di San Sebastiano were the first catacombs to be so called, the name deriving from the Greek *kata* (near), and *kymbas* (cavity), because they were located near a cave. Subsequently, this term was extended to all the other underground burial sites. Over the centuries this catacomb was one of only three to remain open and receive pilgrims. For this reason the first of its three levels is now almost completely destroyed. The public can see the 2nd floor, including areas with frescoes, stucco-work and epigraphs. There are also three perfectly preserved mausoleums and a plastered wall with hundreds of invocations to the Apostles Peter and Paul, engraved by worshippers in the 3rd and 4th centuries.

The church and catacombs (☎ 06 788 70 35) at Via Appia Antica 136, just past the main entrance to the Catacombs of San Callisto, open 8.30 am to midday and 2.30 to 5.30 pm (to 5 pm in winter) daily (except Sunday). Admission to the catacombs is with a guide only and costs €4.13. The catacombs are closed each year from mid-November to mid-December.

Catacombe di Santa Domitilla Among the largest and oldest catacombs in Rome, they were established on the private burial ground of Flavia Domitilla, a niece of Domitian. They contain Christian wall paintings and the underground Chiesa di SS Nereus e Achilleus. The catacombs (☎ 06 511 03 42), Via delle Sette Chiese 283 (take bus No 218), open 8.30 am to noon and 2.30 to 5 pm daily (except Tuesday). Admission costs €4.13. These catacombs close from late December to late January.

Mausoleo delle Fosse Ardeatine

If you walk back to Via Ardeatine and turn right to reach the Mausoleo delle Fosse Ardeatine, you will come to the site of one of the worst Nazi atrocities committed in Italy during WWII.

After a brigade of Roman urban partisans blew up 32 German military police in Via Rasella, the Germans took 335 random prisoners (including 75 Jews) to the Ardeatine Caves and shot them. The Germans used mines to explode sections of the caves and thus bury the bodies. After the war, the bodies were exhumed, identified and reburied in a mass grave at the site, now marked by a huge concrete slab and sculptures.

The massacre continues to anger and distress Italians. The German SS commander, Erich Priebke, who has admitted to killing at least two of the victims himself, was tried and convicted in 1996.

The Mausoleo delle Fosse Ardeatine (☎ 06 513 67 42) open 8.15 am to 5.45 pm Monday to Saturday, and from 8.45 am to 5.15 pm on Sunday and public holidays. Admission is free.

OSTIENSE & SAN PAOLO (Map 1)
Capitoline Museums at Centrale Montemartini

About 500m outside the city walls, heading along Via Ostiense away from the centre, are (on the left) the **Mercati Generali**, Rome's wholesale food markets. Plans are afoot to move the markets to a new site on the periphery of the city and use the present buildings for Rome's third university, Roma Tre.

Beyond the Mercati Generali, on the right, is **Centrale Montemartini**, the former power station, which in 1997 became the temporary home of many pieces of ancient sculpture from the Capitoline Museums, which are undergoing major renovation. Central Montemartini (☎ 06 574 80 30), Via Ostiense 106, opens 10 am to 6 pm Tuesday to Friday and 10 am to 7 pm on Saturday and Sunday. Admission costs €6.19. Take bus No 23 (or walk) from Piramide Metro station (Linea B).

The juxtaposition of early-20th-century industrial machinery and delicately carved marble, which is around 2000 years older, is unusual but surprisingly effective. The move has given the Capitoline Museums curators an opportunity to research the collection, to display sculptures and mosaics which have been hidden for decades in Capitoline storage vaults, and to exhibit together connected pieces (eg, sculptures from the same monument), which have previously been displayed separately. Most of the exhibits came to light during excavations in Rome in the late 19th century, when there was large-scale building and development of the new national capital.

On the ground floor, beyond the entrance, is the Sala Colonne where the oldest pieces in the collection – sculpture and ceramics dating from the 7th century BC – are displayed. These include Etruscan and Greek pieces as well as discoveries from a necropolis on the Esquiline.

Metal stairs lead up to the Sala Macchina, painted a garish blue, where antiquities dating from the late-Republican period to the height of the Empire share the exhibition space with two mammoth 7500HP diesel engines. Of note are several Roman copies of original Greek works, including a number of statues of *Athena* (grouped together), a black-basalt statue of *Orantes* (recently identified as being a portrait of Agrippina, the niece of Claudius), and heads of divinities and statues from the pediment of the Tempio di Apollo Soianus, a temple that once stood near the Teatro di Marcello. These statues depict a battle between Greeks and Amazons and were originally coloured. There are also sculptures found on the Capitoline, in the Area Sacra

di Largo Argentina and near the Teatro di Pompeo (in the Campo de' Fiori area).

The Sala Caldaia, painted a rather sickly hospital green, has the highlights of the collection set against the backdrop of a giant furnace. Many pieces were excavated from imperial and patrician villas and gardens, and represent the taste of the emperors and nobility. The magnificent floor mosaic of hunting scenes has rarely been exhibited before. It was found during excavations near the Porta Maggiore. Two of the most beautiful pieces are statues of young girls, the *Fanciulla Seduta* sitting with her elbow resting on her knee, and *Musa Polimnia* standing, leaning on a pedestal and gazing dreamily into the distance. At the far end of the room, flanked by two attendants and against the backdrop of a giant furnace, is the milky-white *Venus Esquilina* from the 1st century BC discovered on the Esquiline in 1874.

San Paolo Fuori-le-Mura

The Basilica di San Paolo Fuori-le-Mura is in Via Ostiense, about 3km from Porta San Paolo and some distance from the city centre (take Metro Linea B to San Paolo). The original church was built in the 4th century AD by Constantine over the burial place of St Paul and, until the construction of the present-day St Peter's Basilica, was the largest church in the world. The church was destroyed by fire in 1823 and the present structure was erected in its place.

The triumphal arch was part of the former church; its 5th-century mosaics of Christ with angels, St Peter and St Paul and symbols of the Evangelists have been heavily restored. On the other side of the arch are mosaics by Pietro Cavallini. The mosaics in the apse were done by Venetian artists and show the figures of Christ with St Peter, St Andrew, St Paul and St Luke. The 13th-century marble canopy over the high altar was designed by Arnolfo di Cambio together with another artist, possibly Pietro Cavallini. The paintings between the windows of the nave show the life of St Paul. Below are mosaic portraits of all the popes from St Peter to John Paul II.

The beautiful **cloisters** of the adjacent Benedictine abbey survived the fire. These are a masterpiece of Cosmati mosaic work and, along with the cloisters at the Basilica di San Giovanni in Laterano, are generally considered to be the most beautiful example of their kind in Rome. The octagonal and spiral columns supporting the elaborate arcade are arranged in pairs and are inlaid with colourful mosaics. The sacristy contains other objects from the old church, including four fresco portraits of past popes.

EUR

This acronym, which stands for Esposizione Universale di Roma, has become the name of a peripheral suburb of Rome, interesting for its many examples of Fascist architecture, including the **Palazzo della Civiltà del Lavoro** (Palace of the Workers), a square building with arched windows, also known as the 'Square Colosseum'. Mussolini ordered the construction of the satellite city about 5km south of Rome for an international exhibition to have been held in 1942. Work was suspended with the outbreak of war and the exhibition was never held; however, many buildings were completed during the 1950s.

The **Museo della Civiltà Romana** (☎ 06 592 61 35), Piazza G Agnelli 10, reconstructs the development of Rome, so you can see what Rome really looked like before everything fell into ruin. Mussolini established this museum in 1937 to glorify Imperial Rome. There's an excellent model of the city in the 4th century AD and plaster casts of several monuments, including the reliefs on the Colonna Antonia. It opens 9 am to 7 pm Tuesday to Saturday and 9 am to 2 pm on Sunday. Admission costs €4.13.

Also of interest is the **Museo Nazionale Preistorico Etnografico Luigi Pigorini**. This didactic museum displays prehistoric artefacts (human bones, mammoth tusks, shells etc) from all over Italy and ethnological material (weapons, pottery, jewellery etc) from various world cultures. The museum (☎ 06 54 95 21) at Viale Lincoln 1, opens 9 am to 2 pm Tuesday to Saturday, and 9 am to 1 pm on Sunday. Admission costs €4.13.

On the other side of the enormous Piazza Marconi is the **Museo delle Arti e Tradizioni Popolari** (☎ 06 592 61 48), Piazza Marconi 8. Its collection illustrates traditional Italian culture through history and includes agricultural and artisan tools, popular arts and crafts, clothing, furniture, musical instruments and jewellery. It opens 9 am to 2 pm Tuesday to Saturday, and 9 am to 1 pm on Sunday. Admission costs €2.06.

EUR is accessible via Metro Linea B.

PONTE MILVIO & FORO ITALICO (Map 1)
Ponte Milvio

Ponte Milvio was the scene of one of the great events in Rome's history – when Constantine defeated Maxentius in 312 and threw him into the Tiber below. The bridge dates from 109 BC and was built to carry the old Via Flaminia over the river. Nicholas V added the watchtowers in the 15th century. Pius VII commissioned Giuseppe Valadier to build the triumphal arch at its entrance. Garibaldi's troops blew up the bridge in 1849 to stop the advancing French soldiers, and it was rebuilt in 1850 by Pius IX. Today it's just a pretty footbridge, with a colourful market on its northern side (see the boxed text 'To Market, to Market' in the Places to Eat chapter and Markets in the Shopping chapter).

Foro Italico

About 600m from Ponte Milvio, at the foot of Monte Mario, is the Foro Italico, an ambitious project for a sports centre built under the Fascist regime between 1928 and 1931. It was Mussolini's attempt at a modern form of Imperial-Roman architecture. A 17m-high marble obelisk inscribed with the words 'Mussolini Dux' greets arrivals at the complex. If you like Fascist architecture, it's worth a visit.

The **Stadio Olimpico** is the largest stadium in the complex, seating 100,000. It was built in 1960 for the Olympic Games and rebuilt in 1990 for the World Cup. It is home of Rome's two teams, Roma and Lazio (see under Spectator Sports in the Entertainment chapter for further details).

The Vatican

After unification, the Papal States of central Italy became part of the new Kingdom of Italy, causing a considerable rift between the church and state. In 1929, Mussolini signed the Lateran Treaty (or Concordat) with Pius XI, giving the pope full sovereignty over what is now the Città del Vaticano (Vatican City). The Lateran Treaty also granted the privilege of extraterritoriality to the basilicas of San Giovanni in Laterano (as well as the Palazzo Laterano), Santa Maria Maggiore and San Paolo Fuori-le-Mura and to certain other buildings including the Palazzo della Cancelleria.

The Vatican City is the smallest independent state in existence. It has its own postal service, currency, newspaper, radio station and train station (now used only for freight). It also has its own army of Swiss Guards, responsible for the pope's personal security. The corps was established in 1506 by Julius II to defend the Papal States against invading armies. The guards still wear the traditional eye-catching red, yellow and blue uniform (not, as legend would have it, designed by Michelangelo) and brandish unwieldy 15th-century pikes (see the boxed text 'The Pope's Army' later in this chapter).

Dress regulations are stringently enforced at St Peter's and throughout the Vatican. It is forbidden to enter the church in

---

Waiting for the White Smoke

With his health failing, a frail Pope John Paul II stumbled through the Jubilee Year celebrations. Naturally there is constant speculation about his possible successor, with bookmakers offering odds on possible future incumbents, and the world's media poised to descend on Rome for the Conclave of cardinals which elects a new pope.

The Conclave is made up a maximum of 120 cardinals, none of whom may be over 80. They are locked up inside the Vatican, usually in the Sistine Chapel, with no communication to the outside world, until a new pope is chosen through a series of secret ballots. The place chosen is locked both inside and out and it includes rooms for the cardinals and their assistants. The result of the vote is indicated to the outside world by the colour of the smoke which issues from a vent above the Sistine Chapel (black smoke indicates no decision has been made; white smoke indicates a new pope has been elected).

What are the requirements for the Roman Catholic Church's top job? There is a list of unwritten prerequisites. The candidate needs to be well known in the Curia, the papal court and government of the Roman Catholic Church. He must have a reputation as a theologian and must have written prominent Vatican documents. He must also have worked in one of the Church's international organisations. In addition, the candidate must be in good health (to avoid a repeat of John Paul I's month-long papacy); he should be neither too young (there's a feeling that John Paul II's papacy has been too long) nor too old; and he must be media-friendly and capable of projecting a charismatic image. On top of all that, candidates must never appear actually to be campaigning for the job. As one saying goes: 'He who goes into a conclave a *papabile* comes out a cardinal.'

Almost all the current cardinals were appointed by John Paul II, and thus he has ensured the continuation of his own legacy. Although the election of a new pope frees the Church to change its course, the new pope cannot actively contradict the teaching of his predecessor, so even if a more liberal pope is appointed, contradictory proclamations will be curtailed.

Ill health has ruled out a number of former front runners, including the Brazilian Cardinal Lucas Moreira Neves, who suffers from diabetes, and the Belgian Godfried Daneels, archbishop of Brussels, who had a heart attack in late 1997.

One possible contender is the charismatic and clever Nigerian Cardinal Francis Arinze, 68, a pop-

---

shorts (men included), a short skirt or with bare shoulders.

Places mentioned in this section are on Map 4 unless otherwise indicated.

Information & Services

The Centro Servizi Pellegrini e Turisti (tourist office) is in Piazza San Pietro to the left of the basilica (Map 4; ☎ 06 69 88 16 62, fax 06 69 88 16 94). It opens 8.30 am to 7 pm Monday to Saturday and has general information about St Peter's and the Vatican.

The Vatican post office, said to provide a faster and more reliable service than the normal Italian postal system, is a few doors from the tourist office (there is another outlet on the other side of the square and one

in the Vatican Museums). Letters can be posted in blue Vatican post boxes only if they carry Vatican stamps.

PIAZZA SAN PIETRO (Map 4)

Bernini's square is considered a masterpiece. Laid out in the 17th century as a place for the Christians of the world to gather, the immense square is bounded by two semicircular colonnades, each of which is made up of four rows of Doric columns. These are topped with 140 statues of saints by Bernini's pupils and followers. In the centre is an obelisk brought to Rome by Gaius Caligula from Heliopolis in Egypt. When you stand on the dark paving stones between the obelisk and either of the fountains, the

Waiting for the White Smoke

ular figure who has been in charge of the Church's ecumenical relations, with Islam in particular, since 1985. Just as John Paul II has dealt with Communism during his papacy, perhaps Arinze will be the one to be able to handle the Church's relations with other religions in the next century. The media-savvy Arinze is also fiercely orthodox on hot-button Church topics, including his opposition to abortion, female priests and contraception. But is the Catholic world ready for a black African pope? Arinze would not be the first – that honour was taken by Gelasius I who reigned from 492 to 496 – but the excitement and media attention that greeted the first mention of him as a possible candidate in the early 1990s has probably not worked in his favour.

The charismatic archbishop of Milan, Carlo Maria Martini, 74, a brilliant linguist and preacher, famous for his pastoral work, would be a popular choice, but he has several things against him. He has been branded as a liberal (relative to John Paul II's hard-line conservatism), he is prepared to be critical of the Church, and believes in consultation and debate, which the Curia shuns. Secondly, he is a Jesuit; and not only has there never been a Jesuit pope but there has never even been a Jesuit cardinal who was seriously considered as a candidate.

Several of the more recently elected cardinals (who gained their red hats early in 1998) may also be in the running. These include the widely published archbishop of Vienna, Christoph Schönborn (who at 55 is possibly a bit young), another Eastern European, Miloslav Vlk, archbishop of Prague, who has withstood decades of persecution, and Francis George of Chicago.

After so long with a foreigner at the helm of the Church, and given that the pope is also bishop of Rome, it is not unreasonable to assume that an Italian will be given the job. Those whose names have been mentioned (all of whom are in their mid-70s) include: Giacomo Biffi, the ultra-conservative archbishop of Bologna; Giovanni Saldarini, archbishop of Turin; Silvano Piovanelli, 75, archbishop of Florence, who spent years as a parish priest and is known for his pastoral abilities; and Marco Cé, the patriarch of Venice, who has been a seminary director, has taught dogmatic theology and was the church's chief advisor to Catholic Action.

Only one thing is sure. When Pope John Paul II dies and a group of men in red hats get together to elect his successor, the reverberations will be felt around the world, and Rome once again will be the focus of the world's attention.

Building the Vatican

When Pope Symmachus (498–514) was ousted from the Palazzo Laterano by Emperor Theodoric the Great, he had a mansion built for himself on the Vatican hill next to St Peter's Basilica and not far from Castel Sant'Angelo, which had been converted into a papal fortress in the 6th century. Charlemagne stayed at the Vatican during his visits to Rome in 781 and 800. In 846, after a Saracen fleet sailed up the Tiber and attacked Rome, Pope Leo IV built a protective barrier – the Leonine Walls – around the Vatican area.

The Palazzo Vaticano was restored by Pope Eugenius III in 1150 and Pope Celestine made further improvements in 1191. Under Innocent III (1198–1216) and Nicholas III (1277–80) the palace was enlarged and fortified; the latter linked Castel Sant'Angelo to the Vatican palaces in 1277 by a wall and passageway, which allowed the popes to escape to the fortress in times of threat.

During the Great Schism, the Lateran Palace had become uninhabitable, so on his return to Rome from Avignon in 1377, Gregory XI took up residence there. Subsequent centuries saw massive expansion of the palace, with many popes overseeing significant additions.

Nicholas V (1447–55) turned the mansion into a palace which he built around the Cortile dei Pappagalli. Sixtus IV (1471–84) built the Sistine Chapel in 1473.

The Belvedere pavilion was added under Innocent VIII in the late 15th century. It was built as a summer *casino* (house) on the northern summit of the Vatican hill. Julius II situated his impressive collection of classical sculpture in the Belvedere and had Donato Bramante design a new palace entrance with a spiral staircase up which horses could be ridden. Under Julius II, Bramante also created the Cortile del Belvedere when he joined the Belvedere to Nicholas V's palace and the Sistine Chapel with long corridors.

The courtyard was subsequently sliced into three smaller sections with the additions of the Biblioteca Apostolica (Vatican Library) under Popes Sixtus V and the Braccio Nuovo (under Pius VII). The northern courtyard, the Cortile della Pigna, is named after the colossal bronze pine cone dating from the 1st or 2nd century placed there in 1608 by Paul V. As part of the conversion of the Belvedere into a museum in the late 18th century, a monumental staircase (by Michelangelo Simonetti) was added as well as a new entrance, the Atrio dei Quattro Cancelli.

The 20th century saw more additions. Pius XI unveiled a new Pinacoteca and a new entrance to the museums in 1932. Galleries of modern religious art in the Borgia apartments were opened in 1973, and in the same year an Ethnological Missionary Museum was inaugurated. In 2000, under John Paul II, a new museum entrance was opened. The magnificent Simonetti staircase is now the exit.

colonnade on that side appears to have only one row of columns.

On Sunday the pope makes his regular address and recites the Angelus at noon from the building to the right of the square. His office is on the top floor, the second window from the right. At Christmas, a huge nativity scene is erected in the centre of the square.

ST PETER'S BASILICA (Map 4)

In the same area where St Peter's Basilica (Basilica di San Pietro) now stands, there was once the Circo Vaticano, built by Nero. It was probably in this stadium that St Peter

and other Christians were martyred between AD 64 and 67. The body of the saint was buried in an anonymous grave next to the wall of the circus, and his fellow Christians built a humble 'red wall' to mark the site. In 160 the stadium was abandoned and a small monument erected on the grave. Then, in 315, Constantine ordered construction of a basilica on the site of the Apostle's tomb. This first basilica was consecrated in 326.

After more than 1000 years, the church was in a poor state of repair and, in the mid-15th century, Pope Nicholas V put architects, including Alberti, to work on its reconstruction. But it was not until 1506, when Pope Julius II employed Donato Bramante, that serious work began. Bramante designed a new basilica on a Greek cross plan, with a central dome and four smaller domes. He oversaw the demolition of much of the old basilica and attracted great criticism for the unnecessary destruction of many of its precious works of art – including Byzantine mosaics and frescoes by artists including Giotto.

It took more than 150 years to complete the basilica, involving the contributions of Bramante, Raphael, Antonio da Sangallo, Michelangelo, Giacomo della Porta and Carlo Maderno. It is generally held that St Peter's owes most to Michelangelo, who took over the project in 1547 at the age of 72 and was responsible for the design of the dome. He died before the church was completed. The facade and portico were designed by Carlo Maderno, who took over the project after Michelangelo's death. He was instructed to lengthen the nave towards the square, effectively altering Bramante's original Greek cross plan to a Latin cross.

The basilica opens 7 am to 7 pm April to September, and 7 am to 6 pm October to March.

The cavernous interior, superbly decorated by Bernini and Giacomo della Porta, can hold up to 60,000 people. It contains a vast number of incredible treasures. The red-porphyry disk on the floor just inside the main door marks the spot where Charlemagne and later Holy Roman emperors were crowned by the pope. Bronze plates in the marble floor of the central aisle indicate the respective sizes of the 14 next largest churches in the world.

Bernini's Baroque **baldachino** stands 29m high in the centre of the church and is an extraordinary work of art. The bronze used to make it was taken from the roof of the Pantheon. The high altar, at which only the pope can serve, stands over the site of St Peter's grave. The Confessione in front of it, built by Carlo Maderno, is encircled with perpetually burning lamps.

Michelangelo's **dome**, a majestic architectural masterpiece, soars 119m above the high altar (see boxed text 'God's-Eye View' later in this chapter). The solid stone **piers** supporting the dome have niches and balconies designed by Bernini. Each pier is named after the saint whose colossal statue stands in its niches – St Longinus (by Bernini), St Helena, St Veronica and St Andrew. The balconies above are decorated with reliefs depicting the Reliquie Maggiori (Major Relics): the lance of St Longinus, which he used to pierce Christ's side; the cloth of St Veronica, which bears a miraculous portrait of Christ; and a piece of the True Cross, collected by St Helena, the mother of Constantine.

An Audience with the Pope

The pope usually gives a public audience every Wednesday at 11 am in the Aula delle Udienze Pontificie (Papal Audience Hall). For permission to attend an audience, go to the Prefettura della Casa Pontificia (Map 4; ☎ 69 88 46 31), through the bronze doors under the colonnade to the right of St Peter's. The office opens 9 am to 1 pm and you can apply on the Tuesday before the audience (or, at a push, on the morning of the audience). You can also apply in writing to the Prefettura della Casa Pontificia, 00120 Città del Vaticano or fax 06 69 88 38 65.

You should specify the date you'd like to attend and the number of tickets required. If you have a hotel in Rome, the office will forward the tickets there. Individuals shouldn't have too much trouble obtaining a ticket at short notice. Tickets are free.

The pope also occasionally celebrates Mass at St Peter's Basilica and information can be obtained at the same office. You will be required to leave your passport with the Swiss Guards at the bronze doors. People wanting to attend a normal Mass at St Peter's can ask for the times of daily Masses at the tourist office in the square.

The Pope's Army

The Swiss Guards are the pope's private bodyguards. Despite the colourful uniform, which makes them look like they have just stepped out of a television period drama, all Swiss Guards are highly trained soldiers.

The selection process for potential recruits is rigid; they are hand-picked for their total precision, total loyalty and total dedication. Not only must these men be in excellent physical condition, but they must also be Swiss-born, practising Catholics, of impeccable moral standing and they must have completed their national military service in Switzerland.

A full complement of Swiss Guards is 100, although in recent years the Vatican has had problems filling its quota, and few of them tend to make a career out of being one of the pope's guardian angels. The soldiers are paid very low wages; they cannot live outside the Vatican and therefore if they want to marry, they might have to wait years before suitable accommodation is available.

The soldiers do a lot more than guard the entrances to and perimeters of the Vatican. A typical day might include martial arts practice or weapons training (all guards are skilled in using their traditional 15th-century pike) as well as more conventional modern weapons, or sessions on anti-terrorism tactics. The soldiers always accompany the pope when he makes public appearances – a Swiss Guard was at John Paul II's side during the assassination attempt in Piazza San Pietro in 1981 – and two (plain-clothes) guards travel with him whenever he goes abroad.

To the right as you face the high altar, at the base of the Pier of St Longinus, is a famous bronze statue of St Peter, believed to be a 13th-century work by Arnolfo di Cambio. The statue's right foot has been worn down by the kisses and strokes of pilgrims, who patiently queue to touch it. The statue is dressed in papal robes on the Feast Day of St Peter and St Paul, 29 June.

Probably the easiest way to see all the artworks in St Peter's is to begin in the southern nave and work your way around the basilica in an anticlockwise direction (see the St Peter's Basilica floor plan earlier in this chapter).

Michelangelo's superb **Pietà** is at the beginning of the right aisle just inside the **Porta Santa** (Holy Door). It was sculpted when he was only 25 years old and is the only work to carry his signature (on the sash across the breast of the Madonna). It is now protected by bulletproof glass after having been attacked in 1972 by a hammer-wielding vandal.

Beyond the Pietà is the **Cappella del Santissimo Sacramento**. The iron grille separating the chapel from the rest of the basilica was designed by Borromini. Above the altar is a gilt bronze ciborium by Bernini

(modelled on Bramante's Tempietto at San Pietro in Montorio) and behind it an altarpiece, *The Trinity*, by Pietro da Cortona.

At the back of the Pier of St Longinus is a large mosaic of the Communion of St Jerome, after Domenichino. From a distance the medium is unclear and this vast artwork looks very like a canvas. The **Cappella Gregoriana** opposite was built by Gregory XIII from designs by Michelangelo. Part of a marble column from the old basilica was placed here in 1578; the painting on it, the Madonna del Soccorso, can still be made out.

Two notable artworks in the **transept** right of the main entrance are the monument of Clement XIII by Canova, and the bright and garish Altare della Navicella mosaic of Christ Walking on the Waters, after Lanfranco. Of the three mosaics in the **Cappella di San Michele**, the Santa Petronilla after Guercino (a massive canvas of the subject is in the Capitoline Museums) is most impressive.

The **Throne of St Peter** by Bernini (1665) in the Tribune cannot fail to catch your eye. The huge gilted-bronze throne is supported by statues of St Augustine, St Ambrose, St Athanasius and St John Chrysostom. Its wooden seat, inlaid with ivory, is thought to have been St Peter's chair. In a very modernist composition, rays of light shine from the figure of a dove (representing the Holy Spirit) towards a halo of flying angels. To the right of the throne is Bernini's monument to Urban VIII, where the pope is flanked by the figures of Charity and Justice. The design is clearly influenced by Michelangelo's Medici tombs in Florence.

The **Cappella della Colonna**, in the northern aisle, is decorated with figures of angels with garlands of flowers. Above the tomb of St Leo the Great is a particularly fine relief (1650) by the Baroque sculptor Alessandro Algardi. Opposite it, under the

next arch, is Bernini's last work in the basilica, the monument to Alexander VII, in which the sculptor has made heavy red marble resemble soft velvet.

The sacristy entrance leads to the **Museo Storico Artistico** (Treasury) which has sacred relics and priceless artefacts. Highlights include: a tabernacle by Donatello; the Colonna Santa, a 4th-century Byzantine column from the earlier church; the 6th-century Crux Vaticana, made of bronze and beset with jewels – a gift of the emperor Justinian II; and the massive bronze tomb of Sixtus IV by Pollaiuolo. The Treasury

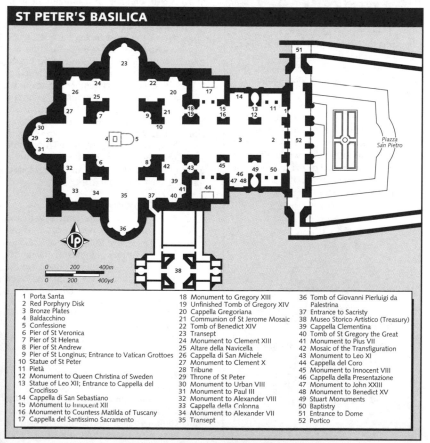

ST PETER'S BASILICA

Piazza San Pietro

0   200   400m
0   200   400yd

1 Porta Santa	18 Monument to Gregory XIII	36 Tomb of Giovanni Pierluigi da
2 Red Porphyry Disk	19 Unfinished Tomb of Gregory XIV	Palestrina
3 Bronze Plates	20 Cappella Gregoriana	37 Entrance to Sacristy
4 Baldacchino	21 Communion of St Jerome Mosaic	38 Museo Storico Artistico (Treasury)
5 Confessione	22 Tomb of Benedict XIV	39 Cappella Clementina
6 Pier of St Veronica	23 Transept	40 Tomb of St Gregory the Great
7 Pier of St Helena	24 Monument to Clement XIII	41 Monument to Pius VII
8 Pier of St Andrew	25 Altare della Navicella	42 Mosaic of the Transfiguration
9 Pier of St Longinus; Entrance to Vatican Grottoes	26 Cappella di San Michele	43 Monument to Leo XI
10 Statue of St Peter	27 Monument to Clement X	44 Cappella del Coro
11 Pietà	28 Tribune	45 Monument to Innocent VIII
12 Monument to Queen Christina of Sweden	29 Throne of St Peter	46 Cappella della Presentazione
13 Statue of Leo XII; Entrance to Cappella del	30 Monument to Urban VIII	47 Monument to John XXIII
Crocifisso	31 Monument to Paul III	48 Monument to Benedict XV
14 Cappella di San Sebastiano	32 Monument to Alexander VIII	49 Stuart Monuments
15 Monument to Innocent XII	33 Cappella della Colonna	50 Baptistry
16 Monument to Countess Matilda of Tuscany	34 Monument to Alexander VII	51 Entrance to Dome
17 Cappella del Santissimo Sacramento	35 Transept	52 Portico

opens 9 am to 6.15 pm April to September (to 5.15 pm October to March). Admission costs €4.13.

The cupola of the **Cappella Clementina** is decorated with mosaics, after Pomarancio. The chapel is named after Clement VIII (died 1605) who had Giacomo della Porta decorate it for the Jubilee of 1600. Beneath the altar is the **tomb of St Gregory the Great** (died 604), and above it a mosaic representing the **Miracle of St Gregory** after Andrea Sacchi. To the left of the altar is a classical monument to Pope Pius VII by Thorvaldsen, whose work at the time was strongly influenced by Canova.

Particularly charming is the **monument to Leo XI** by Alessandro Algardi in the next aisle arch. Beyond it, the richly decorated **Cappella del Coro** shows what happens if you go mad with gilt. Giovanni Battista Ricci carried out the work in the chapel following designs by Giacomo della Porta; Bernini designed the elegant choir stalls. The chapel is usually locked but it's worth sticking your nose through the gate to get a good look. The monument to Innocent VIII by Antonio Pollaiuolo (in the next aisle arch) is a re-creation of a monument from the old basilica.

The **Cappella della Presentazione** contains two of the most modern works in the whole basilica. On the right of the altar is a monument to John XXIII by Emilio Greco and on the left is a monument to Benedict XV by Pietro Canonica. Under the next arch are the so-called **Stuart monuments**. On the right is the monument to Clementina Sobieska, wife of James Stuart, by Filippo Barigioni, and on the left is Canova's superb monument to the last Stuarts. The simple sculpture has two angels flanking a door, and busts of the Old and Young Pretenders and of Henry Cardinal York.

Vatican Grottoes

The entrance to the **Sacre Grotte Vaticane** (Vatican Grottoes), the resting place of numerous popes, is next to the pier of St Longinus (one of four piers supporting the arches at the base of Michelangelo's cupola) to the right as you approach the papal altar. The tombs of many early popes were moved here from the old St Peter's Basilica, and recent popes, including John XXIII, Paul VI and John Paul I, are buried here. The grottoes open 7 am to 6 pm (April to September) and 7 am to 5 pm (September to March) daily.

Tomb of St Peter

The excavations beneath St Peter's, which began in 1940, have uncovered part of the original church, an early-Christian cemetery and Roman tombs. Archaeologists believe they have also found the tomb of St Peter;

God's-Eye View

Entry to the dome is to the right as you climb the stairs to the atrium of the basilica. Access to the roof is by lift (€3.61) or stairs (€3.09). From there, ascend the stairs to the base of the dome for a view down into the basilica. From here, a narrow staircase leads eventually to the top of the dome and St Peter's lantern, from where you have an unequalled view of Rome. It is well worth the effort but bear in mind it is a long and tiring climb and not to be recommended for those who suffer from claustrophobia or vertigo. You can climb the dome 8 am to 6 pm daily April to September, and 8 am to 5 pm daily October to March.

ASA ANDERSSON

the site of the empty tomb is marked by a shrine and a wall plastered with red. Nearby is another wall, scrawled with the graffiti of pilgrims; in 1942 the bones of an elderly, strongly built man were found in a box placed in a niche behind this wall. In 1976, after many years of forensic examination, Paul VI declared the bones to be those of St Peter. John Paul II had some of the relics transferred to his hospital room when he was recovering from the 1981 assassination attempt. The bones were then returned to the tomb and are kept in hermetically sealed perspex cases designed by NASA.

The excavations can be visited only by appointment, which can be made either in writing or in person at the Ufficio Scavi (☎ 06 69 88 53 18, fax 06 69 88 55 18), in Piazza Braschi. Address your letter to Ufficio Scavi, 00120 Città del Vaticano, and stipulate the date you'd like to visit. The office will then contact you to confirm the time and date. You need to book at least one week ahead. The office opens 9 am to 5 pm Monday to Friday. Small groups are taken most days between 9 am and noon and 2 to 5 pm. Admission costs €5.16 with a guide.

VATICAN MUSEUMS (Map 4)

From Piazza San Pietro, follow the wall of the Vatican north to the museums' entrance.

The museums contain an incredible collection of art and treasures accumulated by the popes, and you will need several hours to see the most important areas and museums. One visit is probably not enough to appreciate the full value of the collections and it's worth trying to make at least two visits if you have the time.

Make sure you pick up a floor-plan leaflet. There are four 'one-way' itineraries which have been mapped out with the aim of simplifying visits and containing the huge number of visitors. It is basically compulsory that you follow the itineraries (which vary in duration from 1½ to 5 hours) but you can make some deviations if you want. The new entrance (with every facility a museum visitor could want) leads up to the area known as the Quattro Cancelli, where each of the separate itineraries starts.

Holy Gardens

The Giardini del Vaticano (Vatican Gardens) contain fortifications, grottoes, monuments and fountains dating from the 9th century to the present day, as well as a heliport and manicured gardens in various styles tended by 30 full-time gardeners. There's a formal Italian garden, a flower-filled French parterre and a naturalistic English wood. There is even a kitchen garden which provides produce for the pontifical household, although tour groups don't get close enough to check out the papal tomatoes.

Walking tours take place on Monday, Tuesday, Thursday, Friday and Saturday from March to October but are less frequent at other times of the year. Tickets must be booked in advance through the Ufficio Visite Guidate dei Musei Vaticani (☎ 06 69 88 44 66) and cost €8.78. It's advisable to book well in advance.

Another point to note is that the Sistine Chapel comes towards the end of each itinerary. If you want to spend most of your time in the chapel, or you want to get there early to avoid the crowds, it is possible to walk straight there and then walk back to the Quattro Cancelli to pick up one of the itineraries. Most tour groups (and there are many!) head straight to the chapel and it is almost always very crowded. Of great assistance, and well worth the €10.33 investment, is the *Guide to the Vatican Museums and City*, on sale at the museums. You can also hire CD audio guides which provide a commentary on what you are seeing.

The buildings that house the Vatican Museums, known collectively as the Palazzo Apostolico Vaticano, cover an area of 5.5 hectares. Their construction has been a work in progress since the 5th century (see the boxed text 'Building the Vatican' earlier in this chapter). The buildings to the west of the Quattro Cancelli are the most recent and house the Museo Gregoriano Profano, the Museo Pio-Cristiano, the Pinacoteca, the

Museo Missionario-Etnologico and a carriage museum. These galleries are the last on the longer itineraries and are probably the ones to miss if you run out of time and energy.

The museums are well equipped for disabled visitors; there are four suggested itineraries, several lifts and specially fitted toilets. Ask for a folder at the ticket window or information desk or call in advance on ☎ 06 69 88 43 41. Wheelchairs can be reserved. Parents with young children can take pushchairs into the museums.

The Vatican Museums open 8.45 am to 4.45 pm (last admission at 3.30 pm) Monday to Friday, and 8.45 to 1.45 pm (last admission 12.45 pm) on Saturday. Admission costs €9.29. The museums are closed on Sunday and holidays but open 9 am to 1.45 pm on the last Sunday of every month. Admission is free but be prepared for queues.

Museo Gregoriano Profano
This museum houses classical antiquities and was started by Gregory XVI in 1844. Exhibits include original Greek sculpture dating from the 5th and 4th centuries BC and Roman sculpture from the 1st to 3rd centuries AD.

Museo Pio-Cristiano
The Museo Pio-Cristiano contains early-Christian antiquities, including inscriptions and sculpture from catacombs and basilicas, and sarcophagi decorated with carved reliefs of biblical scenes. The collection was founded by Pius IX in 1854. Both these collections were formerly kept in the Palazzo Laterano and were moved to the Vatican in 1970.

Pinacoteca
The popes' picture gallery was founded by Pius XI and houses a magnificent collection of paintings dating from the 11th to the 19th century. Napoleon carted off many of the pictures in 1797 but they were returned to Rome in 1815. They were hung in chronological order and include works by Fra Angelico, Filippo Lippi, Benozzo Gozzoli, Federico Barocci, Guido Reni, Guercino,

Nicholas Poussin, Van Dyck and Pietro da Cortona.

There are several works by Raphael, who has a room to himself, including the *Madonna di Foligno*, originally kept in the church of Santa Maria in Aracoeli, and the magnificent *La Trasfigurazione* (Transfiguration) completed just before he died in 1520. Other highlights of the collection include Giotto's *Polittico Stefaneschi* (Stefaneschi triptych), which was originally an altarpiece in the Sacristry of St Peter's, Giovanni Bellini's *Pietà*, Leonardo's unfinished *San Gerolamo* and Caravaggio's *Deposizione*.

Museo Missionario-Etnologico
This museum contains ethnological and anthropological material from Africa, the Americas, Asia, Australasia and the Middle East, some of which was gathered during missionary expeditions.

Museo Gregoriano Egizio
The Egyptian museum is on the lower floor of the Belvedere, on the eastern side of the Quattro Cancelli. It was founded by Pope Gregory XVI in 1839 and contains many pieces taken from Egypt in Roman times. The collection is small but there are some fascinating exhibits. The rooms were decorated in the 19th century in Egyptian style and have decorative details such as cornice friezes with inscriptions in hieroglyphics, and midnight-blue ceilings peppered with gold stars.

Of particular note in Room I is the **Trono di Rameses II**, part of a statue of the seated king. Room II contains painted wooden sarcophagi dating from around 1000 BC, whose colours are unbelievably fresh and rich. There are two mummies, one of which is totally bandaged. The other has its blackened hands and feet exposed, and you can see the henna-treated hair and a hole where the mummy's left eye should have been; the eye was probably removed so that the brain could be extracted before mummification. There are also two carved-marble sarcophagi from the 6th century BC. Room III has Egyptian-style Roman sculptures, which were used as decoration at the Villa Adriana in Tivoli (see the Excursions chapter). Of particular note in Room IV is the black-marble statue representing the Nile.

Museo Chiaramonti

From the Egyptian Museum, a short flight of stairs leads down to a long corridor which runs the length of the Cortile della Pigna. It contains hundreds of marble statues of gods, sculptures of playful cherubs and busts of Roman patricians. It's a great way to get an idea of fashionable Roman hairstyles. Near the end of the Museo Chiaramonti, off to the right is the **Braccio Nuovo** (new wing). It contains important works, including a famous statue of Augustus and a statue depicting the Nile as a reclining god with 16 babies, supposedly representing the number of cubits the Nile rose when in flood, playing on him.

Visible through a gate at the end of the Museo Chiaramonti is the **Galleria Lapidaria**, which only opens to scholars on request. It contains over 3000 Christian and Roman inscriptions, mounted into the walls of the gallery. The Christian inscriptions are on the right side and the Classical ones on the left.

Museo Pio-Clementino

This museum is in the Belvedere and accessible through the Egyptian Museum or from the Cortile della Pigna. Entering through the square vestibule, you come to the Gabinetto dell'Apoxyomenos, which contains a 1st-century-AD Roman statue found in Trastevere in 1849. The statue depicts an athlete towelling himself off and is actually a copy of a bronze original thought to date from around 320 BC.

In the elegant **Cortile Ottagono** (Octagonal Courtyard), which forms part of the gallery, are several important ancient statues, bas-reliefs and sarcophagi. To the left as you enter, in a niche in the corner, is the famous *Apollo Belvedere*, a 2nd-century Roman copy in marble of a 4th-century-BC Greek bronze, considered one of the great masterpieces of classical sculpture. Also on the left is an impressive statue of a river god

(Tigris). Beyond it is another notable piece, the *Laocoön*, depicting a Trojan priest of Apollo and his two sons in mortal struggle with two sea serpents. When discovered in 1506 on the Esquiline (Michelangelo was said to have been present), the sculpture was recognised from descriptions by the Roman writer Pliny the Elder and purchased by Pope Julius II.

Back inside the Belvedere is the **Sala degli Animali**, filled with sculptures of all sorts of creatures. The floors of both sides of the gallery contain magnificent mosaics dating from the 4th century AD. Don't miss the delightful crab (made from rare green-porphyry stone) at the far end of the room on the right. Facing it, mounted on the wall, is a charming mosaic showing a cat (which has caught a chicken) with ducks and fruit. There are also two small mosaic landscapes which came from the Villa Adriana. Beyond the Sala degli Animali are the Galleria delle Statue, with several important classical pieces, the Sala delle Buste, which contains portrait busts of important Roman emperors and political figures, and the Gabinetto delle Maschere, which is named after the floor mosaics of theatrical masks; there are several interesting pieces in this room including two statues of Venus and a group representing the three Graces.

In the **Sala delle Muse** (Room of the Muses) is the *Torso Belvedere*, a Greek sculpture of the 1st century BC, which was found in the Campo de' Fiori during the time of Pope Julius II; it was much admired by Michelangelo and other Renaissance artists. The next room, the round **Sala Rotonda**, built by Michelangelo Simonetti in 1780, was inspired by the Pantheon. It contains a number of colossal statues including the gilded-bronze figure of *Ercole* (Hercules). The ancient mosaic on the floor, featuring sea monsters and battles between Greeks and centaurs, is quite exquisite. The enormous basin in the centre of the room was found at the site of Nero's Domus Aurea and is made out of a single piece of red-porphyry stone.

In the **Sala a Croce Greca** (Greek Cross Room) are the porphyry stone sarcophagi of

Constantine's daughter, Constantia, and his mother, St Helena. These were originally in the Mausoleo di Santa Constanza in Via Nomentana.

Museo Gregoriano Etrusco

On the upper level of the Belvedere, off the Simonetti staircase, is the Museo Gregoriano Etrusco (Etruscan Museum), which contains artefacts from Etruscan tombs of southern Etruria. Of particular interest are those in Room II from the Regolini-Galassi tomb, discovered in 1836 south of Cerveteri. Those buried in the tomb included a princess and among the finds on display are gold jewellery and a funeral carriage, with a bronze bed and funeral couch, dating from the 7th century BC. The Etruscan rooms were refurbished and expanded in 1996. The exhibits are arranged by subject matter so it is easy to compare pieces.

The **Sala dei Bronzi** has the *Marte di Todi* (Mars of Todi), a full-length bronze statue of a warrior dating from the 4th century BC, as well as bronze figurines, statuettes of young boys, armour, hand mirrors and candelabras. Beyond it, the **Sala delle Pietre** displays sarcophagi and statues in volcanic stone such as tufa and peperino which were favoured by the Etruscans as they were soft and easy to carve, then hardened over time. The **Sala degli Ori** is devoted to beautifully displayed Etruscan jewellery.

The **Sala delle Terracotte** displays terracotta pieces, including some wonderfully expressive portrait heads. Don't miss the bust of an elderly woman. The Etruscan Museum also incorporates a collection of Greek vases and Roman antiquities, a highlight of which is a vase, signed by the Greek artist Exekias and decorated with an image of Achilles and Ajax playing draughts, dating from around 530 BC. Magnificent views of Rome can be had from the last room at the end of the wing. From here you can also get a glimpse down the full drop of Bramante's spiral staircase which was designed so that horses could be ridden up it. The stairway was built for Julius II inside a square tower which was at one time the entrance to the Belvedere.

Galleria dei Candelabri

The Galleria dei Candelabri (Gallery of the Candelabras) was originally an open loggia and is packed with classical sculpture including several elegantly carved marble candelabras which give the room its name. In the middle section of the long gallery note the fragments of Roman frescoes and the vividly coloured still-life mosaics. Farther on is a charming sculpture of a boy strangling a goose and opposite it a flute player.

Galleria degli Arazzi

You have to walk through the Galleria degli Arazzi (Tapestry Gallery) to get to the Sistine Chapel, and it is worth a brief look. The tapestries on the left (opposite the windows) date from the 16th century. They were designed by students of Raphael and woven in the Brussels workshop of Pieter van Aeist. Note the intricate details of flowers and foliage in the penultimate tapestry showing Christ appearing to Mary Magdalen. The tapestries on the right date from the 17th century and were woven by the Barberini workshop.

Galleria delle Carte Geografiche

Covered from one end to another with fascinating topographical maps, the Galleria delle Carte Geografiche (Map Gallery) also merits more than a cursory glance from the hoards of people heading single-mindedly to the Sistine Chapel. The 40 topographical maps were painted between 1580 and 1583 for Pope Gregory XIII based on cartoons by Ignazio Danti, one of the leading cartographers of his day. The ceiling frescoes, representing the lives of saints and the history of the church, are related geographically to the maps below them.

Next to the Map Gallery is the **Appartamento di San Pio V**, containing some interesting Flemish tapestries, and the **Sala Sobieski**, named after the enormous 19th-century canvas on its northern wall (depicting the victory of the Polish King John III Sobieski over the Turks in 1683). These rooms lead into the magnificent Stanze di Raffaello.

Stanze di Raffaello

The so-called 'Raphael Rooms' were the private apartments of Pope Julius II. Raphael painted the Stanza della Segnatura and the Stanza d'Eliodoro, while the Stanza dell'Incendio was painted by his students to his designs and the ceiling was painted by his master, Perugino.

The far room, the **Sala di Costantino,** was decorated by Raphael's students with some of the works based on his designs. Off this room is the Sala dei Chiaroscuri and the Cappella di Niccolo V. The **Sala dei Chiaroscuri** was decorated in the 16th century and used for ceremonial purposes. Raphael designed the ceiling which, along with the chiaroscuro figures on the walls, was executed by his students. A small door leads to the tiny **Cappella di Niccolo V** which was Pope Nicholas V's private chapel. The superb frescoes were painted by Fra Angelico around 1450 and depict the lives of St Stephen (upper cycle) and St Lawrence (lower level).

Back in the Stanze di Raffaello you enter the **Stanza d'Eliodoro**. Raphael's fine **Cacciata d'Eliodoro** (Expulsion of Heliodorus from the Temple), on the main wall (to the right as you enter from the Sala dei Chiaroscuri), depicts Julius' military victory over foreign powers. To the left is *Mass of Bolsena*, showing Julius II paying homage to the relic of a 13th-century miracle at Orvieto. Next is *Leone X ferma l'invasione di Attila* (Leo X Repulsing Attila), by Raphael and his school, and on the fourth wall is *Liberazione di San Pietro* (Liberation of St Peter), which depicts St Peter being freed from prison but is actually an allusion to Pope Leo's imprisonment after the battle of Ravenna (also the metaphorical subject of the Attila fresco).

In the **Stanza della Segnatura** is another masterpiece by Raphael and perhaps his best-known work: **La Scuola d'Atene** (The School of Athens), featuring philosophers and scholars gathered around Plato and Aristotle. The lone figure in front of the steps is believed to be a portrait of Michelangelo, who was painting the Sistine Chapel at the time. The figure of Plato (pointing to the sky) is said to be a portrait of Leonardo da Vinci. In the lower right, the figure of Euclide (bent over and drawing with a compass) is Bramante. Raphael included a self portrait at the lower right of the fresco (second figure from right). Opposite is *La Disputa del Sacramento* (Dispute over the Holy Sacrament), also by Raphael.

From Raphael's rooms, go down the stairs to the **Appartamento Borgia,** but only to see the ceiling in the first room, decorated with frescoes by Bernardino Pinturicchio. The Vatican collection of modern religious art was installed in the Borgia apartments in 1973 but it's really only worth visiting if religious paintings are your thing.

SISTINE CHAPEL (Map 4)

The Sistine Chapel (Cappella Sistina) is the private papal chapel and was completed in 1484 for Pope Sixtus IV. It is used for some papal functions and for the conclave which elects the popes. But the chapel is best known for one of the most famous works of art in the world: Michelangelo's wonderful frescoes of the *Genesis* (Creation) on the barrel-vaulted ceiling, and the *Giudizio Universale* (Last Judgment) on the end wall. Both have been restored; the ceiling was unveiled after a 10-year restoration project in 1990 and work on the Last Judgment was completed in 1994. The rich, vibrant colours used by Michelangelo were brought back to the surface and surprised many scholars and art historians, who had only ever studied the ceiling when it was covered in centuries of soot and grime.

Michelangelo was commissioned by Pope Julius II to paint the ceiling and although very reluctant to take on the job (he never considered himself a painter), he started work on it in 1508. The complex and grand composition which Michelangelo devised to cover the 800 sq m of ceiling took him four years to complete. He worked on scaffolding which the restorers believe was inserted into holes under the windows. The restorers also learned much about the way in which the artist worked and how his painting skill developed as he progressed through the great project.

Michelangelo in Rome

Michelangelo Buonarotti was born in Caprese near Arrezzo in Tuscany in 1475, the son of a Tuscan magistrate. He was moody and solitary figure, easily offended and irritated. The true Renaissance man, he was a supremely talented architect and painter, but he regarded himself as a sculptor above all else.

It was as a sculptor that Michelangelo achieved his early recognition. One of his greatest early carvings is the *Pietà* in St Peter's Basilica which he completed when he was 25.

Michelangelo came to work in Rome for Pope Julius II who wanted a grand marble tomb which would surpass any funerary monument that had ever been built. Michelangelo was dispatched to the marble quarries of Carrara in northern Tuscany (which still provide stone for sculptors today) and spent eight months selecting and excavating suitable marble blocks which, when brought to Rome, reportedly filled half of Piazza San Pietro.

Although the tomb preoccupied Michelangelo throughout his working life, it was never completed and Julius II lies in an unadorned grave in St Peter's. The original design included 40 statues. The famous figure of Moses as well as statues of Leah and Rachel are in the Basilica di San Pietro in Vincoli. Two of the slaves are now in the Louvre (Paris) and several famous unfinished slaves are in the Accademia (Florence).

Despite claiming to be a reluctant painter, Michelangelo's single greatest artistic achievement – and one of the most awe-inspiring acts of individual creativity in the history of the visual arts – is the ceiling of the Sistine Chapel, painted between 1508 and 1512.

Michelangelo never wanted the commission (also from Julius II) and the project was problematic from the outset. First the artist rejected the scaffolding that Bramante had built for him; then he considered his assistants so incompetent that he dismissed them all, scraped off their work, and ended up painting the entire ceiling by himself. The artist was pushed to his physical and emotional limits, and was continually harassed by the pope and his court, who wanted the job finished.

Michelangelo returned to Rome aged 59 at the request of Pope Clement VII to paint *The Last Judgment* on the altar wall of the Sistine Chapel. Once again he accepted the commission against his will, preferring to continue sculpting figures for Julius II's tomb which he did secretly while he prepared cartoons for the chapel.

On Clement VII's death, his successor Paul III was determined to have Michelangelo working exclusively for him and have the Sistine Chapel completed; in 1535 he appointed Michelangelo as chief

Vasari records Michelangelo's suffering and frustration, as well as his problems with an impatient Pope Julius and the fact that he did the work almost entirely alone, after dismissing in disgust the Florentine masters he had gathered to help him.

Ceiling Paintings

Looking towards the Last Judgment, the scenes down the middle of the ceiling represent nine scenes from the book of Genesis: the Division of Day from Night; Creation of the Sun, Moon and Planets; Creation of the heavens; Separation of land from sea; Creation of Adam; Creation of Eve; Temptation and Expulsion of Adam and Eve from the garden of Eden; Noah's sacrifice; the Flood; the Drunkenness of Noah.

Michelangelo's development as a painter is clearly evident as you look at the ceiling frescoes. He actually worked in reverse order, starting with the *Drunkenness of Noah* (which is fairly stiff and formal) and working back to the *Creation of the Sun, Moon and Planets* and the *Division of Day from Night* (both of which demonstrate the artist at the peak of his powers).

Probably the most famous scene is the image of the *Creation of Adam*, where God points his index figure at Adam, bringing him to life. God's swirling red cape surrounds a group of people, said to represent

Michelangelo in Rome

TRUDI CANAVAN

Michelangelo's *Pietà* sculpture shows the Madonna tenderly holding her crucified son.

architect, sculptor and painter to the Vatican, and the artist started working on *The Last Judgment*, which was unveiled in 1541 and claimed by some as surpassing not only the other masters who had decorated the chapel walls but also his own ceiling frescoes.

Paul III then commissioned Michelangelo to create a new central square for the city on the Capitoline and design a grand approach to it. The work was not finished until the mid-17th century but successive architects closely followed the original plans.

Michelangelo's design for the upper storey of the Palazzo Farnese was also realised posthumously, when Giacomo della Porta completed the building, and his design for the city gateway at Porta Pia was finished a year after his death.

The artist spent his last years working – unhappily – on St Peter's Basilica; he felt that it was a penance from God. He disapproved of the plans that had been drawn up by Antonio da Sangallo the Younger before his death, claiming that they deprived the basilica of light, and argued with Sangallo's assistants who wanted to retain their master's designs. Instead Michelangelo created the magnificent light-filled dome, based on Brunelleschi's design for the Duomo cupola in Florence, and a stately facade.

In his old age he was said to work with the same strength and concentration as he had as a younger man. He continued to direct the work until his death on 18 February 1564. He was buried in the Chiesa dei Santi Apostoli although his remains were later moved to Florence. The dome and facade of St Peter's were completed to his designs by Vignola, Giacomo della Porta and Carlo Fontana.

the future generations to come. In the *Temptation and Expulsion of Adam and Eve from the Garden of Eden*, Adam and Eve are shown (on the left) tasting the forbidden fruit, with Satan represented by a snake with the body of a woman coiled around a tree. On the right, Adam and Eve are expelled from Eden by the red-robed, sword-wielding Angel of the Lord.

The main scenes are framed by the *Ignudi*, athletic male nudes, with which Michelangelo celebrates the male figure. Next to them, on the lower curved part of the vault, separated by trompe l'oeil cornices, are large figures of Hebrew Prophets and pagan Sibyls. These muscular, power-

ful figures – especially the Delphic and Libyan Sibyls – are among the most striking and dramatic images on the ceiling. The bulky arms on the androgynous Cumaean Sibyl are a caseload of steroids short of feminine, and most scholars believe that Michelangelo modelled all his female figures on men. In the lunettes, found over the windows, are the ancestors of Christ.

The Last Judgment

Michelangelo was commissioned by Clement VII to paint *The Last Judgment*, 24 years after he worked on the ceiling (the pope died shortly afterwards and the work was executed under Paul III). Two frescoes by Perugino were destroyed to make way for the new painting, which caused great controversy in its day, and the entire wall had to be replastered, so that it tilted inwards, to avoid dust settling on it.

The painting was done between 1535 and 1541. It is considered to be the masterpiece of Michelangelo's mature years but the artist's finely honed technical proficiency takes second place against the exuberance of the composition. The painting depicts the souls of the dead being torn from their graves to face the wrath of God. The subject was chosen by Paul III as a warning to Catholics to toe the line of their faith in the turmoil of the Reformation then sweeping Europe. It is a dynamic, emotional composition, said to reflect Michelangelo's own tormented attitude to his faith.

Criticism of its dramatic, swirling mass of predominantly naked bodies was summarily dismissed by Michelangelo, who depicted one of his greatest critics, Paul III's master of ceremonies, as Minos with donkey's ears. Michelangelo also includes a self-portrait on the shroud held by St Bartholomew, to the right of Christ.

As with the Creation, *The Last Judgment* was blackened by candle smoke and incense, but it was also damaged by poor restorations and by the addition of clothes to cover some of the nude figures. One of Michelangelo's students, Daniele da Volterra, was commissioned by Pius IV to do the cover-up job.

Wall Paintings

The walls of the chapel were painted by famous Renaissance artists including Botticelli, Domenico Ghirlandaio, Pinturicchio and Luca Signorelli. The restoration of these paintings was completed in 2000. Even if you find it hard to drag your attention away from Michelangelo's frescoes, take time to appreciate these paintings, which were produced in the late 15th century and depict events in the life of Moses (to the left looking at *The Last Judgment*) and Christ (to the right). Anywhere else in the world, these frescoes would be the prime exhibits. As it is many visitors to the Sistine Chapel hardly give them a second glance, focusing all their attention on Michelangelo's work.

The first parts of each cycle, the Finding of Moses and the Birth of Christ, were the Perugino frescoes destroyed to make way for *The Last Judgment*. The second fresco on the right, depicting the *Tentazione di Cristo* (Temptations of Christ) and the *Purificazione del Lebbroso* (Cleansing of the Leper) by Botticelli is particularly beautiful. Note the typical Botticelli maiden in diaphanous dress in the foreground.

In the fifth fresco on the left, which depicts the Punishment of the Rebels, Botticelli uses the Arco di Costantino as a backdrop for the action and includes a self-portrait (the figure in black behind Moses on the far right). Ghirlandaio's *Vocazione di Pietro e Andrea* (Calling of Peter and Andrew), the third fresco on the right, includes among the crowd of onlookers portraits of prominent contemporary figures. Perugino's *Consegna delle Chiavi* (Christ Giving the Keys to St Peter), the fifth fresco on the right, is a superbly composed cityscape also includes a self-portrait (the fifth figure from the right).

VATICAN LIBRARY (Map 4)

Returning to the Quattro Cancelli area from the Sistine Chapel, you pass through the splendid frescoed halls of the **Biblioteca Apostolica Vaticana** (the Vatican library) which was founded by Nicholas V in 1450. The library contains over 1.5 million volumes including illuminated manuscripts, early printed books, prints and drawings, and coins. Selected items from the collection are displayed in the **Salone Sistino**, which has particularly beautiful frescoes on the ceiling and walls. If you haven't run out of time and energy, take a moment to stop and look.

CASTEL SANT'ANGELO (Map 4)

Originally the mausoleum of Hadrian, this building was converted into a fortress for the popes in the 6th century AD. It was named Castel Sant'Angelo by Pope Gregory the Great in 590, after he saw a vision of an angel above the structure heralding the end of a plague in Rome. The fortress was linked to the Vatican palaces in 1277 by a wall and passageway, used often by the popes to escape to the fortress in times of threat. During the 16th-century sacking of Rome by Emperor Charles V, hundreds of people lived in the fortress for months.

The Castel Sant'Angelo (☎ 06 681 91 11), Lungotevere Castello, opens 9 am to 8 pm (last admission 7 pm) Tuesday to Sunday. Admission costs €5.16. The bar built into the battlements has good snacks and a unique peep-hole view of Rome's rooftops.

Hadrian built the **Ponte Sant'Angelo** across the Tiber in 136 to provide an approach to his mausoleum. It collapsed in 1450 and was subsequently rebuilt, incorporating parts of the ancient bridge. In the 17th century, Bernini and his pupils sculpted the figures of angels which now line the pedestrian-only bridge.

The area between the Vatican and the Tiber is known as the **Borgo**. Not much is left of the medieval (and earlier) buildings, as Mussolini had the area virtually razed to the ground to make way for Via della Conciliazione.

On the Lungotevere, beside Castel Sant'-Angelo is the huge **Palazzo di Giustizia** built between 1889 and 1910. It houses the national law courts.

Activities

Walking and cycling are great ways to get around Rome. See the Rome Walks chapter for routes around the city and the Getting Around chapter for details on bicycle rental.

SWIMMING

If you're in Rome during the hot summer months, chances are you'll want to cool off before long. If you can't be bothered making the trek out to the beaches on the Lazio coast (see the Excursions chapter) there are a few public swimming pools you could try.

Generally they are well outside the city centre and can be difficult to reach on public transport (indications are given). Admission costs between €5 and €8, with a

€5.16 annual membership fee payable on the first visit.

Bear in mind that these pools usually close for part of August (some close for the whole month) and opening hours and days vary. Some pools also require a doctor's certificate before you are allowed to swim. Call first to check.

Viale dei Consoli (☎ 06 76 90 06 27), off Via Tuscolana south-east of the city – Take Metro Linea A to Numidio Quadrato then follow Via San Curione to Viale dei Consoli.
Via Bravetta (☎ 06 66 16 09 85), past Villa Doria Pamphilj park – Take bus No 98 from Via Paola at the end of Corso Vittorio Emanuele II.
Via Manduria 21 (☎ 06 259 23 80), off Via Prenestina east of the city – Take tram No 14 from Via Turati near Stazione Termini and alight just after it turns right into Via Togliatti, then follow Via Ascoli Satriano and Via Conversano to Via Manduria.

There are also several privately run pools, which are a little more accessible, including pools run by upmarket hotels where you can swim and lounge – at a price.

Piscina delle Rose (☎ 06 592 67 17), Viale America 20, EUR – Take Metro Linea B to EUR Palasport. It opens 9 am to 7 pm daily, June to September and charges €8.16/6.19 per full/half-day.
Cavalieri Hilton Hotel (☎ 06 350 91), Via Cadlolo 101, Monte Mario. €41.31 Monday to Friday, €49.06 weekends (under-18s are half-price). Take bus No 907 or 991 from Piazza del Risorgimento to Piazzale Medaglie D'Oro.
Hotel Parco dei Principi (☎ 06 85 44 21), Via G Frescobaldi 5, (on the northern side of Villa Borghese). Open 10 am to 6 pm daily, May to September. €25.82 Monday to Friday, €36.15 weekends. Take bus No 910 from Stazione Termini or No 52 from Piazza San Silvestro.

JOGGING

Good places to jog include Circo Massimo, Villa Borghese, Villa Ada and Villa Doria Pamphilj. See the relevant sections earlier in this chapter for details.

HORSE RIDING

Prices at the exclusive Il Galoppatoio equestrian club in Villa Borghese (Map 2;

☎ 06 322 67 97), Via del Galoppatoio 25, make horse riding a costly pursuit. You pay for at least 10 lessons (€155) plus an annual €206 registration fee and €20 insurance.

Courses

LANGUAGE
Centro Linguisitico Italiano Dante Alighieri (Map 1; ☎ 06 44 23 14 00, fax 06 44 23 10 07, 🄴 clidar@tin.it), Piazza Bologna 1, runs courses throughout the year. Four-week courses (four hours per day) cost from €516, with books an extra €19. Groups are kept to a maximum of 12 students. You can get more information from its Web site at www.clidante.it.

Berlitz (Map 8; ☎ 06 683 40 00 or 06 68 80 69 51), Via di Torre Argentina 21, has 60-lesson courses from €300. Visit online at www.berlitz.com.

Centro Studi Flaminio (Map 2; ☎ 06 361 09 03 or 06 361 08 96) at Via Flaminia 21, 50m from Flaminia Metro station (Linea A), has intensive (two hours per day) and extensive (four hours per week) courses, for a total of 32 hours for each of four levels. Courses cost from €196.

Italiaidea (Map 8; ☎ 06 68 30 76 20, fax 06 689 29 97, 🄴 italiaidea@italisidea.com) at Piazza della Cancelleria 85, near Campo de' Fiori, has four-week intensive courses (three hours per day) for around €413.

Torre di Babele Centro di Lingua e Cultura Italiana (Map 5; ☎ 06 700 84 34, fax 06 70 49 71 50, 🄴 info@torredibabele.it) is at Via Bixio 74, near Piazza Vittorio. Intensive courses (four hours per day) are run in two-week blocks and cost €273. There is also a €25.82 enrolment fee covering books and cultural excursions.

COOKING
Well known cookery writer Diane Seed, author of *The Top One Hundred Pasta Sauces* and *Diane Seed's Rome for All Seasons*, runs rather expensive cooking courses four or five times a year from her kitchen in the Doria Pamphilj palace. Week-long courses cost from around €670. For information call ☎ 06 679 71 09, fax 06 679 71 03 or email her at 🄴 dianeseed@compuserve.com.

Rome Walks

Rome is so densely packed with important monuments that it is easy to feel overwhelmed and confused by the juxtaposition of art and architecture from so many different periods in the city's long history. You might, for instance, find yourself looking at a church built in the Middle Ages, which incorporates the precious marble and columns of a Roman temple that once stood on the site. The same church might have been rebuilt several times and could be a mix of architectural styles, from Romanesque to Baroque.

As you dash around the city, taking in the obligatory sights such as the Colosseum, the Roman Forum and the Vatican (certainly more than enough to keep you very busy for a few days), you can too easily overlook the rich architectural and artistic heritage of the city, which is visible in almost every narrow alleyway and square in the form of palaces, fountains and churches.

The three walks outlined in this chapter are designed to help you discover this heritage *con calma* (roughly translated as 'calmly taking your time'). The time needed to complete the following itineraries is not stated because this depends on the number of stops you make en route and your individual pace. Each route can take several hours or a full day – or longer if you want. The itineraries, especially Walk 3 on the Via Appia Antica, can also be done by bicycle (see Bicycle Rental in the Getting Around chapter).

The first walk starts on the Gianicolo, from where you have a glorious panorama of the city centre, takes you through the medieval neighbourhood of Trastevere and across the Tiber to the beautiful Aventine area.

The second walk concentrates on the Ghetto area, takes you up to the Capitoline, the traditional seat of Roman government, and ends with a spectacular view of the Roman Forum.

The third walk is the longest in terms of distance, starting near the Terme di Caracalla and taking you along the Via Appia Antica, the most famous of the ancient-Roman consular roads.

Further information on the main points of interest in this chapter can be found in the Things to See & Do chapter.

WALK 1: PIAZZALE GIUSEPPE GARIBALDI TO PIAZZALE UGO LA MALFA (MAPS 4 & 6)

This is an easy 4.5km route that crosses the south-western confines of Rome's historic centre, taking in gardens and parks, breathtaking views and significant Romanesque churches with centuries-old mosaics. It takes you from the fortified bastions of the Gianicolo, the hill that dominates the centre of Rome, through the lively streets of Trastevere and up to the Giardino degli Aranci on the Aventine hill. It ends at a high point, from where you have a view across the remains of the Circo Massimo to the Palatine, the hill that was once home to the Roman emperors.

ATAC bus No 870 runs up to Piazzale Garibaldi from the terminus in Via Paola at the north-western end of Corso Vittorio Emanuele II, near Ponte Principe Amedeo Savoia Aosta.

In **Piazzale Giuseppe Garibaldi** (Map 4), which sits like a terrace on top of the 17th-century bastions of the Gianicolo (82m above sea level), the bronze equestrian statue of General Garibaldi faces the city of Rome. Its back is turned on Michelangelo's huge dome of St Peter's Basilica as a reminder of the battles fought by the general against the papacy and the Bourbon rulers of Naples, which led to the unification of Italy in 1870.

From here there is a marvellous panorama. It extends from Castel Sant'Angelo to the Villa Borghese park behind the pale facade of the Villa Medici, with its two symmetrical turrets to the left (north-east), and across to the majestic Roman remains of the Palatine and the leafy outline of the Aventine hill with its churches and gardens on the right (south-east).

On a clear day, the domes, palaces and *campanili* (bell towers) of Baroque Rome stand out against the backdrop of the foothills of the Apennines, terminating to the south-east among the outlines of the volcanic Colli Albani. Every day at noon in the square beneath the terrace of Piazzale Garibaldi a troop of gunners notifies the city that it is lunchtime with a single cannon fire.

To your right as you are looking out over the panorama, the *passeggiata del Gianicolo* (Gianicolo walk) divides in two. Take the path to the left, which descends between tall trees, and pass the 17th-century Villa Aurelia (now part of the American Academy in Rome) on your right to emerge into the semicircular square in front of the **Fontana dell'Acqua Paola**, from where there is another famed view of Rome. The fountain is known locally as the *Fontanone del Gianicolo* (big fountain of the Gianicolo) because of its monumental form, inspired by the triumphal arches of ancient Rome. The spot is often frequented by Roman newlyweds and their photographers in search of an appropriate backdrop for their snaps. The fountain was built by order of Pope Paul V in 1608 to showcase the workings of the recently restored aqueduct, originally built by Emperor Trajan.

Go down Via Garibaldi until you reach the nearby **Chiesa di San Pietro in Montorio**, built in the 9th century on the spot thought to have been the site where St Peter was crucified upside down. The current structure dates from the end of the 15th century, when Ferdinand II of Aragon ordered it to be rebuilt. To the right of the elegant Renaissance facade with its Gothic rose window, a gate leads into the modest cloister of the adjoining convent and the famous **Tempietto di Bramante**, built around 1502 and used as a model by numerous architects in the early 16th century. Behind the Tempietto you can view a double flight of stairs, added by Bernini in the 17th century, leading to the crypt; an opening in the floor is all that remains of the place where St Peter was once thought to have been martyred.

A gate to the left as you leave the cloister leads to Via San Pietro in Montorio, a flight of steps lined with the stations of the cross, which cuts down to Via Garibaldi. Turn left and follow Via Garibaldi downhill to reach the intersection with Via della Lungara (Map 4), commissioned by Pope Julius II in the early 16th century to link Trastevere with the Vatican. Go through **Porta Settimiano**, a 16th-century reconstruction of an ancient gate in the Aurelian Wall, adorned with Ghibelline battlements, and you come to elegant Via Corsini on the left.

The road runs alongside the 18th-century Palazzo Corsini to Rome's **Orto Botanico** (botanical gardens), founded in the 19th century in the former gardens of the palace. The gardens are noted for their collections of Mediterranean succulents and tropical species and are an ideal place for a rest.

Back on Via della Lungara, walk the length of **Palazzo Corsini**. Opposite is the early-16th-century **Villa Farnesina**, one of the first examples of a single-standing residence, surrounded by gardens and featuring frescoes by Raphael and others.

Retrace your steps back through the Porta Settimiano and turn left into Via Santa Dorotea to reach the heart of characteristic Trastevere. From the small **Piazza San Giovanni della Malva**, with a church of the same name, turn right into Via Benedetta. Note the two-storey, 15th-century house at Nos 20 and 21, with typical arched windows. Shortly afterwards, turn right into the narrow Vicolo del Bologna (the street sign is a few metres from the corner), to reach a tiny triangular square with a drinking fountain.

From here, take the right-hand fork of Vicolo del Bologna (the left-hand fork has the same name) and you'll soon reach the 17th-century church and adjacent Carmelite monastery of **Santa Maria della Scala** (Map 6). On the 2nd floor of the monastery there is a perfectly-preserved *speziaria* (pharmacy) dating from the 18th century. The monks here are renowned for having commissioned and then rejected Caravaggio's *Il Transito della Vergine* (Transition of the Virgin), now in the Louvre (Paris). Groups of 10 or more can see the pharmacy by prior appointment; for bookings contact Dr Piccioni (☎ 06 440 42 37).

Turn left into Via della Scala and after about 50m turn left again into Vicolo del Cinque. Straight away you come to a five-road junction. Take Via della Pelliccia in front of you to the right, and follow it until you get to the large Piazza de' Renzi, now used as a car park. On the left at No 20 there is a small medieval house and two restaurants, including Da Augusto, which is famous for its informal, Roman-style food (see the Places to Eat chapter). Back on Via della Pelliccia, immediately turn left into Vicolo del Piede, and when this bends to the right turn left into Via Fonte dell'Olio.

Follow a tight s-bend in the road and you'll soon catch sight of a beautiful fountain of Roman origin, which was restored by Carlo Fontana in the 17th century. The fountain stands in the centre of the **Piazza Santa Maria in Trastevere**, the heart of this lively neighbourhood and one of Rome's most picturesque squares. Dominating the square is the basilica of the same name, thought to have been the first church in Rome to be officially dedicated to the Virgin Mary.

From Piazza Santa Maria in Trastevere, walk southwards to Piazza San Calisto and turn left into Via dell'Arco di San Calisto, passing under an arch. Don't miss the tiny medieval house at No 42. Said to be the smallest house in Rome, it has an external staircase and is decorated with a small painted figure of the Madonna. At the end of the street, turn left into Piazza Santa Rufina. From here you can see the graceful 12th-century Romanesque **bell tower** of the Chiesa di SS Rufina e Seconda inside the convent of the same name.

On the far side of the square turn right into Via della Lungaretta and follow it to the busy Viale di Trastevere. On the right is **San Crisogono**, a Baroque reconstruction of a medieval church dating from 1123. The medieval church itself stands on top of a 5th-century early-Christian basilica. The sacristan will take you down to the basilica on request for €1.55. The three naves in the Baroque interior are decorated with a beautiful Cosmati floor dating from the 13th century and are separated by granite columns taken from ancient Roman ruins.

Cross Viale di Trastevere and continue along Via della Lungaretta, past the **Casa di Dante**, a 13th-century towered stronghold once belonging to the patrician Anguillara family, and now a centre for Dante studies. At No 160 is quite a rare sight: an original 14th-century house with Gothic console arches and an external staircase. Just past the house is Piazza in Piscinula, which you cross diagonally. Head towards the right, along Via Arco dei Tolomei, and pass under a characteristic medieval arch named after the Sienese family who lived in this area in the 14th century. On the other side of the arch you will find yourself in Via dei Salumi. Follow this street to the left and turn right at Via dei Vascellari, which soon becomes Via di Santa Cecilia. Continue to square of the same name, from where you can enter the **Basilica di Santa Cecilia in Trastevere**. This basilica contains many artistic treasures and is worth visiting.

From here, go into the adjacent Piazza dei Mercanti, and take Via Santa Maria in Cappella to the left. You will soon find a courtyard containing the small, run-down **Chiesa di Santa Maria in Cappella**, which has a lovely Romanesque bell tower with two orders of mullioned windows dating from the 12th century. Turn left into Via Jandolo, which becomes Via dei Genovesi and turn right into the narrow Vicolo dell'Atleta, so called because of the discovery here in 1844 of the statue of Apoxyomenos, the *Atleta* (athlete) now in the Museo Pio-Clementino in the Vatican Museums. The medieval building at No 14, with a 13th-century loggia, is thought to be the oldest medieval synagogue left in Rome.

Turn left back into Via dei Salumi, then right into Via in Piscinula to return to Piazza in Piscinula near the Tiber. On the side of Piazza in Piscinula closest to river is **Palazzo Mattei**, a medieval building dating from 1300 and restored in 1926. On the opposite side of the square you can see the smallest bell tower in Rome.

The 12th-century Romanesque structure contains a bell dating from 1069. It is part of the **Chiesa di San Benedetto in Piscinula**, which contains the cell where St Benedict, founder of the Benedictine Order, prayed. To visit, ring the doorbell at the convent at No 40. It opens 9 to 11 am and 4 to 6 pm daily.

From the square go right along Via della Lungarina until you get to Piazza Castellani. Taking care of the aggressive Roman traffic, cross over to the Ponte Palatino. To your left is the Isola Tiberina and the surviving arch of the **Ponte Rotto** (broken bridge). This is a Renaissance reconstruction of the ancient Pons Aemilius, the first stone Roman bridge, built in 182 BC. This reconstruction still bears the traces of Pope Gregory XIII's coat of arms featuring a dragon. It collapsed in 1598 during the most violent of the disastrous floods that plagued Rome before the construction of the river embankments in 1900.

On the opposite side of the river you can see a large arch dug out of the wall of the embankment, which marks the mouth of the **Cloaca Maxima**, the drainage system begun by the Romans as early as the 6th century BC to drain the valley of the Roman Forum. It became an extensive sewage system as the ancient city developed.

As you cross the bridge, enjoy the view of the city. On the left you can see the square dome of the synagogue and the large dome of St Peter's Basilica in the distance. On the right, you can see the leafy heights of the Aventine and the long 17th- to 18th-century facade (334m) of the former **Ospizio Apostolico di San Michele a Ripa** on the Trastevere side of the river. This now houses the Ministero per i Beni Culturali e Ambientali (Ministry for Culture and the Environment).

Once across the bridge, turn right into the busy Lungotevere Aventino and follow the river for about 200m. On the other side of the road, off Via Santa Maria in Cosmedin, just past the traffic lights of Via della Greca, you will notice a flight of steps called Clivo di Rocca Savella, leading up onto the Aventine hill through the walls of a 10th-century fortress. The fortress was built by Emperor Alberico II and subsequently inherited by the Savelli family. At the top, a narrow footpath leads to the **Parco Savello**, also known as the Giardino degli Aranci because of its orange trees, where there is a panoramic terrace looking over the Gianicolo and the historic centre. Exiting from the opposite side of the park you will reach the 5th-century **Basilica di Santa Sabina**, one of the most important early-Christian basilicas in Rome.

Turning right into Via di Santa Sabina, you'll pass another panoramic garden and will come to the **Santi Bonifacio ed Alessio**, a medieval church rebuilt on numerous occasions and almost completely restored in 1750. It still has a lovely Romanesque campanile and a cosmati door dating from 1200. The church opens 8.30 am to 12.30 pm and 3.30 to 6.30 pm daily, April to October. It closes at 5 pm November to March.

At the end of Via di Santa Sabina is the **Piazza dei Cavalieri di Malta**, designed by Piranesi, famous for his etchings of Rome, in 1734 for the Order of the Knights of Malta. Join the line of people queuing to peer through the keyhole in the door that leads to the splendid gardens (accessible only on special occasions) of the **Priorato di Malta**, the headquarters of the order.

From the square, take Via di Porta Lavernale, passing the **Chiesa di Sant'Anselmo**, a 20th-century church in Romanesque-Lombard style, to reach Piazza Sant' Anselmo. Here, turn left into Via di San Domenico and follow it until you get to Piazza Giunone Regina. Go past the three arches of a sober Fascist-period building, turn right into Via Sant'Alberto Magno and you come to Largo Arrigo VII. Turn left out of Largo Arrigo on the far side, passing beneath the pine trees in the gardens, and descend to the left along Clivo dei Publicii. Turn right into Via di Valle Murcia, which passes through the city **rose garden** (Roseto Comunale), open to the public in May and June when the flowers are in bloom. A short distance farther is **Piazzale Ugo La Malfa**, the site of a monument to Giuseppe Mazzini, another father of Italian unity.

At the end of the route, turn right out of Piazzale Ugo La Malfa and follow the road downhill to reach the Circo Massimo stop on the Metro Linea B. From here you can take the subway to Stazione Termini. Alternatively, a number of buses serve Piazzale Ugo La Malfa, including bus No 81 going to the Colosseum and San Giovanni in Laterano. On the other side of Circo Massimo on Via dei Cerchi the same bus goes towards Piazza Venezia, Piazza Navona and the Vatican.

WALK 2: LARGO DI TORRE ARGENTINA, THROUGH THE GHETTO TO PIAZZA DEL CAMPIDOGLIO (MAP 4)

This is a short 1.8km route through the heart of Rome, an area dense with important monuments, where Renaissance buildings and the impressive ruins of classical antiquity coexist. It explores the courtyards of patrician palaces and the narrow streets of one of the city's more characteristic areas. You end up at Michelangelo's beautiful Piazza del Campidoglio and nearby there is a breathtaking view over the Roman Forum.

It is easy to get to Largo di Torre Argentina since it is very well-served by public transport, including buses from Piazza Venezia and Stazione Termini (Nos H, 40 and 64), from the Vatican (Nos 40, 62 and 64), from San Giovanni in Laterano and the Colosseum (Nos 87 and J5) and from Via del Corso and Via Veneto (No 63). The No 8 tram from Trastevere–Casaletto terminates at Largo di Torre Argentina.

Start on the southern side of the large and noisy **Largo di Torre Argentina** (Map 4) and archaeological zone, at the corner of Via delle Botteghe Oscure and Via Florida. Cross Piazza della Enciclopedia Italiana, skirting the elegant **Palazzo Mattei di Paganica**, built in 1541, which now houses the Istituto per l'Enciclopedia Italiana. This is one of five palaces built by the patrician Mattei family in the area, causing it to be renamed L'isola dei Mattei (Mattei Island) in the mid-16th century.

If you cross Piazza Paganica and follow Via Paganica you come to the charming **Piazza Mattei** with its elegant **Fontana delle Tartarughe**. In the square at No 10 is the 16th-century **Palazzo Costaguti** and at Nos 17 to 19 **Palazzo di Giacomo Mattei**. The building on the right has a beautiful 15th-century courtyard with a staircase and an open gallery.

Go to the left along Via dei Funari and enter the **Palazzo Mattei di Giove** at No 3. Built by Carlo Maderno in 1598, today it houses the Centro Italiano di Studi Americani Italian Centre for American Studies); sections are open to the public. The palace, which is adorned with numerous pieces of ancient Roman sculpture, bas-reliefs and stuccoes, is a good example of the taste of the Renaissance noble classes for all things classical. The courtyards contain ancient Roman bas-reliefs set into the walls, and busts and statues from what remains of the Mattei collection, once one of the most valuable collections of Roman antiquities. The monumental staircase decorated with classical stucco and ancient sculptures leads to a library. There is a loggia from where you get a better view of the decorative scheme. The balustrade is decorated with 16th-century busts of emperors.

There is a large hall in the library with ceiling frescoes and an interesting Renaissance floor with the family coat of arms at its centre. The palace's entrance area opens to the public Monday to Saturday. The library opens 10 am to 6 pm Monday to Thursday, and 10 am to 2 pm on Friday.

From Piazza Mattei take Via della Reginella, lined with artisan workshops, framers and bookshops. The street is a reminder of what the old Jewish Ghetto area would have once looked like. A few paces to the right along Via del Portico d'Ottavia brings you to the curious **Casa di Lorenzo Manilio** at Via del Portico d'Ottavia 1. The building was constructed in 1468 or, according to the Latin inscription on its facade, 2221 years after the founding of Rome in 753 BC (AB URB CON MMCCXXII). Another Latin inscription on the doors on the ground floor tells us the owner's name: Laur Manlius. There is also an inscription in Greek and fragments of Roman sculpture set into the wall, including a relief depicting a lion killing a fallow deer, a Greek stela with two dogs and a funereal relief with four busts.

Keeping Casa di Lorenzo Manilio on your left, walk down Via del Portico d'Ottavia. Go past the Case dei Fabi with their beautiful 16th-century windows and the 13th-century Torre dei Grassi, until you reach the remains of an entrance to the **Portico d'Ottavia**. In AD 755, the portico was remodelled to incorporate **Chiesa di Sant'Angelo in Pescheria**. A medieval fish market, established in the portico, was operational until the end of the 19th century.

Beyond the portico at Via del Portico d'Ottavia 29 is the 14th-century **Casa dei Valati**, housing the X Circoscrizione of the Comune di Roma, which oversees the city's cultural patrimony. Unusually for this area, the building stands in isolation, since the surrounding buildings were demolished in 1927 during the restoration of the Teatro di Marcello at the rear.

A narrow passage to the left of the portico opens onto the deserted Via Sant'Angelo in Pescheria. Go round the back of the church and then bear right at a water fountain until you come to a dead end. From this isolated spot you get a view of the arches of the **Teatro di Marcello**. Only 12 of the original 41 arches, made of large travertine blocks, remain. You can also see the three marble columns with Corinthian capitals and beams of the Tempio di Apollo Sosiano, dedicated in 431 BC and rebuilt in 34 BC.

Retrace your steps out of the dead-end street, and take Via della Tribuna Campitelli to the right. On the corner, at No 23, there is a house incorporating a medieval portico with granite columns and Ionian capitals. After a short walk you'll come to **Piazza Campitelli**. On the north-eastern and western sides of the square stand a row of fine palaces belonging to five noble families: the Gaetani-Lovatelli family at Via Tribuna Campitelli 16; the Patrizi-Clementi family at Via Cavaletti 2 (16th century); the Cavaletti family at Piazza Campitelli 1 (16th century); the Albertoni family (early 17th century); and the Capizucchi family (late 16th century).

Teatro di Marcello

This theatre was originally planned by Julius Caesar but remained unfinished at the time of his assassination in 44 BC. Augustus then inherited the project and named it after Marcellus, his nephew, who had died prematurely in 23 BC. By 17 BC, the theatre was in use but it was not formally dedicated for a further four to six years.

Capable of holding over 20,000 people, seated according to social status, the Teatro di Marcello was the most important of Rome's three ancient theatres.

The theatre was restored on many occasions following fires and earthquakes, until it finally fell into disuse and became a quarry for building material. In AD 365 the theatre was partially demolished and the stone used to restore the nearby Ponte Cestio.

The Perleone family converted it into a fortress during the 11th and 12th centuries, and in the 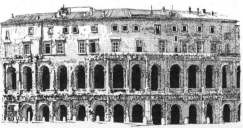 16th century Baldassarre Peruzzi converted the fortress into a luxurious palace for the Savelli family, preserving the original form of the theatre. In 1712 the palace was inherited by the Orsini family who partly restored the theatre.

The theatre and the ruins at its base can only be visited by request (see the boxed text 'Open Only On Request' in the Things to See & Do chapter).

TRUDI CANAVAN

On the other side of the square, the **Chiesa di Santa Maria in Campitelli** was built by Carlo Rainaldi and is a masterpiece of late-Baroque style, with a fine travertine facade. The church was built in 1662 to honour the Virgin Mary, who was believed to have halted the plague of 1656. Inside, on the main altar, there is an image in silver leaf and enamel of the miraculous Madonna.

To the left of the church there is a pretty fountain designed in 1589 by Giacomo della Porta. The 17th-century facade of the building at No 6, was designed by the architect Flaminio Ponzio and once adorned his house near the Roman Forum. It was rebuilt here after the house was demolished in 1933, when the area was cleared to make way for the Via dei Fori Imperiali.

Slightly farther along on Via Montanara is the **Chiesa di Santa Rita da Cascia**, now deconsecrated. It was built by Carlo Fontana in 1665 at the foot of the nearby Scalinata dell'Aracoeli and rebuilt on this spot in 1940 to allow for an urban revamp. Take Via Capizucchi to the left off the square. This takes you through deserted narrow streets into Piazza Capizucchi, and then to the left into Piazza Margana with the **Torre dei Margani**. Together with the surrounding buildings, the tower looks like a fortified medieval residence. Set in the wall is an ancient column with an Ionic capital. In the door next to it are large pieces of cornice from buildings of the late Empire.

Turn right into Via di Tor Margana and then right again into the darkness of Vicolo Margana. Go under an arch and you will emerge on Via Tribuna di Tor de' Specchi. Here at No 3 there is a medieval tower. Turn left to reach the chaotic Piazza d'Aracoeli, from where you have a splendid 180° view extending from Palazzo Venezia to the Capitoline. Turn right and go past the 16th-century facade of Palazzo Pecci-Blunt at No 3 and the 17th-century Palazzo Massimo di Rignano. Cross the busy Piazza Aracoeli using the pedestrian crossing but beware that cars don't always stop! This brings you to **Cordonata di Michelangelo**, the monumental flight of steps designed by Michelangelo, which lead up to the **Capitoline**.

The cordonata is guarded at the bottom by two Egyptian basalt lions (turned into fountains in 1588) and almost touches the older staircase on the left, which leads up to **Chiesa di Santa Maria in Aracoeli**, also accessible from the Capitoline. Climb the stairs, noting the shift in perspective as you approach the colossal Dioscuri, Castor and Pollux, at the top. These statues date from the late Empire and were found in a temple complex dedicated to them near Monte dei Cenci. On the same balustrade in a symmetrical arrangement are the **Trofei di Mario** representing barbarian weapons, which date back to the reign of Domitian, and statues of Constantine and his son Constans, found at the Terme di Costantino. There are also two milestones taken from the Via Appia Antica, which bear inscriptions of Nerva and Vespasian.

Once at the top of the stairs, the square, designed by Michelangelo, will take your breath away. It is bordered by the **Palazzo dei Conservatori** on the southern side, the **Palazzo Senatorio** at the rear, and the **Palazzo Nuovo** on the northern side and in its centre stands a copy of an original bronze equestrian statue of Marcus Aurelius (see the boxed text 'A Case of Mistaken Identity' in the Things to See & Do chapter).

Take the road going downhill to the right of the Palazzo Senatorio. This brings you to a (usually) crowded terrace overlooking the ancient Roman Forum and the Colosseum against the backdrop of the city and the Colli Albani – definitely one of the best views in Rome.

The route ends here. However, if you want to visit the **Roman Forum** (Map 5), there is an entrance to the right of the terrace at Via di Monte Tarpeo. See the Roman Forum map in the Things to See & Do chapter.

WALK 3: PIAZZALE NUMA POMPILIO TO THE TOMBA DI CECILIA METELLA, VIA APPIA ANTICA (MAPS 1 & 7)

This 5km route begins near the Terme di Caracalla (Map 1) and crosses the Aurelian Wall to reach the archaeological area of the Via Appia Antica, all that remains of the

ROME WALKS

romantic Roman countryside extolled by the German writer Goethe and other famous travellers of the past. It takes you to a handful of interesting churches, the fascinating Museo delle Mura, two of the most famous catacombs, the monumental remains of ancient tombs and the ruins of a Roman chariot-racing track. From the end of the walk you can take the bus back into town.

This long route can easily be cycled and by bike you can go beyond the Tomba di Cecilia Metella, which is 5km from the start of Via Appia Antica, to reach the intersection with the GRA (Grande Raccordo Anulare) 6km farther on.

Piazzale Numa Pompilio is easily reached from Piazza Venezia on bus No 628. If you want to shorten the walk, catch bus No 218 from San Giovanni in Laterano to Porta San Sebastiano and start there.

At the end of the route, shortly after the Tomba di Cecilia Metella, at the intersection of Via Appia Antica and Via Cecilia Metella (on the No 660 bus route), there is a snack bar with a garden, outside tables (at the rear) and bicycles for hire.

To head back, you can catch bus No 660 from here to the Colli Albani Metro stop on Linea A (Via Appia Nuova). It is also possible to start here and do the walk in reverse: take Metro Linea A to the Colli Albani stop and then bus No 660 to the intersection.

The section of Via Appia Antica between Via Cecilia Metella and the GRA is not served by public transport. Sunday is the best day to walk the route, when Via Appia Antica is closed to traffic and becomes a haven for pedestrians and cyclists from 9.30 am to 7 pm. During these hours Via di Porta San Sebastiano and Via Appia Antica are served by a small shuttle bus from the Colosseum and Circo Massimo as far as Via Cecilia Metella. Call ATAC ☎ 800-43 17 84 for information (English is spoken).

To gain access to some of the monuments on this route, you will need to fax a request to the Comune di Roma Ripartizione X, specifying the preferred date and time of your visit. You can then phone the following day to be allocated a visiting time according to the availability of wardens; call ☎ 06 67 10 38 19 (fax 06 68 92 115) in the morning and ask for Geometra Rapaccioni.

From the busy Piazzale Numa Pompilio, near the **Terme di Caracalla** (Map 7), go south-eastwards along Via di Porta San Sebastiano. The road begins after a 12th-century circular shrine and is often busy, especially during rush hour. Almost immediately, Via di Porta Latina branches off to the left, but keep to Via di Porta San Sebastiano. Here on the right you will find the **Chiesa di San Cesareo 'de Appia'** or 'in palatio' (to visit ring at the iron gate at No 4). The ancient church was built in the 8th century on top of a Roman building and was rebuilt in the early 17th century in late-mannerist style. The interior was decorated by Cavalier D'Arpino and contains splendid medieval marble pieces with coloured mosaics dating from the 13th century. These come from the transept of the Basilica di San Giovanni in Laterano, which had been restored in preparation for the 1600 Jubilee. In the crypt corresponding to the level of the Roman building, there is still a splendid black-and-white mosaic floor with marine scenes dating from the 2nd century.

To the right of the church is the **Casina del Cardinal Bessarione** (accessible only on request to the Comune di Roma Ripartizione X). This is a delightful example of a 15th-century rural residence. On the side facing the road you can see the Guelph-cross windows typical of the period. The other side is graced with a beautiful frescoed loggia looking out onto a garden visible from the gate.

Via di Porta San Sebastiano is lined with houses and gardens that evoke the long-gone atmosphere of 18th-century suburban Rome. Just under 1km along the road, to the left at No 9, is the entrance to the **Sepolcro degli Scipioni**, a tomb belonging to one of the most important families in Republican Rome. You can see the remains of the brick house built here in the 3rd century, many times restored. The door next to it takes you up a flight of stairs and into the **Parco degli Scipioni**, created in 1929 to embellish the burial ground, that also includes the **Colombario di Pomponio Hylas**, a tomb dating from the early-Imperial period and featuring mosaics and a ceiling painted with leaf motifs. (The tomb is accessible only on request from the Comune di Roma Ripartizione X; see the boxed text 'Open Only on Request' in the Things to See & Do chapter).

On the far side of the park exit onto Via di Porta Latina. Turn left and on your right there is a road leading to the delightful medieval **Chiesa di San Giovanni a Porta Latina**. The church was built by Celestine III in the 12th century, although an earlier church was founded here in the 5th century. An interesting cycle of 12th-century paintings in the central nave, now sadly faded, depicts Old and New Testament scenes. In the presbytery, there are the symbols of the Evangelists and the 24 elders of the Apocalypse dating from the same period. Outside, the beautiful porticoed facade stands in the shade of an ancient cedar tree, which provides a balance to the handsome three-ordered Romanesque campanile. An ancient well bearing 9th-century inscriptions adds the final touch to the picture. The church (☎ 06 772 09 898) opens 8 am to 12.30 pm and 3 to 6 pm.

Once back on Via di Porta Latina, go back past the entrance to the park to reach the oratory of **San Giovanni in Oleo**, founded in the 5th century on the site where the saint was said to have been immersed in a cauldron of boiling oil without being harmed. After this miraculous event, he was pardoned and exiled to the Greek island of Patmos. The octagonal building was restored by Borromini in the 17th century.

Just past the oratory is the **Porta Latina** and the mighty Aurelian Wall (see the boxed text 'Within These Walls' in the Facts about Rome chapter). Unlike other *porte* (entrances) in the walls, this one retains much of its original 3rd-century appearance.

Turn right into Viale delle Mura Latine and follow the wall's perimeter. You will soon reach **Porta San Sebastiano** (Map 1) on Via Appia Antica. This is the largest and the most majestic entrance in the walls and houses the very interesting **Museo delle Mura**. The museum visit includes the pan-

oramic view of Via Appia Antica from one of the towers and a walk along the battlements as far as Porta Ardeatina and Sangallo's 16th-century bastions.

The area inside the museum door is covered by the **Arco di Druso**, a simple arch supporting the Antonius aqueduct, a branch of the Acqua Marcia aqueduct, that passed overhead at this point on its way to the Terme di Caracalla. It was built on a monumental scale to celebrate the importance of Via Appia Antica, an important line of communication with Naples and the port of Brindisi in Apulia, the main departure point for the east. In medieval times the arch was used as an outer door to protect a fortified internal courtyard.

Outside the walls, the Via Appia Antica, used as a short cut by rush-hour traffic, technically begins with the first milestone set into the wall on the right, just after the No 218 bus stop coming from San Giovanni in Laterano. The road is narrow and slopes downwards and there is no pavement. However, if you make it past the modern bridge that passes over an ancient cemetery, the road widens and levels out.

Just past a restaurant on your right, you can see to the left the remains of the **Tomba di Geta**, and above them a 16th-century house. About 100m farther on is the **Tomba di Priscilla**, which is hidden from view by the restaurant at No 68, but you can see it from a gate near the intersection or from the car park behind the restaurant. The tomb was used by the Caetani family in the 13th century as the base for a military tower.

At the intersection where Via Ardeatina goes off to the right, there is a large sign to a private road for visitors to the **Catacombe di San Callisto**. The road opens 8 am to 6.30 pm (to 5.30 pm in winter) daily, except Wednesday. Unless you're doing the walk on a Sunday, it is much better to take this route than to brave the fast-moving traffic on Via Appia Antica, where there is no footpath. It is pleasant to walk this peaceful 2km route on a ridge between fields dotted with tombs and old country residences. About halfway along is the entrance to the Catacombe di San Callisto and the route ends at another gate next to the **Catacombe di San Sebastiano**.

Back on Via Appia Antica, you can see the **Chiesa del Domine Quo Vadis**. The church stands on the spot where Jesus appeared to St Peter who was fleeing Rome to escape the Neronian persecution. It also houses a stone said to bear Jesus' footprints, although it is more likely to be an offering of thanksgiving made by an ancient traveller having escaped from danger.

If you choose not to follow the private road and continue along the Via Appia Antica, you will note the run-down 16th-century **Cappella del Cardinale Reginald Pole** with a circular base leaning against a country house at the corner of Via della Caffarella. The chapel was built as an offering by the cardinal, who had come to Rome after having refused to participate in the Protestant reform in his native England. The chapel stands on the site where in 1539 the cardinal escaped death at the hands of Henry VIII's hired assassins.

As you continue, you will pass another entrance to the Catacombe di San Callisto and then, after the intersection with Via Appia Pignatelli on the left, you will come to the **Jewish catacombs** of Vigna Rondanini (accessible only with permission from

The Catacombs

The catacombs are underground corridors and passageways that were built as communal burial grounds. The best known are the Christian catacombs along the Via Appia Antica, although there are Jewish and pagan ones too. Scholars are divided as to whether the catacombs were also clandestine meeting places for early Christians, as well as useful places for secreting important relics.

The choice of underground graves was probably influenced by contemporary practices (such as using columbariums) and also by practical and economic concerns. Catacombs were often established in areas where there were existing quarries or underground passages: the soft volcanic earth of the Roman countryside enabled the Christians to dig to a depth of 20m or so. They maximised on the land donated by wealthy members of the Christian community by digging on numerous levels, retaining for security purposes only a few entrances.

During the periods of persecution, many martyrs were buried beside the fathers of the Church and the first popes. Many Christians followed suit, wanting to be buried in the same place as the martyrs. Consequently, an increasingly unethical property trade in tombs developed, until Gregory I issued a decree in 597 abolishing the sale of graves. However, Christians had already started to abandon the catacombs as early as 313, when Constantine issued the Milan decree of religious tolerance.

Increasingly, Christians opted to bury their dead near the churches and basilicas that were being built, often above pagan temples. This became common practice under Theodosius, who made Christianity the state religion in 394. The catacombs became sanctuaries for remembering the martyrs buried there.

In about 800 the increasingly frequent incursions by invaders necessitated the removal of the saintly bodies of the martyrs and the first popes to the basilicas inside the city walls. The catacombs were thus left abandoned and eventually many were forgotten and filled up with earth. In the Middle Ages only three catacombs were known about, and those of San Sebastiano were the most frequented as a place of pilgrimage, since they had earlier been the burial place of St Peter and St Paul.

The Catacombe di Priscilla on Via Salaria were discovered by chance at the end of the 16th century, following the collapse of a tufa quarry. From that time on, groups of curious aristocrats began to lower themselves into the dark underground passages on a regular basis, often risking losing themselves permanently in the underground labyrinths. From the mid-19th century onwards passionate scholars of Christian archaeology began a programme of scientific research and more than 30 catacombs in the Rome area have been uncovered.

the Comunitá Ebraica in Rome). Note that there is no sign indicating the catacombs from the road.

After passing the third and final entrance to the Catacombe di San Callisto you'll reach the **Basilica & Catacombe di San Sebastiano**, built in the 4th century on the spot where the bodies of the Apostles Peter and Paul were buried, before being transferred to the respective basilicas built in their honour.

Not much farther along Via Appia Antica, you'll reach the archaeological area of **Villa di Massenzio** on the left. The area encompasses the **Tomba di Romolo**, the **Circo di Massenzio** and the remains of Maxentius' imperial palace.

Continue a short distance and you will reach the imposing **Tomba di Cecilia Metella**. The mausoleum was built, as stated on the inscription, for Cecilia Metella, daughter of Quintus Metellus Creticus and wife of Crassus. The tomb was incorporated into the castle of the Caetani family in the early 14th century. On the other side of the road the roofless **Chiesa di San Nicola a Capo di Bove** is a rare example of Gothic architecture in Rome. The church of 'St Nicola at the Bull's Head' gets its unusual name from the carved bulls' skulls *(bucrania)* that decorate the Tomba di Cecilia Metella.

Not far past the tomb and the church is a section of the actual ancient road, excavated in the mid-19th century.

If you have walked this far, you will most likely want to take the bus back into the city. If you choose to continue, ideally by bicycle, you will encounter more inspiring ruins and an increasingly Felliniesque atmosphere as, moving away from the area frequented by tourists, the road begins to turn into an innocuous but unsettling backdrop for prostitutes plying their trade in cars parked behind tombs and in nearby woods.

Via Appia Antica continues in an unbroken line of tombs and ruined monuments. The vast ruins of **Villa dei Quintili** are on the left after Via di Tor Carbone. The villa was built with a central heating system, a private aqueduct and a hippodrome. Not far from here is the unusual **Casal Rotondo**, a large circular tomb (approximately 35m in diameter) dating from the time of Augustus and now the basement of an old farm house.

On the left, after Via di Torricola you will find the characteristic **Torre in Selce**, built during the 12th century above an ancient tomb. Over many years these monuments were largely ignored and fell into serious decay. Fortunately, extensive restoration work is now underway as part of a plan to restore the entire area of the Parco Archeologico dell'Appia Antica. In the section that was cut off by the Grande Raccordo Anulare, roughly 10km from the start of the road, work is underway to build an underpass that should help to restore the queen of roads, which has been the main road of communication with the east for so long.

Places to Stay

Rome has a vast number of *pensioni* (guesthouses) and hotels but it is always best to book. While spring and autumn are the peak periods, tourists and pilgrims flock to Rome year-round. There is a free hotel reservation service at Stazione Termini opposite platform 21, open 7.30 am to 9 pm (☎ 06 699 10 00). A good alternative is the private tourist office Enjoy Rome (see Tourist Offices in the Facts for the Visitor chapter).

Avoid the people at the train station who claim to be tourism officials and offer to find you a room. They usually lead you to pretty seedy accommodation for which you end up paying more than the official rate.

Most of the budget pensioni and larger hotels which cater for tour groups are located near Stazione Termini. The area south-west (to the left as you leave the platforms) can be noisy and unpleasant. Pickpockets are active in this area and women alone may find it unsafe at night, although the city authorities have gone to some lengths to clean it up in recent years. To the north-east of Termini you can find accommodation in a quieter and more pleasant residential area, and in the streets around Via Nazionale, a busy traffic thoroughfare and shopping area, there are several decent hotels. However, the historic centre of Rome is far more appealing and the area around the Vatican is much less chaotic; both of these areas are only a short bus or Metro ride away.

You will often find three or four budget pensioni in the same building; many are small establishments (12 rooms or less) that fill up quickly in summer. The sheer number of budget hotels in the area should, however, ensure you find a room.

Most hotels accept advance bookings, although some demand a deposit or credit-card details for the first night.

Rome does not have a low season as such but many hotels offer significant discounts in July and August and from November to March (excluding the Christmas/New Year period). A lot of mid-range and top-end hotels also offer special deals for families and discounts for extended stays – so be sure to enquire. There is a terrible lack of on-site parking facilities in the city centre, but your hotel should be able to direct you to a private garage.

All hotels listed here accept credit cards and travellers cheques unless otherwise indicated.

PLACES TO STAY – BUDGET
Camping
All of Rome's camp sites are a fair distance from the centre. *Seven Hills* (☎ 06 303 10 826, Via Cassia 1216) charges €6.97 per person, per day. It costs €4.13 per tent and an extra €3.36 if you have a car; caravan sites cost €7.23. It's a bit of a hike from Stazione Termini: catch the Metro Linea A to Ottaviano, then take bus No 907 (ask the driver where to get off). From Via Cassia it is a 1km walk to the camp site. It opens 15 March to 30 October.

Another possibility is *Village Camping Flaminio* (☎ 06 333 26 04, e info@village flaminio.com, Via Flaminia 821), which is about 30 minutes from the city centre by public transport. It costs €7.23 per person and €4.13 for a tent site. They also have bungalows for €36.15 with shared bathroom or €43.38 with private bathroom. Tents and caravans are also available for rent. From Stazione Termini catch bus No 910 to Piazza Mancini, then bus No 200 to the camp site. At night, catch bus No 24N from Piazzale Flaminio (just north of Piazza del Popolo).

Hostels
Rome has one official youth hostel, the HI (Hostelling International) *Ostello Foro Italico* (Map 1; ☎ 06 323 62 67, e aig@uni .net, Viale delle Olimpiadi 61). Take Metro Linea A to Ottaviano, then bus No 32 to Foro Italico. It has a bar, self-service restaurant and a garden, and is open all year. Breakfast and showers are included in the

Ninth-century sheep mosaics look down from the apse in the Basilica di Santa Cecilia in Trastevere.

MARTIN MOOS

An innocent look beneath St Peter's dome

Lavish detail of Madonna with cherubs

MARTIN MOOS

NEIL SETCHFIELD

The leafy Arco Farnese straddles Via Giulia.

A lion guards the entrance to Bioparco zoo.

You might meet your Latin lover at the Trevi Fountain...

price, which is €12.91 per night for a bed in a segregated dorm. A meal costs €7.23. The hostel accepts bookings a minimum of one month in advance, otherwise you have to turn up at 10 am to be assigned a bed. However you cannot enter the dorm until 2 pm, and there is a midnight curfew. Given its location so far from the action, and these restrictions (hell for someone arriving on an early-morning flight), you will do better heading for the centre of town.

The Italian youth hostels association, Associazione Italiana Alberghi per la Gioventù (Map 5; ☎ 06 487 11 52, Via Cavour 44) has details about all youth hostels in Italy and will assist with bookings to stay at universities in summer. You can also join HI here.

A good option for budget travellers – women, men and couples – is the *YWCA (Map 5; ☎ 06 488 04 60, fax 06 487 10 28, Via Cesare Balbo 4)*, near Piazza dell'Esquilino and Santa Maria Maggiore. This is the place for early risers with a serious sightseeing agenda, but is probably best avoided by night-owls as there's a midnight curfew. Singles cost €36.15 or €46.48 with bathroom, doubles cost €30.99 per person or €36.15 with bathroom, and triples and quads cost €25.82 per person. Breakfast is included and payment is by cash only. Take Via Cavour from Stazione Termini and turn right into Via A Depretis at Piazza dell' Esquilino. Via Cesare Balbo is the second street on the right.

Student Accommodation

People planning to study in Italy can usually organise accommodation through the school or university they will be attending. Options include a room with an Italian family, or a share arrangement with other students in an independent apartment. Some Italian universities operate a *casa dello studente*, which houses Italian students throughout the school year and lets rooms to others during the summer break (July to the end of September).

It can be very difficult to organise a room in one of these institutions. The best idea is to go through your own university or contact the Italian university directly.

Religious Institutions

There are a number of religious institutions in Rome which offer accommodation. To stay in one, you usually apply to the nearest Catholic archdiocese in your home town, although some institutions (including those listed here) will consider independent requests. It is wise to book well in advance.

Bear in mind that all religious institutions have strict curfews and the accommodation, while clean, is of the basic, no-frills variety. Breakfast is included for all prices listed below and almost all rooms include private bathrooms unless stated otherwise.

The *Domus Aurelia delle Suore Orsoline (Map 1; ☎ 06 636 784, fax 06 393 764 80, Via Aurelia 218)*, about 1km from St Peter's Basilica, has singles/doubles/triples for €38.73/59.39/77.47. From Stazione Termini catch bus No 64 to Largo di Torre Argentina, then No 46 to Via Aurelia. Get off the bus after it has done a steep ascent and made a sharp left turn.

The *Padri Trinitari (Map 4; ☎ 06 638 38 88, fax 06 393 66 795, Piazza Santa Maria alle Fornaci 27)*, very close to St Peter's, has singles/doubles/triples for €41.32/72.30/ 92.96.

Nearby, English-speaking and extremely friendly *Franciscan Sisters of the Atonement (Map 1; ☎ 06 630 782, fax 06 638 61 49, Via Monte del Gallo 105)* offer singles/ doubles for €34.60/58.87.

The *Suore Dorotee (Map 4; ☎ 06 688 03 349, fax 06 68 80 33 11, Via del Gianicolo 4a)* is located in the green and leafy area off a steep winding road that leads up from the Lungotevere to the top of the Gianicolo hill. Rooms cost €46.48 per person (half-board) or €51.64 full board.

As far as location is concerned you cannot do better than the convent of the *Suore di Santa Brigida (Map 8; ☎ 06 688 92 596, fax 06 682 19 126, e brigida@mclink.it, Piazza Farnese 96)*, which is run by a Swedish order of nuns. The sisters offer beds for €74.88 per single and €64.55 per person in a double room – which is on the pricier side for religious accommodation. The entrance is at Via Monserrato 54. Note the 11 pm curfew.

PLACES TO STAY

Bed & Breakfast

B&B is a relatively new concept in Rome. Much to the chagrin of many hotel operators, it has taken off thanks to the influx of pilgrims during the Jubilee year and the over-demand for really good budget accommodation.

The bonus of B&B accommodation is that Italian houses are invariably spotlessly clean. The drawback is that you are staying in someone's home, and will probably be expected to operate within the family's timetable. As keys are not always provided, a hotel would be more suitable for those who expect to be coming in late at night.

Most of the accommodation is fairly central but when making the booking (which should be done well in advance of your stay) make sure you fully understand the location of the accommodation that is being proposed, to avoid finding yourself in an outer suburb with limited public transport.

Lists of authorised private B&B operators in and around Rome can usually be obtained from the information desks at the Ala Mazzonina, next to Via Giolitti, and platform 24 at Stazione Termini. The Comune di Roma information desk has lists of B&B operators in Rome, which are also available from the tourist information booths around the city. The APT information desk at Termini also has lists of B&B operators in the province (outskirts) of Rome. However, don't bank on getting your hands on either list – supplies often run out and the staff aren't always overly helpful.

Private B&B operators are also listed in *Wanted in Rome* (see Newspapers and Magazines in the Facts for the Visitor chapter), although not all of these are registered (and therefore insured) by the city authorities.

Bed & Breakfast Italia (Map 4; ☎ 06 687 86 18, fax 06 687 86 19, ✉ md4095@ mclink.it, Corso Vittorio Emanuele II 282) is the longest established of several B&B networks. It offers accommodation in three different price categories and staff are both professional and multilingual. Singles/doubles/triples with shared bathroom cost €30.98/50.61/ 74.88; rooms with private bathroom cost €43.89/81.60/ 108.45; luxu-

rious rooms with private bathroom cost €56.81/97.09/129.11. You can view the apartments and book online through the Web site at www.bbitalia.it – all credit cards are accepted.

Pensioni & Hotels

Rome has a wide range of *pensioni* and hotels in this price range, although real budget establishments are becoming more and more difficult to find. Prices have risen considerably in recent years, and not always with a corresponding upgrade in services and facilities.

Traditionally, a *pensione* was more personal and smaller than a hotel, often occupying one or two floors in a building housing other, similar establishments. However, the distinction is becoming blurred, particularly as pensioni got caught up in the rush to upgrade in preparation for the Jubilee. In fact, most former pensioni now class themselves as hotels.

Unless otherwise stated, the prices quoted for hotels in this section are for rooms without a shower or bath, and do not include breakfast (although this is sometimes available for an extra charge).

North-East of Stazione Termini (Map 5) To reach the pensioni in this area, head to the right as you leave the train platforms onto Via Marsala, which runs alongside the station.

Off Via Vicenza, *Pensione Giamaica* (☎ 06 490 121, fax 06 445 19 63, ✉ md 0991@mclink.it, Via Magenta 13) is fairly basic with frightful decor but it has well-priced singles/doubles for €28.40/43.89. Breakfast costs an extra €2.58. The communal bathrooms are clean and each room has its own basin. Some rooms look onto a dark and grimy internal courtyard; try to get one looking onto the street or out the back of the building instead. There's no curfew and the owners will provide front-door keys for those planning to come in late.

Fawlty Towers (☎ 06 445 03 74, fax 06 445 03 74, ✉ info@enjoyrome.com, Via Magenta 39) offers hostel-style accommodation and is without doubt one of the best budget options in Rome. A bed in a four-person dorm costs €18.07, or €20.65 if the dorm has a private shower, and doubles cost from €51.64, or €72.30 with bathroom. Run by the people at Enjoy Rome (see under Tourist Offices in Facts for the Visitor), it offers lots of information about Rome. Added bonuses are the sunny terrace, satellite TV, communal fridge and microwave. Fawlty Towers only accepts advance bookings for the private (nondorm) rooms. To reserve a dorm bed, you have to call in (either in person or by phone) at 9 pm the night before you wish to stay there, and they'll hold the bed until around 10 the following morning. It's also a good place to go if you've arrived in Rome late at night and the accommodation agencies are closed, as the staff can usually recommend a pensione with vacancies.

Nearby in Via Palestro are a few reasonably priced places. **Pensione Restivo** (☎ *06 446 21 72, Via Palestro 55*) is run by the friendly and helpful Signor Restivo (a former *carabiniere* officer) and his elderly mother. Former guests have been known to send gifts and thank-you letters to the owners, which are proudly displayed. The place is immaculate and has large singles/doubles for €36.15/56.81 and triples for €64.55. Breakfast is not included but Signor Restivo usually offers guests a cup of coffee before they set off. Bookings are only taken in the morning and there is a midnight curfew.

On the ground floor of the same building is **Hotel Cervia** (☎ *06 491 057, fax 06 49 10 56,* e *hotelcervia@wnt.it, Via Palestro 55*). The rooms in this 19th-century building have high vaulted ceilings and seem enormous. They are also very reasonably priced. Singles/doubles/triples/quads cost €28.40/46.48/54.22/61.97. Rooms with bathrooms are available: doubles/triples cost €67.14/77.47. A recent addition are the four- and five-bed dorms on the third floor at €18.08 to €20.65 per person.

Albergo Sandra (☎ *06 445 26 12, fax 06 446 08 46, Via Villafranca 10*), between Via Vicenza and Via San Martino della Battaglia, is a medium-size pensione run by a house-proud Italian mamma and her English-speaking son. The rooms are clean and pleasant and singles/doubles cost in the region of €41/72.

North-West of Stazione Termini The following are all on Map 5 unless stated otherwise. There is paid street parking in this area and reasonably priced garage parking facilities, so ask at your hotel.

Directly north of the station in Via Calatafimi, **Papa Germano** (☎ *06 489 19, fax 06 478 25 02,* e *info@hotelpapagermano.it, Via Calatafimi 14a*) is a popular budget choice. Prices start at €18.07 for dorm beds, singles cost €46.48, doubles (with bathroom) cost €67.14, and triples cost €77.47. The English- and French-speaking management nurture a friendly family atmosphere – and judging by the enthusiastic comments in the visitor's book their efforts are not in vain. Free city maps are available and there are guide books available on loan. There is Internet access, and telephones and TVs in the rooms.

Nearby is **Hotel Floridia** (☎ *06 481 40 89, fax 06 444 13 77, Via Montebello 45*). The elegant entrance area on the ground floor gives a misleading impression of quality; the rooms are quite small and decorated in pseudo-elegant style, but all have telephone and private bath. Singles/doubles/triples/quads cost from €56.81/82.63/92.96/103.29 and prices include breakfast.

Hotel Ascot (☎ *06 474 16 75, fax 06 474 01 65, Via Montebello 22*) has quiet family-run singles/doubles with bathroom for €46.48/67.14. Ask for No 24 which still has its original parquet floor. The hotel itself is fine – as long as you're not concerned about the porn cinemas and sex shops in the area.

Hotel Castelfidardo (☎ *06 446 46 38, fax 06 494 13 78,* e *castelfidardo@ital market.it, Via Castelfidardo 31*), off Piazza dell'Indipendenza, is one of Rome's better one-star pensioni. It has clean and pleasant singles/doubles for €36.15/49.06 and triples for €61.97; a double/triple with private bathroom costs €56.81/77.47. The English-speaking staff are friendly and helpful.

On the other side of Via XX Settembre, 10 minutes' walk from Stazione Termini, is

PLACES TO STAY

Hotel Ercoli *(Map 3; ☎/fax 06 474 54 54, 06 474 40 63, Via Collina 48)*. Refurbished singles/doubles seem expensive at €67.14/92.96 but the price reflects the facilities on offer (private bath, TV, telephone and hairdryer) and includes breakfast in the sunny breakfast room.

Downstairs in the same building is the welcoming *Hotel Tizi* *(Map 3; ☎ 06 482 01 28, ☎/fax 06 474 32 66, Via Collina 48)*, also recently refurbished. The light and spacious single/double rooms are a bargain at €36.15/46.48 or €56.81 for doubles with bath. There are reasonable discounts out of season and for stays of more than five days. Payment is by cash only.

South of Termini (Map 5) This area is seedier than the northern side of the station, but it improves as you head away from the train station and towards the Colosseum and Roman Forum.

Hotel Sandy *(☎ 06 488 45 85, fax 06 445 07 34, @ gi.costantini@agora.stm.it, Via Cavour 136)* is probably the closest thing in Rome to a backpackers' crash pad. Go through the palazzo's entrance and the hotel is on the 5th floor (no lift). Beds are in dorms for between three and five people (eight in summer) and cost €15.49 per person. There are metal lockers but no keys and the hotel lacks adequate bathroom facilities – so be prepared to queue. Reservations are not accepted and payment is by cash only. See for yourself online at www.sandyhostel.com.

Near Via Nazionale (Map 5) Off Via Nazionale is the excellent *Hotel Elide* *(☎ 06 488 39 77 or 06 474 13 67, fax 06 489 043 18, Via Firenze 50)*. Comfortable singles/doubles with bath (and breakfast) cost €61.97/87.79, triples cost €113.62 and prices drop by around €25 from December to March. Ask for room No 18, which has an elaborate, gilded ceiling.

Hotel Galatea *(☎ 06 474 30 70, fax 06 489 04 318, Via Genova 24)*, on the other side of Via Nazionale, is through the grand entrance of an old palace. Its beautifully furnished singles/doubles are good value at €51.64/67.14. A triple costs around €107

and rooms with private bathroom cost an additional €10 to €15. The hotel does a lot of business with school groups so don't be surprised if the place is overrun with kids. The staff speak six European languages.

City Centre The following are all on Map 8 unless otherwise stated. Really economical hotels in Rome's historical centre basically don't exist. But in the areas around Piazza di Spagna, Piazza Navona, the Pantheon and Campo de' Fiori, you do have the convenience and pleasure of staying right in the centre of historic Rome. The easiest way to get to Piazza di Spagna is on the Metro Linea A to Spagna. To get to Piazza Navona and the Pantheon area, take bus No 64 from Piazza dei Cinquecento, in front of Stazione Termini, to Largo di Torre Argentina and walk.

Winning the prize for position is *Albergo Abruzzi* *(☎ 06 679 20 21, Piazza della Rotonda 69)*, directly opposite the Pantheon, but it can be very noisy until late at night when the square is finally deserted. There's nothing fancy about the rooms – basic singles/doubles without bathrooms cost €59.39/87.79 – but the chatty management make it a perennial budget favourite. Credit cards are not accepted.

Hotel Mimosa *(☎ 06 688 01 753, fax 06 683 35 57, @ hotelmimosa@tin.it, Via di Santa Chiara 61)*, off Piazza della Minerva, offers singles/doubles/triples for €56.81/77.47/108.45. There are also doubles/triples with bath for €87.79/123.95. Some rooms are a bit poky but all of them are clean and it's in a great position – hence it is always full and you have to book weeks in advance to get a room. The elderly owners and their son (who speaks English and French) are helpful and friendly and provide free city maps and other information. You can't drink alcohol in the hotel and there are designated smoking areas. Payment by cash is preferred although you might be able to pay by card by prior arrangement.

Albergo della Lunetta *(☎ 06 686 10 80 or 06 687 76 30, fax 06 689 20 28, Piazza Paradiso 68)*, east of Campo de' Fiori, is a Roman pensione of the old school, run by

euro currency converter €1 = L1936.27

three rather cantankerous but somewhat charming *signore*. It is popular with young foreign students who stay for months at a time. The labyrinthine corridors and staircases lead to small but spotless rooms. Simple singles/doubles/triples cost €56.81/77.47/108.45. Doubles/triples with bathroom go for €87.79/123.94. There is a TV in the ground-floor lounge area and a small internal courtyard, and parking is sometimes available in the square (you'll need to obtain a permit from the hotel).

Right in the heart of the ancient city is *Casa Kolbe (Map 6; ☎ 06 679 49 74, fax 06 699 41 550, Via di San Teodoro 44)*. Located in an ex-Franciscan convent, it takes its name from a Polish monk who lived there before his death in Auschwitz during WWII. The 64 spacious rooms are reasonable at €77.46 for a double and €92.96/103.29 for a triple/quad. Meals are available for €5.16 (breakfast) and €12.91 (lunch or dinner) in the huge refectory-style restaurant. The hotel looks onto the Roman Forum on one side and opens onto a large sheltered garden on the other, accessible through an equally large bar-lounge and TV room. It is popular with tour groups.

Near the Vatican Although there aren't many bargains in this area, it is comparatively quiet and still close to the main sights. Bookings are an absolute necessity because rooms are often filled with people attending conferences at the Vatican. In some cases car parking is possible, either in the street or in a nearby garage. The simplest way to reach the area is on the Metro Linea A to Ottaviano. Turn left into Via Ottaviano, and Via Germanico is a short walk away. Otherwise, catch bus No 64 from Stazione Termini to St Peter's and take a five-minute walk from the basilica northwards along Via di Porta Angelica, which becomes Via Ottaviano after the Piazza del Risorgimento.

The cheapest accommodation in the area is the friendly and informal *Pensione Ottaviano (Map 4; ☎ 06 397 38 138, ℮ gi .costantini@agora.stm.it, Via Ottaviano 6)*, near Piazza del Risorgimento and the Vati-

can Museums. It has dorm beds for €15.49 per person and doubles/triples for €46.48/61.97. What it lacks in glamour – the doubles, triples and dorm rooms are pretty basic – it makes up for in friendliness, and the reception area doubles as a backpacker's meeting place. There's no curfew or lock out, the staff speak English and email access is available after 9 pm. See the Web site at www.pensioneottaviano.com.

Another good choice in the area is *Colors Hotel & Hostel (Map 4; ☎ 06 687 40 30, fax 06 686 79 47, ℮ fulang@flashnet.it, Via Boezio 31)*, run by the people at Enjoy Rome (see under Tourist Offices in Facts for the Visitor). It offers both dorm beds and private rooms. Added bonuses are the fully equipped kitchen, mini-gym and Internet access. A bed in a four-person dorm costs €15.49 or €18.07 if the dorm has a private shower. Doubles cost €51.64 or €72.30 with bathroom. There is no curfew and no lock-out period. There are only seven rooms (all painted different colours) but it was about to expand at the time of writing.

In a single building at Via Germanico 198 there are four accommodation options – three of which are in the budget range. On the first floor, *Hotel Giuggioli (Map 2; ☎ 06 324 21 13, Via Germanico 198)*, in one of the more pleasant residential areas of Rome, is a small, old-fashioned pensione, run by a delightful, Italian-speaking *signora*. A double costs €77.46 or €103.29 with bathroom. The decor won't win any awards but it is clean. On the 2nd floor, *Pensione Nautilus (Map 2; ☎ 06 324 21 18, Via Germanico 198)* has clean and simple doubles/triples for €67.14/92.96. Rooms with bathroom cost an extra €15.49, although the 'bathrooms' are in fact just a shower stall in the corner of the bedroom. There is a small lounge/TV area. Payment is by cash only.

Upstairs on the 4th floor, *Hotel Lady (Map 2; ☎ 06 324 21 12, fax 06 324 34 46, Via Germanico 198)* is an old-fashioned, quiet pensione with very pleasant singles/doubles for €61.97/82.63 (€103.29 with bathroom). The bathrooms are new and sparkling and there are stunning wooden doors throughout. Ask for room No 4 or 6,

PLACES TO STAY

both of which still have the original beamed ceiling. The eccentric owner and his wife do not speak English but their eager conversation will give you lots of practice in Italian.

Pensione Paradise (*Map 2; ☎ 06 321 31 84, Viale Giulio Cesare 47*) is in a well-connected position near the Lepanto Metro stop. It has good-value singles/doubles with bathroom for €46.48/82.63. Rooms are simple but bright. Singles and triples with shared bathroom cost €38.73 per person.

PLACES TO STAY – MID-RANGE

All rooms in this section have private bathroom unless otherwise stated.

North-East of Termini (Map 5)

If you can get past the grouchy doorman-cum-receptionist guarding the grand-looking mirrored and wood-panelled entrance of *Hotel Rimini* (*☎ 06 446 19 91, e rimini@ travel.it, Via Marghera 17*), you'll find clean, renovated rooms (all with TV). Its singles/doubles cost €77.47/118.78 including breakfast. The Internet cafe and the left-luggage facility next door are added bonuses.

Via Palestro is a good street for mid-range hotels. The three-star *Hotel Adventure* (*☎ 06 446 90 26, fax 06 446 00 84, e hotel .adventure@flashnet.it, Via Palestro 88*) has been decorated by someone with a particular predilection for pastel pink, fake stucco and reproduction antiques, and there are more chandeliers in the reception area than you'd find in a lighting showroom. However, it's immaculate and very safe, with video cameras and security doors monitoring those who enter and exit each floor. Doubles cost between €93 and €124, triples cost €155 and quads go for €232. One huge room on the top floor has its own private terrace. All rooms have air-con and TV. The rooms looking onto the internal courtyard are quieter than those facing the street.

At the same address, on the 1st and 2nd floors, is two-star *Hotel Gabriella* (*☎ 06 445 01 20, fax 06 445 02 52, e gabriel@ micanet.it, Via Palestro 88*). It's an unassuming and friendly, family-run place. Singles/doubles cost €82.63/103.29 but discounts

are available for longer stays. The hotel has been redecorated fairly recently and all rooms have air-con, although it costs €10.33 per day if you want to use it.

At Via Palestro 49, there are several good mid-range hotels. *Hotel Continentale* (*☎ 06 445 03 82, fax 06 445 26 29, Via Palestro 49*) is on the ground floor on the right. All the rooms are very clean and most have been renovated (try to get one of these). Singles/doubles/triples/quads cost €46.48/ 82.63/108.45/123.94. There are also separate doubles/triples with shared bathrooms in an apartment on the fifth floor of the same building which cost €41.32/61.97 (including breakfast). The owners and staff are friendly and speak several languages, including English and French. See the Web site at www.hotel-continentale.com.

Hotel Positano (*☎ 06 490 360, fax 06 446 91 01, e hotposit@tin.it, Via Palestro 49*) is a family-run hotel next to the Continentale. It is particularly good for families as they don't charge for children under six. Singles/doubles/triples cost €72.30/103.29/ 144.61 and have bathrooms plus all the mod cons. There are also some grim dorm rooms for €18.07 per person – if mattresses on the floor appeal to you. All credit cards are accepted.

Hotel Lachea and *Hotel Dolomiti* (*☎ 06 495 72 56, fax 06 445 46 65, e dolomiti@ hotel-dolomiti.it, Via San Martino della Battaglia 11*) are two hotels in the same building run by the same family. Hotel Dolomiti has been renovated, and offers elegant and airy rooms (all with private bathroom, mini-bar, TV, telephone, air-con, double glazing, safe and hairdryer). Prices are reasonable given the three-star rating: singles cost €61.97 and doubles/triples start at €92.96/108.45 respectively, including breakfast in the delightful marble-panelled bar-breakfast area. Hotel Lachea, which used to be more run-down and cheaper, was undergoing extensive renovations at the time of writing, but by the time you read this work should be completed and the standard and prices the same as Hotel Dolomiti. The owners speak English, French and Spanish.

Hotel Venezia (☎ 06 445 71 01, fax 06 495 76 87, Via Varese 18), on the corner of Via Marghera, is beautifully furnished with antiques and attractive fabrics. Singles/doubles/triples cost €101.22/137.37/185.41. Prices drop by about 10% in the low season. The multilingual staff are charming and it is the nicest place to stay in this area.

Hotel Piemonte (☎ 06 445 22 40, fax 06 445 16 49, ✉ piemonte@italyhotel.com, Via Vicenza 34) is a stone's throw from Stazione Termini and has very pleasant singles/doubles for up to €103.29/144.61. There's double glazing throughout and the bathrooms are particularly pleasant. One room has disabled access.

South-West of Termini (Map 5)

A short distance from the train station is *Hotel Igea* (☎ 06 446 69 11, fax 06 446 69 11, ✉ igea@igearoma.com, Via Principe Amedeo 97). The fancy entrance suggests a great interior which in fact isn't the case. The rooms are simple with basic furniture but all have satellite TV, double-glazed windows and air-con. Singles/doubles cost €82.63/129.11 and triples cost €149.77 not including breakfast.

Hotel Dina (☎ 06 474 06 94, fax 06 48 90 36 14, Via Principe Amedeo 62) is clean and the management is extremely friendly. Singles/doubles are reasonable at €72.30/98.13, not including breakfast (for the extra €3.61 you'd do better to go to a bar). The hotel has two rooms equipped for disabled people, with open showers and hand rails – unusual for hotels in this price range.

Hotel Sweet Home (☎ 06 488 09 54, fax 06 481 76 13, ✉ homesweet@libero.it, Via Principe Amedeo 47) has singles/doubles for €61.97/92.96, not including breakfast. The rooms vary in size and comfort; ask for one facing away from the street as these are larger and quieter.

The stylish *Hotel Contilia* (☎ 06 446 68 87, fax 06 446 69 04, ✉ contilia@tin.it, Via Principe Amedeo 81) is great value in low season but becomes more expensive in the busy months. Singles between €51.64 and €103.28, doubles cost between €77.47

and €129.11 and triples between €92.96 and €165.27. The rooms are spotless and have satellite TV and independent air-con.

Via Nazionale (Map 5)

North-west of the train station, off Via Nazionale, there are a couple of good-value hotels.

Hotel Seiler (☎ 06 488 02 04, fax 06 488 06 88, ✉ acropoli@rdn.it, Via Firenze 48) has friendly, helpful management and clean and comfortable singles/doubles/triples for €82.63/113.62/134.28. There are also family rooms for five people (more if necessary) for between €20.65 and €30.98 per person – ask for room 405, known as *la camera degli angeletti* for its ceiling fresco of angels dating from 1885.

Hotel Oceania (☎ 06 482 46 96, fax 06 488 55 86, ✉ hoceania@tin.it, Via Firenze 38) is an ideal family hotel, located in a quiet 19th-century palazzo. Large singles/doubles cost €98.13/126.53 and triples/family rooms cost between €160.10 and €211.74. There is a 5% discount for stays longer than four days. The hotel stands out for the unbeatable hospitality offered by the delightful owners. There are English newspapers for guests to read and modem plugs for those with computers. There are only nine rooms, so book early.

Hotel Caravaggio (☎ 06 48 59 15, fax 06 474 73 63, ✉ carvagio@mbox.vol.it, Via Palermo 73/75), just off Via Nazionale and a 10-minute walk from Stazione Termini, is a pleasant three-star hotel offering singles/doubles/triples for €108.45/165.26/223.11 and discounts of up to 40% out of season. The reception and bar-breakfast areas are at No 75 and the rooms are next door at No 73, although there are plans to build a connecting corridor. The rooms are small but beautifully furnished, and all have at least one antique piece: No 16 is worth mentioning for its 19th-century mosaic floor. Room services include TV, mini-bar and air-con. The hotel also has a Jacuzzi.

Between the Teatro dell'Opera and Terme di Diocleziano is *Hotel Columbia* (☎ 06 474 42 89, fax 06 474 02 09, ✉ info@hotel columbia.com, Via del Viminale 15), off

Piazza della Repubblica. Singles/doubles/triples cost €101.22/137.37/185.40, including breakfast on the fine roof terrace. Rooms are large and bright and all are fitted with modem plugs. Visit online at www.hotelcolumbia.com.

City Centre

The following are all on Map 8 unless otherwise specified.

Albergo del Sole (☎ *06 687 94 46 or 06 688 068 73, fax 06 689 37 87,* **e** *alb.sole@flashnet.it, Via del Biscione 76)*, very close to Campo de' Fiori, dates from 1462 and is claimed by some to be the oldest hotel in Rome. It has comfortable rooms, some with antique furniture, and prices are reasonable given its position. Singles/doubles cost €82.63/118.78 or €56.81/87.79 without bath. Prices exclude breakfast. There is lots of communal space, including a TV room, internal patio and a roof terrace (open to guests until 11 pm). The hotel provides garage facilities for €20.65 per day. Credit cards are not accepted.

Hotel Campo de' Fiori (☎ *06 688 06 865, fax 06 687 60 03, Via del Biscione 6)* is a peculiar establishment in a six-storey building (no lift) just off Campo de' Fiori. The decor is unique: the narrow entrance is lined with mirrors and columns to create an unsettling kaleidoscopic *trompe l'oeil* effect and the 27 rooms (all doubles) are a decorator's nightmare, with garish blue carpet and clashing floral wallpaper (not recommended if you have a hangover). Singles/doubles cost €103.29/129.11 with bathroom, although in some cases the 'bathroom' is merely a shower stall plonked unceremoniously in the room. There are a few slightly cheaper rooms without bathroom. Prices include breakfast and discounts are negotiable out of season. The hotel has a panoramic roof terrace. It also has nine mini-apartments, which can sleep up to five people. They cost from €129.11 per day.

Also close to Campo de' Fiori, *Hotel Pomezia* (☎/fax *06 686 13 71,* **e** *hotel pomezia@openaccess.it, Via dei Chiavari 12)* is a good lower mid-range choice, especially after its recent renovation. Sin-gles/doubles with private bathroom cost €77.47/113.62 and triples go for €129.11. There is one room equipped for disabled travellers. Prices include breakfast.

The recently opened *Residenza Farnese* (☎ *06 68 89 13 88, fax 06 68 21 09 80, Via del Mascherone)* is located just off Piazza Farnese in a former 17th-century monastery. More a club than a hotel, it is tastefully furnished with tiles rather than carpet throughout. Singles/doubles/triples cost €92.96/123.95/154.93. Some rooms are huge, others are tiny and there's a bar and billiard table. The friendly management can help with tickets to cultural and sporting events.

One of the most centrally located hotels in this area is *Hotel Primavera* (☎ *06 68 80 31 09, fax 06 686 92 65, Piazza San Pantaleo 3)* on Corso Vittorio Emanuele II (good for transport), just south of Piazza Navona. Go through the grand entrance and reception is on the 1st floor. Doubles without/with bathroom cost €82.63/108.45. Triples are a better deal at €113.62/134.28. Prices include breakfast. The rooms are clean and comfortable and all have air-con and double glazing to keep out the (considerable) traffic noise. Bathrooms, added to the rooms as an afterthought, are a bit cramped. Booking is recommended and one night's deposit is requested. Credit cards are not accepted.

On the other side of Piazza di Spagna, *Hotel Forte* (Map 4; ☎ *06 320 76 25, fax 06 320 27 07,* **e** *forte@venere.it, Via Margutta 61)* has pleasant singles from €103.29 to €144.60 and doubles from €129.11 to €196.25. If you like antiques, this is a perfect spot as Via Margutta is lined with antique shops and artists' studios.

Closer to Piazza del Popolo is *Hotel Margutta* (Map 2; ☎ *06 322 36 74, fax 06 320 03 95, Via Laurina 34)*, between Via del Corso and Via del Babuino. The rooms (all doubles) are small and dark, but very clean, and cost €87.79/98.13 for one/two people in a double room. There are two rooms which share a terrace for €123.94 and one with its own terrace for €134.28, but they are often booked up months ahead. Some of the ground-floor rooms have wheelchair access.

Hotel Pensione Merano (Map 3; ☎ 06 482 17 96, fax 06 482 18 10, Via Vittorio Veneto 155) is a quaint old place with dark, heavy furniture. It is surprisingly cheap given the upmarket location. Singles/doubles (all with twin beds) cost €72.30/ 100.70 and triples cost €129.11. The rooms are carpeted and have double glazing to keep out the roar of traffic on the busy Via Veneto, but there's no air-con so they can bake in summer.

Close to busy Piazza Barberini is *Hotel Julia (Map 5; ☎ 06 488 16 37 or 06 487 34 13, fax 06 481 70 44, ⓔ info@hoteljulia.it, Via Rasella 29)*, off Via delle Quattro Fontane. It offers simple comfort in a tranquil environment. Singles (with shower) cost €103.29 and doubles (with bath) cost €154.94. There's a small bar, and all rooms have satellite TV, air-con, hairdryer and safe facilities.

Villa Borghese (Map 3)

The comfortable and friendly *Hotel Villa Borghese (☎ 06 85 30 09 19, fax 06 841 41 00, ⓔ hotel.villaborghese@tiscalinet.it, Via Pinciana 31)* is in an attractive Art Nouveau building notable for being the birthplace and home of the 20th-century Roman writer Alberto Moravia. Homely singles/doubles/triples cost €139.44/185.92/ 216.91 with low-season discounts. There's an attractive garden that also doubles as a summer breakfast area.

Near the Vatican

Hotel Adriatic (Map 4; ☎ 06 688 08 080, fax 06 689 35 52, ⓔ adriatic@ats.it, Via Vitelleschi 25), on the continuation of Via Porcari, off Piazza del Risorgimento, has simple but comfortable singles/doubles for €56.81/77.47 without bathroom or €77.47/ 98.13 with. Breakfast is not included. The large terrace is an added bonus for guests and makes up for the somewhat unfriendly management.

At Via Cola di Rienzo 243 there are two good-quality hotels, both excellent value considering their location. The family-friendly *Hotel Joli (Map 4; ☎ 06 324 18 54, fax 06 324 18 93, Via Cola di Rienzo 243)* is on the 6th floor. It has pleasant rooms

although the bathrooms are small and the hand-held showers are liable to soak everything in the room. Readers have reported that the walls are not well sound-proofed. Singles/doubles cost €61.97/92.96 including breakfast. The breakfast room doubles as a TV lounge. Book well in advance.

Hotel Florida (Map 4; ☎ 06 324 18 72, fax 06 324 18 57, Via Cola di Rienzo 243), on the 2nd floor, is popular with families. It is small and quiet and has nicely furnished singles/doubles for around €77/103 and triples/quads for around €134/155. Breakfast is not included. There are some cheaper rooms with shared bathroom. Discounts are available out of season and if you pay in cash. Air-con costs an additional €15.49 per night and car parking can be arranged in a nearby garage for €15.49 per day.

Hotel Amalia (Map 2; ☎ 06 39 72 33 54, fax 06 39 72 33 65, ⓔ hotelamalia@iol.it, Via Germanico 66), on the corner of Via Ottaviano, is a stone's throw from the Vatican and one of the best-value hotels in the area. Singles/doubles cost €118.78/165.26 including breakfast. There's nothing special about the rooms, although they are bright, spacious and spotlessly clean, with fans rather than air-con.

Also in Via Germanico on the 4th floor of a building with several budget accommodation options is *Residenza dei Quiriti (Map 2; ☎ 06 360 05 389, fax 06 367 90 487, ⓔ quiriti@tiscalinet.it, Via Germanico 198)*, which is quiet and homely with sunny and elegantly decorated rooms. Singles/doubles/triples cost €82.63/123.94/144.61.

Trastevere (Map 6)

Trastevere has surprisingly few hotels. *Hotel Trastevere (☎ 06 581 47 13, fax 06 588 10 16, Via Luciano Manara 24a–25)* used to be a well-located dive but following a major renovation in 1998 it is now one of the area's, if not the city's, best deals, with three-star quality at excellent prices. All immaculate rooms have bathrooms (with hairdryers) and TV, and most of them look out over the market square of Piazza San Cosimato. Attractive frescoes decorate the reception and breakfast areas.

PLACES TO STAY

Singles/doubles/triples/quads cost €67.13/
87.79/108.45/123.94. There are only nine
rooms so book early. They also have apartments sleeping four in the same building for
€154.93.

Hotel Carmel (☎ 06 580 99 21, fax 06
581 88 53, Via Mameli 11) has singles/
doubles for €61.97/92.96 with bathroom.
There is a shady roof terrace which can be
used by guests.

Hotel Cisterna (☎ 06 581 72 12, fax 06
581 00 91, Via della Cisterna 7–9), off Via
San Francesco a Ripa, is another option. It
is located in a quiet, pretty street around the
corner from the busy Piazza Santa Maria in
Trastevere, and close to all the best restaurants, cafes and night spots in the area. The
rooms are unexceptional but comfortable
and clean. Some of the rooms are much larger and airier than others. Singles/doubles/
triples cost €96.57/118.78/153.38.

PLACES TO STAY – TOP END

There is no shortage of expensive hotels in
Rome, but many, particularly the three- and
four-star ones near Stazione Termini, are
geared towards large tour groups and, while
certainly offering all the usual conven-
iences, they tend to be a bit anonymous.
The following hotels have been selected on
the basis of their individual charm, as well
as value for money and location. All rooms
have bathroom, telephone and TV; most
also have a mini-bar, hairdryer and safe.

Breakfast is generally included in the
given price but it is wise to check. Unless
stated otherwise, all these hotels accept
payment by credit card.

Near Stazione Termini (Map 5)
Hotel Palladium Palace (☎ 06 446 69 18,
fax 06 446 69 37, e nox@iol.it, Via Gio-
berti 36) is an expensive choice at €160.10/
206.58/278.88 for a single/double/triple.
There are luxury suites costing up to €428
per night. The hotel has been stylishly refurbished and the comfortable rooms are all
individually decorated with parquet floors
and gilded ceilings. However, with the exception of the cosy pastel-coloured basement breakfast room, the feel of the place is

somewhat impersonal. There are four rooms
for disabled travellers, a bar and a roof garden with sauna.

Hotel d'Este (☎ 06 446 56 07, fax 06
446 56 01, e d.este@italyhotel.com, Via
Carlo Alberto 4b) is a stone's throw from
the Basilica di Santa Maria Maggiore and
is one of the better mid-range hotels in
the area. It has beautifully furnished rooms,
a roof garden, bar, restaurant and laundry
and dry-cleaning service. Singles/doubles
cost up to €134.28/196.25 and triples cost
€216.91, although prices vary considerably
according to the season and are negotiable
– call to check.

Via Nazionale (Map 5)
Hotel Artemide (☎ 06 48 99 11, fax 06 48 99
17 00, e hotel.artemide@tiscalinet.it, Via
Nazionale 22) is an elegant four-star hotel.
The official price for comfortable
singles/doubles is €222.07/299.54 (including breakfast) but there are substantial discounts in low season – it's worth asking.
There is a twin room with facilities for disabled people. Nice extras include free mineral water, soft drinks and daily newspapers.

Roman Forum/Colosseum (Map 5)
Just behind Via dei Fori Imperiali, in the
area once known as the Suburra, are two superb hotels. **Hotel Forum** (Map 5; ☎ 06 679
24 46, fax 06 678 64 79, e info@hotel
forum.com, Via Tor de' Conti 25) is in an
ex-convent and has very comfortable sin-
gles/doubles/triples for €211.74/304.71/
351.19. See the Web site www.hotelforum.
com for any special packages, which are offered periodically – even in high season. Antique furniture abounds in the elegant,
wood-panelled lobby and lounge area. The
hotel's best asset is its delightful roof-garden
restaurant with views to take your breath
away. Over breakfast you can watch Rome
come to life or dine at night against the impressive backdrop of the Forum and Palatine. Above the restaurant is a another small
roof terrace with a bar and lounge chairs.

The nearby **Hotel Nerva** (Map 5; ☎ 06
678 18 35, fax 06 69 92 22 04, Via Tor de'

Conti) is a cosy establishment directly behind the forum, from which it takes its name. Its very pleasant singles/doubles cost €154.94/216.91, with suites for €335.69. Rooms aren't huge but what they lack in size is made up for by the friendly management. Considerable discounts are available out of season and if you pay in cash. There are also two rooms (a single and a double) with facilities for disabled people.

Just south-east of the Colosseum is **Hotel Celio** (Map 7; ☎ 06 70 49 53 33, fax 06 709 63 77, Via dei Santissimi Quattro Coronati 35c), a slice of heaven in an area with few accommodation options. The owners have spent a fortune on meticulous renovations: stunning mosaic floors decorate corridors and rooms, and large-screen TVs feature in most rooms. Art is the theme of this hotel – there are reproduction oils and frescoes throughout – with each room named after a famous artist. The rooms are not huge but all are tastefully decorated. Singles/doubles cost €191.09/204 and superior doubles cost €232.40. One of the two suites (€568.10) has two bedrooms, two bathrooms, terraces with sun-lounges, repro frescoes of Pompeii and views of the Colosseum. There is a private garage for guest parking.

City Centre

Several of Rome's better hotels are located near Piazza di Spagna. One of the newer ones, and a complete delight, is **Casa Howard** (Map 4; ☎ 06 69 92 45 55, fax 06 679 46 44 , e casahowardroma@yahoo.com, Via Capo le Case 18). More guesthouse than hotel, the five rooms are individually decorated with gorgeous fabrics and paintings. Four of them are named after the colour upon which the decor is based – azzurra, rosa, bianca, verde – and one is known as the Chinese room. Two rooms have en-suite bathrooms, the others have their own private bathroom in a separate room next door. Singles cost from €118.78 to €160.10, doubles from €149.77 to €185.92 and triples from €185.92 to €216.91. A room-service breakfast is provided for an additional €7.75. Visit online at www.casahoward.com.

The **Gregoriana** (Map 4; ☎ 06 679 79 88, fax 06 678 42 58, Via Gregoriana 18) has long been an institution for the fashionable set: Naomi Campbell and Claudia Schiffer have both stayed here. Its rooms are not numbered but are instead adorned with letters by the 1930s French fashion illustrator Erté. Everything here seems like a step back in time and it is one of the few hotels in this category that doesn't accept credit cards. Singles start at €123.95 and doubles cost €206.58, including room-service breakfast.

Hotel Manfredi (Map 4; ☎ 06 320 76 76, fax 06 320 77 36, e hmanfredi@tiscalinet.it, Via Margutta 61) is ideally located near Piazza di Spagna on charming Via Margutta, which is lined with antiques shops. The rooms are extremely comfortable and quiet (if somewhat over-decorated) and the hotel staff are amiable and professional. Singles/doubles cost €180.76/232.40, including an American-style buffet breakfast.

Hotel Locarno (Map 2; ☎ 06 361 08 41, fax 06 321 52 49, e info@hotellocarno.com, Via della Penna 22), near Piazza del Popolo, is a friendly alternative to some of the more impersonal top-end hotels. Singles/doubles cost €134.28/204.52 and superior doubles go for €224.14, including breakfast (served in the garden or on the roof terrace during summer). It is popular with both tourists and business travellers (all rooms have modem plugs) and has an attractive Art Deco lounge-bar, free bicycle use and one room equipped for disabled travellers.

The **Fontana Hotel** (Map 4; ☎ 06 678 61 13, fax 06 679 10 56, Piazza di Trevi 96) is appealing because of its location – bang opposite the Trevi Fountain. The establishment, an ex-17th-century convent, is good value given its location: singles/doubles/triples/quads cost €180.76/232.41/258.22/309.87. Some rooms have a view of the fountain but they have their drawbacks – the noise from the crowds around the fountain lasts late into the night.

Also well located, this time behind the Pantheon, is the three-star **Hotel Santa Chiara** (Map 8; ☎ 06 687 29 79, fax 06 687 31 44, e info@albergosantachiara.com, Via Santa Chiara 21). Singles/doubles/triples/

quads cost €139.44/201.42/ 237.57/268.55. Some rooms have small balconies overlooking the street, although the rooms around the internal courtyard are quieter.

Albergo Teatro di Pompeo (Map 8; ☎ 06 687 28 12, fax 06 68 80 55 31, Largo del Pallaro 8), just off Campo de' Fiori, has plenty of old-world charm. Parts of the hotel go back as far as the Roman Republic – guests have breakfast in the remains of Pompey's Theatre (55 BC). It has quiet, comfortable singles/doubles for €153.38/ 198.84.

North of Piazza Navona, superbly positioned in a quiet street lined with craft shops and jewellers, is the lovely *Hotel Portoghesi* (Map 8; ☎ 06 686 42 31, fax 06 687 69 76, e info@hotelportoghesiroma.com, Via dei Portoghesi 1). Singles/doubles cost €129.11/170.43 and suites are available from €185.92, including one with terrace for €309.87. Prices include breakfast on the delightful roof terrace. The hotel does not accept Amex or Diners Club cards.

If it's serious luxury you're after then you'll be spoilt for choice in Rome. Just make sure there's plenty of credit left on your card.

One of Rome's top hotels is the *Minerva* (Map 4; ☎ 06 69 52 01, fax 06 679 41 65, e minerva@pronet.it, Piazza della Minerva 69), just opposite Bernini's *Elefantino* statue near the Pantheon. This deluxe hotel belongs to the Crowne Plaza chain and offers extensive facilities in absolute comfort – as you'd expect given the price. Singles go for around €335 and doubles cost between €413 and €490. Luxury suites, with original coffered wooden ceilings, start at €723. Breakfast is a hefty €23 extra. The hotel is located in a 17th-century palace redesigned in post-modern style by the Italian architect Paolo Portoghesi in the late 1980s. One of his additions was a magnificent Art Deco-style coloured-glass ceiling in the lobby. There are nonsmoking rooms and one room for disabled travellers as well as a restaurant and gym.

Just near the northern end of Piazza Navona, and ideally located for exploring the city centre on foot, is the ivy-clad *Hotel Raphael* (Map 8; ☎ 06 682 831, fax 06 687 89 93, e info@raphaelhotel.com, Largo Febo 2). During the 1980s this hotel was the power base of Bettino Craxi and his cronies. The reception area has fine artworks and antiques, including ceramics by Pablo Picasso. Depending on the season, rates range from €253.07 to €268.55 for a single room and from €371.85 to € 438.98 for a double (some with private terraces). There are also suites from €506.13 and special weekend rates. The roof-terrace restaurant has a stunning view of the city centre. There is also a gym and sauna and three rooms are equipped for disabled people.

Dubbing itself 'Your Home in Rome', the friendly and informal *Hotel Scalinata di Spagna* (Map 4; ☎ 06 679 30 06, fax 06 699 40 598, e info@hotelscalinata.com, Piazza Trinità dei Monti 17) is superbly located at the top of the Spanish Steps. Its pretty roof terrace (where breakfast is eaten) has views over the Roman rooftops. Comfortable singles/doubles cost €206.58/ 284.05 in high season. Room No 18 has a private terrace and connects with an adjoining room to make a family suite costing from €464.81. The hotel is very popular, so book well in advance and try to get one of the rooms that lead onto the terrace. Visit online at www.hotelscalinata.com.

Opposite, the luxurious *Hassler Villa Medici* (Map 4; ☎ 06 699 340, fax 06 678 99 91, e hasslerroma@mclink.it, Piazza Trinitá dei Monti 6) can claim among its guests the royal families of Sweden, Greece and England, President Kennedy and Elizabeth Taylor. However, luxury doesn't come cheap: singles cost €366.68 and doubles cost from €459.65 for standard doubles (which are quite small) to €655.90 for ultra-swanky super-deluxe rooms. You'll have to fork out more for breakfast. Special weekend and 'romance' packages are available at certain times of the year – check online at www.hotelhasslerroma.com. Hotel facilities include a beauty salon, a massage service and free bicycles for touring the historic centre or nearby Villa Borghese. The hotel's rooftop restaurant has views of the city to die for. If nothing else, go there for Sunday brunch.

The nearby **Hotel d'Inghilterra** *(Map 4; ☎ 06 699 81 204, fax 06 679 86 01, e reservation_hir@charminghotels.it, Via Bocca di Leone 14)* was once the guest-house of the Torlonia family, who occupied the palazzo opposite. This building has been a hotel since 1850 and you can literally smell the history emanating from the wood-panelled corridors. Guests have included Liszt, Mendelssohn and Hemingway. Singles range from €198.84 to €216.91 and doubles cost between €258.23 and €335.69. The decor is a mix of dowdy, tasteful, opulent and over the top (depending on whether or not the rooms have been redecorated). The rooms on the fifth floor are smaller with sloping roofs and exposed wooden beams but have their own private balconies.

Right next to Piazza del Popolo is **Hotel de Russie** *(Map 2; ☎ 06 328 881, fax 06 328 88 888, e hotelderussie@hotelderussie.it, Via del Babuino 9)*, Rome's newest luxury hotel and part of Sir Rocco Forte's RF group. The decor is at the same time opulent, minimal and tasteful. That no expense has been spared is evident from the enormous bathrooms (complete with mosaic tiles) and fine linens. But it is the terraced gardens behind the hotel and the various rooftop spaces that take your breath away. If the luxury provided by the hotel isn't enough, you can indulge in any number of treatments in the spa – from aromatherapy to foot reflexology. Luxury doesn't come cheap – prices (not including IVA) start from €304 for a classic single, and cost somewhere between €439 and €604 for a double or suite.

Near the Vatican (Map 4)

You can't get much closer to St Peter's than at **Hotel Columbus** *(☎ 06 686 54 35, fax 06 686 48 74, e hotel.columbus@alfa net.it, Via della Conciliazione 33)*, located in a magnificent 15th-century palace. Quiet and surprisingly homely, given its history and proportions, it is a Renaissance curiosity with its splendid halls, frescoes by Pinturicchio and heavy wooden furnishings. Its attractive internal courtyard doubles as a free car park. It has singles/doubles for

€191.09/294.38 and suites for €387.34. There's a pretty roof terrace and a delightful restaurant in the old refectory of the palace, offering Italian and international cuisine.

Also in the Borgo is **Hotel Bramante** *(☎ 06 688 06 426, fax 06 687 98 81, e bramante@excalhq.it, Vicolo delle Palline 24)*, one of the most charming hotels in Rome. It is located in a restored 16th-century building designed and lived in by the Swiss architect, Domenico Fontana, until he was expelled from Rome by Pope Sixtus V. It has superbly decorated bedrooms, antique furniture and carpets throughout and there's a small terrace on the 1st floor. All of the spacious guest rooms have marble bathrooms (with hairdryers), TV and mini-bar, and are worth every penny at €129.11/ 180.75 for a single/double.

Farther away from the Vatican, between the Lepanto and Flaminio Metro stops, is **Hotel Mellini** *(☎ 06 32 47 71, fax 06 32 47 78 81, e battistini@hotel mellini.com, Via Muzio Clementi 81)*. The rooms are large and comfortable and there are excellent facilities for disabled people, including an external lift for access from the street. Singles/doubles cost €196.25/247.89 and suites start at €309.87. There's a roof terrace overlooking the Palazzo della Giustizia and a snack bar serving light meals. The 5th and 6th floors are reserved for nonsmokers. Check out its Web site at www.hotel mellini.com.

Aventino (Map 6)

The **Aventino – Sant'Anselmo Hotels** *(☎ 06 574 51 74, fax 06 578 36 04, e frpiroli@ tin.it, Piazza di Sant'Anselmo 2)* are five separate turn-of-the-century villas run by one company. They are situated in a predominantly residential area but still only a stone's throw from the historic centre (to the north) and the restaurants of Testaccio (to the south). The Aventino provides two-star single/double/triple accommodation for €87.79/129.11/139.44. The other villas are three star and singles/doubles/triples/quads cost €108.45/165.26/191.09/206.58. All prices include breakfast. These hotels are perfect if you prefer quieter surroundings

Doss Down with the Romantics

If you fancy staying in the building where the poet John Keats died, contact the Landmark Trust in the UK. Established as a charity in 1965, the trust restores and conserves a host of architectural marvels in the UK, as well several in Italy including the 3rd floor apartment where Keats died in Piazza di Spagna, Rome.

For any further information, contact The Landmark Trust (☎ 01628-825 925), Shottesbrooke Maidenhead, Berkshire SL6 3SW, UK.

or if you have a car, as street parking is fairly easy to find. There are pleasant gardens and courtyards where you can have your breakfast or a drink. See the Web site at www.aventinohotels.com.

RENTAL ACCOMMODATION

Apartments near the centre of Rome are expensive and you can expect to pay a minimum of €775 per month for a studio apartment or a small one-bedroom place. On top of the rent there are bills for electricity (which is quite expensive in Italy) and gas. There is usually also a building maintenance charge *condominio*, of between €25 and €155 depending on the size and location of the apartment.

A room in a shared apartment will cost at least €310 per month, plus bills. You will usually be asked to pay a deposit equivalent to one or two months' rent and the first month in advance.

Several of the English-language bookshops in Rome have notice boards where people looking for accommodation or offering a room on a short- or long-term basis place their messages. Try the Economy Book and Video Center (Map 5), Via Torino 136 (near Via Nazionale) or The Corner Bookshop (Map 6), Via del Moro 48 in Trastevere, between Piazza Santa Maria in Trastevere and Piazza Trilussa. Internet cafes around town also have notice boards.

Another good way to find a shared apartment is to buy *Wanted in Rome* (published fortnightly on Wednesday) or *Porta Portese* (published twice weekly on Tuesday and Friday) at newsstands. Bear in mind that many shared apartments in Rome have a communal kitchen and bathroom but no common living space. What was once the living room is often converted into an additional bedroom to keep costs down.

There are many estate agencies specialising in short-term rentals in Rome, which charge a fee for their services. You will also be asked for a deposit of up to one month's rent. They are listed in the telephone directory under *Agenzie immobiliari*. English-speaking agencies are also listed in *Wanted in Rome*.

Places to Eat

FOOD

Eating is one of life's greatest pleasures for Romans so be adventurous. And, if you're not intimidated by eccentric waiters or indecipherable menus, you might well find yourself agreeing with the locals that nowhere in the world is the food as good as in Rome.

Rome offers a pretty good range of eateries: there are some excellent places providing typical Roman fare to suit a range of budgets, as well as some good, but usually fairly expensive, restaurants offering international cuisine such as Indian, Chinese, Japanese and Argentine.

Generally, the restaurants near Stazione Termini are to be avoided if you want to pay reasonable prices for good-quality food. San Lorenzo (to the east of Termini, near the university) and Testaccio (south of the city centre) are popular eating districts with the locals. Trastevere offers an excellent selection of rustic-style eating places hidden in tiny squares, and *pizzerie* where it doesn't cost the earth to sit at an outside table. In the centre, the side streets around Campo de' Fiori and Piazza Navona harbour good restaurants and pizzerie, as does Monti. The Ghetto is the place to go for traditional Roman-Jewish fare.

During summer these areas are lively and atmospheric, with most establishments offering outside tables. Restaurants usually open for lunch from 12.30 to 3 pm but many are not keen to take orders after 2 pm. In the evening, restaurants open from about 8 pm, though they will often open earlier in tourist areas. If you want to be sure of finding a table (especially if you want one outside), either drop into the restaurant during the day and make a booking or arrive before 8.30 pm. Many restaurants close during part of August.

Roman Cuisine

The roots of Roman food are in the diet of the poor and offal has always been an important ingredient. Historically, the ordinary folk ate the *quinto quarto* (fifth quarter) of the animal, which was all that was left after the rich had taken their pickings. Offal eaters shouldn't miss the opportunity to try *coda* (oxtail) or *trippa* (tripe) here, where they are done best. If you can stomach it, try the pasta *pajata*, made with the entrails of very young veal calves, considered a delicacy since they contain the mother's congealed milk.

Deep frying, which has its origins in Jewish cooking, is another important feature of Roman cuisine. Deep-fried fillets of *baccalà* (salted cod), *fiori di zucca* (courgette flowers) stuffed with mozzarella and anchovies, and *carciofi alla giudia* (artichokes) are a must on any Roman gastronomic itinerary, whether they be eaten as a snack, as a prelude to a pizza or as a course in themselves.

In recent years fish has become an important fixture on the menus of Rome's better eateries. More often than not it is grilled whole and then filleted by the waiter at the table. It is, however, more expensive than any other main course. A word of warning for fish eaters: unless you're eating at one of the city's top restaurants, only order it on Tuesday or Friday when the markets sell it fresh.

Antipasto dishes (starters) in Rome are particularly good and many restaurants allow you to make your own mixed selection from a buffet. See the later boxed text 'Pasta al Dente' for typically Roman pasta dishes.

Roman meat dishes to look out for are *saltimbocca alla Romana*, a thin fillet of veal topped with a slice of *prosciutto crudo* (cured ham), white wine and sage, and *abbacchio al forno*, spring lamb roasted with rosemary and garlic – an Easter favourite.

Try these vegetable dishes: *carciofi alla Romana*, artichokes stuffed with mint or parsley and garlic; a salad of curly *puntarelle* (Catalonian chicory) tossed in a garlic, olive oil and anchovy dressing; and, in spring, freshly shelled *fave* (broad beans) served with a slice of *pecorino Romano*, the most famous pecorino (sheep's milk) cheese.

Pasta al Dente

Cooking good pasta according to the Italian way is no mean feat. First, the pasta has to be of the highest quality and second it has to be cooked for precisely the correct length of time, so that it is *al dente* – firm. Italians always salt the boiling water before adding the pasta and they never *buttare* (throw in) the pasta until everyone is present. Don't complain if your pasta takes time to arrive in a restaurant – you'll have to wait 10 to 12 minutes for it to cook.

Italian pasta is infinitely varied. It comes in a dazzling variety of shapes and sizes, ranging from *spaghetti* and *linguini* to tube-shaped *penne* and *rigatoni*, shell-shaped *conchiglie*, bow-shaped *farfalle* (meaning butterflies) or corkscrew-shaped *fusilli* pasta. You can even find 'naughty' pasta on sale in some shops in the shape of human genitalia.

Dried, packet pasta is made with high-quality durum wheat and water. Fresh egg pasta *(pasta all'uovo)* is made with eggs and flour and is used to make stuffed pasta such as *tortellini* and *ravioli*, used in sheets for *lasagne* or cut into strips like noodles called *tagliatelle* (thinner strips are also called *taglionini* or *tagliarini*). Fresh pasta is usually served with richer, creamier sauces than those which accompany dried pasta and are likely to be tomato based.

Pasta sauces traditionally vary quite dramatically between northern and southern Italy. Traditional Roman pasta dishes include *spaghetti alla carbonara* (with egg, parmesan cheese and *pancetta* – cured bacon) and *all'amatriciana* (with tomato sauce, pancetta and a touch of chilli), which originates from Amatrice, a town east of Rome. *Penne all'arrabbiata* (literally 'angry' pasta) has a tomato and chilli sauce.

Another favourite Roman pasta dish is *spaghetti al cacio e pepe*, a deceptively simple dish of piping-hot pasta topped with freshly grated *pecorino Romano*, ground black pepper and a dash of good olive oil. It appears on many Roman menus, traditionally in the more humble *osterie* and *trattorie*, although in recent years there has been a fashion in more up-market eateries for this and other dishes of the *cucina povera* school. *Spaghetti alla gricia* is similar but with the addition of pancetta. It comes from the town of Griciano in northern Lazio.

Although pasta with seafood sauces hails from southern Italy, many Roman restaurants serve delicious *spaghetti alle vongole* (with clams) – best on Tuesday or Friday when the seafood is guaranteed to be really fresh.

In many Roman restaurants, Thursday is the day for *gnocchi* (dumplings). The traditional Roman recipe uses semolina flour and makes quite heavy gnocchi, usually served with a tomato or meat *ragu*.

Nonsqueamish eaters might want to try pasta *pajata*, made with young veal calf intestines. But if you don't fancy that then try the hearty and warming *pasta e lenticchie* (pasta with lentils) – but be prepared for the post-meal anaesthetic effect!

Freshly grated cheese is the magic ingredient for most pasta (although don't try adding it to a seafood sauce unless you want really strange looks and comments). Parmesan *(parmigiano)* is the most widely used, particularly in the north. Look for the name 'Parmigiano Reggiano' on the rind to ensure you're getting the genuine article because there is also the similar, but lower-quality, *grana padano*. In and around Rome (and also in Sardinia) there is a tendency to use the sharp and slightly salty sheep's milk *pecorino*.

The city's neighbourhoods have their own specialities. Testaccio, home of the former slaughterhouse which is now used as a social centre and live music venue (see the Entertainment chapter), is still known as *the* place to go for an authentic Roman dining experience.

Where to Eat
Eateries are divided into several categories. A *tavola calda* (literally 'hot table') usually offers cheap, pre-prepared pasta, meat and vegetable dishes in a self-service style. A *rosticceria* usually offers cooked meats but often has a larger selection of takeaway

Be serenaded by street musicians in the relaxing Piazza Navona.

Sunset over Rome (with a local touch) as viewed from Piazza Garibaldi on the Gianicolo

Out with the new and in with the old at Centrale Montemartini, the former power station

Sculpted bodies pose at the Capitoline Museums.

food. A *pizzeria* will of course serve pizza, but usually also a full menu including antipasto, pasta, meat and vegetable dishes. An *enoteca* is a specialist wine shop which also serves wine by the glass (or bottle), light snacks (such as cheeses or cold meats) and often a couple of hot dishes. An *osteria* is likely to be either a wine bar offering a small selection of dishes or a small *trattoria*. A trattoria is a cheaper version of a *ristorante* (restaurant), which in turn has a wider selection of dishes and a higher standard of service. The problem is that many of the establishments that are in fact restaurants call themselves trattorie or osterie for reasons best known to themselves. It is advisable to check the menu, usually posted by the door, for prices.

Don't judge the quality of a ristorante or trattoria by its appearance. You are likely to eat your most memorable meal at a place with plastic tablecloths in a tiny back street, on a dingy square or on a back road in the country.

And don't panic if you find yourself in a trattoria which has no printed menu: they are often the ones which offer outstanding, authentic food and have menus that change daily to accommodate the availability of fresh produce. Just hope that the waiter will patiently explain the dishes and cost.

After lunch and dinner, head for the nearest *gelateria* (ice-cream parlour) to round off the meal with some excellent *gelati*, followed by a *digestivo* (after-dinner liqueur) at a bar.

For a light lunch or a snack, most bars serve *tramezzini* (sandwiches) and *panini* (rolls), which cost €1 to €3 taken at the bar *(al banco)*. Another option is to go to one of the many *alimentari* (delicatessens) and ask them to make a panino with the filling (usually cold meats and cheeses) of your choice. At a *pasticceria* you can buy pastries, cakes and biscuits. Bakeries *(forni)*, numerous in the Campo de' Fiori area, are another good choice for a cheap snack. Try a piece of *pizza bianca*, a flat bread resembling *focaccia*, which costs from around €1 per slice.

Fast food is becoming increasingly popular in Rome. There are McDonald's outlets throughout the city as well as numerous other chain restaurants and US-style hamburger joints. But seriously, why would you bother when you can pick up a delicious slice of pizza from one of the many *pizza a taglio* or *pizza rustica* outlets. See the Sandwiches & Snacks section later for details.

Costs

Most eating establishments have a cover charge, usually around €1 to €1.50 per person, and a service charge of 10% to 15% which is included in the total bill. There is no obligation to tip on top of this, but most people leave a small tip of €1 to €2.50, unless the service has been particularly bad. Make sure you check the bill *(il conto)* closely, especially in restaurants in touristy areas, as items that were never ordered sometimes mysteriously appear, or the bill can be added up 'incorrectly'.

When you pay your bill you should be given a detailed receipt *(ricevuta fiscale)*. Hang on to it. Technically, if you leave the restaurant without it and are stopped by the *guardia di finanza* (finance police), you could be fined up to €1033.

Never assume that credit cards or travellers cheques are accepted. Budget eateries rarely accept anything other than cash and even some of the mid-range and top-end restaurants accept only cash or debit cards issued by Italian banks. If you want to pay by credit card, check first.

Always remember to check the menu posted outside for prices, cover and service charges. For a three-course meal and wine expect to pay around €10 per person in a pizzeria, €15 at a simple trattoria, up to €26 at a mid-range restaurant and around €50 or more at Rome's top eating places. Eating only a pasta dish and salad and drinking the house wine at a trattoria can keep the bill down. If you order meat or fish you will push the price up substantially.

In this chapter, prices are quoted for full meals: this refers to three courses (chosen from antipasto, *primo, secondo* and *dolce*) with wine.

Numerous restaurants offer tourist menus, with an average price of between €10 and €15, not generally including drinks.

The food is of a reasonable standard but choices will be limited. Again, you can usually pay less if you want only pasta, salad and wine.

Eating Customs
Italians rarely eat a sit-down *colazione* (breakfast). They tend to drink a cappuccino, usually *tiepido* (warm) with a *cornetto* (croissant) or other type of pastry while standing at a bar.

Pranzo (lunch) is traditionally the main meal of the day and many shops and businesses close for three to four hours every afternoon to accommodate the meal and siesta which is supposed to follow.

A full meal will consist of antipasto, which can vary from *bruschetta* (a type of garlic bread with various toppings) to fried vegetables or *prosciutto e melone* (cured ham wrapped around melon). Next comes the *primo piatto* (first plate) – a pasta or risotto – followed by the *secondo piatto* of meat or fish. Italians often then eat an *insalata* (salad) or *contorno* (vegetable side dish) and round off the meal with fruit, or occasionally with a sweet, and *caffè*, often at a bar on the way back to work.

The evening meal *(cena)* is traditionally a simpler affair, but habits are changing because of the inconvenience of travelling home for lunch every day.

Vegetarian
Vegetarians will have no problems eating in Rome. While there are only a few restaurants devoted to them, vegetables are a staple of the Italian diet. Most eating establishments serve a good selection of antipasti, contorni prepared in a variety of ways and salads. Most traditional Roman pasta dishes are suitable for vegetarians. Other dishes to look out for are: *pasta e fagioli*, a thick soup made with borlotti beans and pasta; *pasta al pesto*, pasta with basil, parmesan, pine nuts and olive oil; and *orecchiette ai broccoletti*, ear-shaped pasta with a broccoli sauce, often quite spicy. Risotto is usually a good choice, although sometimes it is made with a meat or chicken stock.

Self-Catering
If you have access to cooking facilities, it is best to buy fresh fruit and vegetables at open markets, and prosciutto, salami, cheese and wine at alimentari or *salumerie*, which are a cross between grocery stores and delicatessens. Fresh bread is available at a *forno* or *panetteria* (bakeries which sell bread, pastries and sometimes groceries) and usually at alimentari. *Latterie* sell milk, yoghurt and cheese. Some bars also sell milk and dairy products. See the Self-Catering section later in the chapter.

DRINKS
Nonalcoholic Drinks
Coffee The first-time visitor to Rome is likely to be confused by the many ways in which the locals consume their caffeine. See the boxed text 'Coffee for all Tastes' later.

Tea Italians don't drink a lot of tea *(tè)* and generally only do so in the late afternoon, when they might take a cup with a few *pasticcini* (small cakes). You can order tea in bars, although it will usually arrive in the form of a cup of warm water extracted from the *espresso* machine (with a strange smell and sometimes a slightly rotten taste) with an accompanying tea bag. If this doesn't suit your taste, ask for the water *bollente* (boiling).

Quality packaged teas, such as Twinings tea bags and leaves, as well as packaged herbal teas, such as camomile, are often sold in supermarkets, alimentari and some bars. You can find a wide range of herbal teas in a herbalist's shop *(erboristeria)*, which sometimes stock health foods too.

Fruit Juices & Nectars Most Italian bars will make you a freshly squeezed fruit juice, known as a *spremuta* for around €1.50 to €3. Orange juice, *spremuta di arancia*, is the most common, but you can also get *spremuta di limone* (lemon juice) and *spremuta di pompelmo* (grapefruit).

Bars also sell small glass bottles of thick, sweet fruit juices *(succhi di frutta)* in flavours including apricot *(albicocca)*, peach *(pesca)* and pear *(pera)*.

Coffee for all Tastes

An *espresso* is a small amount of very strong black coffee. It is also referred to simply as *un caffè*. You can ask for a *doppio espresso,* which means double the amount, or a *caffè lungo* (translated as a slightly diluted espresso). If you want a long black coffee (as in a weaker, watered-down version), ask for a *caffè Americano.*

A *caffè corretto* is an espresso with a dash of grappa or some other spirit and a *macchiato* ('stained' coffee) is espresso with a dash of milk. You can ask for a *macchiato caldo* (with a dot of hot, foamed milk) or *freddo* with a spot of cold milk. On the other hand, *latte macchiato* is warmed milk stained with a spot of coffee. *Caffè freddo* is a long glass of cold, black, sweetened coffee. If you want it without sugar, ask for *caffè freddo amaro. Gran caffè* is a wonderful, almost bubbly, coffee made by beating the first drops of espresso and several teaspoons of sugar into a frothy paste, then adding the coffee on top.

Then, of course, there is the *cappuccino,* coffee with hot, frothy milk. If you want it without froth, ask for a *cappuccino senza schiuma.* Italians tend to drink cappuccino only with breakfast and during the morning. They never drink it after meals – 'How can you put all that hot milk on a full stomach?' – or in the evening and, if you order one after dinner, don't be surprised if the waiter asks you two or three times, just to make sure that they heard correctly.

You will also find it hard to convince bartenders to make your cappuccino hot rather than lukewarm. Ask for it *ben caldo, molto caldo* or *bollente* (boiling) and wait for the same 'tut-tut' response that you got when you ordered a cappuccino after dinner.

Milky coffee variations include *caffè latte*, a milkier version of the cappuccino with less froth. In summer the *cappuccino freddo*, a type of iced coffee, is popular.

JANE SMITH

Granita & Grattachecca Refreshingly cool *granita* is a drink made of crushed ice with fresh lemon or other fruit juices, or with coffee topped with whipped cream. A slightly different kind of ice drink, and uniquely Roman, is *grattachecca*, ice grated off a huge block and flavoured with syrups or juices. There used to be grattachecca kiosks all over Rome but now there is only a handful left (including two in Testaccio, one on the Trastevere side of the Isola Tiberina and one on the Lungotevere near Ponte Umberto I, north of Piazza Navona).

Water Rome's water is among the cleanest in Italy and you can drink the water from any of the ubiquitous street fountains. Most of these run continuously and have a small hole in the spout to facilitate drinking; just hold your finger over the bottom of the

spout and a jet of water will emerge higher up. The water is ice-cold year-round, which is especially refreshing in summer.

The water does contain relatively high levels of calcium and many Romans prefer to drink bottled mineral water *(acqua minerale)*. This is either sparkling *(frizzante* or *gasata)* or still *(naturale)* and you will be asked in restaurants and bars which you prefer. If you want a glass of tap water, ask for *acqua dal rubinetto*, although simply asking for *acqua semplice* will suffice.

Alcoholic Drinks

Beer The main local labels are Peroni, Dreher, Nastro Azzuro and Moretti, all very drinkable and cheaper than the imported varieties. If you want a local beer, ask for a *birra nazionale*, which will be either in a bottle or *alla spina* (on tap). Italy also

PLACES TO EAT

imports beers from throughout Europe and the rest of the world.

All the main German beers are available in bottles or cans and English beers and Guinness are often found on tap in *birrerie* (bars specialising in beer). Australians might be pleased to know that you can even find Foster's and Castlemaine XXXX. Lately there has been a proliferation of pubs which specialise in international beers. See Pubs & Bars in the Entertainment chapter.

Wine & Spirits Wine *(vino)* is an essential accompaniment to any meal. Italians are very proud of their wines and find it hard to believe that anyone else could produce wines as good as theirs. Many Italians drink alcohol only with meals and the foreign custom of going out for a drink is still considered unusual although, in some parts of Italy (mainly the north), it is common to see men starting their day with a *grappa* (a very strong clear grape spirit) for breakfast and continuing to consume strong drinks throughout the day.

Wine is reasonably priced and you will rarely pay more than €10 for a good bottle of wine, although prices can be up to more than €15 for really good quality. There are three main classifications of wine which will be marked on the label: DOCG *(Denominazione di Origine Controllata e Garantita)*, DOC *(Denominazione di Origine Controllata)* and *vino da tavola* (table wine). A DOC wine is produced subject to certain specifications, although the label does not certify quality. DOCG is subject to the same requirements as normal DOC but it is also tested by government inspectors. Table wines can vary considerably in quality; some are very good and others best avoided.

Although some excellent wines are produced in Italy, most trattorie stock only a limited selection of bottled wines and generally only cheaper varieties. Most people tend to order the house wine *(vino della casa* or *vino sfuso)* or the local wine *(vino locale)* when they go out to dine.

The styles of wine vary throughout the country. While many wine buffs would argue that Rome and the Lazio region are poor relations as far as Italian wine production is concerned, some good white wines are produced in the Castelli Romani area (south-east of the city), notably Frascati Superiore. You can taste local and not-so-local wine in many of Rome's *enoteche* (specialist wine shops). See Pubs & Bars in the Entertainment chapter.

Before dinner, Italians might drink a Campari and soda or a fruit cocktail (usually pre-prepared and often without alcohol – *analcolico*). After dinner try a shot of grappa or an *amaro*, a dark liqueur prepared from herbs. If you prefer a sweeter liqueur, try an almond-flavoured *amaretto*, a sweet aniseed *sambucca* or, in the hotter months, a chilled *limoncello*.

PLACES TO EAT – BUDGET
City Centre
Restaurants & Pizzerie For a bargain pizza, try *Pizzeria Il Leoncino (Map 4; ☎ 06 687 63 06, Via del Leoncino 28)* across Via del Corso from Via Condotti. It's cheap, it's hectic, it's not full of tourists and best of all it serves up delicious, thin-crusted pizzas and serves them fast. Bring cash as no cards are accepted. It's closed on Wednesday.

Off Via del Campo Marzio near Piazza del Parlamento is *Da Gino (Map 8; ☎ 06 687 34 34, Vicolo Rosini 4)*, a trattoria of the old school with old-fashioned prices. It's always full and popular with politicians and journalists, especially at lunchtime. Try the home-made fettuccine cooked with peas and *guanciale* (bacon made from the pig's cheek) or the *coniglio al vino bianco* (rabbit cooked in white wine). It is closed on Sunday. Don't mind the old family retainer who slumps over a table at the entrance. He's not dead, just asleep.

Insalata Ricca (Map 8; ☎ 06 856 88 036, Largo dei Chiavari 85), between Piazza Navona and Campo de' Fiori, serves pasta and meal-in-itself salads. It's good value (meals cost around €13) and has become so popular with young Romans that new branches are popping up all over the city. There is another one nearby at Piazza Pasquino 72 *(Map 8; ☎ 06 683 07 881)*. Both have outdoor tables and open daily.

Via del Governo Vecchio is home to countless second-hand clothing stores and two of Rome's most popular budget dining spots. *Pizzeria da Baffetto (Map 8; ☎ 06 686 16 17, Via del Governo Vecchio 11)* is a Roman institution that opens daily. Its large, excellent-value pizzas would feed an army and deserve their reputation as among the most supreme in Rome. Expect to join a queue if you arrive after 9 pm and don't be surprised if you end up sharing a table. Pizzas cost around €4 to €6, a litre of wine costs €4 and the cover charge is about €1. Farther along the street is a tiny, nameless *osteria (Map 8; Via del Governo Vecchio 18)* run by Antonio Bassetti, which has a reputation among locals as one of the top low-cost eats in town. It's a step back in time to the days when it was as cheap to eat out as eat in, and you can tuck into an excellent meal here for around €13. There's no menu – you take your pick from the list the owner rattles off. It is closed on Sunday.

Nearby are three good-value pizzerie. *Pizzeria Corallo (Map 8; ☎ 06 683 07 703, Via del Corallo 10)* is open late. Virtually next door to it, in an atmospheric square, is *Trattoria Pizzeria da Francesco (Map 8; ☎ 06 686 40 09, Piazza del Fico 29)*, which has pizzas and decent pasta from around €4.50 to €7 and a good selection of antipasto and vegetables. Beer costs €3 and wine €5. It is open for lunch and dinner every day except Tuesday, when it is open only for dinner. *Pizzeria La Montecarlo (Map 8; ☎ 06 686 18 77, Vicolo Savelli 11–13)*, off Via del Governo Vecchio, is a very traditional pizzeria, with paper sheets for tablecloths. The pizzas are good and a meal with wine or beer will cost under €10. It opens daily.

Hostaria Giulio (Map 4; ☎ 06 688 06 466, Via della Barchetta 19), in a tiny street between Via Monserrato and Via Giulia, is an excellent-value family-run eatery. The food is consistently good with traditional fare and a few less common dishes sharing space on the menu. Try the fresh porcini mushroom, celery and parmesan salad or the feather-light gnocchi, a home-made speciality. The building dates from the 16th

century, the dining room has a vaulted ceiling and it's decorated cheerfully, with plenty of outdoor tables in summer. It is closed on Sunday.

You don't need to see a menu at *Sergio alla Grotta (Map 8; ☎ 06 686 42 93, Via delle Grotte 27)*, off Via dei Giubbonari near Campo de' Fiori. Decide what takes your fancy by looking at the pictures on the walls, then enjoy enormous helpings of traditional Roman pasta (*cacio e pepe*, carbonara, amatriciana and so on) and good meat and fish dishes. The pizza oven and grill cater to all tastes. It's got a great atmosphere and has tables outside in summer. It is closed on Sunday.

The main item on the menu at *Dar Filettaro a Santa Barbara*, which is also known as *Filetti di Baccalà (Map 8; ☎ 06 686 40 18, Largo dei Librari 88)*, off Via dei Giubbonari, is deep-fried salted cod. The fish fillets, which literally melt in the mouth, are presented wrapped in paper, and you eat them with your fingers rather than with a knife and fork. Various antipasto dishes, salads (including a Roman favourite of puntarelle with an anchovy and garlic dressing) and desserts are also available. It is closed on Sunday.

On the other side of Via Arenula at the start of the Jewish Ghetto is one of Rome's most popular lunch spots (open Monday to Saturday), *Benito (Map 8; ☎ 06 686 15 08, Via dei Falegnami 14)*. There's a daily choice of two pasta dishes and a range of meats and vegetables. A plate of pasta and a salad will set you back €5 or €6. Turnover is fast and furious so don't eat here if a long, leisurely lunch is what you're after.

Sora Margherita (Map 4; ☎ 06 686 40 02, Piazza delle Cinque Scole 30), in the heart of the Jewish Ghetto, is open only for lunch from Monday to Friday. It is so well known and popular with the locals that there isn't even a sign over the door. Don't let the Formica table tops put you off: you're here for the food – traditional Roman and Jewish fare – and the bargain prices. Get here early to avoid a queue (especially on Thursday if you want the fresh gnocchi).

PLACES TO EAT

Vatican

Restaurants & Pizzerie Most establishments around St Peter's and the Vatican are geared towards tourists and can be overpriced for fairly mediocre food. The streetside cafes and restaurants on Via delle Conciliazione are best avoided. If you head north into the Borgo and beyond it through Piazza del Risorgimento, or north-east towards the Tiber, you'll find better options.

Il Mozzicone (Map 4; ☎ 06 686 15 00, Borgo Pio 180) has atmosphere, good Roman fare and great prices. Try the *fettuccini al ragu* or the spaghetti all'amatriciana, and follow it with saltimbocca alla Romana, *scamorza* (grilled cheese) and *trippa alla Romana* (tripe with tomato sauce). It is closed on Sunday.

Osteria dell'Angelo (Map 2; ☎ 06 389 218, Via G Bettolo 24) is a good choice. Seats at the basic wooden tables fill up fast as locals return time and gain for tripe, braised oxtail, or bowls of *picchiapò*, a meaty stew. The *tonnarelli cacio e pepe* (long-strands of home-made pasta with grated pecorino, black pepper and a dash of good olive oil) is a legendary dish. To get there, walk along Via Leone IV from Piazza del Risorgimento.

L'Isola della Pizza (Map 2; ☎ 06 397 33 483, Via degli Scipioni 43–47) is open daily except Wednesday. It's a big place with friendly staff and churns out giant, tasty pizzas and other dishes.

Between Piazza Mazzini and the Tiber is *Cacio e Pepe (Map 2; ☎ 06 321 72 68, Via Avezzana 11)*, a tiny place with a handful of tables. It's not much more than a hole in the wall but you won't find better home-made pasta in the entire city. The spaghetti alla carbonara and namesake al cacio e pepe are sublime. In summer, tables spill onto the street, and in winter hungry Romans will sit outside, wrapped in overcoats and scarves, rather than wait for a table indoors.

Trastevere

Restaurants & Pizzerie In Trastevere's maze of tiny streets there are any number of pizzerie and cheap trattorie. The area is beautiful at night and most establishments have outside tables. It is also very popular, so arrive before 9 pm unless you want to queue for a table.

Osteria Der Belli (Map 6; ☎ 06 580 37 82, Piazza Sant'Apollonia 9–11), just off Piazza Santa Maria in Trastevere, is a reliable trattoria with a great antipasto selection and large helpings of pasta. The main courses are nothing special (don't order the fish unless it's Tuesday or Friday, as it is unlikely to be fresh) but they do good pizzas. A decent meal will cost around €15. It is closed on Monday.

Da Augusto (Map 6; ☎ 06 580 37 98, Piazza de' Renzi 15) is one of Trastevere's favourite mamma's kitchens, dishing up honest fare at prices you only read about. Enjoy your home-made fettuccine or *stracciatella* (clear broth with egg and parmesan) at one of the rickety tables that spill out onto the square in summer. A meal with wine will cost around €13. It is closed on Sunday and every so often closes (without notice) on other days of the week too.

Just across the square is *Casetta di Trastevere (Map 6; ☎ 06 580 01 58, Piazza de' Renzi 31a)*. There's nothing fancy about this neighbourhood trattoria – except that it always seems to be serving just what you fancy, like steaming bowls of *pasta e fagioli* (thick borlotti bean soup) or piquant mounds of penne amatriciana. When it's warm the outdoor tables cram up and service gets slow. It is closed on Monday.

Another very cheap family-run place, hidden behind an anonymous frosted-glass door, a few paces from the square is *Da Corrado (Map 6; Via della Pelliccia)*, where you can choose from two or three pasta and two or three meat dishes daily. You'll pay under €13. This is a traditional workers' canteen with no frills and is a favourite haunt of Trastevere's shopkeepers, especially at lunchtime. It is closed on Sunday and throughout August.

Pizzeria San Calisto (Map 6; ☎ 06 581 82 56, Piazza San Calisto 9a) serves enormous pizzas that fall off your plate for €5 to €7. Dine at one of the outdoor tables in summer and casually watch the passers-by. The mural-decorated front dining area is also pleasant but avoid the basement. It is closed on Monday. For a Neapolitan-style pizza with a thicker base, try *Pizzeria da Vittorio (Map 6; ☎ 06 580 03 53, Via di San Cosimato 14)* between Piazza San Calisto and Piazza San Cosimato. You'll have to wait for an outside table if you arrive after 9 pm, but the atmosphere is great. There are all the regular pizzas plus a few house specials such as the *Vittorio* (fresh tomato, basil, mozzarella and parmesan) and the *Imperiale* (fresh tomatoes, lettuce, cured ham and olives). A bruschetta, pizza and wine costs around €13. It is closed on Monday.

Pizzeria Popi-Popi (Map 6; ☎ 06 589 51 67, Via delle Fratte di Trastevere 45) is a popular haunt among the youth of Rome – hardly surprising since its pizzas are good, big and cheap. Dodge the garlands of garlic in the cavernous interior. The outdoor tables that spill onto the square opposite are a summer attraction. It's closed on Thursday.

Panattoni (Map 6; ☎ 06 580 09 19, Viale di Trastevere 53) is also known as *L'Obitorio* (the morgue) on account of its cold hard marble tables. Open late and always crowded, it is one of the more popular pizzerie in Trastevere. You can eat there for around €8. It is closed on Wednesday and during August.

Testaccio

Restaurants & Pizzerie Testaccio, a traditional working-class area, is a bit off the beaten tourist track but very popular with young Romans as the place to go for a choice, cheap meal.

You won't find a noisier, more popular pizzeria in the city than *Pizzeria Remo (Map 6; ☎ 06 574 62 70, Piazza Santa Maria Liberatrice 44)*. It's a lively place and the pizzas (€4 to €7) are some of Rome's best. They are huge but have a very thin crust. Place your order by ticking your choices on a sheet of paper the waiter gives you. Expect to queue if you arrive after 8.30 pm. It is closed on Sunday.

Augustarello (Map 6; ☎ 06 574 65 85, Via G Branca 98), off the square, specialises in offal. If sweetbreads and oxtail aren't your thing, then don't come here. Vir-

tually every dish (other than the pasta) in this old-fashioned trattoria has some correlation to the innards of an animal. Pasta dishes cost €5 and secondi cost €7 to €8. It is closed on Sunday.

Trattoria da Bucatino (Map 6; ☎ 06 574 68 86, Via Luca della Robbia 84) is a popular Testaccio eating place, decorated with the ubiquitous garlands of garlic and empty chianti bottles. The extensive antipasto buffet is excellent, and there's a good variety of pasta and meat main dishes (€5 or €6). Save room for the desserts which exceed normal trattoria standards. It is closed on Monday and all credit cards are accepted.

Da Felice (Map 6; ☎ 06 574 68 00, Via Mastro Giorgio 29) is a local institution and is especially popular at lunchtime with shoppers and stallholders at the nearby Testaccio market. Ask nicely for a table as the proprietor will only let you sit down if he likes the look of you; he keeps reserved signs on all the tables to cover his tracks! If you're one of the privileged few, you'll enjoy true Roman fare, great pasta and lots of meat and offal, all for a bargain price. It is closed on Sunday.

San Lorenzo

Restaurants & Pizzerie As Rome's university district, eating places in San Lorenzo are influenced by the student population. One of the more popular places, *Pizzeria l'Economia (Map 5; Via Tiburtina 44)*, serves local fare and good pizzas at prices students can afford.

Formula 1 (Map 5; ☎ 06 445 38 66, Via degli Equi 13) is another good-value pizzeria, where you'll pay around €8 for bruschetta, pizza and wine. It is closed on Sunday. *Le Maschere (Map 5; ☎ 06 445 38 05, Via degli Umbri 8)* charges the same sort of prices and both are popular with students.

Stazione Termini

Restaurants & Pizzerie If you have no option but to eat near Stazione Termini, try to avoid the places offering overpriced tourist menus – the food is never any good. There are many *tavole calde* (places which serve ready-to-eat meals such as lasagne) in

PLACES TO EAT

the area, particularly to the west of the train station, which offer panini and pre-prepared dishes for reasonable prices. There are also several bars and self-service places within the station complex.

There are a few good-value restaurants in the area. *Da Gemma alla Lupa (Map 5; ☎ 06 49 12 30, Via Marghera 39)*, northeast of the station, is a simple trattoria with prices to match: a full meal will cost under €16. *Trattoria da Bruno (Map 5; Via Varese 29)* is one of the top places in this (relative) culinary wasteland and has good food at reasonable prices (around €15 for pasta and up to €8 for secondi). Homemade gnocchi is served up on Thursday. *Hostaria Angelo (Map 5; Via Principe Amedeo 104)*, near Piazza Santa Maria Maggiore, is a traditional Roman trattoria that offers reasonably priced fare.

Monti & Caelian
Restaurants & Pizzerie This is a good area for cheap neighbourhood eateries. Stroll around Via del Boschetto, Via dei Serpenti, Via Panisperna, Via Urbana and Via Madonna de' Monti and you're bound to find something to whet your appetite.

Alle Carrette (Map 5; ☎ 06 679 27 70, Vicolo delle Carrette 14) is a decent pizzeria off Via Cavour near the Roman Forum, well placed to rest weary legs after a hard day's sightseeing. A pizza and wine will come to around €10. In the same area, near the Cavour Metro station is *Wanted Il Posto Ricercato (Map 5; ☎ 06 474 22 05, Via Leonina 90)*. The usual pasta and meat dishes are on offer here together with very good pizzas. It is open late and closed on Monday.

Al Giubileo (Map 5; ☎ 06 481 88 79, Via

Cafe Society

Most people hear the word 'bar' and think of beer, wine and cocktails. And that's what Roman bars serve, as well as soft drinks, sandwiches and pastries. However, Roman bars are really about coffee, which accounts for over 80% of their takings. Around the country, more than 70 million espressos are downed each day, an average of 600 espressos per person per year (the highest consumption in the world).

Basically, cafes and bars are one and the same, although there are some cafes that function more like coffee houses or tea rooms, where you can sit down over a leisurely brew, perhaps accompanied by a small cake or pastry. Few Romans would spend more than five minutes in a typical bar – they enter, order, down their coffee at the counter and go.

There's a certain bar etiquette and the usual practice is to pay for what you want at the *cassa* (cash desk) first. If the bar is empty you can usually pay afterwards but if it's busy this rule always applies. Most Romans add €0.05 or €0.10 to ensure the *barista's* attention. Remember that prices skyrocket in cafes as soon as you sit down, particularly near the major tourist haunts such as Piazza di Spagna, Piazza Navona and the Pantheon, where a cappuccino at a table can cost as much as €6. The same cappuccino taken at the bar will cost around €1.

There are countless bars and cafes in Rome. Many operate on the drink-your-coffee-and-run formula and are more active during the day than in the evening. Indeed many bars close at around 8 or 9 pm. For bars that are popular evening drinking spots, see under Pubs & Bars in the Entertainment chapter.

Coffee aficionados have a wealth of choice for their daytime tipplings. There are several excellent bars near the Pantheon, including: *La Tazza d'Oro (Map 8; Via degli Orfani 84–86)*, just off Piazza della Rotonda; *Camilloni a Sant'Eustachio (Map 8; ☎ 06 686 49 95, Piazza Sant'Eustachio 54–55)*; and *Caffè Sant'Eustachio (Map 8; ☎ 06 686 13 09, Piazza Sant'Eustachio 82)*, which makes a wonderful *gran caffè*.

Fashionable (and expensive) places to drink coffee (or tea) are the *Caffè Greco (Map 4; ☎ 06 678 54 74, Via dei Condotti 86)* near Piazza di Spagna, and *Babington's Tea Rooms (Map 4; ☎ 06 678 del Boschetto 44)* is another good bet in the area. Waiters dash around this high-energy pizzeria punching orders into computer handsets, pizza is piled onto wooden slabs and hungry punters dig in. Neapolitan pizza comes to Rome with Al Giubileo's authentic *pizza verace*, although the thin-crust Roman variety is also available. There's plenty of other stuff on the menu, including the delicious melt-in-your-mouth gnocchi *alla sorrentina*.

Off Via Nazionale, *Da Ricci (Map 5; ☎ 06 488 11 07, Via Genova 32)* is reputed to be the oldest pizzeria in Rome. It started up as a wine shop in 1905 and has been run by the same family ever since. The pizzas turned out here have a slightly thicker crust than the normal Roman variety, but some say this is the best pizza in town. There are also good salads and home-made desserts.

Foreign Restaurants The largest of a chain of Argentine restaurants is fun and funky *Baires (Map 5; ☎ 06 692 02 164, Via Cavour 315)*. Try Sardinia-size steaks, meat any which way and flavoursome vegetable- and pulse-based soups. Knock it all back with the excellent organic house wine. It's a good place for a rowdy, hungry group.

If you've got a craving for a curry, try *Il Guru (Map 5; ☎ 06 474 41 10, Via del Cimarra 4–6)*. Gurus in the know and those who just want a good Indian meal eat here. The menu offers tandoori dishes, curries (of every strength) and great vegetarian choices. The exotic decor will transport you eastwards and the friendly proprietor will steer you clear of curries that are too hot to handle.

Mexico al 104 (Map 5; ☎ 06 474 27 72, Via Urbana 104) is hardly Acapulco but it's

Cafe Society

60 27, *Piazza di Spagna 23)*, where you'll pay through the nose for English-style tea and cakes. In summer tables are set up on the square.

Caffè Rosati (Map 2; ☎ 06 322 58 59, Piazza del Popolo 5) has always been popular – especially with left-wing intellectuals including Calvino, Moravia and Pasolini – but has recently become a pleasant spot to catch some afternoon sun and sip a coffee since the 'people's piazza' became fully pedestrianised.

Le Pain Quotidien (Map 4; ☎ 06 688 07 727, Via Tomacelli 24–25) serves French-style coffee, tasty bread and croissants. You can also settle down at the huge communal table and tuck into a hearty brunch on Saturday and Sunday. *Le Bougainville Café (Map 8; ☎ 06 688 04 140, Piazza Rondanini 42)* is a well-located bar near the Pantheon, where it won't cost extra to sit down. The baristas Francesco and Enzo make excellent cappuccini.

Cafe Cafe (Map 7; ☎ 06 700 87 43, Via dei Santissimi Quattro Coronati 44) is *the* place for a pit stop near the Colosseum. Tea connoisseurs will be especially happy, as there are 20 different varieties of tea.

Caffè Farnese (Map 8; ☎ 06 688 02 125, Via dei Baullari 106), on one corner of the lovely Piazza Farnese, is a great spot for people-watching, especially on Saturday morning when the Campo de' Fiori market is at its busiest. At *Caffè Marzio (Map 6; Piazza Santa Maria in Trastevere)*, you will pay €2.50 for a cappuccino if you sit down outside (compared with €0.77 at the counter inside), but it's worth it as it looks onto one of Rome's most beautiful and atmospheric squares.

You won't find a panoramic view or a sun-filled square at *Bar Vezio (Map 3; Via dei Delfini 23)* in the Ghetto (near Piazza Venezia) but you should find some old *compagnia* without much effort. Also known as the *bar comunista* (communist bar), this bar is a local institution and the neighbourhood watering hole for the nearby Democratici di Sinistra Party headquarters. If you start talking politics with the owner, Vezio Bagazzini (who is as much a local legend as the bar itself), expect to be there for quite some time. It's a veritable archive of Italian communist memorabilia; Stalin competes with Che Guevera for space on the walls and there's even Fidel Castro's visiting card.

the closest you'll get in the centre of Rome. Tuck into tacos, burritos, chimichanga, flautas, tamales or enchiladas in a €14.97 set menu.

Shawerma *(Map 7; ☎ 06 700 81 01, Via Ostilia 24)* is half pub, half informal eatery, and serves Egyptian-style comfort food to soak up the lagers. House specialities are vegetable couscous, vegetable tajine, kebabs, taboule and falafels. Come on Friday and Saturday nights for a belly-dancing bonus.

Sandwiches & Snacks

Fast food Roman-style usually consists of a hearty filled panino, a slice of piping hot *pizza bianca* (plain focaccia-like bread) or a tasty slice of *pizza a taglio* (also known as *pizza rustica*). Most bars also serve sandwiches and panini.

At ***Paladini*** *(Map 8; ☎ 06 688 06 662, Via del Governo Vecchio 29)* the staff are glum, there's nowhere to sit and you can wait for ages to be served, but the continuous mass of customers affirms its position as Rome's chief sandwich shop. Fill your piping-hot pizza bianca with cured meats, cheese, artichokes and more – for around €2. It's worth going out of your way for one of these doorstoppers.

M & M Volpetti *(Map 8; Via della Scrofa 31)*, near Piazza Navona, is an upmarket sandwich bar/deli/*rosticcerie* where you can buy gourmet lunch snacks (and take-away dinners) for above-average prices.

Antico Forno *(Map 4; ☎ 06 679 28 66, Via delle Muratte 8)* is right opposite the Trevi Fountain. Your wishes won't necessarily come true by throwing a coin into the Fountain but a few coins spent in this famous bakery will assure you of a delicious slice of pizza or a sizeable filled panino.

Forno di Campo de' Fiori *(Map 8; ☎ 06 688 06 662, Campo de' Fiori 22)* is one of Rome's leading bakeries. People come from all over the city for the pizza bianca here. Drizzled with extra virgin olive oil and sprinkled with crunchy grains of sea salt, it proves the maxim that less is more. The *pizza rossa* with a thin layer of tomato paste is just as good. Buy it by the metre.

Trastevere's ***Forno la Renella*** *(Map 6; ☎ 06 581 72 65, Via del Moro 15–16)* has been producing Rome's finest bread for decades. As the embers die down in the wood-fired ovens, the bakers turn their hand to slabs of thick, doughy pizza with toppings such as tomato, olives and oregano, or potato and rosemary. Pizza by the slice here is worth crossing rivers for.

Another excellent spot for a snack in Trastevere is ***Frontoni*** *(Map 6; Viale di Trastevere)* at the corner of Via San Francesco a Ripa. It makes its panini with both pizza bianca and bread and you can choose from an enormous range of fillings. Sandwiches are sold by weight and a generously filled one will cost around €3. It also has good pizza by the slice.

Zì Fenizia *(Map 4; Via Santa Maria del Pianto 64)* is better known as the kosher pizzeria (Rome's one and only). Zì Fenizia makes outstanding pizza and although there's no cheese on this kosher variety, you don't miss it. The toppings are not the usual suspects either. This is pizza a taglio *par excellence*. It is open Sunday to Friday but closed on Jewish holidays.

It is worth making a special trip to Testaccio to eat lunch at ***Volpetti Più*** *(Map 6; Via A Volta 8)*. It is a tavola calda, so you don't pay extra to sit down. The pizza by the slice is extraordinarily good and there are plenty of pasta, vegetable and meat dishes.

There are hundreds of pizza a taglio outlets all over the city. Usually you can judge the quality of the pizza simply by taking a look. Some good places include: ***Pizza Rustica*** *(Map 8; Campo de' Fiori)*; ***Pizza a Taglio*** *(Map 8; Via Baullari)*, between Campo de' Fiori and Corso Vittorio Emanuele II; and ***Pizza a Taglio*** *(Map 4; Via delle Muratte)*, just off Piazza di Trevi.

If all you really want is a Big Mac, you'll find McDonald's outlets on Piazza della Repubblica (with outside tables), Piazza di Spagna, Piazza della Rotonda (with a view of the Pantheon that many a chic eatery would kill for) and Viale di Trastevere (between Piazza Sonnino and Piazza Mastai).

Gelati

Roman diners will often forsake a restaurant dessert and leg it to the nearest gelateria for a heavenly ice cream instead.

Near the Pantheon is **Gelateria Giolitti** (Map 8; ☎ 06 699 12 43, Via degli Uffici del Vicario 40), which still trades off its (perhaps fading) reputation as the finest gelateria in Rome. At one time it regularly delivered tubs of Pope John Paul II's favourite flavour, *marrons glacé*, to his summer residence. The 70-odd flavours on offer are bound to satisfy less pious sweet-tooths. Nearby is **Gelateria della Palma** (Map 8; ☎ 06 688 06 752, Via della Maddalena 20). You could be forgiven for thinking you'd stumbled into Willy Wonka's factory here, and choosing from the 100 flavours is surprisingly difficult. The house specialities are extra creamy (and rich) mousse gelati and the *meringata* varieties infused with bits of meringue.

The ice-cream cognoscenti say you've never tasted real gelato until you've been to **San Crispino** (Map 4; ☎ 06 679 39 24, Via della Panetteria 42). The fruit-flavoured sorbets change according to season but it's the cream-based flavours – ginger, whisky and pistachio to name a few – that are the real winners. The cinnamon is divine.

Any visit to Piazza Navona should include a pit stop at **Tre Scalini** (Map 8; ☎ 06 688 01 996, Piazza Navona 30). The *tartufo* is the thing to try: it's a rich ball of chocolate gelato filled with huge chunks of pure chocolate, squashed flat and served with mountains of fresh whipped cream. Bernini's achievements in the square fade into insignificance in comparison! Just off the square is **Quinto Bottega del Gelato** (Map 8; ☎ 06 686 56 57, Via di Tor Millina 15), a self-styled 'ice-cream boutique' which does milkshakes, smoothies and fruit salad as well as dozens of gelato flavours.

You'll get better value for money across the Tiber in Trastevere at **La Fonte della Salute** (Map 6; ☎ 06 589 74 71, Via Cardinal Marmaggi 2–6). Whether this gelateria really is a fountain of health (as its name translates) is debatable, although the soy- and yoghurt-based gelati support the theory.

The fruit flavours are superb and the *marron glacé* so delicious that it *has* to be good for you. Scoops are more generous than at gelaterie in the *centro storico*.

Another good spot in Trastevere for gelato is **Bar San Calisto** (Map 6; ☎ 06 583 58 69, Piazza San Calisto). Although there's nothing fancy about this neighbourhood bar, this author's ongoing research suggests that the chocolate gelato – soft and creamy and almost like a mousse – is hard to beat. The coffee flavour's not bad either.

If you're in Testaccio, make sure you stop at **Il Gelato di Antonio** (Map 6; Via Mastro Giorgio, corner Piazza Santa Maria Liberatrice). It's number one in the area.

Pasticcerie

At **Bernasconi** (Map 8; Piazza B Cairoli 16) there's always a tempting selection of cakes and pastries; the *cornetti alla crema* (cream croissants) are to die for. **Bella Napoli** (Map 8; Corso Vittorio Emanuele II 246) is a Neapolitan bar-pasticceria and you won't get much better outside Naples. Try stopping at one ricotta-filled *sfogliatelle*.

The Ghetto is a good place for cakes. **La Dolceroma** (Map 4; Via del Portico d'Ottavia 20), between the Teatro di Marcello and Via Arenula, specialises in Austrian cakes and pastries. It also has American treats such as cheesecake, brownies and chocolate-chip cookies. On the same street is the kosher bakery **Il Forno del Ghetto** (Map 4; Via del Portico d'Ottavia 2). You'll lose all self-control when you see what the all-female team in this tiny corner bakery can produce. People come from all parts of Rome for the ricotta and damson tart. Buy a slice and you'll know why.

Sweet-tooths will also be satisfied west of the Tiber. **Antonini** (Map 2; Via Sabotino 21–29), near Piazza Mazzini in Prati, is one of Rome's top pasticcerie.

Ruschena (Map 4; Lungotevere Mellini 1), also in the Prati area near Piazza Cavour, has excellent cakes, biscuits and pastries, especially the bite-size mignons.

There's no shortage of good pasticcerie in Trastevere. **Valzani** (Map 6; Via del Moro 37) is one of them and displays its mouth-watering chocolate cakes in the window. *Daniela Orecchia (Map 6; ☎ 06 581 00 60, Vicolo del Cinque 40)* is the place to go for a sweet fix at midnight. They bake *cornetti caldi* (hot croissants) from 7 pm until 2 am every night.

A local favourite with shoppers and stall-holders at Piazza San Cosimato market is *Sacchetti (Map 6; Piazza San Cosimato 61)*. Ignore the grumpy proprietors: these cakes – especially the chestnut and cream confection called *monte bianco* are something special. Just around the corner is *Pasticceria Trastevere (Map 6; Via Natale del Grande 49–50)*, where delightful staff sell you delicious cakes and biscuits.

Near Stazione Termini, *Panella l'Arte del Pane (Map 5; Largo Leopardi 2–10)* on Via Merulana has a tempting variety of pastries and breads.

Self-Catering

Rome has no shortage of *alimentari* (delicatessens) selling wide selections of Italian and imported cheeses, salami, olives, bread and other gourmet delights. Only a few of the more notable outlets are listed in this section. If you're looking for food of other nationalities, try the Ghetto area (centred around Via di Portico di Ottavia; Map 4) for shops stocking kosher food and delicious pastries, or the area around Piazza Vittorio Emanuele II (Map 5) for Middle Eastern, Asian and African food stores.

There is also a growing number of supermarkets in Rome's suburbs. Two of the easiest to get to from the centre are the *Standa Supermarkets (Map 6; Viale di Trastevere and Map 2; Via Cola di Rienzo 173)*.

The following are some of Rome's better-known gastronomic establishments. See the boxed text 'To Market, To Market' for details about the daily fresh-food markets in Rome.

Gino Placidi (Map 8; Via della Maddalena 48), near the Pantheon, is one of central Rome's leading alimentari. *Ruggeri (Map 8; Campo de' Fiori 1)* has a good range of cheeses and meats. *Billo Bottarga (Map 4; Via di Sant'Ambrogio 20)*, near Piazza Mattei, specialises in kosher food and is famous for its *bottarga* (tuna or mullet roe).

Castroni (Map 4; ☎ 06 687 43 83, Via Cola di Rienzo 196), in Prati near the Vatican, has a wide selection of gourmet foods, packaged and fresh, including international foods (desperate Aussies will find Vegemite

To Market, To Market

Rome's fresh-produce markets are treasured reminders of a more traditional way of life. There's generally a dazzling array of fresh fruit and vegetables, often meat and fish stalls, the usual delicatessen fare and sometimes stalls selling clothing, shoes or bric-a-brac.

The lively daily market in **Campo de' Fiori** (Map 8) is certainly the most picturesque, but also the most expensive. Prices seem to rise if the shopper has a foreign accent.

Trastevere locals shop at the excellent **Piazza San Cosimato** market (Map 6), a traditional neighbourhood market adjacent to one of the best food-shopping streets in Rome, Via Natale del Grande.

The covered **Piazza dell' Unità** market (Map 4), near the Vatican, is another good place to shop. The **Ponte Milvio** market (Map 1), north of the city centre, caters for well-heeled shoppers.

The huge market at **Piazza Vittorio Emanuele** (Map 5) is Rome's biggest and goes all the way around the square. It is one of the cheapest markets in the city and the place to find exotic ingredients alongside the usual fare, as it is in the most multi-ethnic area of Rome. It is colourful but not the most salubrious of places – watch your handbag. Great bargains can be found on Saturday afternoon when the market is closing.

The **Testaccio** market on Piazza Testaccio (Map 6), is the most Roman of all the city's markets. It is noted for its excellent quality and good prices.

Food markets operate from around 7 am to around 1.30pm, Monday to Saturday.

here, albeit at a huge mark-up). Next door is *Franchi (Map 4;* ☎ *06 687 46 51, Via Cola di Rienzo 198)*, a well-stocked *salumeria* (delicatessen) and takeaway.

Volpetti (Map 6; ☎ *06 574 23 52, Via Marmorata 47)* in Testaccio is famous for its gastronomic specialities, including a large selection of unusual cheeses from throughout Italy. It is always packed with shoppers. There's another branch near the Vatican *(Map 2;* ☎ *06 397 44 834, Via Giulio Cesare 143)*.

Health Food
Buying muesli, soya milk and the like can be expensive in Italy. The following outlets have a good range of products, including organic fruit and vegetables at relatively reasonable prices.

L'Albero del Pane (Map 4; ☎ *06 686 50 16, Via Santa Maria del Pianto 19)* in the Ghetto has a wide range of health foods, both packaged and fresh. *Emporium Naturae (Map 2; Viale Angelico 2)* is a wellstocked health-food supermarket; take Metro Linea A to Ottaviano. *Il Canestro (Map 6; Via Luca della Robbia 47)*, in Testaccio near the market, also has a large selection of health foods, as well as fresh fruit and vegetables and takeaway food. There is a vegetarian restaurant attached to it.

PLACES TO EAT – MID-RANGE
City Centre
Restaurants The fashionable shopping area around Piazza di Spagna is packed with restaurants, some better and bettervalue than others. Roman and regional Italian cooking can be enjoyed at *Otello alla Concordia (Map 4;* ☎ *06 679 11 78, Via della Croce 81)*. The faithful following of local artisans and shopkeepers keeps Otello away from the tourist-trap tag. Cannelloni and *pollo alla Romana* (chicken with capsicums) are among the many dishes they do well. A glassed-in courtyard is used as an attractive winter garden in the colder months – check out the fountain of fruit created daily. It is closed on Sunday.

The very popular *Mario (Map 4;* ☎ *06 678 38 18, Via delle Vite 55)* offers Tuscan

food – fabulous bean soup, grilled meat and game – for around €33. We've had some reports saying the service was fabulous, others that it was dreadful. It's closed on Sunday. *Al 34 (Map 4;* ☎ *06 679 50 91, Via Mario de' Fiori 34)* combines Roman cooking with regional dishes from throughout Italy. It is consistently good and very popular so booking is essential. It is closed on Monday. A full meal will cost around €31. Try the rigatoni with pajata (if you can stomach it) or the spaghetti with courgettes (if you can't). For those with a really large appetite, a *menu degustazione* (gourmand's menu) is also available.

Osteria Margutta (Map 4; ☎ *06 323 10 25, Via Margutta 82)*, off Via del Babuino near Piazza di Spagna, has a good selection of vegetable antipasto dishes and pasta with tasty sauces such as broccoli and sausage. It is closed on Sunday. On the same street, near the corner of Via Alibert, is *Gran Caffè La Caffettiera (Map 4;* ☎ *06 321 33 44, Via Margutta 61a)*, an old-fashioned tea room with Art Nouveau woodwork and fresco-adorned ceilings. It serves delicious light meals such as a rice timbale with vegetables and cheese, or buffalo mozzarella with salad. It is open for lunch Tuesday to Sunday, for early dinners (to 9 pm) Tuesday, Wednesday and Sunday and for dinner (with piano bar) Thursday to Saturday.

Nearby, in a tiny street between Via Margutta and Via del Babuino is *Edy (Map 2;* ☎ *06 36 00 17 38, Vicolo del Babuino 4)*. Residents and shopkeepers of upmarket Via del Babuino make up Edy's regular clientele – they know it's a good bet in an area not known for great value. Try the house speciality, *spaghetti al cartoccio*, a silverfoil parcel of pasta and seafood. Fettucine with artichokes is also worth writing home about; expect to part with around €23 for a three-course meal. It is closed on Sunday.

The trendy *'Gusto (Map 4;* ☎ *06 322 62 73, Piazza Augusto Imperatore 9)*, opposite the Mausoleo di Augusto, has brought a touch of New York to Rome. It's a huge place, with exposed brick walls and a converted warehouse feel. An original concept in Roman dining, it offers several possibilities

PLACES TO EAT

for eating: substantial bar snacks, a pizzeria serving Neapolitan-type pizzas (with a thicker crust than the Roman variety) or a more formal restaurant on the first floor. Bar snacks cost from €5 to €10. A pizza with a bruschetta and drinks will cost around €18, and meals in the restaurant from €31. There's also a bookshop-cookshop, a wine shop and a cigar room. The eating-bar areas are closed on Monday.

Near the Trevi Fountain, in a little street which runs between Via dei Crociferi and Via delle Muratte, is *Al Moro (Map 4; ☎ 06 678 34 95, Vicolo delle Bollette 13)*. A good-quality, traditional Roman meal will come to around €36. It is closed on Sunday.

Tullio (Map 5; ☎ 06 475 85 64, Via San Nicola da Tolentino 26), which runs off Piazza Barberini, is one of the chief restaurants in Rome specialising in Tuscan cuisine such as hearty soups and grilled meats. The food is excellent (you'll pay around €36 for a meal), the place is usually packed and the service fast and efficient. It is closed on Sunday. Also near Piazza Barberini is *Colline Emiliane (Map 5; ☎ 06 481 75 38, Via degli Avignonesi 22)*, a small trattoria which serves superb Emilia-Romagnan food. Try the home-made pasta stuffed with pumpkin and the *vitello* (veal) with mashed potatoes – both are delicious. It is closed on Friday. A meal will set you back around €31.

The designer decor of *Osteria dell'Ingegno (Map 4; ☎ 06 678 06 62, Piazza della Pietra 45)*, near Piazza Colonna, gives the place a modern feel, even though it's located opposite the ancient Hadrian's Temple. The cuisine is central Italian with an international twist. Antipasto dishes include porcini mushroom salad and warm goat's milk ricotta with grilled vegetables. Pastas range from farfalle with leeks and saffron to crepes stuffed with scamorza and radicchio. Meat mains include turkey, veal and Angus beef. There's a good selection of salads and an excellent wine list. Pasta dishes start at €8 and a full meal will set you back around €28. It is closed on Sunday.

Il Bacaro (Map 8; ☎ 06 686 41 10, Via degli Spagnoli 27), around the corner from the Pantheon, is a tiny restaurant where mir-

acles are performed in a minute kitchen. The pasta and risotto dishes are imaginative and delicious and they do great things with beef and veal. As there are only a few tables inside and a couple in the street in summer, booking is essential. It is closed on Sunday. A meal with wine will cost around €31.

Il Primoli (Map 8; ☎ 06 681 35 112, Via dei Soldati 22–23) has deep banquettes, designer lighting and minimalistic white walls, and wouldn't look out of place in London or Melbourne. But the food is definitely Italian – with pasta choices ranging from traditional to innovative and veal, lamb and beef featuring among the mains. Beware of the over-solicitous waiters.

Nowhere in Rome does antipasto better than *L'Orso 80 (Map 8; ☎ 06 686 49 04, Via dell'Orso 33)*. There are bowls of it – vegetables, seafood, meat – which just keep coming until you groan *'basta'* (enough). The *primi* are not great but the chargrilled meats or wood-fired pizza are excellent. Foreigners love this place – just look at the signed photos of Tom and Nicole in happier times, Brad Pitt and others on the walls.

Cul de Sac (Map 8; ☎ 06 68 80 10 94, Piazza Pasquino 73), just off the southern end of Piazza Navona, started life as a wine bar but is better known for its hearty soups, pasta, paté, dips (the babaganoush made with aubergines and garlic is to die for) and its bountiful selection of cheeses and cured meats. The narrow wood-panelled dining room, lined with bottles of wine, is cosy in winter but there are also outdoor tables in summer.

If your tastebuds need a break, the charming *Albistrò (Map 4; ☎ 06 686 52 74, Via dei Banchi Vecchi 140a)* is a nice alternative to Roman cuisine. The Swiss owner blends her culinary heritage with regional Italian and oriental dishes with excellent results. The pretty interior features a tiny open courtyard. It is closed on Wednesday and booking is essential at weekends.

Ristorante Monserrato (Map 8; ☎ 06 687 33 86, Via Monserrato 96) is an unassuming neighbourhood eatery that does marvellous things with fish and seafood. The *spaghetti alle vongole* and *risotto con scampi* are among Rome's most outstanding. Shady outdoor tables and a superb wine list (with excellent whites from northeastern Italy) encourage long, relaxed summer lunches.

La Carbonara *(Map 8; ☎ 06 686 47 83, Campo de' Fiori 23)* takes up virtually one side of Campo de' Fiori. It is a consistently good restaurant, serving traditional Roman fare at honest prices. As the name might suggest, it is known for its spaghetti alla carbonara. Expect to pay around €31 for a full meal. It is closed on Tuesday.

Ditirambo *(Map 8; ☎ 06 687 16 26, Piazza della Cancelleria 72)* has a rustic feel with its wood-beamed ceilings and wooden floors. The food is traditional Italian with a dash of innovation and has a good selection of vegetable dishes. The home-made bread and pasta add to its charms. It is closed Monday lunchtime.

Good food and the Ghetto go hand in hand. **Da Giggetto** *(Map 4; ☎ 06 686 11 05, Via del Portico di Ottavia 21–22)* is a local institution that has been serving Roman-Jewish cooking for years (the deep-fried artichokes are especially good). The location – in the heart of the Ghetto, next to the ancient Portico d'Ottavia – can't be beaten, especially if you get a footpath table. Meals cost around €26. It is closed on Monday.

On the edge of the Ghetto, closer to Piazza Venezia, is **La Taverna degli Amici** *(Map 4; ☎ 06 69 92 06 37, Piazza Margana)*. Its charming terrace, covered with shady market umbrellas, makes this restaurant extremely popular with locals (especially politicians from the nearby Democratici di Sinistra headquarters) and at lunchtime the service can be very slow. However, the antipasto, pasta and risotto dishes are worth the wait. A full meal costs around €26 but expect to pay up to €41 if it includes meat or fish. It is closed on Monday.

Vegetarian Restaurants The Centro Macrobiotico Italiano, also known as the **Naturist Club – L'Isola** *(Map 4; ☎ 06 679 25 09, 4th floor, Via delle Vite 14)*, leads a double life: at lunch it's a semi-self-service

vegetarian eatery serving wholegrain risottos and veggie pies; by night it offers a la carte dining with speciality fish dishes.

Margutta Vegetariano *(Map 2; ☎ 06 678 60 33, Via Margutta 118)* is one of Rome's few completely vegetarian eateries. However, its veggie specialities are bland and disappointing so stick with vegetable versions of Italian staples – pizza and pasta – and you'll eat well. Bizarre decor features black 1970s-style love couches. There's another branch of the same operation near the Pantheon: **Le Cornacchie** *(Map 8; ☎ 06 681 34 544, Piazza Rondanini 53)*.

Foreign Restaurants Hailed as the first 'Tex-Mex' theme restaurant in Rome, **Oliphant** *(Map 8; ☎ 06 686 14 16, Via della Coppelle 31)* is still a winner. If you want a meat fix go Tex with hot dogs or buffalo wings and Mex with tortillas and enchiladas. A good range of beers makes it a popular hang-out.

Thien Kim *(Map 4; ☎ 06 683 07 832, Via Giulia 201)* does an Italian take on Vietnamese cooking, with tasty dishes that are lighter and more strongly flavoured than other Vietnamese restaurants in Rome. A meal will cost around €23. It is closed on Sunday.

Vatican
Restaurants A reliable option in an area not renowned for its eating establishments is **Da Cesare** *(Map 4; ☎ 06 686 12 27, Via Cresenzio 13)*, just off Piazza Cavour. It is a traditional place with a clubby feel and is especially popular in the autumn and winter, when the menu offers game, truffles, porcini mushrooms and wonderful soups made from lentils, chick peas, borlotti and cannellini beans. Expect to part with around €31 to €36 for a full meal. It is closed Sunday evening and Monday.

Diagonally opposite, on the corner of Piazza Cavour and Via Tacito, is **Il Simposio** *(Map 4; ☎ 06 321 32 10, Piazza Cavour)*. It was once a simple enoteca (attached to Costantini, one of Rome's best-known wine-sellers) but has metamorphosed into a top restaurant, with a menu as impressive as the enoteca's Art Nouveau vine decoration and magnificent cellar area. It is closed on Sunday. See also under Entertainment.

Trastevere

Restaurants Trastevere has dozens of good mid-range restaurants. Just wander the streets and you'll find something that appeals.

Il Conte di Montecristo (Map 6; ☎ 06 581 31 89, Vicolo del Bologna 87–89), is hidden away in a tiny lane behind the noise and buzz of the busier Trastevere streets. Start with delicious courgette flowers which are stuffed with mozzarella and anchovies, and then chargrilled rather than fried. Follow them with fabulous lamb, either oven-roasted or grilled chops, called *scottaditto*, 'finger-burners'. Three courses plus wine costs around €20.

In the same area, in a *vicolo* (alley) parallel to Via della Scala is *La Botticella* (Map 6; ☎ 06 581 47 38, Vicolo del Leopardo 39a). In summer you'll eat outside beneath the neighbours' washing, and probably feel you're part of their conversations and arguments too. Rome's yummiest spaghetti all'amatriciana can be had here, as well as typically Roman tripe (oxtail or lamb) and *fritto alla botticella*, a tempura-like dish of deep-fried vegetables, including strangely delicious apple slices.

Nearby is *Da Lucia* (Map 6; ☎ 06 580 36 01, Vicolo del Mattonato 2), which has excellent antipasto and pasta as well as Roman specialities such as *pollo con peperoni* (chicken with peppers) and trippa alla Romana. Many locals return time and again for the *spaghetti alla gricia*. In summer it has outside tables, where you sit beneath a cobweb of washing lines, but it's atmospheric all year. Meals cost around €18. It is closed on Monday.

La Tana di Noantri (Map 6; ☎ 06 580 64 04, Via Paglia 1), between Piazza Santa Maria in Trastevere and Piazza Sant'Egidio, has an extensive menu and is a good place to take the kids, who can tuck into a pizza (from €4) while their parents enjoy more sophisticated fare. The helpings are not enormous so you'll probably want three

or four courses, for which you'll pay around €26. The antipasto, meat and fish dishes are particularly tasty and there's the usual range of pastas. In the warmer months tables are set up under huge umbrellas in the small courtyard opposite the restaurant, tucked into the side of the church of Santa Maria in Trastevere. It makes an excellent spot to watch the passing parade of human (rather than vehicular) traffic. It is closed on Tuesday.

Ferrara (Map 6; ☎ 06 580 37 69, Via del Moro 1a) is a compulsory stop on any foodie's itinerary for dishes such as *orecchiette* (shell pasta) with courgettes and ginger-scented prawns or warm rabbit salad with spicy couscous. Expert advice is on tap for choosing wine from the encyclopedic lists – this is one of Rome's highly acclaimed wine sellers after all (see under Wine Bars in the Entertainment chapter) – and the vaulted, whitewashed dining room is decorated with old barriques. Book a courtyard table. It is closed Tuesday.

Ripa 12 (Map 6; ☎ 06 580 90 93, Via di San Francesco a Ripa 12) is a Calabrian family restaurant serving original pasta, fish and seafood dishes. The food is good – it is credited by some with having invented *carpaccio di spigola* (very fine slices of marinated raw sea bass) – although the service can be haphazard and indifferent. There are some tables on the street but, unless you want your fish smoked by traffic fumes, you'll do better sitting inside. It is closed on Sunday.

Foreign Restaurants For an Indian feast on a delightful garden terrace try *Surya Mahal* (Map 4; ☎ 06 589 45 54, Piazza Trilussa 50) right next to the fountain on Piazza Trilussa in Trastevere. Set menus – vegetarian, meat or fish – provide an opportunity to try almost everything.

The excellent Japanese *ATM Sushi Bar* (Map 4; ☎ 06 683 07 053, Via della Penitenza 7) is in the quiet backstreets of Trastevere. Chill out amid the minimalist decor, soft lighting and relaxed music and chow down on excellent sushi, sashimi, nori rolls, tempura and other Japanese classics.

Fancy a slice of *La Dolce Vita*? The Trevi Fountain is *the* place to woo.

BETHUNE CARMICHAEL

Nibble on your *antipasto* near the Pantheon and wash it all down with a Campari and soda.

MARTIN MOOS

Blend in with the locals: deck yourself out with a Lazio footie kit.

It's not all rock 'n' roll at Julius Caesar, this pub also offers over 40 types of beer.

Testaccio

Restaurants Family-run *Cecchino dal 1887 (Map 6; ☎ 06 574 63 18, Via di Monte Testaccio 30)* is a local institution and provides constant fodder for travel magazines seeking the best places for traditional Roman dining. Its location near the former abbatoir is appropriate, given that offal – from calf's head to pig's trotters and sweetbreads – is its trademark. The great wine cellar is a bonus. Meals cost around €39. It is closed on Monday.

Vegetarian Restaurants It's unusual to find a vegetarian restaurant in the heart of offal territory, but stranger things have happened. *Il Canestro (Map 6; ☎ 06 574 62 87, Via Luca della Robbia 47)* is an informal eatery offering vegetarian food, with a health food shop attached to it. A full meal will cost around €18. It is closed on Sunday.

San Lorenzo

Il Dito e la Luna (Map 5; ☎ 06 494 07 26, Via dei Sabelli 49–51), in the San Lorenzo district, is a cut above your ordinary trattoria and serves a Sicily-inspired menu. Interesting dishes include fresh anchovies marinated in orange juice, a savoury tart made with onions and melted Parmesan, *caponata* (a sort of Sicilian ratatouille) or fish cooked in a potato crust. A meal will set you back around €26. It is closed on Sunday.

You'll understand how *Tram Tram (Map 1; ☎ 06 490 416, Via dei Reti 44)* got its name when you hear the trams rumbling past but don't mind them, as this is a great San Lorenzo haunt. The menu has a southern Italian slant and is reasonably priced. It's also suitable for vegetarians as they dish up several veggie mains. It is closed on Monday.

Monti & Caelian

Just off Via Cavour in the tiny Via dell'Angeletto is *Osteria Gli Angeletti (Map 5; ☎ 06 474 33 74, Via dell'Angeletto 3)*. Consistently good food and outdoor seating on atmospheric Piazza Madonna dei Monti make this an excellent little trattoria. The service can get a bit slow when they're busy, but the prices are reasonable. The menu caters well to both carnivores and vegetarians, with a cluster of fail-safe pasta dishes to satisfy the fussiest of eaters.

La Tana del Grillo (Map 7; ☎ 06 704 53 517, Via Alfieri 4–8), on the corner of Via Merulana, a few streets north of Piazza San Giovanni in Laterano, offers typical cuisine from Ferrara in northern Emilia Romagna. The menu features meat, regional cheeses and pasta such as *cappelacci di zucca*, pouches filled with pumpkin that look vaguely like floppy hats. There is also the usual Roman fare. Meals cost around €26. It is closed Sunday and Monday lunchtime.

The restaurants and bars on the street opposite the Colosseum are overpriced and best avoided. However, if you wander eastwards into the grid of streets behind you'll find a number of options. One of the most appealing is *Pasqualino (Map 7; ☎ 06 700 45 76, Via dei Santi Quattro 66)*, an authentic neighbourhood trattoria frequented by locals. It serves reliable food at honest prices. The pasta with seafood in a creamy tomato sauce is excellent and the fish is usually first-class. It is closed on Monday.

PLACES TO EAT- TOP END
City Centre

Restaurants You cannot find a more perfect setting for a restaurant than that of *Camponeschi (Map 8; ☎ 06 687 49 27)* on the beautiful (and delightfully car-free) Piazza Farnese. It is a favourite with politicians, diplomats and the glitterati, all of whom are happy to pay upwards of €52 for a meal here. It is only open for dinner and is closed on Sunday.

La Rosetta (Map 8; ☎ 06 686 10 02, Via della Rosetta 8–9), near the Pantheon, is without doubt *la migliore* (the best) seafood restaurant in Rome. The menu features innovative combinations – how about shrimp, grapefruit and raspberry salad or fried *moscardini* (baby octopus) with mint? Owner-chef Massimo Riccioli is regarded as one of Italy's greats. Expensive (€67 per person minimum) but memorable. Booking is essential and it's closed on Sunday.

The terrace of *L'Angoletto (Map 8; ☎ 06 686 80 19, Piazza Rondanini 55)* spills out

PLACES TO EAT

onto the picturesque square. This traditional restaurant has a faithful clientele and trades off its long-standing reputation for good food rather than creativity or innovation. The *spaghetti alle vongole* (with clams, olive oil, garlic and chilli) is delicious. Meals cost around €31. It is closed on Sunday. The upmarket *El Toulà (Map 4; ☎ 06 687 34 98, Via della Lupa 29)* features dishes from northern Italy's Veneto region. It is closed on Saturday lunch and Sunday.

Piperno (Map 4; ☎ 06 68 80 66 29, Via Monte de' Cenci 9) in the Ghetto has turned deep frying into an art form; the house special is a mixed platter of deep-fried fillets of *baccalá* (cured fish), stuffed courgette flowers, vegetables and mozzarella cheese. Offal eaters will be well satisfied. It is closed on Sunday evening and Monday.

The terrace of *Vecchia Roma (Map 4; ☎ 06 686 46 04, Piazza Campitelli 18)* is one of the prettiest in Rome and it's an extremely pleasant spot to pass a few hours. The pan-Italian menu is extensive and changes seasonally. In summer there are imaginative salads, in winter lots of dishes based on polenta, and year-round good pasta and risotto. Expect to pay around €44. It is closed on Wednesday.

St Teodoro (Map 6; ☎ 06 678 09 33, Piazza dei Fienili 49–50) is tucked away in a quiet area between the Teatro di Marcello and the Palatine. The extensive menu combines favourite Roman dishes with regional cuisine (the rich cooking of Emilia Romagna features) and a strong emphasis on fish. Pasta dishes with seafood are especially good (the pasta is freshly made each day by the owner's mother). Try the *tonarelli St Teodoro* (incredibly light pasta with a sauce of juicy prawns, courgettes and cherry tomatoes) and save space for *gelatini di frutta* – exquisite fruit-flavoured ice creams. There's an interesting selection of wines from all over Italy in addition to good house wine. The gorgeous terrace is *the* place to be in summer, although the attractive modern art works lining the walls make it pleasant in winter. Meals cost from €41 (significantly more if you order fish). It is closed on Sunday.

Foreign Restaurants For the authentic flavours of classical Japanese food, head for *Sogo Asahi (Map 4; ☎ 06 678 60 93, Via di Propaganda 22)* near Piazza di Spagna. A separate sushi bar, teppanyaki room and sakura (with tatami mats) preserve the atmosphere and ritual of Japanese dining. Tasting menus are excellent value, and sushi lovers shouldn't miss the Saturday evening sushi buffet. It is closed on Sunday.

Trastevere & Testaccio

If it's fish you want and you're in Trastevere, *Alberto Ciarla (Map 6; ☎ 06 581 86 68, Piazza San Cosimato 40)* is the obvious choice. The decor is three decades out of date but so what, you're meant to be concentrating on the food: platters of raw, smoked and marinated fish, herb-scented *spigola* (sea bass); or *mazzancolle al coccio* (king prawn terrine). Expect to pay between €46 and €52 for a meal with wine. It only opens in the evening and is closed Sunday.

Paris (Map 6; ☎ 06 581 53 78, Piazza San Calisto 7) is the best place outside the Ghetto to sample true Roman-Jewish cuisine. The delicate *fritto misto con baccalá* (deep-fried vegetables with salt cod) is memorable, as are simpler dishes such as the *pasta e ceci* (a thick chickpea soup in which the pasta is cooked) and fresh gilled fish. You'll part with around €41 for a full meal. It is closed Sunday evening and Monday.

Stazione Termini

Your tastebuds are in for a treat at *Agata e Romeo (Map 5; ☎ 06 446 61 15, Via Carlo Alberto 45)* near Santa Maria Maggiore. This intimate and elegant restaurant is the benchmark for Roman fine dining. Chef Agata Parisella serves innovative food, which combines the traditional and the unexpected. Try *raviolini* stuffed with aubergine in a goat's cheese sauce, or an aged pecorino tart with fig and honey sauce. Desserts, especially the legendary *millefoglie* (small puffed-pastry sheets filled with jam and cream), are exquisite. You'll pay upwards of €52 per person.

Entertainment

Roma C'è, published every Thursday, is the most comprehensive guide to fun and entertainment in Rome. It is available from newsstands and costs €1.03. For those whose Italian is rather rusty, it has a small English-language section. Two other guides published on Thursday are: *Metro*, a supplement to *Il Messaggero*; and *Trovaroma*, which comes with *La Repubblica*. Both newspapers also print daily cinema, theatre and concert listings.

Wanted in Rome (€0.77) is an English-language news magazine that contains listings and reviews of festivals, exhibitions, dance shows, classical music events, operas and cinema releases. It is published on Wednesday (fortnightly) and is available from central newsstands and at some international bookshops (see under Bookshops in the Shopping chapter). *Time Out Roma* is published weekly in Italian and is packed with up-to-the-minute listings and reviews. It's available from newsstands and costs €1.03.

OPERA

A night at the opera is an unforgettable experience. The functional Fascist-era exterior of the Teatro dell'Opera di Roma does not prepare you for the plush 19th-century interior, smothered in red velvet and gold-leaf paint.

Rome's opera is a poor cousin to Milan's La Scala or Naples' San Carlo, mainly due to a lack of consistent artistic direction and poor management. However, there are some top-class productions and tickets are not impossible to get. The operas *Cavalleria Rusticana* by Mascagnai and Puccini's *Tosca* had their world premieres at the Teatro dell'Opera. Rossini's operas *Il Barbiere di Siviglia* and *La Cenerentola* also premiered in Rome, at Teatro Argentina.

The opera season at the ***Teatro dell' Opera*** (Map 5; ☎ 06 481 60 255 or toll free 800 01 66 65, fax 06 488 17 55, Piazza Beniamino Gigli) starts in December and continues until June. Tickets are expensive: the cheapest upper balcony seats (not recommended for vertigo sufferers) start at around €20 and prices go up to €103. First-night performances cost more.

In summer, opera is performed outdoors and for many years the atmospheric ruins of the Terme di Caracalla were used as a backdrop. More recently the Stadio Olimpico football stadium has been the stage, with tickets starting at €10.33.

Many of the summer festivals include opera performances in their programmes. Check magazines for current events.

THEATRE

If you understand Italian there's a wealth of theatre to enjoy, although Italian theatre is often more melodramatic than dramatic. There are over 80 theatres in the city, many of them worth visiting as much for the architecture and decoration as for the production itself. The ones listed here are merely a selection:

Teatro Argentina *(Map 8; ☎ 06 688 04 601, Largo di Torre Argentina 52)* – State-funded theatre, official home of the Teatro di Roma, stages major theatre and dance productions

Teatro dell'Orologio *(Map 4; ☎ 06 683 087 35, Via dei Filippini 17a)* – Fringe theatre and works by contemporary Italian playwrights

Teatro Quirino *(Map 4; ☎ 06 679 45 85, Via Minghetti 1)* – Classical Italian works such as *Commedia dell'Arte*

Teatro Sistina *(Map 5; ☎ 06 482 68 41, Via Sistina 129)* – Big-budget theatre spectaculars and musicals

Teatro Valle *(Map 8; ☎ 06 688 03 794, Via del Teatro Valle 23a)* – Modern English-language works translated into Italian plus some excellent international productions

Teatro Vascello *(Map 6; ☎ 06 588 10 21, Via Carini 72, Monteverde)* – Fringe theatre, dance, workshops

In summer, many theatre productions are staged outdoors. Classical Greek and Latin works and 18th-century Italian comedies are

ENTERTAINMENT

Rome, Festival Town

From June to November Rome comes alive to the sound and vision of music, dance, theatre, opera and cinema in its many summer and autumn festivals. The most important events are listed below:

Concert a Villa Giulia (☎ 06 688 01 044) – The Accademia di Santa Cecilia orchestra performs a series of concerts in the beautiful Villa Giulia (June and July).

Cosmophonies (☎ 06 373 52 205) – A short season of theatre, music and dance in the Roman theatre, Ostia Antica (June to early July).
Web site: www.fly.to/cosmophonies

Estate Romana – Dozens of events, supported and promoted by city authorities, come under the general umbrella of Estate Romana (June to September).
Web site: www.comune.roma.it

Invito alla Danza (☎ 06 442 92 323) – Long-established modern dance festival in the beautiful grounds of Villa Massimo (July and August).

Isola del Cinema (☎ 06 583 31 13). The Isola Tiberina hosts an international film festival often featuring independent films (July to mid-August).
Web site: www.isoladelcinema.com

Massenzio (☎ 06 428 14 962) – The screen under the stars on the Caelian hill (opposite the Colosseum) has been one of Rome's most popular festivals for decades (July and August).

New Operafestival (☎ 06 561 15 19) – Established and emerging Italian and international talent appears at this festival, held in the courtyard of Basilica di San Clemente (July & August).

Notti di Cinema a Piazza Vittorio (☎ 06 445 12 08) – Open-air cinema in the most multicultural part of town (August to early September).
Web site: www.agisanec.lazio.it

OperaEstate (☎ 06 868 00 125) – Opera concerts and recitals in the courtyard of Sant'Ivo alla Sapienza (July).

Romaeuropa Festival – The city's most with-it festival. Great theatre, dance and opera from around the world (October & November).

Roma Jazz Festival (☎ 06 543 96 361) – Top international jazz performers come to Rome to do their thing, with main concerts taking place at the Auditorium Massimo in EUR and smaller fringe events at venues such as Alexanderplatz and Big Mama (October & November).

Sotto le Stelle di San Lorenzo (☎ 06 996 29 46) – Outdoor film festival held in the gardens of Villa Mercede, Via Tiburtina, in the San Lorenzo district (July to early September).

Teatro dell'Opera Summer Season (☎ 06 48 16 01) – The opera house (orchestra, singers and ballet dancers) goes to the football stadium (July to early August).

Venezia a Roma – Films screened at the Venice Film Festival get a quick pre-release showing in Rome (Early September).

Villa Celimontana Jazz (☎ 06 589 78 07) – The city's most atmospheric jazz festival, under the stars in grounds of the Renaissance Villa Celimontana (June to September).

ASA ANDERSSON

performed from July to September each year in the ancient *Anfiteatro della Quercia del Tasso* (Map 4; ☎ 06 575 08 27) on the Gianicolo. There are also afternoon performances for children. Some theatre productions in the annual Romaeuropa festival are performed outdoors. Check magazines or the daily press for details.

English theatre in Rome is thriving, thanks to the large numbers of expat and bilingual thespians resident in the city. These are usually weekly fixtures or short seasons, and details (even theatres) can change at short notice. Call for information or check the listings press.

Off-Night Repertory Theater is an international theatre company that performs a mix of contemporary one-act plays and full-length dramas in English every Friday. At the time of writing these were staged at *Arte del Teatro Studio* (Map 5; ☎ 06 488 56 08, *Via Urbana 107*). For information on performances, call ☎ 06 444 13 75.

In summer The Miracle Players (☎ 06 446 98 67) perform classic English theatre pieces such as *Everyman* and *Julius Caesar*, usually in abridged form, near the Roman Forum and other atmospheric open-air locations. The performances are of a very high standard and are usually free. Check out the Web site at www.miracleplayers.org.

English-language theatre is presented periodically by the International Theatre at *Teatro Agora* (Map 4; ☎ 06 687 41 67, *Via della Penitenza 33*) in Trastevere. French and Spanish productions are also staged there. Other theatres occasionally stage performances in English. Check *Wanted in Rome* or *Roma C'é* etc for details.

DANCE

There's an active dance scene in Rome and many of the world's best companies tour Italy, although quality home-grown companies are few and far between. See the daily papers and listings press for details.

The Accademia Filarmonica Romana includes several dance events in its annual programme at *Teatro Olimpico* (Map 1; ☎ 06 320 17 52 or 06 326 59 91, *Piazza Gentile da Fabriano 17*), north of Piazza

del Popolo, ranging from classical ballet to ethnic dance and avant-garde performances.

The *Teatro dell'Opera* (see under Opera earlier in the chapter) includes a few classical ballets in its season. These productions are generally only worth seeing if there are important guest stars – the opera's *corps de ballet* has been in a sorry state for many years. The cheapest seats cost around €13 and go up to around €52.

CLASSICAL MUSIC

During the winter months, the *Accademia di Santa Cecilia* (Map 4; ☎ 06 68 80 10 44, *Via della Conciliazione 4*) holds its music season in the Auditorio Pio, although concerts will take place in the new auditorium north of the city centre when it is completed in 2002 (see the boxed text 'A New Auditorium for a New Millennium' later in the chapter). World-class international performers join the highly regarded Santa Cecilia orchestra directed by Myung-Whun Chung. Short festivals dedicated to a single composer feature in the autumn calendar. In June the orchestra and its guest stars move to the beautiful gardens of Villa Giulia (Map 2) for its summer concert series.

The Accademia Filarmonica Romana holds its season at the *Teatro Olimpico* (see under Dance earlier). The academy was founded in 1821 and its members have included Rossini, Donizetti and Verdi. The programme mainly features chamber music, with some contemporary concerts and multimedia events.

From October to May, the *Istituzione Universitaria dei Concerti* (Map 5; ☎ 06 361 00 51, *Piazzale Aldo Moro*) has recitals and chamber-music concerts in the Aula Magna of La Sapienza university. Check out the programme online at www.concertiiuc.it. *Teatro Ghione* (Map 4; ☎ 06 637 22 94, *Via delle Fornaci 37*), near St Peter's, has a varied programme of recitals often featuring major international opera stars. Visit online at www.ghione.it.

The *Associazione Musicale Romana* (☎ 06 39 36 63 22, *Via dei Banchi Vecchi 61*) organises recitals and concerts in various locations throughout the year as well as two

A New Auditorium for a New Millennium

Rome has been in need of a new music auditorium ever since Mussolini knocked down the city's concert hall in Piazza Augusto Imperatore in 1936. A massive project costing over L250 billion (€129 million) should ensure that the city gets it soon – albeit more than three years behind schedule and well over budget.

The new auditorium complex, designed by Italy's leading contemporary architect Renzo Piano, is situated north of the city in a former wasteland. It consists of three scarab-shaped concert halls of varying sizes plus modern facilities such as restaurants and car parks.

Fears that the project might never be realised grew when the site was cleared to lay foundations for the new concert halls. A machine, burrowing 4m below current ground level, hit Roman remains which, hasty excavations showed, were the (quite well-preserved) ruins of a Roman farmhouse villa. Dating from the early to mid-Republic, between the 5th and 2nd centuries BC, the villa is from a period that has very little surviving architecture. As a working farm – possibly a vineyard – it is also important to the history of Roman agriculture.

What this illustrates is the ongoing polemic between the need to build modern facilities for a modern city and the necessity to preserve Rome's extraordinary cultural patrimony. Thankfully, in this instance, the two were able to be combined successfully, though not without significant delays and much hand-wringing.

---

prestigious events: an international organ festival in September (in the Basilica di San Giovanni de' Fiorentini) and an international harpsichord festival in spring.

Free concerts are often held in many of Rome's churches, especially at Easter and around Christmas and New Year, with seats available on a first-come-first-served basis. The programmes are generally excellent. Sant'Ignazio in Loyola is a popular venue for choral masses as are the Pantheon and San Giovanni in Laterano. San Paolo Fuori-le-Mura hosts an important choral mass on 25 January and a *Te Deum* is sung at the Gesù on 31 December. Details are published in daily newspapers, *Roma C'è* or *Trovaroma*.

ROCK

International artists don't always include Rome on their tour schedule, as there is no specialist music venue and the organisation and promotion of events is often haphazard. When top acts do come to Rome, they tend to be part of one of the summer festivals or feature in the line-up of acts at the free May Day rock concert held every year on 1 May in Piazza di Porta di San Giovanni.

If you are into Italian performers, there's plenty of choice. Rock concerts are held throughout the year and are advertised on posters plastered around the city. Concerts by major performers are usually held at the Palazzo dello Sport in the EUR district or Stadio Flaminia, both a good distance from the city centre. The city's *centri sociali* (see the boxed text 'Centri Sociali' later in the chapter) also host major and emerging Italian talent. For information and bookings, see local listings publications or contact the Orbis agency (Map 5; ☎ 06 482 74 03) in Piazza dell'Esquilino 37 near Stazione Termini.

There are plenty of smaller live-music venues; the scene is active and there's something for everyone most nights of the week. See the Live-Music Venues section later in the chapter.

JAZZ

Rome's leading jazz and blues club is *Alexanderplatz (Map 1; ☎ 06 39 74 21 71, Via Ostia 9)*, off Via Leone IV near the Vatican. Top international (especially American) musicians and well-known Italian artists feature on the programme nightly (except Sunday) from October to June. You can also get light meals here. In July and August the club moves to the grounds of the

Renaissance Villa Celimontana (Map 7) on the Caelian hill.

Big Mama *(Map 6; ☎ 06 581 25 51, Vicolo di San Francesco a Ripa 18)* in Trastevere has branded itself as the 'home of the blues', although it also plays host to rock and jazz artists, both Italian and international.

Folkstudio *(Map 5; ☎ 06 48 71 06 30, Via Frangipane 42)*, near Via Cavour, is a Roman-music-scene institution, providing a stage for folk, jazz and world music as well as young artists just starting out.

In the summer, true jazz aficionados head to **Umbria Jazz** in Perugia (1½ hours from Rome), which hosts some of the best international and Italian acts. Umbria Jazz has now expanded and holds a winter edition in Orvieto and an Easter edition (featuring gospel and soul music) in Terni. For information contact ☎ 075 573 24 32 or visit online at www.umbriajazz.com.

For information on the Roma Jazz Festival and Villa Celimontana Jazz see the boxed text 'Rome, Festival Town' earlier.

CINEMA

Film buffs can take delight in Rome's 80-odd cinemas, some of which are multiscreen. Most foreign films are dubbed into Italian; those shown in the original language with Italian subtitles are indicated in listings by *versione originale* or 'VO' after the title. Tickets cost between €4 and €7. Afternoon and early-evening screenings are often cheaper. Check the listings press or daily papers for schedules and ticket prices.

Films are screened daily in English at the **Pasquino** *(Map 6; ☎ 06 580 36 22, Piazza Sant'Egidio)*, just off Piazza Santa Maria in Trastevere, and at the **Quirinetta** *(Map 4; ☎ 06 679 00 12, Via Minghetti 4)* off Via del Corso. **Warner Village Moderno** *(Map 5; ☎ 06 47 77 92 02, Piazza della Repubblica)* has five cinemas showing Hollywood blockbusters (both in English and dubbed into Italian) and major-release Italian films.

On Monday you can see films in English or with English subtitles at **Alcazar** *(Map 6; ☎ 06 588 00 99, Via Merry del Val 14)* off Viale Trastevere. **Nuovo Sacher** *(Map 6; ☎ 06 581 81 16, Largo Ascianghi 1)*, between the Porta Portese area and Trastevere, shows films in their original language on Monday and Tuesday.

For information on the popular open-air cinemas, which take place during the hot Roman summer, see the boxed text 'Rome, Festival Town' earlier in the chapter.

CLUBS & DISCOS

In terms of clubs, Rome falls a long way behind Berlin or London. However, there's still plenty of choice, from grungy clubs with live music or cool DJs to upmarket clubs frequented by jetset types. The latter can be expensive; expect to pay up to €21 to get in, which may or may not include one drink.

Alien *(Map 3; ☎ 06 841 22 12, Via Velletri 13)* is one of the hot spots. The decor is like a set from a science-fiction film and there are dancers on raised platforms. The music is a mix of house, techno and hip-hop, although one of the two dance areas also features 1970s and '80s revivals. **Piper** *(Map 3; ☎ 06 841 44 59, Via Tagliamento 9)* has been around for decades but reinvents itself regularly and appeals to all tastes, depending on the night. It plays house and underground music on Friday and Saturday (admission costs €15.49/20.65, respectively). Its gay night 'Stomp' is on Saturday and there's live music on Thursday.

In the Ostiense area near the Basilica di San Paolo Fuori-le-Mura is **Goa** *(Map 1; ☎ 06 574 82 77, Via Libetta 13)*. It's decked out in ethnic style, with comfy couches to sink into when your feet need a break from the dance floor. The bouncers rule – you might not get in if they don't like the look of you. Admission costs €15.49 (which includes one free drink). Tuesday is 'Gorgeous Goa Gay' night. On Wednesday, it's 'Marrakesh', where eastern atmosphere meets western sounds.

Black Out Rock Club *(Map 7; ☎ 06 704 96 791, Via Saturnia 18)* in the San Giovanni area is home to punk, rock and indie music, with occasional gigs by British and American punk and rock bands. Admission costs €7.74.

Bush *(Map 6; ☎ 06 572 88 691, Via Galvani 46)* in Testaccio has a reputation for its

ENTERTAINMENT

excellent DJs, especially on Thursday which is hip-hop, R&B and soul night. Admission costs €10.32.

Appealing to a slightly older, wealthier (and some might say less than cool) clientele is *Gilda (Map 4; ☎ 06 678 48 38, Via Mario de' Fiori 97)* near Piazza di Spagna, which has plush decor, state-of-the-art lighting and a huge dance floor. Despite all this, it has a sterile, formal atmosphere – not helped perhaps by the dress code, which requires jackets. *Jackie O (Map 3; ☎ 06 42 88 54 57, Via Boncompagni 11)* is a similar joint, with a pricey restaurant tagged on for good measure. Both are good for politician and celeb-spotting.

In summer, many of the larger city discos relocate to Rome's beaches (mainly to Fregene and Ostia) for sultry, open-air dancing.

LIVE-MUSIC VENUES

Admission to most venues costs between €5 and €10. In some cases the charge takes the form of a *tessera* (membership card) that allows cheaper or free admission on subsequent visits.

One of the most popular places in the centre that hosts the hippest Italian and some foreign bands is *Locale (Map 8; ☎ 06 687 90 75, Via del Fico 3)*, off Via del Governo Vecchio near Piazza Navona. On Friday and Saturday nights expect to queue. Admission costs €2.58. *The Groove (Map 8; ☎ 06 687 24 27, Vicolo Savelli 10)*, in the same area, is equally popular among young foreigners and Italians. Home-grown bands play here and it has a reputation for having some of Rome's trendiest DJs.

Fonclea (Map 4; ☎ 06 689 63 02, Via Crescenzio 82a), in the Prati area near the Vatican, is decked out like an English country pub and has jazz, soul, funk, rock music (including cover bands) most nights. Admission is free except on Saturday when you pay €5.16.

Il Controlocale (Map 7; ☎ 06 700 89 44, Via dei Santissimi Quattro Coronati 103) not far from the Colosseum, showcases a variety of live music (Wednesday to Saturday), from Italian folk to blues. There's an unplugged jam session on Monday. Admission costs €2.58 to €5.16.

Testaccio (Map 6) is alive with clubs, most on Via di Monte Testaccio. One of the more interesting and popular places is *Radio Londra (☎ 06 575 00 44, Via di Monte Testaccio 65b)*, decked out like an air-raid shelter, which has live music four nights a week. For Brazilian and Caribbean music head to *Caruso (☎ 06 574 50 19, Via di Monte Testaccio 36)*, which has live music twice a week and good DJs playing

---

Centri Sociali

Italy's independent *centri sociali* (social centres) provide an alternative social life for young people and are often associated with extreme left-wing politics. The entertainment on offer varies from place to place and can include anything from music to theatre and cinema to debates. Entrance is cheap – from €2.58 to €7.74 depending on the location and the event. Many centri sociali also run short courses in film making, theatre, music and art. The artists who perform at the centres, as well as the young people who flock to them, belong to an anti-establishment counter-culture and it's not unusual for prominent bands, who once cut their teeth on the centri sociali circuit, to return to their launching pad to perform at popular prices.

There are around 30 centri sociali in and around Rome, most of which are principally entertainment venues. Most of these are located on the outskirts of the city in disused factories, garages or industrial estates. The biggest and best-known centres are *Forte Prenestino (☎ 06 21 80 78 55, Via F. Delpino, Centocelle)*, east of the city centre, and *Villaggio Globale* in Testaccio *(Map 6; ☎ 06 573 00 39, Lungotevere Testaccio)*. The daily newspaper *Il Manifesto* and the weekly *Roma C'é* usually carry listings of events at the various centri sociali.

Latin, rock and hip-hop the rest of the time. *Caffè Latino* (☎ 06 574 40 20, *Via di Monte Testaccio 96*) has live Latin American music most nights, followed by a disco of Latin, acid jazz and funk. You'll also find cabaret and film screenings here.

In the same area is *Villaggio Globale* (*Map 6; ☎ 06 573 00 39, Lungotevere Testaccio*), in the former slaughterhouse (accessible from Largo G B Marzi at the Ponte Testaccio), an alternative hang-out for people who really know the meaning of 'angst'. This is one of Rome's several centri sociali, a type of squatters' club frequented by ageing hippies, new-age types and people who are still into punk and 'grunge' (see the earlier boxed text 'Centri Sociali'). Many big acts also perform here.

From June until September part of Via di Monte Testaccio is transformed into *Testaccio Village*, an outdoor entertainment complex with several dance areas, bars and live music – international acts, Italian performers, rock, pop, jazz, ethnic sound – every night. A weekly ticket for around €8 allows unlimited entry, although there's an additional charge for some concerts. Check listings magazines and the daily press for details.

PUBS & BARS
Pubs

Pubs – *birrerie* in Italian – are not part of traditional Roman culture but since the first ones were introduced in the early 1990s, they have taken off with a bang. There are over 400 of them, most styled after traditional English or Irish pubs. There are also places with Australian or American themes. They offer a wide selection of draught and bottled beers and many have Guinness on tap. A favourite haunt of young foreigners, they're also popular with the locals.

In the centre, try *The Drunken Ship* (*Map 8; ☎ 06 683 00 535, Campo de' Fiori 20*), a popular haunt for foreign students and locals, which has happy hour from 7 to 9 pm daily. *Trinity College* (*Map 4; ☎ 06 678 64 72, Via del Collegio Romano 6*), off Via del Corso, also has a daily happy hour with a good selection of international beers

and great food. Both get packed to overflowing at the weekend.

Near Largo di Torre Argentina are two very popular English-style pubs: *John Bull* (*Map 8; Corso Vittorio Emanuele II 107a*); and *Mad Jack's* (*Map 4; ☎ 06 68 80 82 23, Via Arenula 20*).

Ned Kelly (*Map 8; ☎ 06 683 22 20, Via delle Coppelle 13*), around the corner from the Pantheon, is an Australian-style bar serving Foster's Lager and other brews. There are TV screens with satellite coverage of sports events. Another pub with an Australian-ish theme is *Four XXXX* (*Map 6; ☎ 06 575 72 96, Via Galvani 29*). This eclectic Testaccio haunt has undergone a bit of 'Latinisation' and has something for everyone: Castlemaine XXXX on tap for homesick Aussies; tequila cocktails if you want something stronger; tasty South American food; and good live jazz or a DJ most nights.

In Trastevere, Irish pub fans will find Guinness and much more at *Molly Malone* (*Map 6; Via dell'Arco di San Calisto 17*). The *Fiddler's Elbow* (*Map 5; ☎ 06 487 21 10, Via dell'Olmata 43*), near Santa Maria Maggiore, was one of the first Irish pubs to hit Rome and its Guinness, darts and chips formula is still very popular. The *Druid's Den* (*Map 5; ☎ 06 488 02 58, Via San Martino ai Monti 28*) is a similar but smaller affair, with live music organised by the owners some nights.

Marconi (*Map 5; ☎ 06 486 636, Via Santa Prassede 9*) serves eclectic pub food – Irish breakfasts, English fish and chips and Hungarian goulash.

There are a few pubs near Stazione Termini including *Julius Caesar* (*Map 5; ☎ 06 446 15 65, Via Castelfidardo 49*), which has over 40 different beers. Down near the Colosseum, you can play darts and knock back a few pints at *The Shamrock* (*Map 7; Via Capo d'Africa 26d*).

Bars

If you're after a more traditional Roman ambience, try *Bar del Fico* (*Map 8; ☎ 06 686 52 05, Piazza del Fico 26*). Open every day until the early hours, it's popular with local actors and artists. Gas heaters allow you to sit outside even in winter, and the place is packed all hours with people just hanging out. Nearby, *Jonathan's Angels* (Map 8; ☎ 06 689 34 26, Via della Fossa 18), off Piazza del Fico, is run by an artist and the whole place – even the loo – is covered with pictures and decorations. It's a relaxed place for a late-night drink and is open till 2 am.

Take some more serious attitude with you to *Bar della Pace* (Map 8; ☎ 06 686 12 16, Via della Pace 5) near Piazza Navona, which is drowning in ivy and has a superb wood-panelled interior. It's a classically trendy place for the 'in' crowd, and as good for an early-evening aperitif outside in summer as for a leisurely nightcap inside in winter.

Baronato Quattro Bellezze (Map 4; ☎ 06 687 28 65, Via di Panico 23), between Via dei Coronari and Corso Vittorio Emanuele II, is quirky and original. Late on Thursday nights, drag-queen owner Dominot dons gown and wig and performs Piaf songs to piano accompaniment. A menu of mainly Tunisian meals and snacks will sustain you through your cocktail tipples, *vin chaud* or *amaro*. Reserve a table for the Piaf show.

Campo de' Fiori is a good place for a drink or just to watch the passing parade, and is especially popular with young Romans and foreign students. The impecunious be warned: the square has been re-zoned as a 'tourist precinct' and some of the bars are charging up to €6.19 for a beer. Not so *Sloppy Sam's* (Map 8; Campo de' Fiori), a cross between an Italian bar and an English pub with several beers on tap. The atmosphere is friendly and relaxed. *Taverna del Campo* (Map 8; ☎ 06 687 44 02, Campo de' Fiori 16) is the new kid on the block and is now as popular as the Vineria (see Wine Bars later) next door. Crowds from both places spill out onto the square in summer and it's always buzzing until the small hours.

In the Ghetto area is *Bartaruga* (Map 4; ☎ 06 689 22 99, Piazza Mattei 9). Named – in a fashion – after the Fontana delle Tartarughe outside, this combined cocktail bar, tea room and pub is decked out in bright colours with oriental furniture, velvet cushions and a Turkish harem feel. It's the type

of place where you can spend hours either sipping tea or scoffing wine.

Trastevere is another popular area for evening entertainment – you can cruise the narrow *vicoli* (alleys) and see what appeals. *Bar San Calisto* (Map 6; ☎ 06 583 58 69) in the square of the same name (next to Piazza Santa Maria in Trastevere) is a Trastevere institution, with tables outside. There's nothing glamorous about it; it is seedy but cheap and you can sit down without paying extra. It is famous for its to-die-for hot chocolate in winter and chocolate gelato in summer.

Also in Trastevere but closer to Ponte Sisto, is *Friends Art Café* (Map 4; ☎ 06 581 61 11, Piazza Trilussa 34), a fashionable drinking spot which also has Internet access. The staff have attitude – be warned. Nearby, *Stardust Live Jazz Bar* (Map 6; ☎ 06 583 20 875, Vicolo dei Renzi 4) is a cross between a bar and a pub. There's often live jazz music and jam sessions and on Sunday there are bagels and American coffee for brunch. It's a real neighbourhood place that tends to close when the last customers fall out the door. *Café della Scala* (Map 6; ☎ 06 580 37 63, Via della Scala 4) is a small, laid-back cafe and a good place to watch the passing parade. Art exhibitions are regularly held here. *La Scala* (Map 6; ☎ 06 580 37 63, Piazza della Scala 60) is crass, loud and busy with several different bar areas. It's always packed but it can't be the music they come for – it's generally awful.

Miscellanea (Map 4; Via delle Paste 110a), near the Pantheon, is one of Rome's longest-running American-style bars, which attracts a good mix of Romans and foreigners (especially American students).

Wine Bars

Wine bars, known as *enoteche* or *vini e oli*, are a feature of most Roman neighbourhoods, especially in the older areas of the city. They sell wine, spirits and olive oil and are often frequented by groups of elderly locals enjoying a glass of wine and a chat, in much the same manner as they might have a coffee at a bar. In recent years, a more sophisticated breed of *enoteca* has appeared on the scene attracting a different crowd from the regular drinkers. Many of these offer snacks or light meals in addition to an extensive range of wines that you can taste by the glass *(alla mescita* or *al bicchiere)* or buy by the bottle. Some have live music and run courses in Italian wines.

The *Vineria* in Campo de' Fiori *(Map 8; ☎ 06 688 03 268)*, also known as *Da Giorgio*, has a wide selection of wine and beers and was once the gathering place of the Roman literati. Today it is less glamorous but still a good place to drink (although cheap only if you stand at the bar) and has some light snacks. Off one end of Campo de' Fiori in Via dei Balestrari, is *L'Angolo Divino (Map 8; ☎ 06 686 44 13)*, a charming place with wooden beams and terracotta floors. For many years it was a simple vini e oli outlet but now serves a variety of interesting dishes, including at least one hot dish daily and an excellent selection of cheeses to compliment its changing selection of a dozen wines by the glass. The owner is well informed and happy to share his knowledge. Themed wine-tasting evenings are held throughout the year.

Atmospheric *Bevitoria Navona (Map 8; ☎ 06 68 80 10 22, Piazza Navona 72)* is one of the more reasonably priced watering holes in this touristy area. You can get a glass of wine at the bar from around €2.50 – although expect to pay much higher prices if you sit outside. In winter mulled wine is available. Ask the owner to take you down to the cellar to see some remains of Domitian's stadium, on top of which Piazza Navona was built.

Enoteca Piccolo (Map 8; ☎ 06 688 01 746, Via del Governo Vecchio 75) has a good selection of Italian wines and also serves snacks.

Across Corso Vittorio Emanuele II is *Il Goccetto (Map 4; ☎ 06 686 42 68, Via dei Banchi Vecchi 14)*, one of Rome's more serious wine bars with a huge selection of well-priced wines from all over the world. There's usually a choice of up to 20 wines by the glass, and plates of cheese or salami are available to soak up what you're tasting. The proprietors are friendly, welcoming and informative. Most of the customers are regulars who live nearby and drop in for a drink after work.

Trimani (Map 5; ☎ 06 446 96 61, Via Cernaia 37), near Stazione Termini, is the city's biggest enoteca and serves excellent soups, pasta and *torta rustica* (quiche). Trimani has a vast selection of Italian regional wines and regularly hosts wine-tasting courses. The popular *Cavour 313 (Map 5; ☎ 06 678 54 96, Via Cavour 313)* is always full of people. You can choose from over 500 bottles, many of which are by the glass, and there are hot and cold snacks to keep you going.

Antica Enoteca (Map 4; ☎ 06 679 08 96, Via della Croce 76b) is a local institution in the Piazza di Spagna area and has always been popular with shopkeepers and shoppers alike. It has a wood-panelled interior and tables outside in summer. Wines by the glass range from €2.06 to €5.16. There's a cold buffet at the impressive, polished wood-and-brass counter and a good selection of wines. There's also a restaurant at the back if you need something more substantial.

Towards the Vatican, on the corner of Piazza Cavour and Via Tacito is *Il Simposio (Map 4; ☎ 06 321 15 02)*. In-the-know Romans now frequent this enoteca for the food as much as the wines; if you can't afford either (it is on the pricey side) it's worth going just to see the vine-and-grape motif decoration that covers the place. Another cheaper option, although less central, is the tiny *Tastevin (Map 2; ☎ 06 320 80 56, Via Ciro Menotti 16)*. The list features around 120 wines, with a weekly selection of a dozen wines that you can taste by the glass (€1.55 to €3.61). The food is good too. You can nibble on cheeses and salamis, tuck into a daily hot dish or chomp on a choice of salads. Save space for a slice of *torta caprese*, a delicious almond and chocolate cake. It's closed for Saturday lunch, all Sunday and Monday evening.

In Trastevere, *Ferrara (Map 6; ☎ 06 580 37 69, Via del Moro 1a)* has an exhaustive list of regional Italian wines and great food (the hearty winter soups and desserts are especially good). There's no messing around here – the wine list is two encyclopedic volumes – one for reds and one for whites. You'll probably have to book to get a table. Nearby, at *Il Cantiniere di Santa Dorotea* (Map 4; ☎ 06 581 90 25, Via di Santa Dorotea 9), there's a lengthy selection of wine by the glass (or beer if you prefer) and a good-value menu. The vaulted ceilings and exposed bricks give the place a cellar feel. The tables outside are inviting in summer although there's a lot of passing traffic.

GAY & LESBIAN VENUES

It's unlikely that you'll find gay and lesbian nightlife in Rome without a bit of research. The fashion for gay and lesbian cafes popular in other parts of Europe has yet to hit Rome, so the scene tends to be nocturnal and can be a bit sleazy. Dark rooms are still a feature of several clubs.

Details of Rome's gay bars and clubs are provided in gay publications and through local gay organisations (see Gay & Lesbian Travellers in the Facts for the Visitor chapter). As clubs come and go and in some places only certain nights are 'gay', it's wise to check the information first.

Popular cruising spots in Rome are listed in the back of *Guide* magazine but cruising is not recommended for unwary travellers as these places are often frequented by hustlers and rent boys – usually impoverished and desperate illegal immigrants.

Gay Bars & Clubs

Admission to clubs usually costs between €5 and €10, although in some places you get in free but are then obliged to buy a drink. Most venues (bars and clubs) require you to have an annual Arci-Gay membership card. These cost €10.33 and are available from any venue that requests them. They are valid throughout Italy for one year from the date of issue.

Many gay bars are springing up in suburban areas, especially on and near Via Casilina, but the longer-established locales are centrally located.

Hangar (Map 5; ☎ 06 488 13 97, fax 06 683 09 081, Via in Selci 69), just off Largo Venosta in the Esquiline area, is run by an American. It is Rome's oldest gay bar and

has a varied clientele, both international and Italian, of all ages but with a significant portion of gym bunnies. Gay videos are shown. It is closed Tuesday. Just around the corner, off Piazza San Martino ai Monti, is *L'Apeiron* (Map 5; ☎ 06 482 88 20, Via dei Quattro Cantoni 5). Club membership costs €2.58 per year. You can choose to hang out in one of several distinct lounge and bar areas or in the basement video and dark room. It's friendly and relaxed.

The long-established *Max's Bar* (Map 5; ☎ 06 702 01 599, Via Achille Grandi 3a) is near Porta Maggiore. An institution in gay Rome, it's an informal place – the ordinary man's bar – with little attitude and great music. It's frequented by young, old and everything in between. Admission costs €7.74.

Edoardo II (Map 4; ☎ 06 699 42 419, Vicolo Margana 14), just off Piazza Venezia, offers amusing decor (it's done up like a medieval torture chamber) and a mixed clientele (mostly dressed in black). There's no dancing, it's just a bar, but a good cruising spot none-the-less.

L'Alibi (Map 6; ☎ 06 574 34 48, Via di Monte Testaccio 44), opposite the former slaughterhouse in Testaccio, has been regarded as Rome's premier gay venue for years but insiders say that it's now attracting an increasingly mixed crowd and that it's in the autumn of its life as the city's top gay disco. There are two levels, each with bar and dance floor and a fabulous roof terrace in summer.

Shelter Discopub (Map 6; Via dei Vascellari 35) in Trastevere is a pub with a dance floor, predominantly for gays and lesbians.

Several mixed clubs have gay nights. *Goa* (Map 1; ☎ 06 574 82 77, Via Libetta 13) in the Ostiense area has 'Gorgeous Goa Gay' on Tuesday. There's a strict door policy and admission costs €10.33. *Alien* (Map 3; ☎ 06 841 22 12, Via Velletri 13) turns gay on Saturday. *Alpheus* (Map 1; ☎ 06 541 39 58, Via del Commercio 271b), off Via Ostiense south of Piramide Metro station, hosts the *Muccassantina* DJ crew from the Mario Mieli centre for a mixed gay and lesbian disco every Friday night.

Lesbian Clubs

There is no permanent lesbian club in Rome but local organisations and bookshops will have information about special events (see Gay & Lesbian Travellers in the Facts for the Visitor chapter). *Goa* and *Alien* (see Gay Bars & Clubs) have lesbian and gay nights on Tuesday and Saturday respectively.

Alpheus (Map 1; ☎ 06 541 39 58, Via del Commercio 271b) has a mixed gay and lesbian disco on Friday.

The *Buon Pastore Centre (Map 4; ☎ 06 686 42 01),* on the corner of Via San Francesco di Sales and Via della Lungara in Trastevere, has a cafe and a women-only restaurant called *Le Sorellastre.*

Gay Saunas

There are several gay saunas in central Rome. Most open 2 pm or 3 pm until very late daily and admission costs around €13 with an Arci-Gay card (which you can buy at the saunas), with discounts for students.

Sauna Mediterraneo (Map 7; ☎ 06 772 05 934, Via Villari 3), off Via Merulana in San Giovanni, is noted for its cleanliness. Its staff speak English, Spanish and Arabic. *Europa Multiclub (Map 5; ☎ 06 482 36 50, Via Aureliana 40)* has good facilities including a popular bar, Alcatraz, which has a leather night on the last Saturday of each month. *Apollion (Map 5; ☎ 06 482 53 89, Via Mecenate 59a)* has a Turkish bath, Jacuzzi, bar and dark room and attracts an older clientele and a few rent boys. Other gay saunas and mixed saunas that have gay nights are listed in the gay press.

Gay Beach

Rome's gay beach, *Il Buco,* is located 9km south of Lido di Ostia (the closest seaside resort to Rome and really an outer suburb) on the road to Torvaianica. Don't expect white sand (it's black) or sparkling clear water (it's often heavily polluted) but at Il Buco you can let it all hang out and check out everyone else doing the same.

The beach isn't exclusively gay – it attracts everything from nudists to fully swimming-costumed middle-aged couples – but the dunes behind the beach are a pop-

ular daytime cruising ground. To get there take the Lido di Ostia train from Porta San Paolo station (right next to Piramide station on Metro Linea B). From there a bus will take you past all the expensive bathing clubs to the *spiaggia libera* (free beach). Ask for directions on the bus.

SPECTATOR SPORTS
Football

Il calcio (football or soccer) excites Italian souls more than politics, religion, good food and dressing up all put together. Football is one of the great forces in Italian life, so if you can get to one of the big games you'll be in for a treat. Spirits run wild and at times overflow but, although outbreaks of violence do occur, the reputation of Italian fans is not as bad as some of the world's worst football hooligans.

Eighteen teams battle it out for the Italian football honours in Serie A (the top division). Serie B teams consist of a further 20 teams, while another 90 teams dispute the medals at Serie C level, itself split up into several more manageable sub-competitions.

Predictably enough, Serie A is dominated by an elite group of *squadre* (teams) that generally take the honours. Among the leading teams, well known to football fans beyond Italy too, are Juventus (based in Turin) that won its 25th league title in 1998, Inter Milan, AC Milan and Parma.

Both local teams, AS Roma and Lazio, play in Serie A. The teams share the Stadio Olimpico at Foro Italico, north of the city centre, and play all their home matches there.

Lazio won the League championship in 2000, having taken home the European Cup Winners' Cup in 1999, and is one of the new powerhouses of Serie A. The club's president is Sergio Cragnotti, head of an international food-processing conglomerate that owns (among other things) Del Monte (makers of tinned fruits and fruit juices). It's regarded as the billion dollar club and has spent huge sums buying leading international players. The purchase (from the Parma football club) of the Argentine player Hernan Crespo in 2000, for a record L110 billion (over US$53 million) was at the time the most expensive

ENTERTAINMENT

signing ever in Italian football history. Time will tell whether the club maintains its success following Swedish coach Sven Goran Eriksson's departure to manage the England team in January 2001.

Lazio fans are traditionally from provincial towns outside Rome although the team is now popular with wealthier middle-class Romans. Lazio supporters do however have an unfortunate (but deserved) reputation for racist abuse of opposition players.

Roma's supporters, known as *romanisti*, are traditionally from the working-class left, from Rome's Jewish community and from Trastevere and Testaccio. Currently, the team is coached in a strict military style. Star players include the Brazilian defender Cafu, Argentine superstar Gabriel Batistuta, poached from Fiorentina in July 2000, and the young Italian Francesco Totti. In the 1980s and early '90s Roma was the stronger of the two local clubs but had, until 2001, been overshadowed by Lazio's European dominance.

There is great rivalry between the teams which sometimes spills over into other facets of life. For example, fans often compare club share prices as both teams are listed on the Italian stock exchange. And when the Lazio president (and then central dairy owner) Cragnotti spent a record sum to secure the services of star Italian striker Cristian Vieri in August 1998 and an increase in the price of milk was announced in the same week, romanisti all over the city boycotted their morning cappuccino in protest!

Reaching the climax of the 2001 season, Rome was leading the national championships, with Lazio two places behind.

Whatever the form or place on the ladder of the teams, a Roma-Lazio derby makes for a particularly hot clash. This is traditionally a sell-out excuse for a little sporting lunacy – with *tifosi* (fans) even more vociferous than usual. At the Stadio Olimpico, true Roma fans flock to the Curva Sud (southern stand) while Lazio supporters sit in the Curva Nord. Tickets for games start at around €15 and can rise to €62. They are best purchased from the Stadio Olimpico box office (☎ 06 323 73 33) or from authorised ticket agencies such as Orbis (☎ 06 482 74 03), Piazza Esquilino 37.

For more details on the clubs, visit online at www.asromacalcio.it and www.sslazio.it.

Basketball

The second most popular spectator sport in Rome is basketball. The arrival of several star players from the United States and from the former Yugoslavia has spiced up the Italian league. The season runs over the winter months and matches are played at the *Palazzo dello Sport* (☎ 06 592 50 06, Viale dell'Umanesimo) in EUR.

Tennis

The Italian International Tennis Championships take place each May on the clay courts at the *Foro Italico* (☎ 06 321 90 64, Via dei Gladiatori 31). The championships attract the world's best players. Tickets can be bought at the Foro Italico each day of the tournament, except for the final days, which are sold out weeks in advance.

Athletics

The Golden Gala athletics meet takes place in June at the Stadio Olimpico. It's organised by the Federazione Italiana di Atletica Leggera. Call ☎ 06 365 81 for information.

Equestrianism

The annual Piazza di Siena show-jumping competition is held in May in Villa Borghese (Maps 2 and 3). Call ☎ 06 322 53 57 for details on obtaining tickets.

Rome Marathon

The Rome Marathon, which starts and finishes at the Colosseum and passes most of the city's major monuments, takes place in late March. If you think you're up to 42km on cobblestones, you should register well in advance with Italia Marathon Club (☎ 06 406 50 64 or 06 445 66 26).

Cycling

Cycling is especially popular in provincial areas. Second only to the Tour de France, the Giro d'Italia is *the* event on Europe's summer cycling calendar. The race usually starts in Rome (near the Colosseum) and finishes in Milan.

Shopping

Don't feel bad if you find that Rome's shop windows are competing with its monuments for your attention. Just make sure there is plenty of time in your itinerary for shopping. You'll find all of the big designer names in Rome and even if your budget doesn't allow for an Armani suit, a Prada bag or a pair of Gucci loafers, you can still have fun trying them on.

If you confine your expeditions to the main shopping districts, you'll find a concentration of clothing and accessories shops that, apart from the designer outlets, sell fairly tacky stuff at inflated prices. By exploring the side streets and seeking the more out-of-the-way shopping areas you will uncover a side of Rome often hidden even from its residents. In this chapter we have tried to cover the main places to shop and things to buy, as well as the more off-beat side to shopping in Rome.

There are several shopping districts in and near Rome's historical centre, many based around particular streets. The area between Piazza di Spagna and Via del Corso (Map 4), including Via Condotti, Via Frattina, Via delle Vite and Via Borgognona, harbours most of the main designer shops for clothing, shoes, leather goods and other accessories, with a fair sprinkling of more affordable shops.

Via Nazionale, Via del Corso and Via dei Giubbonari are good streets for mid-range clothing stores, but quality can be lacking. Second-hand clothes can be found along Via del Governo Vecchio, a winding street that runs from a small square just off Piazza Navona towards the river. If you're looking for antiques or an unusual gift, try Via dei Coronari or Via del Babuino (Maps 2 and 4).

Across the river, near the Vatican (Map 4), is an extensive shopping area. The most interesting street here is Via Cola di Rienzo, where you'll find a good selection of clothing and shoe shops, as well as some excellent fine food outlets. Trastevere (Map 6), just across the river from the historical centre, offers lots of interesting little boutiques and knick-knack shops tucked away down narrow medieval streets and lanes.

Rome has been slower than some of the northern Italian cities to adopt the trend towards department stores, malls and supermarkets. There is only one department store actually in the historical centre (Rinascente, on the corner of Via del Tritone and Via del Corso) but it's hardly a Harrods or Macy's. All of the large shopping malls are quite a distance from the city centre; a couple of them are listed in this chapter.

If you can time your visit to coincide with the sales *(saldi)*, you'll pick up some marvellous bargains. Winter sales run from early January to mid-February and the summer sales run from July to early September.

Shops usually open 9.30 am to 1 pm and 3.30 to 7.30 pm (in winter) or 4 to 8 pm (summer) Monday to Saturday, although a small boutique might not open until 10 am and afternoon hours might be shortened. There is a trend amongst larger shops and department stores towards continuous opening hours from 9.30 am to 7.30 pm. Many shops are closed on Monday morning.

Most shops accept credit cards and many accept travellers cheques. See Money in the Facts for the Visitor chapter for information on value-added tax refunds, known in Italy as IVA. It's also important to remember that you are required by Italian law to ask for a *ricevuta* (receipt) for your purchases.

ACCESSORIES
For accessories by the top designers, see Designer Wear under Clothing later in the chapter.

The prime place in Rome for gloves is Sermoneta (Map 4; ☎ 06 679 19 60), Piazza di Spagna 61. It stocks a kaleidoscopic range of coloured and textured leather and suede gloves with linings ranging from silk to cashmere. There are two other Sermoneta shops on Piazza di Spagna, one stocking ties and scarves and the other handbags and luggage.

Alberta Gloves (Map 4; ☎ 06 678 57 53), Corso Vittorio Emanuele II 18a, has a fascinating selection of handmade gloves, ranging from evening wear to nifty driving gloves. Nearby is Galleria di Orditi e Trame (Map 8; ☎ 06 689 33 72), Via del Teatro Valle 54, where you'll find an interesting, if rather expensive, range of funky handmade hats, scarves, gloves, bags and clothing – all woven from colourful cotton. Credit cards are not accepted.

Troncarelli (Map 8; ☎ 06 687 93 20), Via della Cuccagna 15, just off Piazza Navona, stocks top-brand hats for men and women, including bowlers, top hats, Panama hats, Borsalino hats and Florence's straw hats. Beny (Map 5; ☎ 06 679 58 69), Via Nazionale 164, stocks designer ties and scarves, including a selection reproducing patterns created in the 1950s by the eclectic Italian designer Piero Fornasetti. For cheaper ties and scarves go to the Beny shop next door at Via Nazionale 162.

If you want a pair of glasses or sunglasses with a difference head to Mondello Ottica (Map 8; ☎ 06 686 19 55), Via del Pellegrino 97–8, near Campo de' Fiori. Without doubt, this fabulous store has the grooviest, quirkiest range of eyewear in town – glasses have never looked so good. The owners source spectacle frames by leading European and international designers whose models are not distributed widely in Italy. These include Anne et Valentin, l.a.Eyeworks, Cutler and Gross and the Belgian designer Theo. Mondello Ottica can have your prescription glasses ready in under an hour.

One of the best places in Rome for discount glasses is Moresco Ottica (Map 8; ☎ 06 68 80 50 79), Via dei Falegnami 23a. The tiny shop stocks frames by all the major labels – Gucci, Chanel, Persol, Web and Luxottica to name a few – and the friendly proprietor can organise prescriptions in a couple of hours.

Federico Fellini was a patron of Ottica Spiezia (Map 2; ☎ 06 361 05 93), Via del Babuino 199. This tiny shop, just off Piazza del Popolo, is crammed with stylish, high-quality spectacle frames and sunglasses. Ottica Castri (Map 4; ☎ 06 699 04 80), Via

Frattina 3, is another choice place for specs, with over 2000 frames on display.

Italy is famous for its silk ties and there are shops for all tastes and budgets. One of the more economical ones is Andrew's Ties (Map 4; ☎ 06 679 74 17), Via del Gambero 29, which sells printed, woven and embossed silk ties as well as the wool and cashmere variety, priced from €13 up to about €26. Next door, and giving Andrew's some stiff competition, is Tie Store (☎ 06 679 01 64), which sells similarly priced neck wear. Both shops also sell men's shirts.

Tie connoisseurs should head for Trastevere and La Cravatta su Misura (Map 6; ☎ 06 581 66 76), Via Santa Cecilia 12, for superb custom-made ties from the finest Italian silk and English wool. Choose your fabric, the width and length of the tie and, at a push, it can be ready in a few hours.

ANTIQUES

The main areas to find the best antique shops are around Via Giulia, Via dei Coronari and Via del Babuino. Even if you're just window shopping, it is fascinating to browse – particularly along Via dei Coronari. Most shops specialise in particular periods. The shops mentioned in this section are located throughout the city centre and have been selected for both their originality and more affordable prices.

Lilia Leoni (Map 4; ☎ 06 678 32 10), Via Belsiana 86, has unusual objects and furniture. For example, you'll find collectable Murano drinking glasses and Art Nouveau (known as Liberty in Italy) garden furniture, as well as pieces dating from the early 1900s to the 1950s.

Alinari (Map 4; ☎ 06 679 29 23), Via Alibert 16a, sells photography books and photographic prints (mostly views of Rome) reproduced from the archives of the work of the Alinari brothers. The archives contain more than a million glass-plate negatives of photographs taken by these famous Italian photographers in the late 19th century.

Animalier e Oltre (Map 2; ☎ 06 320 82 82), Via Margutta 47, stocks original bric-a-brac, rustic furniture and a huge selection of animal-shaped antiques (including repro-

Via Condotti is Rome's top shopping patch.

Posing Prada style in Via Condotti

The glitzy La Rinascente, on Via del Corso, is Rome's largest shopping centre.

MARTIN MOOS

Peering into the world of Salvatore Ferragamo, Via Condotti

MARTIN MOOS

Unwinding from mall madness in Caffè Rosati on Piazza del Popolo ductions of French 19th-century *animalier* sculptures). Here you'll find exquisitely made porcelain dogs, animal-shaped salt and pepper sets and bedside lamps.

Antichità Tanca (Map 8; ☎ 06 687 52 72), Salita de' Crescenzi 12, near the Pantheon, has a fascinating atmosphere. In addition to a wide range of antique prints, it has an excellent selection of bronze, silver and chinaware, as well as crystal, jewellery and paintings dating from the 18th century to the turn of the 20th century.

Nardecchia (Map 8; ☎ 06 686 93 18), Piazza Navona 25, is a Roman landmark – although it is perhaps not quite as famous as Bernini's Fontana dei Fiumi just outside. It sells antique prints, including 18th-century engravings of Rome by Giovanni Battista Piranesi, which usually sell for a minimum of €1500. The shop also stocks more inexpensive 19th-century depictions of Rome.

Not far from Campo de' Fiori is Comics Bazar (Map 4; ☎ 06 68 80 29 23), Via dei Banchi Vecchi 127–8, a veritable warehouse of antiques. It's crammed with objects, lamps and furniture dating from the late 19th century to the 1940s, including a large selection of Viennese furniture by Thonet. Lumieres (Map 6; ☎ 06 580 36 14), at Vicolo del Cinque 48, a lane in the heart of Trastevere, has a large collection of lamps, from Art Nouveau and Art Deco to the 1950s.

If you like antique Chinese furniture, head for Yaky (Map 4; ☎ 06 688 07 724, e yakyhome@tin.it) at Via Santa Maria del Pianto 55 in the Ghetto area. It has a range of objects including stunning wooden cabinets and lacquered bowls.

BOOKS
English-Language

The Corner Bookshop (Map 6; ☎ 06 583 69 42), Via del Moro 48 in Trastevere, has an excellent range of English-language books and travel guides. The selection of contemporary novels and nonfiction publications is well chosen, and piles of books cover every spare space of the tiny shop. It opens daily.

The Anglo-American Bookshop (Map 4; ☎ 06 678 96 57) at Via della Vite 102, off Piazza di Spagna, has an excellent range of literature, travel guides, reference books and maps and sells the *Thomas Cook European Timetable* for Italy. There is another branch at Via della Vite 102.

The Economy Book & Video Center (Map 5; ☎ 06 474 68 77) at Via Torino 136, near Stazione Termini, has a good selection of books, as well as second-hand paperbacks. As the name suggests, they also sell and rent videos.

Feltrinelli International (Map 5; ☎ 06 482 78 78) at Via Orlando 84, just off Piazza della Repubblica, has an extensive range of books for adults and children in English, Spanish, French, German and Portuguese, plus lots of guidebooks for Rome, Italy and the rest of the world. Another branch of Feltrinelli is at Largo di Torre Argentina (Map 8; see Italian-Language below).

Italian-Language

Bibli Bookshop (Map 6; ☎ 06 588 40 97), Via dei Fienaroli 28, near Piazza Santa Maria in Trastevere, is a bookshop-cum-cafe-cum Internet cafe, as well as an occasional venue for poetry readings. Open daily until midnight, it's a great place to meet for a chat; the Sunday brunch is also worth checking out. See under Internet Cafes in the Facts for the Visitor chapter.

Mel Bookstore (Map 5; ☎ 06 488 54 05) at Via Nazionale 254–255, near Piazza della Repubblica, is a combination bookshop, music store and coffee shop on three levels. It has a wide selection of literature, fiction, reference books, dictionaries, school books, travel guides and a range of half-price books. It also has some books in English and French. The store opens daily.

Feltrinelli (Map 8; ☎ 06 688 03 248), Largo di Torre Argentina 5a, is a well organised bookshop with a wide range of books on art, photography, cinema and history, as well as an extensive selection of Italian literature and travel guides. The store opens daily. Other Feltrinelli bookshops are at Via del Babuino 39 and Via VE Orlando 84, next to Feltrinelli International.

For something different, there is Franco Maria Ricci (Map 4; ☎ 06 679 34 66), Via

SHOPPING

Borgognona 4d, a small bookshop tucked in between the high-fashion boutiques that sells splendidly produced and illustrated books on art and culture, published by Franco Maria Ricci, as well as the superb glossy *FMR* magazine.

For travellers, Libreria del Viaggiatore (Map 8; ☎ 06 688 01 048), Via del Pellegrino 78, is a real find. This intimate bookshop is devoted to travelling and is crammed with travel guides and travel literature in various languages. It also has a huge range of maps, including hiking maps. Some books are available in English and French.

Other Languages

Herder Buchhandlung (Map 4; ☎ 06 679 46 28), Piazza Montecitorio 117, opposite the Italian parliament building, has German-language books. French-speakers will find a good selection of literature, fiction, non-fiction, general interest and children's books at La Procure (Map 8; ☎ 06 683 07 598), Piazza San Luigi dei Francesi 23. You might like to pop into the church next door to see the paintings by Caravaggio.

Libreria Sorgente (Map 8; ☎ 06 688 06 950), Piazza Navona 90, has a wide range of books and some videos in Spanish. It also stocks some Portuguese-language books.

Feltrinelli International (see the English-Language section earlier) stocks books in a number of languages.

Gay & Lesbian

Libreria Babele (Map 4; ☎ 06 687 66 28) at Via dei Banchi Vecchi 116, parallel to Corso Vittorio Emanuele near the Tiber, is an exclusively gay and lesbian bookshop and has a well stocked English section. The staff are extremely friendly and helpful and it's a good first stop for information about Rome's gay scene, especially as the offices of some of the other organisations are a bit out of the way. Forthcoming gay and lesbian events are listed on the shop's noticeboard. It opens 10 am to 7.30 pm Monday to Saturday. Another gay bookshop is Queer (Map 5; ☎ 06 474 06 91), Via del Boschetto 25, off Via Nazionale, which sells books in

Italian and English as well as videos and gifts. It open 2.30 to 7.30 pm Monday and 9.30 am to 7.30 pm Tuesday to Sunday.

The Libreria delle Donne: Al Tempo Ritrovato (Map 6; ☎ 06 581 77 24), Via dei Fienaroli 31d, in Trastevere, is a women's bookshop with a well stocked lesbian section, including lots of material in English. The shop's notice board is packed with information and details of events.

Children's

The best children's bookshop in Rome is Mel Giannino Stoppani Librerie per Ragazzi (Map 4; ☎ 06 699 41 045), Piazza Santi Apostoli 59–65, which stocks mainly Italian books but has a corner devoted to French, Spanish, German and English books.

The Anglo-American Bookshop (see English-Language) has an excellent kids' selection.

CLOTHING
Designer Wear

Did anyone say 'recession'? For those with a mission, get ready to join the queue for that Prada backpack! Most of the designer-clothing stores, including all of the big names, are located in the area around Piazza di Spagna. Prices are eye-popping; for some more affordable names, see under Diffusion Ranges & Independent Designers.

Following is a list of the main designer stores (Map 4):

Dolce e Gabbana (☎ 06 679 22 94) Piazza di Spagna 82–83
Ermenegildo Zegna (☎ 06 678 91 43) Via Borgognona 7e
Fendi (☎ 06 696 661) Via Borgognona 36–40
Ferre (☎ 06 679 74 45) Via Borgognona 6
Genny (☎ 06 679 60 74) Piazza di Spagna 27
Gianni Versace (for men; ☎ 06 679 50 37) Via Borgognona 24–25; (for women; ☎ 06 678 05 21) Via Bocca di Leone 26
Giorgio Armani Boutique (☎ 06 699 14 60) Via Condotti 77
Gucci (☎ 06 678 93 40) Via Condotti 8
Krizia (☎ 06 679 37 72) Piazza di Spagna 87
Laura Biagiotti (☎ 06 679 12 05) Via Borgognona 43–44
Missoni (☎ 06 679 25 55) Piazza di Spagna 78

Prada (☎ 06 679 08 97) Via Condotti 92–95
Roccobarocco (☎ 06 679 79 14) Via Bocca di
  Leone 65a
Salvatore Ferragamo (for men; ☎ 06 678 11
  30) Via Condotti 66; (for women; ☎ 06 679 15
  65) Via Condotti 73–74
Trussardi (☎ 06 678 02 80) Via Condotti 49–50
Valentino (☎ 06 678 36 56) Via Condotti 13

MaxMara (Map 4; ☎ 06 679 36 38), Via
Frattina 28, is one of Italy's top labels but
its ready-to-wear clothes are somewhat
more affordable. Trademark items include
jackets, trousers, suits and superb winter
coats in luxurious cashmere blends. There
are other branches at Via Condotti 17 and
Via Nazionale 28 (Map 5).

Cenci (Map 8; ☎ 06 699 06 81), Via
Campo Marzio 1–7, stocks an enviable selection of all the top Italian and international
labels for men, women and children and is a
good bet if you prefer classic fashions on the
conservative side (think English country
squire and you get the idea). Etro (Map 4;
☎ 06 678 82 57), Via del Babuino 102, uses
fine printed fabrics including some stunning
paisley prints to create exclusive clothing
and accessories at exclusive prices.

Brioni (Map 5; ☎ 06 485 855), Via Barberini 79–81, is Rome's most elegant tailor.
A creator of costumes for James Bond
films, Brioni also makes classic ready-to-
wear fashions for men and women.

Diffusion Ranges and Independent Designers

Several of the top designers also have
more affordable diffusion ranges aimed at
younger tastes.

The third generation of the Fendi family run Fendissime (Map 4; ☎ 06 696 661,
fax 06 699 40 808), Via della Fontanella
Borghese 56a, which sells clothes and accessories which err on the groovy side of
classic.

Emporio Armani (Map 4; ☎ 06 360 02
197), Via del Babuino 140, is Giorgio Armani's range of ready-to-wear suits and
separates for men and women. Armani
Jeans (☎ 06 360 01 848), diagonally across
the road at Via del Babuino 70a, carries the
Armani jeans and sportswear collection.

King & Queen of Fashion

In the Roman fashion world two names stand
out – Valentino Garavani and Laura Biagiotti.
When Valentino set up his *alta moda* in 1959,
his clientele included Jackie Kennedy, Sophia
Loren and Audrey Hepburn. While his couture collections featuring superb evening
gowns have always been inaccessible to all
but the most wealthy of customers, his ready-
to-wear lines for both men and women, introduced in the 1970s, have become staples
of the fashionable set.

The eternally elegant Laura Biagiotti is
Rome's queen of fashion. Luxurious knitwear,
sumptuous silk separates and lots of white
and cream are her trademarks. Biagiotti is a
generous philanthropist and has funded many
restoration works in Rome. She has even
named a perfume after the city.

ASA ANDERSSON

SHOPPING

SHOPPING

Moschino Jeans (Map 4; ☎ 06 692 00 415), Via Belsiana 53–57, is the diffusion/sportswear range for Moschino.

Valentino (Map 4; ☎ 06 360 01 906), Via del Babuino 61, carries the designer's (slightly) more affordable range, aimed at a younger market than his couture collections. Hipster jeans with embroidered or transparent panels were a big feature at the time of writing.

T'Store (Map 4; ☎ 06 322 60 55), Via del Corso 477–478, is the younger line of Trussardi, and sells jeans, sportswear, chunky knits, jackets, casual trousers and more.

Max & Co (Map 4; ☎ 06 678 79 46), Via Condotti 46, is the youth range of the Max-Mara company; it sells trendy tops and bottoms, coats, leather jackets and accessories.

Baullà (Map 8; ☎ 686 76 70) at Via Baullari 37, between Campo de' Fiori and Piazza Farnese, is a gem of a shop selling good-quality knits, original coats and jackets, skirts, tops, bags, scarves and other accessories.

Angelo di Nepi (Map 4; ☎ 06 322 48 00), Via Cola di Rienzo 267a, has well made skirts, trousers, tops and scarves in stunning fabrics, including bright Indian silks, often embroidered.

Lei (Map 8; ☎ 06 687 54 32) at Via dei Giubbonari 103, near Campo de' Fiori, is the place to go for a pretty dress or an elegant party outfit. Most of the stock is by French designers, although they do have some Italian names.

Wildlife Watching

While you shop, look out for a distinctive breed of Roman – the shop assistant. These curious creatures are imperious, grumpy and rude; they spend hours chatting to colleagues or talking on the phone and have developed the highly skilled art of ignoring customers. Scientists believe that the role of the shop assistant was originally to help shoppers part with their money but in Rome creatures exhibiting these behavioural traits are now virtually extinct.

Mid-Range Boutiques

If designer price tags don't match your budget, head for the shops on Via del Corso, Via Nazionale or, for something a little more original, Via dei Giubbonari (near Campo de' Fiori).

United Colors of Benetton (Map 4; ☎ 06 699 24 010) at Via Cesare Battisti 129, near Piazza Venezia, is as popular as ever for its staples such as wool and wool-mix jumpers in a kaleidoscope of colours, T-shirts, shirts, trousers and jackets at accessible prices. There are several other locations throughout the centre, including the newest and largest store (Map 2; ☎ Via Cola di Rienzo).

Stefanel (Map 4; ☎ 06 679 26 67), Via Frattina 31–32, and Sisley (Map 4; ☎ 06 699 41 787), Via Frattina 19a, are two other mid-range options for reasonably priced casual gear.

Ethic (Map 8; ☎ 06 683 01 063) at Piazza Cairoli 11–12, off Via dei Giubbonari, describes itself as a multiconcept store. It has hip decor to match the groovy clothing it sells (fake-fur trimmed coats, jackets and separates in daring fabrics and finishes) and is extremely popular with young *romane*.

Onyx (Map 4; ☎ 06 360 06 073), Via Cola di Rienzo 225–229, is a good-value shop popular with the hip young things who buy gold lamé shirts, leather jackets and furry handbags.

Lingerie

Brighenti (Map 4; ☎ 06 679 14 84), Via Frattina 7–10, is a favourite of Italian actors and TV personalities for its lingerie and swimming costumes. La Perla (Map 4; ☎ 06 69 94 19 33), Via Condotti 78, is Italy's most famous lingerie range. It's all luxurious, from the lace-trimmed silk bras to the delicious negligées with matching dressing gowns and stiletto-heeled house slippers. Guaranteed to make you feel a million dollars and cost you about half that amount!

Fogal (Map 4; ☎ 06 678 45 66), Via Condotti 55, is a good choice for fancy lingerie and a large variety of highly desirable and very expensive stockings and socks. Schostal (Map 4; ☎ 06 679 12 40), Via del Corso 158, has been selling lavish underwear and lingerie from this elegant shop since 1870. The shop also stocks knitwear and shirts. Tebro (Map 4; ☎ 06 687 34 41), Via dei Prefetti 46–54, is well stocked with underwear and nightwear for men, women and children. It also carries bed and table linen, bath towels and the like.

Second-Hand Clothing

Via del Governo Vecchio is the main street for second-hand clothing outlets. However, you'll pick up better bargains at markets such as Porta Portese and Via Sannio (see Markets later in the chapter).

Distanés (Map 8; ☎ 06 683 33 63), Via della Chiesa Nuova 17, specialises in remainders, second-hand clothes and accessories from the 1960s and '70s. In spring and autumn, apart from normal shop hours, it also opens 10.30 pm to midnight. Around the corner at Via del Governo Vecchio 45 is the trendy Vestiti Usati Cinzia (Map 8), one of Rome's most popular second-hand stores selling pre-loved clothes and a good place to snap up a bargain leather jacket or vintage skirt. Omero e Cecilia (Map 8; ☎ 06 683 35 06), Via del Governo Vecchio 68, is a bit of a Roman institution and specialises in second-hand military wear.

In Monti is Le Gallinelle (Map 5; ☎ 06 488 10 17), Via del Boschetto 76, a former butcher's shop where the meat hooks now hold up good-quality second-hand clothes, as well as interesting clothing created with vintage fabrics.

Children's Clothes

PréNatal (Map 5; ☎ 06 488 14 03), Via Nazionale 45, is one of a number of children's clothing chain stores in Italy. It has its own range of affordable, good-quality clothing for kids aged up to 11 years, as well as for expecting mothers. It also stocks equipment such as prams and pushchairs.

There is a good range of kids' casual wear, as well as a children's hairdresser, on the second floor of United Colors of Benetton (Map 4; ☎ 06 699 24 010), Via Cesare Battisti 129. An added bonus is the view of Piazza Venezia. Among the many other Benetton outlets in Rome is Zerododici of

Benetton (Map 4; ☎ 06 688 09 381), Via Tomacelli 137, which stocks clothing exclusively for children aged 12 and under.

Heading up the price ladder is La Cicogna (Map 4; ☎ 06 678 69 77), Via Frattina 138, which sells a selection of fashionable children's clothes by top designers. It also has its own label. If you're looking for something really special, try Sotto una Foglia di Cavolo (Map 2; ☎ 06 360 02 960), Via del Vantaggio 25. This small shop is crammed with classic and unusual clothing from Italy, France and the Netherlands for babies and children aged up to eight. Nearby but not quite as pricey is Chicco (Map 4; ☎ 06 679 36 66), Via Frattina 146–147, which sells good-quality kids' clothes and toys.

Leri (Map 4; ☎ 06 678 45 16), Via del Corso 344, also stocks classic and sporty gear for sophisticated babies and children with lots of cash.

Department stores are also top places to track down children's wear (see that section later in the chapter).

COSMETICS

The top European brands are widely available in shops called *profumerie* (perfumeries), as well as in department stores. The following outlets have been suggested because they offer something a bit different.

Materozzoli (Map 4; ☎ 06 688 92 686), Piazza San Lorenzo in Lucina 5, is a charming *profumeria* that has become a Roman landmark. It stocks a selection of rare perfumes, particularly from France and England, as well as cosmetics and exquisite beauty accessories. Casamaria (Map 8; ☎ 06 683 30 74), Via della Scrofa 71, is roomy and well stocked with leading cosmetic brands at good prices.

Officina Profumo Farmaceutica di Santa Maria Novella (Map 8; ☎ 06 687 96 08, fax 06 687 9472), Corso del Rinascimento 47, has various scents and unusual cosmetic products based on the original recipes handed down by the Dominican monks of Santa Maria Novella in Florence. Some of the potions and lotions have their origins in the 17th century. Ai Monasteri (Map 8; ☎ 06 688 02 783), Corso del Rinascimento 72, is equally historic. The impressive wood-panelled shop sells herbal essences, spirits, soaps, balms, deodorants, antiwrinkle creams, bubble-bath and various liqueurs. Everything is made by monks in abbeys around Italy.

The trendy and successful international make-up brand MAC (Map 4; ☎ 06 679 21 65) now has a presence in Rome at Via del Babuino 124.

DEPARTMENT STORES

Depending on your point of view, it could be either a good or a bad thing that Romans have begun to embrace the concept of one-stop shopping. Department stores and *centri commerciali* (large shopping centres) are popping up all over the place, although most are on the outskirts of the city. All of the following are open daily and don't close for lunch:

Auchan (Map 1; ☎ 06 432 071) Via Alberto Pollio 50, between Via Tiburtina and Via Prenestina. A *centro commerciale* with 60 shops and a hypermarket. Take Metro Linea B to Tiburtina, from there it's a 20-minute walk (follow the signs).

Cinecittà Due (☎ 06 722 09 10) Via P Togliatti 2 on the corner of Via Tuscolana, near the famous Cinecittà film studios. More than 100 shops, a supermarket and a COIN department store. Take Metro Linea A to Cinecittà.

COIN (Map 7; ☎ 06 708 00 91) Piazzale Appio 7; (Map 2; ☎ 06 36 00 42 98) Via di Cola di Rienzo 173. Good-quality clothing and accessories, cosmetics, children's clothes and a good range of homeware.

I Granai (☎ 06 519 55 890) Via Mario Rigamonti 100 in EUR. Spoilt for choice with 130 shops and a hypermarket.

La Rinascente (Map 4; ☎ 06 679 76 91) Via del Corso. A good range of reasonable quality clothing and accessories, and big-name cosmetics. The Piazza Fiume (Map 3) store also stocks homeware. It opens 9 am to 9 pm Monday to Saturday and 10.30 am to 8 pm on Sunday.

MAS (Map 5; ☎ 06 446 80 78) Via dello Statuto 11. Dirt-cheap goods, from kitchenware to leather jackets and sports shoes, with occasional bargains.

UPIM (Map 5; ☎ 06 678 33 36) Via del Tritone 172 and Via Nazionale 211. Budget store selling clothing and household goods. The quality of stock can be patchy.

GIFTS

If you're looking for something different, you are likely to find it at Amati & Amati (Map 8; ☎ 06 686 43 19), Via dei Pianellari 21, which stocks unusual imported objects and homeware, small pieces of furniture from Morocco, as well as clothing, original jewellery and funky accessories.

Stilo Fetti (Map 8; ☎ 06 678 96 62) at Via degli Orfani 82, near the Pantheon, has a wide selection of antique and new fountain and ballpoint pens, as well as writing desk sets and diaries.

La Chiave (Map 8; ☎ 06 683 08 848), Largo delle Stimmate 28, stocks reasonably priced imported handicrafts, including textiles, rugs, bric-a-brac and some furniture. If you're looking for something special, try the gift shop inside the Palazzo delle Esposizioni (Map 5; ☎ 06 482 80 01), one of Rome's main exhibitions spaces. The shop is accessible from the building's side entrance at Via Milano 9a and has a range of unusual design objects, gadgets and homeware. There's also a bookshop that specialises in art, design and photography books.

Single (Map 5; ☎ 06 679 07 13), Via Francesco Crispi 47, near Via Sistina, has a good selection of designer objects, including unusual watches, Alessi kitchenware and expensive fountain pens. Guaytamelli (Map 6; ☎ 06 588 07 04) at Via del Moro 59, in Trastevere, is a workshop and retail outlet selling hand-crafted compasses, hourglasses, and sundials, based on 16th- to 18th-century designs.

An excellent place to find special gifts is Pandora (Map 6; ☎ 06 581 71 45), Piazza Santa Maria in Trastevere. Here you'll find unusual costume jewellery from around the world but, in particular, gorgeous necklaces made from Murano glass. The shop also sells ceramics, some glassware, photo frames and scarves.

Also in Trastevere and selling stunning hand-printed paper objects – such as storage boxes, photo albums and diaries – is Officina della Carta (Map 4; ☎ 06 589 55 57), Via Benedetta 26b, just off Piazza Trilussa. It's a tiny hole-in-the-wall place but produces superb merchandise and can make to order with enough notice. Near the Pantheon there are another couple of similar stores, including Daniela Rosati (Map 8; ☎ 06 68 80 20 53) at Via della Stelletta 27.

HOMEWARE

De Sanctis (Map 8; ☎ 06 688 06 810), Piazza Navona 82–84, has a good selection of Alessi products (including replacement parts) and other designer kitchenware and tableware. Their Italian ceramics, including the colourful work of the Sicilian ceramicist De Simone, are particularly interesting.

Just around the corner from the Trevi Fountain is Il Tucano (Map 4; ☎ 06 679 75 47), Piazza dei Crociferi 10, where you can pick up anything from home furnishings and haberdashery to kid's toys. Everything is displayed in the shop windows and the staff retrieve your selection from the storeroom. It opens daily; credit cards are not accepted.

Home (Map 8; ☎ 06 686 84 50), Largo di Torre Argentina 8, is a good place to find bargain-priced homeware, including kitchen utensils, candles, glassware, haberdashery and vibrant crockery. It also sells upmarket goods such as rustic antique-repro furniture and oriental rugs.

Leone Limentani (Map 4; ☎ 06 688 06 686), in the basement at Via Portico d'Ottavia 47, is a warehouse-style shop with an unbelievable choice of kitchenware and tableware. Here you'll find high-priced porcelain and fine crystal alongside bargain items. It also stocks plenty of Alessi and a good selection of quality pots and pans.

Near Piazza di Spagna is C.U.C.I.N.A. (Map 4; ☎ 06 679 12 75), Via del Babuino 118a, an underground open space specialising in kitchenware. It has a large selection of stainless-steel items. Don't be put off by the store's not-so-helpful staff.

Stockmarket (Map 4; ☎ 06 686 42 38), Via dei Banchi Vecchi 51, has a huge range of seconds and end-of-series homeware and furnishings at affordable prices. Ecole De (Map 4; ☎ 06 689 2015), Vicolo della Moretta 10–11, is similar but slightly more frivolous. Gifts and eclectic homeware are its business, with everything from buttons to blow-up chairs, all with a strong dose of kitsch.

In the characteristic Monti area is Io Sono un Autarchico (Map 5; ☎ 06 228 66 48), Via del Boschetto 92, a tiny shop full of interesting homeware. The shop's high turnover means that its stock changes continually.

Shops have been selling *passamanerie* (lengths of ribbon, braided cord and colourful tassels used as trimmings for furnishings) in Rome for centuries. Passamanerie Crocianelli (Map 8; ☎ 06 687 35 92), Via dei Prefetti 37–40, has bundles of fringes and cords piled from floor to ceiling.

One of Rome's premier homeware stores is Spazio Sette (Map 8; ☎ 06 688 04 261), Via dei Barbieri 7, just off Largo di Torre Argentina. If you can manage to tear your attention away from the frescoed ceiling at the entrance, you will find three levels of quality designer furniture, kitchenware, tableware and gifts.

Alternatively, you might prefer to spend a small fortune on what might best be described as weirdly stylish furnishings and fabulous fabrics, by some of Italy and Europe's top avant-garde designers, at Contemporanea (Map 4; ☎ 06 688 04 533), Via dei Banchi Vecchi 143. At Tad (Map 2; ☎ 06 360 01 679), Via di S Giacomo 5, you'll find trendy ethnic-style furniture, screens, vases, textiles and linens.

For a reproduction Roman bust, mosaic or an obelisk for the mantelpiece try Maurizio Grossi (Map 2; ☎ 06 360 01 935), Via Margutta 109. His marble objects for interior decoration are cleverly deceptive: the huge bowls of what looks like ripe figs and apricots are in fact heavy sculpted marble, hand painted to resemble fruit.

There are two shops selling top-brand modern lighting near Piazza di Spagna. Artemide (Map 2; ☎ 06 360 01 802), Via Margutta 107, sells lamps and light fittings by Italian and international designers. Flos Arteluce (Map 4; ☎ 06 320 76 31), Via del Babuino 84–85, is like a gallery of lighting fixtures. The 'exhibits' are minimalist, in chrome, steel and simple shades such as black and white.

SHOPPING

JEWELLERY

Bulgari (Map 4; ☎ 06 679 38 76), Via Condotti 10, is Italy's most prestigious and famous jeweller. If you're just window shopping, you can admire the precious and unique pieces of jewellery displayed as though they were in a museum.

Siragusa (Map 4; ☎ 06 679 70 85), Via delle Carrozze 64, creates exceptionally beautiful and unusual jewellery by setting antique coins and gems in gold.

Nicla Boncompagni (Map 4; ☎ 06 678 32 39), Via del Babuino 115, has a charming collection of very expensive vintage jewellery dating from the mid-19th century to the 1960s (including pieces by Van Cleef & Arpels and Cartier) and American jewellery from the 1940s and '50s.

Tempi Moderni (Map 8; ☎ 06 687 70 07), Via del Governo Vecchio 108, stocks a large selection of vintage costume jewellery dating from 1880 to 1970, with an emphasis on pieces from the Art Nouveau and Art Deco periods. Pieces include 19th-century resin brooches, Bakelite from the 1920s and '30s and costume jewellery created by couturiers such as Chanel, Dior and Balenciaga in the '50s and '60s.

Not far from the Colosseum is Fabio Piccioni (Map 5; ☎ 06 474 16 97), Via del Boschetto 148, an artisan who recycles old trinkets to create exquisite handcrafted jewellery (credit cards not accepted).

Hausmann & Co watchmakers (Map 4; ☎ 06 687 15 01), Via del Corso 406, was founded in 1794 and still makes a limited number of its own watches. The shop also stocks a selection of top international brands.

To make your own jewellery using gorgeous coloured crystals and beads, head for Pollicina (Map 4; ☎ 06 322 41 32) at Via Margutta 61c.

MARKETS

Rome's biggest and best-known flea market is Porta Portese (Map 6). It is held every Sunday until around 1 pm in the area extending south from the Porta Portese, an ancient Roman gate on the River Tiber, to Piazza Ippolito Nievo, in the streets parallel to Viale Trastevere. There's a mish-mash of new and old, with everything on sale (including the kitchen sink) from bags to bikes, clothes to furniture. The market has all manner of incredible deals but if you don't bargain, it's boring! Watch out for pickpockets.

There is a covered market selling new and second-hand clothing and shoes in Via Sannio (Map 7), near Porta San Giovanni and the Basilica di San Giovanni in Laterano. It opens 8 am to 1 pm daily (except Sunday). If you're looking for leather jackets or second-hand cashmere at bargain prices, this is your place.

The Ponte Milvio market (Map 1) specialises in antiques and bric-a-brac and is held on the Lungotevere Capoprati, which extends along the Tiber from the Ponte Milvio to the Ponte Duca d'Aosta. It opens 9 am to sunset and takes place on the first Sunday of the month (closed in August).

Underground (Map 5; ☎ 06 36 00 53 45), held in the Ludovisi underground car park at Via Francesco Crispi 96 between Via Sistina and Via Veneto, is a haven for antiques and collectibles. It's held on the second weekend of the month (3 to 8 pm Saturday and 10.30 am to 7.30 pm Sunday). It is closed July and August.

The Borgo Parioli market (Map 3; ☎ 06 855 27 73), Via Tirso 14 off Via Salaria near Piazza Buenos Aires, specialises in original mint-condition jewellery and accessories from the 1950s onwards including brooches, cigarette cases and watches (not at bargain prices). Silverware, paintings, antique lamps and old gramophones are also on sale. It is held the first three weekends of the month (9 am to 8 pm Saturday and Sunday).

For antique prints and an array of second-hand books, head for the Mercato delle Stampe at Largo della Fontanella di Borghese (Map 4). It's held 8 am to sunset daily (except Sunday).

For food markets, see boxed text 'To Market, to Market' in the Places to Eat chapter.

MUSIC

Ricordi Media Store (Map 4; ☎ 06 679 80 22), Via Cesare Battisti 120d, is one of

Rome's biggest music stores. Open daily, it's well stocked with all sorts of music, music videos and original-language films. In the shop next door there's a large selection of classical music, musical instruments, musical scores and music books. Ricordi also has outlets in Via del Corso, Viale Giulio Cesare and Piazza Indipendenza.

Rinascita (Map 4; ☎ 06 699 22 436), Via delle Botteghe Oscure 5, specialises in world and contemporary music and the latest trends. It opens daily.

Disfunzioni Musicali (Map 5; ☎ 06 446 19 84), Via degli Etruschi 4–14, is in the heart of Rome's university area and opens daily. It specialises in alternative, noncommercial music, rare vinyl and bootlegs. There is a second-hand record and CD shop nearby at Via dei Marrucini 1, which sells everything from opera to rock, international to Italian artists.

L'Allegretto (Map 2; ☎ 06 320 82 24), Via Oslavia 44, is off the beaten track in Prati but it's worth seeking out for a smashing selection of opera and classical music.

Caro Vinile...Caro Cinema (Map 8; ☎ 06 687 40 05), Piazza del Paradiso 42 near Campo de' Fiori, is more than a music shop – it's a collector's paradise. There are rare discs from the 1960s, a special section of Beatles memorabilia and film posters and photos. It opens 4 to 7.30 pm daily.

SHOES & LEATHER GOODS
For shoes and leather goods by the top fashion designers see Designer Wear earlier in the chapter.

Mandarina Duck (Map 4; ☎ 06 69 94 03 20), at Via di Propaganda 1, just off Piazza di Spagna, makes popular, trendy handbags, wallets and luggage in leather, rubber and the latest nylon fabrics. Furla (Map 4; ☎ 06 692 00 363), at Piazza di Spagna 22, right next to the Spanish Steps, is another well known brand of first-rate leather bags and accessories, including wallets, belts, sunglasses, watches and costume jewellery. There are various other outlets including those at Via del Corso 481 and Via Tomacelli 136. More original designs at less-expensive prices can be found at Francesco

Biasia (Map 8; ☎ 06 686 50 98), Via di Torre Argentina 7, which sells classic soft-leather wallets, handbags in patent leather, pony skin, leopard skin and fake fur, and accessories such as luggage and fun umbrellas. There is another store at Via Due Macelli 62, near Piazza di Spagna.

Sergio Rossi (Map 4; ☎ 06 678 32 45) has a showroom at Piazza di Spagna 97–100 displaying glamorous day and evening shoes created by this top Italian designer. Fratelli Rossetti (Map 4; ☎ 06 678 26 76), Via Borgognona 5a, is another outlet for classy shoes, bags and leather jackets. Fausto Santini (Map 4; ☎ 06 678 41 14), Via Frattina 120, is famous for his quixotic and truly original shoes, boots and bags. There is another outlet at Via Cavour 106 (Map 5; ☎ 06 488 09 34), near the Basilica di Santa Maria Maggiore, where you can pick up remainders from past (and some current) collections at half-price. There are lots of bargains though it's sometimes hard to find the size you're after.

De Bach (Map 4; ☎ 06 678 33 84), Via del Babuino 123, has stylish women's shoes. One of the better-known Italian shoe-makers is Bruno Magli (Map 5; ☎ 06 488 43 55) at Via Vittorio Veneto 70a. Magli also has outlets in Via del Gambero and at Leonardo da Vinci airport. Raphael Salato (Map 3; ☎ 06 481 76 41), Via Vittorio Veneto 149, stocks a large selection of Italian and foreign-brand shoes, bags and leather clothing, in addition to its own label shoes and leather goods.

For classic, costly but very well made leather loafers try Tod's (Map 4; ☎ 06 678 68 28), Via Borgognona 45. Another shop that sells lots of Tod's products (sometimes at better prices) is Red & Blue (Map 4; ☎ 06 678 07 50) at Via Due Macelli 67, near Piazza di Spagna.

Loco (Map 8; ☎ 06 688 08 216) at Via dei Baullari 22, just off Campo de' Fiori, is a good spot for trendy ladies and gents shoes. Nearby Borini (Map 8; ☎ 06 687 56 70), Via dei Pettinari 86–87, was originally a shoe repair shop but is now crowded with girls looking for fancy footwear at affordable prices.

Couture for Clerics

Whether you're after papal party gear, nun's knickers, incense burners or a life-size painted wooden statue of the Virgin Mary, the streets around Via dei Cestari and Via di Santa Chiara (near the Pantheon) are where you'll find it.

Anniable Gamarelli is the pope's official tailor and is responsible for providing the new pope with a set of clothes long before anyone knows who it will be. So they make three different sizes – tall and thin, short and fat, and average – and hope that one fits.

Close to the Vatican Museums you'll find Grandi Firme (Map 4; ☎ 06 397 23 169), Via Germanico 8, an unassuming outlet where you can stock up on designer bags, luggage, ties, belts, scarves, umbrellas, shoes and similar items at lower warehouse prices.

TOYS

If the kids need a rest from sightseeing, giving them a few hours in a toy shop is not such a bad idea. First choice (although perhaps only for browsing unless you have deep pockets) should be Al Sogno (Map 8; ☎ 06 686 41 98), Piazza Navona 53. Its first floor is a wonderland of expensive dolls and stuffed animals of every shape and size.

On the opposite side of the square is Bertè (Map 8; ☎ 06 687 50 11), selling beautifully made wooden dolls and puppets, finely crafted scooters in wood and metal and high-quality educational games.

Rome's finest toy shop is Città del Sole (Map 8; ☎ 06 688 03 805), Via della Scrofa 65, which stocks only the very best-quality educational and creative toys.

Excursions

Rome demands so much of your time and concentration that most tourists forget that the city is part of the Lazio region. Declared a *regione* in 1934, the Lazio area (Latium) has, since ancient Roman times, been an extension of Rome.

Through the ages, the rich built their villas in the Lazio countryside and many towns developed as the fiefs of noble Roman families, such as the Orsini, Barberini and Farnese. Even today, Romans build their weekend and holiday homes in the picturesque areas of the region (the pope, for instance, has his summer residence at Castel Gandolfo, in the Colli Albani south of Rome) and Romans continue to migrate from their sometimes chaotic and polluted city to live in the green space farther afield. This means the region is relatively well served by public transport, and tourists can take advantage of this to visit places of interest.

Although major tourist destinations do not abound in Lazio, it does offer some worthwhile day trips from the city. A tour of Etruria, the ancient land of the Etruscans, which extended into northern Lazio, is highly recommended. Visits to the tombs and museums at Cerveteri and Tarquinia provide a fascinating insight into Etruscan civilisation. The ruins of Villa Adriana (Hadrian's Villa), near Tivoli, and of the ancient-Roman port at Ostia Antica, are both easily accessible from Rome, as is the medieval town of Viterbo to the north.

In summer, tired and overheated tourists can head for the lakes north of Rome, including Bracciano, Bolsena and Vico, which are preferable to the polluted beaches near the city, or head south of Rome to the relatively clean, sandy beaches of Sabaudia or Sperlonga.

There are some hill-top towns, not far from Rome, which are worth visiting including: Anagni, about 67km east of the city and known for the remarkable frescoes in its Romanesque cathedral; Alatri, about

80km south of Rome; and the Castelli Romani in the hills just past Rome's outskirts.

Rome is also a suitable base for excursions to places outside Lazio. Day-trips to major tourist destinations such as Florence and Naples or the ancient city of Pompeii are easy by train. To the east, the mountains and the Parco Nazionale di Abruzzo, one of the oldest national parks in Italy, provide an ideal escape from the noise and the crowds in an area renowned for its breathtaking scenery and fauna.

When you are making plans bear in mind that in Italy buses and trains stop running early in the evenings, and that services are limited on Sunday and public holidays. For up-to-date timetable information call CO-TRAL (Linee Laziali)/Ferrovia dello Stato (FS; State Railway) toll-free on ☎ 800 43 17 84; the number responds in Italian and you need to press 1 to be connected with an operator (some of whom speak basic English). For details on BIT and BIRG tickets see the Getting Around chapter. If you have your own transport, try to avoid day trips out of Rome at the weekend, particularly during summer, when you will find that the whole of Lazio is on the move. On your return on Sunday evening you are likely to find yourself in traffic jams extending for many kilometres, even on the autostrada.

OSTIA ANTICA

Founded by the Romans at the mouth of the River Tiber in the 4th century BC and functioning as Rome's main port for 600 years, Ostia Antica gives a very fascinating insight into contemporary life in a working ancient-Roman town.

Populated by Roman and foreign merchants, sailors and slaves, it became a strategically important centre of defence and trade, and the ruins of the city provide an interesting contrast to the ruins of the ancient city at Pompeii, which was a resort town for the rich upper classes. The cultural, religious and ethnic diversity of Ostia Antica's

EXCURSIONS

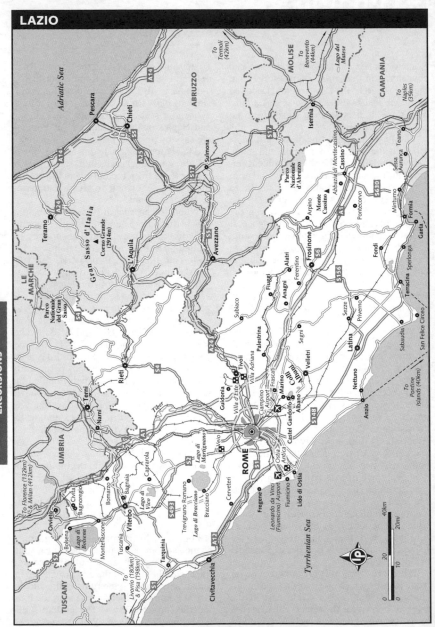

LAZIO

euro currency converter L10,000 = €5.16

inhabitants is attested to in the sanctuaries, temples and shrines dedicated to different deities, and the scope of their activity can be seen in the range of clearly discernible buildings: restaurants, laundries, bakeries, shops, residential properties and meeting places.

Barbarian invasions and the outbreak of malaria led to the city's eventual abandonment and it slowly became buried under river silt, up to 2nd-floor level, which explains the remains' excellent state of preservation. Pope Gregory IV re-established the town in the 9th century. The walls of this borgo (walled village) are still standing, although the town has spread beyond them. It is interesting to visit the borgo and 15th-century castle, which are opposite the entrance to the Roman Ostia Antica ruins.

You need to give yourself several hours to really *do* Ostia Antica. Go early on a sunny weekday to experience the ruins and their leafy park-like setting at their most enchanting. The significant ruins are marked but it is well worth leaving the beaten track and exploring the ruins at random.

Information about the town and ruins is available at the APT office in Rome (see Tourist Offices in the Facts for the Visitor chapter).

Things to See & Do

The ruins are a five-minute walk from the train station and located along the **Decumanus Maximus**, Ostia Antica's main thoroughfare, over 1km long and leading to the sea. Entrance to the city is through the **Porta Romana** to the east, built in the 1st century BC. The **Porta Marina** at the other end of the road marks the exit to the old seafront. The area outside the gate bears evidence of use as an ancient cemetery and then later as a residential area during the Empire.

Of particular note in the area around the Porta Romana are the 2nd-century **Terme di Nettuno** (Baths of Neptune) on the right just after entering the city. Take a look at the large gymnasium and the black-and-white mosaic depicting Neptune and Amphitrite. Next to the baths is a **Roman theatre**, built by Agrippa during the Augustan era and

then enlarged under the Severi. Holding up to 3000 people, it was restored in 1927 and is now used for staging classical performances. Behind the theatre is **Piazzale delle Corporazioni**, the location of the offices of Ostia's merchant guilds, displaying mosaics depicting their different interests.

Returning to the Decumanus Maximus, you come to Via dei Molini containing a large **bakery** dating from the 2nd century, one of several establishments which produced bread for Ostia and Rome. Every stage of production took place here, from the grinding of the corn in the mills made of volcanic stone to the sale of the finished item over the shop counters at the front.

Round the corner in Via di Diana is the perfectly preserved **Casa di Diana**, consisting of three floors, accessible through a central courtyard. It was the ancient-Roman answer to high-density housing, built in the 2nd century when space was at a premium.

Opposite Casa di Diana (across the street) is the **Thermopolium**, a sort of bar with sinks for washing dishes, an adjacent kitchen and courtyard seating. Of interest too are the **forum**, built in the 1st century and then partly demolished in the following century to make way for the existing structures. These include the raised Capitolium (the city's most important temple), the Tempio di Roma e Augusto, with its statue of Roma Virtrix (Rome the Conqueror), and the Tempio Rotondo. Follow the Vico del Pino and Via del Tempio Rotondo to the Cardo Maximus (a wide street lined with arcaded shops) to reach the **Domus Fortuna Annonaria**, the heavily decorated home of one of Ostia's better-off citizens.

Retrace your steps and you get to the Bivio di Castrum and Via della Foce, which leads to the mouth of the River Tiber and pre-dates the foundation of Ostia. Immediately on the right is the sacred area of the Republican temples, the most important of which is dedicated to Hercules Invictus (Hercules the Unconquered).

Cut through the **Terme dei Sette Sapienti** to reach the Cardo degli Aurighi, and then the continuation of the Decumanus Maximus. On the left towards the Bivio is the

Basilica Cristiana, built in the late 4th century and the largest Christian building within the city walls.

The **Ostiense Museum**, housing statues, mosaics and wall paintings found at the site, is at the end of Via dei Dipinti, behind the Casa di Diana.

Near the excavations is the medieval fortified borgo of Ostia Antica, dominated by an imposing, moated castle built between 1483 and 1486 for the future Julius II, from whom it takes its name. The castle opens 9 am to 1 pm Tuesday to Sunday (also open 2.30 to 4.30 pm Tuesday and Thursday). Only groups of 30 people can enter at a time. To get to the town from the excavations go straight on until you get to a main road. Here turn left and follow the road to the right until you get to the town centre.

The excavations (☎ 06 563 58 099) open 9 am to 5 pm (6 or 7 pm in summer) Tuesday to Sunday. Admission to the excavations and archaeological museum costs €4.13. There's a self-service restaurant with hot and cold snacks but picnicking in the ruins is also recommended.

Getting There & Away

Trains leave Rome' Stazione Ostiense (Porta San Paolo) approximately every 30 minutes (more frequently at peak times). Take Metro Linea B to Piramide and follow signs for the Ferroviere Roma-Lido di Ostia. Ostia Antica is seven stops away. The journey takes about 25 minutes and is covered by a standard BIT ticket (see the Getting Around chapter). The ruins, 25km from Rome, are also an easy ride by car. Take the Via del Mare (S8) or the parallel Via Ostiense. There is a car park at the entrance to the site, where you pay a flat fee of €2.07.

TIVOLI

Tivoli, known to the ancient Romans as Tibur, nestles on the lower slopes of the Sabine Hills by the River Aniene, around 30km east of Rome. By the 1st century BC it had become a holiday resort for Roman aristocrats who were attracted by the town's clean air and its beautiful situation among olive groves overlooking the Roman Cam-

pagna, the countryside surrounding Rome that stretches from the Tyrrhenian Sea to the mountains, some 50km inland. The poets Catullus and Horace had villas in or near Tivoli, as did Cassius (one of Julius Caesar's assassins) and the emperors Trajan and Hadrian.

During the Middle Ages, Tivoli was frequently overrun by invaders who used the town as a base from which to attack Rome. During the Renaissance the town became once again a summer playground for the moneyed classes and wealthy cardinals.

The town has long been famous for its travertine marble and the quarries, which line the road from Rome, testify to the continuing flourishing trade. Easily reached by car or public transport, Tivoli is one of the most popular day trips from Rome. It can get quite crowded in summer and the traffic on the approaching road can be very heavy.

Orientation & Information

Buses stop in Piazzale Nazioni Uniti, opposite Largo Garibaldi in the town centre, and continue on to the terminus (☎ 07 743 35 096) in Piazza Massimo, near Villa Gregoriana park. The train station is in Viale Mazzini, about 800m east of Largo Garibaldi on the far side of the River Aniene, and 400m south-east of Largo Sant'Angelo.

The IAT tourist office (☎ 07 743 11 249), Largo Garibaldi, opens 8.30 am to 2.30 pm Tuesday to Saturday (also open 3 to 6 pm Tuesday and Thursday). It provides a useful information leaflet containing a street map indicating Tivoli's main sites and can supply a list of accommodation options in and around the town.

Town Centre

Tivoli is dominated by **Castello Rocca Pia**, an imposing castle built by Pope Pius II in the 1460s to remind the inhabitants who was in charge. The town had a long history of struggles with Rome, once even defeating its neighbour and capturing a pope. The ruins of an ancient-Roman amphitheatre, over which the castle was built, can still be seen. After 1870, the Rocca Pia was a prison and it now houses temporary exhibitions.

Most visitors head straight for the Villa d'Este, next to the Chiesa di Santa Maria Maggiore in Piazza Trento. However, the labyrinthine streets of the rest of the town are definitely worth seeing.

Just north of Villa d'Este, on the narrow and steep Via del Colle, you'll find the 12th-century Romanesque **Chiesa di San Silvestro**. Some interesting early-medieval frescoes representing the legend of Constantine decorate the triumphal arch and the apse.

At the north-eastern end of the town, two Roman temples built during the Republican era share the most picturesque location in Tivoli on the edge of a ravine overlooking a deep valley. The circular **Tempio di Vesta**, dating from the 1st century BC, was converted into a church in the Middle Ages. Next to it is the rectangular **Tempio della Sibilla** built in the 2nd century BC. The temples are now incorporated into the gardens of a restaurant. Ask with a smile and the proprietors might let you in for a closer look.

A better view of the temples can be had from the wooded park of **Villa Gregoriana** below (enter from Largo Sant'Angelo). The waterfalls and gardens of Villa Gregoriana were created when Pope Gregory XVI diverted the flow of the River Aniene to put an end to the periodic flooding in the area. There are two main waterfalls – the smaller one at the neck of the gorge was designed by Bernini. Shady paths surrounded by lush vegetation wind down to various viewpoints over the waterfalls. The park also contains the remains of a Roman villa and there's a picnic area where ancient column capitals double as stools. Villa Gregoriana opens 9 am to one hour before sunset daily. Admission costs €4.13.

Villa d'Este

There's a sense of faded splendour about the Renaissance pleasure palace created in 1550 by Cardinal Ippolito d'Este, the son of Lucrezia Borgia and grandson of Borgia pope Alexander VI. Originally a Benedictine convent, the site was transformed by Ippolito d'Este into a sumptuous villa with a breathtaking formal garden full of elaborate fountains and pools.

Some of the remaining mannerist frescoes in the villa have recently been restored and deserve a quick look, but the residence is totally upstaged by the gardens. These are an almost entirely symmetrical series of terraces, shady pathways and spectacular fountains, powered solely by gravitational force; one fountain once played the organ and another imitated the call of birds.

Not all of the fountains are functional today but the visitor can still get a sense of the fantastic creation that the garden once was. There are delightful features such as the long terrace of grotesque heads, all spouting water, and the Rometta fountain (on the far left going down the terraces), which features reproductions of Rome's major buildings. From 1865 to 1886, the villa was home to Franz Liszt and inspired his composition *Fountains of the Villa d'Este*.

Villa d'Este opens 9 am to 7.30 pm Tuesday to Sunday (April to September) and 9 am to 5.30 pm (October to March). It also opens on Monday afternoons. Admission costs €4.13.

Villa Adriana

Constructed between AD 118 and 134, Villa Adriana was one of the largest and most sumptuous villas in the Roman Empire. It was the country palace of Hadrian and was later used by other emperors. After the fall of the Empire, it was plundered by barbarians and Romans alike for building materials. Many of its original decorations were used to embellish the Villa d'Este.

A model near the entrance gives you some idea of the scale of the complex. The site is enormous and you'll need several hours to see it properly.

Hadrian travelled widely and was a keen architect; parts of the villa were inspired by buildings he had seen around the world. The massive Pecile, through which you enter, was a reproduction of a building in Athens. The Canopo, on the far side of the site, is a copy of the sanctuary of Serapis near Alexandria. Its long canal, originally surrounded

EXCURSIONS

by Egyptian statues, is supposed to imitate the Nile.

Highlights of the excavations include the **fishpond** (probably used less for keeping fish than for creating decorative reflections and plays of light), encircled by an underground gallery where the emperor took his summer walks, the **Piccole e Grandi Terme** (Small and Large Baths), and Hadrian's private retreat, the **Teatro Marittimo**, a small circular palace on an island in an artificial pool, which could be reached only by a retractable bridge. There are also nymphaeums, temples and barracks and a museum displaying the latest discoveries from ongoing excavations. Archaeologists have found features such as a heated bench with steam pipes under the sand, and a network of subterranean service passages for horses and carts.

Villa Adriana opens 9 am to 5 pm daily (November to January), to 6 pm (February to October), to 6.30 pm (March and September), to 7 pm (April) and to 7.30 pm (May and August). Tickets are sold until one hour before closing and cost €6.20.

Local bus No 4 goes to Villa Adriana, leaving Tivoli from Piazza Massimo near Villa Gregoriana park. Otherwise take the COTRAL bus to Rome (from the terminus in Piazza Massimo or from the stop outside the tourist office on Largo Garibaldi) and get off at the town of Villa Adriana, from where it's an easy 1km, signposted walk to the villa itself.

Bagni di Tivoli

You can't ignore the smell of the sulphurous waters of Terme Acque Albule (☎ 07 743 71 007) at Bagni di Tivoli, 8km from Tivoli on the Via Tiburtina. Virgil wrote about these springs in the *Aeneid*, and many Romans built their country villas nearby to benefit from the healing waters. Today's visitors to the baths complex benefit from the same springs which fill the four huge swimming pools. Admission to the baths costs €10.33/ 2.58 for adults/children and a vast array of mud, inhalation and massage treatments is available at extra cost.

To get to Bagni di Tivoli you can take the

COTRAL bus from Tivoli to Rome and get off at the town of the same name.

Places to Eat

Antica Trattoria del Falcone (☎ 07 743 12 358, Via del Trevio 34) serves good pasta and pizza daily. A meal with wine will cost around €13. You can eat outside in the courtyard in the warmer months.

Trattoria L'Angolino (☎ 07 743 12 027, Via della Missione 3) has pizzas (€3.50 to €5.50), pasta (€4.65 to €6.20) and meal-in-itself salads (€5.50). *M31 pub* (☎ 07 74 33 32 43, Via della Missione 56–58) has excellent sandwiches for €2, pasta dishes for €3.10, beer from €1.55 and coffee for €0.50. It's open late and often has live music in the evening.

Close to Villa Adriana, *Villa Esedra* (☎ 07 745 34 716, Via di Villa Adriana 51) has tasty risottos and home-made pasta dishes. It's on the expensive side though and you'll pay about €15 to €18 for a full meal. It is closed on Monday.

Getting There & Away

Tivoli is 30km east of Rome. To get there from Rome, take Metro Linea B to Ponte Mammolo. The COTRAL bus to Tivoli leaves from outside Ponte Mammolo station every 10 minutes Monday to Saturday and every 20 minutes on Sunday and holidays. It also stops at the Rebibbia stop at the end of Metro Linea B before taking Via Tiburtina to Tivoli, stopping at the towns of Bagni di Tivoli and Villa Adriana along the way.

Tivoli can also be reached from Rome by train but it's a slow journey on the Avezzano line from Staziones Termini or Tiburtina. By car take Via Tiburtina (S5) or the Roma–L'Aquila autostrada (A24).

ETRUSCAN SITES

Lazio has a number of important Etruscan archaeological sites, most within easy reach of Rome by car or public transport. These include Tarquinia, Cerveteri, Veio and Tuscania (four of the main city-states in the Etruscan League).

Predominantly navigators and traders, the Etruscans developed a political and social

A splendid Renaissance fountain gushes among the greenery at Villa d'Este, Tivoli.

Fruity Frascati wine is produced south of Rome.

Palatial pleasure at Villa d'Este, Tivoli

SALLY WEBB

Ancient *tumoli* (tombs) dot the Etruscan town of Cerveteri, founded in the 8th century BC.

SALLY WEBB

Ostia Antica's well preserved amphitheatre, built by Agrippa, still stages classical performances today

Etruscan Mysteries

Much of the fascination of the Etruscans comes from the fact that so much about this complex civilisation remains unknown. The jury is still out as to whether the Etruscans were native to Italy, or whether they migrated from somewhere in Asia Minor. The Etruscan language is yet to be fully understood. They did, however, leave a wealth of archaeological remains and had an enormous influence on Roman culture.

The boundaries of Etruria were the River Arno in the north, the Tiber in the south, and the Mediterranean Sea. Many of the major sites are in Tuscany but some, most notably Tarquinia, Cerveteri, Veio, Viterbo, and Tuscania, are in Lazio. Among the surviving Etruscan architectural treasures are the foundations and elaborately decorated wooden tiles of wooden temples and the alluring Etruscan cemeteries, which hold the main attraction.

The grandest tombs were built to resemble houses, even down to their arrangement in neat 'streets'. The wealthy dead were buried in spectacular portrait sarcophagi, which often depicted women as the apparent social equals of their husbands. The tomb walls were painted with cheerful scenes of the afterlife, which like that of the Egyptians, closely resembled the nicest aspects of this existence – the Etruscans looked forward to a boisterous eternity of parties and hunting. They also packed suitable grave goods for a pleasant afterlife, including distinctive black bucchero tableware, bronze mirrors engraved with mythological scenes, and exquisite gold jewellery.

The Etruscans also excelled in bronzework, surviving examples of which include the Capitoline Wolf (originally minus the twins), and the Mars of Todi now in the Vatican Museums.

The deep-seated ambivalence the Romans felt towards the Etruscans is reflected in their legends. Of the three Etruscan kings who ruled Rome, Servius Tullius is credited with building the first walls and organising the political and military systems, while the last, Tarquinius Superbus (Tarquin the Proud), was expelled from Rome after his son raped a nobleman's wife.

The Romans did adopt many Etruscan civil and religious customs, including the study of the flight of birds and the entrails of sacrificed victims to determine the will of the gods, and the fasces, an axe inserted into a bundle of rods which symbolised the State's powers of corporal and capital punishment. A common motif in Roman art, the fasces were also adopted by Mussolini.

system to rival the Romans and their great artistic sense found expression in the tomb paintings and artefacts that have been discovered since excavations began in the 18th century. Profoundly influential on the growing culture in nearby Rome, Etruscan culture reached a peak in the 7th and 6th centuries BC. However, surrender of their trade routes to the more powerful Greeks in the 5th century precipitated a long period of decline that culminated in the eventual absorption of the Etruscan culture by the Republic in the 1st century BC.

Most of what is known about Etruscan culture has been gleaned from the archaeological evidence of tombs and religious sanctuaries. Their belief in life after death gave rise to the practice of burying the dead with everything that he or she might need in the next life: food, drink, clothes, ornaments and jewellery. These items, and the colourful tomb paintings that depict scenes from everyday life, constitute the most important sources of information regarding the Etruscans. Many can now be seen in museums including Villa Giulia and the Vatican Museums. The smaller museums at Tarquinia and Cerveteri are also well worth a visit.

The sheer number of tombs in the area has long supported the illegitimate industry of the *tombaroli* (tomb robbers), who have been plundering the sites for centuries and selling their 'discoveries' on the black market. It is said that, since many tombs are still to be excavated, a good number of tombaroli remain active. Prospective buyers of illicit Etruscan artefacts should, however, beware:

EXCURSIONS

another notorious activity of the tombaroli is the manufacture of fake antiquities.

A few days spent touring at least Tarquinia and Cerveteri, combined with visits to their museums and the Villa Giulia should constitute one of your most fascinating experiences in Italy. A useful guidebook to the area, *The Etruscans*, is published by the Istituto Geografico de Agostini and has a map. If you really want to lose yourself in a poetic journey, take along a copy of DH Lawrence's *Etruscan Places* (published in the compilation *DH Lawrence and Italy*).

Tarquinia

Believed to have been founded in the 12th century BC, and home of the Tarquin kings who ruled Rome before the creation of the Republic, Tarquinia was an important economic and political centre of the Etruscan League. The town has a small medieval centre, with a good Etruscan museum, but the major attractions here are the painted tombs of its burial grounds.

Orientation & Information By car or bus you will arrive at the Barriera San Giusto, just outside the main entrance to the town (see Getting There & Away later in this section). The APT office (☎ 07 668 56 384), Piazza Cavour 1, is on your left as you walk through the medieval ramparts. It opens 8 am to 2 pm Monday to Saturday.

Things to See The 15th-century Palazzo Vitelleschi, located in Piazza Cavour, houses the **Museo Nazionale Tarquiniese** (☎ 07 668 56 036), containing a significant collection of Etruscan treasures, including reconstructions of the Tomba del Triclinio and the Tomba delle Olimpiadi, with the frescoes removed from the original tombs. There is a beautiful terracotta frieze of winged horses, taken from the temple Ara della Regina (see later in this section). Numerous sarcophagi found in the tombs are also on display. The museum opens 9 am to 7 pm Tuesday to Sunday. Admission costs €6.20 and includes entrance to the famous painted tombs at the **necropolis** (☎ 07 668 56 308), 15 to 20 minutes' walk away (ask

for directions from the museum). The necropolis opens 9 am to around one hour before sunset, Tuesday to Sunday. Nearly 6000 tombs have been excavated, of which about 60 are painted, but only a handful are open to the public. Excavation of the tombs began in the 15th century and still continues today. Unfortunately, exposure to air and human interference has led to serious deterioration and many tombs are now enclosed and kept at constant temperatures. The painted tombs can be seen only through glass partitions.

DH Lawrence, who studied the tombs before measures were taken to protect them, wrote extensive descriptions of the frescoes he saw, and it is well worth reading his *Etruscan Places* before seeing the tombs of Tarquinia. Entering the famous Tomba dei Leopardi, Lawrence noted how, despite the extensive destruction of the tombs through vandalism and neglect, the colours of the wall paintings were still fresh and alive. Equally noteworthy are the Tomba della Caccia e della Pesca, the Tomba del Barone, and the Tomba del Guerriero, depicting scenes of convivial life, hunting and fishing scenes and scenes from mythology.

If you have a car, drive to the remains of the Etruscan acropolis of Tarxuna, on the crest of the Civita hill, 5km away on the Monte Romano road running eastwards. There is little evidence of the ancient city – apart from a few limestone blocks that once formed part of the city walls – as the Etruscans generally used wood to build their temples and houses. However, the foundations of a large temple, the **Ara della Regina**, were discovered on the hill and have been excavated this century.

In the pleasant medieval town there are several churches worth a look, including the late-13th-century **Chiesa di San Francesco**, on Via Porta Tarquinia, and the beautiful Romanesque **Chiesa di Santa Maria di Castello**, in the citadel at the north-western edge of town.

Places to Eat There are few places to eat in Tarquinia but for a good, cheap meal go to *Trattoria Arcadia (Via Mazzini 6)* or *Cucina Casareccia (Via Mazzini 5)*.

Getting There & Away COTRAL buses leave for Tarquinia approximately every hour from outside the Lepanto stop on Rome's Metro Linea A, arriving at Tarquinia at the Barriera San Giusto, a short distance from the tourist office. The BIRG (Zone 5) ticket costs €6.71 and the Tarquinia–Rome journey takes about two hours.

If you are travelling by car, take the A12 autostrada for Civitavecchia and then the Via Aurelia (S1). Tarquinia is about 90km north-west of Rome.

Around Tarquinia

Tuscania, 24km north-east of Tarquinia, is worth a visit. The leading Etruscan city after the 4th century BC, it has a good **Museo Archaeologico** (☎ 07 614 36 209), Via Donna del Riposo. The museum opens 8.30 am to 7.30 pm Tuesday to Sunday and admission is free.

Also worth a visit are the churches of **San Pietro** and **Santa Maria Maggiore**, dating from the 8th century AD with 11th and 12th century additions.

Tuscania is an easy drive from Tarquinia. Otherwise catch a COTRAL bus from the Barriera San Giusta just off Piazza Cavour in Tarquina.

Cerveteri

Forty-five kilometres north-west of Rome overlooking the sea, Cerveteri, Caere in classical times, was founded by the Etruscans in the 8th century BC. It enjoyed a time of great prosperity as an important commercial centre in the Mediterranean from the 7th to the 5th century, before entering into a period of decline. In 358 BC, the city was annexed by Rome and the inhabitants were granted Roman citizenship.

This colonisation of the city (as of the other cities in the Etruscan league in the same period) resulted in the absorption of Etruscan culture into Roman culture and its eventual disappearance. After the fall of the Empire the spread of malaria and repeated Saracen invasions caused further decline. In the 13th century there was a mass exodus from the city to the nearby town of Ceri, farther inland; and Caere became Caere Vetus ('old Caere'), from which its current name derives. The first half of the 19th century saw the first tentative archaeological explorations in the area and in 1911 systematic excavations began in earnest.

The main attractions here are the tombs known as *tumoli*, great mounds of earth with carved stone bases laid out in the form of a town with streets and squares. Within the tombs Etruscans reproduced the interior of their homes with doors, ceilings, chairs, beds and other household objects, either illustrated or carved into the rock. This is now an important record of both Etruscan architecture and daily life. Treasures taken from the tombs can be seen in the Vatican Museums, Villa Giulia and the Louvre.

Information The Pro Loco tourist office is at Piazza Risorgimento 19 (☎ 06 99 55 19 71) in the centre of the medieval town. It opens 10.30 am to 12.30 pm and 4 to 6 pm Tuesday to Friday, and 10 am to 12.30 pm on Saturday.

Things to See & Do The medieval town boasts a 16th-century **castle**. A small **archaeological museum** (☎ 06 994 13 54), Piazza S Maria, contains an interesting display of pottery and sarcophagi dating from the 9th century BC, from Cerveteri and the port of Pyrgi. The museum opens 9 am to 7 pm Tuesday to Sunday. Admission is free.

The lovely **Chiesa di Santa Maria Maggiore** is also worth a visit. Behind it, the **Chiesa Vecchia** contains a notable fresco from the school of Antoniazzo Romano and a board painting of the *Madonna and Child* by Lorenzo da Viterbo, produced in 1472.

The main necropolis area is **Banditaccia** (☎ 06 994 00 01), a couple of kilometres from the town centre. If you are in Cerveteri on Saturday or Sunday there is a bus that leaves the medieval town from the main square at 9, 10 and 11 am. The return bus leaves the necropolis at 10.15 and 11.15 am. Otherwise it is an easy and pleasant 20-minute walk and there are signposts from the main square. The necropolis opens 9 am to 4 pm (to 7 pm in summer) Tuesday to Sunday. Admission costs €4.13.

EXCURSIONS

You can roam freely once inside the area, although it is a good idea to follow the recommended routes to see the best-preserved tombs. It is advisable to read the information panels in the didactic centre before exploring the tumoli, which are laid out in the form of a town, with streets, squares and terraced houses.

One of the more interesting tombs is the **Tomba dei Rilievi**, dating from the 4th century BC. The tomb belonged to the Mantuna family and is decorated with painted reliefs of cooking implements and other household items. The tomb has been closed to avoid further damage to its paintings but can be viewed through a glass window.

Follow the signs to the **Tomba dei Capitelli** and the **Tomba dei Vasi Greci**. Ask at the entrance if you can see the **Tomba degli Scudi e delle Sedie**, outside the main area, which has chairs carved out of the tufa rock and bas-reliefs of shields on the walls.

Places to Eat Many Romans make the trip to Cerveteri just to eat at *Antica Locanda Le Ginestre* (☎ 06 994 06 72, *Piazza Santa Maria 5*), near the museum. The *panzerotti in salsa d'ortiche* (stuffed pasta parcels in a creamy, herb sauce) are especially good. There's a nice outdoor area for summer dining.

Getting There & Away Cerveteri is easily accessible from Rome by COTRAL bus from outside the Lepanto stop on Metro Linea A. Buses leave about every half-hour and the journey takes about 75 minutes. Buy a regional ticket (BIRG) for €4.40 covering the return bus journey, public transport in Cerveteri and the Metro and buses in Rome.

By road take either Via Aurelia or the Civitavecchia autostrada (A12) and come off at the Cerveteri-Ladispoli exit. The journey takes approximately 30 minutes.

Around Cerveteri
Ceri is a small medieval town 9km east of Cerveteri. It was founded by the inhabitants of Cerveteri to escape the double threat of malaria and attack by the Saracens. There is a small church notable for its frescoes.

Ceri is an easy drive from Rome or you can catch a bus there from Cerveteri's main square. Timetables are available at the Pro Loco tourist office in Cerveteri.

Veio
Your visit to Etruria should include Veio, 19km north of Rome and best reached by car. This was the largest of the Etruscan League cities and a major rival to nearby Rome. In 396 BC, after a siege lasting 10 years, Furius Camillus entered the acropolis at Veio through a tunnel and conquered and destroyed it. Under Augustus it became a municipium but eventually declined in importance and was abandoned.

Little evidence remains of the city. However, important finds came to light during 18th-century excavations of the site, including the famous statue of Apollo, now in the Museo di Villa Giulia in Rome. In Veio, things to see include the foundations of the temple of Apollo, the remains of a swimming pool and ornamental terracotta pieces. There is also the **Tomba Campana**, a frescoed chamber dating from the 7th and 6th centuries BC, and the **Ponte Sodo**, a tunnel cut out by Etruscans to make a watercourse.

By car, take the Via Cassia out of Rome and exit at Isola Farnese and follow signs for Veio. Otherwise, take bus No 201 for Olgiata from Piazza Mancini, near Ponte Milvio, to Isola Farnese and ask the bus driver to let you off at the road to Veio. It's quite a trek getting there and back and there is probably not enough to see at Veio to warrant the trouble of taking public transport.

VITERBO
Founded by the Etruscans and later taken over by Rome, Viterbo developed into an important medieval centre and in the 13th century became the residence of the popes, offering a safe house during the violent Church–Empire conflict revolving around Rome. Located 75km north of Rome, Viterbo is a very long day-trip from the city.

Papal elections were held in the town's Gothic Palazzo dei Papi, and stories abound about the antics of impatient townspeople anxious for a decision. In 1271, when the

EXCURSIONS

college of cardinals failed to elect a new pope after three years of deliberation following the death of Clement IV, the Viterbesi first locked them in a turreted hall of the palazzo, and then removed its roof and put them on a starvation diet. Only then did the cardinals manage to elect Gregory X.

Although badly damaged by bombing during WWII, Viterbo remains Lazio's best-preserved medieval town, to the extent that the historical San Pellegrino quarter is frequently used as a movie set. Wandering around the narrow streets you will feel as though you have been transported back in time, or into a scene from Dante's *Divina Commedia* (Divine Comedy).

Apart from its historical appeal, Viterbo is famous for its therapeutic hot springs. One of the best known is the sulphurous Bulicame pool, to which Dante refers in his *Inferno*. It is the pool of boiling blood into which Henry of Cornwall's murderer Guy de Montfort is immersed.

Orientation & Information

The town of Viterbo is neatly divided between the newer section to the north and east and the older part to the south, centring on Piazza San Pellegrino and the network of narrow streets that make up the medieval town. Hotels are in the newer part of Viterbo and you must cross the Piazza del Plebiscito, with its 15th- and 16th-century palaces, before reaching the old town and the real reason for your visit.

There are train stations north and southeast of the town centre, at the Porta Fiorentina and Porta Romana entrances to the city, just outside the town walls. The station for intercity buses is located rather inconveniently at Riello, a few kilometres northwest of town. To get to the medieval centre from Stazione Porta Romana take Via Giuseppe Garibaldi in front of you. This brings you to Piazza Fontana Grande. From here bear left and then right into Via Cardinale la Fontaine. Go straight on and in a few minutes you will find yourself in the heart of the medieval quarter.

The phenomenally unhelpful APT office (☎ 07 61 30 47 95) is on Piazza San Car-

luccio in the medieval quarter. It opens 9 am to 1 pm Monday to Saturday. There is a car park in the square.

The main post office is on Via F Ascenzi, just north of Piazza del Plebiscito. The Telecom office is at Via Cavour 28, between Piazza del Plebiscito and Piazza Fontana Grande.

Palazzo dei Priori

Piazza del Plebiscito is enclosed by 15th- and 16th-century palaces, the most imposing of which is the Palazzo dei Priori, or Palazzo Comunale, dating from 1500. The arched entrance leads into a pretty courtyard with an elegant 17th-century fountain and a lovely view over the Faul valley. The staircase on the left as you enter the courtyard leads to the elaborately decorated Senate Rooms on the 1st floor, open to visitors during office hours.

Notable newly restored 16th-century frescoes by Baldassare Croce can be found in the **Sala Reggia**. They give a comic representation of the myths and history of Viterbo. Of interest also is the ornate wooden tribunal supporting the figure of justice in the Sala Consiglio and the small pulpit, or *bigonoia*, between the two windows, into which dissenters had to climb to voice their disagreements during council meetings.

The Palazzo dei Priori opens 9 am to 1 pm and 2 pm to 7 pm daily, though rooms are sometimes used for council business and visitors may find them closed. Admission is free.

Cattedrale di San Lorenzo & Palazzo dei Papi

The black-and-white striped cathedral in Piazza San Lorenzo dates from the 12th century with 16th-century and postwar revisions, although the interior has just been restored to its original Romanesque simplicity. The building contains paintings from various epochs and a 15th-century marble font, as well as the tomb of John XXI, the only Portuguese pope, killed in 1277 when the floor of his room in the Palazzo dei Papi collapsed.

Also on the square is the Palazzo dei Papi (☎ 07 613 25 463), built for the popes

EXCURSIONS

between 1255 and 1267 with the aim of enticing them away from Rome. The graceful loggia with its double row of fine columns to the right of the steps is in the early-Gothic style. The part facing the valley collapsed in the 14th century and you can see the bases of some of the columns. Go up the steps and you come to the hall in which papal conclaves were held, now used frequently for concerts, meetings and exhibitions, including the annual **Mostra dell'Antiquariato** (antiques fare) in October/ November. The palace opens 9 am to 12.30 pm and 3.30 to 7 pm Tuesday to Sunday but only when exhibitions are being held.

Piazza Santa Maria Nuova
From the Palazzo dei Papi, head eastwards to the Piazza della Morte and take Via Cardinale la Fontaine to reach this square. The Romanesque church of the same name dates from the 12th century and as such is one of the oldest churches in Viterbo, although it has been largely restored after sustaining bomb damage in WWII.

On the facade, above the door, there is an ancient relief sculpture of Jupiter's head, adding weight to the theory that the church stands on the pre-existing site of an ancient-pagan temple. The pulpit on the left was used by St Thomas Aquinas. Follow the side wall to the back of the church and you get to the remains of a small Lombard cloister, always open and well worth a visit.

Chiesa del Gesù
Located in the square of the same name, just north of Piazza della Morte, this church supposedly stands at the geographical centre of the old town. Immortalised by Dante in his *Inferno*, it is the site of the murder of Henry, duke of Cornwall, cousin of Edward I, in 1272. He was killed by Guy and Simon de Montfort to avenge their father's murder. Note the crude sculpture of the lion, the symbol of Viterbo, on the roof. It is a comic alternative to the ornate Gothic lion sculptures that abound throughout the city.

Medieval Quarter
Via San Pellegrino takes you eastwards

from Piazza San Carluccio, through the medieval quarter, into **Piazza San Pellegrino**. The well preserved buildings that enclose this tiny square are considered the finest group of medieval buildings in Italy.

Other Things to See
The early-13th-century **Fontana Grande**, in Piazza Fontana Grande, is the oldest and largest of Viterbo's Gothic fountains.

Back at the northern entrance to the town is the **Chiesa di San Francesco**, in the square of the same name, a Gothic building that was restored after suffering bomb damage in January 1944. The church contains the tombs of two popes, Clement IV (died 1268) and Hadrian V (died 1276). Both tombs are lavishly decorated; note the fine Cosmatiesque mosaic work of Hadrian's.

There is no shortage of museums in Viterbo. The **Museo della Macchina di Santa Rosa** (☎ 07 61 34 51 57), Via San Pellegrino, documents the history of the local festival that takes place on 3 September of each year, when the Viterbesi parade a 30m tower around the town. The museum opens 10 am to 1 pm and 4 to 7 pm Wednesday to Sunday, April to September (on Sunday only in winter). Admission is free.

The **Museo Civico** (☎ 07 61 34 82 75) has reopened after a 10-year restoration project. It is housed in the convent of the Chiesa di Santa Maria della Verità, just outside the Porta della Verità on the north-eastern side of town. Among the works in the museum are the lovely *Pietà* by Sebastiano del Piombo (1515), along with a Roman sarcophagus which is said to be the tomb of Galiana, a beautiful woman murdered by a Roman aristocrat after she refused his advances. The museum opens 9 am to 6 pm Tuesday to Sunday, November to March (to 7 pm April to October). Admission costs €3.10.

Places to Eat
Stop for a coffee at *Caffè Schenardi (Corso Italia 11)*, built by the important Ghigi family in the 15th century and used as a bank and then as a hotel before being turned into a cafe in 1818. The Art Deco interior is the setting for frequent art exhibitions.

EXCURSIONS

Nestling under a medieval arch in a delightful square, *All'Archetto (☎ 07 613 25 769, Via San Cristoforo)*, off Via Cavour, offers a selection of dishes in a traditional environment. A full meal costs around €13.

Il Richiastro (☎ 07 61 22 80 09, Via della Marrocca 18) serves good, simple fare using local ingredients in a cosy semi-basement setting (there is outside seating in summer). Soups are a speciality and cost €4.13, or €7.23 for four. Try the lentil and mushroom variety, which is based on an ancient-Roman recipe. The restaurant opens for lunch and dinner Thursday to Saturday, and for lunch only on Sunday. Booking is advisable.

If you fancy a pizza try *Il Ciuffo (☎ 07 613 08 237, Piazza Capella)*, just off Piazza San Pellegrino, in the heart of the medieval quarter. It opens 7.30 to 11.30 pm (closed Tuesday).

Getting There & Away

You can take a COTRAL bus to Viterbo from Saxa Rubra terminus, which is on the Ferrovia Roma-Nord train line in Rome. Take Metro A to Flaminio and follow the blue signs to Roma Stazione Nord (Piazzale Flaminio). The 10-minute journey to Saxa Rubra is covered by the standard BIT ticket. Buses leave Saxa Rubra approximately every 30 minutes (more or less on the half-hour) and a single ticket costs €3.31. The journey to Viterbo takes 1½ hours. The bus terminates at Riello, a few kilometres northwest of Viterbo; however, buses also stop at the Porta Romana and Porta Fiorentina entrances to the town. If you find yourself at Riello, catch city bus No 11 into Viterbo. The journey takes five minutes and costs €0.52.

By train, take the Ferrovia Metro FM3. These trains leave from Roma San Pietro (accessible by bus No 64 from Largo di Torre Argentina and Piazza Barberini) or, more easily, from Valle Aurelia station (which is connected to the Linea A Metro stop of the same name). The BIRG (Zone 5) ticket costs €6.71 and trains from Rome to Viterbo take about 1½ hours. Trains run every hour from 5.47 am to 9.47 pm and,

from Viterbo, they depart (roughly) hourly between 5.53 am and 9.53 pm.

By car, the easiest way to get to Viterbo is on the Cassia-bis (about 1 hour's drive); alternatively take the Autostrada del Sole (A1) and follow signs from Orte. Enter the old town through the Porta Romana onto Via G Garibaldi and follow the street as it becomes Via Cavour, through Piazza del Plebiscito. There are many public car parks scattered throughout the town, although the best is probably Piazza della Rocca.

AROUND VITERBO

Viterbo's **thermal springs** are within a 10km radius of the town. Used by both the Etruscans and the Romans (who built large bath complexes, of which virtually nothing remains), they were then abandoned before being restored by the 13th-century popes. There are both public and private facilities, used by locals and visitors alike. Travellers wanting to take a cure or relax in the hot sulphur baths will find the privately owned Terme dei Papi (☎ 07 613 501) the easiest to reach. A dip in the outdoor thermal pool costs €10.33 (it is open year round) and you can have other treatments (by appointment) at a price. Take city bus No 2 from the bus station on Piazza Martiri d'Ungheria, near the APT office, in Viterbo.

If you have a car, follow the signs from the Terme dei Papi for the Etruscan **necropoli** at Castel d'Asso, 5km away. The ancient tombs are interesting and have recently been restored. Theatrical performances are occasionally staged here in summer.

At Bagnaia, a few kilometres north-east of Viterbo, is the beautiful 16th-century **Villa Lante** (☎ 07 612 88 008), noted for its fine Renaissance gardens. The two, superficially identical, palaces are not open to the public, although you can wander in the large public park (€2.07). Climb to the highest terrace and look down over the gardens as they fall away in front of you. The park opens 8.30 am to one hour before sunset Tuesday to Sunday. From Viterbo, take city bus No 6 from Piazza Caduti.

At Caprarola, south-east of Viterbo, is the splendid **Palazzo Farnese** (☎ 07 616 46 052).

EXCURSIONS

Designed by Vignola, it is one of the most important examples of mannerist architecture in Italy. You need to wait for an attendant to take you through rooms richly frescoed in the 16th century by artists such as Taddeo and Federico Zuccari. Tours leave every 15 minutes. The palace opens to the public 8.30 am to 6.45 pm Tuesday to Sunday. Admission costs €2.07. The ticket includes admission to the lovely gardens (by guided tour only); there are six tours per day from April to October and one (at 3 pm) the rest of the year. Seven daily buses leave from the Riello bus station just outside Viterbo for Caprarola.

The **Parco dei Mostri** or **Sacro Bosco** (☎ 07 619 24 029) at Bomarzo, north-east of Viterbo, will be particularly interesting for people with young children. The park, created for the Orsini family in the 1570s as a private pleasure garden, was brought to light and restored by Giovanni Bettini, the owner since 1954. Gigantic and grotesque sculptures are scattered throughout, including an ogre, a giant and a dragon.

Also of interest are the octagonal *tempietto* (little temple), dedicated to Julia Farnese, and the crooked house, allegedly built without the use of right angles but really the result of the land subsiding. The park opens 8 am to sunset and admission costs €7.75. To get there from Viterbo, catch the CO-TRAL bus from the stop near Viale Trento to Bomarzo, then take a 10-minute walk following the signs to Palazzo Orsini.

Another interesting place near Viterbo is the tiny, hill-top medieval town of **Civita di Bagnoregio**, near its newer Renaissance counterpart, Bagnoregio, (north of Viterbo). In a picturesque area of tufa ravines, Civita is known as the 'dying town' because continuous erosion of its hill has caused the collapse of many buildings. Abandoned by its original residents, who moved to Bagnoregio, most of the buildings in the town were purchased by foreigners and artisans and, in recent years, Civita has been restored and developed into a minor tourist attraction.

Regular COTRAL buses connect Bagnoregio with Viterbo, leaving from the Riello bus station. From the bus stop, ask for directions to Civita, which is connected to Bagnoregio's outskirts by a pedestrian bridge.

THE LAKES

There are four lakes in northern Lazio: Bracciano, Martignano, Vico and Bolsena. The attraction of water and the natural beauty of the surroundings make them popular spots for hot Romans in summer. These former volcanic craters offer a range of activities for sport-lovers including sailing and horse riding. On Saturday and Sunday, especially in summer, the lakes can be crowded.

Lago di Bracciano

Forty kilometres north-west of Rome, this lake is easily accessible by public transport and is ideal if you need a break from the confusion of the city. Occupying a series of craters in the volcanic Monti Sabatini range, it measures 31km in circumference and is the eighth-largest lake in Italy.

The lake is dominated by the pleasant hill-top town of **Bracciano**. To the northeast is **Trevignano Romano**, a picturesque medieval fishing town with a pretty *lungolago* (waterfront) and a modest beach.

The fortified town of **Anguillara** stands on a basalt promontory on the south-eastern shore overlooking the lake and was a popular location for holiday homes in ancient times. Its name is thought to come from the eels *(anguille)* that populate the lake.

Orientation & Information The travel agency (☎ 06 99 84 00 62) at Piazza IV Novembre can supply limited tourist information and will help with hotel bookings. The COTRAL stop for buses to/from Rome and the other towns around the lake is on Piazza Roma near the central Piazza I Maggio, a short distance from the castle.

Things to See & Do The **Castello Orsini-Odelscalchi** (☎ 06 998 04 348) in Bracciano is a must for castle-lovers. Built in 1470 by Napoleone Orsini and decorated by Antoniazzo Romano and the Zuccari brothers, it is an excellent example of Renaissance military architecture. The castle is signposted from Piazza I Maggio. It opens

10 am to noon and 3 to 5 pm Tuesday to Sunday in summer.

In Trevignano Romano there is the **Museo Civico Etrusco-Romano** (☎ 06 999 12 02 01), on the ground floor of the Palazzo Comunale in Piazza Vittorio Emmanuele III. The museum houses a small but interesting collection of Etruscan and Roman pieces testifying to the ancient history of the area. It opens 10 am to 1 pm Thursday to Sunday. Admission is free.

Have a look at the **Chiesa di Santa Maria Assunta** on the hill in the heart of medieval Trevignano. To get there go through the arch on the right of the square as you face the Palazzo Comunale. Follow the narrow road for about 500m until you come to a small square on your left. From here take the path leading up to the church (clearly signposted). This parish church has recently been restored and the apse contains frescoes by the school of Raphael. The **Chiesa di San Bernadino** is also interesting. Dedicated to the patron saint of Trevignano, it dates from the second half of the 15th century.

In Trevignano on the second Sunday of the month there is the Fiera dei Sogni (Dream Fair), a lively market selling local produce and handicrafts. In October and early November the town plays host to a popular series of six classical-music concerts. The concerts take place in the Sala Convegni at the Banca di Credito Cooperativo in Piazza Vittorio Emanuele III next to the Palazzo Comune (for programme details check the *spettacoli* section in the daily papers; see the Facts for the Visitor chapter).

In Anguillara there is an interesting castle with fortified walls, which are 15m thick at their strongest point. Outside the walls there is the pretty **Chiesa di San Francesco**, dating from the 10th century.

About 5km from Anguillara is the picturesque **Lago di Martignano**, an off-shoot of the Bracciano crater. It has a small beach with pedaloes, sailing boats and canoes for hire. You will need to ask for directions to reach this lake.

Places to Eat In Bracciano try the top little trattoria, *Da Regina*, near the castle. To get there from Piazza I Maggio take Via G Palazzi. Follow the road round to the left and then take Via Sant' Antonio on the right. This brings you to a pretty unnamed square and the restaurant is on the left. It has a first-rate selection of dishes including *pasta al forno* (a baked pasta dish using penne) and fresh fish from the lake. Portions are generous and the prices are unbeatable; a full meal including coffee costs less than €11. The restaurant opens for lunch and supper from 7.15 to 9.15 pm (closed Friday). To be sure of a table go early and queue (no reservations).

Trattoria del Castello (☎ 06 998 04 339), in the same square as the castle, has top food. If *funghi porcini* (porcini mushrooms) are on the menu, have them.

In Trevignano Romano a good bet is *La Tavernetta* (☎ 06 999 90 26, Via Garibaldi 62), a rustic, family-run establishment with lakeside seating in summer and lovely niche paintings produced by a local artist. For sensational home-made ice cream try *Bar Sandro* (Via dell'Arena 16a) and enjoy it with the strollers on the promenade or at a shady table by the lake.

Getting There & Away There are two COTRAL buses that go to Bracciano. The first goes directly to Bracciano from Rome (final destination Manziana). The second takes a slightly longer route, stopping at Anguillara and Trevignano on the way. Both buses leave approximately every hour from the Lepanto stop on Metro Linea A. The BIRG (Zone 3) ticket costs €4.39.

You can also get to Bracciano and Anguillara by a combination of train and bus, leaving from Ostiense and changing at Pineto. By car, take Via Braccianense (S493) to Anguillara and Bracciano, and Via Cassia (S2) to Trevignano Romano.

Lago di Vico

Legend has it that the horseshoe-shaped Lago di Vico came into being when Hercules, passing through the area in search of Melissa and Amaltea, thrust his club into the ground to prove his identity. When the local inhabitants failed to meet his challenge to

EXCURSIONS

extract the weapon, Hercules pulled it out himself, leaving a hole which then filled with water to create the lake. In reality, the lake derives from an ancient volcano.

Today it is part of a sizeable nature reserve (☎ 07 616 47 444) that includes an area of marshland popular with migrating birds. For this reason the area around the lake is fairly undeveloped and restaurant facilities are minimal. However, for lovers of the outdoors the lake offers a range of activities, including canoeing and horse riding.

Getting There & Away Lago di Vico is not easily accessible from Rome by public transport. However, the COTRAL bus to Caprarola passes nearby. Catch it from the Saxa Rubra stop on Ferrovia Roma Nord and ask the driver when to get off. If you find yourself in Caprarola, take the local bus to the lake. By road from Rome, take Via Cassia for Viterbo and follow signs to Vico.

Lago di Bolsena & Bolsena

Lago di Bolsena, 100km north of Rome, is a long way to reach in a day. It is, however, easily accessible if you are staying in nearby Viterbo (see that section earlier in this chapter). The elliptical lake is the fifth-largest lake in Italy and, like the others in northern Lazio, it is volcanic in origin. It is surrounded by a number of towns, the most important being its namesake, Bolsena.

The town is renowned for the miracle that took place here in 1263, when a Bohemian priest who harboured doubts about the doctrine of transubstantiation (the miraculous transformation of the Eucharist into the physical body of Christ) saw blood drip from the host that he was holding. Pope Urban IV founded the festival of Corpus Domini to commemorate the event and it was also celebrated by Raphael in his *Miracle of Bolsena* in the Raphael Stanze in the Vatican Museums. The townspeople remember the event in June by holding a 3km procession and filling Bolsena with flowers.

Things to See & Do In the medieval quarter, Castello Monaldeschi has an interesting history. The original structure dates from

between the 13th and 16th centuries. However, it was pulled down by the locals in 1815 to prevent it from being taken by Luciano Bonaparte. It has subsequently been rebuilt to a square design with four towers and it now houses the **Museo Territoriale del Lago di Bolsena** (☎ 07 617 98 630), documenting the geology, and archaeology of the area and a tourist office (☎ 07 617 99 923). The museum opens 9.30 am to 1.30 pm and 4 to 8 pm Tuesday to Friday (mornings only in winter), and 10 am to 1 pm and 3 to 6 pm on Saturday and Sunday.

Also of interest are the 11th-century **Basilica di Santa Cristina** and the **catacombs** beneath it. The basilica houses the remains of Santa Cristina, found in the catacombs in 1070. Tradition says that the young Christian was thrown into the lake tied to a huge stone that miraculously floated her safely to the shore, an event celebrated on 23 July in a theatrical performance staged by Bolsena's young people dressed as Romans. Just before the entrance to the catacombs is the **altare del miracolo**, marking the spot where the miracle of Bolsena occurred. The catacombs are notable because they contain tombs that are still sealed.

Boat trips around the lake and the islands of Martana and Bisentina (tips of the submerged volcanic cone) leave daily from Bolsena. For information and bookings ask at the tourist office.

If you're touring the area by car, it is worth heading on to **Montefiascone**, a hilltop town dominated by the huge dome of the **duomo**, the third largest in Italy. Also of interest is the Romanesque church of **Sant'-Andrea** and, on the town's outskirts on the road to Orvieto, the Romanesque church of **San Flaviano**.

The town is known for its white wine, Est! Est! Est! Local history has it that on his travels a monk wrote 'Est' (it is) to indicate the places where the wine was good. On arriving at Montefiascone he was so overcome by the quality of the wine that he exclaimed 'Est! Est! Est!'.

Getting There & Away In summer CO-TRAL operates a direct bus service to

Bolsena from the Saxa Rubra stop on Ferrovia Roma-Nord (catch the train from the station in Piazzale Flaminio). Otherwise you need to change at Viterbo. There are regular COTRAL buses to Bolsena from Viterbo, Monday to Saturday, leaving from the bus station at Riello. On Sunday there is only one bus that leaves around 9 am (returning at around 6 pm).

By car, take the Via Cassia (S2) to Viterbo and follow the signs.

CASTELLI ROMANI

Just past the southern periphery of Rome are the Colli Albani (Alban Hills) and the 13 towns of the Castelli Romani. A summer resort area for wealthy Romans since the days of the Empire, its towns were mainly founded by popes and patrician families. Castel Gandolfo and Frascati are perhaps the best known; the former is the summer residence of the pope and the latter is famous for its crisp white wine. The other towns are Monte Porzio Catone, Montecompatri, Rocca Priora, Colonna, Rocca di Papa, Grottaferrata, Marino, Albano Laziale, Ariccia, Genzano and Nemi.

Frascati

Of the Castelli, Frascati is the closest to Rome and makes a good starting point for a tour of the area.

Orientation & Information If you arrive by train, go out of the station and up the steps in front of you. Immediately you will find yourself in the main Piazzale Marconi. From here it is a short walk left into the old town and the main sights.

The APT tourist office (☎ 06 942 03 31) is at Piazzale Marconi 1. It opens 8 am to 2 pm Monday to Saturday, and also between 3.30 and 6.30 pm Tuesday to Friday.

Things to See & Do The 16th-century **Villa Aldobrandini**, on the hill overlooking Piazzale Marconi, is one of a number of exquisite villas in the area. Designed by Giacomo della Porta and built by Carlo Maderno in 1598, it contains frescoes by Domenichino. Unfortunately, it is now a private residence and is not open to the public. However, with a permit you can wander through the extensive gardens surrounding the villa from 9 am to 1 pm and 3 to 6 pm in summer (to 5 pm in winter) Monday to Friday. Permits are free from the APT office.

Other places of interest include the **Cattedrale di San Pietro Apostolo**, which dominates the square of the same name, just off the main square. It was built in the 17th century and then restored to its original form after sustaining serious bomb damage during WWII. Take a look at the lovely carved marble altarpiece depicting Christ giving Peter the keys to the church.

Around the corner in Piazza del Gesù is the 16th century **Chiesa del Gesù**, notable for its magnificent painted architecture, executed by Andrea Pozzo in an attempt to compensate for the modesty of the church itself due to the lack of funding. At the heart of the historical centre are the 15th-century **Palazzo Vescovile** and the adjacent **bell tower**, dating from 1305.

Places to Eat There is no shortage of eateries in Frascati, especially in the historic centre. For a decent meal try *Il Pinnocchio (Piazza del Mercato)*, where pizzas cost from €3.52. The restaurant opens for lunch and dinner (closed Tuesday).

For a snack go to *Il Fornaretto* next door. It offers a mouth-watering selection of home-baked bread, pizza, cakes and biscuits, including the famous *ciambelle al vino*, ideally dipped into a glass of chilled local wine. Otherwise, stop at one of the many kiosks selling *porchetta* (roast pork).

If you're after Frascati wine, head for any one of the *cantine*, rustic outlets serving simple food and wine on tap. Some also allow you to bring your own food and even your empty bottles to fill and take away.

Getting There & Away The COTRAL bus drops you in Piazzale Marconi. Buses for the other Castelli also leave from here and there is a timetable posted on the wall of the Palazzo Marconi.

If you arrive by car, follow the road into town and park in a pay-to-park car park.

Around Frascati

Above Frascati is the ancient city of **Tuscolo**, founded in or around the 9th century BC. Imposing and impregnable, it remained independent until 380 BC, when it came under Roman domination. Towards the end of the Republican era, patrician families started to build country residences here, setting a trend that is still going on today. In 1191, it was destroyed and the inhabitants founded the nearby towns of the Castelli.

Today, scant evidence of the city remains. There is a small amphitheatre (reputedly now the site of black masses and satanic rituals), the remains of a villa and a stretch of ancient Roman road leading up to the city. Tuscolo is signposted from Frascati. If you have a car you can drive to the top of the hill. Otherwise it is a short walk through the woods and you can enjoy the view.

At **Grottaferrata** there is the Abbazia di Grottaferrata (☎ 06 945 93 09), in Viale San Nilo, founded in the 11th century and home to a congregation of Greek monks. The abbey also contains an interesting museum containing sculpture, frescoes and icons. It opens 8.30 am to noon and 4.30 to 6 pm Tuesday to Saturday, and 8.30 to 10 am and 4.30 to 6 pm on Sunday.

Nemi is worth a visit to see the pretty **Lago di Nemi**, in a volcanic crater. In ancient times there was a sanctuary beside the lake where the goddess Diana was worshipped. Today, little remains of this massive temple complex but it is possible to see the niche walls of what was once an arcade portico. Excavations at the site are ongoing.

The incongruous-looking building at the edge of the lake, near the ruins of the temple, has an interesting story attached to it. It was built by Mussolini to house two ancient Roman boats (one 73m long, the other 71m), Gaius Caligula's pleasure craft, which were recovered from the bottom of the lake when it was partly drained between 1927 and 1932. The official story is that retreating German troops burned the ships on June 1, 1944. Locals tell a different story, but you'll have to go there to find out! It's now a museum, the Museo delle Navi Romane. Admission costs €2.58.

Nemi is famous for its small wild strawberries (which are in fact cultivated), and the town hosts a strawberry festival in the first weekend of June. There is a delightful trattoria, the **Trattoria la Sirena del Lago** (☎ 06 936 80 20), located literally on the edge of a cliff behind the Palazzo Ruspoli and overlooking the lake. Signs will direct you there from the town centre. Simple but excellent meals cost around €15, with wine.

Getting There & Away

It is really best to tour this area by car: you could see most of the more interesting sights on an easy day-trip from Rome. Take the Via Tuscolana (S5) to Grottaferrata and Frascati and the Via Appia (S7) to Genzano and Nemi. However, most of the towns of the Castelli Romani, including Nemi, are accessible by the regular COTRAL bus from the Anagnina station on Metro Linea A, or from the main square in Frascati if you want to go on from there.

Trains also leave from the Lazio platform at Stazione Termini for Frascati and Castel Gandolfo/Albano Laziale.

PALESTRINA

The present town stands on the site of an ancient temple erected in the 6th century BC and dedicated to the oracle of Fortuna Primigenia, subsequently rebuilt by Sulla after he conquered the town in 87 BC. However, the history of the settlement dates back as far as the 7th century BC, making it one of the oldest in the region. Originally known as Praeneste, it has attracted people since ancient times because of its altitude and healthy air, and it makes an interesting half-day trip out of the city.

Orientation & Information

The tourist office (☎ 06 957 31 76) is next to the Museo Archeologico Nazionale Prenestino on Piazza Santa Maria degli Angeli 2 in the town centre. It opens 9.30 am to 1 pm and 3.30 to 5.30 pm daily.

Things to See

The town of Palestrina is dominated by the **Santuario della Fortuna Primigenia**. Built by the ancient Romans on a series of terraces on the slope of Monte Ginestro, the massive sanctuary was topped by a circular temple with a statue of the goddess Palestrina on the top. On a clear day the view from the sanctuary is sensational. The 17th-century Palazzo Colonna Barberini now stands at this point and houses the **Museo Archeologico Nazionale Prenestino** (☎ 06 953 81 00), open 9 am to around 8 pm (hours are reduced in winter) daily.

The museum houses an important collection of Roman artefacts and is one of Lazio's best. Of particular interest is the spectacular **Nile mosaic**, a masterpiece of Hellenistic art, which came from the most sacred part of the temple (where the cathedral with its Romanesque belfry now stands). It depicts the Nile in flood from Ethiopia to Alexandria.

Apart from its historical and archaeological importance, Palestrina is also renowned for being the birthplace of the 16th-century choral composer, Giovanni Pierluigi da Palestrina (see the boxed text 'God's Choirmaster' in the Facts about Rome chapter). The Casa di Palestrina, his former home, is now a museum and important music library, open 9.30 am to 12.30 pm Tuesday to Sunday. Craft-lovers can purchase locally produced beaten copper work in the shape of shells and 'Palestrina point' embroidery.

Getting There & Away

Palestrina is accessible from Rome by COTRAL bus from the Anagnina stop on Metro Linea A. Buses leave approximately every 30 minutes and the journey (€2.01) takes one hour. At Palestrina, you can either walk uphill to the Santuario or save your legs and take the small local bus.

By road it is a straightforward 39km along the Via Prenestina (S155).

ANAGNI & ALATRI

These medieval towns are in an area about 40 minutes south-east of Rome known as the Ciociaria. **Anagni**, birthplace of a number of medieval popes including Innocent III and Gregory IX, is of particular note for its Lombard-Romanesque cathedral, built in the 11th century. Its pavement was laid by Cosmati marble workers of the Middle Ages. In the crypt is an extraordinary series of vibrant frescoes, painted by three Benedictine monks in diverse periods during the 13th century. Depicting a wide range of subjects, the frescoes are considered a major example of pre-Giotto medieval painting. The frescoes were recently unveiled after a four-year restoration project and certainly deserve a look (free). The crypt's pavement was also laid by the Cosmati.

Alatri has a few of interesting churches, including the 13th-century **Chiesa di Santa Maria Maggiore** in its main square. Its ancient **acropolis** is surrounded by massive 6th-century-BC walls, built by the town's original inhabitants, the Hernici.

To get to Anagni by bus you have to change at Colle Ferro. COTRAL buses for Colle Ferro leave from the Anagnina stop on the Metro Linea A approximately every 30 minutes. From here take the bus to Anagni. Otherwise take the Frosinone train from Rome's Stazione Termini (leaving approximately every hour) and get off at Anagni-Fiuggi. To get to Alatri, catch the train to Anagni and then take the COTRAL bus to Alatri.

THE COAST

There is no shortage of beaches close to Rome if you feel like a swim, although large crowds and heavy pollution make them rather unattractive destinations. Bear in mind that facilities at most coastal resorts operate from May to September only.

Ostia & Anzio

Lido di Ostia is the closest seaside resort for Romans but the beach gets very crowded in summer and the water isn't terribly clean; take a dip at your peril! Take the Lido di Ostia train from the Porta San Paolo station (35 minutes) and get off at Lido Centro. From here cross Piazza della Stazione del Lido in front of the station and go straight on until you hit the sea (five minutes).

The town is characterless and safety, especially at night, is increasingly a problem. The Pro Loco office (☎ 06 562 78 92) is inside the main hall of the train station; it usually opens 5 to 7.30 pm Monday to Friday, summer only.

On either side of Ostia there are long stretches of beach lined with degraded sand dunes. These beaches include **Fregene**, a rapidly expanding but unexceptional seaside resort near Fiumicino airport. South of Ostia, there is the sandy beach at **Torvaianica**. If you choose to stop here don't miss the archaeological excavations in the nearby town of **Pratica di Mare**, a short distance inland. The town stands on the site of the ancient town of Lavinium, allegedly founded by Aeneas after his escape from Troy. You can see 13 archaic altars and a number of tomb sanctuaries. An Iron Age necropolis has also been identified here.

Farther south is the interesting port town of Anzio, which dates back to the Latium civilisation at the beginning of the first millennium BC. **Anzio** was then occupied by the Volsci, before becoming a popular resort and port of call in Roman times. Cicero and Augustus both had residences here, and it was the birthplace of Nero, who built the harbour, now an important archaeological site. Statues from the Imperial Villa, also built by Nero, are on display in museums throughout the world.

After the fall of the Roman Empire, Anzio was plundered by the Barbarians and the Saracens, forcing the population to move out and found the nearby city of Nettuno. The town was re-established by Innocent XII in 1700, when he financed the building of the harbour still bearing his name. On 22 April 1944 the allies landed here before going on to liberate Rome from the Germans. The event is commemorated in the colossal American and British war cemeteries that surround the town.

There is an APT tourist office in Anzio (☎ 06 984 51 47), next to the church, at Piazza Pia 19. If you arrive by train take the road in front of the station and go straight on until you get to the main square. It opens 8 am to 1 pm Tuesday to Saturday and also 3 to 6 pm Tuesday and Thursday.

Buses to Anzio leave Rome from the EUR-Fermi stop on the Metro Linea B, following the coastal road, or from the Cinecittà stop on the Metro Linea A. In both cases the journey takes 1¾ hours and costs around €3.10. Otherwise take the regular train from Stazione Termini. The journey takes 1¼ hours and costs €2.63. By car take Via Pontina (S148) going south.

You'll need to go farther south to Sabaudia and Sperlonga to find more attractive spots for a swim.

Sabaudia

Rivalling the Capalbio coast in Tuscany for the cleanliness of its sea, Sabaudia is an upmarket resort and a favourite with the Italian intellectual elite in summer. It also has the added attraction of sand dunes (protected by an EU initiative) and the **Parco Nazionale del Circeo**, a wetlands nature reserve along the coast encompassing Monte Circeo, the promontory to the south.

The town itself grew up in the 1930s on former marshland and is an important monument to Fascist architecture with large squares and wide avenues. On the fourth Sunday of the month there is the lively **Mercatino di Archimede** on Piazza del Comune selling antiques, books and handicrafts.

You can buy *trecce* (braids) of fresh mozzarella from the dairy on Via Litoranea running parallel to the coast. It is situated approximately 300m before the first major crossroad as you are coming from Rome.

Getting There and Away Sabaudia is accessible by COTRAL bus from outside the EUR-Fermi stop on Rome's Metro Linea B. Take the bus going to San Felice Circeo and get off at Sabaudia. By road take the Pontina (S148) from EUR going south.

Sperlonga

The small coastal town of Sperlonga is a good destination for a weekend break with two long, sandy beaches on either side of a rocky promontory jutting into the sea. The town is divided into two parts. Medieval Sperlonga Alta is on top of the promontory and with it whitewashed buildings it seems more Greek than Italian. Modern Sperlonga Bassa is at sea level.

Other than the beach, the main attraction is the **Grotta di Tiberio**, a cave with a circular pool used by the emperor Tiberius. It used to contain sculpture groups celebrating the adventures of Ulysses and his companions, erected for Tiberius between AD 4 and 26. These were smashed by a group of zealous iconoclastic monks in 511 and the pieces were discovered only in 1957. The sculptures have since been restored and are on show in the nearby **Museo Archaeologico**. Among them is a large group in the style of the *Laocoön* (in the Vatican Museums). The remains of Tiberius' villa are in front of the cave. The museum opens 9 am to one hour before sunset Tuesday to Sunday and admission to both costs €2.58.

In early September the town celebrates the feast of the patron saints Rocco and Leo the Great. There is a religious procession, music and fireworks in the evening. On Saturday, Sperlonga hosts a lively food and second-hand clothes market.

Places to Eat For a snack on the beach go to *Lido da Rocco (☎ 07 715 44 93, Via Spiaggia Angelo 22)* on the seafront, which does tasty rolls filled with mozzarella, tomato and basil. For something a bit more special try *Agli Archi (☎ 07 715 43 00, Via Ottaviano 17)* in the heart of the medieval town. The restaurant specialises in fish and there are a lot of dishes to choose from. A full meal can cost anything between €20 and €60. The restaurant is open for lunch and dinner daily, except Wednesday.

For a snack, try Filippo's *cornetti caldi* (hot croissants) available from *Fiorelli* in Sperlonga Bassa, or from any one of the town's many bars. You need to go early though, as they are popular and run out fast.

Getting There & Away To get to Sperlonga from Rome, take the COTRAL bus from the EUR-Fermi stop on the Metro Linea B. Alternatively, catch the train to Naples (not the Intercity) from Stazione Termini and get off at Fondi. From here take the COTRAL bus to Sperlonga. In theory the bus timetable coincides with the train. Otherwise you can take a taxi. The return

bus leaves from the main square at the top of the hill in the centre of Sperlonga Alta.

Sperlonga is 120km from Rome by car. Take Via Pontina (S148) from EUR going south and follow signs to Terracina. From Terracina it is a short drive on the S213 to Sperlonga.

Pontine Islands

Foreign tourists are only just beginning to discover this group of small islands between Rome and Naples. The archipelago comprises two groups of islands: Ponza, Palmarola, Gavi and Zannone to the north, and Ventotene and Santo Stefano to the south. Only two of the islands, Ponza and Ventotene, are inhabited, and their striking natural beauty and efficient services make them popular summer holiday destinations.

They are especially crowded at weekends, when they fill up with visitors from the nearby cities of Naples and Rome. Prices are not cheap and budget travellers are best to go out of season when the islands are more affordable – although beware that many services shut down.

The history of the islands goes back a long way. Homer refers to Ponza in Book Ten of the *Odyssey*, attesting to the presence of the ancient Greeks, confirmed by the remains of the tombs on the bluff overlooking Chiaia di Luna. In 313 BC, the archipelago came under Roman rule, and later came the building of sumptuous villas for the emperor and his circle. The collapse of the Empire brought about a period of decline on the islands, during which they sustained violent attacks by Saracens and by groups from mainland Italy and the nearby Isole Eolie.

Unfaithful wives, promiscuous daughters and persecuted Christians counted among the large number of people exiled to the islands at this time.

The recent history of the islands begins in 1734, when surrender to the Bourbon ruler Charles III gave rise to a wave of migration to Ponza that was to last the rest of the century. Commerce on the island flourished, at the expense of the natural habitat, largely destroyed in the rush to build and to cultivate. The island of Ponza is ecologically in

EXCURSIONS

pretty poor shape. Almost every inch of the hilly island was terraced and used for farming, causing serious erosion. Bird hunting is an obsession for the locals; migrating birds pass over on their journeys between Europe and Africa. However, all the islands are now under National Park protection.

Orientation & Information Ponza is the largest of the islands and a good base for exploring the archipelago. The port is at Ponza town, the largest settlement on the island. The other main settlement is Le Forna, 8km to the north by road. Both have decent beaches and a good choice of hotels and restaurants. For the most part the coast is steep and the stony beaches are most easily reached by boat (there is an efficient ferry service from the port and a return trip costs around €4). The two major exceptions are Spiaggia di Frontone and Chiaia di Luna, both accessible on foot.

Palmarola is uninhabited but there are facilities for tourists in summer. Zannone, slightly closer to Ponza, is part of the Parco Nazionale di Circeo and is a sanctuary for migratory birds that pass over on their journeys between Europe and Africa.

Ventotene is where Julia, the daughter of Augustus, and Octavia, the divorced wife of Nero, lived in exile (Octavia was killed shortly afterwards.) The remains of their villa can be found near Punta Eolo. Popular with fishing enthusiasts, the island has a small permanent population and limited accommodation facilities. Private vehicles are not permitted on the island, but hotels operate a minibus service to and from the port.

The Pro Loco tourist office (☎ 07 718 00 31), Via Molo Musco, is near the port in the main town on Ponza. It opens 9 am to 1 pm and 4 to 7.30 pm daily in summer, 10 am to noon daily in spring and autumn, and 10 am to noon on Saturday and Sunday only in winter. On Ventotene contact the private travel agency Bemtilem (☎ 07 718 53 65).

Things to See & Do On the west coast of Ponza is **Chiaia di Luna**, a spectacular bay so-called because of the effect produced by the reflection of the 100m-high rock face on

the sea. **Monte Guardia**, in the south, is the highest point on the island and has a breathtaking view. To get there take the path that leads from the road out of Ponza going south. If you continue past Monte Guardia you get to the ruins of an ancient **faro** (lighthouse).

Punta Incenso at the other end of the island is another high point and looks over Ventotene and Zannone. **Grotte di Pilato** on the promontory that dominates Ponza town are the remains of an ancient Roman fish farm, located at the foot of a large residence, also in ruins. The complex consists of five pools (four covered), notable for the skill with which they have been cut out of the rock. The ruins and the tunnel that connects Ponza town and Chiaia di Luna are the only Roman remains on the island.

Places to Eat The Pontine Islands are renowned for their fish-based cuisine and lentil soup is also a local speciality. On Ponza head to *Ristorante da Ciro (☎ 07 718 08 388, Via Calacaparra)*, 1km or so past the town of Le Forna, for a good seafood meal. The restaurant opens for lunch and dinner year round and there is a west-facing terrace with a view of Palmarola.

Getting There & Around The islands are accessible by car ferry or hydrofoil from Anzio, Terracina or Formia. Timetable information is available from most travel agents. During the summer the timetables are also published in the *Cronaca di Roma* section of the national daily newspapers *Il Messaggero* and *Il Tempo*.

The use of cars and large motorbikes is forbidden on Ponza during the high season but there is a good local bus service that covers the main points of interest. Otherwise, you can rent a scooter at the port from one of the numerous outlets, or from a tout who will meet you at the ferry. There is a hydrofoil that runs between Ponza and Ventotene.

The other islands are best visited on an organised day-trip or by hiring a small motor boat. In both cases get information from the port or the Pro Loco office.

Language

Italian is a Romance language related to French, Spanish, Portuguese and Romanian. The Romance languages belong to the Indo-European group of languages, which include English. Indeed, as English and Italian share common roots in Latin, you will recognise many Italian words.

Modern literary Italian began to develop in the 13th and 14th centuries, predominantly through the works of Dante, Petrarch and Boccaccio, who wrote chiefly in the Florentine dialect. The standard Italian of today is closely founded on this Florentine dialect, and although regional dialects are still commonly used by locals in everyday conversation, standard Italian is the national language of schools, media and literature, and is spoken throughout the country.

Visitors to Italy with more than the most fundamental grasp of the language need to be aware that many older Italians still expect to be addressed in the third person polite, *(lei* instead of *tu)*. Also, it's not considered appropriate to use the greeting *ciao* when addressing strangers unless they use it first; it's better to say *buon giorno* (or *buona sera*, as the case may be) and *arrivederci* (or the more polite form, *arrivederla*). We have used the polite address for most of the phrases in this guide. Use of the informal address is indicated by 'inf' in brackets. Italian also has both masculine and feminine forms (they usually end in 'o' and 'a' respectively). Where both forms are given in this guide, they are separated by a slash, the masculine form first.

If you'd like a more comprehensive guide to the language, get a copy of Lonely Planet's *Italian phrasebook*.

Pronunciation

Italian pronunciation isn't difficult to master once you learn a few simple rules. Although some of the more clipped vowels and the stress on double letters require careful practice for English speakers, it's easy enough to make yourself understood.

Vowels

Vowels are generally more clipped than in English:

a	as in 'art', *caro* (dear); sometimes short, *amico* (friend)
e	as in 'tell', *mettere* (to put)
i	as in 'inn', *inizio* (start)
o	as in 'dot', *donna* (woman); as in 'port', *dormire* (to sleep)
u	as the 'oo' in 'book', *puro* (pure)

Consonants

The pronunciation of many Italian consonants is similar to that of their English counterparts. Pronunciation of some consonants depends on certain rules:

c	as 'k' before **a**, **o** and **u**; as the 'ch' in 'choose' before **e** and **i**
ch	as the 'k' in 'kit'
g	as the 'g' in 'get' before **a**, **o**, **u** and **h**; as the 'j' in 'jet' before **e** and **i**
gli	as the 'lli' in 'million'
gn	as the 'ny' in 'canyon'
h	always silent
r	a rolled 'rr' sound
sc	as the 'sh' in 'sheep' before **e** and **i**; as 'sk' before **a**, **o**, **u** and **h**
z	as the 'ts' in 'lights', except at the beginning of a word, when it's as the 'ds' in 'suds'

Note that when **ci**, **gi** and **sci** are followed by **a**, **o** or **u**, the 'i' is not pronounced unless the accent falls on the 'i'. Thus the name 'Giovanni' is pronounced 'joh-**vahn**-nee'.

Word Stress

A double consonant is pronounced as a longer, more forceful sound than a single consonant.

Stress generally falls on the second-last syllable, as in *spa-**ghet**-ti*. When a word has an accent, the stress falls on that syllable, as in *cit-**tà*** (city).

Greetings & Civilities

Hello.	*Buongiorno.*
	Ciao. (inf)
Goodbye.	*Arrivederci.*
	Ciao. (inf)
Yes.	*Sì.*
No.	*No.*
Please.	*Per favore/Per piacere.*
Thank you.	*Grazie.*
That's fine/	*Prego.*
You're welcome.	
Excuse me.	*Mi scusi.*
Sorry (forgive me).	*Mi scusi/Mi perdoni.*
What's your name?	*Come si chiama?*
	Come ti chiami? (inf)
My name is ...	*Mi chiamo ...*
Where are you	*Di dov'è?*
from?	*Di dove sei?* (inf)
I'm from ...	*Sono di ...*
I (don't) like ...	*(Non) Mi piace ...*

Language Difficulties

Please write it down.	*Può scriverlo, per favore?*
I understand.	*Capisco.*
I don't understand.	*Non capisco.*
Do you speak English?	*Parla inglese?*
	Parli inglese? (inf)
Does anyone here speak English?	*C'è qualcuno che parla inglese?*
How do you say ... in Italian?	*Come si dice ... in italiano?*
What does ... mean?	*Che vuole dire ...?*

Paperwork

name	*nome*
nationality	*nazionalità*
date of birth	*data di nascita*
place of birth	*luogo di nascita*
sex (gender)	*sesso*
passport	*passaporto*
visa	*visto consolare*

Getting Around

What time does ... leave/arrive?	*A che ora parte/ arriva ...?*
the boat	*la barca*
the (city) bus	*l'autobus*
the (intercity) bus	*il pullman/corriere*
the plane	*l'aereo*
the train	*il treno*

I'd like a ... ticket.	*Vorrei un biglietto di ...*
one-way	*solo andata*
return	*andata e ritorno*
1st class	*prima classe*
2nd class	*seconda classe*

I want to go to ...	*Voglio andare a ...*
The train has been cancelled/delayed.	*Il treno è soppresso/ in ritardo.*
the first	*il primo*
the last	*l'ultimo*
platform (three)	*binario (tre)*
ticket office	*biglietteria*
timetable	*orario*
train station	*stazione*

I'd like to rent ...	*Vorrei noleggiare ...*
a bicycle	*una bicicletta*
a car	*una macchina*
a motorcycle	*una motocicletta*

Directions

Where is ...?	*Dov'è ...?*
Can you show me (on the map)?	*Può mostrarmelo (sulla carta/pianta)?*
Go straight ahead.	*Si va sempre diritto.*
	Vai sempre diritto. (inf)
Turn left.	*Giri a sinistra.*
Turn right.	*Giri a destra.*
at the next corner	*al prossimo angolo*
at the traffic lights	*al semaforo*
behind	*dietro*
in front of	*davanti*
opposite	*di fronte a*
near	*vicino*
far	*lontano*

Around Town

I'm looking for ...	*Cerco ...*
a bank	*una banca*
the church	*la chiesa*
the city centre	*il centro (città)*
the ... embassy	*l'ambasciata di ...*
my hotel	*il mio albergo*
the market	*il mercato*
the museum	*il museo*
the post office	*la posta*
a public toilet	*un gabinetto/ bagno pubblico*
the telephone centre	*il centro telefonico*

Signs

Ingresso/Entrata	**Entrance**
Uscita	**Exit**
Aperto	**Open**
Chiuso	**Closed**
Informazione	**Information**
Camere Libere	**Rooms Available**
Completo	**Full/No Vacancies**
Proibito/Vietato	**Prohibited**
Polizia/	**Police**
Carabinieri	
Questura	**Police Station**
Gabinetti/Bagni	**Toilets**
Uomini	**Men**
Donne	**Women**

the tourist office	*l'ufficio di turismo/ d'informazione*

I want to change ...	*Voglio cambiare ...*
money	*del denaro*
travellers cheques	*degli assegni per viaggiatori*

Accommodation

I'm looking for ...	*Cerco ...*
a guesthouse	*una pensione*
a hotel	*un albergo*
a youth hostel	*un ostello per la gioventù*

Where is a cheap hotel?	*Dov'è un albergo che costa poco?*
What is the address?	*Cos'è l'indirizzo?*
Could you write the address, please?	*Può scrivere l'indirizzo, per favore?*
Do you have any rooms available?	*Ha camere libere/C'è una camera libera?*

I'd like ...	*Vorrei ...*
a bed	*un letto*
a single room	*una camera singola*
a room with a double bed	*una camera matrimoniale*
a room with two beds	*una camera doppia*

a room with a bathroom	*una camera con bagno*
to share a dorm	*un letto in dormitorio*

How much is it ...?	*Quanto costa ...?*
per night	*per la notte*
per person	*per ciascuno*

May I see it?	*Posso vederla?*
Where is the bathroom?	*Dov'è il bagno?*
I'm/We're leaving today.	*Parto/Partiamo oggi.*

Shopping

I'd like to buy ...	*Vorrei comprare ...*
How much is it?	*Quanto costa?*
I'm just looking.	*Sto solo guardando.*
May I look at it?	*Posso dare un'occhiata?*
I don't like it.	*Non mi piace.*
It's cheap.	*Non è caro/a.*
It's too expensive.	*È troppo caro/a.*
I'll take it.	*Lo/La compro.*
Do you accept credit cards?	*Accettate le carte di credito?*

more	*più*
less	*meno*
bigger	*più grande*
smaller	*più piccolo/a*

Time, Date & Numbers

What time is it?	*Che (ora è/ore sono)?*
It's (8 o'clock).	*Sono (le otto).*
When?	*Quando?*
in the morning	*di mattina*
in the afternoon	*di pomeriggio*
in the evening	*di sera*
today	*oggi*
tomorrow	*domani*
yesterday	*ieri*

Monday	*lunedì*
Tuesday	*martedì*
Wednesday	*mercoledì*
Thursday	*giovedì*
Friday	*venerdì*
Saturday	*sabato*
Sunday	*domenica*

January	*gennaio*
February	*febbraio*
March	*marzo*
April	*aprile*
May	*maggio*
June	*giugno*
July	*luglio*
August	*agosto*
September	*settembre*
October	*ottobre*
November	*novembre*
December	*dicembre*

0	*zero*
1	*uno*
2	*due*
3	*tre*
4	*quattro*
5	*cinque*
6	*sei*
7	*sette*
8	*otto*
9	*nove*
10	*dieci*
11	*undici*
12	*dodici*
13	*tredici*
14	*quattordici*
15	*quindici*
16	*sedici*
17	*diciassette*
18	*diciotto*
19	*diciannove*
20	*venti*
21	*ventuno*
22	*ventidue*
30	*trenta*
40	*quaranta*
50	*cinquanta*
60	*sessanta*
70	*settanta*
80	*ottanta*
90	*novanta*
100	*cento*
1000	*mille*
2000	*due mila*

one million	*un milione*

Emergencies

Help!	*Aiuto!*
Call ...!	*Chiami ...!*
	Chiama ...! (inf)
a doctor	*un dottore/*
	un medico
the police	*la polizia*
There's been an accident!	*C'è stato un incidente!*
I'm lost.	*Mi sono perso/a.*
Go away!	*Lasciami in pace!*
	Vai via! (inf)

Health

I'm ill.	*Mi sento male.*
It hurts here.	*Mi fa male qui.*

I'm ...	*Sono ...*
asthmatic	*asmatico/a*
diabetic	*diabetico/a*
epileptic	*epilettico/a*

I'm allergic ...	*Sono allergico/a ...*
to antibiotics	*agli antibiotici*
to penicillin	*alla penicillina*
to nuts	*alle noci*

antiseptic	*antisettico*
aspirin	*aspirina*
condoms	*preservativi*
contraceptive	*anticoncezionale*
diarrhoea	*diarrea*
medicine	*medicina*
sunblock cream	*crema/latte solare (per protezione)*
tampons	*tamponi*

FOOD

breakfast	*prima colazione*
lunch	*pranzo*
dinner	*cena*
a restaurant	*un ristorante*
a grocery store	*un alimentari*

I'd like the set lunch.	*Vorrei il menù turistico.*
Is service included in the bill?	*È compreso il servizio?*

| What is this? | (Che) cos'è? |
| I'm a vegetarian. | Sono vegetariano/a. |

I don't eat ...	Non mangio ...
meat	carne
chicken	pollo
fish	pesce

Menu Decoder

This glossary is intended as a brief guide to some basics. Most travellers will already be well acquainted with the various Italian pastas, which include spaghetti, fettucine, penne, rigatoni, gnocchi, lasagne, tortellini and ravioli. The names are the same in Italy and no further definitions are given here.

Useful Words

antipasto	starter
affumicato	smoked
al dente	firm (as all good pasta should be)
alla brace	cooked over hot coals
alla griglia	grilled
arrosto	roasted
ben cotto	well done (cooked)
bollito	boiled
cameriere/a	waiter/waitress
coltello	knife
conto	bill/check
caffè	coffee
cotto	cooked
crudo	raw
cucchiaino	teaspoon
cucchiaio	spoon
dolce	dessert
forchetta	fork
fritto	fried
menù	menu
piatto	plate
primo piatto	first course (often pasta or risotto)
secondo piatto	second course (meat or fish)

Common Food Items

aceto	vinegar
burro	butter
contorno	vegetable side dish
farinata	thin flat bread made from chickpea flour

focaccia	flat bread (usually served with a variety of toppings)
formaggio	cheese
insalata	salad
limone	lemon
marmellata	jam
miele	honey
olio	oil
olive	olives
pane	bread
pane integrale	wholemeal bread
panna	cream
pepe	pepper
peperoncino	chilli
polenta	cooked cornmeal
riso	rice
risotto	rice cooked with wine and stock
sale	salt
uovo/uova	egg/eggs
zucchero	sugar

Soups & Antipasti

brodo – broth
carpaccio – very fine slices of raw meat
insalata caprese – sliced tomatoes with mozzarella and basil
insalata di mare – seafood, generally crustaceans
minestrina in brodo – pasta in broth
minestrone – vegetable soup
olive ascolane – stuffed, deep-fried olives
prosciutto e melone – cured ham with melon
ripieni – stuffed, oven-baked vegetables
stracciatella – egg in broth

Pasta Sauces

alla matriciana – tomato and bacon
al ragù – meat sauce (bolognese)
arrabbiata – tomato and chilli
carbonara – egg, bacon and black pepper
crema di pomodori secchi – sauce of sun-dried tomatoes
crema di rucola – creamed rocket, best served with gnocchi
gremolata – chopped parsley, garlic and lemon
napoletana – tomato and basil
panna – cream, prosciutto and sometimes peas

pesto genovese – basil, garlic, oil and pine nuts

salsa di noci – pasta sauce made from ground nuts

vongole – clams, garlic, oil and sometimes with tomato

Pizzas

All pizzas listed have a tomato (and sometimes mozzarella) base.

capricciosa – olives, prosciutto, mushrooms and artichokes

frutti di mare – seafood

funghi – mushrooms

margherita – oregano

napoletana – anchovies

pugliese – tomato, mozzarella and onions

quattro formaggi – with four types of cheese

quattro stagioni – like a capricciosa, but sometimes with egg

verdura – mixed vegetables; usually courgette (zucchini) and aubergine (eggplant), sometimes carrot and spinach

Meat & Fish

acciughe – anchovies

agnello – lamb

aragosta – lobster

bistecca – steak

burrida – fish stew

busecca – tripe slices boiled with beans

calamari – squid

cassoeula – pork and vegetable stew

cozze – mussels

dentice – dentex (type of fish)

fegato – liver

gamberi – prawns

granchio – crab

lumache – snails

manzo – beef

merluzzo – cod

ossobuco – sliced veal shanks

ostriche – oysters

pesce spada – swordfish

pollo – chicken

polpo – octopus

salsiccia – sausage

sarde – sardines

sgombro – mackerel

sogliola – sole

tacchino – turkey

tonno – tuna

triglie – red mullet

trippa – tripe

vitello – veal

vongole – clams

Vegetables

asparagi – asparagus

carciofi – artichokes

carote – carrots

cipolle – onions

fagiolini – string beans

melanzane – aubergines (eggplant)

patate – potatoes

peperoni – peppers

piselli – peas

spinaci – spinach

Fruit

arance – oranges

banane – bananas

ciliegie – cherries

fragole – strawberries

mele – apples

pere – pears

pesche – peaches

uve – grapes

Glossary

See the Food section in the Language chapter for a list of culinary terms

(s) indicates singular, (pl) indicates plural

ACI – Automobile Club Italiano (Italian Automobile Association)
aereo – aeroplane
aeroporto – airport
albergo (s), **alberghi** (pl) – hotel (up to five stars)
alimentari – grocery shop
amaro – bitter herbal digestive liqueur
ambasciata – embassy
ambulanza – ambulance
APT – Azienda di Promozione Turistica (provincial tourist office)
autostrada (s), **autostrade** (pl) – motorway, highway

bagno – bathroom, also toilet
bancomat – ATM (automated teller machine)
bar – cafe
barriere – beer bar
benzina – petrol
benzina senza piombo – unleaded petrol
biblioteca (s), **biblioteche** (pl) – library
biglietteria – box or ticket office
biglietto – ticket
biglietto chilometrico – kilometric ticket
borgo (s), **borghi** (pl) – walled village
BR – Brigate Rosse (Red Brigades; terrorist group)

caffè – coffee; cafe
calcio – football
cambio – currency exchange bureau
camera – room
campanile – bell tower
cappella – chapel
carabinieri – police with military and civil duties
carnevale – carnival period between Epiphany and Lent
carta d'identità – identity card
carta telefonica – phonecard
cartoleria – stationery shop

casa – house, home
casino – mansion
castello – castle
cattedrale – cathedral
centro – city centre
centro commerciali – large shopping centre
centro sociali – social club
centro storico – historic centre, old city
chiesa (s), **chiese** (pl) – church
chiostro – cloister; covered walkway, usually enclosed by columns, around a quadrangle
cimitero – cemetery
circo – circus, chariot racetrack
CIT – Compagnia Italiana di Turismo (Italy's national travel agency)
colazione – breakfast
colle – hill
colonna – column
commissariato – local police station
comune – equivalent to a municipality or county; town or city council; historically, a commune (self-governing town or city)
cordonata – stepped ramp
corso – main street
CTS – Centro Turistico Studentesco e Giovanile (Centre for Student and Youth Tourists)
cuccetta – couchette
cupola – dome

DC – Democrazia Cristiana (Christian Democrats; political party)
digestivo – after-dinner liqueur
domus – house
DS – Democratici della Sinistra (Democrats of the Left; political party)

enoteca – wine bar
ES – Eurostar (very fast train)
espresso – express mail; express train; short black coffee
EUR – Esposizione Universale di Roma, a Fascist-era cultural complex south of the city centre

farmacia – pharmacy
fermo posta – poste restante

ferrovia – train station
festa – feast day; festival
fidanzato – boyfriend
fiume – river
fontana – fountain
forno – bakery
forte – fort
forum (s), **fora** (pl) – public square
francobolli – stamps
FS – Ferrovie dello Stato (State Railways)

gabinetto – toilets, WC
gasolio – diesel
gelateria – ice-cream parlour
guardia di finanza – fiscal police

IAT – Informazioni e Assistenza ai Turisti (local tourist office)
IC – Intercity (fast train)
insula – multistorey apartment block
isola – island
IVA – Imposta di Valore Aggiunto (value-added tax)

lago – lake
largo – (small) square
lavanderia – laundrette
lavaseco – dry-cleaning
Lega Nord – Northern League (federalist political party)
libreria – bookshop
lido – beach
lingua originale – original language
loggia – covered area on the side of a building; porch
lungolago – waterfront

macchina da scrivere – typewriter
marito – husband
mercato – market
Metropolitana (Metro) – suburban underground train system
monte – mountain
mura – city wall
museo (s), **musei** (pl) – museum

necropolis – literally 'city of the dead'; above-ground tomb complex, often Etruscan
numeri verdi – toll-free numbers
orto botanico – botanical gardens

ospedale – hospital
ostello – hostel
osteria – cheap restaurant or wine bar offering a small selection of dishes

palazzo (s), **palazzi** (pl) – mansion or palace; large building of any type (including an apartment block)
panetteria – bakery
parco – park
passeggiata – traditional evening stroll
pasticceria – cake shop
PCI – Partito Comunista Italiano (Italian Communist Party)
PDS – Partito Democratico della Sinistra (Democratic Party of the Left)
pellicola – roll of film
pensione – small hotel, often offering board
permesso di lavoro – work permit
permesso di soggiorno – permit to stay in Italy for a nominated period
pescheria – fish shop
piazza (s), **piazze** (pl) – square
piazzale – (large) open square
pietà – literally 'pity or compassion'; sculpture, drawing or painting of the dead Christ supported by the Madonna
pinacoteca – art gallery
piscina – pool
pizzeria (s), **pizzerie** (pl) – pizza restaurant
poliambulatorio – polyclinic
polizia – police
Polo per le Libertà – Freedom Alliance (right-wing political coalition)
ponte – bridge
porta – city gate
portico – portico; covered walkway, usually attached to the outside of buildings
posta – post office
presepio – model Nativity scene
profumeria – perfumery
pronto soccorso – casualty ward
PRC – Partito Rifondazione Comunista (Refounded Communist Party)
PSI – Partito Socialista Italiano (Italian Socialist Party)

questura – police station

regioni – administrative regions in Italy, such as Lazio

Risorgimento – late-19th-century movement led by Garibaldi and others to create a united, independent Italian state
ristorante – restaurant
rosticceria – restaurant specialising in meat dishes, often takeaway

sala – room in a museum or a gallery
salumeria – delicatessen
scala – staircase
scalinata – staircase
sedia a rotelle – wheelchair
seggliolini – children's highchairs
senza piombo – unleaded petrol
servizio – service charge in restaurants
sindaco – mayor
stazione – station
stazione di servizio – petrol or service station
supplemento – supplement, payable on a fast train

tabaccheria – tobacconist's shop
tarocco – tarot cards
tavola calda – literally 'hot table'; pre-prepared meat, pasta and vegetable selection, often self-service

TCI – Touring Club Italiano
teatro – theatre
tempio – temple
terme – baths
titilus – a private house used for clandestine Christian worship
torre – tower
trattoria (s), **trattorie** (pl) – inexpensive restaurant; less sophisticated version of a *ristorante*
treno – train

UDR – Unione Democratica per la Repubblica (Democratic Union for the Republic; centre political party)
ufficio postale – post office
ufficio stranieri – foreigners office (police)

via – street, road
via aerea – air mail
vicoli – alley, alleyway
vigili urbani – traffic police, local police
villa – town house or country house; also the park surrounding the house
vineria – wine bar
vino – wine

Lonely Planet Guides by Region

Lonely Planet is known worldwide for publishing practical, reliable and no-nonsense travel information in our guides and on our Web site. The Lonely Planet list covers just about every accessible part of the world. Currently there are 16 series: Travel guides, Shoestring guides, Condensed guides, Phrasebooks, Read This First, Healthy Travel, Walking guides, Cycling guides, Watching Wildlife guides, Pisces Diving & Snorkeling guides, City Maps, Road Atlases, Out to Eat, World Food, Journeys travel literature and Pictorials.

AFRICA Africa on a shoestring • Botswana • Cairo • Cairo City Map • Cape Town • Cape Town City Map • East Africa • Egypt • Egyptian Arabic phrasebook • Ethiopia, Eritrea & Djibouti • Ethiopian Amharic phrasebook • The Gambia & Senegal • Healthy Travel Africa • Kenya • Malawi • Morocco • Moroccan Arabic phrasebook • Mozambique • Namibia • Read This First: Africa • South Africa, Lesotho & Swaziland • Southern Africa • Southern Africa Road Atlas • Swahili phrasebook • Tanzania, Zanzibar & Pemba • Trekking in East Africa • Tunisia • Watching Wildlife East Africa • Watching Wildlife Southern Africa • West Africa • World Food Morocco • Zambia • Zimbabwe, Botswana & Namibia
Travel Literature: Mali Blues: Traveling to an African Beat • The Rainbird: A Central African Journey • Songs to an African Sunset: A Zimbabwean Story

AUSTRALIA & THE PACIFIC Aboriginal Australia & the Torres Strait Islands •Auckland • Australia • Australian phrasebook • Australia Road Atlas • Cycling Australia • Cycling New Zealand • Fiji • Fijian phrasebook • Healthy Travel Australia, NZ & the Pacific • Islands of Australia's Great Barrier Reef • Melbourne • Melbourne City Map • Micronesia • New Caledonia • New South Wales • New Zealand • Northern Territory • Outback Australia • Out to Eat – Melbourne • Out to Eat – Sydney • Papua New Guinea • Pidgin phrasebook • Queensland • Rarotonga & the Cook Islands • Samoa • Solomon Islands • South Australia • South Pacific • South Pacific phrasebook • Sydney • Sydney City Map • Sydney Condensed • Tahiti & French Polynesia • Tasmania • Tonga • Tramping in New Zealand • Vanuatu • Victoria • Walking in Australia • Watching Wildlife Australia • Western Australia
Travel Literature: Islands in the Clouds: Travels in the Highlands of New Guinea • Kiwi Tracks: A New Zealand Journey • Sean & David's Long Drive

CENTRAL AMERICA & THE CARIBBEAN Bahamas, Turks & Caicos • Baja California • Belize, Guatemala & Yucatán • Bermuda • Central America on a shoestring • Costa Rica • Costa Rica Spanish phrasebook • Cuba • Cycling Cuba • Dominican Republic & Haiti • Eastern Caribbean • Guatemala • Havana • Healthy Travel Central & South America • Jamaica • Mexico • Mexico City • Panama • Puerto Rico • Read This First: Central & South America • Virgin Islands • World Food Caribbean • World Food Mexico • Yucatán
Travel Literature: Green Dreams: Travels in Central America

EUROPE Amsterdam • Amsterdam City Map • Amsterdam Condensed • Andalucía • Athens • Austria • Baltic States phrasebook • Barcelona • Barcelona City Map • Belgium & Luxembourg • Berlin • Berlin City Map • Britain • British phrasebook • Brussels, Bruges & Antwerp • Brussels City Map • Budapest • Budapest City Map • Canary Islands • Catalunya & the Costa Brava • Central Europe • Central Europe phrasebook • Copenhagen • Corfu & the Ionians • Corsica • Crete • Crete Condensed • Croatia • Cycling Britain • Cycling France • Cyprus • Czech & Slovak Republics • Czech phrasebook • Denmark • Dublin • Dublin City Map • Dublin Condensed • Eastern Europe • Eastern Europe phrasebook • Edinburgh • Edinburgh City Map • England • Estonia, Latvia & Lithuania • Europe on a shoestring • Europe phrasebook • Finland • Florence • Florence City Map • France • Frankfurt City Map • Frankfurt Condensed • French phrasebook • Georgia, Armenia & Azerbaijan • Germany • German phrasebook • Greece • Greek Islands • Greek phrasebook • Hungary • Iceland, Greenland & the Faroe Islands • Ireland • Italian phrasebook • Italy • Kraków • Lisbon • The Loire • London • London City Map • London Condensed • Madrid • Madrid City Map • Malta • Mediterranean Europe • Milan, Turin & Genoa • Moscow • Munich • Netherlands • Normandy • Norway • Out to Eat – London • Out to Eat – Paris • Paris • Paris City Map • Paris Condensed • Poland • Polish phrasebook • Portugal • Portuguese phrasebook • Prague • Prague City Map • Provence & the Côte d'Azur • Read This First: Europe • Rhodes & the Dodecanese • Romania & Moldova • Rome • Rome City Map • Rome Condensed • Russia, Ukraine & Belarus • Russian phrasebook • Scandinavia & Baltic Europe • Scandinavian phrasebook • Scotland • Sicily • Slovenia • South-West France • Spain • Spanish phrasebook • Stockholm • St Petersburg • St Petersburg City Map • Sweden • Switzerland • Tuscany • Ukrainian phrasebook • Venice • Vienna • Wales • Walking in Britain • Walking in France • Walking in Ireland • Walking in Italy • Walking in Scotland • Walking in Spain • Walking in Switzerland • Western Europe • World Food France • World Food Greece • World Food Ireland • World Food Italy • World Food Spain **Travel Literature:** After Yugoslavia • Love and War in the Apennines • The Olive Grove: Travels in Greece • On the Shores of the Mediterranean • Round Ireland in Low Gear • A Small Place in Italy

Lonely Planet Mail Order

L onely Planet products are distributed worldwide.They are also available by mail order from Lonely Planet, so if you have difficulty finding a title please write to us. North and South American residents should write to 150 Linden St, Oakland, CA 94607, USA; European and African residents should write to 10a Spring Place, London NW5 3BH, UK; and residents of other countries to Locked Bag 1, Footscray, Victoria 3011, Australia.

INDIAN SUBCONTINENT & THE INDIAN OCEAN Bangladesh • Bengali phrasebook • Bhutan • Delhi • Goa • Healthy Travel Asia & India • Hindi & Urdu phrasebook • India • India & Bangladesh City Map • Indian Himalaya • Karakoram Highway • Kathmandu City Map • Kerala • Madagascar • Maldives • Mauritius, Réunion & Seychelles • Mumbai (Bombay) • Nepal • Nepali phrasebook • North India • Pakistan • Rajasthan • Read This First: Asia & India • South India • Sri Lanka • Sri Lanka phrasebook • Tibet • Tibetan phrasebook • Trekking in the Indian Himalaya • Trekking in the Karakoram & Hindukush • Trekking in the Nepal Himalaya • World Food India **Travel Literature:** The Age of Kali: Indian Travels and Encounters • Hello Goodnight: A Life of Goa • In Rajasthan • Maverick in Madagascar • A Season in Heaven: True Tales from the Road to Kathmandu • Shopping for Buddhas • A Short Walk in the Hindu Kush • Slowly Down the Ganges

MIDDLE EAST & CENTRAL ASIA Bahrain, Kuwait & Qatar • Central Asia • Central Asia phrasebook • Dubai • Farsi (Persian) phrasebook • Hebrew phrasebook • Iran • Israel & the Palestinian Territories • Istanbul • Istanbul City Map • Istanbul to Cairo • Istanbul to Kathmandu • Jerusalem • Jerusalem City Map • Jordan • Lebanon • Middle East • Oman & the United Arab Emirates • Syria • Turkey • Turkish phrasebook • World Food Turkey • Yemen **Travel Literature:** Black on Black: Iran Revisited • Breaking Ranks: Turbulent Travels in the Promised Land • The Gates of Damascus • Kingdom of the Film Stars: Journey into Jordan

NORTH AMERICA Alaska • Boston • Boston City Map • Boston Condensed • British Columbia • California & Nevada • California Condensed • Canada • Chicago • Chicago City Map • Chicago Condensed • Florida • Georgia & the Carolinas • Great Lakes • Hawaii • Hiking in Alaska • Hiking in the USA • Honolulu & Oahu City Map • Las Vegas • Los Angeles • Los Angeles City Map • Louisiana & the Deep South • Miami • Miami City Map • Montreal • New England • New Orleans • New Orleans City Map • New York City • New York City City Map • New York City Condensed • New York, New Jersey & Pennsylvania • Oahu • Out to Eat – San Francisco • Pacific Northwest • Rocky Mountains • San Diego & Tijuana • San Francisco • San Francisco City Map • Seattle • Seattle City Map • Southwest • Texas • Toronto • USA • USA phrasebook • Vancouver • Vancouver City Map • Virginia & the Capital Region • Washington, DC • Washington, DC City Map • World Food New Orleans **Travel Literature:** Caught Inside: A Surfer's Year on the California Coast • Drive Thru America

NORTH-EAST ASIA Beijing • Beijing City Map • Cantonese phrasebook • China • Hiking in Japan • Hong Kong & Macau • Hong Kong City Map • Hong Kong Condensed • Japan • Japanese phrasebook • Korea • Korean phrasebook • Kyoto • Mandarin phrasebook • Mongolia • Mongolian phrasebook • Seoul • Shanghai • South-West China • Taiwan • Tokyo • Tokyo Condensed • World Food Hong Kong • World Food Japan **Travel Literature:** In Xanadu: A Quest • Lost Japan

SOUTH AMERICA Argentina, Uruguay & Paraguay • Bolivia • Brazil • Brazilian phrasebook • Buenos Aires • Buenos Aires City Map • Chile & Easter Island • Colombia • Ecuador & the Galapagos Islands • Healthy Travel Central & South America • Latin American Spanish phrasebook • Peru • Quechua phrasebook • Read This First: Central & South America • Rio de Janeiro • Rio de Janeiro City Map • Santiago de Chile • South America on a shoestring • Trekking in the Patagonian Andes • Venezuela **Travel Literature:** Full Circle: A South American Journey

SOUTH-EAST ASIA Bali & Lombok • Bangkok • Bangkok City Map • Burmese phrasebook • Cambodia • Cycling Vietnam, Laos & Cambodia • East Timor phrasebook • Hanoi • Healthy Travel Asia & India • Hill Tribes phrasebook • Ho Chi Minh City (Saigon) • Indonesia • Indonesian phrasebook • Indonesia's Eastern Islands • Java • Lao phrasebook • Laos • Malay phrasebook • Malaysia, Singapore & Brunei • Myanmar (Burma) • Philippines • Pilipino (Tagalog) phrasebook • Read This First: Asia & India • Singapore • Singapore City Map • South-East Asia on a shoestring • South-East Asia phrasebook • Thailand • Thailand's Islands & Beaches • Thailand, Vietnam, Laos & Cambodia Road Atlas • Thai phrasebook • Vietnam • Vietnamese phrasebook • World Food Indonesia • World Food Thailand • World Food Vietnam

ALSO AVAILABLE: Antarctica • The Arctic • The Blue Man: Tales of Travel, Love and Coffee • Brief Encounters: Stories of Love, Sex & Travel • Buddhist Stupas in Asia: The Shape of Perfection • Chasing Rickshaws • The Last Grain Race • Lonely Planet ... On the Edge: Adventurous Escapades from Around the World • Lonely Planet Unpacked • Lonely Planet Unpacked Again • Not the Only Planet: Science Fiction Travel Stories • Ports of Call: A Journey by Sea • Sacred India • Travel Photography: A Guide to Taking Better Pictures • Travel with Children • Tuvalu: Portrait of an Island Nation

LONELY PLANET

ON THE ROAD

Travel Guides explore cities, regions and countries, and supply information on transport, restaurants and accommodation, covering all budgets. They come with reliable, easy-to-use maps, practical advice, cultural and historical facts and a rundown on attractions both on and off the beaten track. There are over 200 titles in this classic series, covering nearly every country in the world.

 Lonely Planet Upgrades extend the shelf life of existing travel guides by detailing any changes that may affect travel in a region since a book has been published. Upgrades can be downloaded for free from **www.lonelyplanet.com/upgrades**

For travellers with more time than money, **Shoestring** guides offer dependable, first-hand information with hundreds of detailed maps, plus insider tips for stretching money as far as possible. Covering entire continents in most cases, the six-volume shoestring guides are known around the world as 'backpackers bibles'.

For the discerning short-term visitor, **Condensed** guides highlight the best a destination has to offer in a full-colour, pocket-sized format designed for quick access. They include everything from top sights and walking tours to opinionated reviews of where to eat, stay, shop and have fun.

CitySync lets travellers use their Palm™ or Visor™ hand-held computers to guide them through a city with handy tips on transport, history, cultural life, major sights, and shopping and entertainment options. It can also quickly search and sort hundreds of reviews of hotels, restaurants and attractions, and pinpoint their location on scrollable street maps. CitySync can be downloaded from **www.citysync.com**

MAPS & ATLASES

Lonely Planet's **City Maps** feature downtown and metropolitan maps, as well as transit routes and walking tours. The maps come complete with an index of streets, a listing of sights and a plastic coat for extra durability.

Road Atlases are an essential navigation tool for serious travellers. Cross-referenced with the guidebooks, they also feature distance and climate charts and a complete site index.

LONELY PLANET

OFF THE ROAD

Journeys, the travel literature series written by renowned travel authors, capture the spirit of a place or illuminate a culture with a journalist's attention to detail and a novelist's flair for words. These are tales to soak up while you're actually on the road or dip into as an at-home armchair indulgence.

The new range of lavishly illustrated **Pictorial** books is just the ticket for both travellers and dreamers. Off-beat tales and vivid photographs bring the adventure of travel to your doorstep long before the journey begins and long after it is over.

Lonely Planet **Videos** encourage the same independent, tough-minded approach as the guidebooks. Currently airing throughout the world, this award-winning series features innovative footage and an original soundtrack.

Yes, we know, work is tough, so do a little bit of deskside dreaming with the spiral-bound Lonely Planet **Diary**, the tearaway page-a-day **Day-to-Day Calendar** or a Lonely Planet **Wall Calendar**, filled with great photos from around the world.

TRAVELLERS NETWORK

Lonely Planet Online. Lonely Planet's award-winning Web site has insider information on hundreds of destinations, from Amsterdam to Zimbabwe, complete with interactive maps and relevant links. The site also offers the latest travel news, recent reports from travellers on the road, guidebook upgrades, a travel links site, an online book-buying option and a lively traveller's bulletin board. It can be viewed at **www.lonelyplanet.com** or AOL keyword: lp.

Planet Talk is a quarterly print newsletter, full of gossip, advice, anecdotes and author articles. It provides an antidote to the being-at-home blues and lets you plan and dream for the next trip. Contact the nearest Lonely Planet office for your free copy.

Comet, the free Lonely Planet newsletter, comes via email once a month. It's loaded with travel news, advice, dispatches from authors, travel competitions and letters from readers. To subscribe, click on the Comet subscription link on the front page of the Web site.

LONELY PLANET

You already know that Lonely Planet produces more than this one guidebook, but you might not be aware of the other products we have on this region. Here is a selection of titles that you may want to check out as well:

Europe on a shoestring
ISBN 1 86450 150 2
US$24.99 • UK£14.99

Italy
ISBN 1 86450 352 1
US$24.99 • UK£14.99

Italian phrasebook
ISBN 0 86442 456 6
US$5.95 • UK£3.99

Florence
ISBN 1 74059 030 9
US$17.99 • UK£8.99

Mediterrean Europe
ISBN 1 86450 154 5
US$27.99 • UK£15.99

Read This First: Europe
ISBN 1 86450 136 7
US$14.99 • UK£8.99

Rome
ISBN 1 86450 311 4
US$15.99 • UK£9.99

Venice
ISBN 1 86450 321 1
US$15.99 • UK£8.99

Walking in Italy
ISBN 0 86442 542 2
US$17.95 • UK£11.99

Western Europe
ISBN 1 86450 163 4
US$27.99 • UK£15.99

World Food Italy
ISBN 1 86450 022 0
US$12.95 • UK£7.99

Rome Condensed
ISBN 1 86450 360 2
US$11.99 • UK£5.99

Available wherever books are sold

Index

Text

C

Boxed Text

Rome Map Section

JONATHAN SMITH

ROME METRO MAP

A cobbled Roman road leads the way to the ancient Arco di Tito, built in AD 81 to honour Titus.

In a whirl: the impressive Renaissance gardens of Villa Lante, Bagnaia, north-east of Viterbo

MAP 1 - GREATER ROME

A fine romance on Isola Tiberna

Statue of Giuseppe Garibaldi, Piazza Garibaldi

MAP 2

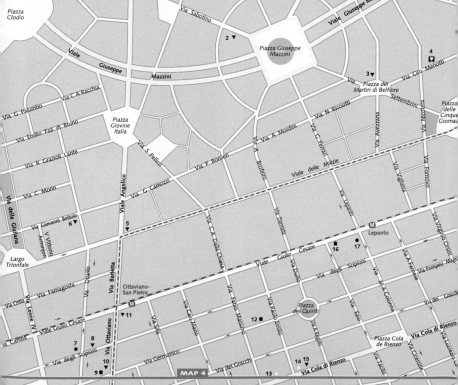

PLACES TO STAY
9   Hotel Amalia
12 Hotel Giuggioli; Hotel Lady;
    Pensione Nautilus; Residenza
    dei Quiriti
16 Pensione Paradise
22 Hotel Locarno
26 Hotel Russie
36 Hotel Margutta

PLACES TO EAT
2   Antonini
3   Cacio e Pepe
5   Emporium Naturae
6   Osteria dell'Angelo
8   L'Isola della Pizza
11 Castroni
12 Volpetti
15 Standa Supermarket
23 Caffè Rosati
32 Margutta Vegetariano
38 Edy

PUBS, BARS & CLUBS
4   Tastevin

SHOPPING
1   L'Allegretto
13 United Colors of Benetton

14 COIN
27 Ottica Spiezia
30 Sotto una Foglia di Cavolo
33 Maurizio Grossi
34 Artimede
37 Tad
39 Animalier e Oltre

OTHER
7   Laundrette
17 Fotoservice
18 Museo Nazionale Etrusco di
    Villa Giulia
19 Villa Giulia; Galleria Nazionale
    d'Arte Moderna
20 Centro Studi Flaminio
21 Chiesa di Santa Maria del
    Popolo
24 Chiesa di Santa Maria dei
    Miracoli
25 Chiesa di Santa Maria in
    Montesanto
28 Nouvelles Frontières
29 Ospedale San Giacomo
31 Casa di Goethe
35 Post Office
40 Villa Medici
41 Il Galoppatio Equestrian
    Club

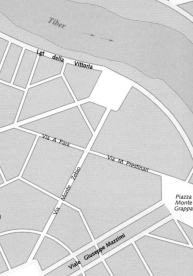

MAP 2

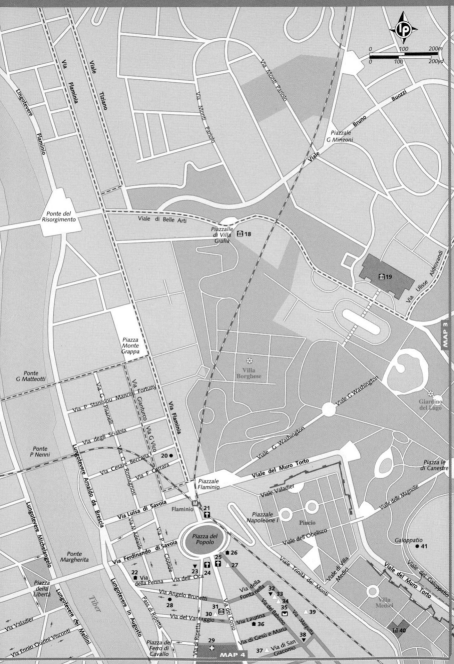

Via Flaminia

Via Tiziano

Viale

Via Monti Parioli

Via Monti Parioli

Buozzi

Lungotevere Flaminio

Lungotevere Flaminio

Piazzale G Minzoni

Viale Bruno

Ponte del Risorgimento

Viale di Belle Arti

Piazzale di Villa Giulia 🏛18

Via Ulisse Aldrovandi

🏛19

MAP 3

Piazza Monte Grappa

Villa Borghese

Ponte G Matteotti

Viale G Washington

Giardino del Lago

Via C Stanislao Mancini

Via C Pisacane

Via P Fortuny

Via Giancurzo

Via G Vico

Via F Carrara

Via degli Scialoia

Ponte P Nenni

Lungotevere Arnaldo da Brescia

Via C Beccaria

Via Cesare Beccaria

Via F Carrara

20 ●

Viale G Washington

Piazza le di Canestre

Viale del Muro Torto

Viale delle Magnolie

Ponte Margherita

Via Luisa di Savoia

Piazzale Flaminio

Viale Valadier

Galoppatio
● 41

Flaminio Ⓜ 21
🚇

Piazzale Napoleone I

Pincio

Viale del Muro Torto

Viale del Galoppatio

Ponte Margherita

Piazza della Libertà

Via Ferdinando di Savoia

Via Adelaide

Piazza del Popolo

26
▪

Viale dell'Obelisco

Viale di Villa Medici

Viale del Galoppatio

Lungotevere Michelangelo

22 ●

Via della Penna

25 ▪
23 ▼ 24

27
▲

Viale Trinità dei Monti

Viale Trinità dei Monti

Villa Medici

Ponte Margherita

Lungotevere in Augusto

Clodia

Via Angelo Brunetti

Via della Fontanella

32 ▼
33

🏛40

Tiber

Pass di Ripetta

28 ●

31
30 ▪

Via del Corso

Via del Babuino

34
35 ▼

📷

39

Via Valadier

Lungotevere dei Mellini

Via di Ripetta

Via del Vantaggio

Via Laurina

36 ▪

Via Margutta

38 ▼

Via Emilio Quinti Visconti

Piazza del Ferro di Cavallo

29 ▽

Via di Gesù e Maria

37 △ Via di San Giacomo

MAP 4

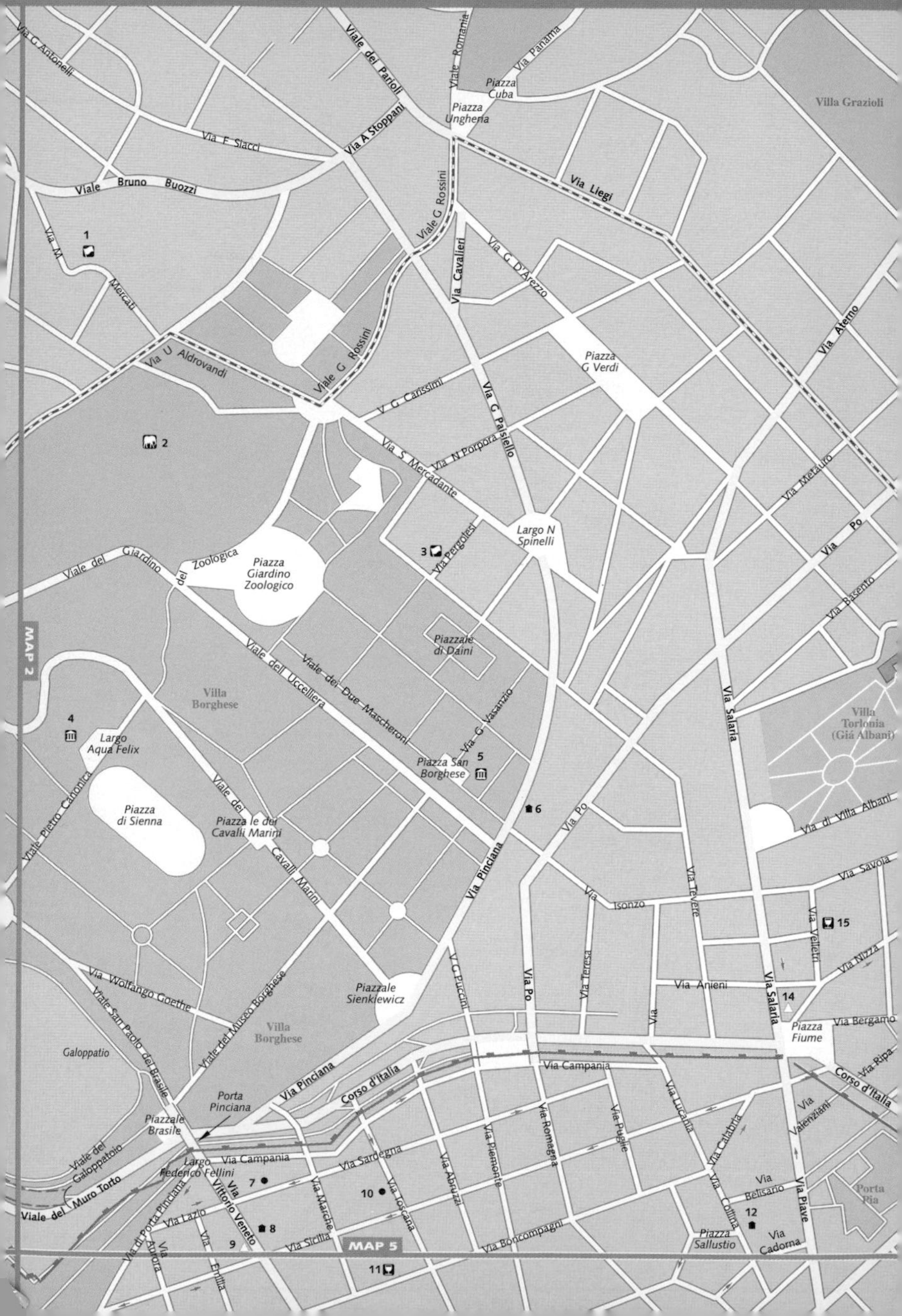

MAP 3

MAP 2

Villa Grazioli

Via L. Antonelli

Viale del Parioli

Via Panama

Piazza Cuba

Piazza Ungheria

Via F. Siacci

Via A. Stoppani

Via G. Rossini

Via Romania

Viale Bruno Buozzi

Via Liegi

Via Mercalli

Via M.

1

Via U. Aldrovandi

Viale G. Rossini

Via Cavalieri

Via G. D'Arezzo

Via Aterno

V. G. Carissimi

Via G. Paisiello

Piazza G Verdi

2

Via S. Mercadante

Via N Porpora

Via Mizzuro

Viale del Giardino del Zoologica

Piazza Giardino Zoologico

3

Via Pergolesi

Largo N Spinelli

Via Po

Via Bisento

Piazzale di Daini

Viale dell'Uccelliera

Viale dei Due Mascheroni

Via G. Vasanzio

Villa Borghese

Via Salaria

Villa Torlonia (Già Albani)

4

Largo Aqua Felix

Piazza di Sienna

Viale Pietro Canonica

Viale dei

Piazza San Borghese

5

6

Via Po

Via di Villa Albani

Piazza le dei Cavalli Marini

Cavalli Marini

Via Pinciana

Via Tevere

Via Savoia

Via Wolfango Goethe

Viale San Paolo del Brasile

Viale del Museo Borghese

Piazzale Sienkiewicz

Via Pinciana

Via Po

Via Teresa

Via Isonzo

Via Anieni

Via Salaria

15

14

Piazza Fiume

Via Bergamo

Galoppatio

Villa Borghese

Porta Pinciana

Via Pinciana

Corso d'Italia

Via Campania

Corso d'Italia

Via Veneto

Porta Pia

Piazzale Brasile

Largo Federico Fellini

Via Campania

7

Via Sardegna

10

Via Romagna

Via Puglie

Via Sicilia

Via Marche

Via Abruzzi

Via Emilia

Via Lucania

Via Calabria

Via Relicario

Via Plave

Viale del Muro Torto

Via di Porta Pinciana

Via Lazio

8

9

Via Sicilia

Via Boncompagni

Piazza Sallustio

12

Via Cadorna

Via Collina

MAP 5

11

MAP 3

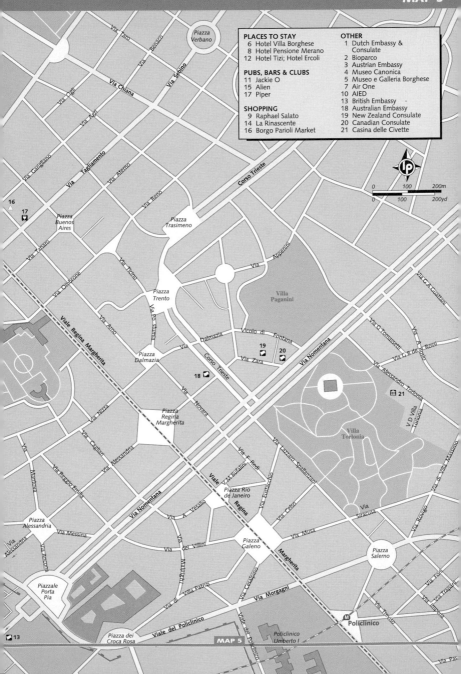

PLACES TO STAY
6 Hotel Villa Borghese
8 Hotel Pensione Merano
12 Hotel Tizi; Hotel Ercoli

PUBS, BARS & CLUBS
11 Jackie O
15 Alien
17 Piper

SHOPPING
9 Raphael Salato
14 La Rinascente
16 Borgo Parioli Market

OTHER
1 Dutch Embassy & Consulate
2 Bioparco
3 Austrian Embassy
4 Museo Canonica
5 Museo e Galleria Borghese
7 Air One
10 AIED
13 British Embassy
18 Australian Embassy
19 New Zealand Consulate
20 Canadian Consulate
21 Casina delle Civette

MAP 5

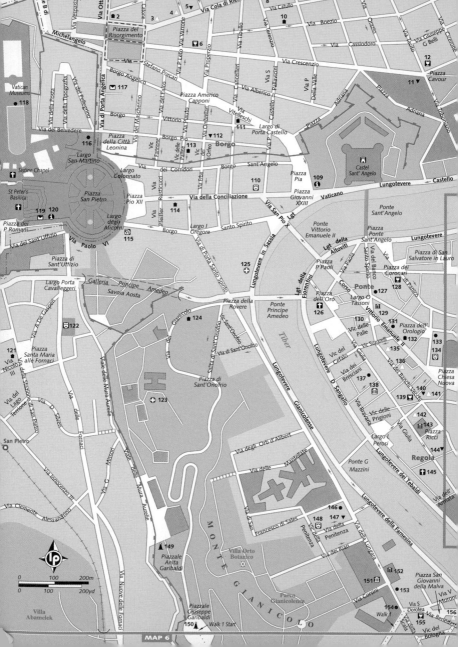

MAP 4

MAP 2

MAP 6

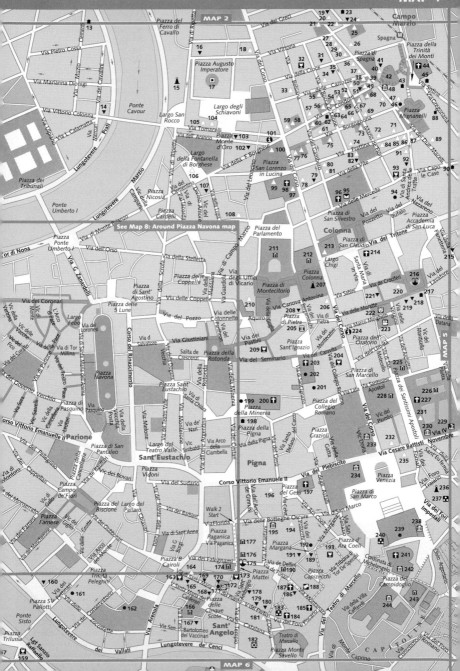

MAP 4

Campo Marzio

MAP 2

Piazza del Ferro di Cavallo

Via di Ripetta

Via dei Greci

Via Vittoria

19 20 21 22 23 24 25

Spagna

Piazza della Trinità dei Monti

Via Pietro Cossa

13

Clementi

16

18

Piazza Augusto Imperatore

104

27 28 29 30

26

Via della Croce

32 31

Via di Spagna 41 40

44 45

Via Marianna Dionigi

Via di Monte di Cavallo

15

17

Via del Corso

33 34

35 36 37

38 39 50 49 48

42 43

Via Sistina

Via Gregoriana

Ponte Cavour

Largo San Rocco

Largo degli Schiavoni

Via della Carrozze

55 52 53 51

Condotti 68

47 46

14

Via Vittorio Colonna

Via Tomacelli

57 56

59 58

Via Borgognona

60 62 61 54 63 64 65 66 67 70

69

Piazza Mignanelli

Via della Fontanella di Borghese

Piazza Monte d'Oro 102

103

101

100

77 76

Via Borgognona

72 73

71

74

84 85 86 87

Via di Due Macelli

88

89

Piazza dei Tribunali

106

Via di Monte Brianzo

Piazza Nicosia

Via di Campo Marzio

Piazza San Lorenzo in Lucina

75

80

83 82

81

91

92

90

Via di Santa Andrea delle Fratte

Via Capo le Case

Ponte Umberto I

107

108

99 98 97

78 79

96 95

93

94

Via della Mercede

Via del Pozzetto

Via del Bufalo

Piazza Accademia di San Luca

Piazza Cardelli

Piazza di San Silvestro

Colonna

Piazza di San Claudio

Via del Tritone

Piazza Ponte Umberto I

or di Nona

See Map 8: Around Piazza Navona map

Via dell'Orso

Via della Stelletta

Piazza del Parlamento

211

213

212

Largo Chigi

214

216

Via de Crociferi

Via di Sant'Agostino

Piazza delle Coppelle

Piazza di Sant'Agostino

Piazza delle 5 Lune

Via degli Uffici del Vicario

210

Piazza Colonna

207

217 218

221

220

219

Piazza di Montecitorio

Via Canova Antonina

208

206

Via delle Muratte

222

223

L'Arco della Pace

Largo dei Lorenesi

Via del Pozzo

Via delle Colonnelle

Aquiro

Via in Aquiro

205

Piazza di Pietra

Via di Pietra

224

Via del Corso

Piazza dell'Oratorio

Piazza Navona

Salita de Crescenzi

Piazza della Rotonda

Via dei Pastini

209

Piazza Sant'Ignazio

204

203

Via dell'Umiltà

225

Sant'Eustachio

Via della Minerva

202

201

Piazza di San Marcello

228

226

227

231

Largo del Teatro Valle

Via Arco della Ciambella

199 200

Piazza della Minerva

198

Piazza della Pigna

Piazza del Collegio Romano

Vic del Piombo

229

230

IV Novembre

232

Pariône

Piazza di San Pantaleo

Largo dei Chiavari

Pigna

Piazza Grazioli

233

235

Corso Vittorio Emanuele II

196

197

Piazza del Gesù

234

Piazza Venezia

236

Piazza Campo de'Fiori

Via dei Giubbonari

Via del Sudario

Walk 2 Start

Via Florida

Via delle Botteghe Oscure

195 194

Piazza di San Marco

237

Via dei Fori Imperiali

Piazza Farnese

Piazza del Biscione

Piazza del Largo del Pallaro

Piazza Paganica

177

176

Piazza Margana

192

191

189

Piazza d'Ara Coeli

238

240

239

160

161

162

Piazza B Cairoli

164

175

174

Piazza Mattei

190

Via di San Marcello

Cordonata di Michelangelo

241

242

Piazza Trinità Pellegrini

163

169 170 172

173

178 179 180

187 186

188

185 184

Piazza del Campidoglio

Ponte Sisto

165 168 171 167 166

181

183

Sant' Angelo

Piazza delle Cinque Scole

Via di San Bartolomeo de' Vaccinari

Teatro di Marcello

182

Piazza Monte Savello

243

244

159

Lungotevere de' Cenci

CAPITOLINE

MAP 6

MAP 4

A handsome detail of Michelangelo's *Moses*, Basilica di San Pietro in Vincoli

MARTIN MOOS

MAP 4

If sleepiness sets in then prop yourself up against one of the 284 columns in Piazza San Pietro.

MARTIN MOOS

MAP 5

MAP 3

Piazza
Sallustio

Sallustiano

Via Boncompagni

Via di Porta Pinciana

Via Lombardia

Via Ludovisi

Via Piemonte

Via Sallustiana

Via Lucullo

Via G Carducci

Via A Salanda

Via Flavia

Via Q Sella

Via XX Settembre

Via Golo

92

Via Castelfidardo

Via degli Artisti

Via Francesco Crispi

Via Vittorio Veneto

16

17

Via Leonida Bissolati

Via Umbria

Piazza
delle Finanze

89

Via delle Purificazione

Via Sistina

Via Molise

Via Versilia

15

Largo di
Santa Susanna

14

18

Via Pastrengo

Via Cernaia

Via Montebello

88
87
86

Castro
Pretor

Via di San Basilio

Via di San Nicola da Tolentino

Salita San Nicola da Tolentino

13

12

10

Largo del
Tritone

9

8

Piazza
Barberini

Barberini

11

Trevi

19

29

Piazza
San Bernardo

20

21

28

27

22

23

Via del Tritone

7

Via d'Avignonesi

4

Via Rasella

6

Giardini

Via dei

30

Via Firenze

31

26
25

Piazza della
Repubblica

24

Via L Einaudi

Largo di
Villa Peretti

83

84

Via Enrico de Nicola

Giardino del
Quirinale

Traforo
Umberto I

MAP 4

Via del Quirinale

Via XX Settembre

Via Modena

Via Firenze

32 33

Torino

Repubblica

Via delle Terme di Diocleziano

34

81

80

82

Termini

5

Piazza del
Quirinale

38

39

40

41

42

Via Genova

Via San Vitale

35

36

37

Via Napoli

79

Piazza
B Gigli

Via
Montalto

Via Massimo D'Azeglio

Via G.
Amendola

Vic
Montecarlo Mazzarino

Via XXIV Maggio

Villa
Colonna

Via della Consulta

Via Panisperna

Via Milano

Via Parma

Via Principe

48

49

50

44

43

45

46

47

Via Agostino de Pretis

Piazza del
Viminale

Ministero
dell'
Interno

Via del Viminale

78

Via Cesare Balbo

Via Urbana

77

Piazza dell'
Esquilino

76

75

124

125

126

Via D Manin

Via Cavour

123

121

122

127

12

Via dell'Esquilino

Via Farini

Via Giolitti

132

133

Piazza
Santa Maria
Maggiore

13

130

57

51

52

53

Via Panisperna

Via Cimara

Via Mazzarino

Via de Serpenti

54
55

Via S di Santa Maria Maggiore

74

135

134

Largo
Magnanapoli

56

58

Largo
Angelicum

Piazza
Zingari

73

Via dei Quattro Cantoni

Via Paolina

Via dell'Olmata

Via

136

137

San Martino ai Monti

Largo di.

Casa dei
Cavalieri
di Rodi

Via Panisperna

Via de Sant'

Via degli Zingari

Piazza
Madonna
dei Monti

Piazza Suburra

Via Giovanni Lanza

Piazza
San Martino
ai Monti

Largo
Brancaccio

59

60

61

62

64

65

66

68

69 70

Via Baccina

Via della Madonna de' Monti

Piazza San
Francesco di Paola

Via Cavour

Via Sforza

Via Cavour

Largo
Visconti
Venosta

Cavour

Via in Selci

72

Monti

138

Parco
di Traiano

Largo della
Madonna
dei Monti

Via del Corso

Largo C Ricci

67

63

Via del Colosseo

Frangipane

Piazza di
San Pietro
in Vincoli

71

Via delle Sette Sale

Parco
di Traiano

Largo
Romolo
e Remo

Roman'
Forum

Via dei Fori Imperiali

Via Alessandrina

Via della
Salara
Vecchia

Largo G
Agnesi

Largo D
Polveriera

139

140

Parco Oppio

141

Viale del Monte Oppio

Via A
Botta

Via Terme di Traiano

Via C
Botta

Via Mecenate

MAP 7

MAP 5

MAP 3

Via Montebello

Via Palestro

Via Castelfidardo

Via Gaeta

Via Goito

95

Piazza dell'Indipendenza

Via San Martino della Battaglia

Via Vicenza

96
97
98
99
100
101

Via Palestro

Via Vittorio Bachelet

108

Via Solferino

109

Via Magenta

Via dei Mille

107
110

Via Marghera

105
106

Via Varese

102

Via Marsala

113
112

Via Milazzo

111

104
103

Piazza dei inquecento

114

115
116
117

118

Stazione Termini

20

119

M Castro Pretorio

Viale del Castro Pretorio

94

Viale del Policlinico

93

Viale Regina Elena

Viale dell'Università

Viale P. Gobetti

Città Universitaria

Piazzale Aldo Moro

155

Via C. De Lollis

Via dei Marrucini

154

153

Via dei Frentani

Via del Castro Pretorio

Via dei Ramni

Piazza dei Siculi

Via Tiburtina

152

Via degli Etruschi

Via dei Sardi

Filippo Turati

Piazza Manfredo Fanti

Via Carlo Cattaneo

Via Principe Amedeo

Via Ratazzi

Via Giovanni Giolitti

Via A. Capuccini

Via Napoleone III

Via Manzoni

143

Via Carlo Alberto

Vito

P. Rossi

142

144

Piazza Vittorio Emanuele II

M Vittorio Emanuele

Via Leopardi

Esquiline

argo opardi

145

Via Merulana

Via Macchiavelli

Piazza Dante

Via Petrarca

Via Ricasoli

Via Labicana

Via Principe Umberto

Via Principe Eugenio

Via Conte Verde

Via Emanuele Filiberto

Via Foscolo

146

Via Niño Bixio

151
150
149
148

Largo Degli Osci

Via dei Volsci

Via dei Latini

Via Degli Equi

Via dei Marsi

Via di Porta Labicana

Via dei Aurunci

Piazza dei Immacolata

Via Campani

Via de Lucani

Via Giovanni Giolitti

Via di Porta Maggiore

147

Piazza di Porta Maggiore

MAP 7

MAP 5

PLACES TO STAY
6 Hotel Julia
30 Hotel Oceania
31 Hotel Seiler
32 Hotel Elide
36 Hotel Artemide
45 Hotel Galatea
46 Hotel Caravaggio
59 Hotel Nerva
62 Hotel Forum
73 Hotel Sandy
78 YWCA
80 Hotel Columbia
86 Hotel Ascot
87 Hotel Floridia
88 Papa Germano
90 Hotel Castelfidardo
96 Hotel Lachea; Hotel Dolomiti
97 Albergo Sandra
100 Hotel Positano; Hotel Continentale
101 Pensione Restivo; Hotel Cervia
102 Hotel Gabriella; Hotel Adventure
105 Hotel Venezia
108 Hotel Piemonte
109 Pensione Giamaica
112 Fawlty Towers
113 Hotel Rimini
121 Hotel Dina
123 Hotel Sweet Home
127 Hotel Palladium Palace
128 Hotel Contilia
129 Hotel Igea
130 Hotel d'Este

PLACES TO EAT
7 Colline Emiliane
13 Tullio
47 Da Ricci
52 Al Giubileo
55 Il Guru
64 Baires
66 Alle Carrette
68 Osteria Gli Angeletti
69 Wanted Il Post Ricercato
75 Mexico al 104
104 Trattoria da Bruno
106 Da Gemma alla Lupa
122 Hostaria Angelo
131 Agata e Romeo
144 Piazza Vittorio Emanuele II Food Market
145 Panella l'Arte del Pane
148 Il Dito e la Luna
149 Formula 1
150 Pizzeria L'Economia
151 Le Maschere

BARS, PUBS & CLUBS
65 Cavour 313
72 Hangar
89 Trimani
91 Julius Caesar
135 Fiddler's Elbow
136 L'Apeiron
137 Druid's Den
147 Max's Bar

SHOPPING
1 Underground
3 Single
4 UPIM
14 Brioni
16 Bruno Magli
27 Feltrinelli International
33 Mel Bookstore
34 Economy Book & Video Center
37 MaxMara
43 PrèNatal
44 Furla
50 Palazzo delle Esposizione Gift Shop
51 Queer
53 Le Gallinelle
54 Fabio Piccioni
57 Beny
74 Fausto Santini
142 MAS
152 Disfunzioni Musicali

OTHER
2 Teatro Sistina
5 Palazzo del Quirinale
8 Fontana del Tritone
9 Fontana delle Api
10 Chiesa di Santa Maria della Concezione
11 Palazzo Barberini; Galleria Nazionale d'Arte Antica
12 Meridiana Airlines
15 US Embassy & Consulate
17 Europa Multiclub
18 Chiesa di Santa Maria della Vittoria
19 Fontana dell'Acqua Felice
20 APT Tourist Office
21 Aula Ottagonale
22 Terme di Diocleziano
23 Chiesa di Santa Maria degli Angeli
24 Fontana delle Naiadi
25 CIT
26 Eurojet
28 Chiesa di San Bernardo alla Terme
29 Chiesa di Santa Susanna; Lending Library
35 St Paul's Within-the-Walls
38 San Carlo alle Quattro Fontane
39 Sant'Andrea al Quirinale
40 Ufficio Stranieri
41 Police Station
42 CTS
48 Tourist Information Kiosk
49 Palazzo delle Esposizioni
56 Villa Aldobrandini
58 Mercati di Traiano
60 Foro di Augusto
61 Foro di Nerva
63 Tourist Information Kiosk
67 Folkstudio
70 Internet Café
71 Basilica di San Pietro in Vincoli
76 Arte del Teatro Studio
77 Chiesa di Santa Pudenziana
79 Teatro dell'Opera
81 Police Station; Bici e Baci
82 Palazzo Massimo alle Terme
83 Museo Nazionale Romano
84 Tourist Information Kiosk
85 Treno e Scooter
92 Zipper Travel Association
93 Policlinico Umberto I
94 Biblioteca Nazionale Centrale Vittorio Emanuele II
95 German Embassy & Consulate
98 Oblo Service Laundrette
99 Bolle Blu Laundrette
103 Splashnet Laundrette & Internet Cafe
107 Enjoy Rome
110 ENIT
111 Bolle Blu Laundrette
114 The Netgate
115 Tourist Information
116 Telephone Office
117 Train Information Office
118 Tourist Information Office
119 Tourist Information; Comune di Roma
120 Ciao Roma
124 Associazione Italiana Alberghi per la Gioventù
125 Happy Rent
126 Green Line Tours
132 Basilica di Santa Maria Maggiore
133 Tourist Information Kiosk
134 Chiesa di Santa Prassede
138 Chiesa di San Martino ai Monti
139 Terme di Tito
140 Domus Aurea
141 Terme di Traiano
143 Chiesa di Sant'Eusebio
146 Torre di Babele Centro di Lingua e Cultura Italiani
153 CTS
154 Internet Café
155 Istituzione Universitaria dei Concerti

The Eternal City's misty skyline masks its modern-day features and offers a timeless spectacle.

Take a relaxing riverbank stroll along the leafy Lungotevere Castello.

MAP 6

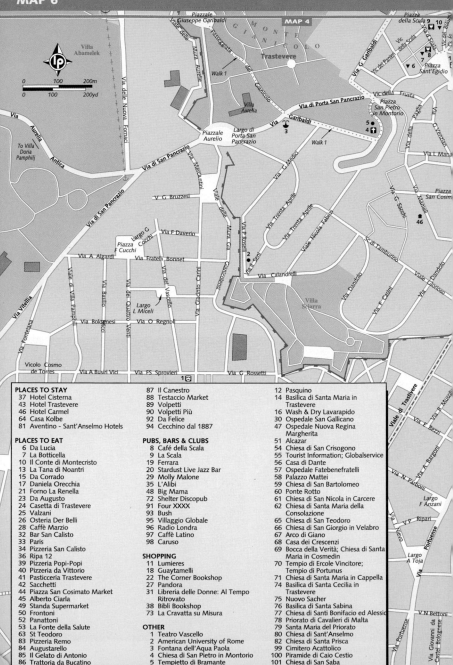

MAP 4

Trastevere

Villa Abamelek

To Villa Doria Pamphilj

Villa Aurelia

Villa Sciarra

Piazzale Giuseppe Garibaldi

Piazza della Scala

Piazza Sant'Egidio

Piazza San Pietro in Montorio

Piazza San Cosima

Piazza San Cosimato

Largo di Porta San Pancrazio

Piazzale Aurelio

Largo G Cocchi

Piazza F Cucchi

Largo L Miceli

Vicolo Cosmo de Torres

Walk 1

PLACES TO STAY
- 37 Hotel Cisterna
- 43 Hotel Trastevere
- 46 Hotel Carmel
- 64 Casa Kolbe
- 81 Aventino - Sant'Anselmo Hotels

PLACES TO EAT
- 6 Da Lucia
- 7 La Botticella
- 10 Il Conte di Montecristo
- 13 La Tana di Noantri
- 15 Da Corrado
- 17 Daniela Orecchia
- 21 Forno La Renella
- 23 Da Augusto
- 24 Casetta di Trastevere
- 25 Valzani
- 26 Osteria Der Belli
- 28 Caffè Marzio
- 32 Bar San Calisto
- 33 Paris
- 34 Pizzeria San Calisto
- 36 Ripa 12
- 39 Pizzeria Popi-Popi
- 40 Pizzeria da Vittorio
- 41 Pasticceria Trastevere
- 42 Sacchetti
- 44 Piazza San Cosimato Market
- 49 Alberto Ciarla
- 49 Standa Supermarket
- 50 Frontoni
- 52 Panattoni
- 53 La Fonte della Salute
- 63 St Teodoro
- 83 Pizzeria Remo
- 84 Augustarello
- 85 Il Gelato di Antonio
- 86 Trattoria da Bucatino

- 87 Il Canestro
- 88 Testaccio Market
- 89 Volpetti
- 90 Volpetti Più
- 92 Da Felice
- 94 Cecchino dal 1887

PUBS, BARS & CLUBS
- 8 Café della Scala
- 9 La Scala
- 19 Ferrara
- 20 Stardust Live Jazz Bar
- 29 Molly Malone
- 35 L'Alibi
- 48 Big Mama
- 72 Shelter Discopub
- 91 Four XXXX
- 93 Bush
- 95 Villaggio Globale
- 96 Radio Londra
- 97 Caffè Latino
- 98 Caruso

SHOPPING
- 11 Lumieres
- 18 Guaytamelli
- 22 The Corner Bookshop
- 27 Pandora
- 31 Libreria delle Donne: Al Tempo Ritrovato
- 38 Bibli Bookshop
- 73 La Cravatta su Misura

OTHER
- 1 Teatro Vascello
- 2 American University of Rome
- 3 Fontana dell'Aqua Paola
- 4 Chiesa di San Pietro in Montorio
- 5 Tempietto di Bramante

- 12 Pasquino
- 14 Basilica di Santa Maria in Trastevere
- 16 Wash & Dry Lavarapido
- 30 Ospedale San Gallicano
- 47 Ospedale Nuova Regina Margherita
- 51 Alcazar
- 54 Chiesa di San Crisogono
- 55 Tourist Information; Globalservice
- 56 Casa di Dante
- 57 Ospedale Fatebenefratelli
- 58 Palazzo Mattei
- 59 Chiesa di San Bartolomeo
- 60 Ponte Rotto
- 61 Chiesa di San Nicola in Carcere
- 62 Chiesa di Santa Maria della Consolazione
- 65 Chiesa di San Teodoro
- 66 Chiesa di San Giorgio in Velabro
- 67 Arco di Giano
- 68 Casa dei Crescenzi
- 69 Bocca della Verità; Chiesa di Santa Maria in Cosmedin
- 70 Tempio di Ercole Vincitore; Tempio di Portunus
- 71 Chiesa di Santa Maria in Cappella
- 74 Basilica di Santa Cecilia in Trastevere
- 75 Nuovo Sacher
- 76 Basilica di Santa Sabina
- 77 Chiesa di Santi Bonifacio ed Alessio
- 78 Priorato di Cavalieri di Malta
- 79 Santa Maria del Priorato
- 80 Chiesa di Sant'Anselmo
- 82 Chiesa di Santa Prisca
- 99 Cimitero Acattolico
- 100 Piramide di Caio Cestio
- 101 Chiesa di San Saba

MAP 6

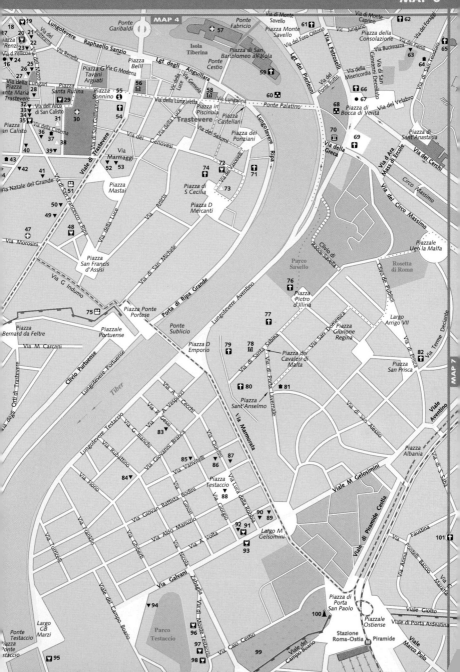

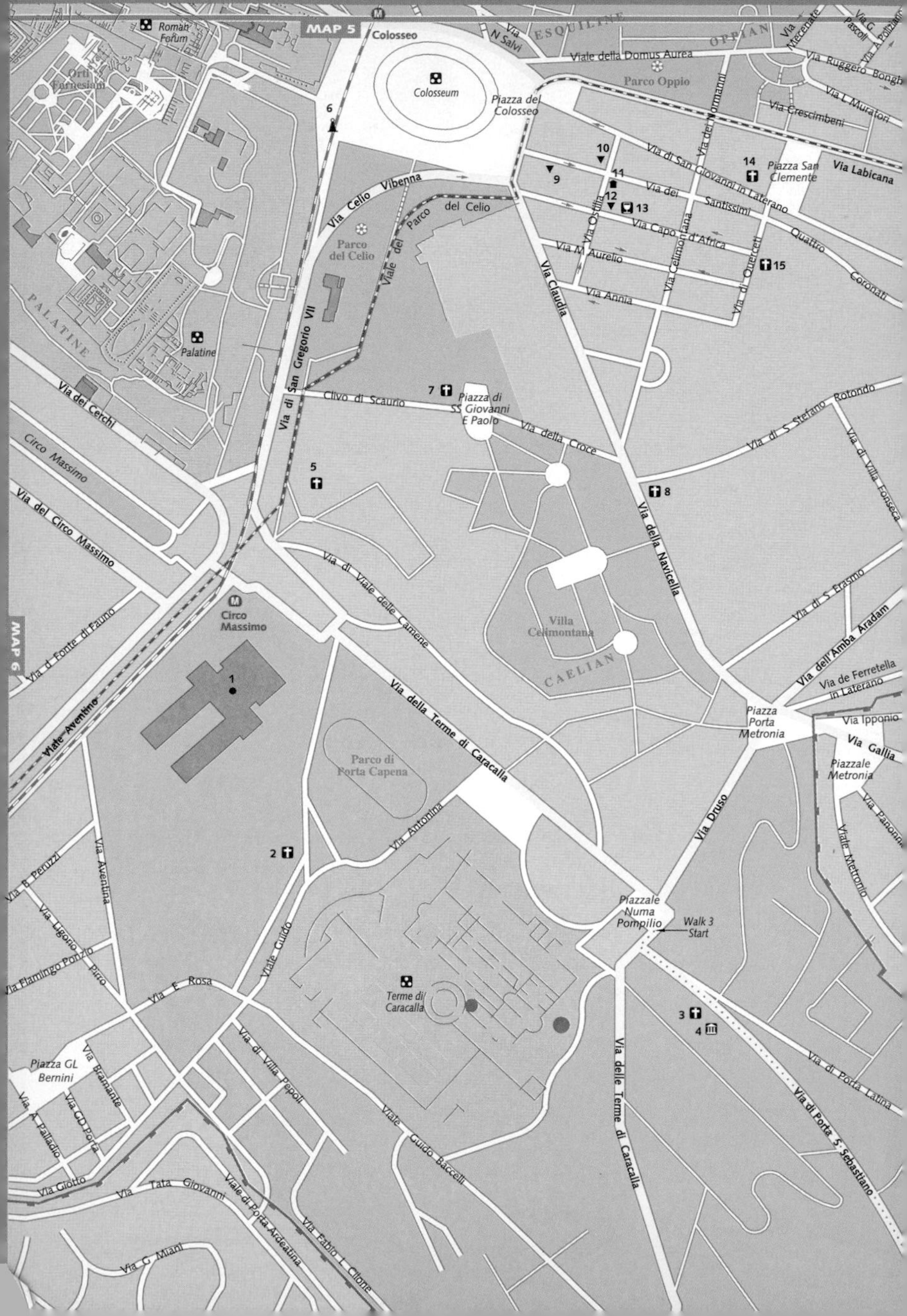

MAP 7

MAP 5

Colosseo

Roman
Forum

Romal
Forum

Orti
Farnesiani

Colosseum

Piazza del
Colosseo

Viale della Domus Aurea

Parco Oppio

ESQUILINE

OPPIAN

Via N Salvi

Via Mecenate

Via G. Lanza
Via G. Pascoli

Via Ruggero Bonghi

Via L. Muratori

Via Crescimbeni

6

10
9

14
11

14 Piazza San
Clemente

Via Labicana

Via di San Giovanni in Laterano

Via di

Santissimi

12
13

13

Via Capo d'Africa

Via M. Aurelio

Quattro

Coronati

15

Via Celio Vibenna

Parco
del Celio

Parco
del Celio

PALATINE

Palatine

Via di San Gregorio VII

Clivo di Scaurio

7 Piazza di
SS Giovanni
E Paolo

Via Claudia

Via Annia

Via della Croce

Via di S. Stefano Rotondo

Via di Villa Fonseca

Via del Cerchi

5

8

Via della Navicella

Via di S. Erasmo

Circo
Massimo

Circo
Massimo

Via del Circo Massimo

Via di viale delle Camene

Villa
Celimontana

Villa
Celimontana

CAELIAN

Via dell'Amba Aradam

Via de Ferratella
in Laterano

Circo
Massimo

Piazza
Porta
Metronia

Via Ipponio

Via Gallia

Piazzale
Metronia

Viale Aventino

1

Via di Fonte di Fauno

Via della Terme di Caracalla

Parco di
Porta Capena

Via Druso

Via Panonia

MAP 6

Via T. Peruzzi

Via Avanina

Via Liporia

Via Flaminio Ponzio

Piro

2

Via Antonina

Piazzale
Numa
Pompilio

Walk 3
Start

Via di Villa Pepoli

Terme di
Caracalla

Via E. Rosa

Piazza GL
Bernini

Via di CM Forà

Via Tata Giovanni

Viale Guido Baccelli

Viale Guido Baccelli

Via di Porta Ardeatina

Via Fabio I. Clone

Via delle Terme di Caracalla

3

4

Via di Porta Latina

Via di Porta S. Sebastiano

Via C. Mianii

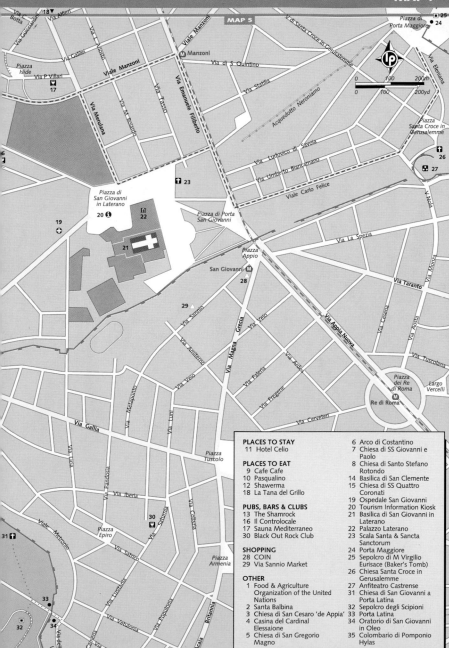

MAP 7

MAP 5

Piazza di
Porta Maggiore

Piazza
Iside

Piazza
Santa Croce in
Gerusalemme

Piazza di
San Giovanni
in Laterano

Piazza di Porta
San Giovanni

Piazza
Appio

San Giovanni

Piazza
dei Re
di Roma

Largo
Vercelli

Re di Roma

Piazza
Tustolo

Piazza
Epiro

Piazza
Armenia

PLACES TO STAY
11 Hotel Celio

PLACES TO EAT
9 Cafe Cafe
10 Pasqualino
12 Shawerma
18 La Tana del Grillo

PUBS, BARS & CLUBS
13 The Shamrock
16 Il Controlocale
17 Sauna Mediterraneo
30 Black Out Rock Club

SHOPPING
28 COIN
29 Via Sannio Market

OTHER
1 Food & Agriculture
 Organization of the United
 Nations
2 Santa Balbina
3 Chiesa di San Cesaro 'de Appia'
4 Casina del Cardinal
 Elessaione
5 Chiesa di San Gregorio
 Magno

6 Arco di Costantino
7 Chiesa di SS Giovanni e
 Paolo
8 Chiesa di Santo Stefano
 Rotondo
14 Basilica di San Clemente
15 Chiesa di SS Quattro
 Coronati
19 Ospedale San Giovanni
20 Tourism Information Kiosk
21 Basilica di San Giovanni in
 Laterano
22 Palazzo Laterano
23 Scala Santa & Sancta
 Sanctorum
24 Porta Maggiore
25 Sepolcro di M Virgilio
 Eurisace (Baker's Tomb)
26 Chiesa Santa Croce in
 Gerusalemme
27 Anfiteatro Castrense
31 Chiesa di San Giovanni a
 Porta Latina
32 Sepolcro degli Scipioni
33 Porta Latina
34 Oratorio di San Giovanni
 in Oleo
35 Colombario di Pomponio
 Hylas

Ponte Umberto I

Piazza Ponte Umberto I

Lungotevere Tor di Nona

Via di Monte Brianzo

Via dell'Orso

Via dei Portoghesi

Via d'Ascanio

Piazza Firenze

Via dei Prefetti

10

1

Piazza della Stelletta

Via di Monte Giordano

4

5

6

7

8

9

Via di Spagnoli

13

Via degli Uffici del Vicar

50   100m

50   100yd

Via C. Zanardelli

2

3

16

Piazza delle Coppelle

Via delle Maddalena

14

Via di Monte

Piazza Lacellotti

Piazza di San Salvatore in Lauro

1

Via dei Tre Archi

Via dei Coronari

Piazza Sant' Apollinare

Piazza Tor Sanguigna

22

Piazza delle Cinque Lune

20

Via dei Sant'

Piazza di Sant' Agostino

Agostino

19

18

17

Via delle Coppelle

54

21

Via San Giovanni d'Arco

Largo G Toniolo

53

Piazza della Maddalena

15

Via di Colonn

Via della

56

Piazza Rondanini

57

58

59

Arco d...

Piazza Monte Vecchio

23

Largo Febo

Via dei Coronari

25

24

Piazza Navona

51

Via delle Vacche

Via delle Vecchie

Piazza del Fico

26

Via del Fico

28

29

Via della Fossa

27

40

41

Via di Tor Millina

43

44

Via de Cupis

Via di Grana

42

46

45

50

48

49

Via del Salvatore

Via Giustiniani

52

55

Via di Sant'Eustachio

68

Salita de Crescenzi

Piazza del Rotondo

Piazza della Mine

63

33

Via del Corallo

31

30

32

34

35

37

36

39

38

Via del Governo Vecchio

Via Sora

Piazza Pasquino

Via della Cancelleria

Via del Pellegrino

Piazza della Chiesa Nuova

79

77

78

Corso Vittorio Emanuele II

Via di Parione

Via di Pasquino

Via della Cuccagna

Via del Canestrari

Via della Vecchie Forte

Via del Teatro Pace

74

75

76

Piazza dei Massimi

73

Piazza di San Pantaleo

80

81

82

83

84

85

Piazza di Sant'Andrea della Valle

Via degli Staderari

70

71

Via dei Sediari

69

Piazza Sant' Eustacchio

67

Via di Santa Chiara

66

Piazza Santa Chiara

65

64

Via de' Nari

72

119

120

Largo del Teatro Valle

Vic Sinibaldi

Via Arco della Ciambella

Largo Stimm

87

86

Vic dei Bovari

116

117

Piazza Vidoni

118

Sant'Eustachio

Corso   Vittorio   Emanuele II

124

123

Via del Monserrato

88

Via dei Baullari

Piazza Pollarola

Via del Sudario

125

Largo di Torre Argent

96

95

91

92

93

94

Piazza Campo de'Fiori

89

90

111

112

114

113

110

Piazza Paradiso

126

Piazza del Biscione

129

Largo del Pallaro

Piazza dei Satiri

128

127

Via del Barbieri

Piazza Farnese

97

108

107

106

109

130

98

99

102

Piazza della Quercia

105

103

104

100

101

Via del Mascherone

Via dei Farnesi

Via San Girolamo della Carità

Via in Caterina

Via dei Cappellari

Via dei Montoro

Via dei Balestrari

Via del Giglio

Via della Corda

Via di Biscione

Via de' Giubbonari

Via dei Chiavari

Via dei Grotte

Via Arco del Monte

Piazza del Monte di Pietà

131

Piazza Trinità Pellegrini

Piazza B Cairoli

133

Via di Sant'Anna

132

Largo Arenula

Via Florida

Via Paganica

Via Arenula

Via dei Falegnami

134

MAP 8 - AROUND PIAZZA NAVONA

PLACES TO STAY
5 Hotel Portoghesi
24 Hotel Raphael
62 Albergo Abruzzi
64 Hotel Santa Chiara
66 Hotel Mimosa
74 Hotel Primavera
95 Suore di Santa Brigida
102 Residenza Farnese
112 Hotel Campo de' Fiori
113 Albergo del Sole
114 Albergo della Lunetta
128 Hotel Pomezia
129 Albergo Teatro di Pompeo

PLACES TO EAT
2 Il Primoli
4 L'Orso 80
7 M & M Volpetti
11 Da Gino
12 Gelateria Giolitti
14 Gelateria della Palma
15 Gino Placidi
16 Il Bacaro
18 Oliphant
30 Trattoria Pizzeria da
   Francesco
31 Pizzeria Corallo
32 Paladini
33 Osteria
34 Pizzeria da Baffetto
40 Quinto Bottega del Gelato
41 Tre Scalini
56 Le Cornacchie
57 L'Angoletto
58 La Bougainville Café
59 La Rosetta
61 La Tazza d'Oro
67 Camilloni a Sant'Eustachio;
   Caffè a Sant'Eustachio
69 Bar Sant'Eustachio
75 Insalata Ricca
76 Cul de Sac
78 Pizzeria La Montecarlo
79 Bella Napoli
86 Pizza a Taglio
87 Ditirambo
89 La Carbonara
90 Forno di Campo de' Fiori
94 Caffè Farnese
96 Ristorante Monserrato
105 Sergio alla Grotta
107 Camponeschi

109 Ruggeri
110 Pizza Rustica
116 Insalata Ricca
130 Dar Filettaro a Santa Barbara
    (Filetti di Baccalà)
131 Bernasconi
134 Benito

PUBS, BARS & CLUBS
17 Ned Kelly's
26 Bar della Pace
27 Jonathan's Angels
28 Bar del Fico
29 Locale
39 Enoteca Piccolo
51 Bevitoria Navona
77 The Groove
91 The Drunken Ship
92 Vineria (Da Giorgio); Taverna
   del Campo
106 L'Angolo Divino
108 Sloppy Sam's
118 John Bull

SHOPPING
6 Amati & Amati
8 Daniela Rosati
10 Passamanerie Crocianelli
13 Cenci
19 Casamaria
21 Ai Monasteri
23 Al Sogno
36 Distanès
38 Tempi Moderni; Omero e
   Cecilia
43 Nardecchia
47 Bertè
48 Libreria Sorgente
49 Officina Profumo Farmaceutia
   di Santa Maria Novella
50 De Sanctis
53 La Procure
54 Città del Sole
60 Stilo Fetti
68 Antichità Tanca
73 Troncarelli
80 Mondello Ottica
82 Libreria del Viaggiatore
93 Baullà
104 Borini
111 Loco
119 Galleria di Orditi e Trame
120 Francesco Biasia

121 La Chiave
123 Home
124 Feltrinelli
127 Spazio Sette
133 Moresco Ottica

OTHER
1 Chiesa di San Salvatore in
   Lauro
3 Palazzo Altemps; Museo
   Nazionale Romano
9 The Netgate
20 Chiesa di Sant'Agostino
22 Tourist Information Kiosk
25 Chiesa di Santa Maria della
   Pace
35 Chiesa Nuova
37 Wash & Dry Lavarapido
42 Fontana dei Quattro Fiumi
44 Chiesa di Sant'Agnese in
   Agone
45 Palazzo Pamphilj
46 Fontana del Moro
52 Palazzo Madama
55 Chiesa di San Luigi dei
   Francesi
63 Pantheon
65 Elsy Viaggi
70 Palazzo della Sapienza
71 Chiesa di Sant'Ivo alla
   Sapienza
72 Teatro Valle
81 Cicli Collati
83 Palazzo della Cancelleria
84 Palazzo Braschi; Museo di
   Roma
85 Museo Barracco
88 Italiaidea
97 Palazzo Farnese; French
   Embassy
98 Palazzo Falconieri
99 Arco Farnese
100 Fontana del Mascherone
101 French Consulate
103 Palazzo Spada; Galleria Spada
117 Chiesa di Sant'Andrea della
    Valle
122 Berlitz
125 Teatro Argentina
126 Area Sacra di Largo Ar-
    gentina
132 Chiesa di San Carlo ai
    Catinari

JONATHAN SMITH

'Mussolini Dux' inscription on the 17m-high marble obelisk at the Fascist-era Foro Italico complex

MAP LEGEND

BOUNDARIES

—··—··—··—··—	International
—··—··—··—··	Provincial, State
—··—··—··—··	Regional, Suburb

HYDROGRAPHY

	Coastline
	River, Creek
	Lake
·—·—·—·—·	Canal

	Building
	Urban Area

ROUTES & TRANSPORT

	Freeway
	Highway
	Major Road
	Minor Road
—————	Unsealed Road
	City Freeway
	City Highway
	City Road
	City Street, Lane

AREA FEATURES

✿	Park, Gardens
	Cemetery

	Pedestrian Mall
⊃═══════	Tunnel
⊢⊢⊢O⊢	Train Route & Station
—·—M·—	Metro & Station
————⊟—·	Tramway & Tram Stop
⊢⊢⊢⊟⊢	Cable Car or Chairlift
—————	Walking Track
············	Walking Tour
————⎅—	Ferry Route & Terminal

	Market
	Beach, Desert

MAP SYMBOLS

◉	**ROME**	Large City	☒	Archaeological Site	⌢⌣ Mountain Range
●	**Latina**	City	⊖	Bank	🏛 Museum
●	**Marino**	Large Town	🏃	Beach	National Park
○	Anzio	Town or Village	🚏 ⊡	Bus Stop, Station	☒ Police Station
			🏰	Castle or Fort	⌂ Post Office
●		Point of Interest	⌂	Cave	🏠 Stately Home
			⊕ ✚	Basilica or Church	Swimming Pool
■		Place to Stay	⊟	Cinema	☒ Synagogue
⬠		Camp Site	🔲	Embassy	⎕ Temple
			🎭	Fountain	⊖ Telephone
▼		Place to Eat	⊕	Hospital	⊟ Theatre
⬛		Pub or Bar	🔲	Internet Cafe	■ Tomb
			🎋	Lighthouse	❶ Tourist Information
☒		Airport	▲	Monument	🚶 Trail Head
⌒		Ancient or City Wall	▲	Mountain or Hill	🗺 Zoo

Note: not all symbols displayed above appear in this book

LONELY PLANET OFFICES

Australia
Locked Bag 1, Footscray, Victoria 3011
☎ 03 8379 8000 fax 03 8379 8111
email: talk2us@lonelyplanet.com.au

USA
150 Linden St, Oakland, CA 94607
☎ 510 893 8555 TOLL FREE: 800 275 8555
fax 510 893 8572
email: info@lonelyplanet.com

UK
10a Spring Place, London NW5 3BH
☎ 020 7428 4800 fax 020 7428 4828
email: go@lonelyplanet.co.uk

France
1 rue du Dahomey, 75011 Paris
☎ 01 55 25 33 00 fax 01 55 25 33 01
email: bip@lonelyplanet.fr
www.lonelyplanet.fr

World Wide Web: www.lonelyplanet.com or AOL keyword: lp
Lonely Planet Images: lpi@lonelyplanet.com.au